The Victorians and English Dialect

The Victorians and English Dialect

Philology, Fiction, and Folklore

Matthew Townend

Great Clarendon Street, Oxford, OX2 6DP,
United Kingdom

Oxford University Press is a department of the University of Oxford.
It furthers the University's objective of excellence in research, scholarship,
and education by publishing worldwide. Oxford is a registered trade mark of
Oxford University Press in the UK and in certain other countries

© Matthew Townend 2024

The moral rights of the author have been asserted

All rights reserved. No part of this publication may be reproduced, stored in
a retrieval system, or transmitted, in any form or by any means, without the
prior permission in writing of Oxford University Press, or as expressly permitted
by law, by licence or under terms agreed with the appropriate reprographics
rights organization. Enquiries concerning reproduction outside the scope of the
above should be sent to the Rights Department, Oxford University Press, at the
address above

You must not circulate this work in any other form
and you must impose this same condition on any acquirer

Published in the United States of America by Oxford University Press
198 Madison Avenue, New York, NY 10016, United States of America

British Library Cataloguing in Publication Data

Data available

Library of Congress Control Number: 2024909673

ISBN 9780198888123

DOI: 10.1093/oso/9780198888123.001.0001

Printed and bound by
CPI Group (UK) Ltd, Croydon, CR0 4YY

Links to third party websites are provided by Oxford in good faith and
for information only. Oxford disclaims any responsibility for the materials
contained in any third party website referenced in this work.

Acknowledgements

For permission to examine and/or quote from unpublished materials in their keeping, I am grateful to the following institutions: Bodleian Libraries, University of Oxford; John Rylands Research Institute and Library, Manchester; and King's College London Archives. A grant from the University of York's 'Culture and Communication' priming fund enabled a small pilot project on the English Dialect Society to be undertaken: I am grateful to Harriet Evans Tang for her superb work as research assistant on this, and to Charlotte Brewer, Matt Campbell, Fiona Douglas, Sue Edney, Jane Hodson, and David Matthews for participating in a very productive discussion day; Charlotte Brewer also gave other forms of help and encouragement in the writing of this book, and I am very grateful for her support. I have also received assistance of various kinds from Richard Dance, Philip Durkin, Beverley McCullough, Matthew Kempshall, Ad Putter, Jonathan Roper, and Jeremy Smith, as well as colleagues in the Department of English and Related Literature, and the Centre for Medieval Studies, at the University of York; I am grateful to all of them. At Oxford University Press, I have been lucky to enjoy the support and editorial guidance of Julia Steer and Jade Dixon, and I would also like to thank Karthiga Ramu and Caroline McLaughlin for their production work.

An earlier and more long-standing debt is to Lynda Mugglestone: it was my good fortune to be taught by her as a student, and in writing this book I have been gratefully conscious of her formative influence. Above all, my greatest and most fundamental debt of gratitude is to my wife, Natasha Glaisyer, and our children, Robin and Kit, for their love and good company.

Contents

Introduction: The Love of Words	1
1. The Pioneers	**15**
Early studies	15
Dignity and danger	28
J. C. Atkinson: the philological turn	47
2. The Phoneticians	**57**
The study of sounds	57
Alexander Ellis	61
The travels of Thomas Hallam	74
The Existing Phonology of English Dialects	83
3. Dialect and Literature	**101**
Fiction	101
Scholars and sources	116
Poetry	121
Remaking poetic diction	133
4. The English Dialect Society	**143**
Origins	143
Activities	150
Membership	163
Glossaries	172
5. Folklore and the Past	**187**
Histories of England	187
Philology and folklore	201
Folkloric fiction	217
6. The *English Dialect Dictionary*	**233**
From Society to *Dictionary*	233
Making the *English Dialect Dictionary*	243
Dialect lexicography (1): contents	252
Dialect lexicography (2): entries	263
Dialect lexicography (3): adjuncts	271
Epilogue: Philology's Aftermath	**279**
Bibliography	289
Index	319

Besom-Bet, the name of the personator of a female in the 'Fond Pleeaf' procession, on Plough Monday.
Black-berries [blaak-ber'·z], [. . .] black-currants. The bramble berry is never so termed, as is usual in the south.
Boggle [baog·l], a hobgoblin.[7]

These five entries exemplify certain patterns or subjects for the dialect vocabulary of Holderness: colloquial intensification (*bangin*), agricultural practices (*belly-band*), folk customs or rituals (*Besom-Bet*), flora and fauna (*black-berries*), and supernatural belief (*boggle*). Such words give a nice indication of some of the discoveries that might be made through the cataloguing of dialect vocabulary, in terms of local practices, mentalities, and expressiveness.

The *Holderness Glossary* suggests that by the 1870s, interest in regional dialect was well developed in Victorian Britain. But this is not dialect as a medium for poetic composition, or for use as a speech style in fiction. Instead, the *Holderness Glossary* attests to the *study* of dialect: it is dialect itself that is being held up as the object of attention, and for its three compilers the study of dialect permits the in-depth, all-round recording of a whole history, culture, and language zone—one that may be geographically remote and politically marginal, but which is well worthy not only of their own attention but also of that of their readers as well.

The word that we need here—the word that was used in the nineteenth century—is 'philology'. To understand the Victorian study and valuation of dialect, and the Victorian *excitement* about dialect, we need to understand what philology was, and what it meant in the nineteenth century: that is the explanatory context for the Victorian discovery of dialect.

'Philology', declared J. R. R. Tolkien in 1957, 'is the foundation of humane letters'.[8] The occasion was Tolkien's 'valedictory lecture' at the University of Oxford, as he retired after three decades as a professor of medieval language and literature. The Professor of Poetry in Oxford in 1957 happened to be W. H. Auden, who had announced in his own inaugural lecture the previous year that 'the most poetical of all scholastic disciplines is, surely, Philology, the study of language in abstraction from its uses, so that words become, as it were, little lyrics about themselves'.[9] These were lavish, extraordinary claims. What was—what is—this discipline that supposedly combines the scholarly with the humane with the poetic? As a term for a discipline, the word is rarely used now, and popularly it has largely fallen into abeyance. Literally, in its constituent elements, *philology* means 'the love of words'. And in the nineteenth and early twentieth centuries, philology was the dominant way of thinking about language—about language in general, and about the English language in particular, both past and present, and national and regional. It was a major intellectual and cultural force.

---

[7] Ross, Stead, and Holderness, *Glossary of Words Used in Holderness*, pp. 26–31.
[8] J. R. R. Tolkien, *The Monsters and the Critics and Other Essays*, ed. Christopher Tolkien (London: Allen and Unwin, 1983), p. 225.
[9] W. H. Auden, *The Dyer's Hand and Other Essays* (London: Faber and Faber, 1963), p. 35.

4   The Victorians and English Dialect

This so-called 'new philology', distinct from what had gone before, was a movement that rose to prominence in Germany and Denmark in the early decades of the nineteenth century, in the work of pioneering scholars such as Jacob Grimm and Rasmus Rask. When it burst upon the scene, it was fresh, exciting, revolutionary. It permeated thought in adjacent or related disciplines, from history to anthropology, folklore to evolutionary biology. It brought about changes in understanding and sensibility that are still with us as part of our core ways of thinking about language and the world—even though we may not now be aware of their ancestry.[10]

Philological thinking, basically, was *historical*: the discipline taught its adherents to view language in terms of change over time, and to make languages and texts the object of historical study in themselves, not just the medium through which the historical study of other subjects might be pursued (as one major scholar, Alexander Ellis, put it, 'We are to study language as a phenomenon, not as an instrument').[11] Nor was this piecemeal: philology sought to identify system and regularity in the processes by which languages changed, prioritizing phonology and grammar as much as vocabulary. As an ambitious and programmatic intellectual endeavour, this was something new; and nineteenth-century philologists believed that they possessed the methods and tools to carry out their ambition, to understand the history of language. For philology also taught that language should be viewed *comparatively*, in terms of family connections between languages, and it was this comparativism that enabled the reconstruction of hypothetical ancestor forms, all the way back to a supposed 'Indo-European' that stood as the origin for many of the languages of Europe and Asia. And these orientations towards the historical and the comparative were accompanied by a third tenet or presupposition, especially important for an engagement with dialect—namely, that *oral* language was primary, and written language secondary. So philologists were not only dedicated to working backwards to early or even prehistoric forms; they were also interested in the unwritten varieties of the present day, above all the regional, non-standard dialects that had been excluded from traditional language study (indeed, Alexander Ellis drew the distinction between Standard English and English dialects by labelling the former as 'Written English' and the latter as 'Unwritten English').[12] Like all disciplines, philology generated many sub-fields and sub-methodologies; but if we are to understand the fundamental tenets and influence of this revolutionary new movement, we

---

[10] See, for example, Hans Aarsleff, *The Study of Language in England, 1780–1860*, 2nd ed. (Minneapolis: University of Minnesota Press, 1983); Anna Morpurgo Davies, *Nineteenth-Century Linguistics*, History of Linguistics IV (London: Longman, 1998); Tom Shippey, *The Road to Middle-earth*, rev. ed. (London: HarperCollins, 2005), pp. 1–31; Haruko Momma, *From Philology to English Studies: Language and Culture in the Nineteenth Century* (Cambridge: Cambridge University Press, 2012); James Turner, *Philology: The Forgotten Origins of the Modern Humanities* (Princeton: Princeton University Press, 2014), esp. pp. 125–46, 236–53.

[11] Alexander J. Ellis, 'First Annual Address of the President to the Philological Society, Delivered at the Anniversary Meeting, Friday, 17th May, 1872', *Transactions of the Philological Society* 1873–4, 1–34, at pp. 20–1.

[12] Alexander J. Ellis, 'On Palaeotype; or, the Representation of Spoken Sounds for Philological Purposes by Means of the Ancient Types', *Transactions of the Philological Society* (1867), Supplement I, 1–52, at pp. 36–7.

Introduction **5**

should hold on to these three principles or priorities: the historical, the comparative, and the oral.

The 1850s and 1860s were the decades in which the discipline of philology, following its earlier continental origins, was adopted and domesticated in Britain, becoming part of the intellectual currency of the times. In the view of James Murray, editor of the *Oxford English Dictionary*, 'etymology began about 1850 in English', and Tolkien later lauded the half century from 1850 to 1900 as being the great 'philological epoch' in England.[13] The *Holderness Glossary* was published in 1877, in the middle of this half century.

One weathervane of this epoch was the success enjoyed by a landmark book of 1861, Friedrich Max Müller's *Lectures on the Science of Language*. Müller (1823–1900) was a German-born scholar of Sanskrit, with a great talent for popularization.[14] Since 1854 he had been Professor of Modern European Languages at the University of Oxford, and in 1868 Oxford created a new chair in Comparative Philology especially for him. This was the first time the university itself (as opposed to individual benefactors) had founded a professorship—another clear signal of the prominence and urgency of philology by this time.

Müller's 1861 book began as a series of lectures, and was followed by a second series in 1864. Delivered at the Royal Institution in London, these lectures were a society sensation, and were attended by such public figures as John Stuart Mill, F. D. Maurice, and Michael Faraday.[15] Müller's lectures are eloquent and assured, delivered with rhetorical flair and a swagger of showmanship, and his claims for the importance of language are visionary:

We cannot tell as yet what language is. It may be a production of nature, a work of human art, or a divine gift. But to whatever sphere it belongs, it would seem to stand unsurpassed—nay, unequalled in it—by anything else. If it be a production of nature, it is her last and crowning production which she reserved for man alone. If it be a work of human art, it would seem to lift the human artist almost to the level of a divine creator. If it be the gift of God, it is God's greatest gift.[16]

---

[13] Quoted in Sarah Ogilvie, 'A Nineteenth-Century Garment Throughout: Description, Collaboration, and Thorough Coverage in the *Oxford English Dictionary* (1884–1928)', in Sarah Ogilvie and Gabriella Safran (eds), *The Whole World in a Book: Dictionaries in the Nineteenth Century* (Oxford: Oxford University Press, 2020), pp. 54–72, at p. 61; J. R. R. Tolkien, 'Philology: General Works', *The Year's Work in English Studies* 4 (1923), 20–37, at p. 37.

[14] On Müller, see Nirad C. Chaudhuri, *Scholar Extraordinary: The Life of Professor the Rt. Hon. Friedrich Max Müller, P.C.* (London: Chatto and Windus, 1974); Linda Dowling, 'Victorian Oxford and the Science of Language', *Publications of the Modern Languages Association* 97 (1982), 160–78; Maurice Olender, *The Languages of Paradise: Race, Religion and Philology in the Nineteenth Century*, trans. Arthur Goldhammer (Cambridge, MA: Harvard University Press, 1992), pp. 82–92; Momma, *From Philology to English Studies*, pp. 137–53; R. C. C. Fynes, 'Müller, Friedrich Max (1823–1900)', in *Oxford Dictionary of National Biography* [www.oxforddnb].

[15] Chaudhuri, *Scholar Extraordinary*, p. 185; see also Turner, *Philology*, pp. 244–7.

[16] F. Max Müller, *Lectures on the Science of Language* (London: Longmans, Green and Co., 1861), p. 3.

6   The Victorians and English Dialect

Soaring eloquence was combined with an awe-inspiring range of reference. Müller's audience were confronted not only with Greek and Latin, but also with Old English, Gothic, and Sanskrit, and a mesmerizing array of world languages, from Africa to Tibet, Iceland to Siberia. Müller sketched out a new domain of knowledge, a new way of thinking, and a new, global perspective.

Müller's arguments about the beginnings of language are probably the most famous element in his work as a linguist; his ambition was to reach 'the extreme limits to which inductive reasoning can carry us in our researches into the mysteries of human speech'.[17] Müller's preference was to see the beginnings of speech in a small number of highly productive 'roots' which, he believed, were fundamentally descriptive, so that 'the word is the thought incarnate'.[18] It is not unfair to say that Müller's claims about the origin of language dated quite rapidly; but it would be ungrateful therefore to undervalue his *Lectures on the Science of Language*. As Müller himself wrote, 'when a new science is to be created, the imagination of the poet is wanted, even more than the accuracy of the scholar'.[19] Müller's *Lectures* offered poetry as well as scholarship: his arguments are imaginative as much as they are learned, and they appealed to the poet as well as the scholar, as we will see in due course.

By 1864 Müller was even giving private lectures on philology to Queen Victoria and her household.[20] In 1867, a decade before the *Holderness Glossary*, a satirical poem called 'Grimm's Law' was published by Charles Neaves, on a famous sound change which had formed the subject of a whole lecture in Müller's second series at the Royal Institution.[21] Neaves was a lawyer, whose other publications included a lecture on comparative philology, and the first four stanzas of his poem on Grimm's Law (out of a total of 17) will give a reasonable taste of its contents:

> Etymology once was a wild kind of thing,
> Which from any one word any other could bring:
> Of the consonants then the effect was thought small,
> And the vowels—the vowels were nothing at all.
> > *Down a down, down, &c.*

> But that state of matters completely is changed,
> And the old school of scholars now feels quite estranged:
> For 'tis clear that whenever we open our jaw,
> Every sound that we utter comes under some Law.

---

[17] Müller, *Lectures on the Science of Language*, p. 344. See further, for example, Paul Salmon, 'Max Müller and the Origin of Language', in Vivien Law and Werner Hüllen (eds), *Linguists and Their Diversions: A Festschrift for R.H. Robins on His 75th Birthday* (Münster: Nodus, 1996), pp. 333–60; Will Abberley, 'Race and Species Essentialism in Nineteenth-Century Philology', *Critical Quarterly* 53 (2011), 45–60.

[18] Müller, *Lectures on the Science of Language*, p. 386.

[19] Müller, *Lectures on the Science of Language*, p. 162.

[20] Chaudhuri, *Scholar Extraordinary*, p. 185.

[21] See F. Max Müller, *Lectures on the Science of Language: Second Series* (London: Longmans, Green, and Co., 1864), pp. 198–222.

Now one of these laws has been named after Grimm,
For the Germans declare it was found out by him:
But their rivals the Danes take the Germans to task,
And proclaim as its finder the great Rasmus Rask.

Be this as it may, few have sought to explain
How it came that this law could its influence gain:
Max Müller has tried, and, perhaps, pretty well;
But I don't understand him, and therefore can't tell.[22]

The poem indicates very nicely the sort of public purchase that philology had gained by 1867. Old-style, free-wheeling etymologizing was no longer respectable, and had been replaced by strict codification ('every sound that we utter comes under some Law'). The prize of philological eminence was a valuable one, and caused international debates about scholarly precedence. And a contemporary figure such as Max Müller was now sufficiently familiar to be the butt of sardonic humour. Above all, the essential point about Neaves' 'Grimm's Law' is that a poem about philology might be thought funny in the 1860s: Neaves could assume that his audience would have a knowledge of the broad outlines of the discipline, and would recognize his targets and allusions. This would not have been the case a decade or two earlier, at least not in Britain; and that the Law retained its cultural recognition for the rest of the century is suggested by Thomas Hardy's passing reference to 'what is everywhere known as Grimm's Law' in *Jude the Obscure* (1895).[23]

Another way of appreciating the centrality of the 1850s and 1860s is by looking at dates of birth. In the 1850s and 1860s, the new philology offered intellectual awakening and excitement, and a new way of thinking about things, to young men and women in their impressionable late teens and early twenties: it was this generation, the beneficiaries of the early pioneers, who would carry the subject forward triumphantly in the second half of the century. Of the great British philologists, Walter William Skeat was born in 1835, James Murray in 1837, and Henry Bradley and Henry Sweet both in 1845. The same is true of some of the most important writers to be influenced by philology: William Morris was born in 1836, Thomas Hardy in 1840, and Gerard Manley Hopkins in 1844. All of these writers and scholars were coming to maturity in the 1850s and 1860s, at precisely the time when philology's potential was being broadcast and recognized.

The *Oxford English Dictionary*, the greatest single achievement of Victorian philology, was begun in 1857, when the Philological Society of London instituted an 'Unregistered Words Committee', and its first instalment (covering *A–Ant*) was

---

[22] [Charles Neaves], *Songs and Verses, Social and Scientific*, 4th ed. (Edinburgh: Blackwood and Sons, 1875), pp. 21–2. See further Lord [Charles] Neaves, *A Glance at Some of the Principles of Comparative Philology as Illustrated by the Latin and Anglian Forms of Speech* (Edinburgh: Blackwood and Sons, 1870); A. H. Millar, 'Neaves, Charles, Lord Neaves (1800–1876)', rev. Robert Shiels, in *Oxford Dictionary of National Biography* [www.oxforddnb].

[23] Thomas Hardy, *Jude the Obscure*, ed. Patricia Ingham (Oxford: Oxford University Press, 1996), p. 26.

8 The Victorians and English Dialect

eventually published in 1884, under the editorship of James Murray.[24] To understand Victorian philology more generally—and, thus, the Victorian study of dialect—there is no better place to look than the prefatory 'General Explanations' which Murray wrote for this first instalment of 1884. The project was originally titled *A New English Dictionary on Historical Principles* (*Oxford English Dictionary* was a later renaming), and the foregrounding of 'Historical Principles' runs right through the dictionary: the *OED* is not simply a dictionary of the English language at the time of its own compilation, but rather is a dictionary of the language from all previous centuries too. Every *OED* entry displays the spelling history of each word in chronological order; demonstrates the sense developments of the word over time; and parades its illustrative quotations for each sense in chronological order too. Murray's 'General Explanations' recognize that time is an 'undefined frontier'. As he writes:

> The living vocabulary is no more permanent in its constitution than definite in its extent. It is not to-day what it was a century ago, still less what it will be a century hence. Its constituent elements are in a state of slow but incessant dissolution and renovation. 'Old words' are ever becoming obsolete and dying out: 'new words' are continually pressing in. And the death of a word is not an event of which the date can be readily determined. It is a vanishing process, extending over a lengthened period, of which contemporaries never see the end.[25]

This sense of time-depth in the language was very powerful. Murray gives the example of the unexceptional Modern English word *acre*: formerly *aker*, this word, he writes, 'is the extant form of Old English *æcer*, this the later form of prehistoric *æcr*, the special English form of *acr*, *akr*, this of West Germanic *akra*, this, through earlier *akra-z*, of Original Teutonic *akro-z*, this of original Aryan or Indo-European *agro-s*; and *agros*, *akroz*, *akraz*, *akra*, *akr*, *æcr*, *æcer*, *aker*, *āker*, *ācre* [. . .] are all merely successive and temporary forms of one and the same word, as employed during successive periods. The word has never died; no year, no day probably, has passed without its being uttered by many'.[26] This is an extraordinary circumstance to contemplate: the words we utter have millennia of continuous history somehow within or behind them. And Murray and the *OED* are only able to trace the backward history of the humble word *acre* because of the reconstructive methodology of comparative philology.

---

[24] See especially K. M. Elisabeth Murray, *Caught in the Web of Words: James A.H. Murray and the Oxford English Dictionary* (New Haven: Yale University Press, 1977); Lynda Mugglestone (ed.), *Lexicography and the OED: Pioneers in the Untrodden Forest* (Oxford: Oxford University Press, 2000); Simon Winchester, *The Meaning of Everything: The Story of the Oxford English Dictionary* (Oxford: Oxford University Press, 2003); Lynda Mugglestone, *Lost for Words: The Hidden History of the Oxford English Dictionary* (New Haven: Yale University Press, 2005); Charlotte Brewer, *Treasure-House of the Language: The Living OED* (New Haven: Yale University Press, 2007); Peter Gilliver, *The Making of the Oxford English Dictionary* (Oxford: Oxford University Press, 2016).

[25] James A. H. Murray, 'General Explanations', in James A. H. Murray (ed.), *A New English Dictionary on Historical Principles: Part 1: A–Ant* (Oxford: Clarendon Press, 1884), pp. xvii–xxiv, at p. xviii.

[26] Murray, 'General Explanations', p. xx.

Murray's discussion of *acre* also shows the priority given to speech over writing, even though the *OED* had to be compiled from written sources ('no year, no day probably, has passed without its being uttered by many'). As he states in his discussion of pronunciation in the *OED*:

> The pronunciation is the actual living form or forms of a word, that is, *the word itself*, of which the current spelling is only a symbolization—generally, indeed, only the traditionally-preserved symbolization of an earlier form, sometimes imperfect to begin with, still oftener corrupted in its passage to our time. This living form is the *latest fact* in the form-history of the word, the starting-point of all investigations into its previous history, the only fact in its form-history to which the lexicographer can personally witness [...] To register the current pronunciation is therefore essential, in a dictionary which deals with the language on historical principles.[27]

Before taking on the *OED* editorship, as we will see, Murray had primarily achieved distinction as a dialectologist: the prioritization of the spoken word, so central to philological thinking, was fundamental to him.

Philology was, however, slow to be institutionalized in English universities.[28] In 1877—the year of the *Holderness Glossary*—Henry Sweet gave his first address as President of the Philological Society (founded in 1842), and lamented that 'in all civilized countries except England' the work of philology 'was done by universities', and that, moreover, 'an undergraduate of an English University who were to announce to the Head of his College his intention of devoting himself to English philology would be regarded as a dangerous lunatic'.[29] At Cambridge, English was at first embedded within the Tripos in Medieval and Modern Languages, instituted in 1878, when W. W. Skeat was appointed the first Professor of Anglo-Saxon—though it did not fully become a separate degree until 1926. The debate at Oxford about the establishment of a School of English, with the relative claims of 'Lit.' and 'Lang.' as alternate approaches, was peculiarly protracted and vitriolic, and a School of English Language and Literature was not created until 1894. By this time, there were new movements afoot in continental philology, especially in the form of the so-called *Junggrammatiker* or 'Neogrammarians', who insisted on the centrality of phonology and the regularity of sound changes.[30]

The development of English philology as a field of study offered hitherto unparalleled opportunities and interest for those who had not experienced a public school or grammar school education—that is, the great majority of the population. It is striking

---

[27] Murray, 'General Explanations', p. xxiv.

[28] See, for example, D. J. Palmer, *The Rise of English Studies: An Account of the Study of English Language and Literature from its Origins to the Making of the Oxford English School* (Oxford: Oxford University Press, 1965); Alan Bacon (ed.), *The Nineteenth-Century History of English Studies* (Aldershot: Routledge, 1998); Carol Atherton, 'The Organisation of Literary Knowledge: The Study of English in the Late Nineteenth Century', in Martin Daunton (ed.), *The Organisation of Knowledge in Victorian Britain* (Oxford: Oxford University Press, 2005), pp. 219–34; Alexandra Lawrie, *The Beginnings of University English: Extramural Study, 1885–1910* (London: Palgrave Macmillan, 2014).

[29] Henry Sweet, *Collected Papers*, ed. H. C. Wyld (Oxford: Clarendon Press, 1913), pp. 82, 90.

[30] See, for example, Morpurgo Davies, *Nineteenth-Century Linguistics*, pp. 229–69.

10 The Victorians and English Dialect

how many of the leading philologists were autodidacts from a working-class, or lower middle-class, background. As we will see in this book, the sub-field of dialect study offered particularly rich opportunities for those excluded from university education, and separation from the traditions of Latinate scholarship also explains why women played such a prominent role in nineteenth-century philology: a classical education was no longer a necessary entry point for engaging in matters of linguistics.

At the same time as it entered the academy, then, English philology also remained democratizing, with an audience outside the universities and the traditional circles of culture. The number of undergraduates formally studying English remained relatively low until after the First World War, though the university extension movement reached many students. Readable, discursive books on the history of the English language, mediating philological learning to a general readership, had as much of a market in the nineteenth century as they do today. A distinguished example of this type of work, spreading linguistic knowledge and enthusiasm far and wide, is Henry Bradley's 1904 volume *The Making of English*: Bradley, the second editor of the *OED*, explained to the poet Robert Bridges that his book 'contain[s] a good many things which, so far as my knowledge goes, have hitherto been presented only in technical language not intelligible to the uninitiated', and it was still selling well a decade after publication.[31]

As we have already seen with the *Holderness Glossary*, at the heart of nineteenth-century philology, at least in Britain, lay the romance of thinking historically, and of discovering the past—as part of what the medievalist R. W. Chambers (1874–1942) called 'the great discovery of the nineteenth century: the historical or evolutionary point of view'.[32] It was philology's historical potential that drew and excited people. Elizabeth Mary Wright (née Lea) studied at Oxford under A. S. Napier, the first Professor of English there, and she later recalled:

> The lectures I really enjoyed were Professor Napier's [. . .] He was extraordinarily clear and precise, and wrote all his philological forms on the black-board, or gave us copies of neatly tabulated lists which we could take home and keep. I remember now being thrilled by hearing what the name 'Canterbury' meant [. . .].[33]

The glamour, in other words, lay in the breathtaking access to the past which philology offered—often, the remote past. The anecdote that Wright gives could hardly be bettered, in terms of the combination of dry detail with emotional excitement: it was the 'neatly tabulated lists' that resulted in her 'being thrilled'.

---

[31] Robert Bridges and Henry Bradley, *Correspondence of Robert Bridges and Henry Bradley 1900–1923* (Oxford: Clarendon Press, 1940), pp. 48, 131–2.

[32] R. W. Chambers, *Man's Unconquerable Mind* (London: Cape, 1939), p. 343. On Chambers, see C. J. Sisson, 'Raymond Wilson Chambers, 1874–1942', in Michael Lapidge (ed.), *Interpreters of Early Medieval Britain* (London, 2002), pp. 221–33 (first published in *Proceedings of the British Academy* 30 (1944), 427–45); Dorothy Everett, 'Chambers, Raymond Wilson (1874–1942)', rev. John D. Haigh, in *Oxford Dictionary of National Biography* [www.oxforddnb].

[33] Elizabeth Mary Wright, *The Life of Joseph Wright*, 2 vols (London: Oxford University Press, 1932), I, 176–7.

W. W. Skeat recalled his own linguistic awakening. One of the history textbooks of his youth gave quotations from Chaucer and *Piers Plowman*, and 'young as I then was, these quotations haunted me'. But this haunting took a particular form:

> The words 'holden' and 'abouten' and 'y-benched' seemed so quaint, that their forms irresistibly invited further consideration. Why and when did people say 'abouten', and what did they mean by the prefix *y*- in 'y-benched'? These were problems to be seriously considered; they could not be beyond human discovery, and discovered they must some day be![34]

Or to take C. S. Lewis as a twentieth-century example, in 1927 he wrote to a childhood friend about the fulfilment of his long-held ambition to learn Old Norse:

> You will be able to imagine what a delight this is to me, and how, even in turning over the pages of my Icelandic Dictionary, the mere name of god or giant catching my eye will sometimes throw me back fifteen years into a wild dream of northern skies and Valkyrie music: only they are now even more beautiful seen thro' a haze of memory.[35]

Lewis' letter offers an extraordinary example of a linguistic excitement that is at the same time intellectual, aesthetic, and even emotional. As Tom Shippey has written, 'for many in the nineteenth century and after, apprehension of the past was made *qualitatively different* by philology'.[36]

The grand affinities between nineteenth-century philology and nineteenth-century evolutionary thought are not hard to perceive.[37] Language had often been spoken of as an organism, in a tradition derived from German romanticism.[38] Henry Sweet wrote that 'in its unceasing alternations of development and decay [. . .] language shows its analogy with the other manifestations of organic life'.[39] Darwin himself, in *The Origin of Species*, used the classification of languages as a parallel to explain the classification of species and varieties, and in *The Descent of Man* he argued that language should be viewed from an evolutionary perspective: for example, 'the formation of different languages and of distinct species [. . .] are curiously parallel'; and 'we see variability in every tongue, and new words are continually

---

[34] Walter W. Skeat, *A Student's Pastime* (Oxford: Clarendon Press, 1896), pp. xiv–xv.

[35] Walter Hooper (ed.), *They Stand Together: The Letters of C. S. Lewis to Arthur Greeves (1914–1963)* (London: Collins, 1979), p. 298 (26 June 1927).

[36] Tom Shippey, 'Goths and Huns: the rediscovery of the Northern cultures in the nineteenth century', in Andreas Haarder et al (eds), *The Medieval Legacy: A Symposium* (Odense: Odense University Press, 1982), pp. 51–69, at p. 67 (italics original).

[37] See, for example, Stephen G. Alter, *Darwinism and the Linguistic Image: Language, Race, and Natural Theology in the Nineteenth Century* (Baltimore: Johns Hopkins University Press, 1999); Abberley, 'Race and Species Essentialism'; Sarah Weaver, 'Victorian Philology and the Metaphors of Language', *Literature Compass* 12 (2015), 333–43.

[38] See Morpurgo Davies, *Nineteenth-Century Linguistics*, pp. 86–94.

[39] Henry Sweet, *A History of English Sounds from the Earliest Period*, English Dialect Society 4 (London: English Dialect Society, 1874), p. 70 (first published in as 'The History of English Sounds', *Transactions of the Philological Society* 1873–4, 421–623).

12   The Victorians and English Dialect

cropping up; but [...] single words, like whole languages, gradually become extinct.[40] As we have seen, James Murray wrote in his 'General Explanations' to the *OED* that: '"Old words" are ever becoming obsolete and dying out: "new words" are continually pressing in.'[41] The affinities here with Darwinian evolution are very plain. It is difficult to know which is chicken and which is egg—philology or evolution?—and perhaps we should simply note that, not only were the two disciplines both products of nineteenth-century historicist thought, but also, by the 1860s and 1870s, both philology and evolution had become part of the common currency of culture and debate.[42] As Patrick Joyce has said, 'it is easy now to lose sight of just how significant for contemporaries was the model of culture and history to be found in language. Notions of language shaped the whole mental framework of nineteenth-century intellectual life.'[43]

In modern scholarship, and outside of histories of linguistics, philology has often received attention in the context of nineteenth-century European nationalism and nation-building. One historian has written that 'in Eastern Europe and the Balkans the first act of awakening nationalism was often a scholar compiling a dictionary'; another, more accusatory, has claimed that European philologists, beginning with Jacob Grimm, encouraged the reckless identification of language, people, and nation state, and through their editing of medieval texts 'provided nationalists with a means of projecting their nations into a distant preliterate past.'[44] But we should proceed with caution here, and avoid overgeneralizations: philology cannot simply be construed as the linguistic wing of nineteenth-century nationalism. By the second half of the nineteenth century, philologists had begun to object loudly to the nationalist or racial misuse of linguistic insights; in his 1861 *Lectures*, for example, Müller insisted:

> The classification of races and languages should be quite independent of each other. Races may change their languages, and history supplies us with several instances where one race adopted the language of another. Different languages, therefore, may be spoken by one race, or the same language may be spoken by different races; so that any attempt at squaring the classification of races and tongues must necessarily fail.[45]

---

[40] Charles Darwin, *The Origin of Species*, ed. Gillian Beer (Oxford: Oxford University Press, 1996), p. 342; Charles Darwin, *The Descent of Man, and Selection in Relation to Sex*, 2nd ed., The Works of Charles Darwin 21–22 (London: Pickering and Chatto, 1989), I, 94–5.

[41] Murray, 'General Explanations', p. xviii.

[42] See, for example, J. W. Burrow, *Evolution and Society: A Study in Victorian Social Theory* (Cambridge: Cambridge University Press, 1966); Morpurgo Davies, *Nineteenth-Century Linguistics*, pp. 196–200; John van Wyhe, 'The Descent of Words: Evolutionary Thinking 1780–1880', *Encounter* 29.3 (2005), 94–100.

[43] Patrick Joyce, *Visions of the People: Industrial England and the Question of Class 1848–1914* (Cambridge: Cambridge University Press, 1991), p. 206.

[44] J. W. Burrow, 'The Uses of Philology in Victorian England', in Robert Robson (ed.), *Ideas and Institutions of Victorian Britain: Essays in Honour of George Kitson Clark* (London: Bell and Sons, 1967), pp. 180–204, at p. 204; Patrick J. Geary, *The Myth of Nations: The Medieval Origins of Europe* (Princeton: Princeton University Press, 2002), pp. 32–3.

[45] Müller, *Lectures on the Science of Language*, p. 329. See further, for example, Chaudhuri, *Scholar Extraordinary*, pp. 313–14; Geoffrey Galt Harpham, 'Roots, Races, and the Return to Philology', *Representations* 106 (2009), 34–62, at pp. 43–6; Momma, *From Philology to English Studies*, p. 152; Chris Manias, *Race, Science, and the Nation: Reconstructing the Ancient Past in Britain, France, and Germany* (London: Routledge, 2013), pp. 33–5.

Introduction   **13**

With their commitment to linguistic comparativism, philologists were, almost by definition, heavily invested in the idea of the multilingual rather than the monoglot; and no group of thinkers could be less likely to assume that language and nation were co-extensive categories. Moreover, as the present book demonstrates in abundance, nineteenth-century philology was frequently directed not towards a national goal but rather to a regional or local one, and this can be paralleled by a similar regionalism in many other fields of Victorian endeavour, from landscape painting and botany to antiquarianism and ethnology.[46] Regionalism and nationalism were not the same thing, and often regional vitality was defined precisely against national norms.[47]

This, then, is a book about the Victorians and the study of English dialect—what we might call 'regional philology', as found in the *Holderness Glossary* and countless other works of the time. Its central claim is that the nineteenth-century discipline of philology is the primary context in which the period's dialect study should be placed and understood. It was Victorian philology which gave the nineteenth-century interest in dialect its impetus, character, and methods; and when, after the turn of the century, the cultural prominence of philology began to decline, so too did the forms of dialect study which the discipline had given rise to, and new ways of thinking about language began to appear in their stead. The philology we shall be looking at was regional not only in the obvious sense that it was concerned with the dialects, past and present, of the regions of Britain; it was also regional in terms of where, and by whom, it was being pursued—that is, in the localities themselves, often remote from the centres of power, rather than at the national level or in major sites of learning. But—to restate—this is a book about the study of dialect, rather than a survey or history of the regional dialects themselves as they were spoken (and sometimes written) in Victorian England.[48] Why, in the nineteenth century, did scholars and enthusiasts turn their attention to local varieties of speech? Why did they place such importance on it? How did they organize themselves, and how did they connect with, and influence,

[46] See, for example, Philippa Levine, *The Amateur and the Professional: Antiquarians, Historian and Archaeologists in Victorian England, 1838–1886* (Cambridge: Cambridge University Press, 1986); K. D. M. Snell (ed.), *The Regional Novel in Britain and Ireland, 1800–1990* (Cambridge: Cambridge University Press, 1998).

[47] See, for example, Robert Colls, 'The New Northumbrians', in Robert Colls (ed.), *Northumbria: History and Identity 547– 2000* (Chichester: Phillimore, 2007), pp. 151–77, at pp. 151–2, 176–7. See further Maiken Umbach, 'Nation and Region: Regionalism in Modern European Nation-States', in Timothy Baycroft and Mark Hewitson (eds), *What is a Nation? Europe 1789–1914* (Oxford: Oxford University Press, 2006), pp. 63–80; Manias, *Race, Science, and Nature*, pp. 41–51; and David Hopkin, 'Regionalism and Folklore', in Xosé M. Núñez Seixas and Eric Storm (eds), *Regionalism and Modern Europe: Identity Construction and Movements from 1890 to the Present Day* (London: Bloomsbury, 2018), pp. 43–64.

[48] See, for example, K. C. Phillipps, *Language and Class in Victorian England* (Oxford: Blackwell, 1984); Richard W. Bailey, *Nineteenth-Century English* (Ann Arbor: University of Michigan Press, 1996); Suzanne Romaine (ed.), *The Cambridge History of the English Language: Volume IV, 1776–1997* (Cambridge: Cambridge University Press, 1999); Manfred Görlach, *English in Nineteenth-Century England: An Introduction* (Cambridge: Cambridge University Press, 1999), esp. pp. 21–43; Susanne Wagner, 'Late Modern English: Dialects', in Alexander Bergs and Laurel J. Brinton (eds), *English Historical Linguistics: An International Handbook*, 2 vols (Berlin: De Gruyter, 2012), I, 915–38; Clive Upton, 'Modern Regional English in the British Isles', in Lynda Mugglestone (ed.), *The Oxford History of English*, rev. ed. (Oxford: Oxford University Press, 2012), pp. 379–414.

14   The Victorians and English Dialect

practitioners in other fields—local historians, folklorists, novelists, poets? The materials available for a history of Victorian dialect study, or regional philology, are very extensive: grammars and glossaries, lectures and monographs, and a great quantity of unpublished notes and correspondence now resting in libraries and archives. But they have never been put together before or examined as a whole; and nor has Victorian dialect study been placed at length within the context which makes most sense of it—namely, nineteenth-century philology.

R. W. Chambers wrote that 'to study language for love of it, is to be a philologist'.[49] Many nineteenth-century philologists felt strongly the romance and glamour of their new discipline, believing that through its historical and comparative methods, it had an extraordinary potential to uncover the mysteries of the past, and to make sense of the patterns of the present. They were conscious that there was an abundance of material waiting to be collected and explored, and an abundance of problems waiting to be solved; and they were animated by a relish for the pleasures and rewards that language study might offer—the irresistible love of words.

---

[49] R. W. Chambers, *Concerning Certain Great Teachers of the English Language: An Inaugural Lecture Delivered in University College, London* (London: Arnold and Co., 1923), p. 8.

1
The Pioneers

Early studies

Prior to the fifteenth century there was, effectively, no standard language in England. People spoke and wrote in their own regional dialect of English, rather than
in some supraregional variety. This changed in the fifteenth and sixteenth centuries,
with the development of a standardized written variety that was focused on the language of London—itself heavily influenced by the language of the East Midlands. A
standardized spoken variety followed later, with a similar tilt towards London and
the south-east.[1]

Awareness of dialectal variation, though, pre-dates the rise of a standard language.
In the twelfth century, William of Malmesbury observed that 'the whole speech of
the Northumbrians, especially that of the men of York, grates so harshly upon the ear
that it is completely unintelligible to us southerners'. He even had an explanation:
'the reason for this is their proximity to barbaric tribes and their distance from the
kings of the land, who, whether English as once or Norman as now, are known to
stay more often in the south than the north'.[2] Later in the century, Gerald of Wales
offered a similar southern view of northern speech: according to Gerald, southern
English was 'purer than elsewhere' because 'it retains more features of the original
language and the old ways of speaking English, whereas the northern regions have
been greatly corrupted by the Danish and Norwegian invasions'.[3] The most celebrated medieval commentary on dialect variation comes two centuries later, in the
conclusion to Chaucer's long poem *Troilus and Criseyde*, in which he remarks that
'ther is so gret diversite / In Englissh and in writyng of oure tonge'.[4] Notable here
is Chaucer's sense that dialect differences exist on the written plane as well as (more
obviously) the spoken.[5]

We can first observe the purposeful collecting of dialect features—above all,
vocabulary—in the seventeenth and eighteenth centuries; it is not a pursuit that

---

[1] See, for example, Lynda Mugglestone (ed.), *The Oxford History of English*, rev. ed. (Oxford: Oxford
University Press, 2012).

[2] David Preest (trans.), *William of Malmesbury: The Deeds of the Bishops of England (Gesta Pontificum
Anglorum)* (Woodbridge: Boydell, 2002), p. 139.

[3] Lewis Thorpe (trans.), *Gerald of Wales: The Journey through Wales and The Description of Wales*
(Harmondsworth: Penguin, 1978), p. 231. See further Mark Faulkner, 'Gerald of Wales and Standard Old
English', *Notes and Queries* 58 (2011), 19–24.

[4] Larry D. Benson (ed.), *The Riverside Chaucer*, 3rd ed. (Oxford: Oxford University Press, 1988), p. 584
(V. 1793–4).

[5] See further David Burnley, *The Language of Chaucer* (Basingstoke: Macmillan, 1989), pp. 108–32.

The Victorians and English Dialect. Matthew Townend, Oxford University Press. © Matthew Townend (2024).
DOI: 10.1093/oso/9780198888123.003.0002

16   The Victorians and English Dialect

began with Victorian philology.[6] Some of the earliest students of what they called Anglo-Saxon were aware that dialect evidence might be relevant for them, but the first scholar to produce a dedicated dictionary of regional vocabulary was John Ray (1627–1705), a botanist and member of the Royal Society, who travelled extensively for the purposes of fieldwork. Ray's *Collection of English Words* was published in 1674, with an expanded edition in 1691.[7] In his introductory address 'To the Reader', Ray explained that 'in my travels through several parts of *England*, besides other things, which I principally minded and pursued, I could not but take notice of the difference of Dialect, and variety of Local words'.[8] Echoing William of Malmesbury, Ray's view was that 'in many places, especially of the North, the Language of the common people, is to a stranger very difficult to be understood'. Hence 'I thought it might be worth the while to make a Collection of such words for my own use'. Soon he was asking friends and colleagues to send him words, and the resultant *Collection of English Words* was published for three reasons:

> *First*, because I knew not of anything that hath been already done in this kind. 2. Because I conceive, they may be of some use to them who shall have occasion to travel the Northern Counties, in helping them to understand the common language there. 3. Because they may also afford some diversion to the curious, and give them occasion of making many considerable remarks.[9]

Ray's collection is miscellaneous in both content and style, mixing austere, minimalist entries with discursive chattiness. He gives localization markers for many of his entries, and even offers etymologies for some, as this sample from the letter B indicates:

> *Bearn-teams*, Broods of Children, as they expounded it to me. I find that *Bearn-team* in the Saxon, signifies Issue, offspring, Children, from *team*, soboles, and Bearn [. . .]
> A *Beck*: a small brook: a word common to the ancient Saxon, high and low Dutch and Danish [. . .]
> To *Bluffe*: To blindfold.
> A *Bondy*: A Simpleton, *York-sh*.
> To *Boke* at one: to Point at one, *Chesh*. i.e. to Poke at one.[10]

---

[6] See Martyn F. Wakelin, *English Dialects: An Introduction* (London: Athlone Press, 1972), pp. 43–6.

[7] See Jo Gladstone, '"New World of English Words": John Ray, FRS, the Dialect Protagonist, in the Context of his Times (1658–1691)', in Peter Burke and Roy Porter (eds), *Language, Self, and Society: A Social History of Language* (Cambridge: Cambridge University Press, 1991), pp. 115–53; John Considine, *Small Dictionaries and Curiosity: Lexicography and Fieldwork in Post-Medieval Europe* (Oxford: Oxford University Press, 2017), pp. 95–113; Robert Penhallurick, 'Dialect Dictionaries', in A. P. Cowie (ed.), *The Oxford History of English Lexicography*, 2 vols (Oxford: Oxford University Press, 2008), II, 290–313, at pp. 294–7; Robert Penhallurick, *Studying Dialect* (London: Bloomsbury, 2018), pp. 6–9; Scott Mandelbrote, 'Ray [*formerly* Wray], John (1627–1705)', in *Oxford Dictionary of National Biography* [www.oxforddnb].

[8] John Ray, *A Collection of English Words* (London: Bruges, 1674), [no pagination].

[9] Ray, *Collection of English Words*, [no pagination].

[10] Ray, *Collection of English Words*, pp. 5–6.

Not all of this is correct (*beck* is from Old Norse, not 'the ancient Saxon'), but Ray's list is remarkably wide-ranging and extensive for a first achievement in the field; W. W. Skeat's view, two hundred years later, was that Ray 'was not only the first to gather together our provincial words, but in some respects has never been surpassed'.[11] What was the ultimate motivation for Ray's word-collecting? As well as the reasons that Ray himself gives in his preface, and in addition to the Royal Society context of curiosity and survey, John Considine suggests that 'it is tempting to see [Ray's *Collection*] as having an autobiographical quality, showing the son of the Essex blacksmith revisiting the rustic linguistic world of his childhood'.[12]

Ray's glossary acted as a stimulus for other word collectors: in the 1690s White Kennett compiled an unpublished *Etymologicon Anglicanum*, and in 1703 the Leeds antiquary Ralph Thoresby sent Ray an important list of northern words.[13] A small number of locally focused glossaries appeared in the eighteenth century before the publication of the next nationally conceived dictionary, Francis Grose's *Provincial Glossary* of 1787 (second edition, 1790). Grose, the son of a Swiss immigrant, had a long career both in the army and as an antiquarian artist, and he began collecting material for his *Provincial Glossary* as far back as the 1750s.[14] Grose's preface declares that words collected from published sources have been 'augmented by many hundred words collected by the Editor in the different places wherein they are used; the rotation of military quarters, and the recruiting service, having occasioned him to reside for some time in most of the counties in England'.[15]

Grose was also a friend of Robert Burns, whose composition of poetry in Scots, and not Standard English, was to prove an inspiration; and mention of Burns invites consideration of Wordsworth and the so-called Romantic poets more broadly. The preface to the 1802 edition of *Lyrical Ballads* famously announces that the subject of Wordsworth's poetry will be 'low and rustic life', and that his language will be drawn from such a station.[16] But Wordsworth himself did not produce dialect poetry, or collect dialect vocabulary; the great breakthrough in the study of Lakeland dialect came in the work of Wordsworth's younger admirer Thomas De Quincey, who wrote articles on dialect in the *Westmorland Gazette* which in turn influenced the later editions of Wordsworth's *Guide to the Lakes*.[17] But Wordsworth's influence

---

[11] Walter W. Skeat, 'Report on the English Dialect Society', in Alexander J. Ellis, 'Eleventh Annual Address of the President to the Philological Society, Delivered at the Anniversary Meeting, Friday, 19th May, 1882', *Transactions of the Philological Society* 1882–4, 1–148, pp. 10–20, at p. 13.

[12] Considine, *Small Dictionaries and Curiosity*, p. 112.

[13] White Kennett, *Etymological Collections of English Words and Provincial Expressions*, ed. Javier Ruano-García (Oxford: Oxford University Press, 2018); see also the review by John Considine in *International Journal of Lexicography* 33 (2020), 504–21.

[14] On Grose, see Richard M. Dorson, *The British Folklorists: A History* (London: Routledge and Kegan Paul, 1968), pp. 25–8; Penhallurick, 'Dialect Dictionaries', pp. 298–300, and *Studying Dialect*, pp. 11–14; Janet Sorensen, *Strange Vernaculars: How Eighteenth-Century Slang, Cant, Provincial Languages, and Nautical Jargon Became English* (Princeton: Princeton University Press, 2017); John H. Farrant, 'Grose, Francis (*bap.* 1731, *d.* 1791)', in *Oxford Dictionary of National Biography* [www.oxforddnb].

[15] Francis Grose, *A Provincial Glossary, with a Collection of Local Proverbs, and Popular Superstitions* (London: Hooper, 1787), p. A2.

[16] Stephen Gill (ed.), *William Wordsworth* (Oxford: Oxford University Press, 1984), p. 597.

[17] See D. S. Roberts, 'Thomas De Quincey's "Danish Origin of the Lake Country Dialect"', *Transactions of the Cumberland and Westmorland Antiquarian and Archaeological Society*, 2nd Series 99 (1999),

18 The Victorians and English Dialect

on Victorian attitudes to rural life—including, potentially, language—was, of course, immense.[18]

In the first half of the nineteenth century, and especially from the 1820s onwards, there was a steady trickle, growing to a stream, of regional glossaries. Let us begin by looking at a couple of distinguished examples: Joseph Hunter's *Hallamshire Glossary* (1829) and George Cornewall Lewis' *Glossary of Provincial Words used in Herefordshire* (1839).

The Rev. Joseph Hunter (1783–1861), the son of a Sheffield cutler, was a Presbyterian minister in Bath who later became Assistant Keeper at the Public Record Office (and vice-president of the Society of Antiquaries).[19] With strong antiquarian interests since his teenage years, in 1819 he published *Hallamshire: the History and Topography of the Parish of Sheffield*, and later a two-volume work on the Doncaster area (1828–31). Hunter's introduction to his *Glossary* begins with a disquisition on language change, both lexical and semantic:

> Custom is for ever introducing new words into our vocabulary, and blotting out others which had kept their station in it with honour for centuries.
>
> Custom is a very capricious power [. . .] She has abolished some of our best words, and introduced others which had no claim to currency amongst us beside the stamp of her authority. Where she has tolerated the continuance of old words, she has often disjoined them from antient senses, thus introducing confusion and uncertainty in the interpretation of our laws, and even of the written records from which we deduce the principles of religious faith.[20]

England, he writes, has suffered especially from the effects of linguistic change: 'the vernacular language of England for the two centuries before and after the Conquest, is to be studied as other antient languages are, by the help of a master, grammars and dictionaries'.[21] What is more, language change can be shockingly rapid: Hunter notes that John Ray gives a Sheffield provenance for six words, but that 150 years later, 'not one of them now remains'.[22]

However—crucially—not all varieties of the language, Hunter claims, have been equally susceptible to change:

257–65; Matthew Townend, *The Vikings and Victorian Lakeland: the Norse medievalism of W. G. Collingwood and his contemporaries*, Cumberland and Westmorland Antiquarian and Archaeological Society Extra Series 34 (Kendal: Cumberland and Westmorland Antiquarian and Archaeological Society, 2009), pp. 17–24.

[18] See Stephen Gill, *Wordsworth and the Victorians* (Oxford: Clarendon Press, 1998).

[19] See David Crook, 'Hunter, Joseph (1783–1861)', in *Oxford Dictionary of National Biography* [www.oxforddnb].

[20] Joseph Hunter, *The Hallamshire Glossary* (London: Pickering, 1829), pp. vii–viii. See further Joan C. Beal, 'The Contribution of the Rev. Joseph Hunter's *Hallamshire Glossary* (1829) to Wright's *English Dialect Dictionary*', in Manfred Markus, Clive Upton, and Reinhard Heuberger (eds), *Joseph Wright's English Dialect Dictionary and Beyond: Studies in Late Modern English Dialectology* (Frankfurt am Main: Lang, 2010), pp. 39–48.

[21] Hunter, *Hallamshire Glossary*, p. ix.

[22] Hunter, *Hallamshire Glossary*, p. xxv.

The empire of custom, or fashion, for that is but another word for the same thing, is however of somewhat limited extent [. . .] The rustic and the mechanic will speak as his father spoke before him, and may be heard therefore using words unknown to the educated classes of society [. . .] Hence amongst them may be found fragments of our antient tongue, relics of what, three or four centuries ago, constituted the language not of the common people only, but of all ranks from the king to the peasant.[23]

As can be seen, Hunter is very keen on the 'antient', and his argument here represents an early example of what was to be a recurrent emphasis in nineteenth-century dialectology—namely, that contemporary dialect words are often of profound historical interest, as 'relics' of the past that can still be encountered in the present. But Hunter also has a literary claim to make, arguing that, since older writers often employed words which are no longer current among the 'educated classes of society', but which do still survive in dialect usage, then 'an extensive and intimate acquaintance with provincial dialects is quite essential to the critic who attempts the explanation of the dark passages occasionally to be found in our early writers'.[24] This is already quite close, we can see, to the claims made later by the authors of the *Holderness Glossary*.

What about Hunter's collection of words, though? 'In preparing collections such as this, there is often difficulty in determining what words to admit and what to reject. A dictionary of archaical words is not a dictionary of *slang* or of mere *vulgarisms*'.[25] The border between dialect and slang was likewise to be a topic that would animate later workers. For Hunter, the criteria are antiquity and literary sanction ('I had long thought [. . .] that the word *egg*, the verb, was mere slang, till I found it in good use in a Chronicle of the reign of Henry VI').[26] Colloquial phrases, such as *back o' beyond* and *Adam's ale* (for 'water') are, however, excluded—suspicious to Hunter on account of their humour.[27]

George Cornewall Lewis (1806–63) later became an eminent Liberal politician, serving as both Chancellor of the Exchequer and Home Secretary, but in the earlier part of his career he was active as a serious scholar of languages (and he continued as a member of the Philological Society's Council even when he was Chancellor).[28] In 1835 he wrote a monograph on the Romance languages, and in 1839 he published, anonymously, his *Glossary of Provincial Words used in Herefordshire* (in 1847 he was elected MP for Hereford). Lewis' *Herefordshire Glossary* shows an attempt to define, categorize, and analyse, and not simply to accumulate, and it marks a clear dawning of philological awareness in dialect collection.

---

[23] Hunter, *Hallamshire Glossary*, pp. xiii–xiv.
[24] Hunter, *Hallamshire Glossary*, p. xiv.
[25] Hunter, *Hallamshire Glossary*, p. xxi.
[26] Hunter, *Hallamshire Glossary*, p. xxii.
[27] Hunter, *Hallamshire Glossary*, p. xxiii.
[28] See Rebecca Posner, 'Sir George Cornewall Lewis: statesman and "new philologist"', *Historiographia Linguistica* 17 (1990), 339–56; D. A. Smith, 'Lewis, Sir George Cornewall (1806–1863)', in *Oxford Dictionary of National Biography* [www.oxforddnb.com].

20 The Victorians and English Dialect

First, definition:

> A provincial word seems properly to mean a word which is not actually used in the written or spoken language of educated persons, but which is current in the familiar language of the inhabitants of some district.[29]

Next, categorization. Lewis suggests that provincial words are of four types: (1) 'Words used by classical [i.e. earlier] writers, but now obsolete'; (2) 'Words not obsolete, but used only in poetry, or as technical terms'; (3) 'Words which are not known to have ever been used in the language of educated persons'; and (4) 'Words substantially the same as words current in the language of educated persons, but modified in form'.[30] These are interesting subdivisions, invoking criteria of archaism, register, class, and pronunciation. In terms of analysis, Lewis has observations to make about distribution ('many, if not most, of the provincial words current in Herefordshire are [. . .] current as provincialisms in other parts of England [. . .] Indeed, few provincial words are confined to one locality'), about language contact (Herefordshire dialect, he says, 'contains few words borrowed from the Welsh'), and about linguistic conservatism ('several ancient preterits (of the form called by Grimm *strong*) are still current in Herefordshire', such as *climb-clomb, shake-shuck,* and *squeeze-squoze*).[31] He is conscious of how a lack of comparative material is hampering his own work, not least in terms of regional patterning: 'no copious provincial Glossary', he laments, 'for any of the midland counties (as Shropshire, Staffordshire, Warwickshire, Worcestershire, Derbyshire, or Leicestershire) has hitherto been published'.[32] He also has a sense of historical change, noting that a number of words recorded in earlier sources are no longer to be found in current usage (such as *beethy* 'soft, sticky, contrary to crisp, overripe: Grose states that underdone meat is so called in Herefordshire; but this sense is not known at present'); so even at this early stage, there is a sense of provincial vocabulary being perishable, and not immutable.[33] Finally, Lewis is explicit about his methodology, and the difficulties of fieldwork. The glossary, he explains, was 'compiled with the assistance of gentlemen resident in various parts of Herefordshire', and all the words 'have been collected from actual usage'; however, 'it is difficult by conversation alone, and that with illiterate persons, to obtain an induction sufficiently wide for fixing the precise import of a word'.[34]

With his early, and explicit, philological interests (we should note the reference to Grimm), Lewis was something of an exception among the dialect collectors of the second quarter of the nineteenth century—as is clear also from an important stock-taking that appeared in 1836. This was a long article on 'English Dialects', published in the *Quarterly Review*. Its author was Richard Garnett (1789–1850), a

---

[29] [George Cornewall Lewis], *A Glossary of Provincial Words used in Herefordshire and some of the Adjoining Counties* (London: Murray, 1839), p. v.

[30] [Lewis], *Glossary of Provincial Words used in Herefordshire*, p. vi.

[31] [Lewis], *Glossary of Provincial Words used in Herefordshire*, pp. vii, x, 121.

[32] [Lewis], *Glossary of Provincial Words used in Herefordshire*, p. ix.

[33] [Lewis], *Glossary of Provincial Words used in Herefordshire*, pp. 9–10.

[34] [Lewis], *Glossary of Provincial Words used in Herefordshire*, pp. viii, 121.

Yorkshire-born clergyman who later became Assistant Keeper of Printed Books at the British Museum (as did one of his sons after him, also called Richard).[35] Garnett was one of the first English writers to perceive the importance of the new, continental philology and to give it a public welcome: in an earlier essay, the year before, he had declared that 'they who are properly qualified to appreciate the matter know that philology is neither a useless nor a trivial pursuit,—that, when treated in an enlightened and philosophical spirit, it is worthy of all the exertions of the subtlest as well as most comprehensive intellect'.[36] Garnett himself was a prodigious linguist: his personal library, according to his son, 'may be said without exaggeration to have contained examples of every printed language, and every species of composition'.[37]

In his 1836 article, he reviews in essayistic manner eleven volumes published over the previous quarter century (including Hunter's *Hallamshire Glossary*), making many points that would be developed more fully by other writers over the coming decades. As with Lewis, there is the issue of definition and terminology ('All agree in calling our standard form of speech the English language, and all provincial deviations from it—at least all that assume a distinct specific character—dialects'), and also the issue of origins and antiquity ('How and when those different forms originated has never yet been fully explained: there is, however, no doubt that some of them existed at a very early period').[38] More pressing is the issue of attrition: since the early modern period, Garnett observes, 'many genuine Saxon words have gradually disappeared from the language of common life, especially in the southern and midland counties'. And so there is now a need to make 'a diligent collection of those which still survive'.[39]

This is the framing spirit of Garnett's review. His knowledge both of languages and of the new philology is, demonstrably, greater by far than that of the authors whose works he is reviewing. But he fully recognizes the value of their endeavours as an act of preservation, even as he corrects their misguided views about etymology, or language history, or linguistic relations. His own preoccupations are northerly: John Trotter Brockett's *Glossary of North Country Words* (1829) is praised as 'the most copious and best executed of our English vocabularies', and in Garnett's view 'the most important of our provincial dialects is undoubtedly the Northumbrian' (and moreover, 'it is unquestionably [. . .] the most pleasing of our provincial forms of speech'). But there is work to be done: 'we have reason to believe that many provincial terms, current in Westmoreland and Cumberland, have never been collected by any glossarist'.[40]

---

[35] See Richard Garnett, 'Memoir of the late Rev. Richard Garnett', in Richard Garnett, *Philological Essays* (London: Williams and Norgate, 1859), pp. i–xvi; David Matthews, *The Making of Middle English, 1765–1910* (Minneapolis: University of Minnesota Press, 1999), pp. 106–7; Richard Garnett, 'Garnett, Richard (1789–1850)', rev. John D. Haigh, in *Oxford Dictionary of National Biography* [www.oxforddnb].

[36] Richard Garnett, *Philological Essays* (London: Williams and Norgate, 1859), p. 2; quoted also in Aarsleff, *The Study of Language in England*, p. 210.

[37] Garnett, *Philological Essays*, p. xvi.

[38] Garnett, *Philological Essays*, p. 42.

[39] Garnett, *Philological Essays*, p. 42.

[40] Garnett, *Philological Essays*, pp. 45, 55.

22 The Victorians and English Dialect

In the 1840s, these views were shared also by the members of the newly founded Philological Society of London. As Peter Gilliver has shown, an early initiative of the Society, launched in 1844, was to compile and collect regional dialect glossaries.[41] Within a decade at most, however, this seems to have petered out. Very few of the collections reported by the Society were ever published, and the brevity of those that did reach print suggests that the initiative may never have been a large-scale enterprise (for example, J. M. Kemble's piece in the Society's *Transactions* on 'Surrey Provincialisms' is only two pages long—'these words are used by old people here in the neighbourhood of Chertsey, Ripley, Weybridge, Pyrford, Guildford').[42] The last and longest to appear—and even this was only ten pages—was Anna Gurney's 'Norfolk Words', published in 1855.[43] Gurney (1795–1857), of North Repps near Cromer, was a remarkable figure, a linguist and medievalist who, at her death, left a trove of unpublished translations from Old English and Old Norse.[44] Her list of Norfolk words, she writes, was 'gathered chiefly on the north-eastern coast', and one of its most conspicuous features is the prominence of terms relating to fishing, ships, and the sea: for example, *brabble* ('a short swell; little waves in quick succession, very unpleasant in a boat'), *driving* ('to go out fishing; letting the herring or mackerel nets drift'), *kittywitch* ('a small crab that makes zigzag tracks on the sand'), *lum* ('the handle of an oar'), *orruck-holes* ('oar-drawing holes, as distinct from thole-pins, which are less used in our boats'), *slug* ('used of a heavy surf tumbling in with an off-shore wind'), and *tangle* ('the thick dark sea-weed beset with little bladders').[45] Gurney's linguistic range is formidable: for parallels and etymologies, she invokes Old English, Celtic, French, German, Greek, and Hebrew. Especially prominent are Scandinavian languages: Danish, Norwegian, and above all Icelandic (often standing in for Old Norse, as the two languages are so similar). Gurney's learning in this area is impressive, as can be gauged from her allusions to medieval Scandinavian law codes, and a strong theme in her word list is the Viking impact on her area of Norfolk.

However, the intellectual framework for many contemporary glossaries in the second quarter of the nineteenth century was not (as it was for Garnett, and also Lewis and Gurney) the new science of language, with its associated medieval learning; rather, it was a more traditional, but still highly capacious, place-based antiquarianism. Local or regional words were regarded as one of the topics that needed recording as part of an antiquarian survey—alongside, for example, ecclesiastical and gentry history, architecture, and flora and fauna. Take, for instance, Pishey Thompson's *History and Antiquities of Boston* (1856), a massive work in every sense.[46] Thompson had begun assembling material in 1804, at the age of 20, and his 1856 preface movingly records that 'in taking leave of this volume, the Author feels he is bidding farewell to

---

[41] Peter Gilliver, 'Harvesting England's ancient treasure: dialect lexicography and the Philological Society's first plans for a national dictionary', *Dictionaries* 32 (2011), 82–92.

[42] J. M. Kemble, 'Surrey Provincialisms', *Transactions of the Philological Society* 1854, 83–4, at p. 83.

[43] Anna Gurney, 'Norfolk Words', *Transactions of the Philological Society* 1855, 29–39.

[44] See M. J. Toswell, 'Anna Gurney: The Unknown Victorian Medievalist', *Poetica* 86 (2016), 69–86.

[45] Gurney, 'Norfolk Words', pp. 30, 31, 33, 34, 36, 37.

[46] On Thompson, see Isabel Bailey, 'Thompson, Pishey (1785–1862)', in *Oxford Dictionary of National Biography* [www.oxforddnb].

an old friend, a pleasing labour, a resource against *ennui* and weariness, a companion in solitude and privation'.[47] After chapters on such subjects as the Anglo-Saxons and Normans, monasteries, commerce, the River Witham, local biography, surrounding villages, the fens, geology, natural history, and agriculture, we eventually come to one on 'Archaisms, &c', filling pages 696–736 of Thompson's giant book.

'It will scarcely be denied', Thompson writes, 'that whatever is peculiar in the language of a district, is as much a portion of its history as the succession of events, or an account of its geology, botany, or natural products. We therefore shall attempt to describe those peculiarities as they exist in the neighbourhood of Boston'.[48] Here is a sample of consecutive entries, again taken from the letter B:

Boggle-bo.—A bug-a-bo; a bugbear to frighten children.
Boggle (to).—"I boggled at it;" I hesitated or demurred; to start as a horse starts at an unaccustomed object.
Boke (to).—To nauseate. A. S., *belcan*.
Bole, or boll. —The trunk of a tree. DANISH, *bul*.
Booning.—"Doing our boons;" repairing the roads.
Boozy. —Stupid with drink. —SKELTON.
Bottle of hay.—A bundle of hay tied together.—*Midsummer Night's Dream*.
Bother.—To tease with questions or tedious details.
Bottom.—A ball of string.—SKELTON.
Bouge.—"I've made a bouge;" a blunder.[49]

As can be seen, Thompson's list mixes words with phrases, and proceeds variously by definition, illustrative quotation, literary reference, and linguistic provenance ('A. S.', of course, means Anglo-Saxon or Old English). And as he explains in his introduction, the claim is not that these words, phrases, and senses are unique to the Boston area—they may well be found, he accepts, in many other areas.

Thompson's antiquarian book on Boston is over seven hundred (folio) pages in length, but only forty are devoted to his dialect word list. But one of the greatest, and largest, of the early-to-mid-century glossaries also arose as part of a wider antiquarian project: Anne Elizabeth Baker's *Glossary of Northamptonshire Words and Phrases*, published in 1854 in two volumes, each of over four hundred pages. (Its most substantial predecessor was probably the 1830 *Vocabulary of East Anglia* of Robert Forby (1759–1825)—also two volumes, but only 560 pages in length.[50]) This work by Baker (1786–1861) had also been decades in the making, and the dedication explains its origins: 'To the memory of a beloved and lamented brother, at whose suggestion this glossary of Northamptonshire words and phrases was originated, and by whose kind encouragement it was fostered, until death deprived her

---

[47] Pishey Thompson, *The History and Antiquities of Boston* (Boston: Noble, 1856), pp. vi, xii.
[48] Thompson, *The History and Antiquities of Boston*, p. 696.
[49] Thompson, *The History and Antiquities of Boston*, p. 700.
[50] On Forby, see Thompson Cooper, 'Forby, Robert (1759–1825)', rev. John D. Haigh, in *Oxford Dictionary of National Biography* [www.oxforddnb].

24   The Victorians and English Dialect

of his cheering support, these volumes are affectionately dedicated by his sister'.[51] Anne Elizabeth Baker's brother was George Baker, and the two unmarried siblings had worked together on his multi-volume *History and Antiquities of the County of Northampton* (1822–41).[52]

Although Baker modestly describes herself as 'a humble gleaner in the philological field', her *Glossary* is noteworthy for several reasons apart from its magnitude.[53] One is her liberal or descriptive approach to inclusion. As we will see later, a number of Victorian collectors wanted to make a distinction between contemporary slang and dialect proper, with only the latter deemed worthy of collection. Not so, Baker: as she writes, 'many may think that the Glossarist retains the rubbish, by perpetuating vulgarisms; and it is often difficult to distinguish between the archaism and the vulgarism'. She continues: 'some of the words which *appear* vulgarisms are only the residuum of our ancient mother tongue; other words admitted into this collection are undoubtedly vulgarisms, or vicious pronunciations; but they are nevertheless curious, as being characteristic of our county phraseology'.[54] Hence, 'my principal aim has been to give full, clear, and accurate definitions of the words and phrases, with familiar colloquial examples of their use'.[55]

A second point of interest is Baker's insistence on the primary nature of her own research: nearly all the words had been collected by Baker herself, in over twenty years of fieldwork ('from the peer to the peasant', she writes), rather than excerpted from prior publications, and similarly the illustrative phrases or quotations 'are all genuine expressions which have either been heard by myself or communicated by friends who have supplied the words to which they are appended'.[56]

And a third point—now, perhaps, her chief claim to fame—is Baker's relationship with the poet John Clare.[57] In her preface, Baker notes that she has frequently quoted from Clare's work to illustrate usage, but it is the next sentence which catches the eye: 'his manuscript poems which are quoted have all been written since his mental aberration, and during his confinement in the Northampton Asylum' (that is, since 1842).[58] So the preface signals that Baker is not simply quoting from Clare's published works, but that she seems to have some personal connection, or communication, with him. This is amply confirmed by the glossary itself: the modern editors of Clare's poetry count no fewer than 34 passages which are known from no other source than

---

[51] Anne Elizabeth Baker, *Glossary of Northamptonshire Words and Phrases*, 2 vols (London: Smith, 1854, I, [iv]). On Anne Elizabeth Baker, see Kennett, *Etymological Collections of English Words*, pp. 84–5; Thompson Cooper, 'Baker, Anne Elizabeth (1786–1861)', rev. Paul Stamper, in *Oxford Dictionary of National Biography* [www.oxforddnb].

[52] On George Baker, see Paul Stamper, 'Baker, George (1781–1851)', in *Oxford Dictionary of National Biography* [www.oxforddnb].

[53] Baker, *Glossary of Northamptonshire Words and Phrases*, I, xvi.

[54] Baker, *Glossary of Northamptonshire Words and Phrases*, I, xiii–xiv.

[55] Baker, *Glossary of Northamptonshire Words and Phrases*, I, xiv–xv.

[56] Baker, *Glossary of Northamptonshire Words and Phrases*, I, xii, xv.

[57] See Valerie Shepherd, 'Anne Elizabeth Baker's *Glossary of Northamptonshire Words and Phrases* and John Clare's "rustic idiom"', *John Clare Society Journal* 15 (1996), 69–75; Jonathan Bate, *John Clare: A Biography* (London: Picador, 2003), pp. 514–15.

[58] Baker, *Glossary of Northamptonshire Words and Phrases*, I, xv.

Baker's *Glossary*.[59] Most of the quotations that Baker gives are very brief, somewhere between one to four lines, as for instance in her comments on *clodhopper* as a name for the wheat-ear:

We have Clare's authority for its present use, in one of his recent MS Poems.

> Where the *clodhopper* on the clods all day,
> Slow moves his tail and TWEETS the winds away.[60]

What such snippets indicate is that Baker possessed copies of a number of poems by Clare which no longer survive (except in the form of such illustrative quotations). As a confirmation of this, Baker's *Glossary* also contains two poems by Clare quoted in their (apparent) entirety, one of which is said to have been 'written expressly for the present work' and is cited as part of a discursive essay on May Day customs.[61]

Baker's *Northamptonshire Glossary* shows us the heights that might be attained by the local and antiquarian school of dialect study in the second quarter of the century. We should now, however, return to the issue of dialect lexicography on a more national scale. Besides the abortive attempt of the Philological Society in the late 1840s and early 1850s, what else had been happening since Francis Grose's *Provincial Glossary* of 1787?

The work that had received most attention from Richard Garnett in his 1836 review, not least because it offered him the greatest scope for holding forth on lexicographical principles, was Jonathan Boucher's *Glossary of Archaic and Provincial Words*—recently published, but in fact the work of an earlier time. Boucher (1738–1804) was a Cumbrian clergyman and teacher, who spent time in America (where he tutored George Washington's stepson), before returning to England to spend the last twenty years of his life as vicar of Epsom in Surrey, and amass an assortment of materials for his *Glossary*, projected as a supplement to the dictionaries of Samuel Johnson and Noah Webster.[62] But only the first two parts of Boucher's gallimaufry were ever published (in 1832–3), edited by Joseph Hunter and his fellow antiquary Joseph Stevenson, and these extend no further than midway through the letter B. Some of Garnett's judgements on these few firstfruits are damning: although Boucher showed 'laudable zeal and industry', he was 'deficient in critical acumen, and imperfectly versed in the various branches of knowledge required'.[63] His learning was also, of course, already out of date by the time his work was published.

Nonetheless, Boucher's *Glossary* is important, as it was—however incomplete— the first attempt at a more national survey of dialect vocabulary to be published

---

[59] Eric Robinson and David Powell (eds), *The Later Poems of John Clare 1837–1864*, 2 vols (Oxford: Clarendon Press, 1984), II, 1107–13.

[60] Baker, *Glossary of Northamptonshire Words and Phrases*, I, 127–8.

[61] Baker, *Glossary of Northamptonshire Words and Phrases*, II, 423–4; Robinson and Powell (eds), *The Later Poems of John Clare*, II, 1108–9.

[62] On Boucher, see Robert M. Calhoon, 'Boucher, Jonathan (1738–1804)', in *Oxford Dictionary of National Biography* [www.oxforddnb.com].

[63] Garnett, *Philological Essays*, p. 56.

26   The Victorians and English Dialect

since Grose's, over forty years earlier. It was followed in 1839 by William Holloway's *General Dictionary of Provincialisms*, a collection of nine thousand words with brief indicators of locality (which also function as references for Holloway's source for the word: the items labelled 'Craven', for example, are taken from William Carr's *Dialect of Craven*, first published in 1824). The collocation of the 'provincial' with the 'archaic' in Boucher's title was also followed by the next, much more important, attempt at a national dictionary, namely James Orchard Halliwell's *Dictionary of Archaic and Provincial Words, Obsolete Phrases, Proverbs, and Ancient Customs, from the Fourteenth Century* (published in parts between 1844 and 1847, and listing over fifty thousand words).[64] Halliwell (1820–89)—who subsequently, for inheritance reasons, changed his surname to Halliwell-Phillipps—was an editor, antiquary, and literary scholar of exceptional industry; later in his career he was to be drawn into a huge row, on Shakespearean matters, between the philologist F. J. Furnivall and the poet Swinburne.[65] The publisher for Halliwell's *Dictionary of Archaic and Provincial Words*, at whose instigation he had undertaken the project, was John Russell Smith (1810–94), whose premises in Old Compton Street, London, were a 'hub of communication' for like-minded antiquaries, and who published many of the dialect glossaries of the mid-nineteenth century.[66] He himself had produced, in 1839, both a *Bibliographical List of the Works that have been published, towards illustrating the Provincial Dialects of England* and a glossary of *Westmoreland and Cumberland Dialects*. Halliwell embarked on a revision of his *Dictionary* a few years after its first publication; but the project then passed to his older friend and supporter, the antiquary Thomas Wright (1810–77)—who had himself given Halliwell help with the original 1847 version.[67] This revised version appeared in 1857, under Wright's name, with the title of *Dictionary of Obsolete and Provincial English*; but the relationship between the two dictionaries is not hard to discern, and they are very similar in their sources and contents.

Both Halliwell and Wright were working within the antiquarian tradition, and Halliwell in particular had little interest in the new philology. What he offered his readers was, basically, a very long alphabetical list, in which no cross-connections

---

[64] On Halliwell, see Dorson, *The British Folklorists*, pp. 66–74; Neil C. Hultin, '"To Shine with Borrowed Splendour": J. O. Halliwell-Phillipps, Thomas Wright, and Victorian Lexicography', *Dictionaries* 16 (1995), 109–50; Marvin Spevack, *James Orchard Halliwell-Phillipps: The Life and Works of the Shakespearean Scholar and Bookman* (New Castle, DE: Oak Knoll, 2001), esp. pp. 174–81; Kennett, *Etymological Collections of English Words and Provincial Expressions*, ed. Ruano-García, pp. 82–4; Penhallurick, *Studying Dialect*, pp. 14–15; Arthur Freeman and Janet Ing Freeman, 'Phillipps, James Orchard Halliwell (1820–1889)', in *Oxford Dictionary of National Biography* [www.oxforddnb].

[65] See William Benzie, *Dr F. J. Furnivall: A Victorian Scholar Adventurer* (Norman: Pilgrim Books, 1983), pp. 203–7; Spevack, *James Orchard Halliwell-Phillipps*, pp. 492–521.

[66] Spevack, *James Orchard Halliwell-Phillipps*, p. 175. On Smith, see Hultin, '"To Shine with Borrowed Splendour"', pp. 124–8; R. J. Goulden, 'Smith, John Russell (1810–1894)', in *Oxford Dictionary of National Biography* [www.oxforddnb].

[67] See Hultin, '"To Shine with Borrowed Splendour"'. On Wright, see further Dorson, *The British Folklorists*, pp. 61–6; Mark Atherton, 'Imaginative Science: The Interactions of Henry Sweet's Linguistic Thought and E. B. Tylor's Anthropology', *Historiographia Linguistica* 37 (2010), 31–73, at pp. 66–8; Michael Welman Thompson, 'Wright, Thomas (1810–1877)', in *Oxford Dictionary of National Biography* [www.oxforddnb].

were made between different words (for example, chronological or regional variants). Inevitably, too, because of its national scope, Halliwell's *Dictionary* was mostly compiled from written sources; he did not engage in extensive fieldwork, though a few entries bear the stamp of having been drawn from life.[68] He did, however, receive information from a variety of correspondents, especially for dialect terms—for the Isle of Wight, Lincolnshire, Norfolk, Somerset, and so on.[69] In spite of this, it is not surprising that, of the dual targets of the 'archaic' and the 'provincial' which his title proclaims, it is the archaic which tends to dominate: what Halliwell's *Dictionary* supplies is a glossary of late medieval and early modern vocabulary, very useful for the reading (or editing) of earlier texts. His preface explicitly confirms this priority. 'The real value of provincial words', he writes, is in 'the important assistance they continually afford in glossing the works of our early writers'. For Halliwell, they are not necessarily of interest in and of themselves: 'the history of provincialisms is of far inferior importance to the illustration they afford of our early language'.[70]

That is what Halliwell's preface states. The introduction that follows, however, seems to have a significantly different set of values, for this is a twenty-eight-page essay titled 'The English Provincial Dialects' (which John Russell Smith also reprinted as a separate work). The nature of this can be gauged from its first two entries:

BEDFORDSHIRE
The dialect of this county has been fully investigated in Batchelor's Orthoepical Analysis of the English Language [. . .] *Ew* takes the place of *ow*, *ea* of *a*, *ow* of the long *o*, *oi* of *i*, &c. When *r* precedes *s* and *e* final, or *s* and other consonants, it is frequently not pronounced. *Ow* final is often changed into *er*; *ge* final, into *dge*; and *g* final is sometimes omitted.

BERKSHIRE
The Berkshire dialect partly belongs to the Western, and partly to the Midland, more strongly marked with the features of the former in the South-West of the county. The *a* is changed into *o*, the diphthongs are pronounced broadly, and the vowels are lengthened. *Way* is pronounced *woye*; *thik* and *thak* for this and that; *he* for him, and *she* for her.[71]

Other county entries are much longer, though their length is due not to a fuller linguistic analysis, but to the quotation of samples of dialect writing, so that Halliwell's introduction functions somewhat as a regional anthology. Nonetheless, what these two short examples of Bedfordshire and Berkshire indicate is that Halliwell's essay is offering something rather different from his actual word list: first, a cataloguing

---

[68] See Hultin, '"To Shine with Borrowed Splendour"', p. 120.
[69] James Orchard Halliwell, *A Dictionary of Archaic and Provincial Words: Obsolete Phrases, Proverbs, and Ancient Customs, from the Fourteenth Century* (London: Smith, 1847), p. viii.
[70] Halliwell, *A Dictionary of Archaic and Provincial Words*, p. vii.
[71] Halliwell, *A Dictionary of Archaic and Provincial Words*, p. [xi].

28   The Victorians and English Dialect

of the main features of both dialect phonology and dialect grammar; and second, an attempt to group the county dialects into larger regional clusters. Both of these issues, needless to say, were to receive a great deal more attention as the philological epoch advanced.

Dignity and danger

Although working within an antiquarian tradition, James Orchard Halliwell had been cautious in his giving of etymologies, confining himself to simple labels without foregrounding word origins in detail.[72] But another version of early dialectology was precisely focused on questions of etymology, and what these revealed; and to trace this tradition we need to track back briefly to its seventeenth-century beginnings.

An interest in 'Saxonism' had been part of English dialect study from the very start. John Ray, in his 1674 *Collection of English Words*, had observed that he found 'a great part of these words to be pure Saxon, or manifestly derived thence', and he gave a derivation from 'AS' for a significant number of items in his word list.[73] White Kennett's unpublished *Etymologicon Anglicanum* had been heavily 'Saxonist' in its priorities.[74] We have also seen that in 1836 Richard Garnett lamented that 'many genuine Saxon words' were disappearing from regional dialects—a lament that indicates Garnett's ability to discern what was 'Saxon' (that is, Old English), and what wasn't.

An important landmark in Anglo-Saxon studies came two years later, with the 1838 publication of the first edition of Joseph Bosworth's *Dictionary of the Anglo-Saxon Language*. Born in 1787 or 1788, Bosworth straddled the philological and pre-philological eras, and in 1858 he became Professor of Anglo-Saxon at Oxford. After his death in 1876, his lexicographical materials were overhauled by Thomas Northcote Toller (1844–1930), resulting in a fuller, more authoritative dictionary in 1898.[75] But even the first edition of Bosworth's 1838 *Dictionary* was bigger and better than any previous resource for the study of Old English—especially for lexical study.

Its impact was immediate. It was promptly cited by the up-to-date George Cornewall Lewis in 1839, and in the same year an excerpt from Bosworth's introduction was quoted by John Russell Smith on the title page of his *Bibliographical List*: 'Much of the peculiarity of dialect prevalent in Anglo-Saxon times, is preserved even to the present day in the provincial dialects of the same districts. In these local

---

[72] See Hultin, '"To Shine with Borrowed Splendour"', pp. 120–3, 128–9.

[73] Ray, *Collection of English Words*, [no pagination].

[74] Kennett, *Etymological Collections of English Words*.

[75] On Bosworth, see John D. Niles, *The Idea of Anglo-Saxon England 1066–1901: Remembering, Forgetting, Deciphering, and Renewing the Past* (Chichester: Wiley Blackwell, 2015), pp. 246–7; Dabney A. Bankert, *Philology in Turbulent Times: Joseph Bosworth, His Dictionary, and the Recovery of Old English* (Turnhout: Brepols, 2023); Henry Bradley, 'Bosworth, Joseph (1787/8–1876)', rev. John D. Haigh, in *Oxford Dictionary of National Biography* [www.oxforddnb]. On Toller, see Donald Scragg (ed.), *Textual and Material Culture in Anglo-Saxon England: Thomas Northcote Toller and the Toller Memorial Lectures* (Cambridge: Brewer, 2003), and 'Toller, Thomas Northcote (1844–1930)', in *Oxford Dictionary of National Biography* [www.oxforddnb].

dialects, then, remnants of the Anglo-Saxon tongue may be found in its least altered, most uncorrupt, and therefore in its purest state'. Moreover, 'Our present polished phrase and fashionable pronunciation are often new, and, as deviating from primitive usage, faulty and corrupt'.[76]

Bosworth's *Dictionary* was an important influence on John Yonge Akerman's *Glossary of Provincial Words and Phrases in Use in Wiltshire* in 1842.[77] Akerman (1806–73) had a wide range of historical and archaeological interests, and later became an important figure at the Society of Antiquaries. His *Wiltshire Glossary* looks back to the language of his childhood:

> Having, in my boyhood, resided in a district of North Wiltshire remote from large towns, I became acquainted with many—I may say nearly all—the provincialisms in use by the rural population; and the cares and anxieties of later life have not been sufficient to efface them from my memory: but, great was my astonishment and delight, when, on my first acquaintance with Anglo-Saxon literature, I discovered that what for many generations past has been considered a barbarous and vulgar jargon, was once the language of Bede, of Alfred, and of Aelfric![78]

He explains further:

> This will scarcely be credited by persons less familiar than myself with these provincialisms; but, I am persuaded that any doubt they may entertain, will be dispelled on comparing the words in the list with those of similar signification in the Anglo-Saxon language. Some of these derivations are palpable and indisputable, while many words are retained to this hour as they originally existed.
>
> Every educated man knows that the basis of our language is the Anglo-Saxon; but, it may be questioned whether many persons are aware of the existence of so many primitive Anglo-Saxon words in the dialects of the West of England.[79]

Nor was it simply a case of words and meanings, but of pronunciation too: 'if I had not aimed at conciseness, I should have inserted many words of well known meaning, which are to this day pronounced in Wiltshire precisely as we may suppose they were pronounced among the Anglo-Saxons' (for example, Wiltshire *sheawe* for *show*, and *sheame* for *shame*).[80] Knowledge of 'Anglo-Saxon', he concludes, is essential if one wishes to understand western dialects. Too many glossaries 'have been published in the last ten years [. . .] which serve to swell the number of words without adding one jot of philological information [. . .] It is evident that several compilers of works of

---

[76] J[oseph] Bosworth, *A Dictionary of the Anglo-Saxon Language* (London: Longmans et al, 1838), pp. xxvi–xxvii.

[77] See W. W. Wroth, 'Akerman, John Yonge (1806–1873)', rev. Nilanjana Banerji, in *Oxford Dictionary of National Biography* [www.oxforddnb].

[78] John Yonge Akerman, *A Glossary of Provincial Words and Phrases in Use in Wiltshire* (London: Smith, 1842), pp. iii–iv.

[79] Akerman, *Glossary of Provincial Words and Phrases in Use in Wiltshire*, p. iv.

[80] Akerman, *Glossary of Provincial Words and Phrases in Use in Wiltshire*, p. viii.

30 The Victorians and English Dialect

this description, have set down to their task in utter ignorance of the Anglo-Saxon language.[81] Not Akerman, though: his glossary, brief though it is, is prefaced conspicuously by a table showing the Anglo-Saxon alphabet (including the use of special typographical symbols, such as 'wynn' for <w>).

Akerman, then, brings to the fore the question of Saxon origins, and uses his new learning (buttressed by Bosworth's *Dictionary*) to assert not only the antiquity of 'the dialects of the West of England', but also their dignity. Furthermore, Bosworth and Akerman were not the only people to be doing this. Richard Garnett had made a similar claim, almost in passing, in his 1836 review article, also on the grounds of a comparison between modern dialect and medieval literary evidence:

> It is worth observing that the language of Layamon—just one step removed from Anglo-Saxon—bears an unequivocal analogy to the present West of England dialect; a pretty strong proof that the distinguishing peculiarities of the latter are not modern corruptions.[82]

'Not modern corruptions' . . . 'in its least altered, most uncorrupt, and therefore in its purest state' . . . 'once the language of Bede, of Alfred, and of Aelfric'. Such statements were a forceful assertion of the historic pedigree and current worthiness of western dialects, and it was only philological learning that enabled collectors to advocate for the dignity of provincial speech in the late 1830s and early 1840s. Moreover, in making such claims, Garnett, Bosworth, and Akerman were preceding a better-known figure who was to argue along very similar lines but at greater length and to greater fame: William Barnes.

Barnes (1801–86) remains an extraordinary and important figure. Born into a farming and labouring family near Sturminster Newton in Dorset, and leaving school at 13, Barnes' self-taught appetite for learning led him, as a young man, to establish himself as a schoolteacher, first in Mere in Wiltshire and later in Dorchester, back in Dorset. In middle age he was ordained as a clergyman, and lived his later decades as rector of Winterborne Came, near Dorchester.[83] As an autodidact and polymath, as a schoolteacher, and as a clergyman, Barnes in his single self exemplifies at least three categories of dialect workers whom we shall meet repeatedly in this book. Through his poetry—to be discussed in Chapter 3—Barnes also became the most significant Dorset writer prior to Thomas Hardy (whose relation to the older man was marked by a filial piety), and his fame and influence were spread through the responses of his more national admirers, such as Alfred Tennyson and Coventry Patmore; he also enjoyed a long relationship with John Russell Smith, as the London-based publisher of many of his works.

---

[81] Akerman, *Glossary of Provincial Words and Phrases in Use in Wiltshire*, p. viii.

[82] Garnett, *Philological Essays*, p. 44 n.

[83] For biography, see Lucy Baxter, *The Life of William Barnes, Poet and Philologist* (London: Macmillan, 1887); Alan Chedzoy, *The People's Poet: William Barnes of Dorset* (Stroud: History Press, 2010); Chris Wrigley, 'Barnes, William (1801–1886)', in *Oxford Dictionary of National Biography* [www.oxforddnb].

The Pioneers   **31**

Barnes' linguistic talents were prodigious, and so we might also note—another recurrent pattern—the manner in which Barnes combines multilingual horizons with a truly intense localism. By his late thirties, Barnes had taught himself at least fourteen languages, including most European languages as well as Persian and Sanskrit.[84] But as his date of birth (1801) indicates, Barnes came from an older generation than most of the major British philologists of the nineteenth century (such as Murray and Sweet), and like Bosworth his language studies both bridged and combined the new philology with the older, less 'scientific' study of the earlier period. His linguistic thinking was thus, in different ways, both progressive and antiquated; as Thomas Hardy put it in his obituary of Barnes, 'in later years academic scholars were sometimes found to remark upon the unsystematic character of his linguistic attainments'.[85] Henry Bradley (the second editor of the *OED*) declared Barnes to have 'no acquaintance whatever' with 'the work of scientific philologists'.[86] Nonetheless, the reach of his learning was undeniably impressive: for example, his comparative *Philological Grammar* (1854), which Barnes regarded as his masterpiece, cites over sixty languages, many of them non-Indo-European, with a range of reference that foreshadows Max Müller's all-conquering *Lectures*.[87] In particular, Barnes was a prominent, and early, enthusiast for Anglo-Saxon or Old English language study: *Se Gefylsta (The Helper)* (1849) supplies a teach-yourself grammar book, complete with 'Questions Philological and Historical' at the end ('Decline guma, *man*, weak form of nouns'; 'How came *her*, from heo, *she*?'; 'Where did Alfred fight with the Danes in 866?'), and later works include *Early England and the Saxon-English* (1869).[88] In his old age, Barnes had envelopes printed bearing an Anglo-Saxon motto (*Bearnas ær Beornas*: seemingly 'Barneses before warriors'); and even in his last illness, his daughter recorded, Barnes was still talking about Alfred the Great and Dorset dialect.[89]

Barnes' eccentricity as a linguist lay not in his pioneering work on dialect, or even in his devotion to Old English, but rather in his subsequent work on Standard English. In his 1862 book *Tiw: or, a View of the Roots and Stems of the English as a Teutonic Tongue*, he advocated a distinctive theory of the 'roots' of English—perhaps not so very far away from Max Müller's views on roots in general, but by no means

---

[84] Chedzoy, *The People's Poet*, pp. 41, 46, 53, 76.

[85] Michael Millgate (ed.), *Thomas Hardy's Public Voice: The Essays, Speeches, and Miscellaneous Prose* (Oxford: Clarendon Press, 2001), p. 68.

[86] Quoted in William Barnes, *Poems in the Broad Form of the Dorset Dialect*, ed. T. L. Burton and K. K. Ruthven, Complete Poems of William Barnes I (Oxford: Oxford University Press, 2013), p. 311.

[87] Chedzoy, *The People's Poet*, pp. 131–5. On Barnes as a linguist, see, for example, Willis D. Jacobs, *William Barnes, Linguist* (Albuquerque: University of New Mexico Press, 1952); Bernard Jones, 'William Barnes, the Philological Society up to 1873 and the New English Dictionary', in Juhani Klemola, Merja Kytö, and Matti Rissanen (eds), *Speech Past and Present: Studies in English Dialectology in Memory of Ossi Ihalainen* (Frankfurt am Main: Lang, 1996), pp. 80–100, and *William Barnes: The Philological Society and the English Dialect Society* (Gillingham: Meldon House, 2010).

[88] William Barnes, *Se Gefylsta (The Helper): An Anglo-Saxon Delectus*, 2nd ed. (London: Smith, 1857), pp. 73–6. On Barnes and Anglo-Saxon, see further Burton and Ruthven, in Barnes, *Poems in the Broad Form of the Dorset Dialect*, pp. xlvi–l; Chris Jones, *Fossil Poetry: Anglo-Saxon and Linguistic Nativism in Nineteenth-Century Poetry* (Oxford: Oxford University Press, 2018), pp. 152–65.

[89] Barnes, *Poems in the Broad Form of the Dorset Dialect*, p. lxxvii, n. 116; Baxter, *The Life of William Barnes*, p. 317.

32   The Victorians and English Dialect

canonical in its details. And in several of his later works, such as *An Outline of English Speech-Craft* (1878), he espoused polemically a lexical nativism, a desire to purge foreign elements from the English vocabulary and replace them with terms generated from Anglo-Saxon resources: *rede-craft* for 'logic', *tie-stroke* for 'hyphen', and so on. Vowels are *breath-sounds*, and consonants *breath-pennings*. 'Philology' itself should become *speechlore*.[90] Such a movement for 'purism' has a long history, going back at least to the sixteenth century, but in terms of nineteenth-century philology it was a distinctly minority view.[91] As Gerard Manley Hopkins wrote to Robert Bridges: 'the madness of an almost unknown man trying to do what the three estates of the realm together could never accomplish! He calls degrees of comparison pitches of suchness: we <u>ought</u> to call them so, but alas!'[92]

But in the present context it is not Barnes' Saxon nativism that is most important, nor his theorizing about language origins, but rather his broader insistence that regional dialect was not inferior to Standard English. Indeed, more than that: in significant respects, Barnes claimed that dialect was superior. The essential text here is Barnes' 1844 'Dissertation on the Dorset Dialect of the English Language', published as an introduction to his first volume of *Poems of Rural Life, in the Dorset Dialect*. A revised version followed in 1847, and then a further essay on Dorset dialect appeared in 1863 as the introduction to Barnes' *Grammar and Glossary of the Dorset Dialect*, published by the Philological Society. Finally, a briefer account appeared in 1886, the year of Barnes' death, as part of an expanded *Glossary of the Dorset Dialect*.

We can take as our basis, though, the 1844 'Dissertation', as the first and fullest of Barnes' acts of advocacy for the Saxon dignity of his local dialect:

> The rustic dialect of Dorsetshire, as the author of this dissertation has some reason to think, is, with little variation, that of most of the western parts of England, which were included in the kingdom of the West Saxons [. . .] and has come down by independent descent from the Saxon dialect which our forefathers, the followers of Cerdic and Cynric, Porta, Stuf, and Wihtgar, brought from the south of Denmark.[93]

So Barnes begins by equating linguistic extent with political geography (and invoking Denmark and Danish as especially important). But that geography is medieval, not contemporary: Dorset dialect is roughly co-extensive with the ancient kingdom of Wessex. The reader expecting the 'Dissertation' to give an account of grammar and vocabulary might be surprised by being confronted at first by several pages of military and political history, with names and events culled from the *Anglo-Saxon Chronicle* ('The founder of the West Saxon kingdom was Cerdic, who landed, in 495, with his

---

[90] William Barnes, *An Outline of English Speech-Craft* (London: Kegan Paul and Co., 1878), p. 74.

[91] See Jacobs, *William Barnes, Linguist*; Dennis E. Baron, *Going Native: The Regeneration of Saxon English*, Publications of the American Dialect Society 69 (Tuscaloosa: University of Alabama Press, 1982), esp. pp. 27–36; Jonathan Roper, 'English Purisms', *Victoriographies* 2 (2012), 44–59; Jones, *Fossil Poetry*.

[92] Gerard Manley Hopkins, *Correspondence*, eds. R. K. R. Thornton and Catherine Phillips, 2 vols, Collected Works of Gerard Manley Hopkins I–II (Oxford: Oxford University Press, 2013), II, 551 (26–27 November 1882, deletions omitted).

[93] Barnes, *Poems in the Broad Form of the Dorset Dialect*, p. 4.

The Pioneers **33**

son Cynric [...]'); but these lead eventually to the conclusion that 'it seems likely that Dorsetshire fell under the power of the West Saxons, and received their language, the venerable parent of its present rustic dialect, with [the battle of] Salisbury, in 552'.[94]

Barnes continues: 'Having said so much of the kingdom of the West Saxons, from whose language the Dorset dialect is directly derived, the author will go on to make a few observations on its structure and features'.[95] Many of these observations are not presented in descriptive, dispassionate fashion, but are cited to serve the central argument of Barnes' 'Dissertation': the superiority of Dorset dialect to modern Standard English. The crucial notion is that of purity:

> Some people, who may have been taught to consider [Dorset dialect] as having originated from corruption of the written English, may not be prepared to hear that it is not only a separate offspring from the Anglo-Saxon tongue, but purer and more regular than the dialect which is chosen as the national speech; purer, inasmuch as it uses many words of Saxon origin for which the English substitutes others of Latin, Greek, or French derivation; and more regular, inasmuch as it inflects regularly many words which in the national language are irregular.[96]

It is, Barnes argues, the standard language which can be accused of irregularity, not Dorset dialect.

There are multiple reasons, Barnes claims, why Dorset dialect is 'purer and more regular' than Standard English (and it is hard not to feel that Barnes is throwing everything possible into this early advocacy; in his later work, by contrast, his arguments for 'purity' come to be more exclusively focused on vocabulary).[97] In Dorset dialect, for example, there is no need to reach for polysyllabic Latin words, when native monosyllables are ready at hand to do the same work (so, for instance, Barnes prefers 'Why b' ye a-cast down?' over 'Why are you dejected?')[98] But Dorset grammar, as well as Dorset word formation, is deemed to be superior too: 'many nouns have in the Dorset dialect the old plural termination *en* instead of *s*'; 'the Dorset dialect retains more than the English of the adjectives ending in *en*'; 'the Dorset dialect is remarkable as retaining in the perfect participle of verbs a *syllabic augment* which is found in Anglo-Saxon [i.e. *a-* for *ge-*]'; and so on.[99] In each instance, Barnes is making the point that it is Dorset dialect that preserves the Old English form, and modern Standard English which has changed (though it should be noted that Barnes' analysis is not always historically correct).[100] Best of all, perhaps, are the forms of the verb *to be*, which Barnes sets out in tabular form:

---

[94] Barnes, *Poems in the Broad Form of the Dorset Dialect*, pp. 5, 6.
[95] Barnes, *Poems in the Broad Form of the Dorset Dialect*, p. 6.
[96] Barnes, *Poems in the Broad Form of the Dorset Dialect*, p. 6.
[97] See Jacobs, *William Barnes, Linguist*, p. 20.
[98] Barnes, *Poems in the Broad Form of the Dorset Dialect*, p.7.
[99] Barnes, *Poems in the Broad Form of the Dorset Dialect*, pp. 8, 13, 15.
[100] See, for example, Jones, *Fossil Poetry*, p. 164 n. 106.

Dorset	*A. Saxon*	*Dorset*	*A. Saxon*
I be	Ic beo	We be	We beoð
Thee bist	Ðu byst	You be	Ge beoð
He is	He is	Thē be	Hi beoð[101]

Taking these and other differences together, Barnes dares to assert that the superiority of Dorset dialect is not only linguistic, but also aesthetic and even moral, claiming that 'from the elisions of harsh consonants, and the frequent use of the syllabic augment (*a*) in participles of verbs, the Dorset dialect has a mellowness which is sometimes wanting in the national speech; and this quality, with its purity and simplicity, makes it a good vehicle for the more tender feelings, as well as for the broader humor of rural life.'[102]

Many of these arguments, presented at length in the 1844 'Dissertation', are replayed repeatedly in Barnes' later works, though there is some evolution in terms of nuance: the 1863 essay, for example, suggests that 'we should not look for a likeness to English in Danish, so much as in Friesic, the speech of the Frieses and Angles of Slesvig and Holstein', and also gives much more attention to questions of Celtic language in the west of England; by 1886, this latter point had led to the conclusion that 'the Britons were much mingled with the English in Dorset.'[103] *Se Gefylsta*, Barnes' primer of Anglo-Saxon grammar and history, also supplements his core argument by implying a triangulation between Anglo-Saxon (Old English), modern Standard English, and Dorset dialect. For Barnes, Old English was, like Dorset dialect, 'purer and more regular' than Modern English: in terms of both grammatical and lexical change, the English language 'has not been cultivated into a better form, but has been corrupted for the worse, since King Alfred's days.'[104] The affinities between Old English and Dorset dialect combine to point up their own mutual superiority, and thus the comparative inferiority of Modern English. In the introduction to *Tiw*, Barnes declares that 'the provincial dialects are not jargons but true and good forms of Teutonic speech.'[105]

The 1844 'Dissertation' (which introduces, we should remember, Barnes' first collection of poetry) reaches its climax with a very long peroration—an exemplification of Barnes' willingness to deploy both complex syntax and an ironic tone:

As [the author] has not written for readers who have had their lots cast in town-occupations of a highly civilized community, and cannot sympathize with the rustic mind, he can hardly hope that they will understand either his poems or his intention; since with the not uncommon notion that every change from the plough

[101] Barnes, *Poems in the Broad Form of the Dorset Dialect*, p. 14.
[102] Barnes, *Poems in the Broad Form of the Dorset Dialect*, p. 18.
[103] William Barnes, *A Grammar and Glossary of the Dorset Dialect* (Berlin: Philological Society, 1863), p. 1; William Barnes, *A Glossary of the Dorset Dialect with a Grammar of its Word Shapening and Wording* (London: Trübner, 1886), p. 27. On Barnes and Frisian, see Jonathan Roper, 'William Barnes and Frisian Forefathers', *Leeds Studies in English* 43 (2012), 9–20.
[104] Barnes, *Se Gefylsta*, pp. iii–iv.
[105] William Barnes, *Tiw; or, A View of the Roots and Stems of the English as a Teutonic Tongue* (London: Smith, 1862), pp. xvii–xviii.

towards the desk, and from the desk towards the couch of empty-handed idleness, is an onward step towards happiness and intellectual and moral excellence, they will most likely find it very hard to conceive that wisdom and goodness would be found speaking in a dialect which may seem to them a fit vehicle only for the animal wants and passions of a boor; though the author is not ashamed to say that he can contemplate its pure and simple Saxon features with gratification after reading some of the best compositions of many of the most polished languages, and has heard from the pithy sentences of village patriarchs truths which he has since found expanded, in the weak wordiness of modern composition, into paragraphs.[106]

Clearly, there is a lot going on here—rural is being set against urban, oral against written, the worth of labour against the vice of leisure, and folk wisdom against writerly emptiness—and we will return to some of these issues when we examine Barnes' dialect poetry. For the present, though, what matters is Barnes' insistence on the dignity of dialect, its 'pure and simple Saxon features': as Thomas Hardy was later to summarize, Barnes' essential demonstration was that 'far from being, as popularly supposed, a corruption of correct English, it [i.e. Dorset dialect] is a distinct branch of Teutonic speech, regular in declension and conjugation.'[107] It was only philology—historicist and comparative—which could reveal this, and which could rescue dialectal varieties from condescension and scorn.

As we have seen, Barnes was not the first to argue for the ancient Anglo-Saxon dignity of west-country language—Akerman, for one, had preceded him in terms of major publications. But his advocacy soon became the best-known and most influential; Müller, for example, cited him with approval in his *Lectures on the Science of Language*, though he took a cooler view of Barnes' campaign for language reform ('the attempts of single grammarians and purists to improve language are perfectly bootless').[108] And Thomas Wright, in his 1857 *Dictionary of Obsolete and Provincial English*, informed his readers not only that 'we find in the provincial dialects [. . .] considerable numbers of old Anglo-Saxon and even Anglo-Norman words', but also that 'in many cases, as far as regards the Anglo-Saxon, [such words] are not even found in the necessarily imperfect vocabulary of the language in its pure state which we are enabled to form from its written monuments.'[109] This would seem an insight, or paradox, to gladden Barnes himself—namely, that modern regional dialects are a better witness to the Old English language than Anglo-Saxon texts themselves.

We will return to the connection between regional philology and nineteenth-century interest in Old English in a later chapter. But for now, in the light of this mid-century shift that asserted the dignity of local varieties of English, we should consider what one of the period's great popularizers of the new philology had to say on the subject of dialect—namely, Richard Chenevix Trench.

---

[106] Barnes, *Poems in the Broad Form of the Dorset Dialect*, pp. 18–19.
[107] Millgate (ed.), *Thomas Hardy's Public Voice*, p. 67.
[108] Müller, *Lectures on the Science of Language*, pp. 51 n., 66, 233, 257 n.
[109] Thomas Wright, *Dictionary of Obsolete and Provincial English* (London: Bohn, 1857), p. v.

36 The Victorians and English Dialect

Trench (1807–86) was a theologian and clergyman who later became Dean of Westminster (1856) and Archbishop of Dublin (1864).[110] He was also a prolific poet, and a well-connected man of letters. In 1851 he published *On the Study of Words*, a work which found an even greater audience than Müller's *Lectures on the Science of Language*. *On the Study of Words* communicates many of the key ideas and inquiries of nineteenth-century philology, at least with respect to vocabulary: the historical value of lexical study; the competitions and relationships within individual semantic fields; the importance of language contact. Not only ideas and inquiries, though, but also emotions: one of the most radiant features of Trench's book is his strong sense of the joy of etymology, the romance and excitement of word studies. Like Müller's, Trench's view of language is poetic, even visionary, and he sees language as the key to understanding almost everything: morality, religion, politics, even the human condition itself. 'Language is the amber', he writes, 'in which a thousand precious and subtle thoughts have been safely embedded and preserved'.[111]

Above all, Trench sees that the study of words is historicist. In a celebrated phrase, Ralph Waldo Emerson had, in 1844, described language as 'fossil poetry'.[112] It was Trench who picked up on this phrase and gave it wider currency, and in doing so he expanded the scope of Emerson's insight formidably:

> The phrase is a striking one; the only fault which one might be tempted to find with it is, that it is too narrow. Language may be, and indeed is, this 'fossil poetry'; but it may be affirmed of it with exactly the same truth that it is fossil ethics, or fossil history. Words quite as often and as effectually embody facts of history, or convictions of the moral common sense, as of the imagination or passion of men.[113]

The great comparison underlying the 'fossil poetry' idiom is of course, as Chris Jones has explored, with the burgeoning field of palaeontology—another form of Victorian engagement with the past.[114] But parallels with a further (related) historicist discipline could also be made, namely geology—with Trench declaring that 'here too are strata and deposits, not of gravel and chalk, sandstone and limestone, but of Celtic, Latin, Saxon, Danish, Norman, and then again Latin and French words'.[115] Anticipating W. H. Auden by over a century, Trench writes that 'a single word is often a concentrated

---

[110] On Trench, see Aarsleff, *The Study of Language in England*, pp. 230–47; Tony Crowley, *The Politics of Discourse: The Standard Language Question in British Cultural Debates* (Basingstoke: Macmillan, 1989), pp. 51–90; Matthew Sperling, 'Richard Chenevix Trench (1807–1886)', in Jay Parini (ed.), *British Writers XIX* (New York: Cengage Gale, 2013), pp. 317–34, and *Visionary Philology: Geoffrey Hill and the Study of Words* (Oxford: Oxford University Press, 2014), pp. 41–71; Kenneth Milnes, 'Trench, Richard Chevenix (1807–1886)', in *Oxford Dictionary of National Biography* [www.oxforddnb].

[111] Richard Chenevix Trench, *On the Study of Words. English Past and Present*, Everyman's Library 788 (London: Dent, no date of publication), p. 22.

[112] See Jones, *Fossil Poetry*, p. 5.

[113] Trench, *On the Study of Words*, p. 11.

[114] Jones, *Fossil Poetry*. See, for example, Michael Freeman, *Victorians and the Prehistoric: Tracks to a Lost World* (New Haven: Yale University Press, 2004).

[115] Trench, *On the Study of Words*, p. 46. See further, for example, Crowley, *The Politics of Discourse*, pp. 57–9; Dennis Taylor, *Hardy's Literary Language and Victorian Philology* (Oxford: Clarendon Press, 1993), pp. 281–4; Megan Perigoe Stitt, *Metaphors of Change in the Language of Nineteenth-Century Fiction: Scott, Gaskell, and Kingsley* (Oxford: Clarendon Press, 1998).

poem', and he stands as the focal point of a whole host of nineteenth-century writers and thinkers about the history of the language, from Walter Scott to Gerard Manley Hopkins.[116]

In some ways, however, Trench represents a form of philology that would soon come to look decidedly old-fashioned. For one thing, he writes throughout as a Christian moralist (his second chapter is titled 'On the Morality in Words'), and his philology would soon seem out-of-date on account of its lack of technical expertise. Trench was writing at the dawn of the discipline, and his excitement is generated almost entirely at the lexical or semantic level—words not sounds. Moreover, his core languages, for the etymologizing of English, are Latin and Greek, and not the Germanic languages, and he rarely tracks back further than the sixteenth century; so although he is a historian, Trench is no medievalist. But pretty much everyone with an interest in the English language read *On the Study of Words*, and it went through multiple editions, both before and after his death.

A sequel followed in 1855, called *English Past and Present*, and this work—unlike *On the Study of Words* itself—includes an important discussion of English dialect. The third chapter of *English Past and Present* is on 'Diminutions of the English Language' (that is, losses and extinctions), and he notes, almost in passing, that a number of words that were 'good Saxon-English once, still live on in some of our provincial dialects': his examples are *nesh, leer, eame,* and *flitter-mouse.*[117] A few paragraphs later, Trench returns to the observation, this time to pause and emphasize the principles which follow from it:

> The fact is one connected with so much of deep interest in the history of language that I cannot pass it thus slightly over. It is one which, rightly regarded, may assist to put us in a just point of view for estimating the character of the local and provincial in speech, and rescuing it from that unmerited contempt and neglect with which it is often regarded.[118]

Trench explains that linguistic divergence between two speech communities may arise from physical, geographical barriers or separation, and then he applies this explanation to English non-standard dialects:

> Nor is it otherwise in respect of our English provincialisms. It is true that our country people, who in the main employ them, have not been separated by distance of space, nor yet by insurmountable obstacles intervening, from the main body of their fellow-countrymen; but they have been quite as effectually divided by deficient education. They have been, if not locally, yet intellectually, kept at a distance from the onward march of the nation's mind.

---

[116] Trench, *On the Study of Words*, p. 13.
[117] Trench, *English Past and Present*, p. 76.
[118] Trench, *English Past and Present*, p. 78.

38   The Victorians and English Dialect

In short, speakers of dialect 'have not kept abreast with the advance of the language and nation, but have been left behind by it'.[119]

This is a fascinating, if somewhat fantastical, explanation, and whether inadvertently or not Trench is collapsing together regional dialects and class dialects, as if they are one and the same. He is also plain wrong in the implication that, once upon a time, everyone spoke the same form of English: before the emergence of a standard variety in the late medieval and early modern period, what existed was not a uniform, omnipresent language, but a whole host of regional dialects.

He continues:

> The usages are only local in the fact that, having once been employed by the whole body of the English people, they have now receded from the lips of all except those in some certain country districts, who have been more faithful than others to the traditions of the past.[120]

Again, this is far from wholly correct: while some forms that were dialectal in the nineteenth century may indeed once have been 'employed by the whole body of the English people' (as Barnes might also have argued), many forms were always dialectal, or geographically restricted. Trench's tone is perhaps rather pejorative or even patronizing: non-standard dialects are 'intellectually [. . .] at a distance'; they have been 'left behind'; they are now 'more or less antiquated and overlived'.[121] He is adamant, too, that his readers should not themselves start to use dialectal forms.

And yet, in spite of his misprisions and condescension, Trench's comments in *English Past and Present* represent an important championing of the value of dialect, a public assertion of the fundamental dignity of provincial English. Provincial varieties contain 'a multitude of isolated words, which were excellent Anglo-Saxon, which were excellent early English, and which only are not excellent present English, because use, which is the supreme arbiter in these matters, has decided against their further employment'.[122] It is nothing to do with quality, with being better or worse; only 'use'. There are thus no grounds, Trench states, for viewing dialectal words—or indeed, dialectal pronunciations, such as *contrāry*, or dialect grammar, such as 'we singen'—as inferior to Standard English. Indeed, provincial speakers, Trench asserts, in a somewhat Barnesian formulation, have been 'more faithful than others to the traditions of the past'. The dignity of the dialectal forms is vouchsafed through their antiquity. What they are not, Trench insists, are corruptions of Standard English.

Trench hammers this point home, with assertion after assertion, example after example. 'You would probably set these phrases down for barbarous English. They are not so at all'. *Afeard* is 'quite as good English' as *afraid*. *Axe* for *ask* is 'a genuine English form'. Even such apparently unacceptable phrases as 'put *them* things away' or 'The man *what* owns the horse' are, Trench declares, 'not bad, but only antiquated,

---

[119] Trench, *English Past and Present*, p. 80.
[120] Trench, *English Past and Present*, p. 80.
[121] Trench, *English Past and Present*, p. 127.
[122] Trench, *English Past and Present*, p. 80.

English'. Examples such as these 'represent past stages of the language, and are not barbarous violations of it'.[123] Provincial English, in other words, 'is often *old* English rather than *bad* English'.[124]

Again, we should pause to appreciate what a quintessentially philological insight this is, the product of new nineteenth-century attitudes to language. It was philology which brought knowledge of past states of the language, so that older forms could be recognized for what they are; but philology also helped to effect the change in values which meant that what was old was now also, *ipso facto*, venerable, and to be treasured. It was the nineteenth-century 'science of language' which rescued the dialects from scorn, and asserted not only their historicity but also their dignity and value. A further implication was that the dialects might therefore prove a rich source for the study of the past, and this is a theme that will be developed further in Chapter 5 of this book.

These were the dominant grounds on which philologists were to champion regional dialects for the rest of the century. Müller in his 1861 *Lectures* also asserted the integrity of dialects:

> It is a mistake to imagine that dialects are everywhere corruptions of the literary language. Even in England, the local patois have many forms which are more primitive than the language of Shakespeare, and the richness of their vocabulary surpasses, on many points, that of the classical writers of any period.[125]

W. W. Skeat wrote that 'in direct contradiction of a common popular error that regards our dialectal forms as being, for the most part, "corrupt", it will be found by experience that they are remarkably conservative and antique'.[126] If regional dialects are 'conservative' and 'antique', and if they differ from modern Standard English, then it follows that it must be the standard language which is new-fangled and inconsistent, not the dialects; as the phonetician Alexander Ellis pointed out, 'the elder cannot possibly be a corruption of the younger'.[127] To quote Skeat again: 'the speaker of the "standard" language is frequently tempted to consider himself as the dialect-speaker's superior, unless he has already acquired some elementary knowledge of the value of the science of language'.[128] Knowledge of philology brought linguistic humility, and rebalanced the perceptual relationship between standard and non-standard forms. For James Murray, it was Standard English which was in danger of 'corrupt[ing]' the dialects, rather than *vice versa*—a stunning reversal of earlier attitudes.[129]

---

[123] Trench, *English Past and Present*, p. 81.

[124] Trench, *English Past and Present*, p. 84.

[125] Müller, *Lectures on the Science of Language*, p. 51.

[126] Skeat, *English Dialects*, p. 9; see also p. 98.

[127] Alexander J. Ellis, 'Eleventh Annual Address of the President to the Philological Society, Delivered at the Anniversary Meeting, Friday, 19th May, 1882', *Transactions of the Philological Society* 1882–4, 1–148, at p. 21.

[128] Skeat, *English Dialects*, p. 2.

[129] James A. H. Murray, *The Dialects of the Southern Counties of Scotland: Its Pronunciation, Grammar, and Historical Relations* (London: Philological Society, 1873), p. v.

40 The Victorians and English Dialect

Similar points were later made by Elizabeth Mary Wright in her book *Rustic Speech and Folk-Lore* (1913). So, for example, in her preface Wright announces that 'dialect-speaking people obey sound-laws and grammatical rules even more faithfully than we do, because theirs is a natural and unconscious obedience'.[130] This is perhaps something of a back-handed compliment, downgrading dialect speakers from the status of self-reflective agents to that of birds or local fauna—instinctual songsters, unhampered by book learning—but the praise is heartfelt: later in her work she rhapsodizes over 'the wonderful uniformity and regularity of the sound-system of modern dialects'.[131] Similarly Wright explains that, when it comes to old words and senses, modern dialect preserves 'a wealth of historical words familiar to us in our older literature, but lost to our standard speech'.[132] But she often goes even further than this, arguing, like William Barnes, for the superiority of dialect: for example, 'it is surprising to find what a number of cases there are where a word in literary English has become corrupt, whilst in the dialects it has followed its normal development'; or 'what may sound to us [in dialect] like a perverted sense is often historically correct', so that 'it is we of the literary speech who use a word in a perverted or specialized sense'.[133] This is a reversal of earlier attitudes in quite a strange form.[134] As can be seen, Wright retains a strong sense of 'correct' and 'incorrect' usage, primarily to be judged on historical grounds: she seems to have little desire to query the principle of linguistic prescriptivism in itself, or to move towards a less prescriptive, and more descriptive, attitude towards language, as we can sometimes see James Murray doing (as in his well-known declaration that 'we do not all think alike, walk alike, dress alike, write alike, or dine alike; why should not we use our liberty in speech also [...]?').[135]

Trench was also the founding theorist for the *Oxford English Dictionary*, and in this context too his comments on dialect vocabulary were important and influential. In November 1857, shortly after it had instituted an 'Unregistered Words Committee', Trench gave a pair of lectures to the Philological Society. These were afterwards printed as a pamphlet: *On Some Deficiencies in Our English Dictionaries*. These lectures were to be crucial not only for the Philological Society's dictionary itself (that is, what became the *OED*), but also for the subsequent history of Victorian dialect study. In this manifesto, Trench expounds seven failings in prior dictionaries, and theorizes the seven actions needed to remedy them.[136] Deficiency no. 1, at the head of the list, begins by stating: 'Obsolete words are incompletely registered'.[137] Nothing could be clearer. The Society's dictionary should seek to be a dictionary not solely of contemporary English, but of past English as well: it should be philological and historicist. Of

---

[130] Elizabeth Mary Wright, *Rustic Speech and Folk-Lore* (London: Oxford University Press, 1913), p. iii.
[131] Wright, *Rustic Speech and Folk-Lore*, p. 126.
[132] Wright, *Rustic Speech and Folk-Lore*, p. 36.
[133] Wright, *Rustic Speech and Folk-Lore*, pp. 77, 84.
[134] See also, for example, Wright, *Rustic Speech and Folk-Lore*, pp. 85, 90, 91.
[135] Murray, *Caught in the Web of Words*, p. 189.
[136] See Gilliver, *The Making of the Oxford English Dictionary*, pp. 16–21.
[137] Richard Chenevix Trench, *On Some Deficiencies in Our English Dictionaries* (London: Parker and Son, 1857), p. 3.

The Pioneers **41**

his third deficiency, for example, Trench complains: 'Our Dictionaries do not always take sufficient care to mark the period of the rise of words, and where they have set, of their setting'.[138] And 'a Dictionary is an historical monument', he states, 'the history of a nation contemplated from one point of view'.[139] Trench's two lectures were not the cause of the *OED*—the project had already been launched—but they served as a founding charter, the first clear statement of the principles which would underpin it.

As for dialect words, though, Trench's view is as follows:

> Let me observe here that *provincial* or *local* words stand on quite a different footing from *obsolete*. We do not complain of their omission. In my judgment we should, on the contrary, have a right to complain if they were admitted, and it is an oversight that some of our Dictionaries occasionally find room for them, in their avowed character of provincial words; when indeed, *as such*, they have no right to a place in a Dictionary of the English tongue.[140]

He continues, returning to the argument made in *English Past and Present*:

> I have placed an emphasis on '*as such*'; for while this is so, it must never be forgotten that a word may be local or provincial now, which was once current over the whole land. There are many such, which belonging once to the written and spoken language of all England, and having free course through the land, have now fallen from their former state and dignity, have retreated to remoter districts, and there maintain an obscure existence still; citizens once, they are only provincials now. These properly find place in a Dictionary, not, however, in right of what they now are, but of what they once have been; not because they now survive in some single district, but because they once lived through the whole land.[141]

Trench's historical claims here are debatable. But his insistence that the Philological Society's dictionary should contain only those dialect words that 'once had nothing local about them' placed an impossible burden of proof on much regional vocabulary.[142] Trench's attitude to the regional dialects, both here and in *English Past and Present*, seems almost paradoxical, a strange combination of sympathy and snootiness. The sympathy came in the insistence that dialects are 'often *old* English rather than *bad* English', and hence were fully worthy of respect and study. But the snootiness came in his accompanying prescription that dialect language was in some way separate from Standard English—not to be adopted or used by speakers of Standard English, and not to be included in a dictionary of the English language.

We can see this as a pivotal moment, a proposed parting of the ways. Boucher and Halliwell had collocated the 'Provincial' and the 'Archaic' in their early attempts

---

[138] Trench, *On Some Deficiencies*, p. 22.
[139] Trench, *On Some Deficiencies*, p. 6.
[140] Trench, *On Some Deficiencies*, p. 12.
[141] Trench, *On Some Deficiencies*, p. 12.
[142] Trench, *On Some Deficiencies*, p. 14.

42 The Victorians and English Dialect

at national dictionaries (and Thomas Wright the 'Provincial' and the 'Obsolete'). Trench's intervention attempts to sever the two, with the provincial being cordoned off and kept separate from the study of Standard English. Under Trench's terms, any systematic attempt at dialect collecting and lexicography would have to be pursued outside of the grand enterprise of the Philological Society's dictionary—an enterprise which was likely to use up a high proportion of English philology's available energy. The decades-long path from Trench's *On Some Deficiencies* to the final editorial policies of James Murray's *OED* was to be by no means direct or unswerving, and, as we will see in Chapter 6, the *OED*'s policy on the inclusion or exclusion of dialect vocabulary wavered several times. Nonetheless, such a clear and influential call to exclude provincial words could hardly be beneficial for the prospects of dialect lexicography.

But for now, we must move from dignity to danger. What we have seen so far is that the rise of the new philology was the catalyst for a revaluation of English dialects. But a second, concurrent factor was also crucial, and this was the sense that these dialects were under threat. 'The local dialects are passing away': these are the opening words of Murray's *The Dialect of the Southern Counties of Scotland*, published in 1873; and such anxieties had been being expressed, with increasing urgency, for at least thirty or forty years.[143]

Barnes' 1844 'Dissertation' begins, in its first paragraph, with a warning of the dangers to dialect:

> As increasing communication among the inhabitants of different parts of England, and the spread of school education among the lower ranks of the people, tend to substitute book English for the provincial dialects, it is likely that after a few years many of them will linger only in the more secluded parts of the land, if they live at all.[144]

Such concerns can be found appearing in the 1820s and 1830s as well. So, for example, William Carr, in his *Craven Glossary* of 1824, wrote:

> Pent up by their native mountains, and principally engaged in agricultural pursuits, the inhabitants of this district had no opportunity of corrupting the purity of their language by the adoption of foreign idioms. But it has become a subject of much regret that, since the introduction of commerce, and, in consequence of that, a greater intercourse, the simplicity of the language has, of late years, been much corrupted.[145]

---

[143] Murray, *Dialect of the Southern Counties of Scotland*, p. v. See further P. J. Waller, 'Democracy and Dialect, Speech and Class', in P. J. Waller (ed.), *Politics and Social Change in Modern Britain: Essays Presented to A. F. Thompson* (Brighton: Harvester Press, 1987), pp. 1–33; Joan C. Beal, *An Introduction to Regional Englishes* (Edinburgh: Edinburgh University Press, 2010), pp. 3–5.

[144] Barnes, *Poems in the Broad Form of the Dorset Dialect*, p. 3.

[145] [William Carr], *Horæ Momenta Cravenæ, or, the Craven Dialect* (London: Hurst, Robinson, and Co., 1824), p. iv.

The Pioneers **43**

And Joseph Hunter, in his 1829 *Hallamshire Glossary*, warns that 'this process of extinction [of dialect words] is going on more rapidly at the present moment than at any former period'—and hence 'the importance that the work of collecting them should be commenced without delay'.[146] This was not just a perennial lament for a supposed golden age, always in the past: there was now hard evidence that words really were disappearing. Pishey Thompson, looking at John Ray's *English Proverbs* from 1737, discovered that 'many of the words which are mentioned as being at that time in use in Lincolnshire, have [...] "perished" within the last 120 years. No doubt this work of demolition continues, and will continue'.[147]

Carr attributes the loss of dialect to increased commerce and communication; Hunter to the spread of education. These were to be the two main reasons cited repeatedly in the nineteenth century, and it is worth looking at each of them in turn. Collectively there was a sense of a great impending loss, as of an ecosystem under threat.[148]

A poem published in 1875 articulates well this sense of threat and loss. Mary Powley's 'Difference of Opinion about our Mudder Tongue' was included in her collection *Echoes of Old Cumberland*, and imagines a local conversation in the year 1850. Powley (pronounced 'Pooley') was born in 1811 and lived in Langwathby, near Penrith in Cumberland, and she was active in her local historical society, the Cumberland and Westmorland Antiquarian and Archaeological Society, being the first woman to publish an article in its journal.[149] *Echoes of Old Cumberland* was her only book-length publication, and several of its poems turn on questions of language, especially as a route into the local past; Powley's preface explains that some of her poems 'were written to preserve in remembrance, and in their proper connection, expressive old words which seemed then in danger of being lost'.[150]

'Difference of Opinion about our Mudder Tongue' begins as follows:

> A grey-haired dweller of the dale
> With his far-travelled friend, behold;—
> In converse calm, till difference rose,—
> One lauds new things—one loves the old.

---

[146] Hunter, *Hallamshire Glossary*, p. xxvi.

[147] Thompson, *The History and Antiquities of Boston*, p. 697.

[148] See also Burton and Ruthven, in Barnes, *Poems in the Broad Form of the Dorset Dialect*, pp. lxi–lxvi.

[149] On Powley see Alexander J. Ellis, *On Early English Pronunciation, with Especial Reference to Shakspere and Chaucer*, 5 vols, Early English Text Society, Extra Series 2, 7, 14, 23, 56 (London: Philological Society, Early English Text Society, and Chaucer Society, 1869–89), V, 561–2; Robin Acland, 'Mary Powley (1811–1882)', *Cumberland and Westmorland Antiquarian and Archaeological Society Newsletter* 40 (Summer 2002), 9–10; Townend, *The Vikings and Victorian Lakeland*, p. 189, and 'The Vikings and the Victorians and Dialect', in Richard Dance, Sara Pons-Sanz, and Brittany Schorn (eds), *The Legacy of Medieval Scandinavian Encounters with England and the Insular World* (Turnhout: Brepols, forthcoming).

[150] Mary Powley, *Echoes of Old Cumberland* (London: Bemrose and Sons, 1875), p. iv.

44   The Victorians and English Dialect

> "You see, the railways, uncle, stretch
>   Across the land, from town to town,
> And equal privileges bring
>   To spots like this—once drear and lone.
>
> "They'll soften life's asperities
>   In manners—customs—where they reach;
> We soon shall hear, the kingdom through,
>   Smooth uniformity of speech."
>
> "What! Do they think to larn fwok, aw—
>   To talk alike, aw England through?
> Is Cummerland to throw away
>   Auld words like ours, for sūm 'at's new?"[151]

The first major threat to the regional dialects, then, was increased mobility, in the shape of the new railways that were criss-crossing Britain: a line reached Carlisle, near Powley's Langwathby, as early as 1836. In Powley's poem, the well-travelled interlocutor, who 'lauds new things' and speaks the standard language, enthuses how the new mobility will spread 'equal privileges' across the country and will 'soften life's asperities'. But one of the things to be softened, it seems, is regional language: rugged, local differences will disappear, and the result will be a 'smooth uniformity of speech'. The aged dialect-speaker is appalled. Why should everyone speak 'alike'? And why should Cumberland be deprived not only of 'auld words' in general, but specifically of old words that are 'ours'—a regional possession? Anne Elizabeth Baker, in Northamptonshire, had similarly pointed to 'the frequent and increasing intercourse occasioned by railroads' as the cause of dialect diminishment.[152]

The second threat to the dialects was education. As we have seen, William Barnes, writing in 1844, attributes the decline of dialect to 'the spread of school education among the lower ranks of the people'. (We should remember that Barnes himself was a schoolteacher when he wrote this. Might there, conceivably, even be an element of guilt or compensation in his promotion of dialect?) The lament of James Murray (also a schoolteacher at his time of writing) continues: '[The dialects] are passing away: even where not utterly trampled under foot by the encroaching language of literature and education, they are corrupted and arrested by its all-pervading influence, and in the same degree rendered valueless as witnesses of the usages of the past and the natural tendencies of the present'.[153] The authors of the *Holderness Glossary* assert that 'the Holderness peasant' is 'separated by lack of education, as much as by geographical remoteness', and hence 'has retained words and phrases which have elsewhere become obsolete'.[154] Education, it was agreed, was damaging,

---

[151] Powley, *Echoes of Old Cumberland*, pp. 139–40.
[152] Baker, *Glossary of Northamptonshire Words and Phrases*, I, xii.
[153] Murray, *Dialect of the Southern Counties of Scotland*, p. v.
[154] Ross, Stead, and Holderness, *A Glossary of Words Used in Holderness*, p. 4.

even destroying, the regional dialects, with a rift opening up between those who had received a modern education and those who had not.[155]

This consciousness pre-dated the 1870 Education Act, as Barnes' comments indicate; but that landmark legislation, and the other acts that followed, served to accelerate the trend, and to increase concern at the erosion of regional dialects. The 'spread of school education' led both to an awareness of generational differences, and also to situations which linguists would now label as 'diglossia'—that is, the use of two different speech varieties by the same speaker according to circumstances. Powley's dialect speaker, imagined in 1850, declares that 'We mainly talk to finer fwok [folk] / I' t'buik-wurds [book-words]'.[156] In the 1880s, another dialect collector, Fred Elworthy in Somerset, judged that 'at the present moment our people are learning two distinct tongues—distinct in pronunciation, in grammar and in syntax'.[157] And Barnes, at the end of his life, predicted that 'the old speech of the West, will be holden for some time, as the language of the house, though the children may learn English, and speak it to their betters abroad'.[158]

The best-known account of the generational shift effected by changing standards of education comes in the third chapter of *Tess of the D'Urbervilles*:

> Mrs Durbeyfield habitually spoke the dialect: her daughter, who had passed the sixth standard in the National school under a London-trained mistress, spoke two languages; the dialect at home, more or less; ordinary English abroad and to persons of quality [. . .] Between the mother, with her fast-perishing lumber of superstitions, folk-lore, dialect, and orally transmitted ballads, and the daughter, with her trained National teachings and Standard knowledge under an infinitely Revised Code, there was a gap of two hundred years as ordinarily understood. When they were together the Jacobean and the Victorian ages were juxtaposed.[159]

Again, this was not a wholly new, post-1870 phenomenon (and in any case, the precise chronological setting of *Tess*, as for many of Hardy's novels, is unclear). But by the close of the century there was a sense not just of change, but of a fundamental disruption, a chasm that was opening up between the present and the past. And when the older speakers had died, much would be lost on the far side of that chasm. Writing in 1908, Hardy looked back over the previous two decades or so:

> Education in the west of England as elsewhere has gone on with its silent and inevitable effacements, reducing the speech of this country to uniformity, and obliterating

---

[155] See further John Honey, '"Talking Proper": Schooling and the Establishment of English "Received Pronunciation"', in Graham Nixon and John Honey (eds), *An Historic Tongue: Studies in English Linguistics in Memory of Barbara Strang* (London: Routledge, 1988), pp. 209–27.

[156] Powley, *Echoes of Old Cumberland*, p. 140.

[157] Frederic Thomas Elworthy, *The West Somerset Word-Book: A Glossary of Dialectal and Archaic Words and Phrases Used in the West of Somerset and East Devon*, English Dialect Society 50 (London: English Dialect Society, 1886), p. xliv.

[158] Barnes, *A Glossary of the Dorset Dialect*, p. 34.

[159] Thomas Hardy, *Tess of the D'Urbervilles*, ed. Juliet Grindle and Simon Gatrell (Oxford: Oxford University Press, 1988), p. 26, 28. See further Simon Gatrell, *Thomas Hardy's Vision of Wessex* (London: Palgrave Macmillan, 2003), pp. 222–3.

46 The Victorians and English Dialect

every year many a fine old local word. The process is always the same: the word is ridiculed by the newly taught; it gets into disgrace; it is heard in holes and corners only; it dies; and, worst of all, it leaves no synonym.[160]

To quote again James Murray's 'General Explanations' to the *OED* (but this time extending the quotation): '"Old words" are ever becoming obsolete and dying out: "new words" are continually pressing in. And the death of a word is not an event of which the date can be readily determined. It is a vanishing process, extending over a lengthened period, of which contemporaries never see the end. Our own words never become obsolete: it is always the words of our grandfathers that have died with them'.[161]

And yet: mobility and education were not, self-evidently, harmful things in themselves—quite the opposite. The encroachment of the modern world was painful, and deleterious to the dialects; but clearly education and mobility were not to be resisted in and of themselves, let alone to be denied to dialect speakers for the sake of preserving the language. Consciousness of this could give an elegiac poignancy to the erosion of the dialects. As Hardy wrote in his 1883 essay on 'The Dorsetshire Labourer': 'It is only the old story that progress and picturesqueness do not harmonise. They [i.e. the labouring classes] are losing their individuality, but they are widening the range of their ideas, and gaining in freedom. It is too much to expect them to remain stagnant and old-fashioned for the pleasure of romantic spectators'.[162]

But was it too late to record what was disappearing? Should one despair? Max Müller struck an optimistic note:

Before there is a national language, there have always been hundreds of dialects in districts, towns, villages, clans, and families; and though the progress of civilization and centralisation tends to reduce their number and to soften their features, it has not as yet annihilated them, even in our own time.[163]

Others were less sanguine: Henry Sweet lamented in 1884 that English dialects were 'perishing fast, leaving either no record at all behind them, or at best, very imperfect ones'.[164] The obvious conclusion was that no time was to be lost. Trench in 1855 had urged his audience to collect 'provincial words and inflexions, local idioms and modes of pronunciation'. He cautioned: 'Count nothing in this kind beneath your notice. Do not at once ascribe anything to the ignorance or stupidity of the speaker'.[165] And he continued:

There is the more need to urge this at the present, because, notwithstanding the tenacity with which our country folk cling to their old forms and usages, still these forms

---

[160] Millgate (ed.), *Thomas Hardy's Public Voice*, p. 292.
[161] Murray, 'General Explanations', p. xviii.
[162] Millgate (ed.), *Thomas Hardy's Public Voice*, p. 49.
[163] Müller, *Lectures on the Science of Language*, p. 57.
[164] Sweet, *Collected Papers*, p. 50.
[165] Trench, *English Past and Present*, p. 82

The Pioneers   **47**

and usages must now be rapidly growing fewer; and there are forces, moral and mate-rial, at work in England, which will probably cause that of those which now survive the greater part will within the next fifty years have disappeared.[166]

Fifty years to record the dialects—the half-century which Tolkien was to term the 'philological epoch'.

J. C. Atkinson: the philological turn

We will end this chapter by looking at one particular collector who, in the 1850s and 1860s, was doing exactly what Trench had urged: the Rev. John Christopher Atkinson (1814–1900).

Atkinson was born in Essex, and educated at Cambridge. In 1847, in his early thir-ties, he became vicar of the parish of Danby, on the North York Moors. And there he was to stay for the next fifty years, where, as one obituarist put it, 'he loved his parish as a lofty patriot might love his country, in no provincial or parochial spirit, but with a liberal and enlightened affection'.[167] He was married three times, with fourteen children and multiple grandchildren (one of whom, Edward L. Atkinson, took command of Captain Scott's polar expedition after Scott's death). He had a wide range of interests, and his extensive writings include natural history and fic-tion as well as dialect and antiquarianism (and we will examine some of his fiction in Chapter 5).[168] William Sheils has studied Atkinson's career and convictions as a minister ('socially conservative but theologically liberal'), and has argued that Atkin-son may have viewed his own record as vicar, at a difficult time for the Established Church, with a sense of disappointment or even failure.[169]

In 1891, when he was in his mid-seventies, Atkinson published *Forty Years in a Moorland Parish*, immediately acclaimed as a classic of folkloric antiquarianism; and the fame of *Forty Years* has since occluded Atkinson's other activities and distinc-tions. As we will see later in this book, there was often a close connection between folklore and philology; but to Atkinson's contemporaries, for most of his career, he was known primarily as a philologist and antiquary rather than a folklorist. When he was awarded an honorary doctorate at Durham University in 1887, this was given in recognition of his 'life-long researches in archaeology and of his books of eminent

---

[166] Trench, *English Past and Present*, p. 83.

[167] Alice Stopford Green, 'Canon Atkinson: Scholar, Thinker, and Lover of the Country', *The Bookman* May 1900, 49–51, at p. 50. On Atkinson, see Tom Scott Burns, *Canon Atkinson and his Country* (Leeds: Rigg, 1986); William Joseph Sheils, 'Church, Community and Culture in Rural England, 1850–1900: J. C. Atkinson and the Parish of Danby in Cleveland', in Simon Ditchfield (ed.), *Christianity and Community in the West: Essays for John Bossy* (Aldershot: Ashgate, 2001), pp. 260–77, 'Nature and Modernity: J. C. Atkinson and Rural Ministry in England c. 1850–1900', in Peter Clarke and Tony Claydon (eds), *God's Bounty? The Churches and the Natural World* (Woodbridge: Boydell and Brewer, 2010), pp. 366–95, and 'Atkinson, John Christopher (1814–1900)', in *Oxford Dictionary of National Biography* [www.oxforddnb]; and Michael Stainsby, *More than an Ordinary Man: Life and Society in the Upper Esk Valley, 1830–1910* (Helmsley: North York Moors National Park Authority, 2006).

[168] For bibliography, see Burns, *Canon Atkinson and his Country*, pp. 100–12.

[169] Sheils, 'Nature and Modernity', p. 395.

48 The Victorians and English Dialect

value on natural history and also on philology in reference to some of the ancient dialects of England.[170] More briefly, when he was granted a Civil List pension a decade later, in 1898, this was simply 'in recognition of the value of his philological writings and researches.'[171]

Atkinson's 1868 *Glossary of the Cleveland Dialect* is one of the great Victorian dialect glossaries, and it was undertaken and printed, he said, 'in the cause of philology.'[172] Atkinson was self-taught as a linguist, having studied Mathematics at Cambridge (gaining a First), and we should remember that when he was undertaking his core dialectal research, in the 1850s and 1860s, the study of English philology was still at the pre-university stage. At some point Atkinson made the acquaintance of F. J. Furnivall, long-serving secretary of the Philological Society and a prime mover of the *OED*, and he also corresponded with James Murray; but these contacts seem to have arisen subsequent to his core period of research, through membership of the Philological Society and publication of his *Cleveland Glossary*.[173] Viewed in retrospect, the *Glossary of the Cleveland Dialect* can look like the start of Atkinson's public career as a scholar; and later works included several editions of medieval records, a number of volumes on the history of Whitby, and an incomplete *History of Cleveland*. But when the *Glossary* was published, Atkinson was already in his fifties—it was by no means the work of a junior or apprentice scholar.

W. W. Skeat wrote that 'the man who has been educated to use the language of books [. . .] finds that the dialect-speaker frequently uses words or modes of expression which he does not understand.'[174] Atkinson's Cleveland *Glossary* arose directly from this circumstance. As he recalled in his introduction, two decades after his arrival in Danby:

> The difficulties and whimsicalities attendant on the efforts after mutual comprehension between myself and the countryside northerners, with whom my clerical and other duties brought me into continual contact, were great enough, and often amply quaint enough, of themselves to induce, even had there been no natural liking and inclination, some notice of the circumstances in which our mutual complications originated. I did not comprehend their spoken dialect, and they did not understand my Southern English and pronunciation: and the reason was, not only that a very large proportion of their stock of current words, and especially in the case of elderly and

---

[170] Burns, *Canon Atkinson and his Country*, pp. 70–1.

[171] *The Times* 16 July 1898.

[172] J. C. Atkinson, *A Glossary of the Cleveland Dialect: Explanatory, Derivative, and Critical* (London: Smith, 1868), p. v.

[173] See John James Munro (ed.), *Frederick James Furnivall: A Volume of Personal Record* (Oxford: Oxford University Press, 1911), pp. 106–7; Benzie, *Dr F. J. Furnivall*, pp. 152–3; Atkinson, *Glossary of the Cleveland Dialect*, p. vi; Oxford, Bodleian Library, MS Murray 1/2, Folder 1 (letters from J. C. Atkinson to James Murray). On Furnivall, see further Munro (ed.), *Frederick James Furnivall*; Benzie, *Dr F. J. Furnivall*; Derek Pearsall, 'Frederick James Furnivall (1825–1910)', in Helen Damico (ed.), *Medieval Scholarship: Biographical Studies on the Formation of a Discipline. Volume 2: Literature and Philology* (New York: Garland, 1998), pp. 125–38; Richard Utz, 'Enthusiast or Philologist? Professional Discourse and the Medievalism of Frederick James Furnivall', *Studies in Medievalism* 11 (2001), 189–212; William S. Peterson, 'Furnivall, Frederick James (1825–1910)', in *Oxford Dictionary of National Biography* [www.oxforddnb].

[174] Skeat, *English Dialects from the Eighth Century to the Present Day*, p. 1.

The *Glossary of the Cleveland Dialect* was published more than twenty years after Atkinson's arrival at Danby, and more than ten years after he had embarked on a systematic survey of the dialect. Atkinson was a member of the clergy, and also an 'off-comer' to the Danby region. Both of these characteristics were paradigmatic: as part of their day-to-day commitments, local clergymen interacted with dialect speakers more regularly and closely than arguably any other group within the educated professional classes, and did so over a sustained period of time; and (as we will see repeatedly) many collections or celebrations of local dialect were made by workers who were not themselves natives of the places they studied.[176]

The publication of Atkinson's Cleveland *Glossary* was preceded (but only just) by a summarizing paper to the Philological Society in 1867 (the year in which Atkinson was elected a member), and followed by a similar paper to the Ethnological Society of London in 1870.[177] But it is the 1868 *Glossary* which is the core publication, and which we can here examine as an eloquent indication of what exactly the 'philological turn' meant for dialect study. Locally, Atkinson's most important predecessor was the Whitby pharmacist and antiquary Francis Kildale Robinson (1809–82), whose *Glossary of Yorkshire Words and Phrases, Collected in Whitby and the Neighbourhood* was published in 1855 by John Russell Smith. This was a valuable work—to be enlarged and republished twenty years later for that very reason. But the individual entries in Robinson's *Glossary* are simple: he gives only a terse definition and, for many but not all words, a brief unattributed quotation to illustrate contemporary usage. There is, thus, no historical dimension. So a typical entry reads as follows:

BELLY-TIMBER, food.[178]

And that is it—all one learns about the word. Let us contrast such brevity with the comparable entry in Atkinson's *Glossary*:

> **Belly-timber**, sb. Food; a supply of material for the belly or stomach.
> A. S. *timbrian* is employed in a metaphorical way which is worthy of notice, and gives point to the accommodation existing in our word—'to prepare wood for building; to build with

---

[175] Atkinson, *Glossary of the Cleveland Dialect*, p. ix.

[176] See Jonathan Roper, 'The Clergyman and the Dialect Speaker: some Sussex examples of a nineteenth century research tradition', in Laura Wright (ed.), *Southern English Varieties Then and Now* (Berlin: De Gruyter, 2018), pp. 110–31.

[177] J. C. Atkinson, 'On the Dialect of Cleveland in the North Riding of Yorkshire', *Transactions of the Philological Society* 1867, 326–57; J. C. Atkinson, 'On the Danish Element in the Population of Cleveland, Yorkshire', *Journal of the Ethnological Society of London* 2 (1869–70), 351–66; see also J. C. Atkinson, 'On the Danish Aspect of the Local Nomenclature of Cleveland', *Journal of the Anthropological Institute of Great Britain and Ireland* 3 (1874), 115–20.

[178] [F. K. Robinson], *A Glossary of Yorkshire Words and Phrases, Collected in Whitby and the Neighbourhood* (London: Smith, 1855), p. 12.

50 The Victorians and English Dialect

timber or wood; the first building being probably of wood: hence, generally, to build, to erect. From this the sense passes to that of *building up the mind*; to instruct, to edify'. The transition of idea in **Belly-timber** is not nearly so startling as in the notion of *mind-timbering*. Comp. also the following, *Flat.* ii.11:—'*Gerdizst ok suo at fullkomliga framkuæmduzst ord ok atquæde þessa goda guds astuinar Olafs konungs Trygguasonar at hans samnafne Olafr Haralldzson upp* TIMBRADE *þat sama smide hæilagrar truar sem adr var giftuliga grunduallat:*' and so it came to pass that fully accomplished was the word and saying of the good God's fast friend King Olaf Tryggvason, that his namesake Olaf Haraldsson built up the same fabric (literally, *timbered* up the same smith-work) of Holy Faith, of which had the foundation before been happily laid. Comp. also '*timbrunge* touward blisse'. *Ancr. Riwle*, p. 124.[179]

The difference is overwhelming. Atkinson not only gives grammatical information ('sb.' = substantive, or noun) and a fuller definition; he also offers a lengthy disquisition on the word, motivated by historical principles. He gives citations or parallels in three medieval languages, Old English or Anglo-Saxon ('A. S.'), Middle English (the thirteenth-century text *Ancrene Riwle*, now better known as *Ancrene Wisse*), and Old Norse (*Flateyjarbók*, a fourteenth-century compendium of sagas). He is, moreover, interested in semantic change over time—not just in the various meanings attested, but in how such meanings may most plausibly have evolved one from another.

Let us take a second example. Here is another entry from Robinson's *Glossary*:

LANDLOUPER, an adventurer; one who goes from place to place, gains the confidence of the community, and then elopes without paying his debts.[180]

And here is the entry for the same word from Atkinson's *Glossary*:

Landlouper, sb. One who flies the country to escape his debtors or the penalty of his crimes; thence one who leaves any part of the country without paying the debts he owes in it [. . .]

O. N. *land-hlaupari*, a vagabond, a wandering knave; Dan. *landløber*, a vagrant, one with no fixed residence.

'Get I those *land lepars* I breke ilka bone:' *Townel. Myst.* p. 144;
where the word is applied to Joseph and Mary when they fled with 'the young child' into Egypt.

'None renneris aboute,

Ne no *leperis* ouer *lond*· Ladies to shryue'.

P. Ploughm. (E. E. T. S.) p. 132.[181]

---

[179] Atkinson, *Glossary of the Cleveland Dialect*, p. 40.
[180] [Robinson], *Glossary of Yorkshire Words and Phrases, Collected in Whitby*, p. 100.
[181] Atkinson, *Glossary of the Cleveland Dialect*, p. 304.

As before for *belly-timber*, Atkinson supplies an etymology (from Old Norse); but here he also adds a cognate or parallel from contemporary Danish. Also as before, he attempts to understand the semantic evolution of the word ('thence'), and to put the meanings in chronological order. But here, additionally, he gives illustrative quotations for the word—from medieval texts, however, not current Cleveland usage. These are the Towneley mystery plays (fifteenth-century, probably from Wakefield in west Yorkshire) and *Piers Plowman* (fourteenth-century, from the West Midlands). For these texts he gives precise page-references, from up-to-date editions. The text of *Piers Plowman* from which Atkinson is quoting was edited by W. W. Skeat for the Early English Text Society (a society founded by Furnivall in 1864), and only published in 1867—a point which will be returned to shortly.[182]

Robinson's word list is 202 pages in length and includes about 2680 words. Atkinson's word list is 590 pages in length (and larger pages, too, in smaller type) and includes about 3920 words. What makes the difference, then, as can be seen from the two examples above, is the scale of treatment that each word receives—it is not simply the case that Atkinson contains more words. It is as if, all of a sudden, there is just so much that one can say about, and learn about, every word—the provision of a definition alone would by no means suffice.

Let us take one more entry, this time not to demonstrate questions of language but rather those of locality (and without a precedent in Robinson, for reasons which will be obvious):

> **Beacon**, sb. A name applied to the highest hill on the Danby North Moors, and of remote imposition.
>
> A. S. *beacen, beacn, becen*, a sign, token. '*Cneorisse yflo and árg soecas becon: and hire ne bið nán becon gesald, buta Jones becon ðæs witgo;*' literally, a generation evil and arf seeks a sign, and to it there to no sign given be-out Jonah's sign the prophet. The beacon-fire was lighted as a token or sign, of an attack or invasion, suppose; and thence the word became applied to the fire itself, or that which contained or supported the fire. Cf. *Pr. Pm.* '*Beekne, or fyrebome. Far, Pharus*'. 'Danby Beacon'—in Danby itself, 'T' Beacon'—a Celtic tumulus of large dimensions originally: and it is quite possible that it may have been the site of sacrificial fires (see **Bally-bleeze**) long ages before it received the Saxon epithet *beacon*.[183]

Like many other dialect collectors, Atkinson is here blurring the lines between the study of dialect vocabulary and the study of minor place names: both reflect, and record, local linguistic usage. As usual, the entry for *beacon* (or *Beacon*?) gives an etymology, and a parallel from medieval texts (here, the Northumbrian gloss to the Lindisfarne Gospels, and the fifteenth-century *Promptorium Parvulorum*, both of which had recently been edited). But what is conspicuous in this entry is the intense

---

[182] On the Early English Text Society, see Benzie, *Dr F. J. Furnivall*, pp. 117–57; Charlotte Brewer, *Editing Piers Plowman: the evolution of the text*, Cambridge Studies in Medieval Literature 28 (Cambridge: Cambridge University Press, 1996), pp. 65–90; Matthews, *The Making of Middle English*, pp. 138–61; Antony Singleton, 'The Early English Text Society in the Nineteenth Century: An Organizational History', *Review of English Studies* New Series 56 (2005), 90–118.

[183] Atkinson, *Glossary of the Cleveland Dialect*, p. 34.

52 The Victorians and English Dialect

localism of both the definition and the discussion—the word is localized not sim-ply to Cleveland in general, but to a particular spot in the Danby area, Atkinson's own parish (and cross-reference elsewhere in Atkinson's *Glossary* reveals that *arf* means 'afraid or fearful; reluctant, backward', while *bally-bleeze* is 'a bonfire').[184] The explanation is not merely topographical, though; it is antiquarian also, reaching back speculatively beyond the accession of Germanic speech to the Celtic world and possi-ble practices of sacrifice. So this entry shows us how the new dialect study of workers such as Atkinson, undertaken in the 1850s and 1860s, could combine the linguis-tic with the antiquarian within its overall historicist world view and method—and could at the same time be both philologically and chronologically wide-ranging and also highly localized and specific. We are surely not wrong also to perceive a note of pride or affection in Atkinson's familiar designation of 'T' Beacon', and this entry is not unusual in the *Glossary* as a whole: one learns a great deal from its entries about the local places and practices of Danby parish—anticipating the more famous *Forty Years* by over two decades.

So much for the entries themselves. But Atkinson's six-hundred-page word list is preceded by fifty tightly packed pages of introductory matter, and this also enables us to see very clearly what was distinct about the philological approach to dialect study. Robinson's 1855 forerunner, by comparison, has a five-and-a-half-page preface. This is modest in tone and scope, leaving to 'abler hands' the full study of the dialect, but noting anxiously that 'provincial peculiarities are fast disappearing before the advancement of an assimilating intelligence, and the effects of a rapid and universal communication'.[185]

Atkinson's introduction has the customary sense of loss and fragility (a railway had reached part of his parish in 1861, and Danby itself in 1865).[186] 'It is a com-mon remark among many of the more intelligent of the Cleveland Dalesmen', he writes, 'when led to speak on the subject, that their dialect has lost not only sensibly but very considerably within their own recollection—a fact that I am myself able to bear personal testimony to'.[187] But this lament is not the main substance of Atkinson's introduction—indeed, the observation is only made in a footnote. What fills the pages instead is an exercise in sustained historical reconstruction, followed by detailed linguistic analysis. Atkinson begins with language—of course—but, in classic philo-logical style, language acts as a doorway into larger historical explorations. Here, those explorations are into the Scandinavian contribution to Cleveland's history and inheritance: Atkinson's realization of the Old Norse origins of much Cleve-land dialect leads him on into an investigation of Scandinavian elements in local place-names, in Domesday Book, and in medieval personal names.[188] Dialect is the evidence that unlocks the local past; and as we will see in Chapter 5, Atkinson was by no means the only worker who was excited to uncover his region's Viking heritage.

---

[184] Atkinson, *Glossary of the Cleveland Dialect*, pp. 9, 26–7.
[185] [Robinson], *Glossary of Yorkshire Words and Phrases, Collected in Whitby*, pp. vi, viii.
[186] See Stainsby, *More than an Ordinary Man*, pp. 23–45.
[187] Atkinson, *Glossary of the Cleveland Dialect*, p. xxv n.
[188] See further Townend, 'The Vikings and the Victorians and Dialect'.

Then in the second half of the introduction Atkinson returns more narrowly to linguistic questions: whether the definite article (*the* or *t'*) has an English or Norse origin; the high number of Norse loanwords among functional parts of speech such as prepositions and adverbs; and whether Cleveland dialect has an especially close parallel in the dialect of Jutland. 'In all the particulars specified', Atkinson concludes, 'the Cleveland dialect is indebted to the Old Danish tongue, and, in a marked manner and no small degree, to the Jutland forms in particular'.[189]

Most remarkable in this section, though, is the word-counting that Atkinson undertakes. He reports that, in order to assay his local vocabulary, he has carefully scrutinized a series of medieval texts, word by word, to discover the proportion of vocabulary shared with Cleveland dialect. The texts examined (as seen in the examples given above) include *Ancrene Wisse*, *Piers Plowman*, the Towneley plays, and also Layamon's *Brut*: many thousands of lines of dominantly Middle English writing which Atkinson has worked his way through—quite apart from Old English and Old Norse texts as well. The labour involved is extraordinary, in the counting of words and calculation of percentages. The point to stress, in terms of method and orientation, is how thoroughly medievalist this enterprise is—how closely Atkinson's dialect studies are tied up with new, contemporary investigations into Old and Middle English and Old Norse. For Atkinson, the study of present-day dialect and the study of medieval languages go hand in hand; indeed, they are the same thing. The best comparative materials for understanding the dialect are medieval materials, not contemporary ones, and the specific conclusion is that Cleveland dialect, compared to Standard English, is very often archaic.

This extensive programme of collation also draws attention to Atkinson's reading, and his access to materials. In his preface, Atkinson presents an image of himself as a solitary but devoted scholar—'working alone and unassisted [. . .] in a singularly remote district, far from any accessible collection of books which might have been of aid'.[190] But it is clear that the contents of his library, or at least the books he was able to access one way or another, were formidable—and this can give us a good sense of what works were available to the regional philologist in the 1850s and 1860s. From his list of abbreviations and other references, we can see that Atkinson was just as well supplied with dictionaries and grammars of Icelandic, Swedish, Danish, and Norwegian—and Scandinavian dialects—as he was of Old and Middle English (and of course he was reading these and other works of Scandinavian scholarship in their original languages, not in translation). He was also thoroughly up-to-date, as we have seen, with the latest editions of medieval texts—and again, for Old Norse as well as Old and Middle English. He was familiar with major scholarship, from Jacob Grimm's *Deutsche Mythologie* to Max Müller's lectures on language.[191] Atkinson's

---

[189] Atkinson, *Glossary of the Cleveland Dialect*, p. xxxiii.
[190] Atkinson, *Glossary of the Cleveland Dialect*, p. v.
[191] See Atkinson, *Glossary of the Cleveland Glossary*, pp. xlvii–liv.

54 The Victorians and English Dialect

reading, far away up on the North York Moors, was extensive, international, and up-to-the-minute; his provincial location proved no hindrance to being contemporary and connected.[192]

As observed previously, the fame of Atkinson's later work, *Forty Years in a Moorland Parish*, has served to eclipse the memory of his earlier publications. But his fellow workers immediately recognized his *Glossary of the Cleveland Dialect* as a brilliant and monumental piece of work, and for the rest of the century it held its place as one of the key reference points in dialect lexicography. Atkinson also found himself in demand as the executor of other scholars' work, as the Philological Society turned to him to bring to publication the incomplete *Glossary of the Dialect of the Hundred of Lonsdale* (in north Lancashire) by Robert Backhouse Peacock. F. J. Furnivall memorialized his fellow lawyer Peacock (who died in 1864) as one of the very best contributors to the Philological Society's dictionary (that is, the *OED*) in the early days of the project.[193] At Furnivall's encouragement, Peacock switched from reading general books for the dictionary to collecting provincialisms, and what he soon became interested in was etymology and historical grammar: what proportion of Lonsdale words and constructions were from Old English, what proportion from Old Norse, or from Celtic. The firstfruits of Peacock's work was a long essay 'On Some Leading Characteristics of Northumbrian; and on the Variations in its Grammar from that of Standard English, with their Probable Etymological Sources', produced in 1863; but his much lengthier word list was unfinished, or at least unrevised, at the time of his death the following year.[194] Furnivall came and went as an editor, as did Hensleigh Wedgwood—philologist and lexicographer, and brother-in-law of Charles Darwin—before Atkinson was approached to finish the job.[195]

J. C. Atkinson's *Dialect of the Glossary of Cleveland*, and associated activity such as his editing of Peacock's work, can therefore stand as a strong representative example of the kind of word-based, philological approach to dialect study that had come to prominence in the 1860s; and in Chapter 4 we shall return to this strand of research to see how it developed in the 1870s and 1880s. But before we do that, there are two other issues to be considered, which will form the subject of the next two chapters.

One of these is a parallel engagement with dialect that was going on between the 1840s and 1870s, alongside the work of pioneering glossarists such as Atkinson. At one point in his *Cleveland Glossary*, Atkinson comments on the use of dialect in Elizabeth Gaskell's novel *Sylvia's Lovers*, published only a few years earlier in 1863.

---

[192] See also John Plotz, 'The Provincial Novel', in Stephen Arata et al (eds), *A Companion to the English Novel* (Oxford: Wiley Blackwell, 2015), pp. 360–72, esp. pp. 369–71.

[193] Frederick J. Furnivall, 'Prefatory Notice', in Robert Backhouse Peacock, *A Glossary of the Dialect of the Hundred of Lonsdale, North and South of the Sands, in the County of Lancaster* (London: Philological Society, 1869), pp. iii–vi, at p. iii.

[194] Robert Backhouse Peacock, 'On Some Leading Characteristics of Northumbrian; and on the Variations in its Grammar from that of Standard English, with their Probable Etymological Sources', *Transactions of the Philological Society* 1862–3, 232–63 (title expanded on republication to 'On Some Leading Characteristics of the Dialects Spoken in the Six Northern Counties of England (or Ancient Northumbria)').

[195] On Wedgwood, see C. H. Herford, 'Wedgwood, Hensleigh (1803–1891)', rev. John D. Haigh, in *Oxford Dictionary of National Biography* [www.oxforddnb].

The Pioneers   55

'The dialect in *Sylvia's Lovers*', he writes, 'the scene of which is supposed to be laid in or near Whitby, would certainly not recommend its speaker to the kindly notice of the Dalesmen as a fellow-Clevelander'.[196] In this brief remark, we can recognize not only that Victorian novelists were active in using regional dialect in their fictions (of course), but also that the dialect representations of such novelists did not always meet with approval from contemporary scholars. The connection between dialect and literature therefore—poetry as well as prose—and the effects of philology on creative practice, will be the subject of Chapter 3, after we have looked at another pressing issue.

This is the question of pronunciation and phonetics. Some six hundred pages of Atkinson's mighty *Glossary* are taken up with the word list, but pronunciation—the sounds of the dialect—receive less than three pages of explicit attention in the fifty-page introduction. Even these three pages only occur right at the end, and they have a singularly diffident tone: Atkinson suggests that 'a few remarks upon the vowel and consonant sounds may, perhaps, be not quite uncalled for'.[197] An example of such remarks is as follows:

> *O* has five sounds:—
> 1. Long, as *eea* dissyllable; the *ee* as in 'feet', but with a quick impulse of the voice, the *a* as in *missal*, or the short *a* at the end of Latin words; as stone, **steean**, bone, **beean**, &c.
> 2. Short, as in 'hot'.
> 3. Before *r*, as with *i* before *r*, when the sound is as in 'word', not in 'lord'.
> 4. Long, before *l*, as *au*, suppressing the consonant, as **cau'd**, **bau'd**, for 'cold', 'bold'.
> 5. Short before *l*, as in 'sod', suppressing the consonant, as **ho'd** for 'hold'.[198]

There are some careful distinctions being made here, but Atkinson is not at his clearest, and the difficulty he is struggling under is the lack of some sort of phonetic notation or alphabet to communicate unambiguously the sounds he wishes to indicate. But in the 1860s and 1870s there arose a whole other class of dialectologist for whom it was precisely the sounds that were important, not the words, and for whom the use of phonetic alphabets was second nature; and it is to their work that we will turn in the next chapter.

---

[196] Atkinson, *Glossary of the Cleveland Dialect*, p. xxxv.
[197] Atkinson, *Glossary of the Cleveland Dialect*, p. xlii.
[198] Atkinson, *Glossary of the Cleveland Dialect*, p. xliii.

2
The Phoneticians

The study of sounds

The most famous phonetician of the Victorian and Edwardian period is a fictional one: Henry Higgins in George Bernard Shaw's *Pygmalion* (first staged in 1913). When we encounter Higgins for the first time, the stage directions state that he has his back turned from a group on whom he is eavesdropping, 'wholly preoccupied with a notebook in which he is writing'.[1] He reveals himself to have a Sherlock Holmes-like trick of being able to deduce the life history of new acquaintances ('Brought up in Hounslow. Mother Welsh, I should think'), amply justifying his famous boast that 'I can place any man within six miles. I can place him within two miles in London. Sometimes within two streets'.[2] And although he has some interest in vocabulary, it is the sounds of speech, and above all vowels, which are at the heart of his endeavours. When Eliza, overwhelmed at the start of Act I, wails 'Ah-ah-ah-ow-ow-ow-oo!', Higgins whips out his notebook: 'Heavens! What a sound! [*He writes; then holds out the book and reads, reproducing her vowels exactly*] Ah-ah-ah-ow-ow-ow-oo!'[3] There is no-one to compete with Higgins: Pickering, his new friend and conspirator, quickly declares himself defeated ('I rather fancied myself because I can pronounce twenty-four distinct vowel sounds; but your hundred and thirty defeat me. I can[']t hear a bit of difference between most of them').[4]

The early studies that we considered in the previous chapter were all dominantly word-based, and usually organized in alphabetical order. A recurrent dilemma for many glossarists was whether or not to include words which differed in pronunciation from Standard English but were not semantically distinct. It may be recalled that some examples of George Cornewall Lewis' type 4 (in 1839) fell into this category, of 'Words substantially the same as words current in the language of educated persons, but modified in form'.[5] Did a different, or distinctively regional, accent turn a word—any word—into an item of dialect vocabulary, or did the word itself, as a lexical item, need to be restricted or localized in order to qualify?

This is not to say that, among the pioneers, there was a lack of interest in pronunciation as opposed to vocabulary. Some early glossaries did address sounds as well as words. *A View of the Lancashire Dialect* (1746) by John Collier (1708–86),

---

[1] George Bernard Shaw, *Pygmalion: A Romance in Five Acts* (London: Penguin, 2000), p. 9.
[2] Shaw, *Pygmalion*, pp. 41, 17.
[3] Shaw, *Pygmalion*, p. 18
[4] Shaw, *Pygmalion*, p. 24.
[5] [Lewis], *Glossary of Provincial Words used in Herefordshire*, p. vi.

The Victorians and English Dialect. Matthew Townend, Oxford University Press. © Matthew Townend (2024).
DOI: 10.1093/oso/9780198888123.003.0003

58 The Victorians and English Dialect

writing under the pseudonym of 'Tim Bobbin', begins with a set of 'Observations' on the subject ('The following Observations may be useful to those who are Strangers to the Lancashire Pronunciation').[6] Joseph Hunter's *Hallamshire Glossary* contained an appendix by the Rev. John Watson on the dialect of Halifax (reprinted from a 1775 publication), and this begins with a series of 'Rules for Pronunciation':

> Rule 1st. After oo add an i, pronouncing brisk, which will give the usual sound in the following monosyllables: for soon, sooin; for noon, nooin [...]
> Rule 8th. The letter o is frequently changed into a, as belangs for belongs, lang for long [...]
> Rule 17th. Letters are frequently transposed, as girn for grin, skrimish for skirmish.[7]

Elsewhere in the country, Robert Forby's posthumous *Vocabulary of East Anglia* of 1830 included a lengthy introductory essay 'On the principal characteristics of East Anglian Pronunciation'.[8] And as we saw in the previous chapter, James Orchard Halliwell's 1847 essay on 'The Provincial Dialects of England' also commented on dialect pronunciation, county by county. Moreover, Richard Chenevix Trench, in his 1855 call to arms, urged his listeners and readers to collect not just 'provincial words and inflexions', but also 'local idioms and modes of pronunciation'.[9] But we can also see that, in the first half of the nineteenth century, the tools had not yet been properly developed to enable this type of work, either conceptually or technically. John Watson talks about 'letters' rather than 'sounds', and he needs to proceed by analogy and circumlocution. The absence of a suitable phonetic alphabet or notation, as we have just seen, can also be observed in J. C. Atkinson's *Cleveland Glossary*.

By the time we come to *Pygmalion*, however, and to the fictional Henry Higgins—dedicated to 'the science of speech', as he calls it—more than half a century of dedicated phonetic study had revolutionized the situation.[10] The discipline's origins, in the 1840s, are intertwined with those of spelling reform, shorthand notation, and elocution.[11] Isaac Pitman (1813–97), with his innovative system of shorthand, is one of the giant figures here, but even more important for the present story is Alexander Melville Bell (1819–1905, and father of Alexander Graham Bell, inventor of the telephone).[12] Melville Bell's 'Visible Speech Alphabet' of 1867 was a landmark in phonetic notation, hailed by W. W. Skeat as 'singular and wonderful' and by Henry Sweet

---

[6] [John Collier], *The Works of Tim Bobbin, Esq. in Prose and Verse* (Manchester: Heywood, 1862), pp. xxxi–xxxii.

[7] Hunter, *Hallamshire Glossary*, pp. 131–4.

[8] Robert Forby, *The Vocabulary of East Anglia; an attempt to record the vulgar tongue of the twin sister counties, Norfolk and Suffolk, as it existed in the last twenty years of the eighteenth century, and still exists; with proof of its antiquity from etymology and authority*, 2 vols (London: Nichols and Son, 1830), I, 76–119.

[9] Trench, *English Past and Present*, p. 82.

[10] Shaw, *Pygmalion*, p. 17.

[11] On nineteenth-century elocution, see Lynda Mugglestone, *'Talking Proper': The Rise of Accent as Social Symbol*, 2nd ed. (Oxford: Oxford University Press, 2007).

[12] See Tony D. Triggs, 'Pitman, Sir Isaac (1813–1897)', in *Oxford Dictionary of National Biography* [www.oxforddnb].

as being 'of priceless value'.[13] Visible Speech uses what has been termed an 'organic-iconic' system, in which each symbol supposedly represents the articulatory shape of the mouth; it does not employ alphabetic notation, whether Roman or otherwise.[14]

But although their origins are intertwined, it is important to distinguish between advocacy for spelling reform and the development of an agreed phonetic alphabet: it was possible to take an interest in the one without following the other; and they were, moreover, only part of the overall interest in phonetics in the nineteenth century. But dialect posed a special set of challenges, and it is worth reflecting on these by way of preface. To begin with, one couldn't really talk about spelling reform for varieties that had scarcely, if ever, been written down; in effect, what one was devising was a spelling system from scratch. But since in Standard English the spelling and pronunciation of many words had diverged from one another on account of English spelling having become fixed while pronunciation continued to change, it was inevitable that the brand-new representation of dialect in written form was likely to use a more phonetic spelling system than Standard English—even when writers simply used the resources of the Roman alphabet, with no additions.[15]

We can view this challenge from the other side as well. How should dialect words be communicated to those who had never encountered them before, or who had no sense of the accent to help them construe the symbolic representation on the page? The balance between broadness or narrowness of transcription is highly problematic. The broader the phonetic notation, the more intelligible it might be to a general reader; but then the dialect would be being represented less accurately or closely. Or the other way round: the more narrow the phonetic notation, the greater the need for more specialist symbols and conventions—which are more likely to be incomprehensible to the same general reader. So questions of dialect spelling—of the representation of dialect in writing—were clearly and complexly different from the situation in Standard English.

In the 1870s, there was a sharpening of interest in both phonetics and spelling reform.[16] There were always far fewer workers in the field of dialect phonetics rather than dialect vocabulary, not least because of the technical expertise required; nonetheless, a small number of influential scholars were absolutely central in defining the nature of Victorian regional philology. And as we will see in future chapters, there could, at times, be a tug-of-war over the discipline between the phoneticians and the glossarists.

---

[13] Walter W. Skeat, 'Preface', in Henry Sweet, *A History of English Sounds from the Earliest Period*, English Dialect Society 4 (London: English Dialect Society, 1874), pp. v–xi, at p. vi; Sweet, *History of English Sounds*, p. 4.

[14] See Barry Heselwood, *Phonetic Transcription in Theory and Practice* (Edinburgh: Edinburgh University Press, 2013), pp. 79–80, and Simon Horobin, *Does Spelling Matter?* (Oxford: Oxford University Press, 2013), pp. 26–8.

[15] See Horobin, *Does Spelling Matter?* See also Burton and Ruthven, in Barnes, *Poems in the Broad Form of the Dorset Dialect*, pp. lvi-lxi.

[16] See, for example, Morpurgo Davies, *Nineteenth-Century Linguistics*, pp. 160–4; Sarah Ogilvie, *The Dictionary People: the unsung heroes who created the Oxford English Dictionary* (London: Chatto and Windus, 2023), pp. 84–91.

60   The Victorians and English Dialect

One of these key workers was James Murray—from 1879 the lead editor of the *Oxford English Dictionary*, but in the 1860s and 1870s a hard-pressed schoolmaster in London, drawn into the activities of the Philological Society.[17] Murray's 1873 monograph *The Dialect of the Southern Counties of Scotland* (published by the Society) makes very clear how Shaw's Higgins was correct in his sense of his discipline: really, it was all about vowels. As Murray wrote: 'In comparing words in kindred languages or dialects, the chief differences which present themselves to our notice concern the *vowels*; even in idioms which have been long severed from each other, and have had quite different histories, the *consonantal skeleton* of such words is found to remain more or less identical.'[18] Murray distinguishes, and describes, no fewer than fifty-seven different vowel realizations in the dialects of southern Scotland.[19] But unlike Higgins', Murray's phonetics are not simply descriptive or analytic; they are also historicist or evolutionary. So, for instance, a complex table in Murray's book traces the evolution of vowels and diphthongs from (using Murray's terms) Anglo-Saxon through Early Scotch and then Middle Scotch to Modern Scotch.[20] More expansively, part of Murray's core justification for dialect study lies in the importance of the history of sounds:

> As a part of the great series of phonetic changes by which the modern Teutonic tongues have come to differ so widely from their ancient sources, and from each other, the *Laut-verschiebung* or systematic vowel-change from Anglo-Saxon to Modern Scotch, and the different forms which the same original vowels have assumed in Southern English and Modern Scotch, possess interest for every student of language.[21]

Although the perspective is historicist, it is phonology, and not vocabulary, which is being studied: for Murray, it is 'systematic vowel-change' which should 'possess interest for every student of language'. In order to talk about sounds, in his *Dialect of the Southern Counties of Scotland* Murray used other scholars' systems of phonetic notation; but when he became editor of the *Oxford English Dictionary*, he devised his own, as part of an unparalleled project to record the pronunciation of English words.[22]

The most famous (real) phonetician of the nineteenth century was Henry Sweet. In his pen portraits of eminent phoneticians in his later preface to *Pygmalion*, it is Sweet whom Shaw reminisces about at by far the greatest length. Sweet was 'a man of genius', and 'the best of them all' as a phonetician, but he lacked 'sweetness

---

[17] On Murray, see especially Murray, *Caught in the Web of Words*.
[18] Murray, *The Dialects of the Southern Counties of Scotland*, p. 93.
[19] Murray, *The Dialects of the Southern Counties of Scotland*, pp. 142–3.
[20] Murray, *The Dialects of the Southern Counties of Scotland*, pp. 142–3.
[21] Murray, *The Dialects of the Southern Counties of Scotland*, p. 140.
[22] See Michael K. C. MacMahon, 'James Murray and the Phonetic Notation in the *New English Dictionary*', *Transactions of the Philological Society* 1985, 72–112, and 'Pronunciation in the *OED*', in Lynda Mugglestone (ed.), *Lexicography and the OED: Pioneers in the Untrodden Forest* (Oxford: Oxford University Press, 2000), pp. 172–88.

The Phoneticians **61**

of character' and was argumentative and denunciatory: 'he would not suffer fools gladly', Shaw recalled, 'and to him all scholars who were not rabid phoneticians were fools'.[23] Sweet was arguably the central figure in the development of phonetic study in Britain in the late nineteenth century (as Shaw recognized: 'the future of phonetics rests probably with his pupils', he wrote), from the publication of his *Handbook of Phonetics* in 1877, through his ceaseless advocacy for the discipline, to his belated appointment as Reader in Phonetics at the University of Oxford in 1901.[24] He was a key theorist in the so-called 'Reform Movement' in modern language teaching in the 1880s, which prioritized spoken language and longer texts over book learning and short, invented sentences; he also developed his own phonetic notation, called Romic, which in turn influenced the design of the alphabet of the International Phonetic Association (which first appeared in 1889).[25] Sweet's expertise was wide, but English regional dialects were not, in truth, one of the areas to which he made an especial contribution—even though his influence was to be felt in various ways.[26]

Alexander Ellis

Much more important for dialect study than either Sweet or Murray was another, older figure, Alexander John Ellis (1814–90).

Ellis amply qualifies as an eminent Victorian, but regrettably no capacious 'Life and Letters' biography was published after his death, and the fullest account of his works remains Robert Sanders' 1977 PhD thesis (founded on a very thorough study of Ellis' abundant writings, both published and unpublished).[27] Born A. J. Sharpe, at the age of 11 the young Alexander John was prevailed upon to change his surname to Ellis, in order to receive an inheritance. After an education at Eton and Cambridge, the resultant wealth set him up into an adulthood in which he was never required to earn his living, but rather could devote himself to his passions: as well as phonetics and dialect, these included music and mathematics (and Ellis claimed that he always

---

[23] Shaw, *Pygmalion*, pp. 3–6.

[24] On Sweet, see Charles Wrenn, 'Henry Sweet', *Transactions of the Philological Society* 1946, 177–210; Michael K. C. MacMahon, 'Henry Sweet (1845–1912)', in Helen Damico (ed.), *Medieval Scholarship: Biographical Studies on the Formation of a Discipline. Volume 2: Literature and Philology* (New York: Garland, 1998), pp. 167–75, and 'Sweet, Henry (1845–1912)', in *Oxford Dictionary of National Biography* [www.oxforddnb]; Robert Henry Robins, 'Against the Establishment: Sidelines on Henry Sweet', in Mark Janse (ed.), *Productivity and Creativity: Studies in General and Descriptive Linguistics in Honor of E. M. Uhlenbeck* (Berlin: De Gruyter, 1998), pp. 167–78; Mark Atherton, '"To observe things as they are without regard to their origin": Henry Sweet's General Writings on Language in the 1870s', *Henry Sweet Society for the History of Linguistic Ideas Bulletin* 51.1 (2008), 41–58, and 'Imaginative Science'.

[25] See A. P. R. Howatt and H. G. Widdowson, *A History of English Language Teaching*, 2nd ed. (Oxford: Oxford University Press, 2004), pp. 187–209; Heselwood, *Phonetic Transcription in Theory and Practice*, pp. 111–12.

[26] See, though, Sweet, *Collected Papers*, pp. 120–32.

[27] Robert Alan Sanders, 'Alexander John Ellis: A Study of a Victorian Philologist' (unpublished PhD, Memorial University, 1977). See also Murray, *Caught in the Web of Words*, pp. 72–6; Ogilvie, *The Dictionary People*, pp. 41–53; Michael K. C. MacMahon, 'Ellis [*formerly* Sharpe], Alexander John (1814–90), in *Oxford Dictionary of National Biography* [www.oxforddnb].

62 The Victorians and English Dialect

looked at words 'as a mathematician or a physicist').[28] He also published a volume of poetry as a young man. George Bernard Shaw was to recall Ellis as 'a London patriarch, with an impressive head always covered by a velvet skull cap, for which he would apologize to public meetings in a very courtly manner'.[29]

As Sanders has written, throughout his long life Ellis showed a 'passion for graphic symbols', and even as an undergraduate, he was highly alert to variations in spoken language: he later recalled that William Whewell, Master of Trinity College, Cambridge, 'was called (Juu·el) or (Jhuu·el) by the undergraduates in 1833, but (Whuu·el) or (Whiuu·el) nearly (Whyy·el) sometimes simply (Wuu·el), by his contemporaries'—no fewer than six different pronunciations, all of which needed distinguishing and which Ellis could remember over thirty years later.[30] In the 1840s he began to work closely with Isaac Pitman, and the climax of their work together was the 'English Phonotypic Alphabet' of 1847; at the same time, Ellis was publishing many independent works with titles such as *A Plea for Phonetic Spelling* and *The Essentials of Phonetics* (both 1848).[31] Over the decades Ellis proposed a series of phonetic alphabets and reformed spelling systems (his commitment was to so-called phonotypy, the phonetic representation of speech in print, rather than phonography, its representation in writing). In the 1840s, he developed what he called his 'Ethnical Alphabet'; in the 1850s, the 'Latinic Alphabet' and 'Travellers' Digraphic Alphabet'; in the 1860s, 'Palaeotype' and 'Glossotype'; in the 1870s, 'Glossic' and 'Engytype'; and in the 1880s, 'Dimid'iun' and the 'Europik Alfabet'.[32] All were distinct from one another, revisions or repurposings in one way or another. Few forms of language can have shown such rapidity of change as Ellis' phonetic alphabets—an irony, perhaps, for a scholar who wished to reform and fix spelling for the good of education. This was not lost on his contemporaries: James Murray noted that Ellis' 'hobby [was] to invent systems and discard them', while Sweet observed 'the dislike with which every phonetician regards all phonetic notations except the one evolved by himself'.[33] It is hard not to think that Ellis' books and articles on spelling reform and phonetic alphabets—including many which are actually written in such notations—were in their own way as doomed and quixotic as William Barnes' concurrent attempts to re-Saxonize the English vocabulary. But Ellis never lost his zeal for spelling reform, nor his conviction that radical reform was needed to benefit the illiterate.[34]

---

[28] Ellis, 'First Annual Address', p. 5. See, for example, Jonathan P. J. Stock, 'Alexander J. Ellis and His Place in the History of Ethnomusicology', *Ethnomusicology* 51 (2007), 306–25.

[29] Shaw, *Pygmalion*, p. 3.

[30] Sanders, 'Alexander John Ellis', p. 8; Ellis, 'On Palaeotype', p. 16 n.1.

[31] See J. Kelly, 'The 1847 Alphabet: An Episode of Phonotypy', in R. E. Asher and Eugénie J. A. Henderson (eds), *Towards a History of Phonetics* (Edinburgh: Edinburgh University Press, 1981), pp. 248–64.

[32] See Sanders, 'Alexander John Ellis', pp. 17–181, and Heselwood, *Phonetic Transcription in Theory and Practice*, pp. 109–11.

[33] Quoted in MacMahon, 'James Murray and the Phonetic Notation in the *New English Dictionary*', p. 90; Sweet, *Collected Papers*, p. 290.

[34] See Alexander J. Ellis, 'Tenth Annual Address of the President to the Philological Society, Delivered at the Anniversary Meeting, Friday, 20th May, 1881', *Transactions of the Philological Society* 1881, 252–321, at pp. 269–319.

The Phoneticians   63

By far the most important of Ellis' alphabets, for the present book, were Palaeotype and Glossic.[35] The first of these, Palaeotype, was presented to the Philological Society in 1867. Ellis' lengthy exposition begins in arresting fashion: 'A word is not known till its sound is known', he asserts, and a single written word may have 'many distinct pronunciations', so that 'one apparent word thus becomes several words to the philologist'.[36] It is thus futile, he argues, to study language on the basis of spellings alone, especially when spelling may be far from representing pronunciation in any close phonetic manner. 'Impressed with these convictions', Ellis writes, 'I have for many years endeavoured to ascertain what were the sounds of human speech, and reduce them to a set of symbols'. Palaeotype represents the fruits of his studies, and its unique selling point, Ellis declares, is that it is 'an alphabet consisting entirely of those types which we may expect to find in every printing office'.[37] In other words—and here we see the importance of Ellis' distinction between phonography and phonotypy—no new symbols or letters needed to be cut or cast for printers (unlike for the rival systems of Pitman and Melville Bell); instead, a remarkable range of symbols could be generated by using italic as well as Roman type, small capitals as well as large capitals, numerals and punctuation marks, and even standard letters printed upside down. Hence the name *Palaeotype* ('old type', already at hand), to distinguish it from what Ellis calls *neotypic* systems.[38]

One of the cleverest features of Ellis' Palaeotype is that it exists in both a 'complete' and an 'approximative' version (transcriptions using the complete version, Ellis explains, should be placed in curved brackets (), and approximative transcriptions in square brackets []). So, for example, the letter (b) represents the familiar English sound at the start of *be*. In the complete version of Palaeotype, this (b) is to be distinguished from four similar (but not identical) sounds: in Ellis' descriptions, 'the sonant of p' (represented as (*b*)), '(b) with the lower lip pressed more firmly against the upper teeth than for (f)' (represented as (B)), 'flat (b) common in Saxony, and in the North American Indian languages' (represented as ('b)), and '[German] *w*, as pronounced in the middle and south of Germany' (represented as (bh)). In the approximative version, however, all five of these similar sounds can be represented simply as [b].[39] Altogether, approximative Palaeotype uses 46 different symbols, but complete Palaeotype requires over 180—and many of these, of course, can be combined in various permutations.[40]

In 1871 Ellis unveiled his second major alphabet to the Philological Society: Glossic, a much simpler system with a significantly different purpose. This time, his mission statement practised what it was attempting to preach, using its own reformed

[35] See Sanders, 'Alexander John Ellis', pp. 401–49; S. S. Eustace, 'The Meaning of the Palaeotype in A. J. Ellis's *On Early English Pronunciation 1869–89*', *Transactions of the Philological Society* 1969, 31–79; John K. Local, 'Making a Transcription: the evolution of A. J. Ellis's Palaeotype', *Journal of the International Phonetic Association* 13.1 (1983), 2–12.

[36] Ellis, 'On Palaeotype', pp. 1–2.

[37] Ellis, 'On Palaeotype', p. 3.

[38] Ellis, 'On Palaeotype', p. 4.

[39] Ellis, 'On Palaeotype', pp. 11–12.

[40] Ellis, 'On Palaeotype', p. 35.

64   The Victorians and English Dialect

spelling; the paper was called 'On Glosik, A Neu Sistem ov Ingglish Spelling, Proapoa·zd faur Konkur·ent Eus, in Aurder too Remidi dhi Difek·ts, widhou·t Ditrak·ting from dhi Valeu ov Our Prezent Aurthog·rafi [On Glossic, A New System of English Spelling, Proposed for Concurrent Use in Order to Remedy the Defects without Distracting from the Value of Our Present Orthography]'. Glossic was pitched less as a system of phonetic transcription, and more as a reformed spelling system—but importantly, one to be introduced alongside the current system, rather than being proposed as a replacement. English spelling, Ellis writes, 'waz oarij·ineli foanet·ik [was originally phonetic]', but has since become, on account of various changes in the language, 'peurli konven·shenel [purely conventional]' (in Ellis' Glossic notation, a superscript point after a syllable indicates stress).[41]

The purpose of Glossic was educational: 'In daiz leik dheez when grait eferts aar being maid too improo·v elimen·teri edeukai·shen, dhi speling difikelti iz ov preim impoa·rtens [In days like these when great efforts are being made to improve elementary education, the spelling difficulty is of prime importance]'.[42] The introduction of Glossic, Ellis claims, will 'fasil·itait Lerning too Reed [facilitate Learning to Read]' and 'maik Lerning too Spel unnes·eseri [make Learning to Spell unnecessary]'.[43] But Modern English spelling was equally problematic for dialect: 'It iz kweit inkai·pabl ov egzib·iting dhi vairrius egzis·ting faurmz ov our langgwej, in dhoaz proavin·shel deialekts which aar absoaleutli deiing out bifoa·r wee kan fiks dhem in print [It is quite incapable of exhibiting the various existing forms of our language, in those provincial dialects which are absolutely dying out before we can fix them in print]'.[44] Ellis' earlier Palaeotype was also judged to be unsuitable: even as its deviser, Ellis had come to the conclusion that, because Palaeotype was intended as a universal system of transcription (that is, it was not specific to English), and because he had taken Latin (rather than English) as its foundation, Palaeotype was 'eusles, when apleid too dhi kolek·shen ov proavin·shel werdz and soundz [useless, when applied to the collection of provincial words and sounds]'. Those attempting to use it, as dialect collectors, 'had too studi sumthing entei·rli neu, which krost dhair habits at everi staij [had to study something entirely new, which crossed their habits at every stage]'.[45] Subsequent evidence suggests that Ellis was right in his instinct here: among dialect collectors, a small number of advanced phoneticians did use Palaeotype (such as James Murray in his *Dialect of the Southern Counties of Scotland*), but Glossic was by far the more popular notation. Ellis also produced a short-lived intermediate alphabet, Glossotype, intended specifically for 'the writing of provincial Glossaries', but this received little use.[46]

Like Palaeotype, Glossic uses only standard letter forms—no new types or symbols are needed—but unlike the earlier system it uses plain, lower-case Roman

---

[41] Ellis, 'On Glosik', p. 90. See further Atherton, '"To observe things as they are"', pp. 47–52.
[42] Ellis, 'On Glosik', p. 92. See further Horobin, *Does Spelling Matter?* pp. 243–5.
[43] Ellis, 'On Glosik', p. 113.
[44] Ellis, 'On Glosik', pp. 92–3.
[45] Ellis, 'On Glosik', p. 100.
[46] Ellis, *On Early English Pronunciation*, I, 13, 16, II, 610–17.

The Phoneticians **65**

throughout, and does away with the need for capitals, accents, inversions, and all the other paraphernalia of the earlier alphabet. But Ellis keeps open the option of Glossic being 'exte·nded bei simbelz [extended by symbols]', first to be able to represent 'nashenel deialek·tik [national dialectic]', and later for being a vehicle of 'euniver·sel foanet.iks [universal phonetics]'—that is, being an alphabet suitable for all languages, not just English.[47]

So Ellis sees Glossic as having great potential for regional philology:

It wuod enai·bl neumerus kontrib·euterz too undertai·k dhi task ov fiksing our feujitiv deialekts, and in dhus endev·ering too reit un·rit·n soundz from dhi lips ov dhi ilit·eret, wuod akeu·meulait a stoar ov foanet·ik nolej that must matee·rrieli inflooens aul sub-sikwent filoaloj·ikel inkwei·rri. Dhis riduk·shen ov our deialekts too reiting iz a mater in which ei taik dhi deepest interest.[48]

[It would enable numerous contributors to undertake the task of fixing our fugitive dialects, and in thus endeavouring to write unwritten sounds from the lips of the illiterate, would accumulate a store of phonetic knowledge that must materially influence all subsequent philological inquiry. This reduction of our dialects to writing is a matter in which I take the deepest interest.]

We should note the ambition of Ellis' goal here (there will be 'neumerus kontrib·euterz'), and also the year of his paper: 1871. As we will see in Chapter 4, the English Dialect Society was founded only two years later—with Ellis himself involved in its founding—and it then functioned for the next twenty years as the main collaborative organization for the collecting of dialect. Ellis' recommendation of his system is breezily upbeat: even though, he claims, 'dhi konsep·shen ov glosik iz aultoagedh·er neu [the conception of Glossic is altogether new]', nonetheless 'glosik iz eezi too reed and neerli az eezi too reit [Glossic is easy to read and nearly as easy to write]'.[49] And his closing peroration makes plain the centrality of dialect to his purposes. There are 'neumerus deialekts skaterd oaver dhi fais ov our kuntri [numerous dialects scattered over the face of our country]', he writes, 'widh ·noa ·wun ·intel·ijibl system ov reiting dhem [with no one intelligible system of writing them]'. But now that a 'eunifaurm methud [uniform method]' of recording them is available—namely Glossic—then the great goal is attainable, at the time of their greatest peril, of 'dhi prezervai·shen ov our Ingglish deialekts, air dhi railway whisl skairz dhem out ov egzis·tens [the preservation of our English dialects, ere the railway whistle scares them out of existence]'.[50] However, as we will see at the end of this chapter, by 'prezervai·shen' Ellis does not necessarily mean 'continued existence', but only 'recording in writing', for he believed that one of the necessary corollaries of a

[47] Ellis, 'On Glosik', p. 98.
[48] Ellis, 'On Glosik', p. 104.
[49] Ellis, 'On Glosik', pp. 109, 111.
[50] Ellis, 'On Glosik', p. 112.

66   The Victorians and English Dialect

reformed spelling system—educationally urgent, in his view—was also a reformed, or standard, form of pronunciation, common to all.

Those are the two main alphabets; but now we should step back to appraise Ellis' larger viewpoint and purpose. In 1872, having become President of the Philological Society for a three-year period, Ellis inaugurated the practice of an annual presidential address. The addresses of 1873 and 1874 are composite affairs, an assemblage of reports from various workers; but in his first year, on Friday 17 May 1872, Ellis took the opportunity to set forth his own particular views on philology and linguistic study. It soon becomes clear that he has strong opinions, and he wastes no time in telling his (no doubt startled) audience that 'we have no real science of language at present', and only 'a collection of materials', which are in fact 'utterly insufficient' and 'mostly of the wrong sort'.[51]

Why does Ellis say this? The answer is because of the importance he places on spoken language—on sound—over written language. The great philological breakthrough in the late eighteenth and early nineteenth century, the crucible of the discipline itself, was the encounter of European linguists (such as Sir William Jones) with Sanskrit: it was this contact which enabled the discovery, and comparative reconstruction, of the Indo-European group of languages. But for Ellis, this was all the wrong way round:

> We are under the greatest obligations to those distinguished men who have undertaken to unravel its secrets and to shew its connection with the languages of Europe. Yet I must repeat, that for the pure science of language, to begin with Sanscrit was as much beginning at the wrong end as it would have been to commence zoology with palæontology,—the relations of life with the bones of the dead. And I am afraid that one of the consequences will be an extreme unwillingness to undertake that long and troublesome living examination of living speech wherein alone, as it seems to me, can we hope to find the key to the mystery.[52]

By 'the mystery', Ellis means nothing less than an understanding of what exactly language is, how it works, how it came into being. But a whole new discipline or methodology is needed to study living speech:

> Laborious as it may be to pore over manuscripts, to compare letter by letter, to exhume, as it were, bone after bone of long interred skeletons, and place them side by side for comparison, carefully studying every little projection and depression, the labour is as nothing compared to the patient watching of habits, registering of usages, slow acquirement of uncongenial thought, accurate appreciation of living changing sounds, in thousands of thousands of instances, on which we must base our real science of language.[53]

---

[51] Ellis, 'First Annual Address', pp. 2–3.
[52] Ellis, 'First Annual Address', p. 22.
[53] Ellis, 'First Annual Address', p. 22.

The same point is made elsewhere in the address: 'speech sounds must be studied in the living speaker, and not in the dead alphabet', and 'the whole of language [is] to be studied in the living speaker, and not in fossil books'.[54]

This might sound like a plea for a purely synchronic linguistics, making contemporary language the core object of study; but we must be careful how we proceed here. While Ellis is certainly castigating his fellow philologists for their neglect of current speech as the appropriate focus for their endeavours, he is also arguing that it is present language which offers the truest, most dependable access to the past. A study of the current state of language will reveal knowledge of its prior states, or, at least, of the most important things that Ellis wants to know about its prior states: how and why language changes, even (ultimately) where language comes from. The desire to understand the origins of language was one of the great themes of Max Müller, and in his presidential address Ellis reviews the theories of Müller and others, with no great enthusiasm for any of them.[55] Although he does not use the word, what Ellis is effectively proposing is what has come to be known as the 'uniformitarian' principle in language study—that is, the idea that the processes of change in the past are likely to be have been the same as the processes of change in the present, and so we can understand past change by observing present language.

'Language teems with life', he announces.[56] So in the light of this aphorism, Ellis argues that philologists should direct their efforts towards the study of the changing contemporary language, in its spoken form, rather than the unchanging records of earlier states, or the fixed, fossilized features of standard languages. In other words, Ellis writes, philologists need to examine the language—and also the thought—of 'untutored men, uneducated peasants, savage tribes, growing children': that is to say, 'we must discover the genesis of language, if at all, in the continuous genesis of patois, dialects, jargons, lingue franche, camp speech, savage talk'.[57] Regional dialect, as a form of non-standard language, here comes into view as a key component in Ellis' project—but not, it seems, in an especially flattering light.

At this point, we need to contextualize Ellis' remarks within a number of frames of reference. Firstly, we should place his comments in the linguistic, disciplinary context of an emergent Neogrammarianism—though if anything, Ellis is slightly ahead of the curve chronologically. The 1870s saw the *Junggrammatiker*, especially in Germany, rescrutinizing and retheorizing the nature of language change, and arguing that sound changes were regular and exceptionless—and also that sound changes in progress might be observed in the contemporary spoken language.[58] In Germany and France, individual scholars (Georg Wenker and Jules Gilliéron) launched ambitious projects to observe—and, for the first time, to map—the phonology of local

---

[54] Ellis, 'First Annual Address', p. 5.
[55] Ellis, 'First Annual Address', pp. 10–15; see also Alexander J. Ellis, 'Second Annual Address of the President to the Philological Society, Delivered at the Anniversary Meeting, Friday, 16th May, 1873', *Transactions of the Philological Society* 1873–4, 201–52, pp. 248–52.
[56] Ellis, 'First Annual Address', p. 18.
[57] Ellis, 'First Annual Address', pp. 7, 19; see also pp. 19–20.
[58] See Wakelin, *English Dialects*, pp. 6–7; K. M. Petyt, *The Study of Dialect: An Introduction to Dialectology* (London: Deutsch, 1980), pp. 55–7; Penhallurick, *Studying Dialect*, pp. 80–3.

68   The Victorians and English Dialect

dialects, though their results did not confirm the Neogrammarian hypothesis in any straightforward manner.[59]

Secondly, we might place Ellis' preoccupations within the context of debates about Darwinian evolution. To compare Latin, Greek, and Sanskrit, Ellis avers, is to compare 'full-grown skeletons', while 'the fœtal system escapes us'.[60] Ellis asks:

> Could Darwin have drawn his theory of evolution from geological data? Geologists all exclaim that geology furnishes no transitional forms [. . .] Can we then see the transition between these languages?[61]

The answer to the question, for Ellis, is self-evidently negative, and the search should be directed elsewhere than to standard and canonical languages: 'what we want is to find real transitional forms between living language'—in other words, to observe linguistic change in progress.

And thirdly and most fully, we should note that the early 1870s was the period in which the new discipline of anthropology began to exert its intellectual influence. E. B. Tylor's *Primitive Man* was published in 1871, as was Darwin's *The Descent of Man*. Tylor was well read in the new philology, and devotes two chapters to language in *Primitive Man*.[62] In this evolutionary model of human culture, which posited a development from 'savageness' to civilization, many features of contemporary existence were adduced either as evidence of 'primitive' culture or as relic 'survivals' (as we will explore further in Chapter 5).[63] It was inevitable that, for some scholars, language should be drawn into the argument, and Ellis' claim here, that philologists should pay attention to 'untutored men, uneducated peasants, savage tribes, growing children', indicates which human groups were thought to be able to give access to language still in an early or unfixed state.

In this context, it is also worth lingering, for clarity's sake, on two of the terms most often used to describe dialect speakers in the nineteenth century: 'natives' and 'peasants'. Clearly, the evidence of 'natives'—geographically rooted, or localizable, speakers of dialect—was essential for any form of geographical linguistics, such as the 'comparative dialectal phonology' which Ellis wished to attempt.[64] Although its classificatory use inevitably correlates closely with the rural working class, 'natives' was not a class term in itself or simply synonymous with 'peasants', and Ellis often refers to members of the professional classes as 'natives', on the grounds of the location of their

---

[59] See further Petyt, *The Study of Dialect*, pp. 40–9; J. K. Chambers and Peter Trudgill, *Dialectology*, 2nd ed. (Cambridge: Cambridge University Press, 1998), pp. 15–17; Morpurgo Davies, *Nineteenth-Century Linguistics*, pp. 237–9, 244–5, 251–5; William A. Kretzschmar, Jr, 'Dialectology and the History of the English Language', in Donka Minkova and Robert Stockwell (eds), *Studies in the History of the English Language: A Millennial Perspective*, Topics in English Linguistics 39 (Berlin: De Gruyter, 2002), pp. 79–108, at pp. 79–85; Penhallurick, *Studying Dialect*, pp. 55–77. See also Ellis, 'Eleventh Annual Address', pp. 25–32.

[60] Ellis, 'First Annual Address', p. 25.

[61] Ellis, 'First Annual Address', p. 25.

[62] See Atherton, 'Imaginative Science'.

[63] See, for example, George W. Stocking, Jr, *Victorian Anthropology* (New York: Free Press, 1987); Adam Kuper, *The Invention of Primitive Society: Transformations of an Illusion* (London: Routledge, 1988).

[64] Ellis, *On Early English Pronunciation*, IV, 1244.

birth or upbringing. Nor should we misconstrue the term as primarily a colonial one, here being redeployed for inward usage: as the *Oxford English Dictionary* confirms, a domestic reference for the term 'native' is standard in nineteenth-century English (as in the title of Hardy's *The Return of the Native*); and in any case, as a number of scholars have observed, many of the discourses of Victorian anthropology were developed out of the study and classification of European peoples and cultures as much as non-European.[65] As for the idea of the 'peasant', Ellis wrote in 1874:

> The illiterate peasant, speaking a language entirely imitative, unfixed by any theoretic orthography, untrammelled by any pedant's fancies, is the modern representative of our older population, which, confined to small districts by feudal superiors, the custom of villanage, and the difficulty of travelling, and entirely untaught, kept up their language by the mere necessity of talking.[66]

'Peasant' language, then, represents for Ellis an element of the past within the present, and one that is (most importantly) relatively untouched by literacy and the Roman alphabet. It is important to stress, though, that Ellis is not arguing that peasant culture, at least linguistically, preserves this past in any sort of unchanged or 'pure' state. As he states: 'it would be rash to assume that [sounds] were originally the same as now, because the Saxon and Danish tribes which came to our shores of course already spoke dialectally, and present habits are the result of a fusion, subject to many influences though many generations'.[67] But still, the evidence of unwritten dialects, as a point of access to the past, was qualitatively different and highly precious.

Such contexts—Neogrammarian, evolutionary, and linguistic-anthropological—therefore enable us to see more clearly the grounds and purpose of Ellis' precocious argument in his first presidential address. He affirms:

> Language is a living thing, the outcome of the social connection of two or more beings capable of hearing and producing sound, and [. . .] it must be watched and registered as it now grows [. . .] Our only hope of really catching the laws of its formation is to study it in its present life, and not, as hitherto almost exclusively, in its past death.[68]

It is not difficult, therefore, to see where dialect fits into Ellis' scheme. He instructs his listeners at the Philological Society that they should 'fix great and marked attention on existing forms of speech, not merely on those possessing a literature', and

---

[65] See, for example, Robert J. C. Young, *The Idea of English Ethnicity* (Oxford: Blackwell, 2008), pp. 13–14; Chris Wingfield, 'Is the Heart at Home? E. B. Tylor's Collections from Somerset', *Journal of Museum Ethnography* 22 (2009), 22–38; Manias, *Race, Science, and the Nation*, pp. 114–21.

[66] Ellis, *On Early English Pronunciation*, IV, 1317.

[67] Ellis, *On Early English Pronunciation*, IV, 1318.

[68] Ellis, 'First Annual Address', p. 31. See further Robert Penhallurick, 'On Dialectology', in Robert Penhallurick (ed.), *Debating Dialect: Essays on the Philosophy of Dialect Study* (Cardiff: University of Wales Press, 2000), pp. 116–24.

70 The Victorians and English Dialect

'especially on those not possessing a literature, and the peasant dialects of those which do possess one, as the real fermenting mass whence language grows.'[69]

Ellis' two main convictions, then, were that spoken language ('growing living organic speech') is primary over written language, and that one should work from the present to the past, rather than vice versa.[70] Such convictions were not unique to Ellis, though he was among the first to enunciate them so clearly. Most significantly, he exerted a major influence on Henry Sweet: the two scholars admired each other greatly, though they were not without their disagreements. Ellis, as the senior man, supported Sweet's early work, not least through giving him a platform at the Philological Society, and Sweet's major mission statements of the 1870s and 1880s articulate a very Ellis-like set of presuppositions and goals. 'Words, Logic, and Grammar', Sweet's manifesto paper of 1876, begins as follows:

> One of the most striking features of the history of linguistic science as compared with zoology, botany, and the other so-called natural sciences, is its one-sidedly historical character. Philologists have hitherto chiefly confined their attention to the most ancient dead languages, valuing modern languages only in as far as they retain remnants of older linguistic formations—much as if zoology were to identify itself with palaeontology, and refuse to trouble itself with the investigation of living species, except when it promised to throw light on the structure of extinct ones.[71]

This echoes closely what Ellis had said in his first presidential address, as do Sweet's counter-claims that follow, that 'before history must come a knowledge of what now exists' and that 'the first requisite is a knowledge of phonetics'.[72] With 'the warm breath of living phonology', Sweet wrote elsewhere, the 'dead mass' of historical data could be 'thaw[ed] into life'.[73] Similarly, the best part of a decade later, we find Sweet reasserting to the Philological Society the 'general axiom' that 'the living spoken form of every language should be made the foundation of its study', as well as that 'the first and indispensable condition of a rational study of a dead language is the adoption of an accurate and consistent pronunciation', and that what is needed above all is 'a science of *living*, as opposed to dead, or antiquarian philology'.[74]

This was the phonetics revolution of the 1870s, at least in Britain—pioneered by Melville Bell, spearheaded by Ellis, and driven home and popularized by Sweet. Phonetics should be the primary theory and method, and contemporary spoken language the primary data. Moreover, all of this was reinforced by the Neogrammarian focus on the processes of sound change, the uniformitarian principle in linguistic study, and some of the assumptions of Victorian anthropology. As a result, unwritten, regional dialects were placed at the centre of attention for a small number of highly accomplished, and energetically influential, philologists. It was time, they believed, to

---

[69] Ellis, 'First Annual Address', pp. 32–3.
[70] Ellis, 'First Annual Address', p. 20.
[71] Sweet, *Collected Papers*, p. 2.
[72] Sweet, *Collected Papers*, pp. 2–3.
[73] Sweet, *History of English Sounds*, p. 2.
[74] Sweet, *Collected Papers*, pp. 35, 48, 49.

The Phoneticians **71**

rescue dialect study definitively from the antiquarianism and amateurism of the previous decades. Ellis used his final address as President of the Philological Society to call on his fellow philologists to join him in the rigorous study of dialect phonology, and to 'drain [. . .] dry the pestiferous marshes of dilettanteism'.[75]

All this being the case, we might be surprised to find just how historically focused Ellis' main philological publications were in this period. For here we first encounter the multi-volume work which was to be Ellis' main achievement and legacy: *On Early English Pronunciation, with Especial Reference to Shakspere and Chaucer*. Published jointly by the Philological Society, the Early English Text Society, and the Chaucer Society, the first two parts appeared in 1869, and the third in 1871. All three were firmly historical in content. Part I examines the pronunciation of English between the fourteenth and eighteenth centuries, largely using the evidence of rhymes for the Middle English period and that of 'orthoepists' (writers on spelling) for the early modern. Part II starts further back in time, tracing pronunciation and orthography from the Anglo-Saxon period to the thirteenth century. Part III retreads much of the material (and chronology) of Part I, presenting an anthology of evidence from the fourteenth and sixteenth centuries, and endeavouring to reconstruct the pronunciation of Chaucer and Shakespeare in particular (including a forty-five-page transcription of Chaucer's 'General Prologue' into Palaeotype).[76] These first three volumes show an increasing tendency on Ellis' part towards digressions and excursuses, with sections on (for example) the pronunciation of Old Norse and Modern Icelandic (with guidance supplied by Eiríkr Magnússon, William Morris' collaborator), German dialects in Pennsylvania, and 'faulty rhymes' in the works of Tennyson.[77] These volumes also demonstrate, amply, Ellis' habit of conducting long and detailed arguments in footnotes that often take up more of the page than the main text itself. The scale was enormous, as Ellis' publishers soon realized, and by the end of Part III the continuous pagination had already reached page 996. This was becoming a great Gothic cathedral of a book, as capacious and elastic in its notions of coherence as other vast, multi-volume works of the period such as John Ruskin's *Modern Painters* (1843–60) and E. A. Freeman's *History of the Norman Conquest* (1867–79). 'It may be thought at first that too wide a range has been taken', Ellis acknowledged in a later volume, before countering with his own justifications for why his approach, both expansive and microscopic, was correct after all.[78] Elsewhere he insisted on 'the necessity of attending to what outsiders are apt to consider as absurdly minute distinctions'.[79]

All of these features make *Early English Pronunciation* a difficult work to navigate and use, and they may well have contributed to its declining prominence in

---

[75] Alexander J. Ellis, 'Third Annual Address of the President to the Philological Society, Delivered at the Anniversary Meeting, Friday, 15th May, 1874', *Transactions of the Philological Society* 1873–4, 354–460, at p. 451.

[76] Ellis, *On Early English Pronunciation*, III, 680–725; see further David Crystal, 'Early Interest in Shakespeare: Original Pronunciation', *Language and History* 56 (2013), 5–17, at pp. 7–9.

[77] See Ellis, *On Early English Pronunciation*, II, 537–60, III, 652–63, 858–62.

[78] Ellis, *On Early English Pronunciation*, IV, 1432.

[79] Ellis, 'Second Annual Address', p. 206.

72   The Victorians and English Dialect

later scholarship. Nonetheless, the opinion of Henry Sweet, writing when these first three volumes had appeared, gives us a good assessment of how Ellis' massive work was received by his contemporaries. Ellis' great achievement, Sweet writes, 'was to determine generally the phonetic values of the Roman alphabet in England at the different periods, and to establish the all-important principle that the Middle Age scribes wrote not by eye, but by ear'.[80]

Right from the start of *Early English Pronunciation*, Ellis had promised that contemporary, nineteenth-century pronunciation would be treated at the end of the work, in a projected Chapter XI. But the appearance of this promised chapter was repeatedly delayed. Originally, *Early English Pronunciation* was intended as a two-volume work, and Chapter XI was announced as being the final chapter in Part II. Then, as the two-volume design turned into a four-volume design, it was postponed, and reallocated to appear as the final chapter in Part IV. In his presidential address to the Philological Society of May 1873, Ellis was hopeful that 'the fourth part *ought* to be ready' by the same time the following year.[81] But at his 1874 address, Ellis again had to apologize for its non-appearance: 'I have worked at it incessantly', he assured his listeners, and 'have literally allowed myself no holiday at all'.[82] But there had been yet another change of plan: Part IV now had to be split into two separate publications, with the first appearing by the end of 1874 (or so Ellis projected) and the second (as Part V) in 1877. It appears, then, that it was only in the period 1873–4 that Ellis conceived of a volume exclusively dedicated to contemporary pronunciation.[83] And although Part IV did appear in 1874 as pledged, Part V was not published until 1889: it was to take fifteen years to complete, not the mere three that Ellis had envisaged.

What caused this repeated enlargement and deferral? Partly it was Ellis' inclination to encyclopaedism, and his expansive attitude to questions of relevance: topics kept coming up, and studies by other scholars kept appearing, which Ellis felt he had to incorporate and answer in his *magnum opus* (at one point, he even had plans for a sixth volume, in which he would go back to the beginning and cover the early material again in the light of subsequent work). But the more profound reason was the lack of data for Ellis' pioneering project: although the evidence of elocutionists, poets, and other writers on language might enable Ellis to make some progress with what he called 'educated' pronunciation in the present day, there wasn't a remotely sufficient body of contemporary dialectal material available—especially not of phonology, as opposed to vocabulary. It wasn't simply that dialect studies hadn't been undertaken in many places, though this was true; but those which had been undertaken were, for Ellis' stringent phonetic purposes, inadequate or unhelpful. In a footnote in Part II, for example, Ellis praised the studies of Robert Backhouse Peacock in the Lonsdale area (which J. C. Atkinson had brought to publication): in

---

[80] Sweet, *History of English Sounds*, p. 161. See also Atherton, '"To observe things as they are"', pp. 52–3.
[81] Ellis, 'Second Annual Address', p. 244, n. 2.
[82] Ellis, 'Third Annual Address', 360.
[83] See also Ellis, 'Third Annual Address', p. 447.

spite of its shortcomings, Ellis writes, Peacock's work 'is a gem compared to most which I have met with, for they generally leave me in a state of utter bewilderment'.[84] Ellis wanted to understand the phonology of contemporary dialects; but there was very little material for him to use.

One might inquire, of course, why Ellis regarded the study of contemporary dialects to be such a necessity: could he not just stop his great work in the eighteenth century? The answer he gives is that a survey of English dialects is needed 'as a necessary basis for understanding the pronunciation underlying our Early English orthography, which was wholly dialectal'.[85] That is to say, it was not possible to understand the spelling systems of Middle English texts on the basis of Modern English spelling or 'educated' pronunciation alone, because those texts had been written in the period before a standard spelling system arose, and thus each was written in the dialect of its own author or scribe; and Ellis' whole project, we should recall, had begun with a focus on Chaucer as the key author. This reason, then, and the historicist impulse behind it, was what had led Ellis to this point, and to the realization that contemporary spoken dialects preserved a mass of data that was of prime relevance to his project; but it is impossible not to think also that, as Ellis went ever onwards, the study of present-day dialects became more and more an end in itself, a grand intellectual puzzle, and not merely the contemporary means to a medievalist end.

So we can now see that some of the ideas promoted in Ellis' presidential address of 1872 were probably not well-established convictions of many years standing, but rather were fresh realizations, newly theorized as Ellis attempted to plan and promote his project. If not exactly thinking aloud, Ellis was certainly endeavouring to persuade his audience of the rightness of the decisions he was taking, and of the soundness of the methodological assumptions he was starting from: namely, as we have seen, that spoken language is primary; that philologists should work from the present to the past, not the other way round; and that the 'unwritten languages' of the provinces offered the richest, most untapped potential for the study of English.

The story of Parts IV and V of *Early English Pronunciation*, which gathered and presented Ellis' researches into contemporary dialects, will be told in the final section of this chapter. But before then, we have to attend to the problem that Ellis found himself confronted with, in the late 1860s and early 1870s, as he attempted to expand the scope of his great work: how could he accomplish his ambitious and unprecedented survey of contemporary English dialects? The answer, as we will now see, was by means of the invention of the linguistic fieldworker or specialist informant. And to Ellis' great good fortune, one of the informants he was able to make contact with was a man whose genius for linguistic fieldwork was matched only by his extraordinary industry and accuracy: Thomas Hallam.

---

[84] Ellis, *On Early English Pronunciation*, II, 613 n. 1.
[85] Ellis, *On Early English Pronunciation*, IV, xv.

74 The Victorians and English Dialect

The travels of Thomas Hallam

In the churchyard of St Thomas Becket church in Chapel-en-le-Frith, Derbyshire, one can find a gravestone with the following inscription:

> Here rests the body of/Thomas Hallam/a member of the/Council of the/English Dialect Society./Born 26th December 1819/at Raglow, Chapel-en-le-Frith. Died 7th September 1895/at Ardwick, Manchester./He devoted the leisure moments/of a long and busy life/to a patient and diligent enquiry/into all that is noteworthy/in the various dialects/of northern England./The results of his study are/placed in Bodley's Library/in the University of Oxford.

By any standards, this is an unusual memorial inscription, and even more extraordinary are the 'results of his Studies' now preserved in the Bodleian Library: thousands and thousands of pages of notes, letters, reports, and tables, and a singularly remarkable collection of pocket notebooks. This deposition was deliberately planned by Hallam: his will, drawn up two days before his death and at the end of many decades of phonetic and dialectal study, requests that all his manuscript materials should pass to the scholarly Oxbridge trio of W. W. Skeat, Joseph Wright, and A. L. Mayhew, for them either to 'publish at their absolute discretion' or deposit in the Bodleian Library.[86] The brief obituary that marked Hallam's passing in the *Manchester City News* explains how all this material was generated: Hallam, it records, 'spent all his holidays for thirty years in travelling over the country, listening to the speech of rustics and old people in the market place and at solitary farmhouses, noting down the peculiarities and variations, and reproducing them afterwards with an accuracy which was perfectly marvellous'.[87]

If Ellis, as we have seen, did not receive a biography after his death to commemorate him, Hallam does not yet even have an entry in the *Dictionary of National Biography*, and the record of his life must be pieced together from various sources. Scholarship on Hallam is also slender, though Robert Sanders tracked the ups and downs of Ellis and Hallam's relations through the hundreds of letters preserved in the Bodleian Library, and a groundbreaking article by Michael MacMahon, published in 1983, starts to make sense of Hallam's dialect studies.[88] Yet he should beyond doubt be regarded as the most industrious dialect collector of the nineteenth century, and an absolute pioneer in the techniques of linguistic fieldwork.

The most important record of Hallam's early years is a brief unpublished memoir which is now preserved among his papers, headed 'Rough autobiographical notes'.[89] The son of a farmer, Hallam recalled that 'from early childhood I was strongly

---

[86] Will of Thomas Hallam, 5 September 1895 (probate granted 3 October 1895).

[87] [Anon], 'Thomas Hallam', *Manchester City News* 5 October 1895.

[88] Sanders, 'Alexander John Ellis'; Michael K. C. MacMahon, 'Thomas Hallam and the Study of Dialect and Educated Speech', *Transactions of the Yorkshire Dialect Society* 83 (1983), 19–31. See also Annmarie Drury, 'Aural Community and William Barnes as Earwitness', *Victorian Poetry* 56 (2018), 433–53, at pp. 442–7.

[89] Oxford, Bodleian Libraries, MS Eng. lang. d. 21, fols 1–6.

inclined to books'. However, in spite of great academic promise, especially in mathematics, Hallam left school at the age of 10, and worked on the family farm in Fernilee for over a decade, where his especial responsibility was keeping the farm accounts and undertaking errands rather than heavy manual labour ('I was not so strong or robust as the rest of my brothers', he explains).

But alongside this, on 'winter nights' and other opportunities, Hallam 'commenced a course of what I may certainly term self-tuition'. Such study was partly mathematical, and partly linguistic. In 1833 he acquired an abridged version of Samuel Johnson's eighteenth-century dictionary, and in 1840 he began an intense study of John Walker's *Dictionary of the English Language*, especially its prefatory section on 'Principles of English Pronunciation'.

At this point these autobiographical notes can be complemented by a second document, titled 'History of Thos. Hallam's Observations and researches in the Phonology of Educated English and of English Dialects'.[90] These record that 'at the beginning of 1838, when just over 18 years of age, I began to notice, in the speech of preachers, the difference in the pronunciation of unaccented i after the primary & secondary accent, in such words as, <u>family</u>, <u>visible</u>, <u>eternity</u>, <u>immortality</u>, &c some speakers pronouncing this letter as obscure <u>u</u>, and others as obscure <u>i</u>'. The next milestone came on 5 January 1841, when Hallam heard Isaac Pitman lecture in Chorlton Town Hall; not only did Hallam 'after the lecture [have] a few words with him about what he termed the "natural vowel"', but he also set himself to learn Pitman's phonographic system thoroughly, so that he could make verbatim records of talks or sermons that he heard. By 1843, Hallam had become sufficiently self-educated, and self-motivated, to leave the family farm and become a schoolteacher at Flagg, near Taddington in Derbyshire. Hallam's career to this point is strongly reminiscent of that of William Barnes—an autodidactic progress from farming to teaching—but in 1845 he entered the employment of the Manchester, Sheffield, and Lincolnshire Railway, and after brief stints in Ashton-under-Lyme and Whaley Bridge, Hallam moved to Manchester in 1846, where he lived for the rest of his life. In 1869, in his late forties, Hallam married Martha Chadwick, but their marriage was short-lived: she died in 1873, and he did not remarry. For more than forty years Hallam worked as a bookkeeper or audit clerk for the railway company; but he continued to think of himself as a native of the Peak District, keeping in touch with friends and relatives; and at his death most of his books were bequeathed to the Chapel-en-le-Frith Institute (which also received a financial bequest for the purchase of the remaining instalments of the *Oxford English Dictionary* and the future *English Dialect Dictionary*).

Where did this initial interest in language and pronunciation come from? Hallam's autobiographical notes contain a single, poignant sentence to give us a clue. This is included to explain his leaving school in 1830, in spite of his academic promise: 'I might have gone to school longer', he writes, 'but a slight impediment in speech at that time caused me to elect to remain at home'. That is all, and we should not overinterpret; but when Hallam also records that his teacher came to the farm to try to arrange

---

[90] Oxford, Bodleian Libraries, MS Eng. lang. d. 32, fols 1–9.

76   The Victorians and English Dialect

his return to school, and this—because of his talent—at no charge to his parents, we may well wonder about the nature and severity of Hallam's 'slight impediment in speech', and how it affected his growing sensitivity to language and pronunciation. (It is possible that Ellis also experienced speech difficulties in his youth. In a single footnote in *Early English Pronunciation*, he reveals that 'it cost me much trouble and years of practice to obtain (kl-) with ease and certainty, and the same for (gl-). As a consequence, my attention has been constantly drawn to this defect of speech in others'.)[91]

In Manchester, Hallam joined an essay and discussion society (a friend, he remembered, introduced him as someone 'who reads Dictionaries through'), and started to learn Greek and Latin and Old English. His notes contain lists of some of the books that he acquired in the 1850s and 1860s, and these include classic works of mid-century philology (by Garnett and Trench) and an unusually wide range of dialect glossaries (for example, by Forby, Carr, Hunter, Akerman, William Gaskell, and Barnes—as well as Barnes' poems).[92] On 5 November 1863, he took down his 'first dialectal speech recorded from audition or dictation [. . .] from Mr Robert Bagshaw of High Lane in Norbury, Cheshire, a native of Chapel-en-le-Frith'. Next, he rendered the Biblical 'Song of Solomon' into two different Peak dialects, those of Chapel-en-le-Frith and Taddington. When he embarked on this practice of dialect transcription, Hallam was using a phonetic notation of his own devising; later, he would switch to Ellis' Palaeotype and Glossic.

Hallam and Ellis made contact in the following way—and the circumstances also clarify further the steps by which Ellis turned from the study of medieval phonology to contemporary. In attempting to reconstruct the pronunciation of Chaucer, Ellis found the varying realizations of long and short *i* to be especially problematic—not least before the consonant cluster *nd*. As one possible way forward, and alongside consultation with James Murray, Ellis decided to gather information about the value of the vowel in present-day pronunciations. Accordingly, in July 1868 Ellis published a call for help in the *Athenaeum* magazine, announcing that he 'would feel obliged to any gentleman personally acquainted with any provincial dialect in any part of the United Kingdom, if he would communicate with him respecting varieties in the pronunciation of the pronoun I, and of long I generally, as a more extensive knowledge of these varieties than Mr Ellis can at present command is desirable for the purpose of illustrating the sound attributed to this letter in the time of Chaucer'.[93] This is a significant moment: the first, tentative attempt to 'crowdsource' a survey of English dialects, and we should remember that Ellis was already familiar with this mode of seeking help through his involvement with the Philological Society and its intended dictionary. A number of correspondents responded, and Ellis recorded his gratitude, and their names, in *Early English Pronunciation*, designating them his 'dialectic correspondents'.[94] Among these was Thomas Hallam.

---

[91] Ellis, *On Early English Pronunciation*, IV, 1326 n. 1.
[92] Oxford, Bodleian Libraries, MS Eng. lang. d. 21, fols 10–11.
[93] *The Athenaeum* 18 July 1868, 86.
[94] Ellis, *On Early English Pronunciation*, I, 271, n. 1, 277, n. 1.

After an extensive correspondence, Hallam and Ellis first met in person, at the latter's house in London, in April 1869. They had a brief meeting the first day (the first of the month), but the next day they spent five hours together, from afternoon to evening, taking tea in Ellis' study and 'convers[ing] on the Peak Dialect and other provincial sounds, words and phrases; especially Cheshire and Lancashire'.[95]

At a number of moments in the early volumes of *Early English Pronunciation*, the reader can almost see Ellis realizing the importance of contemporary dialect evidence before their very eyes.[96] But while Ellis, in his London home, interviewed servants, workers, and provincial visitors (such as Hallam), he rarely travelled himself; so he needed a network of informants to keep him supplied with transcriptions and data.[97] By the time of the preface to Volume III in 1871, therefore, Ellis was 'invit[ing] all those into whose hands these pages may fall to give me their assistance, or procure me the assistance of others, in collecting materials for this novel and interesting research'.[98]

Ellis quickly developed a set of prescriptions as to what was required in a good fieldworker. His 1872 address to the Philological Society explains the need, and also the difficulty. For one thing, it is a wholly different form of study to the usual book-based endeavour: 'the bookman has to be converted into a natureman; the chair and library have to be forsaken for the horse and hut'.[99] Quite apart from the technical skills required (linguistic and phonetic), there were also unexpected traps to beware of: 'the great difficulty in making observations is to abstain from inferences'; and 'another difficulty is that of eliminating the habits of the observer himself, so as to record as much as possible the habits of the person observed without alloy'.[100] In other words, 'even in collecting European patois, a cultivated man converses with the people, and almost necessarily misconceives their thoughts and misrepresents their words'.[101]

So nineteenth-century dialect collectors such as Ellis and Hallam were perfectly aware of what was later to be labelled the 'observer's paradox'. 'Peasants do not speak naturally to strangers', Ellis remarked, and so arguably 'the only safe method is to listen to the natural speaking of some one who does not know that he is observed'.[102] The problem, as many collectors commented, is that speakers were often diglossic even within their own dialect—speaking two distinct varieties depending on their interlocutor.

Just like later surveyors, Ellis soon developed a sense of a hierarchy of sources, in terms of which speakers the fieldworker should seek to draw evidence from:

---

[95] Oxford, Bodleian Libraries, MS Eng. lang. d. 21, fol. 48.
[96] See especially Ellis, *On Early English Pronunciation*, I, 284–94.
[97] See Murray, *Caught in the Web of Words*, pp. 75–6.
[98] Ellis, *On Early English Pronunciation*, III, v.
[99] Ellis, 'First Annual Address', p. 23.
[100] Ellis, 'First Annual Address', p. 10.
[101] Ellis, 'First Annual Address', p. 20.
[102] Ellis, *On Early English Pronunciation*, III, vi, IV, 1086. See further, for example, Jacques Van Keymeulen, 'The Dialect Dictionary', in Charles Boberg, John Nerbonne, and Dominic Watt (eds), *The Handbook of Dialectology* (Oxford: Wiley Blackwell, 2017), pp. 39–56, at pp. 47–52.

78   The Victorians and English Dialect

No pronunciation should be recorded which has not been actually heard from some speaker who uses it naturally and habitually. The older peasantry and children who have not been at school preserve the dialectic sounds most purely. But the present facilities of communication are rapidly destroying all traces of our older dialectic English. Market women, who attend large towns, have generally a mixed style of speech. The daughters of peasants and small farmers, on becoming domestic servants, learn a new language, and corrupt the genuine Doric of their parents.[103]

This is the view from the centre, from Ellis' London base. As a record of Hallam's own methods as a fieldworker, we can turn to another memorandum in his papers, this one titled 'T. Hallam's mode of introduction to working people to obtain dialectal information'.[104] This document begins as if it is a draft letter, to be sent in advance; but it soon transitions into a set of practical guidelines:

I am away from Manchester for a holiday of a fortnight, and this year I am visiting –shire, –shire, &c. When I am away for a holiday I have a curious pursuit, or mode of employing my time; that is, at any village or town which I visit, after making inquiries, I get into conversation with one or two elderly working people who are natives, in order to ask how various words are spoken by working people, when conversing amongst themselves without "talking fine", what we call the dialect of the place or district.

There is nothing startling here so far, though Hallam's specification of elderly informants is worth noting. The next section of the document, however, takes us more closely into Hallam's explanations, and the conversations that often ensued:

I then observe—There's a great deal of attention being paid to dialects now, for the purpose of taking down (recording) the different ways of speaking words before they are lost. You see with the spread of schools & education (learning), a great many of the old ways of speaking, & numbers of old words, will be left off (go out of use), in another generation or two; so that we are only just in time to take down many of these pronunciations and words.

I next assure them—"This information is not collected for the purpose of putting any squibs or jokes in newspapers, or to make fun of dialects in any way; but for comparing dialects one with another in all parts of the country["].

After that, Hallam's document reveals that he introduced Ellis by name ('there is a gentleman in London, A. J. Ellis Esq'), and the nature of his great project, and the three learned societies that were publishing his results—clearly to create a sense of the importance of the research, and the value of the speaker's contribution. Hallam

---

[103] Ellis, *On Early English Pronunciation*, III, vi.
[104] Oxford, Bodleian Libraries, MS Eng. lang. d. 21, fols 31–3. See also Ellis, *On Early English Pronunciation*, V, 1436–7/4–5; Drury, 'Aural Community and William Barnes as Earwitness', pp. 445–6.

also indicated his own provinciality and accessibility ('I was bro[ugh]t up in the Peak of Derbyshire'), and his own status as a speaker of dialect, giving some examples of his own regional accent. The document concludes:

> By this time, my informants generally feel at home. I then begin to ask how representative words are spoken in the dialect without any refining, and they give the pronunc[iatio]n willingly & freely, & very often with marked pleasure. They frequently give an appropriate dialectal phrase or sentence illustrating the use of the respective words.

Hallam's document was written in 1887, after two decades of intensive fieldwork. There is probably no better record to be found of how Victorian dialect collecting was actually done—although as we shall see in a moment, Hallam's own notebooks provide us with equally precious evidence of a complementary sort.

So let us now turn to Hallam's travels, and his actual field notes. To begin with, we should observe a fundamental paradox in Hallam's dialect-collecting travels. As we have seen, Ellis had lamented, in an evocative phrase, that the railway whistle was scaring the dialects out of existence, and many other commentators also pointed the finger at increasing mobility as one of the main causes of dialect loss.[105] However, it was precisely the network of railways that enabled this greatest of Victorian fieldworkers to record all the dialects that he did. For Hallam, we should recall, was a railway employee: for most of his adult life he worked for the Manchester, Sheffield, and Lincolnshire Railway, and this seems to have enabled him to acquire travel passes (perhaps free) for his annual two weeks of journeying. An 1882 document is preserved which records the request for that year's travels: 'Please procure for me the following passes for my annual holiday', Hallam writes, and then lists the journeys he intends to take on the Great Western Railway, London and North Western Railway, Great Eastern Railway, and Great Northern Railway.[106] So the railways facilitated Hallam's dialect studies: without them, and without his privileged access as a railway employee, he couldn't have surveyed the dialects that he did. As Hallam's notes also record, he 'travel[led] 3rd Class generally', in order to maximize 'contact with working people'.[107]

As he travelled the country, Hallam, like Henry Higgins, was busy scribbling in his pocketbook, both as an interviewer and an eavesdropper. As physical, archival objects, Hallam's notebooks, preserved as a collection in the Bodleian Library, are powerfully evocative. Most of them measure just over 5 inches by 3 inches, and are fastened with a metal clasp. On the front cover of each—there are nearly 80 in all— Hallam has pasted a numbered label, to mark the place of each volume in his series: number 29, for example, covers the period from 19 April to 5 August 1878.[108] When Hallam was travelling, he could get through a whole notebook in less than a week; at

[105] Ellis, 'On Glosik', p. 112.
[106] Oxford, Bodleian Libraries, MS Eng. lang. d. 21, fol. 94.
[107] Oxford, Bodleian Libraries, MS Eng. lang. d. 21, fol. 93.
[108] Oxford, Bodleian Libraries, MS Eng. lang. d. 22, fols 88–90 ('List of my Metallic Note Books').

80   The Victorians and English Dialect

other times, a notebook could last him for months. These notebooks, written on the spot, were the records of raw material from which later copies and digests could be made, and out of which patterns could be observed and conclusions drawn. It was thus a catastrophe when, on one occasion, Hallam lost one of his notebooks (number 54, for the period 25 to 30 August 1883), when he was near Buxton in Norfolk; in spite of earnest appeals in local newspapers, the notebook was never retrieved, and there is a break in Hallam's run of records.

Let us catch the atmosphere of Hallam's travels by dipping into his notebooks for one (typical) annual holiday. In two weeks in late August and early September 1881, on a long tour, he gathered dialect information in Shropshire, Worcestershire, Herefordshire, Northamptonshire, Huntingdonshire, and Cambridgeshire (notebooks number 41, 42, and 43).[109] Much of the time he was overhearing, jotting down words and pronunciations from the speech he was listening in on: his notebooks include a 'man in lane', 'boys playing cricket', 'man with milk cart', 'in the market [at Northampton], man selling fruit', 'several girls and boys', 'boys playing about the fountain in Market Place' (again, in Northampton), and 'several tradesmen of the town in the Smoke room of the White Lion Inn [in Oundle]'. Many of these overhearings took place on trains and at stations, such as 'man, 35 in train' (Hallam often tried to estimate the age of speakers, alert to age as a linguistic variable), '3 market women [who] got in for Market Drayton', and more than one 'porter at station'. Sometimes Hallam used the railway as the grounds for elicitation: 'what station's this?' he asked a 'working man' at Crudgington in Shropshire, in order to hear the local pronunciation of the place name.

These were eavesdropped encounters, fleeting and nameless. Alongside such snatched phonetic reportage, Hallam conducted a fuller series of interviews with individuals whose names and personal histories he took care to discover and record. In Bridgnorth in Shropshire he talked with Francis Preece, a 70-year-old boot and shoemaker, in Hardingstone in Northamptonshire with 'Miss Alice Fitzhugh—say 45—has lived with one or more well-to-do families', and in Holme in Huntingdonshire with 'Will[ia]m Knighton, 31, born July 13th 1850—has a horse and trap for hire'.[110] In conversation with one especially elderly informant, the hundred-year-old Mary Ashcroft of Bewdley in Worcestershire, he filled pages of his notebook with her biography, childhood memories, family trees, and even her clothes and actions ('has on a brown stuff dress she made [...] had darned a small hole [...] at 12 o'clock threaded a needle').[111] Hallam jotted down her children's dates from her family bible, and noted that 'in speaking of [the] Bible [she] used <u>him</u> for <u>it</u> several times'.

As can be seen, then, Hallam's notebooks constitute an unparalleled (and unexploited) record of a large number of individuals in Victorian England and their

---

[109] Oxford, Bodleian Libraries, MS Eng. lang. g. 41–3. See also Oxford, Bodleian Library, MS Eng. lang. d. 21, fol. 93.

[110] Oxford, Bodleian Libraries, MS Eng. lang. g. 41, fol 84; MS Eng. lang. g. 42, fol. 90; MS Eng. lang. g 43, fol. 92.

[111] Oxford, Bodleian Libraries, MS Eng. lang. g. 41, fols 91–106, and MS Eng. lang. g. 42, fols 4–15; see also MS Eng. lang. g. 38, fol. 42, and Ellis, *On Early English Pronunciation*, V, 59∗, 1545/113.

speech styles (recorded on specific, datable days), individuals whose life-details can be confirmed and supplemented by other sources, such as censuses; they are also a record of ephemeral moments of everyday life ('several girls, and one of them running after a boy, to hit him playfully & probably for slight mischief'—in Stourport on 4 October 1880).[112] Hallam was scrupulous about the informants he interviewed at greater length, and he would write up biographical sketches when he transferred his material from notebook to document. On 13 April 1879, for example, he interviewed 18-year-old John Mullett, from Sawston in Cambridgeshire: 'Mr J. M. left home three years ago, and is now a clerk with the Newstead Colliery Company [. . .] I met with him at the Globe Temperance Hotel, 3, Hound's Gate, Nottingham'. Hallam subsequently wrote to Mullett to check his dialect history and 'to ask what is the business or calling of his father: He courteously replied [. . .] that he (his father) is foreman at a Paper Mill, and added: "Of course living there all my life time up to three years ago, I heard a very great deal of the labouring class's dialect"'.[113]

It is important to remember that Hallam was mostly collecting phonetic evidence, not vocabulary or folklore. His notebooks are full of the transcriptions of individual words, and only rarely record longer snatches of speech. But sometimes, it seems, he couldn't resist: the notebooks for his tour of 1881, for example, contain points of dialect grammar ('us went to Ledbury' in Much Cowarne in Herefordshire, and 'I knew nothing about it while yesterday' in Great Stukeley in Huntingdonshire) and also show a recurrent interest in distinctive local surnames (Dalloway in Bewdley, for example, and Dann, Mackness, and Clare around Huntingdon).[114] In one of his later fits of indexing, Hallam made a list of some of the types of miscellanea recorded in his notebooks: these included 'Epitaphs', 'Tautology in Local Nomenclature', and 'Old people whom I have seen' (such as Mary Ashcroft).[115]

In the 1870s and 1880s Hallam was mostly collecting according to Ellis' agenda and needs, usually in a narrowly targeted way. Hallam's phonetic interests were not wholly determined by Ellis, though; he had, after all, commenced his own surveying before he ever came into contact with the London patriarch, starting with unaccented *i* back in the late 1830s. He seems to have placed especial value on the collection he had made of 'Educated English Pronunciation' (much of it gathered prior to his association with Ellis), specifying this material in particular in his will. This collection provides an interesting, and perhaps unexpected, contrast to his work on regional dialect: for the latter, Hallam sought out older, more locally rooted speakers, but for his research on 'Educated English Pronunciation', it was public eminence that formed the criterion for inclusion. Michael MacMahon has made a study of Hallam's 'Educated English' material, and has concluded that, as with his work for Ellis, he was listening for a small number of phonetic features (word-initial *cl-* and

---

[112] Oxford, Bodleian Libraries, MS Eng. lang. g. 38, fol. 27.

[113] Oxford, Bodleian Libraries, MS Eng. lang. d. 1, fol. 159; see also Ellis, *On Early English Pronunciation*, V, 1682/250.

[114] Oxford, Bodleian Libraries, MS Eng. lang. g. 42, fols 2, 59; MS Eng. lang. g. 43, fols 46, 57.

[115] Oxford, Bodleian Libraries, MS Eng. lang. d. 27, fols 61–77.

82   The Victorians and English Dialect

gl-, syllable-initial *cy*- and *gy*-, unaccented *i*, post-vocalic *r*, and word-final -*ed*).[116] Hallam's provisional conclusion was that, even among users of 'Educated Pronunciation', there was 'no common standard', and all were 'local in some degree'. The language of the pulpit, he suggested, was especially 'local', that of the bar 'archaic', and that of the stage 'too imitative—not safe as second hand'. As for the speech of 'professors of language', he judged that was 'too laboured'.[117]

These 'Educated English' transcriptions exist side by side with the regional dialect transcriptions in Hallam's notebooks, but an index (made in 1882, then updated in 1895) enables us to see whose speech Hallam recorded for this project.[118] These were transcriptions made at public performances, not private interviews: Hallam listened to politicians (such as the Earl of Derby, Lord Shaftesbury, and Benjamin Disraeli), various bishops and preachers (such as William H. Booth, D. L. Moody, and Samuel Wilberforce), and assorted other public figures (such as Thomas Huxley and the Prince of Wales). There are over four hundred speakers listed in Hallam's index, and again, this is a unique repository of the voices of a certain section of Victorian Britain, mostly dating from before the advent of sound recording. One of the speakers whose language Hallam observed was Charles Dickens—'The Great Writer', as he labels him. Hallam went to hear him read twice, on 12 April 1866 and 16 February 1867, on both occasions at Manchester's Free Trade Hall. At the first reading, Hallam's notes reveal, the repertoire included *Nicholas Nickleby* ('niculus'), and Hallam noticed that in words such as *odd* and *off* Dickens' 'lips [were] a little more pushed out than Manchester &c—as London generally'. At the second performance, the readings included *A Christmas Carol* and 'The Boy at Mugby' (only recently published). Alert to his particular phonetic concerns, Hallam observed a 'pure' *gl*- in *glee* and a 'pure' *cl*- in *clerk* and *clear*, a 'cyan' pronunciation in the first syllable of *candle*, and a recurrent *i* in unaccented syllables, with 'ĭs', 'ĭd', and 'ĭst' at the end of verbs. The first syllable of *neither* was noted as 'nĭ', and the middle syllables of *particular* as 'tikkĕ'.[119] Although there are many eye-witness accounts of Dickens' highly dramatic readings, these seem to be the only known transcriptions of Dickens' actual speech.

As his index to 'Educated English Pronunciation' reminds us, Hallam was professionally an accountant or bookkeeper. He possessed, to a high degree, skills in the organization, presentation, and appraisal of complex data. He was also, seemingly, a compulsive record-keeper: one of Hallam's autobiographical notes states that 'On the 1st March 1833 I commenced to keep a record of the weather, which I have continued to this day. It is a plain account of 2 to 4 lines per day'.[120] Sadly, this weather diary is not preserved among his extant papers; what is preserved, however, is an abundance of shorter documents which record and tabulate various activities—for example, adding up the dates, timings, and durations of Hallam's meetings with Ellis (between 1869 and 1884 there were nineteen meetings in all, adding up to ninety-seven hours of

---

[116] MacMahon, 'Thomas Hallam and the Study of Dialect', pp. 25–9.
[117] Oxford, Bodleian Libraries, MS Eng. lang. d. 17, fol. 211.
[118] Oxford, Bodleian Libraries, MS Eng. lang. d. 17, fols 70–98.
[119] Oxford, Bodleian Libraries, MS Eng. lang. g. 6, fols 14, 98–9. See also MS Eng. lang. d. 17, fol. 115.
[120] Oxford, Bodleian Libraries, MS Eng. lang. d. 21, fol. 7.

contact time).[121] It is therefore no surprise that Hallam copied, indexed, catalogued, abridged, collated, tabulated, and rearranged the raw material of his dialect note-books in multiple ways; and these copyings and reorganizations swell his Bodleian papers to an enormous volume. But before we fix upon a stereotype of Hallam as some sort of obsessive loner, we should also note that he evidently possessed consid-erable social skills. The success with which he engaged multiple casual acquaintances in conversation attests to this, as does his voluminous correspondence: he was clearly a sympathetic letter-writer (and letter-receiver), and Ellis, Murray, and a host of local dialect collectors confided in him over the years. His obituary in the *Manchester City News* states that 'his exceptionally modest and quiet demeanour [...] enabled him to make himself at home with the humble folk whose utterances he was chiefly anxious to hear and record'.[122]

It is not easy to establish the total number of places for which Hallam gathered dialect specimens. His papers offer a number of different calculations: one list comes to a total of 942 locations, another to 982, a third to as many as 1,109.[123] About three-quarters of these were places actually visited by Hallam: the other quarter is accounted for by interviews with dialect speakers in a place other than their home region (as, for example, in Hallam's meeting with John Mullett of Sawston in a hotel in Nottingham). He interviewed speakers from all thirty-nine of the historic coun-ties of England, with the highest totals for Derbyshire, Lancashire, Lincolnshire, Northamptonshire, Staffordshire, and Yorkshire. These are astonishing figures, the record of an unparalleled programme of research, sustained over decades.

So what did it all add up to, all of Hallam's travels and notebooks and transcriptions and indexes? To try to answer that question, we need to get to grips with the final, gargantuan volume of Ellis' *Early English Pronunciation*.

The Existing Phonology of English Dialects

The long-awaited and much-delayed Chapter XI of *On Early English Pronunciation* had appeared in 1874, as the final chapter of Part IV. Its title was 'Illustrations of the Pronunciation of English during the Nineteenth Century', and it was divided into two main sections (themselves with subsequent subdivisions and even sub-subdivisions), on 'Educated English Pronunciation' (pages 1085–243) and 'Natural English Pronunciation' (pages 1243–432), the first part of which shared some affini-ties with Hallam's private project of the same name.[124] But the two hundred pages on 'Natural English Pronunciation' in Part IV were now presented as merely 'introduc-tory matter', a prolegomenon to the presentation of 'the new collections of English Dialects which have been made [...] in order to register dialectal pronunciation with

---

[121] Oxford, Bodleian Libraries, MS Eng. lang. d. 21, fols 47–9.
[122] [Anon], 'Thomas Hallam'.
[123] Oxford, Bodleian Libraries, MS Eng. lang. d. 64, fol. 8; MS Eng. lang. d. 21, fols 21–2.
[124] See Ellis, *On Early English Pronunciation*, IV, 1208–14.

84   The Victorians and English Dialect

a completeness hitherto unattained and even unattempted'.[125] By 'natural' pronunciation, Ellis meant 'a pronunciation which has been handed down historically, or has changed organically, without the interference of orthoepists, classical theorists, literary fancies, fashionable heresies, and so forth, in short "untamed" English everywhere, from the lowest vulgarity [...] to the mere provinciality'.[126] These two hundred introductory pages were concerned with questions of principle, comparison, and phonetic theory (such as vowel length, types of sound changes, and difficulties of transcription); Ellis did not, yet, cite much of the evidence which Hallam and others had begun to gather for him.

Nonetheless, he confidently declared in Part IV that 'the materials for Part V are [...] all collected', and two years later, in his presidential address of 1877 to the Philological Society, Henry Sweet was evidently expecting the appearance of Volume V that very year—a publication 'which will contain an immense mass of precious information on our living English dialects'.[127] But it didn't appear that year after all, or the next, or indeed in the next decade; and Ellis had to keep making apologies for the non-publication of his final volume.

Progress was slow, then; but it was definitely thorough. Through the late 1870s and 1880s Hallam continued to travel the country, and Ellis continued to accumulate material both from the Manchester man and his other assistants.[128] James Murray was a particular help, especially in the earlier years. In 1881 and 1882 Ellis served a further turn as President of the Philological Society, delivering two further presidential addresses, and in 1886 and 1887 he presented to the Society two major reports on the progress of his dialectal work.[129] Part of the difficulty, as Ellis later explained, was 'the necessity of completing [the research] in all its details before a page of the book could be printed, or the maps drawn'.[130] But by late 1887 the first proof sheets of Volume V could be printed for checking, though it must have been a stunningly complex volume to typeset and check (thankfully, as one might have imagined, Hallam was an exceptionally sharp-eyed proofreader). In 1888, however, Ellis' wife died, and he felt a grim consciousness of his own time running out as well: he was anxious to see his work printed before his death.[131]

In 1889, Volume V of *Early English Pronunciation* finally appeared, bearing the separate title of *The Existing Phonology of English Dialects*, and it was co-published, as the earlier volumes had been, by the Philological Society, the Early English Text Society, and the Chaucer Society. It was enormous. The main text was 835 pages in length, preceded by over one hundred pages of 'preliminary matter', and it weighed

---

[125] Ellis, *On Early English Pronunciation*, IV, xv.

[126] Ellis, *On Early English Pronunciation*, IV, 1243–4.

[127] Ellis, *On Early English Pronunciation*, IV, xx; Sweet, *Collected Papers*, p. 86.

[128] See Sanders, 'Alexander John Ellis'.

[129] Ellis, 'Tenth Annual Address', 'Eleventh Annual Address', *Report on Dialectal Work*, English Dialect Society 49 (London: English Dialect Society, 1885), *Second Report on Dialectal Work*, English Dialect Society 55 (London: English Dialect Society, 1887).

[130] Ellis, *On Early English Pronunciation*, V, 2266/834.

[131] See A. J. Ellis to Thomas Hallam 25 August 1888, Oxford, Bodleian Libraries, MS Eng. lang. d. 13, fol. 281v.

5½ lbs. 'It is quite a thick volume', Hallam observed to Ellis when he received his copy, though Ellis was insistent that 'I have in every instance studied brevity and compression'.[132] But Hallam also added: 'It will be a memorial for all time, of the immense labour bestowed upon it, and of the vast stores of most valuable dialectal information obtained and secured just in time'.[133]

The first sentence of Ellis' introduction supplies a mission statement:

> The object of this treatise is to determine with considerable accuracy the different forms *now*, or *within the last hundred years*, assumed by the descendants of the same original word in passing through the mouths of uneducated people, speaking an inherited language, in all parts of Great Britain where English is the ordinary medium of communication between peasant and peasant.[134]

The two distinguishing features of Ellis' project, compared to other dialect studies to date, were, first, that it was concerned with 'geographical distribution', and, second, that its evidence was drawn from 'living speakers'—hence, unlike most previous students of dialect (and also unlike himself in the first four volumes of *Early English Pronunciation*) Ellis had resolved 'to reject almost all printed books'.[135] Of course, he couldn't simply collect everything, in an indiscriminate manner, and Ellis had quickly realized that what he needed was a passage of text, or selection of words, for which variant pronunciations could be collected from different parts of the country; for studying phonology rather than word distribution, the collection of variant forms of the same word was much more useful than the collection of different words. The first passages of text he chose for this purpose, bizarrely, were extracts from *The Two Gentlemen of Verona* ('selected for their rustic tone').[136] But soon, with help from Murray, Ellis developed a much better collecting tool, his so-called 'Comparative Specimen' (devised 1873, revised 1875). Sometimes known as 'Why John Has No Doubts' after its title, this curious text narrates a short comic tale filled with odd details; those details were included, though, not for their narrative value but in order to give examples of certain sounds or sound sequences which Ellis wanted to gather evidence for ('She swore she saw him with her own eyes, lying stretched at full length, on the ground, in his good Sunday coat, close by the door of the house, down at the corner of yon lane').[137]

In 1879, Ellis supplemented the Comparative Specimen with another text known as the 'Dialect Test', considerably shorter than the Comparative Specimen (it begins, 'So I say, mates, you see now that I am right').[138] Ellis sent it out to his various

---

[132] Thomas Hallam to A. J. Ellis 10 September 1889, Oxford, Bodleian Libraries, MS Eng. lang. d. 13, fol. 475r; Ellis, *On Early English Pronunciation*, V, xviii.

[133] See also Ellis, *Report on Dialectal Work*, p. 45.

[134] Ellis, *On Early English Pronunciation*, V, 1433/1.

[135] Ellis, *On Early English Pronunciation*, V, 1439/7.

[136] Ellis, *On Early English Pronunciation*, III, xi.

[137] Ellis, *On Early English Pronunciation*, V, 7*, 1433–4/1–2; see also Ellis, *On Early English Pronunciation*, IV, 1247; Sanders, 'Alexander John Ellis', pp. 583–8.

[138] Ellis, *On Early English Pronunciation*, V, 8*–16*, 1435/3.

86 The Victorians and English Dialect

collectors and informants with minute instructions as to what they were to listen for. For the first word, 'So', Ellis' helpers were instructed: 'Note whether *s* or *z*. Note whether *o* has a vanishing *ŏŏ* after it as in London. Mark the various fracture sounds, frequently used in the north, as *ee*, *ay*, or *oo*, followed by *a* in China'. For the opening sound of 'right', there were elaborate instructions: 'First mark the *r*, whether it is trilled with the tip of the tongue as in Scotch or Italian, or whether the tip of the tongue is merely raised without being trilled as frequently in London and Spain. Note if the effect is produced by a rattle of the uvula at the back of the mouth as in Paris, or else by the same accompanied by a considerable closure of the lips as in Northumberland. Note also if the effect is produced by turning the tongue up so as almost to point down the throat as in Dorsetshire, or by retracting the tongue very much as in Oxfordshire, both sounds being very harsh and but slightly if at all trilled'. All this just for the first sound in the word! Ellis wanted his informants to be alert to dialect grammar and vocabulary as well as phonology: for 'am', he advised them; 'Use *am*, *is*, *are*, or *be*, according to the habit of the district, always selecting an uneducated person, such as an old native man or woman, because all young people have been *taught* to use *am*'.[139]

Ellis' third collecting tool, alongside the Comparative Specimen and Dialect Test, was his use of word lists. To 1,700 clergymen he sent out a survey of words (drawn from Sweet's *History of English Sounds*, first published in 1874) and received about five hundred copies back, though only a tenth of these, he judged, were of high quality; and he later added to this word survey all the words included in his Comparative Specimen and Dialect Test, to arrive at a 'Classified Word List'.[140] This complete list contained 971 words, subdivided by language of origin into 'Wessex and Norse' (that is, Old English and Old Norse: 712 words), 'English' (common words of uncertain etymology; 96 words), and 'Romance' (163 words), and then further organized according to the main vowel sound. Ellis did not expect his fieldworkers to collect examples of all 971 words; rather, these lists supplied a repertoire of possible words to elicit according to the feature being studied (usually a vowel). Hallam's notebooks are full of short, Ellis-derived word lists which vary according to where or what he is collecting. Ellis' clergymen-informants were also encouraged to 'characterise the nature of the singsong of the speech, underlining as may be, rough, smooth, thick, thin, indistinct, clear, hesitating, glib, whining, drawling, jerking, up and down in pitch, rising in pitch at end, sinking at end, monotonous'.[141]

A decade and a half of targeted fieldwork, coordinated by Ellis and led by Hallam, resulted in a great corpus of Comparative Specimens, Dialect Tests, and assorted word lists. Presented in systematic order, it was the printing of this raw material which made up the bulk of the eight hundred pages of *The Existing Phonology*; and it was largely from the evidence of these three types of source that Ellis produced his analysis of dialect distributions—though inevitably, Volume V of *Early English*

---

[139] Ellis, *On Early English Pronunciation*, V, 8*–9*.
[140] Ellis, *Report on Dialectal Work*, pp. 47–8, and *On Early English Pronunciation*, V, 16*–31*, 1434–5/2–3.
[141] Ellis, *On Early English Pronunciation*, V, 25*.

Pronunciation, like all the earlier volumes, also contains a lot of material which doesn't adhere closely to the main goals of the investigation.

According to Ellis, 104 versions of the Comparative Specimen are included in *The Existing Phonology*, and 116 versions of the Dialect Test.[142] Ellis doesn't give a total for the number of word lists, but since *The Existing Phonology* is based on evidence for speakers from 1,145 different places, we may assume that at least several hundred were utilized.[143] Ellis prints the transcriptions of the Specimens and Tests in full, and the word lists in smaller print, in almost overwhelming mass and detail. His presentational techniques—as befits a volume co-published by the Early English Text Society—resemble those of an editor of medieval manuscripts. Where multiple versions of the Specimen or Test exist from a particular area, he selects one to print in full as the base text, and then beneath this leading version he prints (in full or in part) the samples from nearby places: thus, for instance, the Comparative Specimen for three locations near Durham places Edmondbyers at the top ('sii a SEE, mEEts'), and then Lanchester ('*soo* aa see, meets') and Annfield Plain ('sii a see, marɐz') below—with nineteen other versions from the north-east to follow.[144] (We can see that lexical variation is recorded as well as phonological, with *marrows* in place of *mates* in Annfield Plain.)[145] The printing of Dialect Tests and Comparative Specimens for areas where multiple versions had been collected takes up a great many pages in *The Existing Phonology*, though Ellis justifies such a space-hungry layout on the grounds that it provides 'a remarkably easy method of comparison'.[146] Similarly, Ellis prints his word lists as if they are variant readings in a multi-manuscript edition, or a composite edition of medieval glosses, with comparable use of capital letters as sigla: so, for example, recording variant pronunciations of the word *son* in the Leicester area, Ellis's terse catalogue states 'SE *su*ₒn, LGM sùₒn, Lr sun', where S is Syston, E a Miss Charlotte Ellis living in Belgrave, L is Loughborough, G Glenfield, M Market Harborough, and Lr Leicester.[147]

The 1,145 places are distributed fairly evenly across England (as Ellis' methodology required), with a less thorough treatment of Wales and Scotland (heavily reliant on the works of Murray and Melville Bell for the latter), and only a single location included for Ireland. As the largest county, it is not surprising that Yorkshire receives the highest number of samples (ninety-three locations), but also treated thoroughly are Derbyshire (sixty-seven), Lancashire (sixty-one), Lincolnshire (fifty-five), Northamptonshire (fifty-two), and Staffordshire (fifty-one); the correspondence with Hallam's areas of greatest activity is not, of course, coincidental. Least fully recorded, at least in terms of number of locations, are Suffolk (twelve), Westmorland (ten), Middlesex (seven), Rutland (five), and—counted as an English county—Monmouthshire (three). For most places, there is a single source of

---

[142] Ellis, *On Early English Pronunciation*, V, xvii; but see Hallam's calculations in Oxford, Bodleian Libraries, MS Eng. lang. d. 27, fols 126–9.
[143] Ellis, *On Early English Pronunciation*, V, xvii, xix.
[144] Ellis, *On Early English Pronunciation*, V, 2088/656.
[145] See Wright, *English Dialect Dictionary*, IV, 41–3, sense 4.
[146] Ellis, *On Early English Pronunciation*, V, 1440/8.
[147] Ellis, *On Early English Pronunciation*, V, 1924/492.

88   The Victorians and English Dialect

evidence—a word list, or a Specimen or Test—but for some, Ellis was able to utilize a number of separate sources (for Rothbury in Northumberland, for example, Ellis was able to draw on two Dialect Tests and a Comparative Specimen, as well as some separate notes on words).[148] The materials for Hallam's home town of Chapel-en-le-Frith were especially abundant, 'with the minute particulars which TH prefers'.[149] It is also worth noting that, in his catalogue of places surveyed, Ellis often includes the local pronunciation of the place name, if this is not deemed obvious, and this now amounts to a fascinating collection of forms, many of which have since receded at the rise of what are called 'spelling pronunciations': Ellis records, for example, that Chelmsford was locally pronounced as '(:tʃɛmzfɛd)', Garstang as '(:gjaa·stɪn)', and Oswestry as '(:hɔdʒestri)'. (Like the Tests, Specimens, and word lists, these are all given in Ellis' Palaeotype notation.)

Hundreds of figures such as Charlotte Ellis of Belgrave (no relation) are glimpsed fleetingly in her namesake's teeming pages. Ellis' preface states that no fewer than 811 persons supplied him with information, and an alphabetical roll-call allows us to see who they were. Many, such as Charlotte Ellis, are credited with having supplied dialect content for only a single location—normally, of course, their own: Ellis' acknowledgements thus supply an invaluable commemoration of a vast network of local dialect collectors, most of whom would otherwise be wholly forgotten in this regard.[150] The list of names contains many individuals whom we have met already in this book—J. C. Atkinson, Mary Powley, F. K. Robinson of Whitby, Richard Stead of the *Holderness Glossary*—and many more whom we shall meet in due course; and we shall return more fully to this cadre of local enthusiasts in Chapter 4, when we examine the membership of the English Dialect Society. But we should pause on the three individuals (each labelled 'a chief helper') and one institution that Ellis singles out for special gratitude.

In pride of place, rightly, is Thomas Hallam, whose 'unflagging diligence', 'accuracy of report', and 'trustworthiness of detail' are praised on the very first page of Ellis' book.[151] *The Existing Phonology* could never have been brought to completion without Hallam's 'main excursions to gain phonetic knowledge during nearly twenty years', and we should remember that most of these travels were undertaken with Ellis' research agenda in mind, gathering information and filling in gaps in a strictly targeted manner. Hallam was responsible for some or all of the material for over 500 of Ellis' 1,145 places, a remarkable proportion; Hallam himself, precise as ever, recorded that over the years he had procured for Ellis 26 Comparative Specimens and 66 Dialect Tests, and had sent him 1,344 sheets of 'miscellaneous words and phrases'.[152] Ellis did not always agree with Hallam's judgements, but the book could not have been written without him.[153]

---

[148] Ellis, *On Early English Pronunciation*, V, 51*.
[149] See Ellis, *On Early English Pronunciation*, V, 36*, 1749–61/317–29.
[150] Ellis, *On Early English Pronunciation*, V, xvii, 67*–76*.
[151] Ellis, *On Early English Pronunciation*, V, xvii; see also 1902/470.
[152] Oxford, Bodleian Libraries, MS Eng. lang. d. 27, fols 108–18, 126–7; MS Eng. lang. d. 32, fols 5–6. See also Ellis, *On Early English Pronunciation*, V, 71*.
[153] See for example Ellis, *On Early English Pronunciation*, V, 1748–9/316–17, 1755–6/323–4.

In second place came James George Goodchild, whose work in north-west England, in Ellis' view, left 'scarcely anything to be desired in minute accuracy and repeated careful verification'.[154] Goodchild (1844–1906) was a geologist, who engaged in extensive fieldwork for the national Geological Survey of Great Britain.[155] 'Stay[ing] weeks, or months, at a time in the most out-of-the-way parts of the country', Goodchild had 'abundant opportunities of hearing the most archaic forms of speech yet lingering in the district'.[156] As well as supplying Ellis with information, Goodchild published some of his own researches into the local, dialectal pronunciations of Cumbrian place names (later reprinted in *The Existing Phonology*): his philological conviction, prioritizing spoken language over written, was that 'the traditional names of places are the original forms and their literary forms [are] their corruptions'; and in addition to his north-western material, Goodchild also provided extensive transcriptions of his step-mother's Wiltshire dialect, and his own middle-class East London variety (which he distinguished both from his '"studied" pronunciation, as in lecturing' and from 'low East London talk').[157]

Ellis' third 'chief helper' was C. Clough Robinson, about whom less is known. A long-standing expert on Yorkshire dialect, he had published a glossary of Leeds dialect in 1862 and of what he called 'Mid-Yorkshire' dialect in 1876.[158] Robinson was not as proficient a phonetician as Hallam and Goodchild, and used the simpler system of Glossic rather than the more complex Palaeotype. However, one reason why Ellis valued Robinson was because he was a 'natural dialect speaker' (Hallam retained a 'diglossic' competence alongside his use of Standard English). This competence, Ellis believed, enabled Robinson—and Hallam—to elicit true dialect from his contacts. This was one reason why Ellis was conscious of his own unsuitability as a fieldworker, and valued the work of his collaborators so highly ('If I, having no kind of dialectal speech, were to go among the peasantry, they would of course use their "refined" speech to me').[159] Just occasionally Ellis did engage in some sustained fieldwork, such as his visit to the Newcastle area in early 1879; but this is presented as rather an adventure ('snow was on the ground, and the vicarage lay four miles from a station, road uphill, with no conveyance'), and Ellis remained conscious of the inadequacy of his work.[160]

Many of his other informants, by contrast, caused Ellis to despair, as he lamented in one of his addresses to the Philological Society:

---

[154] Ellis, *On Early English Pronunciation*, V, xvii.

[155] See Ellis, *On Early English Pronunciation*, V 70*, 1436/4, 1798/366, 1826/394; Sanders, 'Alexander John Ellis', pp. 650–2, 759–60; Michael K. C. MacMahon, 'Palaeozoic and Palaeotype: A Note on John George Goodchild (1844–1906)', *The Henry Sweet Society Newsletter* 10 (1988), 7–9.

[156] J. G. Goodchild, 'Traditional Names of Places in Edenside', *Transactions of the Cumberland and Westmorland Antiquarian and Archaeological Society* 6 (1881–3), 50–76, at p. 50.

[157] Goodchild, 'Traditional Names of Places in Edenside', p. 51; Ellis, *On Early English Pronunciation*, V, 1474/42, 1483–90/51–8, 1665–6/233–4, 1971–5/539–43, 2034–9/602–7.

[158] See Ellis, *On Early English Pronunciation*, V, 74*, 1436/4; Sanders, 'Alexander John Ellis', pp. 579–80.

[159] Ellis, *On Early English Pronunciation*, V, 1436/4; see also Ellis, *On Early English Pronunciation*, IV, 1086–7.

[160] Ellis, *On Early English Pronunciation*, V, 2085/653, 2087/655.

90 The Victorians and English Dialect

> The utter helplessness of educated men and women in conveying even the ghost of a feeling of the sounds they have heard, has caused me personally such immense labour and difficulty in my dialectal studies, that I cannot too strongly urge the educational necessity of teaching people to speak, and to hear what they say.[161]

In *The Existing Phonology*, a pained Ellis often reports that he has had to jettison material he has been sent because 'I have found it quite impossible to determine the pron[unciation] from this writing' (in this case, a Comparative Specimen for Milverton in Somerset, written by 'Mr H. Randolph, surgeon', using his own orthography).[162] Evidence drawn from a middle-class speaker's remembered rural origins was also problematic: 'transcripts from natural dialect speakers are always more satisfactory than from gentlemen who can only speak from memory, based possibly upon an originally incorrect appreciation'.[163]

It is important to emphasize that the 811 names listed in Ellis' acknowledgements are, on the whole, his informants, and not the actual speakers whose language is preserved and analysed. It is true that often in *The Existing Phonology*, and especially in material supplied by Hallam, the speakers are named and acknowledged (such as Mary Ashcroft of Bewdley); but they are not collected together and indexed by Ellis in the same way as his informants are. And very many of the dialect speakers—or 'natives', as Ellis often terms them—remain anonymous: Ellis' great volume preserves the language of, among others, butchers, carpenters, carters, colliers, grocers, labourers, lock-keepers, miners, porters, potters, shepherds, shoemakers, waggoners, and wheelwrights (the job descriptions are Ellis'), but very frequently it does not individualize such people by naming them. Many speakers are noted as being servants, housemaids, or gardeners at rectories or other grand houses, but usually they are not named either.[164] Even W. W. Skeat's cook—cited as the source for dialect speech from Thaxted, Essex—is not identified by name.[165] (From census records, she can be identified as Sarah Tyrrell, born in Thaxted.) At the very least, then, we can say that many of the paradoxes of Victorian dialect collection—the coexistence of a strong interest in demotic culture with an equally strong framework of class hierarchies—are fully in evidence in the acknowledgements of *The Existing Phonology*. Dialect collectors were not, of course, blind to such social stratification; indeed, from one point of view their whole project and methodology turned on their awareness of it (as one writer put it, 'the drawing-room and the servants' hall have each their own vocabulary and grammar, and a philological gulf is fixed between the two').[166] Ellis records, for example, that the place name Kineton in Warwickshire was pronounced '(:kjinten) by working men' but '(:káint'n) by the middle class'.[167] Vicars made word lists from the speech of

---

[161] Ellis, 'Third Annual Address', p. 449; see also Ellis, 'Eleventh Annual Address', p. 27.
[162] Ellis, *On Early English Pronunciation*, V, 54*
[163] Ellis, *On Early English Pronunciation*, V, 1882/450.
[164] See further Roper, 'The Clergyman and the Dialect Speaker', esp. pp. 111–12.
[165] Ellis, *On Early English Pronunciation*, V, 40*.
[166] William E. A. Axon, *George Eliot's Use of Dialect*, English Dialect Society 33 (London: English Dialect Society, 1881), p. 39.
[167] Ellis, *On Early English Pronunciation*, V, 40*, 44*, 45*, 54*, 58*.

their labouring parishioners.[168] Lords of the manor transcribed their servants. Herbert Knatchbull-Hugessen, a 'landed proprietor' in Kent (also MP for Faversham, a writer of fairy stories, and a great-nephew of Jane Austen), 'learned the dialect well from his tenants, bailiff, and farm-labourers'; another 'extensive landed proprietor', Susan Maria Ffarington of Worden Hall, near Leyland in Lancashire, who was an antiquarian and artist, also 'took great interest in the language of the people'.[169]

A fourth key provider of material to Ellis, alongside Hallam, Goodchild, and Robinson, was an institution rather than an individual: Whitelands Training College in Chelsea. This was a teacher training college for women, and in the early 1880s, Ellis' friendship with the Principal, the Rev. John Pincher Faunthorpe, enabled him to take dialect transcriptions from many students—twenty-eight in all—who had left their home regions to train at the college. These 'young women generally about twenty years old, fresh from the country', form an unusual subgroup of dialect speakers for Ellis' project, on the grounds of their age, sex, and class or education.[170] Equally unusually, we know them all by name: Miss Beeby, for example, 'since 8 years old living at Aylesbury and Buckingham', supplied Ellis with dialect evidence for Wendover in Buckinghamshire; Miss Buckle for Mattishall in Norfolk; Miss Calland for Strood in Kent; and so on. There were also four (female) teachers who supplied Ellis with dialect evidence, and Faunthorpe himself provided a word list for Scotter, near Gainsborough in Lincolnshire, where he had lived till the age of 15.[171] It is interesting to note that Ellis' association with Faunthorpe and Whitelands was contemporaneous with that of an even more eminent Victorian, namely John Ruskin, whom Faunthorpe venerated as a prophet and with whom he instituted annual 'May Queen' festivities at Whitelands.[172]

These were the materials, the informants, and their dialect sources. What, then, were Ellis' main conclusions, and how did he arrange this material to provide a survey of 'the existing phonology'? In many respects, Ellis' conclusions may seem unstartling to a modern audience, but of course this is because his work was good, and later research has not reached radically different conclusions.

On the basis of dialect phonology, Ellis subdivided the country into six principal Divisions, which he labelled Southern, Western, Eastern, Midland, Northern, and Lowland (presented in that order in the main part of his book, pages 23 to 820). These six principal Divisions he subdivided into forty-two numbered Districts, such as D11 southern West Southern or D34 eastern Mid Lowland. But this was not the end of the classification: Districts could be in turn subdivided into a number of Varieties, so that D11, for example, comprised (i) North Devon, (ii) South Devon, and (iii)

---

[168] See Roper, 'The Clergyman and the Dialect Speaker'.
[169] Ellis, *On Early English Pronunciation*, V, 1569/137, 1764/332; see also Dorson, *The British Folklorists*, pp. 322–3.
[170] Ellis, *On Early English Pronunciation*, V, 1436/4; see also Ellis, *Report on Dialectal Work*, pp. 55–6, and Roper, 'The Clergyman and the Dialect Speaker', p. 129.
[171] Ellis, *On Early English Pronunciation*, V, 34*, 44*, 47*, 49*, 75*.
[172] See Malcolm Cole, *'Be Like Daisies': John Ruskin and the Cultivation of Beauty at Whitelands College*, Ruskin Lecture 1992 (St Albans: Guild of St George, 1992); Tim Hilton, *John Ruskin: The Later Years* (New Haven: Yale University Press, 2000), pp. 441–3.

92 The Victorians and English Dialect

Camelford. Yet Ellis was conscious that not even this was the end of the story, and that really there were, effectively, countless sub-varieties to be found, 'recognized by dialect speakers themselves, who will pick out the village that owns the speech' (at this level, Ellis' phonological criteria—what he called the 'Character' of each area—start to be complemented by what is now termed 'perceptual dialectology', that is, the attribution of contrastive varieties to different speakers or places).[173]

The best way to present such conclusions and subdivisions was by means of a map; and in this respect too Ellis was a pioneer.[174] He was not quite the first person to attempt to map the dialects of English, but the two maps that were published with *The Existing Phonology* (one of England and Wales, and one of Scotland) were by far the most important dialect maps of Britain to be produced until well after the Second World War.

Ellis' most important predecessor in England was, in fact, a French aristocrat, Prince Louis Lucien Bonaparte (1813–91), Napoleon's nephew. Born in Worcestershire when his family were interned, Bonaparte returned to England as an adult, and, with strong philological and scientific interests, directed some of his attention and patronage to the study of English dialects. One of Bonaparte's early initiatives was to have the Old Testament book of the Song of Songs (the Song of Solomon) translated into multiple rural dialects; William Barnes, for example, supplied a version for Dorset, and Thomas Hallam one for Chapel-en-le-Frith. He also acquired a very substantial library of works in dialect. In summer 1875 he 'made several excursions in some of the English counties, with the object of ascertaining the general nature of the dialect therein spoken amongst the uncultivated peasants', and the results of these 'excursions' were presented to the Philological Society the following year, in a paper with the geographically exhaustive title of 'On the Dialects of Monmouthshire, Herefordshire, Worcestershire, Gloucestershire, Berkshire, Oxfordshire, South Warwickshire, South Northamptonshire, Buckinghamshire, Hertfordshire, Middlesex, and Surrey, with a New Classification of the English Dialects'.[175] The most innovative feature of Bonaparte's paper is his map, the first attempt to demarcate spatially the major dialect groups of England. Bonaparte's map takes an unusual dot-to-dot approach, marking dialect sites with large red dots and then connecting comparable dialects by red lines to indicate groupings; and by such means he constructs thirteen major dialect areas (I Eastern, II South Eastern, III South Western, IV Devonshire, and so on). But the materials out of which Bonaparte devised his map were extremely modest, especially compared to Ellis' later work, both in terms of the number of

---

[173] Ellis, *On Early English Pronunciation*, V, 2254/822. See Penhallurick, *Studying Dialect*, pp. 245–75; Chris Montgomery and Emma Moore (eds), *Language and a Sense of Place: Studies in Language and Region* (Cambridge: Cambridge University Press, 2017).

[174] See Penhallurick, *Studying Dialect*, pp. 55–170, esp. pp. 109–24; see also William A. Kretzschmar, Jr., 'Linguistic Atlases', in Charles Boberg, John Nerbonne, and Dominic Watt (eds), *The Handbook of Dialectology* (Oxford: Wiley Blackwell, 2017), pp. 57–72, esp. pp. 60–3.

[175] Prince Louis Lucien Bonaparte, 'On the Dialects of Monmouthshire, Herefordshire, Worcestershire, Gloucestershire, Berkshire, Oxfordshire, South Warwickshire, South Northamptonshire, Buckinghamshire, Hertfordshire, Middlesex, and Surrey, with a New Classification of the English Dialects', *Transactions of the Philological Society* 16 (1876), 570–81, at p. 570.

samples and the range of variables: one or two features of grammar (such as *I be* vs *I am*), and one or two features of phonology (such as 'the sound of *r* peculiar [...] to the South-Western Dialect', or the 'change of *o* into *a* before *ng*' in northern English).[176] James Murray for one took the view that Bonaparte's researches were deeply inadequate for the conclusions he wished to draw, writing ironically to Ellis that 'another & equally good [principle] would be to classify dialects according to the colour of the eyes of the speakers'.[177] Bonaparte's claim that 'no more than a secondary value can be attributed to the permutation of vowels in determining the principal English Dialects' could hardly be more antagonistic to Ellis' own convictions and methods, while his view that 'the Midland characters are negative, and consist in the absence of the Southern as well as the Northern ones' is hardly likely to have commended his conclusions to Hallam, the great recorder of Midland dialects.[178] Nonetheless, Ellis was always careful to speak politely of Bonaparte in his own work, acknowledging that 'to him I owe especially my first conceptions of a classification of the English Dialects'.[179]

Ellis' maps were conceptually more advanced than Bonaparte's, as well as being founded upon far more extensive research. They not only marked his classification of the country into dialectal Divisions and Districts; they also indicated 'the Celtic Border' in Wales and Scotland (discussed at length within the book), and included ten 'Transverse Lines' which cut across the system of Divisions and Districts in a groundbreaking attempt to map the boundaries of major dialect features at a national level.[180] Although there are ten lines, Ellis was really only tracking four particular features: four lines track the distribution of *some* as either northern '(sŏŏm)' or southern or Scottish '(səm)' or '(sɐm)' (in Palaeotype; in IPA, [sʊm] vs [sɜm] or [sʌm]); three lines track various forms of the definite article *the*; and one each are given to southern 'reverted' (retroflex) *r* and to the northern pronunciation of *house* as '(huus)'. The tenth line marks more generally the border between Northern English and Lowland Scots. Rob Penhallurick has acclaimed these Transverse Lines as 'the first isoglosses of British English', but Ellis never explains why he has chosen these features in particular, and it is curious that he does not map what is the most obvious marker between northern and southern English, namely vowel length in words such as *last*.[181] The precision with which Ellis attempts to follow the course of his lines is also striking, and testifies to some exceptionally dogged fieldwork by Hallam: for example, in trying to discover the southern limit of '(sŏŏm)', Hallam, like a linguistic bloodhound, 'visited expressly numerous villages along the route here laid down (30 places in Norfolk

---

[176] Bonaparte, 'On the Dialects of Monmouthshire [...]', pp. 571, 576.
[177] Quoted in Murray, *Caught in the Web of Words*, p. 81.
[178] Bonaparte, 'On the Dialects of Monmouthshire [...]', pp. 575, 576; see also, though, Ellis, *On Early English Pronunciation*, V, 1728/296.
[179] See Ellis, *On Early English Pronunciation*, V, 1437/5.
[180] Ellis, *On Early English Pronunciation*, V, 1447–54/15–22.
[181] Penhallurick, *Studying Dialect*, p. 110.

94   The Victorians and English Dialect

only)'.[182] Ellis' descriptions read like medieval charter bounds: to track retroflex *r* through Gloucestershire and Herefordshire, for example, you should 'start in England from the mouth of the Wye on the Severn R[iver] and proceed n[orth] by the w[est] b[order] of Gl[oucestershire] till you meet the b[order] of He[refordshire] just e[ast] of Monmouth [. . .] Then run in a n[orth]n[orth]e[ast] direction so as to leave Ross, Ledbury [. . .], and Much Cowarne [. . .] on the e[ast]. At Much Cowarne turn more to n[orth]e[ast], leaving on the w[est] Stoke Lacy [. . .]', and so on.[183]

Such microscopic precision suggests—and suggests rightly—that the value and pleasures of Ellis' work are to be found as much in the small features as in the big picture. Like Hallam's notebooks, *The Existing Phonology* is full of astonishing detail, fugitive moments of Victorian life, captured like an early photograph or sound recording. Goodchild's view was that Ellis' Palaeotype 'will enable even a stranger to reproduce the precise shade of each sound with accuracy years after every vestige of the old dialects has gone'.[184] Quite apart from Ellis' classificatory schemes, we can now hear a variety of forgotten voices preserved in his pages: the accents of Folkestone fishermen and Northumberland pitmen; the street cries of Norwich vendors ('new bloaters here, fine bloaters, Yarmouth bloaters here!'); homely phrases from Wedmore in Somerset ('(hæst dhi lʊkt in dhɐ krɔk tɐ zii if dhɐ teetiz bi dɑn?) hast thou looked in the pot to see if the potatoes be done?'); or 'the cry of a woman watching two other women fighting', entrusted to Ellis as 'a specimen of genuine Sunderland' ('(deg) ɐr in)dhɐ mɛl)ɐr)iin, :bɛt), dig = hit her in the mid of her eyes, Bet').[185] The book is a cornucopia of Victorian speech.

It also contains countless human histories, half-glimpsed through Ellis' terse commentary. 'Each spot has a history', Ellis told the members of the Philological Society as he came to the end of his fieldwork.[186] It would be nice to know more, for example, about the conversation that Hallam had with a married couple near King's Lynn, originally hailing from villages just a few miles apart, where 'the woman called *cup* (kɐp), the man (kuₒp), and they had never noticed that they spoke differently, so that TH had the greatest difficulty in making the woman recognise the distinction'.[187] One senses similarly that a whole narrative lies behind the statement that in Cockayne Hatley in Bedfordshire 'the dialect has been nearly exterminated by the action of a former Rector, the Hon. and Rev. H. C. Cust, and his wife'.[188] Furthermore, in what it reveals of the quests and desires of Ellis and his co-workers, *The Existing Phonology* is a type of detective story, containing frustrations and disappointments, moments of breakthrough, and even nailbiting races against time. Would Ellis ever find a speaker

---

[182] Ellis, *On Early English Pronunciation*, V, 1449/17. See also *English Dialect Society: Ninth Annual Report, for the Year 1881* (no place or date of publication), pp. 7–9; *English Dialect Society: Tenth Annual Report, for the Year 1882* (no place or date of publication), pp. 9–10.

[183] Ellis, *On Early English Pronunciation*, V, 1449/17.

[184] Goodchild, 'Traditional Names of Places in Edenside', p. 53.

[185] Ellis, *On Early English Pronunciation*, V, 1521–2/89–90, 1574–7/142–5, 2077–83/645–51, 2085/653, 2106–9/674–7.

[186] Ellis, *Report on Dialectal Work*, p. 45.

[187] Ellis, *On Early English Pronunciation*, V, 1693/261.

[188] Ellis, *On Early English Pronunciation*, V, 1641/209.

who could confirm Sam Weller's Dickensian dialect ('I have never yet heard (v) used for (w) in good faith, though I have much wanted to do so')?[189] Where in the west did the 'Land of Utch' lie (home of a distinctive form of the pronoun *I*), and would Ellis encounter a living example, or at least a witness, before the form finally went extinct, like a linguistic equivalent of the last great auk?[190] (The answer to this question is yes: on 17 August 1880, two native speakers from Montacute in Somerset, George Mitchell and Stephen Price, visited Ellis in his London home, like rare birds coming to an ornithologist.)

Such, then, were the contents, scope, and conclusions of Ellis' stupendous book. 'I can only say that I have done my best', he wrote in his Introduction; and the final words of the book, on page 835, poignantly declare: 'Here I stop. Time and space fail me, and my long task must come to an end'.[191] As we move towards a conclusion for this chapter, we can say that many paradoxes attend Ellis' dialect researches, especially when we reposition *The Existing Phonology of English Dialects* within the larger scheme of *Early English Pronunciation*. First, it is very curious that the biggest, most ambitious Victorian study of dialect phonology, on a scale not paralleled again until the second half of the twentieth century, should be motivated ostensibly by an interest in medieval orthography and pronunciation, and not, in fact, in contemporary language. 'I have long entertained the opinion', Ellis declared in Volume IV, 'that a knowledge of our living dialects is the only foundation for a solid discrimination of our Anglo-Saxon [i.e. Old English] varieties of speech'; and perhaps this might now seem the wrong way round.[192] As he observed wonderingly in 1887, 'all this inquiry arose from my investigation of the sound of long *i* in Chaucer'.[193]

Second, Ellis seems to have had an ambivalent vision of the status and value of regional dialects. On the one hand, it may be recalled, he grouped together 'patois, dialects, jargons, lingue franche, camp speech, savage talk' as examples of uncivilized speech that might be able to reveal language in evolution (an anthropological perspective, one might say). But on the other hand, he also valued modern dialects as precious preservers of historical tradition, the uncompromised descendants of the pre-standard dialects of the medieval period (a more classically philological perspective). So were regional dialects to be regarded as 'primitive' or Chaucerian?

And a third paradox is this. Ellis differs from most of the figures who feature in the present book in that he was not tied to a particular place or region. Most collectors or writers on dialect in the nineteenth century had a distinctive patch of the country to which they were wedded, and to which they showed diligence or devotion—usually, of course, their home region, either by origins or adoption. But Ellis seems to have had no such local piety, and from his London home in Argyll Road, Kensington, he coordinated and digested a national survey in seemingly impartial fashion. Indeed,

---

[189] Ellis, *On Early English Pronunciation*, V, 1564/132.
[190] See Ellis, *On Early English Pronunciation*, V, 8*, 1475/43, 1516–18/84–6; see also Barnes, *Poems in the Broad Form of the Dorset Dialect*, p. lxiv.
[191] Ellis, *On Early English Pronunciation*, V, 1440/8, 2267/835.
[192] Ellis, *On Early English Pronunciation*, IV, 1248.
[193] Ellis, *Second Report on Dialectal Work*, p. 84.

96 The Victorians and English Dialect

one might even go further and say that the elements which gave regional philology its distinctiveness—its motivation of local patriotism, and its frankly variable scholarship—were the very elements which, for Ellis, normally vitiated its value. Ellis does not seem to have held any particular sentiment towards dialect; the emotional strength of local attachment to dialect, or the power of dialect as a badge or vector of identity, seem barely to have registered with him. In his view, regional accents would have to be sacrificed for the greater good of intelligibility and spelling reform on a national scale: 'recognizing the extreme importance of facilitating intercourse between man and man', he wrote at the end of Part II of *Early English Pronunciation*, 'we should feel no doubt, and allow no sentimental regrets to interfere with the establishment of something approaching to a general system of pronouncing, by means of a general system of indicating our pronunciation in writing, as far as our own widespread language extends'.[194] He did not think that 'Received Pronunciation', of which he was one of the leading theorists, was inherently superior to regional dialect: 'It is an opinion held by many that "received speech is pure, and dialectal speech impure", forgetting that received speech has been highly "doctored" in the course of ages from some form of dialectal hereditary speech, and hence is really the impurest possible form of speech'.[195] He was well aware that the selection of one variety to be a standard language was for political and social reasons, not linguistic: 'the sounds that prevail are those used by the conqueror, the ruler, the noble, the wealthy [. . .]'.[196] Nonetheless, in 1874, in Part IV of *Early English Pronunciation*, he wrote bluntly that 'for the advance of our people, dialects must be extinguished', and in his 1881 address to the Philological Society he reiterated that wholesale, radical spelling reform (to which he remained passionately committed) would necessitate the adoption of a standardized pronunciation, and so would 'sweep away that dialectal pronunciation which I have been working so hard for some years to discover and embalm'.[197] It is not evident that Ellis ever changed his mind on this subject, and so this grim paradox—the competing desires both to record English dialects for the sake of phonological research, and also to abolish them for the greater good of spelling reform and education—haunts the pages of Ellis' writings. This was a minority view among English philologists: most, such as James Murray, took a more incremental, and less radical, approach towards spelling reform, and thus regarded the potential loss of regional dialects as a matter of grave regret, not as the necessary collateral damage of a root-and-branch reinvention.[198]

---

[194] Ellis, *On Early English Pronunciation*, II, 630.

[195] Ellis, *On Early English Pronunciation*, V, 1686/254. See further MacMahon, 'James Murray and the Phonetic Notation in the *New English Dictionary*', pp. 78–9; Lynda Mugglestone, 'A. J. Ellis, "Standard English" and the Prescriptive Tradition', *Review of English Studies* New Series 39 (1988), 87–92, 'Alexander Ellis and the virtues of doubt', in M. J. Toswell and E. M. Tyler (eds), *Studies in English Language and Literature: 'Doubt Wisely': Papers in Honour of E. G. Stanley* (London: Routledge, 1996), pp. 85–98, and 'John Walker and Alexander Ellis: Antedating *RP*', *Notes and Queries* 44 (1997), 103–7; Michael K. C. MacMahon, 'Phonology', in Suzanne Romaine (ed.), *The Cambridge History of the English Language: Volume IV, 1776–1997* (Cambridge: Cambridge University Press, 1999), pp. 373–535, at pp. 390–2.

[196] Ellis, 'Tenth Annual Address', p. 282.

[197] Ellis, *On Early English Pronunciation*, IV, 1247, Ellis, 'Tenth Annual Address', p. 306.

[198] See, for example, Murray's comments in *Transactions of the Philological Society* 1881, 320–1.

The Phoneticians **97**

'The great object of this work', Ellis wrote in the postscript to Volume IV of *Early English Pronunciation*, 'has been [...] to trace the living form, with the pure philological purpose of arriving at scientific theories which shall help us to derive the present from the past of language'.[199] Ellis' name does not now enjoy the recognition of others among the great Victorian philologists, such as Murray and Sweet. But the five volumes of *Early English Pronunciation*, and *The Existing Phonology* in particular, amount to a titanic achievement, both in terms of their data and their arguments. Again and again, within the pages of his great work as well as in ancillary lectures, Ellis seems to be on the verge of inventing not just dialectology and phonetics—he may well have been the creator of the first of these terms—but sociolinguistics as well.[200] Thus: 'Spoken language is born of any two or more associated human beings. It grows, matures, assimilates, changes, incorporates, excludes, developes, languishes, decays, dies utterly, with the societies to which it owes its being'.[201] And so: 'Uniformity of pronunciation, necessarily depends upon the proximity of speakers'.[202] Language, he argued, is defined by an *'essential sociability'*, and his investigations into 'the living modifications of speech-sounds' were leading him to believe that such changes 'are due especially to [...] social influences'.[203]

Moreover, Ellis thought that 'age and sex [have] much influence' on pronunciation, and through both variables he believed he could observe sound change in progress. Of course, a concern with change over time was constitutive of nineteenth-century philology, but Ellis was able to point to many precise examples of linguistic change, either in terms of forms that had died out or (more excitingly) sound changes that were currently happening. He observed generational shifts, noting features that were either 'more antiquated forms [used by] old folk' or 'coming into use among the younger people'.[204] Ellis' observations on differences in language use between men and women were even more innovative, and point the way to some of the studies of twentieth-century sociolinguistics.[205] At Ardeley in Huntingdonshire, Hallam and Ellis noticed that, among a group of elderly informants, the men pronounced the word *mate* as (meet), but their wives said (mɛ′it) or (méit). In Ellis' view 'it is certain then that this (éi, ɛ′i), which is now so characteristic of [District 16 Mid Eastern], is of recent growth'.[206] Determining the exact phonetic values indicated by Ellis' notation is not the issue here; the important point is that, as Ellis perceived, the men preserved the older form, while the women used the newer.

Ellis could see clearly that what he was studying was a set of linguistic systems. 'A dialect considered phonetically', he wrote, 'is not a series of mispronunciations, as

---

[199] Ellis, *On Early English Pronunciation*, IV, 1432.
[200] Penhallurick, *Studying Dialect*, pp. 24, 175–6.
[201] Ellis, *On Early English Pronunciation*, I, 17.
[202] Ellis, *On Early English Pronunciation*, II, 626.
[203] Ellis, 'Third Annual Address', p. 459 (italics original).
[204] See for example Ellis, *On Early English Pronunciation*, V, 1710/278, 1879–80/447–8, 1929/497, 1933/501, 1990/558, 1992/560.
[205] Ellis, *On Early English Pronunciation*, IV, 1089. See, for example, Jennifer Coates, *Women, Men and Language: a sociolinguistic account of sex differences in languages* (London: Longman, 1986).
[206] Ellis, *On Early English Pronunciation*, V, 1628/196; see also 1633–4/201–2.

98 The Victorians and English Dialect

the supercilious pseudo-orthoepist is apt to believe. It is a system of pronunciation.[207]
But he was conscious also of the limits of system-building, and of the countervailing
richness and diversity of human language:

> Properly speaking there is no uniformity. Not only will a practised ear tell the village
> in a district from which a speaker hails, but a more accurate examination will shew
> that families in the same village do not speak exactly alike, nay, that the individual
> members of the same family will have generally some differentiating peculiarity.[208]

What is more, the greater the 'minute accuracy' in transcription, as favoured by Hallam and Goodchild, the greater the 'perpetuation of individualisms'.[209] So Ellis was
aware of a tension in his work between the dialect evidence being valuable, on the
one hand, only insofar as it enabled a scheme of classifications to be made, and,
on the other, as a self-justifying capture of contemporary language, to be esteemed,
like its users, for its own individuality ('no two persons reproduce exactly the same
speech-sounds').[210]

Sweet's view of *Early English Pronunciation* as a whole was that 'this colossal work
is far too elaborate for general students', though he defended Ellis' supposed 'hair-splitting' on the basis that 'sound generalizations can only be based on a minute study
of details'.[211] For many decades, Ellis' daunting masterpiece languished in a state of
neglect by specialists as well, little cited in post-World War II dialectology. But more
recently, a number of modern dialectologists and phoneticians, especially Warren
Maguire, have begun to return to its riches as a repository of material, and have also
begun to reassert the dependability of its data and the value of its conclusions. It
may well be that *The Existing Phonology of English Dialects* still has a good deal of
illumination yet to give.[212] Nonetheless, Sweet's phrase 'a minute study of details' is
a very good description of *The Existing Phonology*, and so one of the last works to
be prepared for publication by Ellis, shortly before he died on 28 October 1890, was
an abridgement and simplification into a much more modest volume titled *English*

---

[207] Ellis, *On Early English Pronunciation*, IV, 1245.

[208] Ellis, *On Early English Pronunciation*, V, 1438/6.

[209] Ellis, *On Early English Pronunciation*, V, 1483/51.

[210] Ellis, 'Tenth Annual Address', p. 281.

[211] Sweet, *Collected Papers*, p. 86.

[212] See Peter M. Anderson, 'A New Light on *Early English Pronunciation*', *Transactions of the Yorkshire Dialect Society* 14 (1977), 32–41; Petyt, *The Study of Dialect*, pp. 70–6, and 'A survey of dialect studies in the area of Sedbergh & District History Society', pp. 11–14 [http://centre-for-english-traditional-heritage.org/TraditionToday6/TT6_Petyt_Dialects.pdf]; Peter Wright, 'Alexander J. Ellis: On Early English Pronunciation Part V: Key Dialect Tool or Forgotten Antique?', *Journal of the Lancashire Dialect Society* 34 (1985), 3–10; Graham Shorrocks, 'A. J. Ellis as Dialectologist: A Reassessment', *Historiographia Linguistica* 18 (1991), 321–34; Patricia Poussa, 'Ellis's "Land of *Wee*": A Historico-Structural Re-evaluation', *Neuphilologische Mitteilungen* 96 (1995), 295–307; Wagner, 'Late Modern English: Dialects'; Warren Maguire, '"Mr A. J. Ellis—the pioneer of scientific phonetics in England" (Sweet 1877, vii): an examination of Ellis's data from the northeast of England' [http://www.lel.ed.ac.uk/EllisAtlas/Maguire2003.pdf], 'Mapping *The Existing Phonology of English Dialects*', *Dialectologia et Geolinguistica* 20 (2012), 84–107, and 'An Atlas of Alexander J. Ellis's *The Existing Phonology of English Dialects*' [http://www.lel.ed.ac.uk/EllisAtlas/]; Paul Kerswill, 'Dialect Formation and Dialect Change in the Industrial Revolution: British vernacular English in the nineteenth century', in Laura Wright (ed.), *Southern English Varieties Then and Now* (Berlin: De Gruyter, 2018), pp. 8–38, at pp. 29–33.

The Phoneticians **99**

Dialects—Their Sounds and Homes.[213] Intended as a companion volume, this reduced the eight hundred crowded pages of the original to less than two hundred pages of larger print, and also converted all the transcriptions from the challenging Palaeotype to the more accessible Glossic (Sweet's view of Palaeotype had been that 'its extreme complexity and arbitrariness make it [. . .] quite unfitted for popular exposition').[214] This briefer book, as the title page declared, was published by the English Dialect Society, a society that Ellis himself had been instrumental in establishing nearly twenty years earlier, and whose activities, more lexical and cultural, had been running alongside the phonetic researches of Ellis and Hallam. But before we can turn to the history of the English Dialect Society (in Chapter 4), we need to double-back somewhat, and follow another thread in the Victorian engagement with English dialect: namely, the fertile connection between the burgeoning of regional philology and the creative practice of poets and novelists.

---

[213] Alexander J. Ellis, *English Dialects—Their Sounds and Homes*, English Dialect Society 60 (London: English Dialect Society, 1890).
[214] Sweet, *History of English Sounds*, p. 6; see also Ellis, *Report on Dialectal Work*, pp. 67–8.

3
Dialect and Literature

Fiction

When we think about dialect in nineteenth-century literature, we are likely to think first of individual characters in novels, such as the servant Joseph in *Wuthering Heights*, Jo the crossing-sweep in *Bleak House*, and the ale-house choruses in Hardy's fiction. In fact, dialect is everywhere in Victorian and Edwardian fiction. From *The Moonstone* to *The Secret Garden*, it is present in many works in which the dialect element is likely to be forgotten or overlooked, and not just in works (such as those by the Brontës, Dickens, and Hardy) where the dialect component is one of the more prominent or memorable features. So, to give one example where hundreds are possible, in Charles Kingsley's *The Water-Babies* (1863), the young chimney sweep Tom and his master Mr Grimes speak northern dialect ('Mr Grimes touched his hat to [Sir John of Harthover Place] when he rode through the town, and called him a 'buirdly awd chap', and his young ladies 'gradely lasses', which are two high compliments in the North country'), while the narrator draws attention to his use of vocabulary from 'dear old North Devon', Kingsley's own locality ('stogged in a mire you never will be, I trust').[1] The use of dialect as a marker of character or speech style was not an innovation of the Victorian period, though the flourishing of the nineteenth-century novel—and, as we will see, the rise of regional philology—greatly affected practice in both quantity and quality. As Jane Hodson has shown, pre-Victorian fiction also had its fair share of dialect speakers (servants, Irishmen, rustics), and the process of what linguists now call 'enregisterment'—the development of a recognized repertoire of linguistic forms associated with different linguistic identities—was already well advanced.[2]

The deliberate use of dialect as a means of marking the speech of certain characters goes back to the late medieval period. Two examples are especially celebrated: the

---

[1] Charles Kingsley, *The Water-Babies*, ed. Robert Douglas-Fairhurst (Oxford: Oxford University Press, 2013), pp. 8, 34. See further Stitt, *Metaphors of Change*.

[2] See Jane Hodson and Alex Broadhead, 'Developments in Literary Dialect Representation in British Fiction 1800–1836', *Language and Literature* 22 (2013), 315–32; Jane Hodson, 'Talking Like a Servant: What nineteenth century novels can tell us about the social history of the language', *Journal of Historical Sociolinguistics* 2 (2016), 27–46, and "Did She Say Dinner, Betsey, at This Taam o'Day?': Representing Yorkshire Voices and Characters in Novels 1800–1836', in Patrick Honeybone and Warren Maguire (eds), *Dialect Writing and the North of England* (Edinburgh: Edinburgh University Press, 2020), pp. 188–210. On enregisterment, see, for example, Joan C. Beal, 'Northern English and Enregisterment', in Sylvie Hancil and Joan C. Beal (eds), *Perspectives on Northern Englishes*, Topics in English Linguistics 96 (Berlin: De Gruyter, 2017), pp. 17–39; Paul Cooper, 'Russian Dolls and Dialect Literature: The Enregisterment of Nineteenth-Century "Yorkshire" Dialects', in Patrick Honeybone and Warren Maguire (eds), *Dialect Writing and the North of England* (Edinburgh: Edinburgh University Press, 2020), pp. 126–46.

The Victorians and English Dialect. Matthew Townend, Oxford University Press. © Matthew Townend (2024).
DOI: 10.1093/oso/9780198888123.003.0004

102   The Victorians and English Dialect

Towneley or Wakefield *Second Shepherds' Play* and Chaucer's *The Reeve's Tale*. The first is a northern text representing southern speech for a comic purpose, the second a southern text representing northern speech.[3] In neither case, however, is the use of a different dialect associated with backwardness or bumpkin status: in the *Second Shepherds' Play*, it is a government official's speech which is so distinguished (and mocked: the character doing an impersonation of southern speech is told to 'take outt that sothren tothe, / And sett it in a torde [turd]'), while in *The Reeve's Tale*, the distinctive dialect is that of the most educated characters, two northern students in Cambridge. Not surprisingly, philologists took a keen interest in both texts, for what they might reveal about the history of dialect: for *The Reeve's Tale*, Richard Garnett wrote a perceptive early analysis of Chaucer's northernisms, W. W. Skeat provided detailed notes in his multi-volume edition of Chaucer's works, and J. R. R. Tolkien later made a sustained study of the dialect.[4] F. W. Moorman, Tolkien's predecessor at the University of Leeds, took the *Second Shepherd's Play* as the basis for a modern dialect drama, *The Ewe Lamb*, refashioning the speech above into 'Tak that southern tooth out o' thy mouth, an' speak plain Yorkshire, wilta?'[5]

As observed at the start of Chapter 1, the standard language that developed in the late medieval and early modern period was southerly and London-centric, but it also bore the imprint of East Midland varieties. These historical origins of Standard English are important in the present context, for they meant that, on the whole, the regional dialects of the north and the west were the varieties of English most markedly different from the standard language: even today, when we think of dialect, we are more likely to think of Yorkshire and Lancashire, or Somerset and Devon, than we are to think of, say, Surrey and Hertfordshire—though of course such areas did and do have their own dialect features. The spread of Standard English, therefore, not only made people more conscious of regional differences; it made some dialects seem more different than others. This is a significant factor as we move on to look at dialect in Victorian fiction.[6]

---

[3] See, for example, N. F. Blake, *Non-Standard Language in English Literature* (London: Deutsch, 1981), pp. 28–33, 65–6; Kathleen Irace, 'Mak's Sothren Tothe: A Philological and Critical Study of the Dialect Joke in the *Second Shepherd's Play*', *Comitatus: A Journal of Medieval and Renaissance Studies* 21 (1990), 38–51; Katie Wales, *Northern English: A Cultural and Social History* (Cambridge: Cambridge University Press, 2006), pp. 70–5.

[4] Garnett, *Philological Essays*, pp. 70–2; Walter W. Skeat (ed.), *The Complete Works of Geoffrey Chaucer: Volume 5: Notes to the Canterbury Tales* (Oxford: Clarendon Press, 1894), pp. 120–2; J. R. R. Tolkien, 'Chaucer as a Philologist', *Transactions of the Philological Society* (1934), 1–70. See further Simon Horobin, 'J. R. R. Tolkien as a Philologist: A Reconsideration of the Northernisms in Chaucer's *Reeve's Tale*', *English Studies* 82 (2001), 97–105, and John M. Bowers, *Tolkien's Lost Chaucer* (Oxford: Oxford University Press, 2019), esp. pp. 187–221.

[5] F. W. Moorman, *Plays of the Ridings* (London: Elkin Mathews, 1919), p. 81. See also J. Hanson Green, 'Yorkshire Dialect as Spoken in the West Riding During the Fifteenth and Nineteenth Centuries', *Transactions of the Yorkshire Dialect Society* 2 (1899), 54–68. On Moorman, see C. Vaughan, 'Memoir', in F. W. Moorman, *Tales, Songs and Plays of the Ridings* (London: Elkin Mathews, 1921), pp. 7–20; William Marshall, 'An Eisteddfod for Yorkshire? Professor Moorman and the Uses of Dialect', *Yorkshire Archaeological Journal* 83 (2011), 199–217.

[6] On dialect and literature (especially Victorian), see, for example, Blake, *Non-Standard Language in English Literature*; Norman Page, *Speech in the English Novel*, 2nd ed. (London: Palgrave Macmillan, 1988), pp. 55–96; Graham Shorrocks, 'Non-Standard Dialect Literature and Popular Culture', in Juhani Klemola, Merja Kytö, and Matti Rissanen (eds), *Speech Past and Present: Studies in English Dialectology*

A summary of regional dialect in Victorian fiction, chronologically ordered, is as follows. In the late 1840s, coinciding with the first spreading of philological culture in Britain, a number of famous novels were published in which spoken dialect plays a prominent and memorable role: Emily Brontë's *Wuthering Heights* (1847), Elizabeth Gaskell's *Mary Barton* (1848), and Charlotte Brontë's *Shirley* (1849). Charles Dickens' *Hard Times* (1854), and other works by Gaskell, continued this association between the use of dialect and novels set in the working-class north. Alongside such industrial novels, we see a cluster of 'provincial' novels: works set in the (fictional) small towns of England, remote from the metropolis, but which do not anchor their mood or language in quite such a strong sense of regionality and hence tend to offer less in the way of dialect (pre-eminent examples are Gaskell's *Cranford* (1853), Anthony Trollope's Barchester novels (1855–67), and George Eliot's *Middlemarch* (1872)).[7] In the north of England, there also flourished a more local tradition of dialect writing, often of a humorous sort, printed in newspapers, almanacs, and other regional formats; here the leading authors included Ben Brierley and Edwin Waugh.[8] Partly through the example of Eliot's *Adam Bede* (1859), the 1860s and 1870s then saw the development of a more self-conscious body of regional fiction, presented for a national readership, where the distinctive features of a region are precisely the point of the setting and story.[9] R. D. Blackmore's *Lorna Doone* (1869) is arguably the seminal work here, and in the later decades of the century, this regional historicism became more and more interwoven with a folkloric or even ethnological approach; here, Hardy is the supreme exemplar.

in Memory of Ossi Ihalainen (Frankfurt am Main: Lang, 1996), pp. 385–411; Susan L. Ferguson, 'Drawing Fictional Lines: Dialect and Narrative in the Victorian Novel', *Style* 32 (1998), 1–17; Sylvia Adamson, 'Literary Language', in Suzanne Romaine (ed.), *The Cambridge History of the English Language: Volume IV, 1776–1997* (Cambridge: Cambridge University Press, 1999), pp. 589–692, at pp. 598–606; Mugglestone, *'Talking Proper'*, pp. 173–211; Taryn Hakala, 'Working Dialect: Nonstandard Voices in Victorian Literature' (unpublished PhD, University of Michigan, 2010), and 'Dialect', *Victorian Literature and Culture* 46 (2018), 649–52; Sue Edney, 'Recent Studies in Victorian English Literary Dialect and its Linguistic Connections', *Literature Compass* 8/9 (2011), 660–74; Jane Hodson, *Dialect in Film and Literature* (Basingstoke: Macmillan, 2014); Jane Hodson (ed.), *Dialect and Literature in the Long Nineteenth Century* (Abingdon: Routledge, 2017); Patrick Honeybone and Warren Maguire (eds), *Dialect Writing and the North of England* (Edinburgh: Edinburgh University Press, 2020).

[7] See Robin Gilmour, 'Regional and Provincial in Victorian Literature', in R. P. Draper (ed.), *The Literature of Region and Nation* (New York: Palgrave Macmillan, 1989), pp. 51–60; Ian Duncan, 'The Provincial or Regional Novel', in Patrick Brantlinger and William B. Thesing (eds), *A Companion to the Victorian Novel* (Oxford: Blackwell, 2002), pp. 318–35; Plotz, 'The Provincial Novel'; Josephine McDonagh, 'Rethinking Provincialism in Mid-Nineteenth-Century Fiction: *Our Village* to *Villette*', *Victorian Studies* 55 (2013), 399–424; Amy J. Robinson, 'The Victorian Provincial Novel', *Literature Compass* 12 (2015), 548–54.

[8] See, for example, Martha Vicinus, *The Industrial Muse: A Study of Nineteenth Century Working-Class Literature* (London: Croom Helm, 1974), esp. pp. 185–237; Patrick Joyce, 'The People's English: Language and Class in England c. 1840–1920', in Peter Burke and Roy Porter (eds), *Language, Self, and Society: A Social History of Language* (Cambridge: Polity Press, 1991), pp. 154–90, and *Visions of the People*, esp. pp. 193–211, 256–304; Dave Russell, *Looking North: Northern England and the National Imagination* (Manchester: Manchester University Press, 2004), pp. 111–31; Hakala, 'Working Dialect', pp. 66–117, and 'A Great Man in Clogs: Performing Authenticity in Victorian Lancashire', *Victorian Studies* 52 (2010), 387–412.

[9] See Snell, *The Regional Novel in Britain and Ireland*, and *The Bibliography of Regional Fiction in Britain and Ireland, 1800–2000* (Aldershot: Routledge, 2002).

104 The Victorians and English Dialect

The question to be explored in this chapter is not so much, what is the nature and significance of the dialect representation in such fiction—there already exists a good deal of scholarship on this issue—but rather, what was the connection between dialect writing and philological thinking? Were novelists and poets writing in separation from the contemporaneous labours and arguments of regional philology, or were these literary and scholarly endeavours interrelated? This section will consider dialect in fiction up to and including *Adam Bede* and its influence; the later historical and folkloric fiction will be explored in Chapter 5.

Elizabeth Gaskell (1810–65) offers in many ways the best place to begin, and in its conscientiousness and linguistic accuracy, her Manchester novel *Mary Barton* marks an important step forward in the depiction of northern industrial dialect in fiction.[10] A typical passage of dialogue from the character Alice Wilson, reporting her mother's death, can serve as an illustration:

> 'I cried many a night at after; I'd no time for crying by day, for that missis was terrible strict; she would not hearken to my going to th' funeral; and indeed I would have been too late, for George set off that very night by th' coach, and the letter had been kept or summut (posts were not like th' posts now-a-days), and he found the burial all over, and father talking o' flitting; for he couldn't abide the cottage after mother was gone.'[11]

There is no Ellis-style adoption of a phonetic alphabet to indicate pronunciation here; but Gaskell offers enough linguistic features to represent a variety distinct from Standard English. In Alice's speech we find so-called 'definite article reduction' from 'the' to 'th'', and the related reduction of 'of' to 'o''; 'terrible' as an adverb; the idiom 'at after' and the lexical items 'summut' and 'flitting', in addition to the mildly archaic flavour of 'hearken' and 'abide'; and 'missis' as both a respelling (for 'Mrs') and a distinctive meaning (for 'the mistress'). Moreover, *Mary Barton* as a whole does not hold up dialect as something odd or divergent: all the major characters speak varying degrees of Lancashire dialect, so that the northern variety of English is taken as normative. One of the few explicit comments on language to be found in the novel is John Barton's claim that 'Londoners are mostly all tongue-tied, and can't say their a's and i's properly'.[12] In other words, it is southern or metropolitan English which is curious, not northern varieties, an assumption which recurs when Mary mistakes her aunt's voice for that of her dead mother: 'They were the accents of her mother's voice; the

---

[10] See Gunnel Melchers, 'Mrs Gaskell and Dialect', in Mats Rydén and Lennart A. Björk (eds), *Studies in English Philology, Linguistics and Literature, Presented to Alarik Rynell 7 March 1978*, Stockholm Studies in English 46 (Stockholm: Almqvist & Wiksell, 1978), pp. 112–24; Stitt, *Metaphors of Change*; Hakala, 'Working Dialect', pp. 21–65, and 'Linguistic Self-Fashioning in Elizabeth Gaskell's *Mary Barton*', in Jane Hodson (ed.), *Dialect and Literature in the Long Nineteenth Century* (Abingdon: Routledge, 2017), pp. 146–61.

[11] Elizabeth Gaskell, *Mary Barton*, ed. Shirley Foster (Oxford: Oxford University Press, 2006), p. 32.

[12] Gaskell, *Mary Barton*, p. 99.

very south-country pronunciation, that Mary so well remembered; and which she had sometimes tried to imitate when alone, with the fond mimicry of affection.'[13]

But from a philological point of view, there is another reason to give *Mary Barton* our attention, namely the linguistic paratexts, or side comments, which surround the presentation of dialect in the novel. A series of footnotes (of increasing detail in successive editions) provides glosses or other commentary on dialect words and expressions, and from the fifth edition onwards (1854) the novel was followed by an appendix of 'Two Lectures on the Lancashire Dialect' by Gaskell's husband William. (One member of the audience for these lectures seems to have been Thomas Hallam, who transcribed William Gaskell's speech as part of his record of 'Educated English Pronunciation.'[14]) It is likely that William Gaskell was largely responsible for the footnotes in *Mary Barton*: a letter from Elizabeth Gaskell to her publisher states that 'it is so difficult living in Lancashire to decide upon words likely to be unintelligible in another county; but my husband has put notes to those we believe to require them.'[15]

William Gaskell taught English at Manchester's Working Men's College in the 1850s, including Old English and etymology, and the Gaskells were friendly with F. J. Furnivall.[16] In a Hallam-like anecdote, one acquaintance recalled seeing William Gaskell 'leave a first-class railway carriage and join a number of Lancashire workmen in a third-class compartment, in order to hear them speak in the true Lancashire dialect.'[17] The attitude towards dialect revealed in the Lancashire lectures and *Mary Barton* footnotes is, from beginning to end, profoundly philological. William Gaskell's first lecture begins with a sequence of historicist attitudes towards language: 'These words, which now seem to us so dead and strange, have once been things of living power'; and 'Language thus ever runs backward, and very often, in order clearly to understand what it *is*, we must know what it *was*.'[18] He also makes the same claim as other writers for the dignity of dialect: the distinguishing features of Lancashire dialect are 'not, as some ignorantly suppose, mere vulgar corruptions of modern English, but genuine relics of the old mother tongue.'[19] The bulk of his two lectures is atomistic rather than systematic, commenting on a miscellany of linguistic features, and citing earlier textual parallels, but his organizing groups are historical in principle: features that may be attributable to Celtic influence, or Anglo-Saxon origins, or Scandinavian impact. As David Matthews has observed, William Gaskell's notes and lectures show a remarkable familiarity, for his period, with medieval texts,

---

[13] Gaskell, *Mary Barton*, p. 225.

[14] Oxford, Bodleian Libraries, MS Eng. lang. d. 17, fol. 79.

[15] J. A. V. Chapple and Arthur Pollard (eds), *The Letters of Mrs Gaskell* (Manchester: Manchester University Press, 1966), p. 56.

[16] Benzie, *Dr F. J. Furnivall*, p. 53; Munro, 'Biography', p. xx.

[17] Ellis H. Chadwick, *Mrs Gaskell: Haunts, Homes, and Stories*, rev. ed. (London: Pitman and Sons, 1913), p. 210, quoted in Harriet Guest, 'The Deep Romance of Manchester: Gaskell's *Mary Barton*', in K. D. M. Snell (ed.), *The Regional Novel in Britain and Ireland, 1800–1990* (Cambridge: Cambridge University Press, 1998), pp. 78–98, at p. 78 n. 1.

[18] Gaskell, *Mary Barton*, p. 384.

[19] Gaskell, *Mary Barton*, p. 394.

106 The Victorians and English Dialect

and thus can be placed within the context of nineteenth-century medievalism.[20] But Gaskell also quotes Shakespeare and Spenser as frequently as he quotes Chaucer, after the fashion of the early philology represented by Trench, in which the focus was as much on early modern English as it was on Old and Middle English.

As for the footnotes themselves, these demonstrate the same concerns, and cite the same range of sources, as the lectures that were eventually to join them in the 1854 edition. It was not an innovation in itself to include footnote glosses for dialect terms, and some of the notes simply give a brief explanation of the unfamiliar word: for example, '"Gloppened", amazed, frightened', or '"Cricket", a stool'.[21] But many go a good deal further than this. Some offer etymologies: for example, '"Dree", long and tedious. Anglo-Saxon "dreogan", to suffer, to endure'.[22] Many more offer parallel citations from medieval or early modern texts: for example, the past participle 'getten' is illustrated by a quotation from Chaucer's 'General Prologue' to *The Canterbury Tales* ('For he had *geten* him yet no benefice'), and the idiom 'at after', in the passage quoted above, is illustrated by Shakespeare's *Richard III* ('Come to me, Tyrrel, soon, *at after* supper').[23] Some combine both, as with the first note in the final version of the novel:

> 'Nesh'; Anglo-Saxon nesc, tender
> 'It semeth for love his herte is tender and neshe'.
> CHAUCER – '*Court of Love*'.[24]

In footnotes such as this, the dialect is being viewed diachronically, not synchronically, with a strong air of a Halliwell-style 'Archaic and Provincial' about them. If one gathered all these notes together, and rearranged them into alphabetical order, then the result would be a dialect glossary—but one that showed the philological turn of the 1840s and 1850s rather than the dialect-collecting of an earlier period. The treatment of dialect in *Mary Barton*, then, is significant not only for its attempt at authenticity but also for the framework of philological thinking within which it is pursued.

Let us examine two more of Gaskell's novels: *North and South* (1855) and *Sylvia's Lovers* (1863). In *North and South*, a sympathetic interest in local dialect is one of the features that distinguishes Gaskell's heroine, Margaret Hale, from the rest of her family, as she grows up, a clergyman's daughter, in the New Forest in Hampshire (prior to her family's relocation to 'Milton-Northern', a thinly disguised Manchester):

> This life—at least these walks—realised all Margaret's anticipations. She took a pride in her forest. Its people were her people. She made hearty friends with them; learned and delighted in using their peculiar words; took up her freedom amongst them; nursed

---

[20] David Matthews, *Medievalism: A Critical History* (Cambridge: Brewer, 2015), pp. 153–6. See also Hakala, 'Working Dialect', pp. 30–5, 53–4.
[21] Gaskell, *Mary Barton*, pp. 108, 259.
[22] Gaskell, *Mary Barton*, p. 104.
[23] Gaskell, *Mary Barton*, pp. 14, 32.
[24] Gaskell, *Mary Barton*, p. 8; see also Matthews, *Medievalism*, p. 154.

their babies; talked or read with slow distinctiveness to their old people; carried dainty messes to their sick; resolved before long to teach at the school [. . .][25]

This positive attitude towards local vocabulary continues to animate Margaret after her move up north. The narrator reports that, after a time in Milton, she 'knew enough now to understand many local interests—nay, even some of the technical words employed by the eager mill-owners', and this openness to dialect brings her into conflict with her more decorous mother:

'But, Margaret, don't get to use these horrid Milton words. "Slack of work": it is a provincialism. What will your aunt Shaw say, if she hears you use it on her return?'

'Oh, mamma! don't try and make a bugbear of aunt Shaw,' said Margaret, laughing. 'Edith picked up all sorts of military slang from Captain Lennox, and aunt Shaw never took any notice of it.'

'But yours is factory slang.'

'And if I live in a factory town, I must speak factory language when I want it.'[26]

Not only does Margaret employ and champion local vocabulary, she also sees no qualitative difference between the rural, southern dialect of her youth, and the industrial, northern dialect of her adulthood. 'Mamma is accusing me of having picked up a great deal of vulgarity since we came to Milton', she explains to her father; however, 'if using local words is vulgar, I was very vulgar in the Forest,—was I not, mamma?'[27] *North and South* is filled with the same attention to Lancashire (or, as Gaskell calls it, 'Darkshire') dialect as *Mary Barton*, from distinctive features of grammar (such as *hoo* for *she*) to representative vocabulary (*nesh, fettle, gradely*) to observations on the 'strong Darkshire accent'.[28] But it is the attitude towards dialect on Margaret's part, clearly presented by Gaskell as admirable, which is most worthy of notice here. However, dialect, like country life in general, is not set in aspic, as Gaskell also recognizes. When Margaret revisits her Hampshire home late in the novel, in company with her godfather Mr Bell, she finds that 'there was change everywhere', including in terms of language: at the village school, the new vicar's wife 'went as near as a lady could towards holding Mr Bell by the button, while she explained the Phonetic system to him, and gave him a conversation she had had with the Inspector about it'.[29]

Sylvia's Lovers is set not in Lancashire but in the Yorkshire coastal town of 'Monkshaven', modelled closely on Whitby. The handling of dialect is ambitious and assured, with variation and hierarchy among the dialect speakers in the novel: Sylvia's father has a strongly marked idiolect, surpassed only by that of Kester the farmworker, while Sylvia's own language is less dialectal and that of her cousin Philip

---

[25] Elizabeth Gaskell, *North and South*, ed. Angus Easson (Oxford: Oxford University Press, 1998), p. 17.

[26] Gaskell, *North and South*, pp. 163, 237.

[27] Gaskell, *North and South*, p. 238.

[28] Gaskell, *North and South*, pp. 91, 102, 225, 307.

[29] Gaskell, *North and South*, pp. 391, 394.

108 The Victorians and English Dialect

even less so; but Sylvia's mother is given a different form of northern dialect, as she is repeatedly said to be Cumbrian, 'from Carlisle-way'.[30] Dialect vocabulary is more prominent in *Sylvia's Lovers* than in the Manchester novels, even though Gaskell was not on her home ground: *bingy, clem, fash, gaum-like, hoasts, marlock, melling, moithering, raxes, shippen, throng*, and many more.[31] Gaskell seems to have spent only ten days in Whitby, in 1859: this seems at the same time both an inadequate foundation and also a testament to her receptiveness—though she did need to make tweaks to some of her dialect phonology between the first and second editions, making it less Lancashire and more Yorkshire.[32] It is not clear whether she looked at any publications in her treatment of the Monkshaven dialect, though we do know that she read some works on Whitby history: the obvious word list to have consulted would have been F. K. Robinson's *Whitby Glossary* of 1855, but of the eleven dialect terms given above (at random), only *fash, gaum(-like)*, and *rax* feature in Robinson's book, and the first two words are widespread in the north of England.

It is, moreover, worth noting that, within the narrative of *Sylvia's Lovers*, dialect terms are often flagged in some way. So the farmhouse kitchen of Sylvia's mother is introduced as follows:

> Flitches of bacon and 'hands' (*i.e.*, shoulders of cured pork, the legs or hams being sold, as fetching a better price) abounded; and for any visitor who could stay, neither cream nor finest wheaten flour was wanting for 'turf cakes' and 'singing hinnies', with which it is the delight of the northern housewives to regale the honoured guest, as he sips their high-priced tea, sweetened with dainty sugar.[33]

In *Mary Barton*, dialect terms were treated as normative within the main text, but were glossed through William Gaskell's philological footnotes. Here, they are marked as different within the main text, either by the use of punctuation, or by the presence of a narratorial gloss. Agricultural terms are signalled as being non-standard: 'never were cows that required such "stripping", or were expected to yield such "afterings", as Black Nell and Daisy that night'.[34] Elsewhere in the novel we have the narrator explaining: 'what is called in the district a "dab-wash" of a few articles'; 'a beck (or small stream)'; 'a noggin of gin [. . .] called in Yorkshire "dog's-nose"'; '"humbugs" being the north-country term for certain lumps of toffy, well-flavoured with peppermint'.[35] Parenthetical glosses even intrude into character's speeches: 'Well! yo' lasses will have your conks' (private talks), 'a know'.[36] Why is this? Is it because Gaskell is presenting the language and culture from the point of view of an outsider?

---

[30] Elizabeth Gaskell, *Sylvia's Lovers*, ed. Francis O'Gorman (Oxford: Oxford University Press, 2014), p. 75.

[31] Gaskell, *Sylvia's Lovers*, pp. 110, 127, 156, 159, 165, 211, 213, 232, 237, 415.

[32] See Brian Spencer, 'Elizabeth Gaskell and the Dialect of Whitby', *Transactions of the Yorkshire Dialect Society* 20/101 (2001), 40–5; Melchers, 'Mrs Gaskell and Dialect'; Gaskell, *Sylvia's Lovers*, pp. xv–xvi, xxix.

[33] Gaskell, *Sylvia's Lovers*, p. 35.

[34] Gaskell, *Sylvia's Lovers*, p. 160.

[35] Gaskell, *Sylvia's Lovers*, pp. 53, 188, 339, 409.

[36] Gaskell, *Sylvia's Lovers*, p. 54.

Is it because the novel is set in the past (in the late eighteenth century) and so offers the reader a certain sort of historical distance? Gaskell explains the culture of Monkshaven to the reader in the manner of a historian or ethnologist ('"cleaned" was the word then, "dressed" is that in vogue now').[37] It may be that we can discern the influence of Eliot's *Adam Bede* here, as we shall see shortly; and some of these questions, of the ethnographic or even anthropological treatment of dialect in fiction, will be returned to more fully in Chapter 5.

For Gaskell, then, we can observe certain changes in her treatment of dialect in the fifteen years between *Mary Barton* and *Sylvia's Lovers*; and we can track some, but not all, of the means by which she acquired and checked her knowledge of dialect. For other writers, we are much less sure of their routes into dialect, and, lacking knowledge of their reading or connections, we have to fall back on the assumption of personal observation. The Brontës are the most obvious example in this category, with Yorkshire dialect featuring in the works of all three sisters. The use of regional speech in *Wuthering Heights* in particular has been probed and approved by dialectologists, often with accompanying disapproval of the changes which Charlotte Brontë made after her sister's death; we should also observe that the use of a dialect term in the very title of *Wuthering Heights* is especially bold, and liable to be overlooked now on account of the book's familiarity.[38]

It is, however, worth pausing over the fact that the Brontës were the daughters of a clergyman—the Rev. Patrick Brontë, vicar of Haworth. It has long been suggested that the wives and daughters of clergy, because of the habit of home-visiting parishioners and ministering to the poor and sick, were in an unusual position in the Victorian social order, in that they enjoyed more interaction and familiarity with the lower classes than most middle-class men, let alone women (Elizabeth Gaskell's husband William, we may note, was a Unitarian minister). In the present context, there is good evidence that clergy wives and daughters were unusually familiar with regional dialect—quite apart from the presence of such dialect in the fiction of Gaskell and the Brontës, and in the depiction of the young Margaret in *North and South*, learning the language of her father's Hampshire parishioners. In *The Existing Phonology of English Dialects*, Ellis repeatedly records clergy daughters as being his informants—often, presumably, as a result of his word-list questionnaire being passed to them by their fathers ('I am much indebted to many daughters of clergymen', he told the Philological Society).[39] So, for example, for Tilshead in Wiltshire, Ellis received extensive help (including a face-to-face meeting) from 'the then Vicar's daughter, Miss Louisa H. Johnson, who was born and had resided there above forty years', and for Tetbury in Gloucestershire, from 'Miss Frampton, daughter of the then vicar', who answered 'a

---

[37] Gaskell, *Sylvia's Lovers*, p. 53.

[38] See K. M. Petyt, *Emily Bronte and the Haworth Dialect: A Study of the Dialect Speech in 'Wuthering Heights'* (Keighley: Yorkshire Dialect Society, 1970); Ferguson, 'Drawing Fictional Lines', pp. 4–7; John Waddington-Feather, 'The Dialect of *Shirley*', *Brontë Studies* 27 (2002), 235–9; Christine Alexander and Margaret Smith (eds), *The Oxford Companion to the Brontës* (Oxford: Oxford University Press, 2006), pp. 573–82 ('Dialect and Obsolete Words').

[39] Ellis, *Report on Dialectal Work*, p. 54. See further Roper, 'The Clergyman and the Dialect Speaker', pp. 128–9.

110   The Victorians and English Dialect

very long series of questions' for him. A Dialect Test for Hartlebury in Worcestershire was sent to Ellis by 'the Misses Haviland, daughters of the then Rector', and for Wood Ditton in Cambridgeshire, Ellis took dictation from 'Miss Walker, native, daughter of the then vicar'. Similar help is also recorded for Hannington in Northamptonshire ('Miss Downes, daughter of the Vicar'), Harrington in the same county ('Miss Tollemache, daughter of the Rector'), and Easington in Durham ('Miss E. P. Harrison, daughter of the Rector').[40] The connection between clergy daughters and dialect familiarity, depicted in fiction in *North and South* and to be assumed in the biography of the Brontës, is made especially clear by Ellis in recording the Norfolk help he received from 'Miss Cecilia M. Day, daughter of Rev. Edward Day, then rector of Kirby Bedon [. . .], where she had resided from childhood, and had frequent opportunities of conversing with the peasants'.[41]

For Dickens in *Hard Times*, it has been shown that, in addition to his flying visit to Preston in early 1854 as he began composition (recorded in the article 'On Strike', with dialogue), he drew much of his 'Coketown' dialect from the eighteenth-century Lancashire glossary of 'Tim Bobbin' or John Collier.[42] The Lancashire dialect of *Hard Times* is associated especially with the hard-done-by mill-worker Stephen Blackpool, and the heaviness of Dickens' dialectal colouring varies in the course of the novel, being sometimes thicker and sometimes lighter ('Who can look on 't, Sir, and fairly tell a man 'tis not a muddle?' as Stephen says of the situation he finds himself in).[43] Dickens had earlier had similar recourse to printed authorities for his use of East Anglian dialect for the Peggottys in *David Copperfield* (1849–50), as well as making his own observations.[44] London Cockney is, of course, the most frequently attested dialect in Dickens' works, though it seems uncontroversial to suggest that, with all his regional varieties, Dickens' representation is less close-to-life than that of Gaskell or Emily Brontë, and is heightened by an element of bravura staginess; moreover, his regional voices are often melded into individual idiolects—as Ellis found when he tried (unsuccessfully) to match Sam Weller's language with contemporary dialect speech.[45]

---

[40] Ellis, *On Early English Pronunciation*, V, 1490/58, 1492/60, 1544/112, 1648/216, 1649/217, 1682/250, 2049/617.

[41] Ellis, *On Early English Pronunciation*, V, 1707/275; see also Ellis, *Report on Dialectal Work*, p. 46.

[42] See Patricia Ingham, 'Dialect as "Realism": *Hard Times* and the Industrial Novel', *Review of English Studies* New Series 37 (1986), 518–27; Katie Wales, 'Dickens and Northern English: Stereotyping and "Authenticity" Re-considered', in Sylvie Hancil and Joan C. Beal (eds), *Perspectives on Northern Englishes*, Topics in English Linguistics 96 (Berlin: De Gruyter, 2017), pp. 41–60; Charles Dickens, *'Gone Astray' and Other Papers from Household Words 1851–59*, ed. Michael Slater, Dent Uniform Edition of Dickens' Journalism 3 (London: Dent, 1998), pp. 196–210.

[43] Charles Dickens, *Hard Times*, ed. Paul Schlicke (Oxford: Oxford University Press, 2006), p. 141.

[44] See Patricia Poussa, 'Dickens as Sociolinguist: Dialect in *David Copperfield*', in Irma Taavitsainen, Gunnel Melchers, and Päivi Pahta (eds), *Writing in Nonstandard English* (Amsterdam: Benjamins, 1999), pp. 27–44.

[45] Ellis, *On Early English Pronunciation*, V, 1564/132. See also G. L. Brook, *The Language of Dickens* (London: Deutsch, 1970), pp. 117–37; Page, *Speech in the English Novel*, pp. 64–70; Mugglestone, *'Talking Proper'*, pp. 194–201; Patricia Ingham, 'The Language of Dickens', in David Paroissien (ed.), *A Companion to Charles Dickens* (Oxford: Oxford University Press, 2008), pp. 126–41, at pp. 128–31; Hakala, 'Working Dialect', pp. 118–73.

Dialect and Literature **111**

The great novelist of rural life in the late 1850s and early 1860s is George Eliot—supremely in *Adam Bede* (1859), but also in *Scenes of Clerical Life* (1858), *The Mill on the Floss* (1860), and *Silas Marner* (1861). The daughter of a Warwickshire estate manager, Eliot—Mary Ann or Marian Evans—was late in turning to fiction, after a distinguished decade as a translator, reviewer, and essayist. Her preparatory manifesto for rural fiction is the essay 'The Natural History of German Life', published in the *Westminster Review* in July 1856. This is a review of a series of ethnographic volumes by the German scholar Wilhelm Heinrich von Riehl, but it also acts as a vehicle for Evans—soon to rename herself George Eliot—to analyse and explain the culture of the 'peasantry', which she approaches from the perspective of the social historian or folklorist rather than the storyteller.[46] 'How little the real characteristics of the working classes are known to those who are outside them', she writes, 'how little their natural history has been studied, is sufficiently disclosed by our Art as well as by our political and social theories', and the essay contains some of Eliot's most famous formulations on the value of art: 'The greatest benefit we owe to the artist, whether painter, poet or novelist, is the extension of our sympathies [. . .] Art is the nearest thing to life; it is a mode of amplifying experience and extending our contact with our fellow-men beyond the bounds of our personal lot'.[47] Eliot sees the character of working-class culture as resting with the community rather than the individual, and this includes language: 'among the peasantry it is the race, the district, the province, that has its style; namely, its dialect, its phraseology, its proverbs and its songs, which belong alike to the entire body of the people'.[48] Moreover, Eliot argues that 'the peculiarity of the peasant's language consists chiefly in his retention of historical peculiarities', and she stresses more generally that language is a historical medium: if you were to devise a brand new, 'universal' language, she suggests, what you would end up with would be 'a language which has no uncertainty, no whims of idiom, no cumbrous forms, no fitful shimmer of many-hued significance, no hoary archaisms "familiar with forgotten years", a patent deodorized and nonresonant language'.[49] We know that Eliot had well-developed interests in philology and medievalism, and in this essay we can see her bring a philological perspective to bear on 'the peasant's language'.[50]

Less than six months after the appearance of 'The Natural History of German Life', she started to write fiction: first, *Scenes of Clerical Life*, and then *Adam Bede*, set in the fictional Midlands county of 'Loamshire'. 'With this drop of ink at the end of my pen', she begins, 'I will show you the roomy workshop of Mr Jonathan Burge, carpenter and builder in the village of Hayslope, as it appeared on the eighteenth

---

[46] On Riehl, see, for example, Celia Applegate, *A Nation of Provincials: The German Idea of Heimat* (Berkeley: University of California Press, 1990), pp. 34–9.

[47] George Eliot, *Selected Critical Writings*, ed. Rosemary Ashton (Oxford: Oxford University Press, 1992), pp. 261, 263–4.

[48] Eliot, *Selected Critical Writings*, p. 268.

[49] Eliot, *Selected Critical Writings*, p. 282.

[50] See Judith Johnston, *George Eliot and the Discourses of Medievalism*, Making the Middle Ages 6 (Turnhout: Brepols, 2006); Momma, *From Philology to English Studies*, p. 28 n. 2.

112   The Victorians and English Dialect

of June, in the year of our Lord 1799.'[51] Eliot's stance towards her story is that of a social historian, humane and antiquarian, and it is easy to see how *Adam Bede* acted as a point of departure for more consciously 'folkloric' fiction later in the century: for example, in the explanation of old customs, in the attempt to understand rather than disapprove of them, and in the consciousness of mechanization and railway mobility having set a gulf between mid-century England and two generations earlier ('leisure is gone—gone where the spinning-wheels are gone, and the pack-horses, and the slow waggons, and the pedlars who brought bargains to the door on sunny afternoons').[52]

Eliot's representation of dialect in *Adam Bede* is careful and gradated (and the result of much labour).[53] The most prominent dialect speakers in the novel are Mrs Poyser and Adam's mother Lisbeth, and the speech of the former in particular teems with the 'phraseology' and 'proverbs' which Eliot had mentioned in 'The Natural History of German Life'. Pronunciation is indicated by ellipses as much as respelling, and grammar and morphology are also integral to the presentation (for example, 'I wonna ha' no tay: I carena if I ne'er ate nor drink no more. When one end o' th' bridge tumbles down, where's th' use o' th' other stannin'?').[54] The amount of distinctive dialect vocabulary is actually quite modest, and most such words are uttered by Lisbeth Bede or Mrs Poyser: *clemmed, dratchell, geck, queechy*.[55] Only a couple of times does the narrator offer a gloss for a local term ('the "whittaw", otherwise saddler', and 'a small pond full of tadpoles, alias "bullheads"').[56] The idiolect of Adam himself, as protagonist, is less strongly marked than that of his mother, and his use of dialect is context-sensitive: 'whenever he wished to be especially kind to his mother, he fell into his strongest native accent and dialect, with which at other times his speech was less deeply tinged'.[57] But both the narrator, and the characters themselves, are interested in dialect differences. Mr Casson, the innkeeper in Hayslope, has opinions on this matter:

'I'm not this countryman, you may tell by my tongue, sir. They're cur'ous talkers i' this country, sir; the gentry's hard work to hunderstand 'em. I was brought hup among the gentry, sir, an' got the turn o' their tongue when I was a bye. Why, what do you think the folks here says for 'hevn't you?'—the gentry, you know, says, 'hevn't you'—well, the people about here says 'hanna yey'. It's what they call the dileck as is spoke here-

---

[51] George Eliot, *Adam Bede*, ed. Carol A. Martin (Oxford: Oxford University Press, 2008), p. 5.

[52] Eliot, *Adam Bede*, p. 459.

[53] See, for example, Patricia Ingham, 'Dialect in the Novels of Hardy and George Eliot', in George Watson (ed.), *Literary English Since Shakespeare* (Oxford: Oxford University Press, 1970), pp. 347–63; Blake, *Non-Standard Language in English Literature*, pp. 153–5; Hakala, 'Working Dialect', pp. 21–65; Melissa Raines, 'Language', in Margaret Harris (ed.), *George Eliot in Context* (Cambridge: Cambridge University Press, 2013), pp. 176–82; and Carol A. Martin, 'Rural Life', in Margaret Harris (ed.), *George Eliot in Context* (Cambridge: Cambridge University Press, 2013), pp. 256–63; Hodson, *Dialect in Film and Literature*, pp. 201–3.

[54] Eliot, *Adam Bede*, p. 96.

[55] Eliot, *Adam Bede*, pp. 89, 101, 195, 295.

[56] Eliot, *Adam Bede*, pp. 66, 174.

[57] Eliot, *Adam Bede*, p. 40.

about, sir. That's what I've heared Squire Donnithorne say many a time, it's the dileck, says he.'[58]

There is no need to labour the point that Mr Casson's own speech is full of its own non-standard features, including hyper-correct *h*-addition ('hunderstand' and 'hup'). In Windsor, whither the farm-girl Hetty Sorrel has fled in her attempt to find her upper-class lover Arthur Donnithorne, the innkeeper's wife is similarly observant: she not only perceives—what has escaped other characters—that Hetty is pregnant, but also that her dialect is different ('She looks like a respectable country girl, and she comes from a good way off, to judge by her tongue. She talks something like that ostler we had that come from the north').[59] Much earlier in the story, the narrator tells us that 'while Arthur gazed into Hetty's dark beseeching eyes, it made no difference to him what sort of English she spoke.'[60] Sexual desire, in other words, is going to override the social significance of linguistic difference—with catastrophic effects.

Martha Vicinus proposed the years 1860 to 1885 as the 'outstanding period' for northern dialect writing.[61] As a final example of dialect fiction, then, let us return to Lancashire, and consider the work of an author conspicuously different from the likes of Gaskell and Eliot. Ben Brierley (1825–96, pronounced 'Brearley') was born in Failsworth, between Manchester and Oldham.[62] His father, formerly a soldier who had fought at Waterloo, was a handloom weaver, and Brierley received barely any formal schooling, starting work at the age of six. After a youthful period working in mills, he too became a handloom weaver, and then a 'silk warper'. But his keen intelligence was recognized from an early age: one mill manager lent him issues of *The Pickwick Papers* as they appeared, and as a teenager he discovered the poetry of Burns and Byron (his younger brother, he later recalled, was also an enthusiast for Pitman's phonography).[63] Joining up with a group of like-minded young men, Brierley co-founded the Failsworth Mechanics Institution, and dreamed of assembling a library ('I remember the late Elijah Ridings [a poet] once saying to me—"If I'd fifty pounds I'd go to Lunnon, an' buy a ton o' books"; what a magnificent spectacle that presented to me'); and when he later started working in Manchester, he enjoyed the four-mile walk each way as it gave him undisturbed reading time.[64] In his thirties and forties, Brierley established himself as a sketch-writer, storyteller, and journalist, and from 1869 to 1891 he edited his own periodical, *Ben Brierley's Journal*. He was acclaimed in his own lifetime as one of the leading Lancashire writers of his generation, and after his death a statue was erected, by public subscription, in Queen's Park, Manchester.

---

[58] Eliot, *Adam Bede*, p. 14; see also pp. 307–8.

[59] Eliot, *Adam Bede*, p. 338.

[60] Eliot, *Adam Bede*, p. 120.

[61] Vicinus, *The Industrial Muse*, p. 185.

[62] See C. W. Sutton, 'Brierley, Benjamin [Ben] (1825–1896)', in *Oxford Dictionary of National Biography* [www.oxforddnb]. See further Vicinus, *The Industrial Muse*, pp. 201–3, 206–7; Joyce, *Visions of the People*, pp. 284–7, 293–4, 297–9, 302–4; David Huk, *Ben Brierley 1825–1896* (Manchester: Richardson, 1995); Hakala, 'Working Dialect', pp. 66–117, and 'A Great Man in Clogs'.

[63] See Ben Brierley, *Home Memories and Out of Work* (Bramhall: Reword, 2002), pp. 21–2, 30–1.

[64] Brierley, *Home Memories*, pp. 35, 50.

114   The Victorians and English Dialect

The type of northern prose writing exemplified by Brierley (and also the associated poetry which we will come to shortly) had less extensive connections with nineteenth-century philology than most other types of literature discussed in the present book. Nonetheless, the connections are still there to be observed, and are of various kinds. Most obviously: in addition to other social factors, it is not likely to be a coincidence that dialect compositions came to be more frequently printed, and more widely valued, during the same decades when philological thinking was prominent in Britain. Philology enhanced the general standing of dialect, not only its collection and analysis. Furthermore, all written dialect literature must be in some way artificial, in that its literate composers, even if they are dialect speakers themselves, begin with a pre-knowledge of Standard English as their first written language, and thus they have to devise a new system of spelling to represent their dialect: a significant degree of self-conscious linguisticism is involved.

Brierley's early fictions are similar in method to the other novels and stories surveyed in this section: dialect is normally confined to the speech of characters, with the narrator using Standard English, while various methods of glossing are employed to ensure intelligibility (especially parenthetical translations and explanatory footnotes). He also wrote non-fiction in Standard English, again with glosses for dialect terms. But his most famous stories, those of Ab-o'th'-Yate, a handloom weaver from 'Walmsley Fowt [Fold]', are narrated in the first person, and thus written wholly in Lancashire dialect; and it is the use of dialect for narration as well as dialogue that marks the biggest formal difference between northern dialect writing and the more national traditions represented by Gaskell and Eliot. But even within a narrative of total dialect, Brierley (as Ab) has methods for explaining unfamiliar words to his audience: for example, 'Aw never knew th' meeanin' o' bein' hob-shackled before, but it wur bein' cheeaned to th' hob', or 'We'rn havin' a "fender" at eaur heause one neet, a gradely Lancashire "fender" [. . .] But what, yo'n ax, is a fender? It's a getherin' reaund th' foire o' childer, or neighbours, sittin' i'th' form ov a hauve moon, an raichin' fro' hob to hob'.[65] Among Brierley's most popular works was *Ab-o'th'-Yate in London*, a series of letters in which Ab relates his adventures to his wife back home in Lancashire (letters dated 1868; book publication, 1881); Brierley had himself worked in London for six months in the early 1860s. The narrative dynamic involves a succession of contrasts between Lancashire ways and London ways, in which the former almost invariably emerge as better than the latter—more honest, more homely, more 'gradely'. This preference is linguistic as well as social and cultural. By presenting Ab's Lancashire dialect as normative—the default setting—Brierley is able to turn the linguistic tables, so that other varieties of English appear as marked or even divergent, including Standard English itself. There are regular comments about the incomprehensibility of London speech, such as 'aw didn' know what he meant by that', and '[he] said some soart o' gibberish ut aw couldno' have understood if aw'd had four

---

[65] Ben Brierley, *Ab-o'th'-Yate Sketches and Other Short Stories*, ed. James Dronsfield, 3 vols (Oldham: Clegg, 1896), I, 156, III, 239.

pair o' ears'.[66] Moreover, in Ab's letters home from London, Brierley—a Dickens enthusiast—has fun in rendering a range of speech-styles from the capital, including the foppish swells whom Ab meets in Hyde Park ('Pwobably John Bwight!') and the poor crossing-sweep, modelled obviously on Jo of *Bleak House*, whom he takes for breakfast ('Bad time for sveepers! [. . .] Aint nothink for myself. Jolly good feed this, guv'nor').[67] We might say, perhaps, that Brierley does the *polis* in different voices.

At the end of his career, Brierley published *Home Memories* (1885), a volume of reminiscences. These memoirs say little about the craft of dialect writing, and much more about Brierley's experiences in publishing, but they do record a telling anecdote concerning the editorial assistance he attempted to give to the elderly Samuel Bamford (1788–1872)—radical writer, Peterloo veteran, and author of *The Dialect of South Lancashire* (1854). Brierley recalled that 'I had a tough job with him. He would adhere to quaint forms of spelling that jarred on my ear', indicating something of the challenges of devising spellings that were both dialectally faithful and readily intelligible; the disagreement was surprising in the light of Bamford's earlier judgement that '[Brierley's] orthography of the Lancashire dialect is as good as any I have read'.[68] Most importantly, *Home Memories* closes with an account of the 'testimonial fund' which was presented to Brierley in 1885. The longest speech on the occasion was given by George Milner (1829–1914), a highly active figure in the cultural, political, and educational life of Victorian Manchester, and President of the Manchester Literary Club—a society of which Brierley had himself been one of the founders in 1862. Milner's speech demonstrates well the desire of regional litterateurs, often of a higher social class, to position dialect writing within the respectful framework of historicist philology:

> He sometimes heard it urged against such writing as that of Mr Brierley's that it was in a dialect which was not common to the whole of this country, and it was not at all unusual to hear observations of a depreciatory nature with regard to the Lancashire dialect. He was never disposed to defend a corrupt and debased form of the Lancashire dialect (hear, hear) but the dialect in itself, written as it ought to be, and spoken as it still was in some of the far-off valleys of the county, was not a thing to be despised or to be ashamed of. (Hear, hear.) It was a dialect which drew its words from the most ancient English sources, it was a dialect that was full of words of great strength and beauty, and it was only those who knew the dialect thoroughly, and who had also some philological information, who were able to judge how very many of its words were to be found in our earliest and finest poetic writing. Therefore, Mr Brierley need not be ashamed of having spoken in a tongue which was and is understood of the people to whom he addressed his words.[69]

---

[66] Brierley, *Ab-o'th'-Yate Sketches*, I, 27, 28–9.
[67] Brierley, *Ab-o'th'-Yate Sketches*, I, 29, 73.
[68] Brierley, *Home Memories*, p. 65; Bamford quoted in James Dronsfield, 'Preface: Ben Brierley', in Ben Brierley, *Ab-o'th'-Yate Sketches and Other Short Stories*, ed. James Dronsfield, 3 vols (Oldham: Clegg, 1896), I, v–xxv, at p. xviii.
[69] Brierley, *Home Memories*, pp. 85–6.

116 The Victorians and English Dialect

Milner's speech may not tell us how Brierley thought about his use of dialect at the start of his career, but Brierley's inclusion of this peroration as the climax to his memoirs seems to indicate an end-of-career contentment at being celebrated in such terms.

There is undoubtedly less evidence for Brierley's engagement with 'philological information' than there is for other authors we have considered so far, but another late work does show his familiarity with the genre of lexicography. *Ab-o'th'-Yate's Dictionary* (1881) is effectively a dialect glossary in reverse, with headwords in Standard English and definitions, usually humorous and sometimes politically satirical, in Lancashire dialect:

> METROPOLIS. Th' chief teawn of any country. It gets its name fro' bein th' principal *meetin* place for th' biggest thieves an' scamps ut any country con furnish. There may be a few good folk to be fund i' sich places, but they're generally poor [. . .]
>
> PAUPER. *A poor person.* Generally understood to be folk ut conno' get their own livin, or, ut *dunno'* get their own livin. If that's th' gradely meeanin I see no difference between a poor *pauper* an' a rich un – a warkheause an' a palace [. . .]
>
> RURAL. Smellin o' country life an' fleawers an' green hedges. What we're fast losin through so mony folk creawdin abeaut. There'll be nowt for poets to do in a while nobbut write abeaut blackin, or sewin machines. There'll be nowt *rural* left.[70]

One word, though, that is immune to Brierley's sardonic wit is *folk*, the vehicle of much sentiment and significance:

> FOLK. *People.* A very whoamly word, an' meeans a great deeal. We liken sayin – 'eaur folk', 'gradely folk', 'owd folk', an' 'young folk'. We seldom say 'bad folk'. We liken to meean *good*, when th' word's used.[71]

Scholars and sources

What we have seen so far is that not only did Victorian writers fill their fictions with dialect speech, and sometimes with dialect narration—that is hardly news—but also that novelists often approached the representation of dialect from the point of view of the scholar as well as the artist, drawing on philological resources, or adopting philological positions, in their work. But how did this relationship work from the other side? What use did philologists make of the writings of novelists (and poets), and what did they think of such authors' endeavours? We have seen how Victorian philologists bent their attention to the use of literary dialect in medieval texts such as Chaucer's *The Reeve's Tale*; how were the contemporary works of Gaskell and Eliot, for example, received and valued?

---

[70] [Ben Brierley], *Ab-o'th'-Yate's Dictionary; or, Walmsley Fowt Skoomester* (Manchester: Heywood, 1881), pp. 149–50, 181, 206.

[71] [Brierley], *Ab-o'th'-Yate's Dictionary*, p. 81; quoted also in Joyce, *Visions of the People*, p. 303.

As far back as the 1830s, Richard Garnett had urged the study of dialect glossaries on 'our dramatists and novelists, who, when they introduce a Yorkshire character, generally make him speak something much more like Hampshire—occasionally even broad Somersetshire'.[72] J. C. Atkinson, in his 1868 *Cleveland Glossary*, quotes Garnett's comments with approval, and observes that 'I am afraid this recommendation is as much needed still as when it was written': too often the result is simply a form of 'ordinary English in masquerade'. Sorry to say, not even Gaskell escapes Atkinson's censure, as we saw at the end of Chapter 1: 'the dialect in *Sylvia's Lovers*,' he writes, 'the scene of which is supposed to be laid in or near Whitby, would certainly not recommend its speaker to the kindly notice of the Dalesmen as a fellow-Clevelander'.[73] James Murray in turn approved of Atkinson's comments, and applied them to his 1873 review of Scots dialect in literature: while Walter Scott used the 'pure and genuine' vernacular, for many other writers 'it is hardly too much to adopt the phrase of the author of the Cleveland Glossary, and say that their Scotch is only "ordinary English in masquerade", and of about the same value philologically as the snuff-shop Highlander is in ethnology'.[74] Alexander Ellis took offence at the phonetic spellings whereby dialect was represented in fiction and poetry: 'our litereri men [. . .] heep toogedh·er leterz in dhi moast pripos·terus, inkomprihen·sibl, inkonsis·tent maner [our literary men [. . .] heap together letters in the most preposterous, incomprehensible manner]'.[75] (As we will see shortly, it may be that Ellis had one particular literary man in mind.) W. W. Skeat, with more equanimity, could see both good and ill: 'Very numerous are the specimens of dialect which various authors, with very various ideas on the subject of spelling, have supplied; and the value of these specimens is of all degrees, from the ill-composed productions of ill-educated twaddlers, to the racy sketches of clever and skilful writers who know how to put the right word in the right place'.[76] Another dialect collector thought that contemporary writers were 'unconsciously, but steadily, building up a sort of conventional literary dialect, containing a little of several, but not confined to any one in particular'.[77] And a few decades later, Elizabeth Mary Wright, hardened by her novel-reading labours on the *English Dialect Dictionary*, complained of 'dialect stories by authors who have no personal knowledge of any dialect whatever, and who have never studied any language scientifically. All they have done, perhaps, is to have purchased the Dialect Glossary of some district, or maybe they have asked a friend to supply a little local colouring'.[78]

This is only half of the story, the side (mostly) of exasperation and scholarly purism; and the very fact lamented by Wright, that novelists had been busy

---

[72] Garnett, *Philological Essays*, p. 55.
[73] Atkinson, *Glossary of the Cleveland Dialect*, p. xxxv.
[74] Murray, *Dialect of the Southern Counties of Scotland*, p. 75.
[75] Ellis, 'On Glosik', p. 93.
[76] Walter W. Skeat and J. H. Nodal (eds), *A Bibliographical List of the Works that have been Published, or are Known to Exist in MS, Illustrative of the Various Dialects of English*, English Dialect Society 3, 8, 18 (London: English Dialect Society, 1873–7), p. vii.
[77] Elworthy, *The West Somerset Word-Book*, p. v.
[78] Wright, *Rustic Speech and Folk-Lore*, p. xix.

118   The Victorians and English Dialect

consulting glossaries, is in itself a significant, and positive, piece of evidence for the importance of regional philology to creative writers. The other side of the story, as indicated by the activity that provoked Wright's pique, is the fact that philologists were busy turning to the works of the writers, as evidence for dialect, just at the same time as the writers were turning to the works of the philologists as research resources. The scrutinizing of literary texts for linguistic evidence was not restricted to remote periods such as Chaucer's. We saw in Chapter 1 how Anne Elizabeth Baker, in her 1854 *Glossary of Northamptonshire Words and Phrases*, drew heavily on the writings of John Clare, and made use of unpublished poems. In compiling the *English Dialect Dictionary*, Joseph Wright, as we will see in Chapter 6, chose to make very extensive use of dialect fiction and poetry. Indeed, so routine did this scholarly sampling of fiction become that E. Nesbit ironically states in her preface to *In Homespun* (1896) that her book, although a collection of rural tales, 'is of no value to a Middle English scholar, and needs no glossary'.[79]

Alexander Ellis was often dismissive of fiction and poetry in his dialect researches—frequently, the phonetic representation did not meet his stringent standards—but he did not indulge in a blanket condemnation, and there are many moments in *The Existing Phonology* when he suspends his usual ban. So while he did not allow the use of Yorkshire annuals and almanacs ('The numerous comic publications, such as the *Bairnsla Foaks' Annual* (published at Leeds) and the *Saunterer's Satchel* and *West Riding Almanac* (published at Bradford) are neither accurate nor local enough to be of any service in such an investigation as the present'), there are some authors whose works he does praise and utilize.[80] And although Ellis' quest to find someone who really talked like Sam Weller was frustrated, he still included a section on 'Dickens' London Speech'.[81]

So, for example, while the evidence of northern annuals and almanacs is not admitted into *The Existing Phonology*, a number of Yorkshire and Lancashire poets do meet Ellis' standards. Dialect words in the works of the Bradford poet Ben Preston (1819–1902) are excerpted, and Ellis remarks that Preston's poems 'are generally praised for their dialectal accuracy [. . .] Mr Preston's orthography is on the whole very careful, and I have seldom been at a loss for the interpretation'; furthermore, Ellis quotes from correspondence between Preston and his helper C. Clough Robinson in a manner that seems to recognize the poet as an authority (Preston's view, reported by Ellis, is that 'There are I think no rules for the guidance of dialect writers. Each one does what seems good in his own eyes [. . .]').[82] Other northern writers who contributed to Ellis' work include Joseph Steel, 'well known as a verse writer' in Kirkby Stephen, Westmorland, and the Rev. James Jackson Wray, author of the 1876 novel *Nestleton Magna* ('an admirable Methodist dialect tale', in Ellis' view),

---

[79] E. Nesbit, *In Homespun* (London: Lane, 1896), p. vi.

[80] Ellis, *On Early English Pronunciation*, V, 1798/366.

[81] Ellis, *On Early English Pronunciation*, V, 1660–1/228–9.

[82] Ellis, *On Early English Pronunciation*, V, 1820/388, 1823/391. On Preston, see William Scruton, 'Ben Preston', *Transactions of the Yorkshire Dialect Society* 4 (1902), 41–3.

who gave assistance for Market Weighton in Yorkshire.[83] For Stanhope in Durham, Ellis received a Dialect Test from William Morley Egglestone, 'author of those excellent dialect books *Betty Podkins' Visit to Auckland Flower Show*, and her *Letter to the Queen on Cleopatra's Needle*', and for his 'North Northern' District, Ellis made use of Thomas Wilson's well-known *The Pitman's Pay* (first published 1826–30).[84] Elsewhere in the country, Ellis' contributors included (for Stretton in Rutland) the Rev. Edward Bradley, better known as 'Cuthbert Bede', author of *The Adventures of Mr Verdant Green* (1853) and other comic tales.[85] But there are also conspicuous absences, especially for the leading Lancashire writers of Ben Brierley and Edwin Waugh: although Hallam supplied Ellis with transcriptions of Brierley taken from public readings, they were not cited in *The Existing Phonology*, while Waugh receives only a single, brief mention.[86]

Skeat also took the step of directly consulting George Eliot about her use of dialect. Her response is worth quoting at length:

> It must be borne in mind that my inclination to be as close as I could to the rendering of dialect, both in words and spelling, was constantly checked by the artistic duty of being generally intelligible. But for that check, I should have given a stronger colour to the dialogue in "Adam Bede", which is modelled on the talk of N[orth] Staffordshire and the neighbouring part of Derbyshire [...]
>
> The district imagined as the scene of "Silas Marner" is in N[orth] Warwickshire. But here, and in all my other presentations of English life, except "Adam Bede", it has been my intention to give the general physiognomy rather than a close portraiture of the provincial speech as I have heard it in the Midland or Mercian region. It is a just demand that art should keep clear of such specialities as would make it a puzzle for the larger part of its public; still, one is not bound to respect the lazy obtuseness or snobbish ignorance of people who do not care to know more of their native tongue than the vocabulary of the drawing-room and the newspaper.[87]

Another dialect student who took a keen interest in Eliot was William E. A. Axon, a Manchester librarian and man of letters, who spoke to the Manchester Literary Club in 1881 on 'George Eliot's Use of Dialect'.[88] Axon's view was that 'most dialect

---

[83] Ellis, *On Early English Pronunciation*, V, 1933/501, 1992/560.

[84] Ellis, *On Early English Pronunciation*, V, 2049/617, 2071–2/639–40. See further Rod Hermeston, 'Metaphor and Indexicality in *The Pitman's Pay*: The Ambivalence of Dialect', in Patrick Honeybone and Warren Maguire (eds), *Dialect Writing and the North of England* (Edinburgh: Edinburgh University Press, 2020), pp. 168–87; Warren Maguire, 'Phonological Analysis of Early-Nineteenth-Century Tyneside Dialect Literature: Thomas Wilson's *The Pitman's Pay*', in Patrick Honeybone and Warren Maguire (eds), *Dialect Writing and the North of England* (Edinburgh: Edinburgh University Press, 2020), pp. 243–65.

[85] Ellis, *On Early English Pronunciation*, V, 1688/256.

[86] See Ellis, *On Early English Pronunciation*, V, 44∗, 1747/315, 1779/347.

[87] Skeat and Nodal (eds), *Bibliographical List*, p. viii.

[88] On Axon, see Margaret Beetham, '"Healthy Reading": The Periodical Press in late Victorian Manchester', in Alan J. Kidd and K. W. Roberts (eds), *City, Class and Culture: studies of social policy and cultural production in Victorian Manchester* (Manchester: Manchester University Press, 1985), pp. 167–92, at pp. 173–4, 190; Penhallurick, 'Dialect Dictionaries', pp. 297–8; Brian Hollingworth, 'Axon, William Edward Armytage (1846–1913)', in *Oxford Dictionary of National Biography* [www.oxforddnb].

120   The Victorians and English Dialect

writers aim as a first object at the display of the dialect itself, and this not infrequently leads them into exaggeration.'[89] As an example he cites the Lancashire writer Tim Bobbin (John Collier), who crammed his work with 'all the uncommon and quaint-sounding phrases that he heard anywhere', so that as a result 'his work cannot be taken as a faithful representation of the common speech of the county at any particular time or place'. But Eliot is different, Axon argues, showing 'skill and discretion' and including 'just so much [dialect] as was necessary to give point and finish' to her rural characters. 'With the slightest possible expenditure of material', Axon writes, 'she contrives to give the impression of provincial speech without importing any great number of unfamiliar words.'[90] Philologists such as Skeat and Axon, then, were alert to the particular achievement of George Eliot, and appreciated how artistic priorities might temper the desire for a more narrow dialect transcription.

As the catalogue of assistance given to Ellis indicates, sometimes—perhaps quite often—the scholar and the writer could be one and the same person. We will turn more fully to William Barnes in a moment—at the same time, both Victorian England's leading dialect poet and also a pioneering scholar of Dorset dialect. (He is also, needless to say, a significant figure in *The Existing Phonology*, supplying a Comparative Specimen and word list for his home parish of Winterborne Came, and also advising on Dorset dialect more generally.[91]) What is especially worth noticing is how Barnes sometimes placed scholarship and poetry within the pages of the same book: his landmark volume of 1844, *Poems of Rural Life, in the Dorset Dialect*, contained not only 124 poems, but also a lengthy glossary and the philological 'Dissertation on the Dorset Dialect of the English Language'. Awareness of such a publication format, like William Gaskell's footnotes in *Mary Barton*, should help us to guard against an excessively rigid division between scholarly and creative activity in regional philology, and this combination of poems and grammar/glossary was by no means unique to Barnes. Another author praised by Ellis was G. P. R. Pulman (1819–80), who, according to Ellis, 'made a certain small portion of Sm., Dv., and Do. [i.e. Somerset, Devon, and Dorset] his own dialect ground'.[92] Pulman was a printer, bookseller, and newspaper editor in Crewkerne; he was also a keen fisherman, who won a medal for his artificial flies at the Great Exhibition of 1851 and whose best-known work was his *Rustic Sketches*, a collection of dialect poems about fishing, first published in 1842 and reprinted several times.[93] This volume, although slighter than Barnes', also sandwiches its poems between an introductory account of the local dialect at the start and a glossary of local words at the end, and the perspective is again firmly philological, influenced by the 'Saxon' arguments which John Yonge Akerman had advanced for Wiltshire ('the language of the West Saxons', Pulman writes, 'is undoubtedly the parent of the rustic dialects of those parts of the West of England in which that

---

[89] Axon, *George Eliot's Use of Dialect*, p. 37.

[90] Axon, *George Eliot's Use of Dialect*, p. 39.

[91] Ellis, *On Early English Pronunciation*, V, 1471–4/38–42, 1507–15/75–83.

[92] Ellis, *On Early English Pronunciation*, V, 1519/87; see also Elworthy, *The West Somerset Word-Book*, pp. viii–ix.

[93] W. P. Courtney, 'Pulman, George Philip Rigney (1819–1880)', rev. Ian Maxted, in *Oxford Dictionary of National Biography* [www.oxforddnb].

people established their rule'). The introduction is also unexpectedly spiky in its championing of working-class dialect speakers—'those who are too often set down as ungrateful, immoral, and unimprovable, because forsooth, their real character is little known, or else because they have been criminally neglected and despised.'[94] Many similarly hybrid books, mixing poetry and philology, were published by other authors, such as Alexander Craig Gibson's well-regarded *The Folk-Speech of Cumberland* (1869), a collection of poems and prose pieces which concludes with some 'Remarks on the Cumberland Dialect' and a glossary.[95] And as we will see in the next chapter, at least two participants in the English Dialect Society, active in the 1870s and 1880s, were at the same time both regional novelists and compilers of regional glossaries: Edith Chamberlain in Worcestershire and Edward Peacock in Lincolnshire.

Poetry

It is appropriate to begin this section with the reading of a poem, and the poem that has been chosen is William Barnes' 'The Vield Path'. But the goal, as throughout this chapter, is not to characterize dialect writing in the nineteenth century as an end in itself, but rather to probe the connections between dialect writing and dialect study. So this poem has been chosen because it also exists in an alternate version, written in Standard English, called 'The Field Path'. This second version, composed subsequent to the first, is also by Barnes. A comparison of the two versions should help us to understand what it is that Barnes sees as being distinctive about dialect writing.[96] Moreover, Barnes' ability to stand outside of dialect, as it were, should also tell us something about the status of dialect as a literary medium, and about the significance of its coexistence with Standard English.

As a preface to 'The Vield Path' (or 'The Field Path'), let us consider what Thomas Hardy had to say about Barnes' poetry. The important relationship between Hardy and Barnes, as his most significant predecessor as a regional Dorset writer, has been well explored.[97] Compared to most of the major Victorian novelists, Hardy wrote very little non-fictional prose; but in addition to his obituary of Barnes, he also published a review of a new edition of *Poems of Rural Life in the Dorset Dialect* in 1879 and edited and introduced a *Select Poems of William Barnes* in 1908 (the only editorial

---

[94] G. P. R. Pulman, *Rustic Sketches; being Rhymes on Angling and Other Subjects Illustrative of Rural Life, &c, in the Dialect of the West of England; with Notes and a Glossary* (London: Bell, 1853), pp. vi, ix.

[95] Alexander Craig Gibson, *The Folk-Speech of Cumberland and Some Districts Adjacent* (London: Smith, 1869). See further Townend, *The Vikings and Victorian Lakeland*, p. 185; Albert Nicholson, 'Gibson, Alexander Craig (1813–1874)', rev. Angus J. L. Winchester, in *Oxford Dictionary of National Biography* [www.oxforddnb].

[96] See also Emilie Loriaux, 'From "Zome Other Geäme" to "Another Joy" in William Barnes's Poetry: Composing, Translating and/or Rewriting', *The Hardy Society Journal* 10 (2014), 61–71.

[97] See, for example, Paul Zietlow, 'Thomas Hardy and William Barnes: Two Dorset Poets', *Publications of the Modern Language Association* 84 (1969), 291–303; Taylor, *Hardy's Literary Language and Victorian Philology*, pp. 159–72; Michael Millgate, *Thomas Hardy: A Biography Revisited* (Oxford: Oxford University Press, 2004), pp. 252–4, 422–3.

122   The Victorians and English Dialect

work he ever undertook).[98] Two key points that Hardy emphasizes in his introduction are the functionality of dialect and its localization. On the first issue, he stresses that the emotional and communicative potential of dialect should not be restricted to the merely humorous:

> For some reason or none, many persons suppose that when anything is penned in the tongue of the country-side, the primary intent is burlesque or ridicule, and this especially if the speech be one in which the sibilant has the rough sound, and is expressed by Z. Indeed, scores of thriving story-tellers and dramatists seem to believe that by transmuting the flattest conversation into a dialect that never existed, and making the talkers say 'be' where they would really say 'is', a Falstaffian richness is at once imparted to its qualities.[99]

Hardy continues, crucially: 'But to a person to whom a dialect is native its sounds are as consonant with moods of sorrow as with moods of mirth: there is no grotesqueness in it as such'. In other words, dialect is as appropriate a medium as Standard English for the expression of a full range of human experiences and emotions. Barnes' dialect words, Hardy writes, possess a 'delicate ability to express the doings, joys and jests, troubles, sorrows, needs and sicknesses of life in the rural world as elsewhere'.[100]

On the second issue of localization, Hardy's comments are also worth attending to, in the final paragraph of his introduction:

> As by the screen of dialect, so by the intense localization aforesaid, much is lost to the outsider who by looking into Barnes's pages only revives general recollections of country life. Yet many passages may shine into that reader's mind through the veil which partly hides them; and it is hoped and believed that, even in a superficial reading, something more of this poet's charm will be gathered from the present selection by persons to whom the Wessex R and Z are uncouth misfortunes, and the dying words those of an unlamented language that need leave behind it no grammar of its secrets and no key to its tomb.[101]

According to Hardy, what dialect writing encapsulates and articulates is not simply 'general recollections of country life'—a sort of unspecific pastoralism—but rather 'intense localization': every variety of language is particular to a specific spot or area, and to write in such a localized variety is to say something about precise, individual, unique places. It might be argued therefore—to develop Hardy's thinking—that the exploration of the specificities of place might be best achieved by means of the form of language specific to that place. So let us explore these issues further by means of Barnes' poem, 'The Vield Path'.

---

[98] See Millgate (ed.), *Thomas Hardy's Public Voice*, pp. 16–27, 291–7; W. J. Keith, 'Thomas Hardy's Edition of William Barnes', *Victorian Poetry* 15 (1977), 121–31.

[99] Millgate (ed.), *Thomas Hardy's Public Voice*, p. 294.

[100] Millgate (ed.), *Thomas Hardy's Public Voice*, p. 295; see also p. 25.

[101] Millgate (ed.), *Thomas Hardy's Public Voice*, p. 297.

Here oonce did sound sweet words, a-spoke
  In wind that swum
  Where ivy clomb,
About the ribby woak;
An' still the words, though now a-gone,
Be dear to me, that linger on.

An' here, as comely vo'k did pass,
  Their sheädes did slide
  Below their zide,
Along the flow'ry grass,
An' though the sheädes be all a-gone,
Still dear's the ground they vell upon.

But could they come where then they stroll'd,
  However young
  Mid sound their tongue,
Their sheädes would show em wold;
But dear, though they be all a-gone,
Be sheädes o' trees that linger on.

O ashèn poles, a-sheenèn tall!
  You be too young
  To have a-sprung
In days when I wer small;
But you, broad woak, wi' ribby rind,
Wer here so long as I can mind.

Here sounded words of dear old folk,
  Of this dear ground,
  Where ivy wound
About this ribbèd oak.
And still their words, their words now gone,
Are dear to me that linger on.

And here, as comely forms would pass,
  Their shades would slide
  Below their side,
Along the flow'ry grass.
And now, their shades, their shades now gone,
Still hallow ground they fell upon.

But could they come where then they stroll'd,
  However young
  Might sound their tongue,
Their shades would show them old.
So sweet are shades, the shades now shown,
The shades of trees they all have known.

These ashen poles that shine so tall,
  Are still too young
  To have upsprung
In days when I was small;
But you, stout oak, you, oak so stout,
Were here when my first moon ran out.[102]

Both the features mentioned by Hardy as stereotypical of Dorset dialect are evidenced here (/z/ for /s/, for example in 'zide'/'side' in stanza 2, and the wider use of 'be', for example in 'Be dear to me'/'Are dear to me' in stanza 1). But this is not stereotyping: it is the conscientious representation of local dialect, and all the subsystems of language show divergence from Standard English: phonology (for example, 'woak'/'oak' in stanza 1), morphology (the verbal prefix 'a-' in 'a-gone'/'gone' in stanza 3), syntax ('did sound'/'sounded' in stanza 1), and lexis ('ribby'/'ribbèd' in stanza 1). Many more instances might be offered in all of these subsystems, and some of the more prominent include: phonological variants such as 'vo'k'/'folk', 'wold'/'old', 'sheädes'/'shades', and the dialectal reductions of 'an'', 'o'', and 'wi'' (for 'and', 'of', and 'with'); further examples of the verbal prefix 'a-' in 'a-gone', 'a-sheenèn', and 'a-sprung'; the distinctive auxiliary form 'mid' in stanza 3 (for 'might'); and the Dorset pronoun 'em' instead of 'them' in stanza 3 (not, in fact, a reduction of 'them', but rather an archaic form descending from Old English *he(o)m*). In some cases, the difference between dialect usage and Standard English means that Barnes has to change his rhyme scheme, or rework the syntax and content of his sentences: in the first line, for example, the dialectal past participle 'a-spoke' correlates with Standard English 'spoken', but this undoes Barnes' subsequent rhyme with '(w)oak', and so extensive rewriting is required, involving not only the introduction of 'dear

---

[102] Text from Valentine Cunningham (ed.), *The Victorians: An Anthology of Poetry and Poetics* (Oxford: Blackwell, 2000), pp. 88–9.

124 The Victorians and English Dialect

old folk' but also 'this dear ground' in the following line (generated also from the fact that the dialect rhyme of 'swum'/'clomb' will not work with Standard English 'swam'/'climbed'). The closing rhyme-words of the last stanza are also unworkable in Standard English: 'rind' as a term for 'bark' might just about be possible, but the sense of 'remember' for the intransitive verb 'mind' is not, and so Barnes has to produce a new closing couple, introducing cliché (the notion of a 'stout oak'), repetition ('you, stout oak, you, oak so stout'), and a rather empty idiom ('when my first moon ran out'). Some of the changes remain a little mysterious: why, for example, if Barnes was happy to introduce 'folk' in the first line of stanza 1, did he replace 'vo'k' with 'forms' in the first line of stanza 2? Does Barnes' spelling of 'wer' indicate a phonetic difference from Standard English 'were', and if not why does he respell 'wer' but retain the standard spelling for 'tongue' (complete with silent letters)?

So far this analysis has been purely descriptive, and has sought to demonstrate the philological thoroughness with which Barnes represents the Dorset dialect. But what difference does the rewriting make to the reading and interpretation of the poem? The tendency towards more conventional 'poetic' idioms and effects, seen in the closing couplet of the final stanza, can be found elsewhere in the poem too. There is a comparable repetition in the penultimate line of each of the first three stanzas of the Standard English version which has no counterpart in the dialect version ('still their words, their words now gone'; 'now, their shades, their shades now gone'; 'sweet are shades, the shades now shown'). There is an elevation of diction in the last line of the second stanza: the dialect version states that the ground where the shadows fell is still 'dear', whereas the Standard English version, in a syntactic reordering, declares that the now-absent shadows still 'hallow [the] ground they fell upon'—with the religious term 'hallow' suggesting a rather different register than the much plainer 'dear'.

Less obtrusive parts of speech are also significant. It is noticeable how the Standard English version replaces the simple definite article 'the' with either the demonstrative 'this' or the possessive 'their': 'the ribby woak' in stanza 1 becomes 'this ribbed oak' and 'the words' becomes 'their words', while in stanza 2 'the shades' are changed to 'their shades'. We can perhaps link these alterations to the changes that are made to certain verb constructions. As Barnes noted in his 1844 'Dissertation', Dorset dialect was characterized by the prominent use of *do* as an auxiliary, not least to mark the past tense.[103] In 'The Vield Path' we have 'did sound' in stanza 1, and 'did pass' and 'did slide' in stanza 2. All three are changed in the Standard English version: as noted, 'did sound' becomes 'sounded' in the opening line, but in the other two instances the auxiliary verb is changed to *would*—'would pass' and 'would slide'. The effect of these changes, one may suggest, is a move away from the concrete, matter-of-fact particularity of the dialect version, towards something more habitual and universalizing: we are being told about the sort of thing that might, customarily, have used to happen in this sort of place, rather than specific things that did happen.

The cumulative effect of Barnes' changes is one of distancing. The replacement of dialect as a medium by Standard English, the shift towards a more elevated 'poetic'

---

[103] Barnes, *Poems in the Broad Form of the Dorset Dialect*, p. 14.

register, and the movement from the actual to the habitual, all serve to hold the landscape at a greater arm's length. If we think about the narrator of the poem, in the dialect version he or she seems to be close to the object of contemplation, both physically and emotionally, on the inside rather than the outside. In the Standard English version, by contrast, we have a more external narrator, more distant from their object, in many ways on the outside looking in and less personally invested. In short, what we can see is an exemplification of Hardy's claim about the use of dialect: the dialect version offers us 'intense localization', an elegiac meditation on a particular tree-shadowed footpath; the Standard English version, while not marking a sharp or absolute break, moves us perceptibly towards more 'general recollections of country life'.

But we have to come back to the fact that two versions of this poem exist. For Barnes, it was an active, deliberate choice to write in dialect rather than Standard English. Barnes, like his poem, was diglossic or bidialectal. This means that an explicit linguistic knowledge, philologically self-conscious, shapes and informs his dialect poetry; the instincts that generated his 'Dissertation' and glossaries were the same as those that produced the poems. We cannot make a sharp distinction between philology and poetry.

One way in which Barnes argued for the use of Dorset dialect as a literary medium was through the concept of the 'Doric':

> The Dorset dialect is a broad and bold shape of the English language, as the Doric was of the Greek. It is rich in humour, strong in raillery and hyperbole, and altogether as fit a vehicle of rustic feeling and thought, as the Doric is found in the Idyllia of Theocritus.[104]

However, as Joseph Hunter had remarked in his *Hallamshire Glossary*: 'custom in England allows of no Doric dialect'.[105] So Barnes and his followers had to work hard to establish dialect as a medium for poetry—an endeavour that was strengthened significantly by the rise of philology, and the dignity and value it placed on non-standard varieties. Barnes' 1844 'Dissertation' ends as follows:

> If his [i.e. the author's] verses should engage the happy mind of the dairymaid with her cow, promote the innocent evening cheerfulness of the family circle on the stone floor, or teach his rustic brethren to draw pure delight from the rich but frequently overlooked sources of nature within their own sphere of being, his fondest hopes will be realized.
>
> The dialect in which he writes is spoken in its greatest purity in the villages and hamlets of the secluded and beautiful Vale of Blackmore. He needs not observe that in the towns the poor commonly speak a mixed jargon, violating the canons of the pure dialect as well as those of English.[106]

---

[104] Barnes, *Poems in the Broad Form of the Dorset Dialect*, p. 6.
[105] Hunter, *Hallamshire Glossary*, p. xxi.
[106] Barnes, *Poems in the Broad Form of the Dorset Dialect*, p. 19.

126 The Victorians and English Dialect

These closing paragraphs draw together many of Barnes' key ideas or desires: the opposition of country and town, and of dialect and Standard English; the moral earnestness of his ambitions for rural life; and the uniting of poetry and philology in a single publication.[107]

Alfred Tennyson (1809–92) was one of those who read and admired Barnes' Dorset poems. The two men met on a number of occasions in the 1860s, and there seems little reason to doubt that it was Barnes' example which led Tennyson to compose in the dialect of his native Lincolnshire—even though he had ceased to live there over 20 years previously.[108]

But first, again, we should place Tennyson's dialect activities within the contexts of philology and medievalism. Among the major writers of the Victorian period, Tennyson was exceptionally early both in embracing the new philological learning, and also in turning to medieval subjects for his poetry.[109] As a student at Trinity College, Cambridge, he was a close friend of John Mitchell Kemble, one of the first champions of German philology in Britain.[110] But Kemble was not the only influence: the library of Tennyson's father at Somersby in Lincolnshire was unusually filled with medieval literature. As early as the late 1820s, Tennyson was trawling through Old English dictionaries, editions of medieval drama, and the works of Chaucer to produce a long list of old or rare words that he might one day use in his own writings.[111] He was among the first subscribers to F. J. Furnivall's Early English Text Society, was an eager buyer of dictionaries, and became friendly with Max Müller; and he retained his interest in philology and medieval literature to the end of his life (in 1891, the year before he died, he produced a four-line stanza to accompany an edition and translation of the Middle English poem *Pearl*).[112]

---

[107] See further T. L. Burton and K. K. Ruthven, 'Dialect Poetry, William Barnes and the Literary Canon', *English Literary History* 76 (2009), 309–41; Sue Edney, '"Times be Badish vor the Poor": William Barnes and his Dialect of Disturbance in the Dorset "Eclogues"', *English* 58 (2009), 206–29, and 'William Barnes's Place and Dialects of Connection', in Kirstie Blair and Mina Gorji (eds), *Class and the Canon: Constructing Labouring-Class Poetry and Poetics, 1780–1900* (Basingstoke: Palgrave Macmillan, 2013), pp. 190–210; Marcus Waithe, 'William Barnes: Views of Field Labour in Poems of Rural Life', in Matthew Bevis (ed.), *The Oxford Handbook of Victorian Poetry* (Oxford: Oxford University Press, 2013), pp. 460–74; Drury, 'Aural Community and William Barnes as Earwitness'.

[108] See Chedzoy, *The People's Poet*, pp. 169, 172–3.

[109] See, for example, Patrick Greig Scott, '"Flowering in a Lonely Word": Tennyson and the Victorian Study of Language', *Victorian Poetry* 18 (1980), 371–81; Richard Marggraf Turley, 'Tennyson and the Nineteenth-Century Language Debate', *Leeds Studies in English* New Series 28 (1997), 123–40; Michael Alexander, *Medievalism: the Middle Ages in Modern England* (New Haven: Yale University Press, 2007), pp. 114–26.

[110] On Kemble, see, for example, Raymond A. Wiley (ed.), *John Mitchell Kemble and Jakob Grimm: A Correspondence, 1832–1852* (Leiden: Brill, 1971); Raymond A. Wiley, 'Anglo-Saxon Kemble: The Life and Works of John Mitchell Kemble, 1807–1857: Philologist, Historian, Archaeologist', *Anglo-Saxon Studies in Archaeology and History* 1 (1979), 165–263; Aarsleff, *The Study of Language in England*, pp. 191–210; Momma, *From Philology to English Studies*, pp. 60–94, and 'The Newly-Found Kemble Notebook and an Old English *Hildebrandslied*: A Mirror of the New Philology in the 1830s', *Poetica* 86 (2016), 87–106; John D. Haigh, 'Kemble, John Mitchell (1807–1857)', in *Oxford Dictionary of National Biography* [www. oxforddnb].

[111] See Jones, *Fossil Poetry*, pp. 235–69; Sarah Weaver, *Tennyson's Notebook Glossary and Rhyme Lists*, Tennyson Society Monographs 17 (Lincoln: Tennyson Society, 2019).

[112] Munro, 'Biography', p. xlvi; Alfred Tennyson, *Poems*, ed. Christopher Ricks, 3 vols, 2nd ed. (London: Longman, 1987), III, 232.

Although most of the items in the early word list are drawn from Old and Middle English, a few dialect terms are included—*cratch*, *himsen*, and *owry*—all of which are labelled 'Lincl.' by Tennyson.[113] But the dialect poems themselves—in which *owry* at least features—did not appear until some decades later, and Tennyson published seven in all, from 'The Northern Farmer (Old Style)', written in 1861 and published in 1864, through to 'The Church-Warden and the Curate', written in 1890 and published posthumously in 1892.[114] Tennyson's commitment to dialect writing, then, extended over nearly 30 years; it was no brief fad, and the early word list reveals an interest going back for another 30 years before that. Moreover, these are lengthy poems: all are composed in the same conversational metre (in contrast to the stanzaic forms favoured by Barnes and many northern poets), and they add up to a total of over six hundred lines. All are first-person poems, humorous and even comic, spoken by local figures of a certain class or type: the title of one of Hardy's story series, 'A Few Crusted Characters', would work well as a general label for Tennyson's dialect monologues. As with other first-person narrative poetry of this period, the influence of the contemporary realist novel is unmistakable, and it is not hard to trace a debt to *Adam Bede* as well as to Barnes' *Poems of Rural Life*.

Since the earliest of these poems dates from the 1860s, it is also worth making the obvious point that all of Tennyson's dialect poems were composed and published during the period when he was Poet Laureate (having been appointed in 1850)—a striking assertion of the dignity and worth of dialect. Tennyson's book sales were prodigious, so it seems safe to claim that these were among the most frequently read dialect poems of the nineteenth century.[115] Tennyson's engagement with dialect poetry also shows the philological self-consciousness typical of the 1860s onwards. He experimented with various forms of orthography to represent regional phonology, sought out second opinions from local experts back home in Lincolnshire, and even included explanatory notes.[116] There is self-consciousness, also, in the sense that Tennyson is ventriloquizing an oral culture for the sake of a literate, non-dialectal readership, as for instance in the ironic mockery of 'booöklarnin" in 'The Village Wife' (the old Squire, she says, was 'Hallus aloän wi' 'is booöks, thaw nigh

---

[113] Weaver, *Tennyson's Notebook Glossary*, pp. 15, 23, 29, 46.

[114] Tennyson, *Poems*, II, 619–21, 688–90, III, 41–5, 58–61, 115–9, 169–73, and 227–30. See further Philip M. Tilling, 'Local Dialect and the Poet: A Comparison of the Findings in the *Survey of English Dialects* with Dialect in Tennyson's Lincolnshire Poems', in Martyn F. Wakelin (ed.), *Patterns in the Folk Speech of the British Isles* (London: Athlone Press, 1972), pp. 88–108; G. Edward Campion, *A Tennyson Dialect Glossary, with the dialect poems*, 3rd ed. (Lincoln: Lincolnshire and Humberside Arts, 1976); Roger Ebbatson, *Landscape and Literature 1830–1914: Nature, Text, Aura* (London: Palgrave Macmillan, 2013), pp. 50–61; Gunnel Melchers, '"An" I 'oäps as 'e beänt booöklarn'd: but 'e dosn' not coom fro' the shere: Alfred Tennyson's dialect poetry and insider/outsider readers and writers', in Jane Hodson (ed.), *Dialect and Literature in the Long Nineteenth Century* (Abingdon: Routledge, 2017), pp. 51–64; Sue Edney, 'The "Boggle" in the "Waäste": Meaning and Mask in Tennyson's Dialect Poems', in Claire Hélie, Elise Brault-Dreux, and Emilie Loriaux (eds), *No Dialect Please, You're A Poet: English Dialect in Poetry in the 20th and 21st Centuries* (London: Routledge, 2019), pp. 26–37.

[115] See Jim Cheshire, *Tennyson and Mid-Victorian Publishing: Moxon, Poetry, Commerce* (London: Palgrave Macmillan, 2017).

[116] See Tennyson, *Poems*, III, 42, note to 'The Northern Cobbler' line 1.

128 The Victorians and English Dialect

upo' seventy year. / An' boooks, what's boooks? thou knaws thebe neither 'ere nor theer').[117]

Linguistically, these are dense poems. Tennyson has not simply varied the orthography a little and dropped in a few unusual words; rather, he has attempted to engage systematically with the representation of dialect, as the opening lines of 'Owd Roä' (published 1889) can show as an example:

> Naäy, noä mander o' use to be callin' 'im Roä, Roä, Roä,
> Fur the dog's stoän-deäf, an' 'e's blind, 'e can neither stan' nor goä.
> But I means fur to make 'is owd aäge as 'appy as iver I can,
> Fur I owäs owd Roäver moor nor I iver owäd mottal man.[118]

Not counting the name of the dog (Roä or Rover), there are forty-nine words in these opening four lines: no fewer than thirty of them—nearly two-thirds—are respelled according to Tennyson's scheme, leading to a thick, profoundly unfamiliar reading experience (or, in Gunnel Melchers' description, 'a staggering array of outlandish vowel symbols').[119] It is tempting to conclude that Alexander Ellis had been thinking very specifically of Tennyson when he complained that 'litereri men [. . .] heep toogedh·er leterz in dhi moast pripos·terus, inkomprihen·sibl, inkonsis·tent maner [literary men heap together letters in the most preposterous, incomprehensible, inconsistent manner]'.[120]

Ellis' lament was made in 1871. But there was to be a pleasing twist: on 23 March 1881, in a meeting facilitated by Furnivall, Ellis and Tennyson met to discuss Lincolnshire dialect (the encounter lasted one hour and forty minutes, Ellis scrupulously recorded; it is not clear where it took place).[121] Tennyson read to Ellis parts of the two 'Northern Farmer' poems, presumably so that Ellis could study Tennyson's phonology and work out his orthography (and for good measure, Tennyson also referred Ellis to yet another vicar's daughter—Mrs Douglas Arden, whose father had been rector of Halton Holegate near Somersby—who was later able to guide Ellis further through questions of Lincolnshire dialect). But Ellis could not subsequently transcribe any of Tennyson's poems into Palaeotype 'on account of the copyright', and so his record of the meeting in *The Existing Phonology* is an assemblage of short extracts of individual observations, both phonological and orthographic: 'T[ennyson] pronounced the diphthong written *oi* not quite as (*A'i*), but rather as (*ái*) [. . .] Throughout, *ä* is used for diphthongising (ɐ)', and so on; but even under such restrictions, this is an unparalleled record of Tennyson's dialect pronunciation. There are also some flashes of human insight: for example, 'The peasants speak slowly, and T[ennyson] read [. . .] very slowly, with lengthened final consonants'; and 'I asked

---

[117] Tennyson, *Poems*, III, 58 (lines 27–8).
[118] Tennyson, *Poems*, III, 169 (lines 1–4).
[119] Melchers, '"An" I 'oäps as 'e beänt boooklarn'd', p. 52.
[120] Ellis, 'On Glosik', p. 93.
[121] See Ellis, 'Tenth Annual Address', p. 259, and *On Early English Pronunciation*, V, 1734–8/302–6 (and *English Dialects*, pp. 71–6).

T[ennyson] whether the people of Li[ncolnshire] ever said (sháiɐ) [i.e. *shire*], he said he hoped so, for the sake of the rhyme'.

Although Tennyson's complex orthography is the most pervasive divergence from Standard English in his dialect poems, the seven poems also demonstrate dialect grammar ('moor nor I iver' in the opening lines of 'Owd Roä') and, in some abundance, dialect vocabulary. In addition to including many simplex terms (for example, *fettle*, *huck*, *slaäpe*, *squad*, *hawmin'*, and *sloomy*, all taken from 'The Northern Cobbler'), Tennyson offers a sequence of alliterative, proverbial-seeming doublets: 'scrawmed an' scratted' ('The Northern Cobbler'), 'a-dallackt an' dizened out' ('The Village Wife'), 'a-twizzened an' twined' ('Owd Roä'). He also shows an imaginative relish for expressive compounds: for example, 'buzzard-clock' and 'butter-bump' in 'The Northern Farmer (Old Style)', 'tongue-banger' in 'The Northern Cobbler', and 'glimmer-gowk' in 'The Village Wife'. And finally, it is worth noting Tennyson's frequent use of invented place names in these poems: Thurnaby in 'The Northern Farmer (Old Style)', Wrigglesby in 'The Northern Farmer (New Style)', Thursby, Harmsby, and Hutterby in 'The Northern Cobbler', Gigglesby in 'The Spinster's Sweet-Arts', Howlaby in both 'Owd Roä' and 'The Church-Warden and the Curate', and Owlby and Scratby, also in 'The Church-Warden and the Curate'. Old Norse -*by* is a common second element in Lincolnshire village names (often with an Old Norse personal name ending in -*s* as the first element): Tennyson is finely attuned to this onomastic regional flavouring—he grew up at Somersby near Spilsby—and evokes it through his own repertoire of plausible-sounding coinages. This is, one may say, a very philological form of linguistic creativity.

Let us now go north from Lincolnshire, into Lancashire and Yorkshire. A somewhat different tradition of dialect poetry existed in the north of England. Like the use of dialect in fiction in the same period, mid-century dialect poetry shows both an industrial and a rural distribution, articulating—or ventriloquizing—the working-class voices in both the cities and the countryside, and often with a similar emphasis on the 'homely'.[122] Although we can observe its beginnings in the eighteenth century, the conscious flourishing of regional dialect literature in Lancashire and Yorkshire was a nineteenth-century phenomenon. Brian Hollingworth, editor of an important modern anthology, has suggested the decade and a half between about 1855 and 1870 as the golden age for its production. Why then? Hollingworth has proposed that these decades mark a propitious period of equipoise, in which a poetic culture with its origins in oral tradition moved into print and found a significant readership; later poetry, in his view, 'moved away from a living expression of the "songs of the people" to an antiquarian and rather nostalgic attempt to conserve a dying culture and language'.[123] This may well be true, though some recent work on Lancashire and

---

[122] See Vicinus, *The Industrial Muse*; Brian Hollingworth (ed.), *Songs of the People: Lancashire Dialect Poetry of the Industrial Revolution* (Manchester: Manchester University Press, 1977); Joyce, *Visions of the People*, pp. 256–304; Larry McCauley, '"Eawr Folk": Language, Class, and English Identity in Victorian Dialect Poetry', *Victorian Poetry* 39 (2001), 287–300; Wales, *Northern English*, pp. 114–41.

[123] Hollingworth (ed.), *Songs of the People*, p. 5; see also Brian Hollingworth, 'From Voice to Print: Lancashire Dialect Verse, 1800–70', *Philological Quarterly* 92 (2013), 289–308.

130 The Victorians and English Dialect

Yorkshire dialect poets has turned away from estimating them for their supposed authenticity, to stressing how dialect poetry could be part of a 'performance'—rehearsed and artful, rather than some sort of natural effusion. Other scholars have pointed to the so-called 'Lancashire Cotton Famine' of the early 1860s, provoked by the American Civil War, as being an unusually productive context for composition and publication.[124] In the context of the present book, of course, the new discipline of philology, and the consequent revaluation of dialect in the 1850s to 1870s, can be advocated as another key factor.

Like Barnes in Dorset—and like Ben Brierley in prose—many of the leading northern poets were diglossic, and wrote in Standard English as well as in Lancashire or Yorkshire dialect; some also wrote studies or defences of the dialect itself. A further sign of linguistic self-awareness can be seen in the literature's sense of tradition, and the vogue for reverencing and reprinting earlier dialect writings: the works of 'Tim Bobbin', for example, went through a number of editions in the nineteenth century; Ellis read *The Pitman's Pay* in an 1872 reprint; and Mary Powley's *Echoes of Old Cumberland* concludes with an appreciation of Josiah Relph (1712–43) as the pioneering poet of 'the rugged speech of Cumbria's vales'.[125] One of the templates here may have been the Victorian cult of Robert Burns, to whose dialect both Ellis and Murray pay appropriate attention.[126] Samuel Bamford wrote a poem that makes explicit this sense of literary heritage. It begins, 'I stood beside Tim Bobbin's grave / 'At looks o'er Ratchda' [i.e. Rochdale] teawn', and imagines the great forerunner emerging from his resting place to share a companionable jug of beer.[127] W. E. A. Axon, the Manchester writer who lectured on George Eliot's use of dialect, published in 1870 a volume called *Folk Song and Folk-Speech of Lancashire*, which attempts a historical overview of the field; Axon himself also published dialect poetry as well as several antiquarian works.[128]

Edwin Waugh (1817–90) is the most famous of these northern dialect poets (his surname may well have been pronounced 'Woff', and not necessarily like that of Evelyn Waugh). Waugh's eminence was amply recognized during his lifetime, being expressed, for example, in his receipt of a Civil List pension in his old age, instituted by Gladstone in 1881.[129] Waugh's life was tumultuous, and he worked as a printer and

---

[124] Edney, 'Recent Studies in Victorian English Literary Dialect', p. 664; Hakala, 'A Great Man in Clogs'. See Simon Rennie, 'This "Merikay War": Poetic Responses in Lancashire to the American Civil War', *Journal of Victorian Culture* 25 (2020), 126–43; http://cottonfaminepoetry.exeter.ac.uk/.

[125] Powley, *Echoes of Old Cumberland*, p. 241. See further Stephen Matthews, *Josiah Relph of Sebergham: England's First Dialect Poet* (Carlisle: Bookcase, 2015).

[126] See Murray, *Dialect of the Southern Counties of Scotland*, pp. 75–7; Ellis, *On Early English Pronunciation*, V, 2163–73/731–41, 2180–1/748–9.

[127] Hollingworth (eds), *Songs of the People*, pp. 125–6, 150. See further D. M. Horgan, 'Popular Protest in the Eighteenth Century: John Collier (Tim Bobbin), 1708–1786', *Review of English Studies* New Series 48 (1997), 310–31, at pp. 327–9.

[128] William E. A. Axon, *Folk Song and Folk-Speech of Lancashire, on the Ballads and Songs of the County Palatine, with Notes on the Dialect in which many of them are written, and an Appendix on Lancashire Folk-Lore* (Manchester: Tubbs and Brook, 1870).

[129] On Waugh see, for example, Martha Vicinus, *The Ambiguities of Self-Help: Concerning the Life and Work of the Lancashire Dialect Writer Edwin Waugh* (Littleborough: Kelsall, 1983); Patrick Joyce, *Democratic Subjects: The Self and the Social in Nineteenth-Century England* (Cambridge: Cambridge University

educationalist before becoming a full-time writer and public performer. He became famous through his poem 'Come whoam to thy childer an' me', a woman's plea for her wandering husband to return (written in 1856, by which time Waugh himself had long been separated from his wife). Like Brierley, he was a prolific writer—an 1880s edition of his collected works runs to eleven volumes, and an 1890s edition to eight— and he wrote prose as well as verse, fiction as well as non-fiction (his best-known stories are those of 'Besom Ben').

Waugh was diglossic. He later recalled that 'in his youth he was so habitually in contact with the people in whose mouths that dialect lived, that he learned it and used it habitually'.[130] But although he grew up in an environment rich in dialect, it was not his usual mode of language in adulthood: when Thomas Hallam went to hear Waugh give a public reading and transcribed his speech in 1866, he noted *awt* for 'anything' and *nawt* for 'nothing', but also the mixed pronunciations of *mâster* and *plāster*.[131] Waugh wrote extensively in Standard English as well as dialect, and his 'Besom Ben' tales are narrated in Standard English, with dialect reserved for the dialogue (just like Gaskell and Eliot, say, but unlike Brierley's 'Ab o' the Yate' stories). Moreover, Waugh moved in antiquarian circles throughout his life, from his early patronage under the Rev. F. R. Raines, vicar of Milnrow in Lancashire and a leading light in Manchester's Chetham Society, to his own later involvement in Manchester's literary and historical clubs.

The close connection between Waugh's creative writings and the regional philology of Lancashire becomes especially apparent when we look at the 1890s edition of his collected works, published in Manchester. With dialect glosses in footnotes, these volumes were edited by George Milner, the speech-maker on the occasion of Ben Brierley's 1885 testimonial. Among his other publications, Milner was co-author, with J. H. Nodal, of a substantial *Glossary of the Lancashire Dialect* (1875–82), produced by the Manchester Literary Club (of which he was President), an important society for the championing of Waugh and other dialect writers.[132] In this glossary, not only are Waugh's works listed as by far the most extensive authorities under the heading of 'Writers in the Dialect', but Waugh himself is recorded as the chief contributor of dialect material for Rochdale.[133] Nodal and Milner praise Waugh as being, among Lancashire writers, 'pre-eminent, on account not only of his genius and knowledge, but of his minute observation and scholarly study of the dialect'.[134] In fact, Waugh is a

---

Press, 1994), pp. 23–82; Hakala, 'A Great Man in Clogs'; Brian Hollingworth, 'Edwin Waugh: The Social and Literary Standing of a Working-Class Icon', in Kirstie Blair and Mina Gorji (eds), *Class and the Canon: Constructing Labouring-Class Poetry and Poetics, 1780–1900* (Basingstoke: Palgrave Macmillan, 2013), pp. 174–90; John A. Hargreaves, 'Waugh, Edwin (1817–1890)', in *Oxford Dictionary of National Biography* [www.oxforddnb].

[130] *English Dialect Society: Fifteenth Report, for the Year 1888* (no place or date of publication), p. 8; see also Hakala, 'Working Dialect', pp. 91–5, and 'A Great Man in Clogs', pp. 396–7.

[131] Oxford, Bodleian Libraries, MS Eng. lang. g. 6, fols 15–6.

[132] See Vicinus, *The Industrial Muse*, pp. 204–5; Hakala, 'Working Dialect', pp. 69–79; Steve Roud, *Folk Song in England* (London: Faber and Faber, 2017), pp. 571–7.

[133] John H. Nodal and George Milner, *A Glossary of the Lancashire Dialect* (Manchester: Manchester Literary Club, 1875–82), pp. vii, xii–xiii.

[134] Nodal and Milner, *Glossary of the Lancashire Dialect*, p. ix.

132   The Victorians and English Dialect

pervasive presence on most pages of the *Glossary*, as the leading source of illustrative quotations. So, for example, the last three entries in the work, on the last page, are for *yowl*, *yure*, and *yurey*, and Waugh is the only source cited for any of them. Waugh's writings dominate the *Glossary*.

Milner supplied a biographical introduction for the first volume of Waugh's collected works (*Lancashire Sketches: First Series*), but his fullest appreciation of Waugh's dialect poetry comes in an essay prefaced to the volume *Poems and Songs*, titled 'On the Dialect of Lancashire Considered as a Vehicle for Poetry'—a reprint of an essay originally published in 1875. This attempts to address 'what is the real nature of folk-speech, and how far the particular dialect of Lancashire, for instance, lends itself to the expression of such ideas as are usually associated with the forms of verse'.[135] The first point Milner wishes to stress is that there has, of late years, been a profound change of attitude towards dialect. The older view, he says, was that 'all folk-speech was uncouth and vulgar—a thing to be got rid of, by the aid of the school-master, with as little delay as possible'. But such prejudices have now been abandoned 'by educated persons', and Milner has no doubt as to the cause of this:

> The true nature and importance of dialects having been apprehended, they have become objects of investigations to many of the ripest scholars of our time. To study philology in a scientific spirit was to be forced back, as a necessity, upon the exami-nation of dialects, because in them were so frequently to be found the very roots and springs of the modern literary language.

Milner then attempts to define what a dialect is, and to correct a few false impres-sions: 'words peculiar to a particular district', he writes, 'are but few in number', whereas it is in 'idioms and phrases' that 'the distinction and the Doric flavour of each dialect' can best be discovered'.[136] Milner's claim for dialect poetry is that 'the truest poetry requires for its expression only the simplest words; and in poetical com-position the nearer we are to the roots of language the safer we are from jarring notes and false associations'.[137] Milner links this with the preponderance of (often monosyl-labic or disyllabic) words derived from Old English, Old Norse, and Celtic in regional dialect, especially Lancashire dialect, and the relative paucity of (often polysyllabic) words derived from French or Latin. This is not a Barnes-style argument for lin-guistic nativism as a general principle (indeed, Milner insists that 'the wider and the more polyglot our vocabulary is the better', and he also believes that 'the Celtic element is particularly strong in Lancashire'); but it is a claim for the idea of simplic-ity and rootedness in the language of poetry.[138] Milner attempts to demonstrate this with a quirky translation of Wordsworth's 'Lucy' into Lancashire dialect—'But hoo is in her grave, an' oh, / What change it's browt to me'—but (perhaps thankfully) his

---

[135] George Milner, 'Introductory Essay, On the Dialect of Lancashire Considered as a Vehicle for Poetry', in Edwin Waugh, *Poems and Songs*, ed. George Milner (Manchester: Heywood, no date of publication), pp. xiii–xxxii, at p. xiv.

[136] Milner, 'Introductory Essay', p. xv.

[137] Milner, 'Introductory Essay', p. xvi.

[138] Milner, 'Introductory Essay', pp. xviii, xxviii.

argument doesn't stand or fall on the basis of this experiment.[139] Instead, he changes tack and argues that the use of dialect 'allows the employment of many fine archaic and now forgotten words, which are not so easily admissible into ordinary modern poetry': examples which Milner cites from Waugh's verse include *marrow* (for 'match, mate'), *shoon* ('shoes'), and *welkin* ('sky'). Milner's conclusion is that 'the genius of our provincial poetry is so nearly allied to that of the older literature that any skilful writer of the dialect might enrich his verse by introducing into it any, or all, of those antique, and now disused, but most expressive words which are to be found in the earlier poets'.[140] This marriage between the dialectal and the antique is, of course, one that is made through philology, and thus for Milner the work of the dialect poet, 'if carefully done, will always possess an historical interest and a philological value'. In his eulogy for Ben Brierley, Milner insisted 'how very many of its [i.e. Lancashire dialect's] words were to be found in our earliest and finest poetic writing', and here he makes a similar claim, offering an invitation to contemporary poets writing in Standard English:

> As we have seen, the words of the older poets are often retained in the dialects; and these, the modern poet might reclaim: and further, he could often find in the pages of his humbler brother an original word or phrase, strong and picturesque, with which he might materially enrich his own vocabulary.[141]

Although there is no reason to think that either of them read Milner's essay, we will turn in the final section of this chapter to two poets who endeavoured, in their different ways, to do precisely what the Manchester writer was calling on poets to attempt: Thomas Hardy and Gerard Manley Hopkins.

Remaking poetic diction

Hardy was born in 1840 and Hopkins in 1844; they were just the right age to catch the excitement of philology's rise in the 1850s and 1860s. We know that, in their different social and educational contexts, both read widely in the new discipline. Neither knew each other's poetry, of course: only a few of Hopkins' poems were published prior to his death, and Hardy's first collection did not appear until 1898. But they were working in decidedly similar ways, as they both responded to the opportunities that philology offered for the remaking of poetic diction—including the potential of dialect.

Milner's propositions that dialectal speech offered access to 'the roots of language', and that 'the modern poet' might reclaim words which are 'often retained in the dialects' in order to 'materially enrich his own vocabulary', were not unique. Back

---

[139] Milner, 'Introductory Essay', p. xxii. See further Hakala, 'Working Dialect', pp. 73–4, and 'A Great Man in Clogs', pp. 398–9.
[140] Milner, 'Introductory Essay', p. xxvi.
[141] Brierley, *Home Memories*, p. 86; Milner, 'Introductory Essay', p. xxvi.

134 The Victorians and English Dialect

in the sixteenth century, Edmund Spenser had been praised for rehabilitating in his *Shepheardes Calender* 'such good and naturall English words, as haue ben long time out of vse and almost cleane disherited'.[142] Joseph Hunter, writing about dialect and poetic diction in his 1830 *Hallamshire Glossary*, dared to hope that 'sometimes a daring spirit may arise, who shall venture to recall to public view some word grown obsolete'.[143] In his *Lectures on the Science of Language*, Max Müller proposed 'dialectical regeneration' as one of the fundamental forces in language change, suggesting that 'when literary languages have stereotyped one general term, their dialects will supply fifty, though each with its own special shade of meaning'.[144] What local, professional, and class dialects thus offer, according to Müller, are 'unbounded resources'. And in an 1865 essay in the *Cornhill Magazine* entitled 'The Poetry of Provincialisms', J. R. Wise proposed that 'in some respects provincialisms form the unwritten poetry of a nation. They contain the germs of poems', so that since 'our language requires both enriching and purifying [. . .] we can best do this by drawing on our rich mines of dialects'; Wise believed that 'in the hands of a poet [provincialisms] may be made to yield fresh beauty'.[145] Wise (1831–90) was a historian and nature writer, best known for an influential book on the New Forest; later in life, he also published a 'fairy masque', *The First of May*, which was dedicated to Charles Darwin and illustrated by Walter Crane.[146]

Let us consider Hardy first, and then Hopkins (and we will return to Hardy's fiction in Chapter 5). For both poets it is crucial to stress that recourse to dialect is only one of their philological strategies: in their different ways, they turned also to the resources of Old and Middle English, Old Norse, and early modern English (insofar as these can be distinguished from dialectal survivals), and to the possibilities for word-formation that such earlier states of the language revealed.[147] Hardy grew up in full familiarity with Dorset dialect, and he was an assiduous reader of dialect glossaries, making his own lists of unrecorded words.[148] We can distinguish a number of types of dialect presence in Hardy's poetry. First, 'The Bride-Night Fire' is in a category of its own for being a narrative poem wholly in dialect: written in 1866, it

---

[142] Edmund Spenser, *Poetical Works*, ed. J. C. Smith and E. De Selincourt (Oxford: Oxford University Press, 1912), p. 417. See further, for example, Hannah Crawforth, *Etymology and the Invention of English in Early Modern Literature* (Cambridge: Cambridge University Press, 2013), pp. 19–45.

[143] Hunter, *Hallamshire Glossary*, p. xii.

[144] Müller, *Lectures on the Science of Language*, p. 62.

[145] [John R. Wise], 'The Poetry of Provincialisms', *Cornhill Magazine*, July 1865, 30–42, at pp. 38, 40–1. See further McCauley, '"Eawr Folk"', pp. 294–6.

[146] See Paul Readman, *Storied Ground: Landscape and the Shaping of English National Identity* (Cambridge: Cambridge University Press, 2018), pp. 167, 175; Sidney Lee, 'Wise, John Richard de Capel (1831–1890)', rev. Giles Hudson, in *Oxford Dictionary of National Biography* [www.oxforddnb].

[147] On Hardy, see especially Norman Page, 'Hardy and the English Language', in Norman Page (ed.), *Thomas Hardy: The Writer and his Background* (London: Routledge and Kegan Paul, 1980), pp. 151–72; Ralph W. V. Elliott, *Thomas Hardy's English* (Oxford: Blackwell, 1984); Raymond Chapman, *The Language of Thomas Hardy* (Basingstoke: Macmillan, 1990); Dennis Taylor, 'Victorian Philology and Victorian Poetry', *Victorian Newsletter* 53 (1978), 13–16, *Hardy's Literary Language and Victorian Philology*, and 'The Victorian Philological Contexts of Hardy's Poetry', in Phillip Mallett (ed.), *Thomas Hardy in Context* (Cambridge: Cambridge University Press, 2013), pp. 231–41.

[148] See Millgate, *Thomas Hardy*, pp. 30–1, 77, 383; Taylor, *Hardy's Literary Language and Victorian Philology*, pp. 165–6.

was published as early as 1875. The poem went through many mutations over successive printings, as Hardy revised the vocabulary and orthography (and even the title), and added lexical glosses in some editions.[149] Second, Hardy sometimes uses heavily dialectal language as a feature of dialogue (but not of narrative). An example of this second type is the poem 'Friends Beyond', which overhears the voices of those buried in 'Mellstock churchyard': these include Farmer Ledlow, who declares that 'Ye mid zell my favourite heifer, ye mid let the charlock grow, / Foul the grinterns, give up thrift' (the *Oxford English Dictionary*, in an entry first published in 1900, takes its definition of *grintern*, as 'a compartment in a granary', from Barnes' 1863 *Grammar and Glossary of the Dorset Dialect*, and gives one illustrative quotation: this example from 'Friends Beyond').[150] Under this second heading we might also notice a number of poems in which the presence or absence of dialect is explicitly held up for contemplation: here, a symptomatic poem is 'The Ruined Maid' (written in 1866, but not published till 1901), where a 'country girl' in town meets an old friend who has since been 'ruined', presumably through a sexual liaison:

> "At home in the barton you said 'thee' and 'thou',
> And 'thik oon' and 'theäs oon', and 't'other'; but now
> Your talking quite fits 'ee for high com-pa-ny!"
> "Some polish is gained with one's ruin," said she.[151]

Third—moving from passages of dialect to isolated words—a number of Dorset words, readily familiar from Hardy's fiction, feature regularly in his poetry, especially as part of the vocabulary of landscape or agriculture: for example, *barton*, *coomb*, and *ewe-leaze*.

But it is the fourth category which offers something different, and shows Hardy engaging in the kind of renovation of the poetic vocabulary which Milner was urging. Recurrent in Hardy's poetic practice is a willingness to use dialect words within a poem which one would otherwise say is written in Standard English, albeit a Standard English drawing on diverse sources of vocabulary; and those dialect words are not flagged within the poems as belonging to a different or discordant register (let alone to a different speaker, as in category two). Or rather, it might be better to say that Hardy is making a new register, one which does not recognize the usual oppositions, or proprieties, that govern different types of vocabulary—not only standard and non-standard, or national and regional, but also contemporary and archaic, scientific and non-scientific, and so on. Take, for example, the title of Hardy's famous poem about the loss of the *Titanic*, 'The Convergence of the Twain'.[152] According to the usual

---

[149] Thomas Hardy, *Complete Poetical Works*, ed. Samuel Hynes, 5 vols (Oxford: Clarendon Press, 1982–95), I, 93–8. See further Simon Gatrell, 'Dialect', in Norman Page (ed.), *Oxford Reader's Companion to Hardy* (Oxford: Oxford University Press, 2001), pp. 96–8, and Gatrell, *Thomas Hardy's Vision of Wessex*, pp. 224–5.

[150] Hardy, *Complete Poetical Works*, I, 78–9.

[151] Hardy, *Complete Poetical Works*, I, 197–8. See further Emilie Loriaux, 'Thomas Hardy's Use of the Dorset Dialect: "A Memory of William Barnes"', *The Thomas Hardy Journal* 32 (2016), 104–12.

[152] Hardy, *Complete Poetical Works*, II, 11–13.

136 The Victorians and English Dialect

customs of register, this is an extraordinary title: *twain* (as the *OED* recognizes) is an archaic or dialectal word, and standard modern English would of course be *two*, or perhaps *pair*. Why is the poem not called 'The Convergence of the Pair'? Perhaps the idiom 'never the twain shall meet' is lurking behind the title (as in Rudyard Kipling's 'Ballad of East and West')—because in this case the two do meet, do converge. But this is likely to be only a partial answer; and the conjunction of the title seems even stranger when we realize (from the *OED*) that, in Hardy's time, *convergence* was a term that was still heavily scientific in its register, used to describe rays of light, for example, rather than being purely metaphorical or register-free. In fact the point may be that there isn't a proper, or propriety-based, answer as to why Hardy chose to pair *convergence* with *twain*: his vocabulary choices aren't governed by the usual rules of stylistic appropriateness that prescribe that a writer should choose an archaic word or an archaic style because that is linguistically appropriate to the subject matter, or a scientific style for a different subject, and so on. Arguments that attempt to justify Hardy's stylistic oddities in this way are in danger of making him seem a more conventional writer than he was.[153] But nor should we attribute this mixing of registers to some sort of imperfect education on the part of the (heavily) autodidactic Hardy; there seems no reason to doubt that this is a deliberate style, not the result of incompetence or a failure of taste.

Hardy's poetry is full of this unexpected yoking together of words that would normally exist in separate registers: in 'A Singer Asleep', for example, Hardy's elegy for the poet Swinburne, the words *fulth* and *orts* co-exist with *hydrosphere* and *subterrene*; in 'To Sincerity', we find both *foredeeming* and *unilluded*.[154] Dialect terms are among the types of vocabulary that co-exist like this in Hardy's poetic language, along with the archaic, the colloquial, the scientific, and the philosophical. Although for many words it is uncertain whether they should primarily be regarded as archaic or dialectal (as in the case of *twain*), probable dialectal examples include the following: 'In *lewth* of leaves to throne her bride' ('Postponement'), 'as one *wanzing* weak / From life's *roak* and *reek*' ('He Revisits His First School'), and 'The troubled skulls that heave / And *fust* in the flats of France' ('A Night of Questionings').[155] Critics have long recognized this element in Hardy's writing, pointing out his 'lifelong resistance to the strict division of British language styles into standard and dialect', his 'poetic language which does not try to make itself a homogenous idiom', and his practice of 'dialectal cherry-picking'.[156] This observation goes back at least as far as William Archer's celebrated comment of 1898, in reviewing *Wessex Poems*, that 'there are times when Mr Hardy seems to lose all sense of local and historical perspective in language, seeing all the words in the dictionary on one plane, so to speak, and regarding them all as equally available and appropriate for any and every literary

---

[153] See, for example, Taylor, *Hardy's Literary Language and Victorian Philology*, pp. 269–77.
[154] Hardy, *Complete Poetical Works*, I, 336, II, 31–3.
[155] Hardy, *Complete Poetical Works*, I, 12, II, 258–9, III, 35–7. See further Elliott, *Thomas Hardy's English*, pp. 36–109; Taylor, *Hardy's Literary Language and Victorian Philology*, pp. 179–85.
[156] Ferguson, 'Drawing Fictional Lines', p. 14; Taylor, *Hardy's Literary Language and Victorian Philology*, p. 69; Burton and Ruthven, in Barnes, *Poems in the Broad Form of the Dorset Dialect*, p. xli.

response'.[157] Hardy was clearly taken by this observation, quoting it back to Archer in a subsequent letter; but he had, in any case, already said as much himself, in his preface to *Wessex Poems*: 'Whenever an ancient and legitimate word of the district, for which there was no equivalent in received English, suggested itself as the most natural, nearest, and often only expression of a thought, it has been made use of, on what seemed good grounds'.[158]

Here it is important to make a distinction which is also germane for Hopkins. Many 'philological' writers, such as William Morris, saw their mission as the reclamation or re-introduction of words that had grown obsolete, and were now only to be recovered from old (and often medieval) writings; and Hardy did this too to a significant extent. But when he chose to renovate his literary language from the resources of local dialect, Hardy was not reaching back into the past, to retrieve forgotten words; rather, he was drawing his vocabulary from current local usage—though as the philologists had been pointing out, such contemporary dialect was especially valuable precisely because it preserved old words and expressions that had vanished from the standard language. As Hardy observed in a 1901 interview with William Archer:

> [Some] critics seemed to me to take unnecessary objection to my use of local Wessex words, which they declared to be obsolete. But they are not obsolete here; they are understood and used by educated people. And if they supply a want in the language—if they express an idea which cannot otherwise be so accurately or so briefly expressed— why may not one attempt to preserve them?[159]

Hardy's specification of 'educated people' seems a defiant insistence either that local dialect usage was not restricted to the working class, and/or that the working class should not be dismissed as uneducated. And his further comment to Archer, 'I have no sympathy with the criticism which would treat English as a dead language—a thing crystallised at an arbitrarily selected stage of its existence, and bidden to forget that it has a past and deny that it has a future', indicates that, for Hardy, the use of dialect is a living, future-oriented activity, and not simply a preservationist one. But readers unfamiliar with dialect might well regard a word as archaic or medieval, rather than contemporary and dialectal, as it was to Hardy; and this misapprehension, as we will now see, seems especially to have been the case among readers of Hopkins.

Hopkins' incessant compounding, his creative redeployment of prefixes and suffixes, and his pervasive alliteration, are all practices that could only have come into being in the time of philology.[160] As a number of scholars have shown, it makes more

---

[157] Quoted in Taylor, *Hardy's Literary Language and Victorian Philology*, p. 42.

[158] Hardy, *Complete Poetical Works*, I, 5 (original version).

[159] William Archer, 'Real Conversations', in Martin Ray (ed.), *Thomas Hardy Remembered* (London: Routledge, 2007), pp. 28–37, at pp. 36–7.

[160] See James Milroy, *The Language of Gerard Manley Hopkins* (London: Deutsch, 1977); Taylor, 'Victorian Philology and Victorian Poetry'; Cary H. Plotkin, *The Tenth Muse: Victorian Philology and the Genesis of the Poetic Language of Gerard Manley Hopkins* (Carbondale: Southern Illinois University Press, 1989); Alexander, *Medievalism*, pp. 180–95; Jones, *Fossil Poetry*, pp. 192–234.

138   The Victorians and English Dialect

sense to see Hopkins as a 'philological' writer than a 'medievalist' one—even though, of course, the study of medieval texts lay close to the heart of Victorian philology. The influences of Old English, Middle English, and Old Norse (and Welsh as well) reached him more through the reading of philological scholarship than through extensive engagement with medieval sources; and George Marsh's *Lectures on the English Language* (1860) were especially fertile for him.[161] Moreover, the impact of philology on Hopkins' poetry was not merely decorative—tricks of style, aural adornments—but foundational and shaping: as James Milroy has said, '[it is not] correct to say that it was Hopkins who breathed life into philology; on the contrary, it was philology that helped to breathe life onto Hopkins's poetry'.[162] Echoes of Müller in particular appear to be heard in many places in Hopkins' works. Müller's root-based belief, for example, that 'there is a law which runs through nearly the whole of nature, that everything which is struck rings', prefigures quite startlingly the poem 'As kingfishers catch fire'.[163] Hopkins' early diaries, full of lists of similar-sounding words, reveal a serious engagement with questions of word roots and the origins of language, sometimes in terms of a debate with Müller: 'I think the onomatopoetic theory has not had a fair chance. Cf. crack, creak, croak, crake, graculus, crackle. These must be onomatopoetic'.[164] This commitment to a search for roots—seen also in his sympathetic reading of Barnes—means that, in his later, densely aural poetry, full of alliteration and half-rhyme, Hopkins was not simply putting together words that sounded similar, in a pleasingly euphonious manner: he may have believed that such words were often semantically or conceptually linked.[165]

Hopkins responded eagerly to Müller's argument that dialects offered the potentiality of 'unbounded resources'. His diaries of the early 1860s include notes on dialect terms ('Cranky, provincial, out of sorts, wrong [. . .] Clarty, North Country—sticky'), as do his journals of the early 1870s, concerning both vocabulary and pronunciation ('Stickles / Devonshire for the foamy tongues of water below falls [. . .] They say here th'hee road for the high road and steel for stile').[166] But what dialect was this? Where was he? Hardy is indelibly associated with 'Wessex', Edwin Waugh with Lancashire, and so on; but Hopkins is not associated with a particular part of the country in the same way, and the dialect element in his writings shows traces from a number of the different places where he lived (such as Lancashire and Dublin), as well as from book learning. Hopkins took words from everywhere; the dialectal element in his poetry is not geographically restricted, and so does not offer the 'intense localization' of Barnes, for example.

---

[161] See Plotkin, *The Tenth Muse*, pp. 123–30; Jones, *Fossil Poetry*, pp. 208–11. On Marsh, see David Lowenthal, *George Perkins Marsh: Prophet of Conservation* (Seattle: University of Washington Press, 2003).

[162] Milroy, *The Language of Gerard Manley Hopkins*, p. 39.

[163] Müller, *Lectures on the Science of Language*, p. 387. See further Plotkin, *The Tenth Muse*, pp. 38–40, 103–9.

[164] Gerard Manley Hopkins, *Diaries, Journals, and Notebooks*, ed. Lesley Higgins, Collected Works of Gerard Manley Hopkins III (Oxford: Oxford University Press, 2015), p. 111.

[165] See Plotkin, *The Tenth Muse*, pp. 109–23.

[166] Hopkins, *Diaries, Journals, and Notebooks*, pp. 112, 137, 528.

A few examples are as follows. '*Degged* with dew, dappled with dew' ('Inversnaid'); 'so fagged, so *fashed*, so *cogged*, so cumbered' ('The Leaden Echo and the Golden Echo'); 'When thou at the *random* grim forge, powerful amidst peers, / Didst *fettle* for the great grey drayhorse his bright and battering sandal' ('Felix Randal'); 'Cloud-puffball, torn tufts, tossed pillows | flaunt forth, then *chevy* on an air- / Built thoroughfare' ('That Nature is a Heraclitean Fire').[167] In all of these examples (except, perhaps, for the notably northern 'Felix Randal'), the dialect-derived word is simply deployed as a lexical resource; it is not chosen because of its non-standard status or appropriate regionality. 'Felix Randal' also gives us the phrase 'God rest him *all road* ever he offended'; but here the dialect idiom lurking behind Hopkins' expression is *(at) any road*, so that what this example suggests is that Hopkins' attitude to dialect was not reverential or curatorial, but creative and open, willing to adapt existing expressions.[168] Similarly, 'That Nature is a Heraclitean Fire' offers the compound *shivelight(s)*.[169] *Shive* is a widespread dialect term (meaning 'slice, splinter'), but *shivelight* is a unique Hopkins formation, again showing the use of dialect as a resource for active language-making, not simply a closed glossary.[170] A parallel to Hopkins' practice can be found in Richard Morris' presidential address to the Philological Society in 1876, drawing attention to the morphological possibilities that contemporary dialects offer:

> In the provincial dialects word-making seems to have been in active operation, and is still so wherever the old idioms are in full play; and we find no repugnance to such formations as *lowths* (lowlands), *footh* (=fullth, abundance), *foothy* (well-off) [. . .], *teamful* (brimming), *deftish* (dexterous), *betterment* (amendment), *growsome* (applied to weather favourable for growing crops), *lixom* (=*liksome*, amiable), *skathy* (mischievous).[171]

This 'word-making' is precisely Hopkins' own, and a number of Morris' examples sound as if they have been taken out of Hopkins' poetry. So dialect offered to Hopkins principles of creative morphology as much as specific lexical resources.

Let us conclude with a famous letter from Hopkins to Robert Bridges, written in August 1879. Among other topics, Hopkins gives Bridges his views on the poetry of William Barnes, and the associations of dialect more generally:

---

[167] Gerard Manley Hopkins, *The Major Works*, ed. Catherine Phillips (Oxford: Oxford University Press, 2002), pp. 150, 153, 156, 180. See further Milroy, *The Language of Gerard Manley Hopkins*, pp. 232–48; Plotkin, *The Tenth Muse*, pp. 75–91.

[168] Hopkins, *The Major Works*, p. 150; Joseph Wright (ed.), *English Dialect Dictionary*, 6 vols (Oxford: Frowde, 1898–1905), V, 133; Milroy, *The Language of Gerard Manley Hopkins*, pp. 141, 243.

[169] Hopkins, *The Major Works*, p. 181.

[170] Wright (ed.), *English Dialect Dictionary*, V, 391–2.

[171] Richard Morris, 'Fifth Annual Address of the President to the Philological Society, Delivered at the Anniversary Meeting, Friday, the 19th of May, 1876', *Transactions of the Philological Society* 1876, 273–397, at p. 285 (partly reprinted as Richard Morris, *On the Survival of Early English Words in Our Dialects*, English Dialect Society 11 (London: English Dialect Society, 1876), p. 2).

140 The Victorians and English Dialect

> I was almost a great admirer of Barnes' Dorset (not Devon) poems [...] A proof of their excellence is that you may translate them and they are nearly as good—I say nearly, because if the dialect plays any lawful part in the effect they ought to lose something in losing that [...] But [dialect's] lawful charm I take to be this, that it sort of guarantees the spontaneousness of the thought and puts you in the position to appraise it on its merits as coming from nature and not books and education. It heightens one's admiration for a phrase just as in architecture it heightens one's admiration of a design to know that it is old work, not new [...] Now the use of dialect to a man like Barnes is to tie him down to the things that he or another Dorset man has said or might say, which though it narrows his field heightens his effects. His poems used to charm me also by their Westcountry "instress", a most peculiar product of England.[172]

But it is not because of his thoughts on Barnes that this letter is famous. Rather, its importance is due to the section that follows, in which Hopkins explains his antipathy to the conventional archaisms of poetry such as *ere* and *o'er*:

> I cut myself off from the use of [such words], because, though dignified, they neither belong to nor ever cd. arise from, or be the elevation of, ordinary modern speech. For it seems to me that the poetical language of an age shd. be the current language heightened, to any degree heightened and unlike itself, but not (I mean normally: passing freaks and graces are another thing) an obsolete one.[173]

The sequence of thought is noteworthy here. This celebrated discussion of poetic diction follows directly from Hopkins' reflections on Barnes and rural dialect, suggesting a central role for dialect in Hopkins' thinking about diction—a centrality also suggested by his repeated use of the term 'heighten[ed]' to communicate both the nature of dialect and his desired poetic language. There is no reason to doubt the fundamental truthfulness of Hopkins' diagnosis of his own practice ('the current language heightened'), and Hopkins' champions have sometimes wished to insist that, unlike other Victorian poets, he cannot be accused of (supposedly undesirable) archaism, or of a literary diction that is remote from contemporary speech.[174] But if we consider the status and perception of dialect vocabulary at the time, then we can see that there is, perhaps, an element of disingenuousness in his formulation. To a Standard English audience, as Hardy's comments to William Archer indicate, words which are dialectal will often be perceived as archaic, and in the mid nineteenth century the 'archaic' and the 'provincial' were habitually bracketed together, not least in a number of influential dictionaries; moreover, Hopkins' own letter to Bridges seems to acknowledge and value this, when he compares dialect speech to architectural 'old work'. The 'unbounded resources' of dialect, then, enabled Hopkins to create a poetic language that was indeed, strictly speaking, 'current'—even if

---

[172] Hopkins, *Correspondence*, I, 364 (14–21 August 1879); on Barnes, see also II, 743–4, 824–5.
[173] Hopkins, *Correspondence*, I, 365.
[174] See Milroy, *The Language of Gerard Manley Hopkins*, pp. 75, 80–1.

to many of his contemporaries some of the diction he was redeploying would have seemed 'obsolete'.

Hopkins' dialect activities as a collector lasted all his life, and reached their sharpest focus in the late 1880s, when he was living in Dublin and noting Irish words and phrases. These he was gathering for a purpose: they were intended for the great *English Dialect Dictionary* which was then being planned—even though the first volume of the dictionary did not finally appear until nearly a decade after Hopkins' death, as we will see in Chapter 6.[175] The *English Dialect Dictionary* was an outgrowth of the English Dialect Society, out of whose collections it was partly compiled. Most of the other poets discussed in this chapter also had a connection with the English Dialect Society: Hardy's opinions were sought out, like those of George Eliot, at an early stage in the Society's existence, and Barnes, Tennyson, and Waugh were all members of the Society—indeed, Waugh was even a committee member. So it is to the English Dialect Society, the main organization for regional philology in Victorian England, that we must turn in the next chapter.

---

[175] Wright (ed.), *English Dialect Dictionary*, I, xii; Hopkins, *Correspondence*, II, 923–5. See further Norman White, 'G. M. Hopkins's Contribution to the *English Dialect Dictionary*', *English Studies* 68 (1987), 325–35, and *Hopkins: A Literary Biography* (Oxford: Oxford University Press, 1992), pp. 437–8.

4

The English Dialect Society

Origins

The English Dialect Society is the forgotten society of Victorian language study. Whereas other societies, such as the Philological Society and the Early English Text Society, are still in existence and are fêted in modern scholarship (not least on account of their role in the making of the *Oxford English Dictionary*), the English Dialect Society was a fixed-term enterprise which has left behind little historiography and no institutional archive. But in many ways the activities of the English Dialect Society, and above all the regional glossaries that the Society produced, represent the high-water mark of the Victorian engagement with dialect, and distil the clearest essence of the regional philology which is the subject of this book. It is a society that is worth making our acquaintance with.[1]

The weekly journal *Notes and Queries*, in its issue for 12 March 1870, contained an item headed 'Provincial Glossary', written by William Aldis Wright. This begins as follows:

> It has long been my conviction that some systematic effort ought to be made for the collection and preservation of our provincial words. In a few years it will be too late. Railroads and certificated teachers are doing their work. Not a year passes but some words pass beyond the reach of recovery.[2]

Aldis Wright acknowledges that some good regional glossaries have been published, but 'some counties are almost unrepresented, and, so far as I am aware, nothing like a systematic attempt has yet been made to sweep into one complete collection all the provincialisms in England'. This could only be done by 'a division of labour', and the solution lies in the largest possible team effort, not unlike the reading and collecting that had been undertaken for the Philological Society's great dictionary-in-progress:

> The work is one in which all may assist, clergy and laity alike, societies and individuals. Let each provincial word, and usage of a word, be recorded, with an example of its

---

[1] For prior scholarship, see G. L. Brook, *English Dialects* (London: Deutsch, 1963), pp. 155–6; Wolfgang Viereck, 'The English Dialect Society and its Dictionary', *Transactions of the Yorkshire Dialect Society* 70 (1970), 28–33; Petyt, *The Study of Dialect*, pp. 76–8; Crowley, *The Politics of Discourse*, pp. 105–6; Penhallurick, *Studying Dialect*, pp. 16–18; Jonathan Roper, 'Folklore in the Glossaries of the English Dialect Society', in Jonathan Roper (ed.), *Dictionaries as Sources of Folklore Data*, Folklore Fellows' Communications 321 (Helsinki: Suomalainen Tiedeakatemia, 2020), pp. 189–208.

[2] William Aldis Wright, 'Provincial Glossary', *Notes and Queries*, 12 March 1870, 271.

The Victorians and English Dialect. Matthew Townend, Oxford University Press. © Matthew Townend (2024).
DOI: 10.1093/oso/9780198888123.003.0005

144 The Victorians and English Dialect

application if necessary, and a note of the place where it is so used [...] While we have our Early English Text Society, our Chaucer Society, and our Philological Society, why should we not have a society for collecting and preserving provincial words? In such a work I shall be glad to give the best help in my power.

William Aldis Wright (1831–1914)—no relation of either Thomas Wright or Joseph Wright—was, at the time of this invitation, the librarian of Trinity College, Cambridge. Born in Suffolk, and the son of a Baptist minister, he was a Biblical scholar, and an editor of medieval and early modern literature (especially Shakespeare). One of his friends was the poet Edward FitzGerald, with whom he shared an interest in local dialect, and for whom he later acted as literary executor (although he is best known for his *Rubáiyát of Omar Khayyám*, in 1869 FitzGerald also published a short work entitled *Sea Words and Phrases along the Suffolk Coast*). Wright's obituarist records that he was distinguished for 'the austere precision of his manner', but his 'somewhat rigid sincerity' concealed 'a warm heart and great depth of feeling'.[3]

A flurry of correspondence followed in the pages of *Notes and Queries*, with half a dozen contributors chipping in. Joseph Payne, an educationist and member of the Philological Society, feared that 'the railway whistle will certainly prove the death-knell of our patois, and it becomes, therefore, increasingly important to gather up, while we may, the fragments of the old speech which still remain'.[4] Moreover, Payne offered an analogy that makes unwritten dialect sound like Hardy's John Durbeyfield: 'properly viewed, the patois of a country may be considered as the natural owners of an estate who have been ousted of their original right, and who, though obliged to descend to a lower rank, still retain the indubitable tokens of their earlier and better days'. J. C. Atkinson wrote from Danby on the North York Moors, offering thoughts on collection and verification, drawn from his own experience of what he called 'word-hunting': 'as a rule', he explains, 'I found a great shyness among the people about using their true dialect words, idioms, and tone in my presence', so that various elicitation techniques were required ('shorter lists, containing half a dozen or a dozen words, I gave my own sons, telling them to ask so-and-so or so-and-so about them').[5] Similar advice came from George Fielding Blandford (physician and psychiatrist, about to publish *Insanity and its Treatment* (1871)), who suggested that whoever 'wishes to pick up provincial words and expressions must listen to the workpeople *as they talk to one another*—to the "chaff" which goes on in the workshop, in the harvest-field, at the washtub'.[6]

---

[3] D. N. Smith, 'Wright, William Aldis (1831–1914)', rev. David McKitterick, in *Oxford Dictionary of National Biography* [www.oxforddnb].

[4] Joseph Payne, 'Provincial Glossary', *Notes and Queries*, 9 April 1870, 362–3, at p. 362. See Richard Aldrich, 'Payne, Joseph (1801–1876)', in *Oxford Dictionary of National Biography* [www.oxforddnb].

[5] J. C. Atkinson, 'Provincial Glossary', *Notes and Queries*, 9 April 1870, 363.

[6] George Fielding Blandford, 'Provincial Glossary', *Notes and Queries*, 9 April 1870, 363–4, at p. 363. See Ogilvie, *The Dictionary People*, pp. 160–4; D'A. Power, 'Blandford, George Fielding (1829–1911)', rev. Nick Hervey, in *Oxford Dictionary of National Biography* [www.oxforddnb].

Aldis Wright did not propose a name for the new society that he wished to summon into existence. But a name was suggested a few months later, in a short item ('A New Society') in the *Athenaeum* magazine:

Mr W. Aldis Wright having lately suggested the collection of our provincialisms on a systematic plan, Mr Alexander J. Ellis, the well-known authority on English pronunciation, has proposed the formation of an English Dialect Society, under the presidency of Mr Aldis Wright, to take the matter in hand, and secure the representation of all the provincial sounds on one system, his newly-proposed Glossic, which is specially adapted to the purpose. As without such a scheme of writing down our provincial words the collection of them can be but of little use, we hope that Mr Ellis's proposal may be adopted and carried out. To have an accurate representation of the whole of the speech-sounds of our Victorian England, for the use of ourselves and our posterity, would be, indeed, a gain to all linguistic students, and is well worth an effort to secure.[7]

It may be suspected that Ellis himself was behind this item in the *Athenaeum*, with its insistence that phonetic priorities, and the use of his own Glossic system, should underpin the society's activities; and we know that only a week earlier he had written at length to Aldis Wright, setting out his own detailed plan about how such a society should be organized.[8] Ellis repeated the call the following year, in his introduction to the third volume of *On Early English Pronunciation*:

It is highly desirable that a complete account of our existing English language should occupy the attention of an ENGLISH DIALECT SOCIETY, and I solicit all correspondents to favour me with their views on this subject, and to state whether they would be willing to join such a body.[9]

However, as someone who devoted a good deal of attention to his health, Ellis confessed that he did not feel 'vigorous enough to carry it out'.[10] Nor did Aldis Wright take on the task, as Ellis had publicly proposed that he should. But eventually, after a lapse of a couple of years, another of the contributors to the 1870 discussion did so: namely, Walter William Skeat—'with his usual promptitude and vigour', as Ellis gratefully recognized.[11]

Skeat has been mentioned a number of times already in this book as one of the great English philologists of the nineteenth century, but until this point he has not come centre stage in our narrative.[12] Born in London in 1835, and educated at King's College School (where he was taught by the Anglo-Saxon scholar Thomas Oswald

---

[7] [Anon], 'A New Society', *The Athenaeum* 14 May 1870, 643.
[8] See Sanders, 'Alexander John Ellis', pp. 532–52.
[9] Ellis, *On Early English Pronunciation*, III, xii.
[10] Ellis, 'Second Annual Address', p. 248.
[11] Ellis, 'Second Annual Address', p. 247. See Walter W. Skeat, 'Provincial Glossary', *Notes and Queries*, 19 March 1870, 302–3.
[12] On Skeat, see Skeat, *A Student's Pastime*, pp. vii–lxxxiv; Brewer, *Editing Piers Plowman*, pp. 91–178, esp. pp. 91–105; Charlotte Brewer, 'Walter William Skeat (1835–1912)', in Helen Damico (ed.), *Medieval Scholarship: Biographical Studies on the Formation of a Discipline. Volume 2: Literature and Philology*

146 The Victorians and English Dialect

Cockayne) and Christ's College, Cambridge (where he studied mathematics), Skeat began his career in the church, as a curate in Norfolk, before ill health led him to abandon ministry and return to Cambridge. F. J. Furnivall recruited him for the Early English Text Society, and over the decades that followed he became one of Britain's most eminent editors of Old and Middle English texts: especial landmarks include his editions of the *Anglo-Saxon Gospels* and Ælfric's *Lives of Saints*, the seven-volume *Oxford Chaucer*, and above all his pioneering multi-volume edition of *Piers Plowman*. He also produced a major *Etymological Dictionary of the English Language*, as well as numerous other editions, books, and articles. In 1878 he became the first Professor of Anglo-Saxon at Cambridge. Two statements by Skeat himself can be quoted to gloss his productivity. The first is the explanation in the preface to his *Etymological Dictionary* that 'in very difficult cases, my usual rule has been not to spend more than three hours over one word. During that time, I made the best I could of it, and then let it go'.[13] The second is his reflection in his brief memoirs that 'it is astonishing how much can be done by steady work at the same subject for many hours every day, and by continuing the same during most months in the year'.[14] But he adds: 'It is also necessary to be an enthusiast, working with an ever-present hope of doing something to increase our knowledge in every available direction'. So this was not 'drudgery', Skeat insisted, but 'a sincere pleasure'.[15]

As we have seen, a number of factors combined to make the study of English dialect an issue of pressing importance in the 1870s: the cultural and intellectual prominence of the new philology; the revaluation of spoken dialects that philology brought with it; and the growing anxiety, caused by mobility and education, that the dialects were disappearing fast. These factors are more than enough to account for a vibrant regional philology. But further contexts help to explain the specific decision to found an 'English Dialect Society'. One is the well-recorded proliferation of historical and antiquarian societies at this time: the third quarter of the nineteenth century saw the creation of many such clubs and enterprises, most with some sort of publication programme attached.[16] It was coming to seem natural, as well as strategic, for historically minded enthusiasts to band together to advance their area of study. And in the later decades of the nineteenth century, as a number of scholars have argued, we can also see a development in the idea of Englishness and English history, so that national identity came to be located more with the common people than the elite, and

---

(New York: Garland, 1998), pp. 139–49; Matthews, *The Making of Middle English*, pp. 171–85; Michael Lapidge, 'Walter William Skeat, 1835–1912', in Michael Lapidge (ed.), *Interpreters of Early Medieval Britain* (London: British Academy, 2002), pp. 37–47; Kenneth Sisam, 'Skeat, Walter William (1835–1912)', rev. Charlotte Brewer, in *Oxford Dictionary of National Biography* [www.oxforddnb]. See also Michael Lapidge, 'Introduction: The Study of Anglo-Saxon, Norse and Celtic in Cambridge, 1878–1999', in Michael Lapidge (ed.), *H. M. Chadwick and the Study of Anglo-Saxon, Norse and Celtic in Cambridge* (Aberystwyth: Department of Welsh, Aberystwyth University, 2015), pp. 1–58, at pp. 5–13.

[13] Walter W. Skeat, *An Etymological Dictionary of the English Language* (Oxford: Clarendon Press, 1882), p. xi.

[14] Skeat, *A Student's Pastime*, pp. liii–liv.

[15] Skeat, *A Student's Pastime*, p. liv.

[16] See Levine, *The Amateur and the Professional*; David Wetherall, 'The Growth of Archaeological Societies', in Vanessa Brand (ed.), *The Study of the Past in the Victorian Age* (Oxford: Oxbow, 1998), pp. 21–34.

more in everyday, traditional culture than in grand political or aristocratic history.[17] But this renovated sense of Englishness was not in conflict with regional preoccupations: indeed, it was often expressed in the form of 'regional Englishness', in the appreciation of precious landscapes, or long-established local culture, or 'storied' associations—or language.[18]

It is not possible to reconstruct Skeat's leadership of the English Dialect Society in the same detail as we can follow the partnership of Ellis and Hallam over *The Existing Phonology of English Dialects*: after his death, Skeat's family destroyed most of his private papers, and only a small amount of correspondence now survives (preserved in the Skeat archive at King's College London).[19] But the documents that do exist include a full run of the Society's annual reports and these allow us to track the Society's year-by-year programme of research. Moreover, we should think of the English Dialect Society and Ellis' *Existing Phonology* as parallel and complementary endeavours. As we saw in Chapter 2, it was in 1871 that Ellis set about the serious collecting of dialect, and in 1873–4 that he planned a separate volume on the subject—finally published in 1889. So the work on *The Existing Phonology* extended across the 1870s and 1880s, while the English Dialect Society was founded in 1873 and disbanded in 1896.

In May 1873 Skeat called for helpers and subscribers, at half a guinea per annum.[20] By September, he was able to issue a twelve-page pamphlet that set out his goals as a numbered manifesto:

The objects of the "ENGLISH DIALECT SOCIETY" are:—(1) to bring together all those who have made a study of any of the Provincial Dialects of England, or who are interested in the subject of Provincial English; (2) to combine the labours of collectors of Provincial English words by providing a common centre to which they may be sent, so as to gather material for a general record of all such words; (3) to publish (subject to proper revision) such collections of Provincial English words as exist at present only in manuscript; and (4) to supply references to sources of information which may be of material assistance to word-collectors, students, and all who have a general or particular interest in the subject.[21]

---

[17] See, for example, Robert Colls and Philip Dodd (eds), *Englishness: Politics and Culture 1880–1920* (London: Croom Helm, 1986); Robert Colls, *Identity of England* (Oxford: Oxford University Press, 2002), pp. 256–7, 289–99; Krishan Kumar, *The Making of English National Identity* (Cambridge: Cambridge University Press, 2003), pp. 205–6; Anthony Brundage and Richard A. Cosgrove, *British Historians and National Identity: From Hume to Churchill* (London: Pickering and Chatto, 2014), pp. 125–43; Readman, *Storied Ground*, pp. 272, 278, 307.

[18] See Paul Readman, 'The Place of the Past in English Culture c.1890–1914', *Past and Present* 186 (2005), 147–99, at pp. 175–9, and *Storied Ground*, pp. 20, 45, 86–8, 305.

[19] Brewer, 'Walter William Skeat', p. 140. See also Clara L. Skeat to Elizabeth Mary Wright 23 November 1926, and Elizabeth Mary Wright to unknown recipient 29 November 1928, King's College London Archives, GB0100 KCLCA Skeat 1/15.

[20] Walter W. Skeat, 'English Dialects', *Notes and Queries*, 10 May 1873, 385–6, and 'English Dialect Society', *Notes and Queries* 17 May 1873, 406–7.

[21] [Walter W. Skeat], *English Dialect Society* (no place or date of publication), p. 1 (King's College London Archives, GB0100 KCLCA Skeat 11/1).

148 The Victorians and English Dialect

As the first of these goals suggests, the name of the English Dialect Society had an appropriate, and helpful, ambiguity about it. Is the phrase 'the Provincial Dialects of England' synonymous with 'Provincial English'? Was this a society for the study of dialect in England, or a society for the study of English dialect? Both meanings seem to have been operative for Skeat, and this flexibility applied also to the Society's geographical remit: according to nineteenth-century terminology, dialects of English were to be found in Scotland, Wales, and Ireland, and not just in England— even though, as with Ellis' *Existing Phonology*, it was England that was to receive the lion's share of the attention. It is notable that the three great works of Victorian dialectology—Ellis' *Existing Phonology of the English Dialects*, the English Dialect Society itself, and the later *English Dialect Dictionary*—all include the word 'English' in their titles, in the phrase 'English Dialect' or 'English Dialects', and it is clear that the very idea of 'English dialect' was important to Victorian philologists, not just in terms of discipline and methodology, but also inspiration and identity. 'English dialect' was a concept as well as a description.

Skeat's pamphlet of September 1873 also reveals that, in less than four months, the fledgling society had managed to recruit 149 members—indeed, over 40 had signed up, by word of mouth, before Skeat even made a public announcement (fewer than ten of these were institutional subscriptions, although these did include the Royal Library at Windsor Castle).[22] Questions of membership will be discussed more fully later, but for now we can note that among this initial 149 were many of the dialect workers whom we have met so far in this book, including J. C. Atkinson, W. E. A. Axon, William Barnes, Prince Louis Lucien Bonaparte, Alexander Ellis (of course), J. G. Goodchild, James Orchard Halliwell, George Milner, James Murray, C. Clough Robinson, and F. K. Robinson. (Thomas Hallam is not found in this earliest list: his wife died in 1873.) William Barnes' letter of application seems to have been deliberately preserved by Skeat's family as a memento of this period, even though its contents are trivial.[23] But Barnes' commitment was well worth having; a decade earlier, he had not joined the Early English Text Society, he told Furnivall, because he could not afford the fee.[24] The first subscription Skeat ever received for the English Dialect Society, he recalled, was also from a poet—Edward FitzGerald, Aldis Wright's friend.[25]

Also issued at an early stage was a document titled *Rules and Directions for Word-Collectors*. This sets out Skeat's seven 'rules' for word-collecting, and all seven merit quotation:

---

[22] Skeat, 'English Dialect Society' (17 May 1873), p. 406.

[23] William Barnes to W. W. Skeat 7 May 1873, King's College London Archives, GB0100 KCLCA Skeat 1/14; see also Elizabeth Mary Wright to unknown recipient 29 November 1928, King's College London Archives, GB0100 KCLCA Skeat 1/15.

[24] Benzie, *Dr F. J. Furnivall*, p. 268. See further Jones, *William Barnes*.

[25] Walter W. Skeat, 'The English Dialect Dictionary', *Notes and Queries* 10th Series 4 (11 November 1905), 381.

The English Dialect Society **149**

1. First comes the WORD ITSELF. It should be one that is not found in ordinary smaller dictionaries of standard English. Spell it carefully, according to some intelligible system [...]
2. Next, between square brackets, comes the EXACT PRONUNCIATION, according to the Glossic System invented by Mr A. J. Ellis [...]
3. Thirdly, write down the part of speech to which the word belongs, and underline it for italics [...]
4. Fourthly, define or explain the word, as clearly as possible.
5. Fifthly, state, *not only* the name of the county to which the word belongs, *but also* the name of the place where, to your personal knowledge (or on the trustworthy authority of others) you know or have known it to be in use. Words *only* heard in towns, or *only* heard in the country, should be marked as 'town' or 'country' words [...]
6. Sixthly, add an illustration of the word, viz., either a quotation or a scrap of talk which you have really heard, not one invented for the occasion [...] *This* rule need only be observed where the word really requires illustration, to bring out the sense of it.
7. (*a*) Lastly, if you cite the word from your own observation, add, in the right-hand bottom corner, your name, if you send in only two or three slips; or your initials, if you send in many [...] (*b*) If you cite the word, &c., from a book, add your authority, in the same place, and in a sufficiently intelligible manner.[26]

Skeat offered supplementary guidance for a number of these rules. Under rule (5), for example, he was keen to stress that 'it is not at all necessary for you to ascertain that this word which you "locate" is *so peculiar* to the town or district mentioned as *not* to be in common use elsewhere'; the danger, he explained, was that such an approach could lead to an incomplete picture of distribution or even to common words being left out altogether.[27] And he also gave some illustrative examples of content and layout, drawn from his own knowledge:

STAITHE [staidh] *sb.* a landing-place for goods unloaded from a barge. *Norf.* Acle. BANGE [banj] *v. impers.* To rain slightly; to mizzle. *Ess*, Chelmsfd. 'It *banges*'. [it banjez].[28]

(Here '*sb.*' means substantive or noun, and '*v. impers.*' means impersonal verb.) Each of the words submitted had to be written on a separate slip of paper, that fundamental device for the making of Victorian dictionaries, as Skeat emphasized with a liberal use of italics: 'Each word, with its meaning, &c., must be written down on a *separate half-sheet of note-paper of the ordinary size* (about 7 in. by 4½ in.) *lengthwise, and on*

---

[26] [Walter W. Skeat], *English Dialect Society: Rules and Directions for Word-Collectors* (no place or date of publication), pp. 2–3 (King's College London Archives, GB0100 KCLCA Skeat 11/1).
[27] [Skeat], *Rules and Directions for Word-Collectors*, p. 2.
[28] [Skeat], *Rules and Directions for Word-Collectors*, pp. 3–4.

one side of the paper only [. . .] If this rule is not observed, the result is *useless*, as the slips cannot be sorted together.[29]

Those were the instructions; it was time to get to work. In his 1873 manifesto, Skeat re-quoted much of Aldis Wright's 1870 rallying cry, and italicized the sentence *In a few years it will be too late*.[30] He further emphasized: 'this is, from the nature of the case, the *last* appeal on behalf of the preservation of our provincial words that can ever be made,—the *last* chance of saving the fast-fading relics of those forms of archaic English which have lingered on in country places.'[31] Ellis was President of the Philological Society at the time of the English Dialect Society's launch, and he used his presidential addresses to stress how short the time was, warning (in 1873) that 'intercommunication is drawing a wet sponge over the living records of our nascent tongue', and (in 1874) that 'the work really to be done in England is enormous, and it must be done quickly too, for the railway whistle, and, worse than all, the School-boards, are screaming down every chirp, and grubbing up every stump of dialectality'.[32] But although the clock was ticking, it was not too late. J. R. Wise, in his 1865 essay 'The Poetry of Provincialisms', had communicated the excitements of word-hunting—like a sort of field sport, perhaps—and indicated the finds that might still be made:

Many, too, of those [pre-1865] glossaries, on which much labour has been expended, will still bear supplementing. A curious illustration of this occurred to ourselves when lately staying in a country village. The ground had been twice worked over by two different collectors. The later, too, had gleaned a thousand words, which his predecessor had neglected. The spot did not, therefore, seem very promising. We, however, in the course of a month bagged some hundred and fifty new specimens. This gives an average of five a day, which may be looked upon as very fair sport.[33]

So something could yet be done, and Skeat was the person to do it.

Activities

The organizational history of the English Dialect Society falls into three clear phases, according to its leadership and location. The first, formative phase ran from 1873 to 1875, when Skeat was in charge as Director and Honorary Secretary, and the Society's base was Cambridge (or, to be more precise, Skeat's house, on Cintra Terrace). The second phase began in 1876, when Skeat handed over his leadership role to J. H.

---

[29] [Skeat], *Rules and Directions for Word-Collectors*, p. 1. On slips, see further Walter W. Skeat, in Munro (ed.), *Frederick James Furnivall*, pp. 174–80, at pp. 175–6, 179; Gilliver, *The Making of the Oxford English Dictionary*, p. 261.

[30] [Skeat], *English Dialect Society*, p. 2.

[31] [Skeat], *English Dialect Society*, p. 4.

[32] Ellis, 'Second Annual Address', p. 248, and 'Third Annual Address', p. 447.

[33] [Wise], 'The Poetry of Provincialisms', p. 32.

Nodal, and the Society moved from Cambridge to Manchester. And the third phase—to be narrated in Chapter 6—ran from 1893, when Joseph Wright took over from Nodal and the Society moved to Oxford, until 1896, when the Society was formally wound up. As even this skeleton timeline indicates, therefore, the Society was marked by a cooperation—and sometimes a tension—between university and metropolitan scholars on the one hand, and regional or 'provincial' enthusiasts on the other; and the character of the Society varied significantly as it moved from Cambridge to Manchester to Oxford.

To begin with, though, it really does seem to have been a one-man show. For the first three years, there was no formal committee for the Society, and in early publications only two officers are listed: Skeat as Director and Honorary Secretary, and the Rev. James Cartmell (1810–87), Master of Christ's College, Cambridge (where Skeat was a Fellow) as Treasurer. The bank used was Mortlock and Co., Cambridge.

The best way to track the activities and aspirations of the Society is through its annual reports, which were usually issued in January each year. The first annual report, which appeared in January 1874, chronicled the developments of 1873, and recorded that dialect collections of various sizes were already coming in, such as the following:

> From J. G. Goodchild, Esq. A collection of words used in the neighbourhood of Sittingbourne.
> From E. French, Esq. A neat packet of words used in various counties, but chiefly relating to Farndon, Cheshire [. . .]
> From Miss Douglas, of Clifton. Word-lists, including some very interesting remarks, with examples, on the dialect of South Pembrokeshire.
> From Mrs Francis. A list of some Warwickshire words, especially of words used at Tysoe.[34]

Not everyone, regrettably, was on message about the importance of filling in the slips properly: 'the most cruel thing of all', Skeat complained, 'is to write on both sides of the paper'.[35] Each year, these invaluable reports recorded recent and future publications, work that was in progress or contemplation, and miscellaneous other matters relating to dialect study (such as the appearance of non-Society publications, or dialect research in other countries). They also included a financial statement and a list of members, and from 1879 an annual digest from Thomas Hallam, detailing the places he had visited that year and the number of dialect samples he had taken down. Alexander Ellis also used the reports as a means of communicating progress on *The Existing Phonology.*

The English Dialect Society was primarily a publications society, financed through a subscription system—like Furnivall's Early English Text Society. Also like the Early English Text Society, but unlike the Philological Society or regional antiquarian

---

[34] *English Dialect Society: First Report, for the Year 1873* (no place or date of publication), p. 10 (King's College London Archives, GB0100 KCLCA Skeat 11/1).
[35] *English Dialect Society: First Report,* p. 5.

152   The Victorians and English Dialect

societies, it did not hold meetings at which papers were given and debate could be joined. In return for their annual subscription, members received three or four publications a year (and one consequence of this system is that the date given on the title page of each volume was sometimes the subscription year rather than the actual date of publication, and hence a year or two out; but such dates have been followed here out of consistency). The Society's publications, in octavo format, were designed to be uniform with the outputs of the Early English Text Society and the Chaucer Society, with whom they shared a publisher (Trübner and Co.). From the start, Skeat had a system for a number of different 'series' within the Society's publications: Series A would be bibliographical, Series B would be reprints, Series C would be original glossaries, and Series D would be 'miscellaneous'.[36]

One of Skeat's first activities as Director of the Society was to attend to Series A, and compile 'a new list of books in the English dialects', to replace that prepared by John Russell Smith in 1839; and he called on readers of *Notes and Queries* to send him examples.[37] Especially useful was access to Bonaparte's extensive private library.[38] *A Bibliographical List of the Works That Have Been Published, or Are Known to Exist in MS, Illustrative of the Various Dialects of English* was issued as part of the subscription for 1873, and covered England (131 pages), Wales (half a page), and the Isle of Man (nine lines). The disparity in coverage was mostly due to the England-centric nature of the Society, but it was also partly due to the nature of the help that Skeat received. Where no expert assistance was forthcoming, Skeat had to put together the entry for the county (or country) himself, and some entries proved very meagre indeed (Buckinghamshire: six lines). But other counties received very extensive treatment, especially when a regional expert was able to relieve Skeat of the task: there were nine pages on Cornwall by G. C. Boase and W. P. Courtney, fourteen pages on Cumberland by William Dickinson, twenty-three pages on Yorkshire by C. Clough Robinson, and a mighty thirty-six pages on Lancashire by W. E. A. Axon (including a full five pages listing the various editions of Tim Bobbin, from the 1740s to 1860s). William Barnes had a hand in the entry for Dorset, and eight of the twenty-one items listed for the county were authored by him. In keeping with Skeat's expertise, medieval evidence for dialects was valued highly: the 'best example of Kentish', for instance, is said to be the fourteenth-century *Ayenbite of Inwyt*.[39] But mostly, the *Bibliographical List* catalogues works much more recent than this, with the usual combination of the creative and the scholarly—ballads, novels, dialogues, glossaries, histories, and articles.

The reprinting of important earlier works on dialect—as Series B—was one of Skeat's central intentions right from the start.[40] Skeat's 1873 manifesto enunciated four 'objects' for the Society, but these had expanded to five by the time of the first

---

[36] *English Dialect Society: First Report*, pp. 14–15; see also Walter W. Skeat, 'English Dialect Society', *Notes and Queries*, 1 November 1873, 341–2, and 'Report on the English Dialect Society', pp. 11–13.

[37] Skeat, 'English Dialects', p. 385, and 'English Dialect Society'.

[38] Skeat and Nodal, *A Bibliographical List*, p. 2; Ellis, 'Second Annual Address', p. 248.

[39] Skeat and Nodal, *A Bibliographical List*, p. 54.

[40] Skeat, 'English Dialect Society', p. 406.

annual report, to include a specific commitment to reprinting: the new number (3) was 'to reprint various useful Glossaries that have appeared in scarce or inconvenient volumes'. In fact, because it took time to collect and prepare brand new material for publication, in the first couple of years the Society's publication list was dominated by reprints; as Skeat explained to members, 'in order to fill up the intervening time usefully, as many as seventeen Glossaries have been reprinted'.[41] Such glossaries, usually of eighteenth-century date, tended to be short, so several could be combined into a single volume: the first volume to appear, in 1873, contained no fewer than seven glossaries, ranging from Devon to Yorkshire.

But the core activity was always intended to be the collection and publication of original glossaries—Series C. As Skeat explained: 'the publication of local glossaries is the very work to be done by a Society; for it is not seldom unprofitable, and tends to burden the author with expense; whilst the buyer of locally printed glossaries finds the volumes which he purchases are of all dates and sizes, printed at different presses in different country towns, and often with title-pages which give no sort of clue to the real contents of the volumes'.[42] Over the course of its existence, the Society published over forty original glossaries. Some of these were thematic, such as James Britten and Robert Holland's *Dictionary of English Plant Names* or Charles Swainson's volume on bird names. But the majority were geographically focused, which raised (and raises) the question of subdivision and organization. What was the appropriate unit of geography, for publication as well as research? In *The Existing Phonology of English Dialects*, Ellis had insisted, as a point of methodological principle, that his geographical subdivisions had been made 'mainly, if not always, entirely on pron[unciation], with the least possible admixture of considerations founded on vocabulary and grammar [. . .], and none at all on history'.[43] But Ellis was making his subdivisions, and drawing his map, at the end of his project, after years of data collection was complete. Skeat and the English Dialect Society, on the other hand, needed to make decisions at the start, in order to have a steady stream of publications.

One obvious approach would have been to parcel up the survey work into county units, as the English Place-Name Society (for example) was later to do, and for reporting purposes, in his annual bulletins, Skeat did indeed record work in progress on a county-by-county basis (as he had similarly catalogued previous work in his *Bibliographical List*). He also set up a system whereby 'editors' were appointed for many counties—not for the goal of compiling a county volume, but to act as a single recipient for relevant material, rather than all of it going to Skeat. Inevitably, such a piecemeal approach led to haphazard coverage: some counties got lots of activity and some got none. As in *The Existing Phonology*, Yorkshire received the most attention. Here, for example, is the long record of work in progress for the county in 1875:

---

[41] *English Dialect Society: Second Report, for the Year 1874* (no place or date of publication), p. 5 (King's College London Archives, GB0100 KCLCA Skeat 11/1).
[42] *English Dialect Society: First Report*, p. 4.
[43] Ellis, *On Early English Pronunciation*, V, 1438/6.

154 The Victorians and English Dialect

An additional list of Cleveland words, by the Rev. J. C. Atkinson, author of the Cleveland Glossary, is already in type, and will be issued early in 1876. Mr F. K. Robinson has completed his large collection of Whitby words, and most of it is already in type, Part I forming a number for 1875. Mr J. G. Goodchild hopes soon to complete his list of Swaledale words. The Rev. A. Easther has all but completed his list of Huddersfield words. With respect to the Glossaries in preparation by Mr C. C. Robinson, see the letter by him, printed at the end of Capt. Harland's Swaledale Glossary. Mr Isaac Binns, of Birstall, has contributed some valuable material to them. The Glossary of Sheffield Words is to be edited by Mr R. E. Leader. A list of Holderness words has been undertaken by Mr Ross and Mr Stead.[44]

Two glossaries for Swaledale alone! At the other end of the scale, some counties received little or no attention: no county editor was ever appointed for Middlesex, for example, or Northamptonshire, or Huntingdonshire (and in this regard, there was a mismatch between the English Dialect Society and *The Existing Phonology*: Huntingdonshire, for example, was an important hunting ground for Hallam and Ellis). So the Society's coverage was patchy, because it relied on volunteers.

County divisions were thus employed for organizational purposes. But as the list of Yorkshire work suggests, regional philologists were well aware that dialects did not correlate naturally with county boundaries, in terms of either being unified within them or stopping when they came to them. As William Barnes remarked, 'the forms of folk speech do not change at the map boundaries of Counties, but rather at ridges of hills and streams', and Robert Holland, a glossarist for the English Dialect Society, similarly observed that 'county boundaries are but imaginary lines, very useful for ecclesiastical or parliamentary purposes, but totally inadequate to confine dialect or rural customs'.[45] Distribution patterns could be larger than any individual county; but they could also be smaller. Anne Elizabeth Baker had commented that 'the limited locality of many words is worthy of remark; many archaisms retained in one parish are unknown at the distance of a few miles', and the editors of the *Holderness Glossary* similarly observed, when their work appeared, that 'there are some very perceptible differences in the dialect, geographically; words which are common in some parts of Holderness being wholly unknown in others; and it is the same in pronunciation'.[46] William Jackson, discussing Westmorland dialect, observed that 'minute differences of expression between adjacent localities are appreciable. I have heard an old inhabitant of Grasmere declare that he could detect by his speech a native of Wythburn, and these valleys are not more than six miles apart'.[47] Skeat's *Rules and Directions*, as we have seen, asked for all words to be attributed to a county, but he

---

[44] *English Dialect Society: Third Report, for the Year 1875* (no place or date of publication), p. 10 (King's College London Archives, GB0100 KCLCA Skeat 11/1).

[45] Barnes, *Glossary of the Dorset Dialect*, p. vi; Robert Holland, *A Glossary of Words Used in the County of Chester*, English Dialect Society 44, 46, 51 (London: English Dialect Society, 1884–6), p. iii. See further Burton and Ruthven, in Barnes, *Poems in the Broad Form of the Dorset Dialect*, pp. l–lvi.

[46] Baker, *Glossary of Northamptonshire Words and Phrases*, I, xv; Ross, Stead, and Holderness, *Glossary of Words Used in Holderness*, p. 4.

[47] Quoted in Skeat and Nodal, *Bibliographical List*, p. 104.

also recognized that other units of 'country' might sometimes be equally important: 'Intelligible abbreviations of districts or towns are permissible', he wrote, 'as Furn. (Furness), Exmr. (Exmoor), Newc. (Newcastle)'.[48] So the geographical unit might be the county, or the region, or even the city.

In the event, the determining factor for most glossaries seems to have been the glossarist's own preference and area of operation. Certainly the English Dialect Society went on to publish many glossaries conceived on the county scale: for example, for Cheshire (by Robert Holland), Hampshire (by William H. Cope), Lancashire (by J. H. Nodal and George Milner), Leicestershire (by A. B. Evans and Sebastian Evans), Northumberland (by R. Oliver Heslop), Surrey (by G. Leveson Gower), and Wiltshire (by G. E. Dartnell and E. H. Goddard). But other Society glossaries restricted themselves to a portion of a county, often defined by a compass point: examples include 'South Cheshire' (by Thomas Darlington), 'South-West Lincolnshire' (by R. E. Cole), and 'West Worcestershire' (by Edith L. Chamberlain). One Society volume, issued in 1880, bound together a glossary for 'West Cornwall' (by Margaret A. Courtney) with one for 'East Cornwall' (by Thomas Quiller Couch). Other glossaries, by contrast, defined themselves by reference to a place rather than a county: cities such as Huddersfield (by A. Easther and Thomas Lees) and Sheffield (by Sidney Oldall Addy), or small towns or villages such as Upton-on-Severn (by Robert Lawson, in Worcestershire) and Hartland (by Richard Pearse Chope, in Devon).

Some of the 'original glossaries' printed by the Society were not, in fact, brand new, but rather had lain unpublished for many years. In 1873, using Society funds, Skeat purchased at auction a manuscript compiled by the Derbyshire antiquary Samuel Pegge (1704–96). Skeat briskly published Pegge's collection of 'Kenticisms' in 1876, but cooperating with Thomas Hallam over an edition of Pegge's Derbyshire collections proved a more drawn-out affair, and the work finally reached print only in 1896, following Hallam's death. As part of his highly conscientious approach to his labours, Hallam even engaged in contemporary fieldwork, taking one of Pegge's word lists to Whittington near Chesterfield (where Pegge had been rector), and there testing its contents against the knowledge of four elderly locals: Hallam excitedly reported to Skeat that although 300 of Pegge's words were now obsolete, and a further 24 doubtful, no fewer than 574 were still in use—an empirical demonstration of the rate of lexical attrition over the century or more since Pegge had collected the words.[49]

There was also cooperation with other societies and initiatives. When the English Dialect Society was founded, the Manchester Literary Club was already at work on its own *Glossary of the Lancashire Dialect*, so some tweaks were made to bring it in line with the agreed policies (such as publication in an identical octavo format), and

---

[48] [Skeat], *Rules and Directions for Word-Collectors*, pp. 2–3.
[49] Thomas Hallam to W. W. Skeat 30 May 1891, King's College London Archives, GB0100 KCLCA Skeat 1/7; see further Walter W. Skeat and Thomas Hallam (eds), *Two Collections of Derbicisms, Containing Words and Phrases in a Great Measure Peculiar to the Natives and Inhabitants of the County of Derby, by Samuel Pegge, A. M.*, English Dialect Society 78 (London: English Dialect Society, 1896), pp. xv–xvi, lviii–lx.

156 The Victorians and English Dialect

the glossary was issued to Society members when it appeared.[50] Hilderic Friend's volume on *Devonshire Plant Names* (1882) was a reprint from the *Transactions of the Devonshire Association for the Advancement of Science, Literature, and Art.* Charles Swainson's *The Folk Lore and Provincial Names of British Birds* (1886) was a production of the Folklore Society, but was included in the English Dialect Society's publication list. And W. D. Parish's *Dictionary of the Sussex Dialect*, published in Lewes, was simply issued to members as a bonus, non-Society publication in 1874.[51] Other volumes had a curiously roundabout publication history. Jesse Salisbury's *Glossary of Words and Phrases Used in South East Worcestershire* was announced to members as being complete, and ready for printing, in 1883. However, 'owing to various causes, its publication was from time to time deferred', so that in 1893 Salisbury decided to publish it by himself, after which the Society then (re-)issued Salisbury's edition to its members the following year.[52]

Such practices of co-publication, reissuing, and distribution mean that it is not really possible to give a definitive number of volumes that the Society 'published'. Usually this number is given as 80: this is because 80 volumes were given a publication number in the Society's records and catalogues (so, for example, the *Holderness Glossary* was volume 16, and Salisbury's *South East Worcestershire Glossary* was volume 72), but this list of 80 inconsistently includes some items that were distributed but not printed by the Society (such as the *Lancashire Glossary*) and excludes others (such as Parish's *Sussex Glossary*). Nor does the number of volumes published correlate at all closely with the number of different works produced: some glossaries were published in instalments, across several volumes (such as Holland's *Cheshire Glossary*, which appeared in three parts—Society volumes 44, 46, and 51), while some single volumes contained multiple short glossaries all published within the same wrappers (such as Society volume 5, which contained seven reprinted glossaries, or volume 32, which contained five original glossaries). Moreover, the Society was very happy to publish 'supplement' volumes—either supplements to published glossaries that pre-dated the Society, or later supplements to glossaries that the Society itself had published.

As one might expect, the annual reports also reveal that there were a number of works which never appeared. Sometimes a single reference is all that records a now-lost intention, but in other cases the ongoing history of a work in progress is tracked across various reports, until suddenly it disappears from view, either due to the author's death or some other cause. So, for example, the intention for Nodal and Milner's *Lancashire Glossary*, perhaps rashly, was that Thomas Hallam would render all the words included into Glossic, and then the whole work would be immediately

---

[50] *English Dialect Society: First Report*, pp. 9–10; *English Dialect Society: Second Report*, pp. 9–10.

[51] *English Dialect Society: Second Report*, pp. 5–6. On Parish, see further Roper, 'The Clergyman and the Dialect Speaker', pp. 113–15, and 'Folklore in the Glossaries of the English Dialect Society', pp. 190–1.

[52] *English Dialect Society: Eleventh Annual Report, for the Year 1883* (no place or date of publication), p. 5 (King's College London Archives, GB0100 KCLCA Skeat 11/1); Jesse Salisbury, *A Glossary of Words and Phrases used in S. E. Worcestershire* (London: Salisbury, 1893), p. vi.

The English Dialect Society   **157**

reprinted in a second edition, or with an extra volume; but this never happened.[53] A Bedfordshire glossary, edited by the Rev. W. F. Rose, was repeatedly promised in report after report, until Rose eventually had to acknowledge that 'since my removal from Bedfordshire [. . .] the work has been at a standstill, for the compilation of a provincial Glossary can only be carried on in the district which it is proposed to represent'.[54] (But then Rose immediately embarked on a glossary of North Somerset words which he also failed to complete.) James Britten had grand plans for a *Dictionary of Mining Terms* and then a volume on *Animal, Reptile, and Insect Names*, but increasing devotion to the cause of the Catholic Truth Society led him away from philological pursuits.[55] A proposed volume on *Public School Words* was promised by A. Percy Allsopp, but later his parliamentary duties as an MP meant that he had to withdraw, and he 'forwarded the whole of his materials' to another compiler.[56] In the end, *Public School Words* had to be abandoned when the Society, towards the end of its history, needed to trim its commitments ('a choice will have to be made', members were informed); such was also the fate of a particularly fascinating project, a new edition of Edward FitzGerald's *Sea Words*, using both FitzGerald's own revisions (supplied by his literary executor, Aldis Wright) and also a second 'annotated copy prepared by Mr Fitzgerald' (loaned by its owner, J. R. Wise).[57] But some non-completions remain unexplained, and some projects, sadly, appear only fleetingly and are never heard of again. In 1874, for example, Skeat received 'an interesting communication by the Rev. W. T. Webb, principal of Codrington College, Barbados, concerning the use of certain provincial English words in Barbados', but there is no further reference to this, and nor does Thomas Hallam's *Words Used in the Chapel-en-le-Frith District of the Peak of Derbyshire*, trailed in 1892, ever seem to have advanced.[58] Some reprints also fell by the wayside: Joseph Hunter's *Hallamshire Glossary* was never reprinted as planned, and nor was a revised edition of Murray's *Dialect of the Southern Counties of Scotland* ever produced.[59] So alongside the impressive publications list of the Society, we can also glimpse a shadow catalogue of tantalizing works that never appeared.

[53] See for example *English Dialect Society: Third Report*, p. 8–9; *English Dialect Society: Fourth Report, for the Year 1876* (no place or date of publication), p. 9 (King's College London Archives, GB0100 KCLCA Skeat 11/1); *English Dialect Society: Ninth Annual Report*, p. 4.

[54] *English Dialect Society: Seventh Annual Report, for the Year 1879* (no place or date of publication), p. 4 (King's College London Archives, GB0100 KCLCA Skeat 11/1).

[55] *English Dialect Society: Eleventh Annual Report*, p. 4; A. Roy Vickery, 'James Britten: A Founder Member of the Folklore Society', *Folklore* 89 (1978), 71–4.

[56] *English Dialect Society: Tenth Annual Report*, pp. 5–6; *English Dialect Society: Fourteenth Report, for the Year 1887* (no place or date of publication), p. 3 (King's College London Archives, GB0100 KCLCA Skeat 11/1).

[57] *English Dialect Society: Thirteenth Report, for the Years 1885 and 1886* (no place or date of publication), p. 4 (King's College London Archives, GB0100 KCLCA Skeat 11/1); *English Dialect Society: Fifteenth Report*, p. 2; *English Dialect Society: Sixteenth Report, for the Year 1889* (no place or date of publication), p. 2 (King's College London Archives, GB0100 KCLCA Skeat 11/1).

[58] *English Dialect Society: Second Report*, p. 11; English Dialect Society circular, dated 29 February 1892, in Manchester, John Rylands Research Institute and Library, GB 133 JHN 4/1.

[59] See *English Dialect Society: Second Report*, p. 11; *English Dialect Society: Twelfth Annual Report, for the Year 1884* (no place or date of publication), p. 3 (King's College London Archives, GB0100 KCLCA Skeat 11/1).

158 The Victorians and English Dialect

For some works, there was uncertainty over whether the Society would, in the end, act as publisher or not. One of the biggest and best-regarded of all Victorian glossaries was Georgina Jackson's *Shropshire Word-Book*, published in instalments between 1879 and 1881. Jackson (1823/24–95) was a schoolteacher in Chester, who spent the 1870s collecting the vocabulary of Shropshire, the county where she grew up. She became an acquaintance of Ellis, of Hallam, and—importantly—of Skeat, who advised her to learn Glossic in order to record pronunciation as well as vocabulary and who also, characteristically, advised her on the appropriate use of slips.[60] Skeat left an affectionate portrait of her in his memoirs, recalling how, Hallam-like, she 'travell[ed] in a third-class railway-carriage on a market-day' in order to collect dialect, how she sought out Skeat (and later Ellis) for 'a long and amusing argument [about dialect-collecting], conducted on both sides with due spirit and vigour', and how in her later years she was 'a sad invalid [. . .], being confined to one room and often to bed for long periods, and suffering much pain; but she bore her trials with much courage and even cheerfulness, and at all times took much interest in English dialects and etymology' (in her illness, Jackson was supported both by an award from the Royal Literary Fund and also a Civil List pension).[61] In the light of such a close association, it might have seemed natural that Jackson's *Shropshire Word-Book* should be intended for the English Dialect Society, and Skeat reported Jackson's work in progress to Society members.[62] But for whatever reason this didn't happen, and the 1878 annual report included a cryptic statement to members that 'it is due to Miss Jackson to say that she has always intended to publish the Glossary on her own account', together with a more explicitly confessional footnote from Skeat that 'I fear I must take the blame of any false impression that may have been given to the contrary'.[63] The reasons for non-appearance remain unclear, especially when one adds that Jackson dedicated her *Word-Book* to Skeat, and also gifted its copyright to him, so that it could later be used for the projected *English Dialect Dictionary*.[64] The excellence of Jackson's *Shropshire Word-Book* was recognized by all fellow dialect workers, for both its quantity (over five hundred pages) and its quality. Skeat appraised it as 'one of the best of its kind', and Robert Holland, working away at his own Cheshire glossary, informed Society members, in a spirit of competitiveness as well as admiration, that 'I fancy I have more words than Miss Jackson in her Shropshire Word Book.'[65]

So there were numerous challenges facing Skeat as he endeavoured to organize the Society as both a research organization and a publishing enterprise. But the Society's

---

[60] See Georgina F. Jackson, *Shropshire Word-Book: A Glossary of Archaic and Provincial Words, Etc, Used in the County* (London: Trübner, 1879), pp. x, xiii; George C. Baugh, 'Jackson, Georgina Frederica (1823/4–1895)', in *Oxford Dictionary of National Biography* [www.oxforddnb].

[61] Skeat, *A Student's Pastime*, pp. lxviii–lxx; see also Ellis, 'Third Annual Address', p. 448 n. 1.

[62] See, for example, *English Dialect Society: First Report*, pp. 13–14; *English Dialect Society: Second Report*, p. 10.

[63] *English Dialect Society: Sixth Report, for the Year 1878* (no place or date of publication), p. 12 (King's College London Archives, GB0100 KCLCA Skeat 11/1).

[64] Skeat, *A Student's Pastime*, p. viii.

[65] *English Dialect Society: Ninth Annual Report*, p. 3; see also Skeat, 'Report on the English Dialect Society', p. 19.

publications were warmly welcomed: appreciative reviews appeared in such journals as the *Academy*, the *Athenaeum*, and *Notes and Queries*, and the progress of the Society was often noted in the annual addresses of the President of the Philological Society. One member of the English Dialect Society (Henry Mathwin) later reported that 'he enjoyed half hours with the best authors, and half hours with the microscope, but the best half hours he spent were when one of the new books issued by the Society entered his house'.[66] As another member (Joseph Thompson) declared, 'whatever change may come about in the English language the members of the Society will be able to see through its publications what the folk-speech of England was in the reign of Victoria'.[67]

After three years of conscientious labour, Skeat was ready to hand over sole control of the Society. As he explained to members, the work was just too great for one person, especially the combination of what he called 'literary work' (overseeing the Society's research, editing submissions, steering publications through the press) with 'business arrangements' (collecting subscriptions, updating the membership list, organizing mailings).[68] Oversight of the Series B 'Reprinted Glossaries' had in particular been a drain: 'the editing of these', Skeat confessed as early as 1874, 'has proved far more tedious and laborious than might have been supposed, and a burden has been laid upon the Director [i.e. Skeat] which he cannot, for sheer lack of time, not of good will, easily undertake to the same extent in future years'.[69] It was time to reorganize the Society's mode of operations, and Skeat called for help. As he recorded (in what seems a rather pointed tone):

> In the first instance, I found that most of our London members were far too busy to render assistance, notwithstanding their anxiety for the Society's welfare; but, the Society being strongly represented in the North of England, offers of help came from Manchester.[70]

What was proposed in Manchester was a 'Committee of Management' (which Skeat himself would continue to serve on), under new leadership. 'The increase in the working power of the Society will be really useful to us', Skeat declared, as he handed over the reins, and the Society entered the second phase of its existence.

As Paul Readman has argued, the usual grim-up-north view of Victorian Manchester is only part of the story: the city was also viewed as one of the wonders of the age, and even a tourist hotspot, where visitors might tour the manufactories and marvel at the power and ingenuity of modern industry.[71] It was also a city whose civic identity and culture were intimately bound up with a sense of its own history: in

---

[66] *English Dialect Society: Fifteenth Report*, p. 8.
[67] Joseph Thompson in *English Dialect Society: Fourteenth Report*, p. 8.
[68] *English Dialect Society: Notice to Members. March, 1876* (no place or date of publication), p. 1.
[69] *English Dialect Society: Second Report*, p. 5.
[70] *English Dialect Society: Notice to Members. March, 1876*, p. 2.
[71] Readman, *Storied Ground*, pp. 226–33; see also Josephine M. Guy, '"The Chimneyed City": Imagining the North in Victorian Literature', in Katherine Cockin (ed.), *The Literary North* (Basingstoke: Palgrave Macmillan, 2012), pp. 22–37.

160 The Victorians and English Dialect

nineteenth-century Manchester, the past mattered a great deal. Antiquarian organizations such as the Chetham Society, libraries such as the Manchester Free Library and later the John Rylands Library, and civic architecture such as the Italianate Free Trade Hall and the Gothic Town Hall (complete with historical murals by Ford Madox Brown), all demonstrate that Victorian Manchester was a city not only of industrialists and workers, but of historians and medievalists as well.[72]

The new leadership for the English Dialect Society was provided by John Howard Nodal as Honorary Secretary, assisted by George Milner as Treasurer. Nodal (1831–1909) was Milner's co-editor on the Manchester Literary Club's *Glossary of the Lancashire Dialect* then in progress. Professionally, he was a journalist and a man of letters, and he was editor of the *Manchester City News*.[73] Resident in Heaton Moor, Stockport (Milner lived in Moston, Manchester), Nodal was a Quaker, and the Society's shift from Cambridge to Manchester can be viewed not only in terms of a change in balance between the south and the north, and between university scholarship and civic educationalism, but also between the Established Church and Nonconformism. Even the Society's bank account was moved, to the Manchester and County Bank. In addition to Nodal and Milner, there were nineteen other members of the Committee of Management as first constituted, nearly all of them connected to the Manchester area: antiquaries such as John Eglinton Bailey, James Crossley, and Henry Fishwick, and academics such as the classicist A. S. Wilkins and the Old English scholar Thomas Northcote Toller (both of whom were at Owens College, later the University of Manchester). The following year, the dialect writer Edwin Waugh joined the committee, all the members of which were male.

Money had always been tight during Skeat's directorship (though Skeat himself, it should be stressed, did all his work for the Society unpaid). By the end of 1875 there had been more material to publish than there were resources to pay for it: 'we are now at work in very earnest', Skeat wrote, 'and require at least 300 or 400 new subscribers to enable us to push on faster'.[74] This seems to have been a high priority for Milner and Nodal. In 1876, the 'simple fact [was] that during the last four years rather more books have been issued than the number of members and the amount of subscriptions have justified', but in 1877 the news was much better, and 'the financial position of the Society [had] been materially improved'.[75] Two measures had effected the change: first, a recruitment drive, especially with the goal of getting more libraries and institutions to subscribe; and second, more importantly, a decision to raise the annual subscription from half a guinea (10s 6d) to £1—almost a hundred per cent increase. The Society's income from subscriptions accordingly shot up from £169-14-6 in 1876 to £320-16-10 in 1877.

---

[72] See Alan J. Kidd and K. W. Roberts (eds), *City, Class and Culture: studies of social policy and cultural production in Victorian Manchester* (Manchester: Manchester University Press, 1985), and Joyce, *Visions of the People*, pp. 181–3; for parallels, see Colls, 'The New Northumbrians', esp. pp. 167–70.

[73] See Lynda Mugglestone, 'Nodal, John Howard (1831–1909)', in *Oxford Dictionary of National Biography* [www.oxforddnb].

[74] *English Dialect Society: Third Report*, p. 13.

[75] *English Dialect Society: Fourth Report*, p. 8; *English Dialect Society: Fifth Report, for the Year 1877* (no place or date of publication), p. 9 (King's College London Archives, GB0100 KCLCA Skeat 11/1).

Once established in Manchester, the Society enjoyed a decade of secure progress, gathering materials and issuing publications. Nodal soon realized that Skeat's crisp four-series arrangement for publications was not perfect, as 'no provision [was] made in the Society's scheme' for 'a series of occasional papers'.[76] So Nodal instituted a new category of 'Miscellanies', to cover such publications as the reprinting of W. E. A. Axon's essay on George Eliot's use of dialect and the abridgement of Ellis' *Existing Phonology* as *English Dialects—Their Sounds and Homes* (1890). He also began a new subseries of reprints, re-editing older works of dialect literature (as opposed to glossaries) under the heading of 'Specimens of English Dialects'. And he completed Skeat's *Bibliographical List* by issuing a second part which covered Scotland and Ireland, as well as 'Cant and Slang', 'Americanisms', 'English Gypsy Dialect', 'The English Language in India', and 'China-English Dialect'. Just as Skeat had consulted George Eliot when compiling the first part of the *List* (as quoted in the previous chapter), so Nodal wrote to a younger novelist who was now making his name: Thomas Hardy. *Far From The Madding Crowd* and *The Hand of Ethelberta* were added to the *List* for Dorset (though not, oddly, *Under the Greenwood Tree*), and Hardy's reply to Nodal was quoted at length: 'the dialect of the peasants in my novels is, as far as it goes, that of this county [Dorset] [. . .] But though I have scarcely preserved peculiarities of accent and trifling irregularities with such care as could have been wished for purposes of critical examination, the characteristic words which occur are in every case genuine, as heard from the lips of the natives'.[77] The printing of this letter in the Society's *Bibliographical List* represents Hardy's first public statement on the use of dialect in his fiction.

Although the Society's core mission continued to be the collection and publication of dialect materials, there were some other changes that were instituted following the move to Manchester. One was the practice of holding an annual general meeting of the Society in Manchester Town Hall (or sometimes the Manchester Free Library). An AGM may sound a minor innovation, but it was in fact the first time that the Society existed as a physical gathering of members, as opposed to simply a subscription society. The committee meetings were sociable, too: Nodal's first annual report dared to assert that 'the selection of Manchester, in preference to Cambridge or London [. . .] has been justified by the circumstance that each of the committee meetings of the year has been attended by from ten to twelve of the number'.[78] From 1882 onwards, the yearly reports issued to the Society also contain accounts of these meetings, with a precis of the speeches given. These are marked by a fair degree of Mancunian pride. Speaking in 1882, the Mayor of Manchester, Alderman Thomas Baker, bragged that 'the subject of dialects [. . .] had always been popular in this county; and certainly the work of the English Dialect Society, since it had been located here, had met with a large amount of success'.[79] W. W. Skeat, chairing the meeting two years later, knew

---

[76] *English Dialect Society: Fourth Report*, p. 11.
[77] Skeat and Nodal, *A Bibliographical List*, p. 174; reprinted in Millgate (ed.), *Thomas Hardy's Public Voice*, p. 11.
[78] *English Dialect Society: Fourth Report*, p. 7.
[79] *English Dialect Society: Ninth Annual Report*, p. 14.

162   The Victorians and English Dialect

exactly what to give his northern audience. He told them that he had 'never seen Manchester before this occasion', but that he 'hoped to visit it again'.[80] Looking back to the Society's transfer from Cambridge, he recalled that he had 'never received a letter with greater thankfulness' than he did 'one from Mr Nodal, intimating that he was willing to take the honorary secretaryship', and he 'did not think any other town would have come to their relief as Manchester did'. In 1885, Edwin Waugh was in the chair, urging the Society to 'pursue this work to its conclusion with as great care and attention as we possibly can, [so] that these ancient rills of language which we call dialects may be taken up, recorded, and examined for the benefit of future philologists before they become utterly dried up'.[81] Thomas Hallam also received praise on these occasions: 'there was no doubt', said the chair in 1887, Joseph Hall, 'that fifty or a hundred years hence the labours of Mr Hallam would be more highly appreciated even than they are now'.[82]

Another initiative was the establishment of an English Dialect Society Library. From the start, Skeat had asked members of the Society to send in any relevant publications, especially of a scarce nature, and the annual reports of the Society record many of the works that were gifted: donations from Axon, Bonaparte, Ellis, and many others, and also a host of northern annuals, almanacs, and comic tales. A proposal that the Society should conceptualize its book holdings as a 'special collection' and deposit it with a public library then came from one of philology's larger-than-life figures: Professor George Stephens of Copenhagen (or 'Cheapinghaven', as he preferred to call it). Stephens was a passionate believer in the idea of an 'Anglo-Scandic' or 'Old Northern' culture, and a passionate opponent of what he saw as German aggression and claim-staking in the scholarly world of historical language study.[83] A subscriber to the English Dialect Society from the start, in February 1877 Stephens wrote to the committee with his bright idea:

> I have not been in Manchester for many years, and have forgot many things about it; but I suppose you have a great free library there. In this case allow me to suggest that our Society—which, I suppose, has no large rooms of its own, and which at any time may dissolve [. . .]—forms, as a perpetual deposit and section in the Manchester Book Board, a special Dialect Library for the languages and grammars and dialectica of all lands, especially Great Britain and Ireland. Special libraries are more wanted than ever; they are enormously useful, and attract endless gifts. Birmingham has its Shakspere Library. Why should not Manchester have its Dialect Library?[84]

---

[80] *English Dialect Society: Eleventh Annual Report*, pp. 10–11.

[81] *English Dialect Society: Twelfth Annual Report, for the Year 1884* (no place or date of publication), p. 11 (King's College London Archives, GB0100 KCLCA Skeat 11/1).

[82] *English Dialect Society: Thirteenth Report*, p. 17.

[83] See Andrew Wawn, 'George Stephens, Cheapinghaven and Old Northern Antiquity', *Studies in Medievalism* 7 (1995), 1–42, *The Vikings and the Victorians: Inventing the Old North in Nineteenth-Century Britain* (Cambridge: Brewer, 2000), pp. 215–44, and 'Stephens, George (1813–1895)', in *Oxford Dictionary of National Biography* [www.oxforddnb].

[84] *English Dialect Society: Fifth Report*, p. 11.

The English Dialect Society   **163**

Nodal opened negotiations with the Manchester Public Libraries Committee, and appealed to civic pride as he relayed Stephens' suggestion, cunningly reporting that there had been some talk of the collection going instead to a Cambridge college: 'the Council [of the English Dialect Society] in Manchester were of opinion, however, that a public institution in a more central town would be a preferable location'.[85] An agreement was reached, and the Society's collection was deposited at the Manchester Free Library, then housed in the old Town Hall on King Street (and the collection still exists, in the Free Library's successor, Manchester Central Library). The collection was available for all members of the public to consult, but English Dialect Society members had borrowing rights as well.[86] And the establishment of the library then stimulated a new round of donations: from Bonaparte, twenty-five separate translations of the Song of Solomon into dialect (one of his pet projects from the late 1850s and early 1860s); from Skeat, 'about fifty books and pamphlets'; and from one Manchester member, Robert Holt, a great quantity of Lancashire and Yorkshire dialect writings.[87] The largest single donation received for the Society's library came in 1887, when J. R. Wise presented 162 books and 27 pamphlets, many of them with Warwickshire words annotated by him.[88]

A catalogue for what was now badged as the 'English Dialect Library' was issued in 1880: this followed the organizing principles of Skeat and Nodal's *Bibliographical List*, with sections on 'Dictionaries' and 'English Dialects Generally', followed by county entries (with that for Lancashire by far the fullest), and then 'Scotland', 'Isle of Man', 'Ireland', 'Slang', 'Gipsy', 'America', and finally 'China' (but not, oddly, Wales). In 1880 the Library included 567 volumes (352 on individual English counties).[89] This had risen to 820 in 1888, when a supplementary catalogue was issued, and then 886 in 1893 (542 on English counties).[90]

Such were the activities, publications, and even library of the English Dialect Society. Who, then, were the members?

Membership

In his first annual report, Skeat announced with some delight that 'the very first result of the Society's formation was the discovery of the names and residences of many workers'.[91] The membership lists in the Society's annual reports represent the first

---

[85] *English Dialect Society: Fifth Report*, p. 10.
[86] *English Dialect Society: Sixth Report*, pp. 11–12.
[87] *English Dialect Society: Sixth Report*, pp. 10–11; *English Dialect Society: Seventh Annual Report*, p. 9.
[88] *English Dialect Society: Fourteenth Report*, p. 9.
[89] *English Dialect Society: Seventh Annual Report*, p. 8.
[90] *English Dialect Society: Seventeenth Report, for the Three Years, 1890, 1891, and 1892* (no place or date of publication), pp. 2–3 (King's College London Archives, GB0100 KCLCA Skeat 11/1); *Catalogue of the English Dialect Library* (Manchester: English Dialect Society, 1880); *The English Dialect Library: Catalogue Part II (Works Added from 1880 to 1888)* (London: English Dialect Society, 1888) (King's College London Archives, GB0100 KCLCA Skeat 11/3).
[91] *English Dialect Society: First Report*, p. 3.

164 The Victorians and English Dialect

national census of dialect enthusiasts, a decade and a half before Ellis' roll-call in *The Existing Phonology*.

In spite of efforts by Nodal and Milner, the membership of the Society remained doggedly between the 300 and 350 mark for most of its existence; no wonder there was a sense of funding always being short, and ambition outstripping capacity. In 1874, after less than a year of existence, the Society had 205 members—196 individual, and 9 institutional.[92] This number rose rapidly over the next half decade to reach a high point of 345 in 1879 (Nodal and Milner's push on institutional subscriptions took the number of such subscribers from twenty-six in 1877 to forty-five in 1879). But some shrinkage occurred after that, and membership hovered around three hundred for much of the 1880s, until in 1888 Milner overhauled the membership list, and removed members who had silently discontinued their subscriptions: this reduced the number of individual members to below the figure of two hundred.[93] The last report is for the years 1890–2, and this records 178 individual members—lower than in the first report for 1873. Only institutional subscriptions continued to climb in these final years, and in fact they reached their highest level (sixty-seven) in this final report, thus marking a shift in the proportion of individual and institutional members in the Society's membership from the 1870s to the 1890s—a sign, perhaps, of the increasing academicization of English philology.

A review of the Society's membership lists—and counting the total number of different members across the two decades of the Society's existence, regardless of length of membership—reveals some clear patterns and clusters. Geographically, London was numerically dominant, with over one hundred members having a London address (one reason, presumably, for Skeat's disappointment that London members did not step forward to take over in 1876). Manchester came second, with forty-two members, narrowly beating Cambridge (thirty-nine). This Cambridge number far outstripped that for Oxford (eleven), and may be attributable to Skeat's early energies. County-wise, the distribution of members was haphazard: most counties had at least half a dozen members (and some had many more), but only one each is recorded for Cornwall, Essex, and Rutland, and none at all for Bedfordshire, Berkshire, and Huntingdonshire.

Let us turn to professions. When appealing for informants for *On Early English Pronunciation*, Alexander Ellis had identified, as particularly promising helpers, 'Resident Clergymen, Nonconformist Ministers, National and British Schoolmasters, and Country gentlemen with literary tastes'.[94] If we count from the personal titles given in the annual reports, we can see that by far the most common profession was indeed the church: no fewer than ninety members are styled as 'Rev.' in the annual lists—approximately one-third of all individual members.[95] There were

[92] Membership figures have been calculated by Harriet Evans Tang from English Dialect Society annual reports.

[93] *English Dialect Society: Fifteenth Report*, p. 3.

[94] Ellis, *On Early English Pronunciation*, III, vi; see also IV, 1088.

[95] See also Jonathan Roper, 'England—The Land Without Folklore?', in Timothy Baycroft and David Hopkin (eds), *Folklore and Nationalism in Europe During the Long Nineteenth Century* (Leiden: Brill, 2012), pp. 227–53, at pp. 246–8, and 'The Clergyman and the Dialect Speaker'.

also two archbishops: Richard Chenevix Trench, as Archbishop of Dublin, and the Archbishop of Canterbury, Edward White Benson, who had begun his membership when he was earlier Bishop of Truro (where he invented the famous Festival of Nine Lessons and Carols). The majority of these clergy were Anglican, but there were also a number of Nonconformists, such as the Methodist Hilderic Friend. There were at least eighteen professors, as well as a number of lawyers, doctors, and surgeons, and a cluster of military men (two Captains, one naval Captain, one Lieutenant-Colonel, and one Colonel). Twenty-six of the thirty-nine Cambridge members have college addresses in the annual reports, indicating that this was a membership rooted in university circles, and a number of these were ordained clergy, such as Skeat himself. At least half a dozen members of the Society were Members of Parliament, either at the time of joining or at a later date. There were several knights of the realm, at least two lords, and one prince (Louis Lucien Bonaparte).

But the profile even of its more privileged members was not necessarily the same as that of the county antiquarian societies. Quite a number of those with wealth or grand addresses were in fact industrialists rather than landed gentry, such as William Harrison of Samlesbury Hall (Lancashire) and Joseph Jones of Abberley Hall (Worcestershire). Other industrialists and businessmen include the publisher Alexander Macmillan, Thomas Turnbull, head of the Whitehall Dockyard in Whitby, and R. Oliver Heslop, a Northumberland iron merchant, as well (one assumes) as the E. French whose address is given simply as 'Lead Works, Hull'. But the gentry were also present, in the form of members such as Granville Leveson Gower of Titsey Place, Surrey.

Schoolmasters and educationists were very prominent. Among the schools whose staff were members of the Society were Almondbury Grammar School near Huddersfield, Eton College, Folkestone Grammar School (where the Society member was the headmaster, Richard Stead, co-author of the *Holderness Glossary*), Hulme Grammar School in Oldham, King's College School, London, Sheffield Grammar School, Skipton Grammar School (member and headmaster: F. G. Fleay, spelling reformer and Shakespeare controversialist), Surrey County School in Guildford, the United Services College at Westward Ho in Devon (famous as Rudyard Kipling's *alma mater*), and Yarmouth Grammar School (again the member was the headmaster, John James Raven, an authority on church bells). The prominence of provincial grammar schools in this list is notable. Special mention should be made of Mill Hill School, north of London, which boasted three members of the Society: the headmaster R. F. Weymouth (member of the Philological Society), J. Nettleship, and, pre-eminently, James Murray (prior to his move to Oxford to become a full-time lexicographer).[96] Other educationists in the membership lists include Joseph Payne, the Quaker John Stephen Rowntree of York, Thomas Darlington (who compiled a 450-page glossary of *The Folk-Speech of South Cheshire* while still a student, and later became a school inspector), and Henry Morley (from 1865, Professor of English

---

[96] See Murray, *Caught in the Web of Words*, pp. 102–17.

166 The Victorians and English Dialect

at University College London, but before that one of the staff on Dickens' journals *Household Words* and *All the Year Round*).[97]

Almost by definition, many members of the English Dialect Society were distinguished philologists or antiquarians. In addition to the obvious names of Skeat, Ellis, Sweet, and so on, the former group includes Joseph Bosworth, John Earle, F. J. Furnivall, Henry Hucks Gibbs and Fitzedward Hall (both important for the history of the *Oxford English Dictionary*, among much else), W. P. Ker, T. L. Kington-Oliphant, Eiríkur Magnússon, A. S. Napier, and Hensleigh Wedgwood. Antiquarians, palaeographers, and medieval editors included Henry Bradshaw, H. O. Coxe, Edward Hailstone, James Orchard Halliwell, J. R. Lumby, James Raine, and W. G. Searle.

Institutional subscriptions were mostly libraries. A few of these were grand—the Royal Library at Windsor, the Royal Institution, the London Guildhall—and some were college libraries in Oxford and Cambridge, but the majority were public and civic, in towns such as Blackburn, Bolton, Bradford, Brighton, Nottingham, and West Bromwich, as well as big cities such as Birmingham, Leeds, and Liverpool. There were also philosophical and literary societies in Bristol, Newcastle, and Sheffield, and museums in Torquay and Warrington. Overseas institutions were split between universities and libraries, and were dominated by Germany and the USA (in the latter, there was a variety of subscribers ranging from the Boston Athenaeum, Yale University, and the Library of Congress, to Cincinnati and Detroit Public Libraries). Most remote were the subscriptions from Melbourne Public Library and Sydney Free Public Library in Australia, and Canterbury College Library in New Zealand. Individual overseas subscribers were dominantly philologists of the Germanic languages—such figures as Dr F. H. Stratmann of Krefeld in Germany, Professor Richard Paul Wülker of Leipzig, and Professor Julius Zupitza of Berlin (not to forget Professor George Stephens of Copenhagen).

It may well have been noticed that all the names of members given so far, in this profession-based survey, have been male. The report of the 1884 annual general meeting in Manchester notes demurely that 'there were also two ladies present', but it does not identify them.[98] Such a record seriously undervalues the importance of the contribution of women members to the Society's success—in spite of their absence from its committee, and therefore from speech-making at the AGMs. The absolute numbers were modest. In 1873, there were 12 women members and 184 men; in 1876, 18 women and 293 men (the highest number for each); in 1890–2, 9 women and 169 men. Over the two decades of the Society's existence, 24 different women are recorded as having been members. But although they never formed more than six per cent of the membership, many of the women members of the Society were highly active; they did not simply send off their annual subscription and wait for the publications to come in.

---

[97] See Fred Hunter, 'Morley, Henry (1822–1894)', in *Oxford Dictionary of National Biography* [www.oxforddnb].

[98] *English Dialect Society: Eleventh Annual Report*, p. 10.

Ellis' view, as expressed to the Philological Society, was that women might actually be better fitted for being philologists than men, rhapsodizing 'how very apt women are in the use of language [. . .], how easily they acquire foreign tongues, and how peculiarly adapted for feminine occupation is all the work of the philologist'.[99] As we saw in Chapter 2, female informants had a crucial role to play in Hallam and Ellis' phonetic researches, and there is no evidence that in *The Existing Phonology* (in contrast to some later dialect surveys) male informants were systematically preferred to female ones.[100] Of the twenty-four women members of the English Dialect Society, eight are also listed in *The Existing Phonology* as having given help to Ellis, and the identity of these eight is worth attending to. Georgina Jackson was one of these, as was Isabella Francis (1839/40–1922) of Tysoe near Stratford-upon-Avon, daughter of the Warwickshire MP, Edward Bolton King. Her husband was vicar of Tysoe, and her 'list of some Warwickshire words' was one of the first collections sent in to the Society; it was then published in 1876 as *South Warwickshire Provincialisms*.[101] Both Mary Powley and her sister Ann Atkinson, who lived at Winderwath House near Penrith, were also among this group of eight (they were praised by Ellis in 1889 as 'two old ladies, Mrs Atkinson and Miss Powley, since deceased, who had had a life's knowledge of the dialect'; it is also Ellis who records that the surname was pronounced with an *oo* not an *ow*, as in *pool*).[102] Early annual reports record that 'Miss Powley has promised some Cumberland words', and also that she sent the Society a copy of her *Echoes of Old Cumberland* when it was published.[103] In the 1878 report it was communicated that 'Miss Powley, well known as a careful observer, has promised to prepare for the Society her collection of Cumberland words, with notes on the old customs and old industries of the county on which the words throw light'.[104] Sadly, this had not been accomplished by the time of her death in 1882, and Society members were informed that 'Miss Powley has left in MS a large quantity of material which she had prepared for the English Dialect Society, but how far it will be available for publication is not at present known'.[105]

Three other women who were members of the English Dialect Society and also contributed to Ellis' *Existing Phonology* were Isabella Banks, Mrs G. M. E. Campbell, and Bessy Curteis. Isabella Banks (1821–97), better known by her husband's name as Mrs G. Linnaeus Banks (George Banks was a journalist), was a well-known novelist, often on northern and political themes, and also a campaigner for women's rights. Her treatment of regional dialect was well regarded by her contemporaries, her most famous novel bearing the title *The Manchester Man* (1876); and it was for Manchester that she supplied Ellis with dialectal information (as one of only three

---

[99] Ellis, 'Tenth Annual Address', p. 252.
[100] See Coates, *Women, Men, and Language*, pp. 41–51.
[101] *English Dialect Society: First Report*, p. 10, See Ellis, *On Early English Pronunciation*, V, 58*, 1613/181, 1910–12/478–80; Sanders, 'Alexander John Ellis', pp. 763–4.
[102] Ellis, *On Early English Pronunciation*, V, 1987/555, 1993–4/561–2.
[103] *English Dialect Society: Third Report*, p. 6; *English Dialect Society: Fourth Report*, p. 11.
[104] *English Dialect Society: Sixth Report*, p. 6.
[105] *English Dialect Society: Tenth Annual Report*, p. 7.

168 The Victorians and English Dialect

informants).[106] We know less about Georgiana Mary Elizabeth Campbell (1816–82). Born in Madras, India, and the widow of a naval officer, in the annual reports of the English Dialect Society she has an address in Plymouth and then in London, as confirmed by ten-yearly census returns; but in Ellis' *Existing Phonology*—if it is the same person—she is to be found in Wiltshire, at Corsley House near Warminster.[107] She is also recorded as having submitted over four thousand quotations to the *Oxford English Dictionary*.[108] And Bessy Curteis (1845–91; Elizabeth Charlotte d'Arley by her married name), another contributor of quotations to the *OED*, was the daughter of a Sussex MP, and supplied Ellis with dialect information for Leasam near Rye.[109]

The last of the eight, Charlotte Ellis (1836–1917), we have already met briefly in Chapter 2, submitting to Ellis a dialect sample from her home in Belgrave in Leicestershire.[110] She was also the daughter of an MP—John Ellis, who was a Quaker, a businessman, an anti-slavery campaigner, and a railway entrepreneur (and no relation of Alexander Ellis). After John Ellis' death, five of his children, all unmarried sisters, lived on at Belgrave Hall, from where they engaged in local political and social causes, such as education and the poor law—and contributing to the *OED*.[111] Among the earliest collections of material received by Skeat for the English Dialect Society was 'a capital collection of Leicestershire words, with their pronunciations added in "Glossic", by Miss C. Ellis'. This collection was submitted in the form of an interleaved copy of Arthur Benoni Evans' *Leicestershire Words, Phrases, and Proverbs* (1848), and it was subsequently forwarded to Evans' son Sebastian, who prepared a new and enlarged version of his father's work for the Society.[112] Sebastian Evans recorded that he had incorporated 'nearly the whole' of Ellis' list into his expanded glossary, and that 'often when I have been in doubt as to the exclusion or inclusion of a word, I have been decided by finding it entered in her list'.[113]

But the membership total of twenty-four women does not quite capture the full number involved, in that three dialect collectors had their glossaries published by the Society without, it seems, ever formally being members, namely Margaret A. Courtney, Angelina Parker, and Edith L. Chamberlain. The first of these, Margaret Ann Courtney of Alverton House, Penzance, was a member of a well-connected Cornish

---

[106] Ellis, *On Early English Pronunciation*, V, 45*; Rosemary T. Van Arsdel, 'Banks, Isabella Varley [*née* Isabella Varley; *known as* Mrs G. Linnaeus Banks] (1821–1897)', in *Oxford Dictionary of National Biography* [www.oxforddnb].

[107] Ellis, *On Early English Pronunciation*, V, 59*.

[108] Lindsay Rose Russell, *Women and Dictionary Making: Gender, Genre, and English Language Lexicography* (Cambridge: Cambridge University Press, 2018), p. 154.

[109] Ellis, *On Early English Pronunciation*, V, 1566–8/134–6; Russell, *Women and Dictionary Making*, p. 154.

[110] See Ellis, *On Early English Pronunciation*, V, 1904/472, 1921–5/489–93.

[111] See Russell, *Women and Dictionary Making*, p. 155; Miller Christy, 'Ellis, John (1789–1862)', rev. Alan R. Griffin, in *Oxford Dictionary of National Biography* [www.oxforddnb].

[112] Skeat, 'English Dialect Society' (November 1873), p. 342; *English Dialect Society: First Report*, p. 10; *English Dialect Society: Second Report*, p. 10; Skeat and Nodal, *Bibliographical List*, p. 89.

[113] Arthur Benoni Evans, *Leicestershire Words, Phrases, and Proverbs*, ed. Sebastian Evans, English Dialect Society 31 (London: English Dialect Society, 1881), p. 13.

The English Dialect Society   **169**

family, much involved in public service (one of her brothers, Leonard Henry Court-ney, was a campaigning Liberal MP and was later ennobled as Baron Courtney of Penwith), and the English Dialect Society published her West Cornwall glossary in 1880.

Although Angelina Parker (1843–1922) is not listed as a member of the Society, her husband is. George Parker was an employee of the Bodleian Library, Oxford, and acted as a checker or copyist of manuscripts for (among others) Skeat, Furnivall, and Ellis.[114] George Parker produced an index for an English Dialect Society volume of *Five Original Glossaries* in 1881, but it was his wife who was the dialect collec-tor.[115] She was a central informant for Alexander Ellis' coverage of Oxfordshire, and in English Dialect Society records she is first mentioned in the report for 1875, hav-ing submitted 'some Oxfordshire words': these were published as part of a composite volume in 1876, and then a supplement (three times as long as the original) appeared in the 1881 volume which her husband indexed.[116] Angelina Parker also cooperated with Thomas Hallam: his papers record a stay at the Parkers' house in Oxford in 1884, sitting up till midnight talking about dialect, and his notebooks preserve the speech he heard while dialect-gathering during his visit—in colleges, in the Bodleian Library, and at the market and railway station.[117]

Edith Laxon Chamberlain (1849–1931) first appears in the Society's records in the annual report for 1879, with the rather coy communication that 'towards the close of the year, a lady wrote to the Honorary Secretary [i.e. Nodal] informing him that she has for some years been collecting the dialectal words in use in West Worcestershire, and placing her Glossary at the service of the Society'.[118] The following year this 'lady' was revealed to be 'Mrs Chamberlain, of Hagley', and her glossary was praised for being 'an extensive collection, compiled with great industry and scrupulous care, and well illustrated with colloquialisms'.[119] Hallam's papers, once again, preserve a cache of correspondence with Chamberlain, and his pocket notebook includes his impression of her appearance: 'full brow indicative of mental power—thoughtful & serious cast of countenance, bordering on the pensive'.[120]

The English Dialect Society published Chamberlain's *Glossary of West Worcester-shire Words* in 1882 (subsequently, she started collecting words from the south of the county, but these never reached print).[121] This contains a thirty-five-page word list,

---

[114] Ellis, *On Early English Pronunciation*, I, 279 n. 2; Brewer, *Editing Piers Plowman*, pp. 116, 124, 140; Helen Spencer, 'F. J. Furnivall's Six of the Best: The *Six-Text Canterbury Tales* and the Chaucer Society', *Review of English Studies* New Series 66 (2015), 601–23, at p. 606 n. 24.

[115] *English Dialect Society: Ninth Annual Report*, p. 2.

[116] Ellis, *On Early English Pronunciation*, V, 73*, 1524–5/92–3, 1554–60/122–8; *English Dialect Society: Third Report*, p. 10. See further Javier Ruano-García, 'The Contribution of Angelina Parker to the *English Dialect Dictionary*', *Dictionaries* 41.2 (2020), 1–24.

[117] Oxford, Bodleian Libraries, MS Eng. lang. d. 21, fols 149–53; Oxford, Bodleian Libraries, MS Eng. lang. g. 59, fols 27–41.

[118] *English Dialect Society: Seventh Annual Report*, p. 6.

[119] *English Dialect Society: Eighth Annual Report, for the Year 1880* (no place or date of publication), p. 4 (King's College London Archives, GB0100 KCLCA Skeat 11/1).

[120] Oxford, Bodleian Libraries, MS Eng. lang. g. 62, fols 17–18.

[121] *English Dialect Society: Eleventh Annual Report*, p. 5.

170 The Victorians and English Dialect

topped and tailed by notes on grammar and pronunciation (with a Glossic supplement by Hallam) and a record of local proverbs and superstitions. But Chamberlain was also a writer of fiction, who published two novels (and later, an influential book on gardening), and her glossary gains added interest when set beside her fiction, especially her first novel, *Up Hill and Down Dale: A Tale of Country Life* (1884). Set in a fictional 'Brookshire' (a name with echoes of Elizabeth Gaskell's 'Darkshire' and George Eliot's 'Loamshire'), it seems likely that the scenes of the novel are modelled on a number of real-life locations in Chamberlain's own Worcestershire. *Up Hill and Down Dale* is a mix of provincial novel, soap opera, and melodrama, and most of the distinctive dialect features found in the language of its working-class characters can be looked up in Chamberlain's glossary—individual words such as *gallus* 'wicked; impudent', *gripple* 'miserly', *mullock* 'dirt; litter', *rodney* 'an idle, loafing fellow', and *wimmy* 'giddy', and rhyming proverbs as well.[122] As in Gaskell's *North and South*, in Chamberlain's novel an interest in local dialect is a mark of sympathy and openness: the young gentleman-farmer Armell Dawes, we are told, 'had lived so much away from his own county as to be able to appreciate and enjoy the peculiarities of its dialect and custom'.[123] For Armell, then, social and geographical mobility actually increase, rather than decrease, his capacity for local attachment; by contrast, his more conventional wife Lettice, with whom deep tensions emerge, takes a disapproving view, complaining that the salt-of-the-earth Joe Porter 'does talk so dreadfully broad'.[124] The novel is full of passing observations about the perception and performance of dialect; an arrival from Yorkshire, for example, finds that his fellow diners in the local pub 'began by laughing at him, on account of his north-country accent, yet it was a good-natured laugh, and came of a pleasurable feeling of superiority, and correcter form of speech; for Brookshire folks generally deem other dialects than their own "oncultivated"'.[125]

The example of Edith Chamberlain leads us to a final group of English Dialect Society members to be considered here: writers. There were northern dialect writers, of course, such as Isaac Binns and Edwin Waugh (though Ben Brierley never joined), as well as regional novelists such as Chamberlain and Isabella Banks. Samuel Smiles, author of the paradigmatic Victorian text *Self-Help* (1859) was a subscriber. And one very eminent novelist joined in 1877: George Eliot (under the name 'Mrs G. H. Lewes'), who remained a member until her death in 1880. She did not, alas, engage in any word-collecting or editorial activity, though a letter to William Allingham, also in 1877, indicates a recurring, or continuing, interest in dialect at this time ('dialect, like other living things', she writes, 'tends to become mongrel, especially in a central,

---

[122] Edith L. Chamberlain, *Up Hill and Down Dale: A Tale of Country Life*, 3 vols (London: Remington, 1884), I, 105, II, 36, 47, 96, III, 7; Edith L. Chamberlain, *A Glossary of West Worcestershire Words*, English Dialect Society 36 (London: English Dialect Society, 1882), pp. 13, 14, 20, 25, 34.

[123] Chamberlain, *Up Hill and Down Dale*, II, 67; see also II, 107.

[124] Chamberlain, *Up Hill and Down Dale*, II, 58; see also II, 96–7, 106.

[125] Chamberlain, *Up Hill and Down Dale*, II, 140–1.

The English Dialect Society   171

fertile, and manufacturing region, attractive of migration; and hence the Midland talk presents less interesting relics of elder grammar than the more northerly dialects').[126]

There were poets too among the membership. Although he was professionally a journalist and lawyer, Sebastian Evans, the recipient of Charlotte Ellis' Leicestershire words, published a number of volumes of poetry, moved in literary and artistic circles, and became an expert on the Arthurian legend, both as scholar and translator.[127] Edward FitzGerald and William Barnes, as we have seen, joined the Society on its foundation. And Alfred Tennyson, the Poet Laureate, was also a member: he is recorded in the membership lists from 1875 to 1887, but then disappears; was he one of the casualties, perhaps, of Milner's 1888 purge of members whose subscriptions had lapsed?

A final poetic member, who is worth lingering over in this survey, was Arthur Joseph Munby (1828–1910), a member of the Society from its beginning to its end. Born in York, Munby became a barrister and civil servant in London, and published a series of volumes of poetry. But he is now famous for being revealed as a 'man of two worlds'. Munby's will specified that three boxes of his papers, deposited at Trinity College, Cambridge, should not be opened until forty years after his death. What the diaries and documents revealed was an entirely secret history for this respectable lawyer: an obsession with Victorian working-class women, especially manual workers such as housemaids and fisherwomen, and a concealed marriage with his servant, Hannah Cullwick.[128] Munby's published poetry was, in any case, already full of such subjects, such as *Ann Morgan's Love* (1896), a long narrative poem which tells a thinly disguised version of Munby and Cullwick's own story: a gentleman marries his maid-of-all-work, but after a brief unsuccessful attempt at moving in genteel society, they choose to revert to their earlier relations of master and servant, as well as (now) husband and wife.

Many of Munby's poems about working-class women use dialect for their female voices; the implication is that the language of such women is one of the features that drew Munby to them. As a member of the English Dialect Society, Munby presented to the Society's library a copy of his 1865 volume *Verses New and Old* (containing such poems as 'T' Runawaa Lass', 'The Serving Maid', and 'Mary Ann'), and Nodal praised the volume in his supplement to Skeat's *Bibliographical List*.[129] Over the years Munby submitted a steady stream of Yorkshire and Shropshire words for the Society's collections, and also supplied Georgina Jackson with materials for her *Shropshire Word-Book*.[130] Yorkshire is understandable—Munby came from York—but

---

[126] J. W. Cross (ed.), *George Eliot's Life as Related in her Letters and Journals*, 4 vols (Leipzig: Tauchnitz, 1885), IV, 185.

[127] F. L. Bickley, 'Sebastian Evans (1830–1909)', rev. Rowena Williams, in *Oxford Dictionary of National Biography* [www.oxforddnb].

[128] See Derek Hudson, *Munby: Man of Two Worlds. The Life and Diaries of Arthur J. Munby 1828–1910* (London: Murray, 1972); Diane Atkinson, *Love and Dirt: The Marriage of Arthur Munby and Hannah Cullwick* (London: Macmillan, 2003); Liz Stanley, 'Munby, Arthur Joseph (1828–1910)', in *Oxford Dictionary of National Biography* [www.oxforddnb].

[129] *English Dialect Society: Second Report*, p. 7; Skeat and Nodal, *A Bibliographical List*, p. 179.

[130] *English Dialect Society: Third Report*, p. 10; Jackson, *Shropshire Word-Book*, p. xiii.

172 The Victorians and English Dialect

why Shropshire? The answer is Hannah Cullwick, who grew up in Shifnal. *Ann Morgan's Love* also gives the protagonist a Shropshire background, and the poem ends with the two married lovers relocating to a rural cottage in the fictional village of Burlinghope. A scene between Ann and her (unnamed) husband, early in their marriage, deserves to be quoted at length:

> Her speech too—could she alter it at will?
> 'No', said her husband, 'and you shall not try!'
> For he derided grammar; and he loved
> The folkspeech of the Marches, full of words
> Vivid, expressive, picturesque; unknown
> To southern ears, but old and accurate
> As Chaucer's English; aye, and older far.
> She was no gosterer, yet he knew full well
> How she could snape a rodney, hiking him
> Back to his work; and how with lusty arms
> She bested other women, when agate
> Keeving her barrer, thrutching at the coals;
> And how, on Easter Tuesday, she would oss
> To clip and heave her sweetheart up on high.
> Ah, and he knew that she was never fause,
> Nor fratchety, nor pizy; she was still
> Herself, as peart and jannock as the best.
> Therefore said he, "You shall not change your note;
> It is your own: these many hundred years
> Your peasant fathers spoke as you speak now:
> Why should you change? Your dialect, my wench,
> Is part of England's history". She laugh'd.[131]

No doubt many members of the English Dialect Society would have shared this historicist estimate of the value of rural dialect, even if they would have hesitated to contract a marriage such as that of Ann and her husband—let alone to share Munby's own secret life. Most of the dialect terms here attributed to Ann can be readily checked in Georgina Jackson's *Shropshire Word-Book* and other sources: *fratchety* 'peevish; irritable', *goster* 'swagger; vapouring talk', *snape* 'to check or rebuke hastily', and so on.[132] Munby's poetry is a rich resource.

Glossaries

J. R. Wise, in his 1865 essay 'The Poetry of Provincialisms', had written in praise of glossaries: 'Dictionaries can, we fear, never become popular; but terrible as is

---

[131] Arthur Munby, *Ann Morgan's Love: A Pedestrian Poem* (London: Reeves and Turner, 1896), pp. 32–3.
[132] Jackson, *Shropshire Word-Book*, pp. 162, 182, 394.

The English Dialect Society **173**

the popular idea about them, far worse is it about glossaries [. . .] Yet, in spite of this prejudice, we venture to say that any one of our glossaries of provincialisms is far more amusing than ninety-nine out of a hundred novels'.[133] (And Wise should know: he had written an unsuccessful novel himself.) With the glossaries issued by the English Dialect Society we come, in many regards, to the absolute heart of Victorian dialect study: high-quality regional philology, produced at a moment of balance between the earlier, somewhat haphazard amateur tradition, and the later, more austere professionalization of the field.

The publication of original glossaries—Series C—was the core commitment of the English Dialect Society. So we will finish this chapter by taking a closer look at three of the Society's major glossaries, chosen both to give a more sustained experience of the contents of such glossaries, and also to bring into focus some of the questions of method which dialectologists—and the directors of the Society—had to grapple with. These three glossaries are Edward Peacock's *Glossary of Words Used in the Wapentakes of Manley and Corringham, Lincolnshire* (first edition, 1877; second edition, in two volumes, 1889), Robert Holland's *Glossary of Words Used in the County of Chester* (published in three parts, 1884–6), and F. T. Elworthy's *West Somerset Word-Book* (1886): one volume from the east of the country, one from the north, and one from the west. It is not a coincidence that, in their final form, all three glossaries appeared in the 1880s, after more than a decade of Society activity: all required a great deal of time and labour to bring them to completion. All three works were highly regarded, and we will begin by meeting their authors.

In the Society's membership lists, the address of Edward Peacock (1831–1915) is given as the grand-sounding Bottesford Manor in north-west Lincolnshire. But, as Eileen Elder's research on the Peacock family has shown, he was really more gentleman-farmer than landed gentry, though from 1874 he let out his estate to tenants rather than farming it himself; later still, financial exigency meant he had to give up Bottesford and move to a lesser property in Kirton in Lindsey.[134] In 1865, Peacock had built a new library wing on Bottesford Manor, and there, often assisted by one or more of his children, he pursued his antiquarian and philological interests (all five of Peacock's children published articles in the journal *Notes and Queries*, and Mabel Peacock in particular became an important Lincolnshire writer).[135] Largely self-educated, by the time of his *Manley and Corringham Glossary*, Peacock had published books on such diverse topics as *The Army Lists of the Roundheads and Cavaliers* and *A List of Roman Catholics in the County of York in 1604*, and he had edited a text for the Early English Text Society (John Mirk's *Festial*, a late medieval book of sermons). He had also established himself as a keen contributor to the *Oxford English Dictionary*.[136] He was an acquaintance of Arthur Munby, who records him 'talk[ing]

---

[133] [Wise], 'The Poetry of Provincialisms', p. 30.

[134] See Eileen Elder (ed.), *The Peacock Lincolnshire Word Books 1884–1920* (Scunthorpe: Scunthorpe Museum Society, 1997).

[135] Elder (ed.), *The Peacock Lincolnshire Word Books*; Robert Pacey (ed.), '*Yours Sincerely Mabel Peacock': Fragments of a Lincolnshire Friendship. Letters from Mabel Peacock to John Ostler Nicholson written between 1893 and 1915*, rev. ed. (Burgh le Marsh: Old Chapel Lane Books, 2001).

[136] See Ogilvie, *The Dictionary People*, pp. 326–8.

174   The Victorians and English Dialect

archaeology' and 'pouring out miscellaneous learning antiquarian and philosophical, talking Spinoza and Berkeley, reading Kingsley's poems aloud, reciting ballads of his own.'[137] And Peacock was another member of the English Dialect Society who was active as a regional novelist, publishing three novels in the early 1870s, and a fourth in 1891; the first two, *Ralf Skirlaugh, The Lincolnshire Squire* (1870) and *Mabel Heron* (1872) were set in his home county. Peacock, it has been suggested, had a strongly romantic strain in his antiquarian work; he was devoted to the works of Scott and looked back to earlier and (he believed) happier times when classes mixed together more freely and no-one 'despise[d] home-spun words.'[138] When Peacock's *Manley and Corringham Glossary* was first published in 1877, Nodal explained to Society members that it was 'composed of materials which he [i.e. Peacock] has been engaged in collecting for upwards of a quarter of a century.'[139] When the two-volume revised edition appeared in 1889, Nodal further explained that it was 'the first instance of the Society undertaking to put forth a second edition of one of its books.'[140] So the glossary was clearly flagged to members as a major work.

Information about Robert Holland (1829–93) is less readily forthcoming; he did not move in antiquarian circles in the way that Peacock (and Elworthy) did, and his publication trail is much sparser. His ancestors had farmed at Damhead in Mobberley, Cheshire, since the seventeenth century, and the 1871 census records Robert too as a farmer there (holding 135 acres and employing five men and one boy).[141] But Holland sold the Damhead estate in 1887, and later became a land agent in Frodsham.[142] He married twice, and had at least fourteen children. Various branches of the Holland family could be found throughout Cheshire, including Knutsford, and Robert Holland was a second cousin of Elizabeth Gaskell, whose mother's maiden name had been Holland.[143]

Robert Holland's first publication with the English Dialect Society had been the three-part *Dictionary of English Plant-Names* which he co-authored with James Britten (1846–1924), a member of the Department of Botany at the British Museum. They worked together on the project from 1868 to 1886—it pre-dated the foundation of the English Dialect Society—and made use of the familiar Victorian method of crowdsourcing material through public appeals ('The subject of Plant-names appeared to have created a wide-spread interest, and lists were sent to us from all parts of the kingdom').[144] Holland also published a volume on *Air Pollution as Affecting Plant Life* (1888), but he was not a prolific author, unlike some of the other

---

[137] Hudson, *Munby: Man of Two Worlds*, pp. 364–5.
[138] Elder (ed.), *The Peacock Lincolnshire Word Books*, p. 4.
[139] *English Dialect Society: Fifth Report*, p. 1.
[140] *English Dialect Society: Thirteenth Report*, p. 4.
[141] Information from *Ancestry* (www.ancestry.co.uk).
[142] Edgar Swinton Holland, *A History of the Family of Holland of Mobberley and Knutsford in the County of Chester*, ed. William Fergusson Irvine (Edinburgh: Ballantyne Press, 1902), pp. 47–8.
[143] Bernard Holland, *The Lancashire Hollands* (London: Murray, 1917), pp. 295, 299.
[144] James Britten and Robert Holland, *A Dictionary of English Plant-Names*, English Dialect Society 22, 26, 45 (London: English Dialect Society, 1886), p. x; *English Dialect Society: First Report*, p. 13.

The English Dialect Society **175**

antiquaries who populated the English Dialect Society; the *Cheshire Glossary* is his major single-authored work.

Frederic Thomas Elworthy (1830–1907), usually known as 'Fred', was the son of a wealthy woollen manufacturer in Somerset, and lived comfortably at his house, Foxdown, in Wellington, where he served as a magistrate and churchwarden, and pursued his linguistic and antiquarian interests.[145] In the 1870s, through the Philological Society, he became a close friend of James Murray, and over the years he gave Murray invaluable support in his travails as *OED* editor; Murray's biographer characterizes the Somerset man as 'sensible, cheerful and sympathetic', and 'always a good influence'.[146] Elworthy also sub-edited part of the letter 'D' for the dictionary, and he and his family contributed over ten thousand quotations.[147] His connection with Murray arose via the Philological Society (of which Elworthy became a council member), on account of his work on Somerset dialect: in 1875 he presented a paper to the Society on 'The Dialect of West Somerset', which was subsequently published in its *Transactions* and then reprinted by the English Dialect Society as a self-standing pamphlet. The same happened with the next instalment in Elworthy's three-step study of his local dialect, his *Outline of the Grammar of the Dialect of West Somerset*, in 1876–7. But the third and largest step required another ten years to complete: *The West Somerset Word-Book*, which appeared in 1886 and which, at over nine hundred pages and 25 shillings, was both the longest book the English Dialect Society published and also the most expensive to non-subscribers. In the ten-year interim, Elworthy had also edited a trio of earlier Somerset and Devon texts, as part of an 1879 volume on *Specimens of English Dialects*.

Elworthy's more general observations on dialect, presented especially in his Philological Society papers, show independence and clarity of thinking; Henry Sweet thought that his publications demonstrated 'a fineness and accuracy of observation still rare among dialectologists'.[148] Yes, Elworthy acknowledged in 1875, the usual forces of education and mobility are causing the erosion of dialect, but 'this process is slow, and at present very far from complete'; moreover, if one attends to pronunciation rather than vocabulary, then, in Elworthy's view, 'the changes are far slower than those which are constantly going on in what we call received English itself'.[149] This conviction only deepened as Elworthy went on with his studies: 'our hereditary pronunciation will survive', he wrote a decade later, 'together with our grammatical peculiarities, long after board schools and newspapers have brought English as a written language to one dead level'.[150] As part of his evidence for the endurance of

---

[145] See T. W. Mayberry, 'Elworthy, Frederic Thomas (1830–1907)', in *Oxford Dictionary of National Biography* [www.oxforddnb].

[146] Murray, *Caught in the Web of Words*, pp. 77–8, 219–20, at p. 219; see also Ogilvie, *The Dictionary People*, pp. 75–81.

[147] Peter Gilliver, 'Appendix II: *OED* Personalia', in Lynda Mugglestone (ed.), *Lexicography and the OED: Pioneers in the Untrodden Forest* (Oxford: Oxford University Press, 2000), pp. 232–52, at p. 237.

[148] Sweet, *Collected Papers*, p. 97.

[149] Frederic Thomas Elworthy, *The Dialect of West Somerset*, English Dialect Society 7 (London: English Dialect Society, 1875), p. 4 (first published in *Transactions of the Philological Society* 1876, 197–217).

[150] Elworthy, *The West Somerset Word-Book*, pp. v–vi. See also Burton and Ruthven, in Barnes, *Poems in the Broad Form of the Dorset Dialect*, pp. lxii–lxiii.

176   The Victorians and English Dialect

regional phonology, Elworthy points out that new words continue to enter the dialect from outside, and are phonetically nativized in the process:

> We in our benighted regions have now *raa·ylroa·ŭds, tuul·igraamz,* and *traak·shun ee·njinz,* bringing with them new ideas and enlarged knowledge; but we do not find that the *au·p kuun·trĕe mai·n* who come with them are in sufficient number to make any impression upon local pronunciation; and we find, too, that the words which they import into the district are adopted as words, but with more or less different sounds attached to them.[151]

So Elworthy had a keen intelligence as well as fine powers of observation; these are innovative comments on dialect contact, the linguistic consequences of internal migration, and the processes operative in interdialectal borrowing.

In reviewing and comparing the English Dialect Society glossaries of these three men, we should begin descriptively with size and contents. The word list for Peacock's glossary (second edition) runs to 680 pages, Holland's to 426, and Elworthy's to 854 (the comparison is legitimate: all three glossaries have a similar, though not identical, *mise-en-page*; they were also all issued in instalments). The titles are also worth noting: Holland deliberately called his work *A Glossary of Words Used in the County of Chester*, and not *A Glossary of Cheshire Words*, because (he explained) 'I do not, for a moment, claim that all, or even the majority of the expressions I have collected, are absolutely peculiar to Cheshire [. . .] There are, in reality, very few words which belong exclusively to any county, and which are used nowhere else'.[152] This formulation was used very frequently by the English Dialect Society, dating right back to very first original glossary (*A Glossary of Words Used in Swaledale, Yorkshire*, 1873), and adopted by Peacock also (*A Glossary of Words Used in the Wapentakes of Manley and Corringham, Lincolnshire*). Although Elworthy's work is titled *The West Somerset Word-Book*, he shared the same perception as Holland, explaining that 'I have in no case considered whether a word was widely known, or peculiar to this district'.[153]

The best way both to gain an impression of the contents and flavour of these three glossaries, and also to facilitate comparison between them, is to quote a sample of entries from each. So here are the last five words from each glossary for words beginning with *bu-*, a sample that has been chosen more or less at random, except for the requirement that it should not contain multiple derivatives from the same root word.

What follows are the complete, unabridged entries, with unchanged abbreviations and typography. First, Peacock (second edition):

BUTTON UP, *v.*—To be silent.
BUTTRISE (but·ris).—A blacksmith's tool used for paring horses' feet before they are shod.

---

[151] Elworthy, *The Dialect of West Somerset*, p. 5.
[152] Holland, *Glossary of Words Used in the County of Chester*, p. iii.
[153] Elworthy, *The West Somerset Word-Book*, p. vii.

The English Dialect Society   177

BUTTS.—The ends of ridges in an open field which abutted on other ridges that were at right angles to them.

BUTTY-SHOP.—A shop where goods are given on account of wages.

BUZZARD-CLOCK.—A kind of beetle, a cockchafer.

> "Au 'eerd un a bummin' away loike a *buzzard-clock* ower my yeäd".—Tennyson, *Northern Farmer,* 18.[154]

Next, Holland:

BUTTY, *adv.* Conjointly.

> To go *butty* with one is to act conjointly.

BUTTYBREW, *s.* a social meeting at which each person pays for his own share of the drink. BREDBURY.

BUTTY-PIECE, *s.* a field belonging to two owners, but which is undivided by any fence.

BUY A FATHER, *idiom.* Hatting term. To give a shilling for beer as a treat to workpeople.

BUZZOCK, *s.* a donkey. RUNCORN.[155]

And finally, Elworthy:

BUTTON-STOCKINGS [buut·n stau·keenz], *sb.* Gaiters—either of cloth or leather; leggings. (Very com.)

BUTTONS [buut·nz], *sb.* 1. The flowers of the Feather-few (*q.v.*). *Pyrethum Parthenium.*

2. Senses; intellect. Very com. In the *phr.* He've a-got all his (her) *buttons.*

I never don't sim thick there boy 've a-got all his *buttons*—*i.e.* he is half-witted.

Sharp little maid—her 've a-got all her *buttons*, I'll warn her (warrant).

3. Sheep's droppings.

4. The burs of various plants; such as of *Clivers, Burdock, Thistles,* &c.

BUTTRACE, BUTTRESS [buut·rees]. A farrier's tool for paring horses' hoofs. It cuts like a chisel, but has a bent handle; it is used by pushing the instrument away from the operator, while the *parer* is drawn towards the user. *See* RACE-IRON.

> Boutoir, m., a Farrier's *buttress.—Cotgrave.*
>
> Boutoir (far.), *buttoris,* parer.—*Spiers.*
>
> A *buttrice* and pincers, a hammer and naile,
>
> An aperne and siszers for head and for taile.—*Tusser,* 17.

BUZZ [buuz], *v. i.* To fuss about; to run to and fro; to gossip; to be a busy-body.

[Uur·z au·vees u *buuz·een* ubuw·t waun plae·us ur nuudh·ur,] she is always buzzing about one place or another.

---

[154] Edward Peacock, *A Glossary of Words Used in the Wapentakes of Manley and Corringham, Lincolnshire,* 2nd ed., English Dialect Society 58, 59 (London: English Dialect Society, 1889), p. 85.

[155] Holland, *Glossary of Words Used in the County of Chester,* pp. 52–3.

178 The Victorians and English Dialect

BUZZNACKING [buuz·naak·een], *sb.* Same as *buzzing.* Heard sometimes in this district; common in South Devon.[156]

All three glossaries were published during the directorship of Nodal, but followed practices laid down by Skeat; and the first thing to note, even before we consider questions of content, is how the English Dialect Society did not impose a uniform template on its glossarists, either in terms of what an individual entry should look like or even what its typography should be. Phonetic information is given in round brackets in Peacock's glossary, in square brackets in Elworthy's. 'Substantive' (that is, noun) is abbreviated as 's.' in Holland, 'sb.' in Elworthy. Although headwords are given in capitals in all three glossaries, in Peacock's first edition (and in many other Society glossaries) they appear in bold. Policies on hyphenation may also be inconsistent. These are just presentational differences; we haven't yet considered questions of content.

Of the words sampled here, there is only one case of overlap: *buttrise/buttrace/buttress* occurs in both Peacock and Elworthy. The fifteen words include vocabulary drawn from farming (*buttons* sense 3, *butts*, *butty-piece*, and perhaps *buzzock*), craft and manufacture (*buttrise/buttrace/buttress*, and *buy a father*), the natural world (*buttons* senses 1 and 4, and *buzzard-clock*), and human behaviour and sociability (*buttons* sense 2, *buttybrew*, *buy a father* again, *buzz*, and *buzznacking*). Peacock's *butty-shop*, Holland's *butty*, and Elworthy's *button-stockings* are perhaps the words least able to be fitted into general patterns, at least in such a small sample. In our fifteen words, there are eleven nouns, three verbs, and one adverb.

This therefore raises the question of how much grammatical information the three glossarists give. Peacock gives the least: he signals that *button up* is a verb, but leaves nouns (substantives) unmarked. Holland labels all his words (though he categorizes *buy a father* as an 'idiom' rather than a verb), and so does Elworthy, except for *buttrace/buttress* (perhaps an oversight). All three of these glossaries have prefaces or introductions of varying lengths, but none of these introductions includes a specific section on grammar (as some other English Dialect Society glossaries do, such as the *Holderness Glossary* which we examined in the Introduction). For Peacock and Holland, this seems to be on account of a relative lack of interest—for them, words are what is important—but for Elworthy, this is because he had already anatomized local grammar at great length in his 1877 *Outline of the Grammar of the Dialect of West Somerset.* This hundred-page analysis was consciously modelled on Murray's *Dialect of the Southern Counties of Scotland,* and Murray obliged by praising Elworthy's effort as 'the first grammar of an English dialect of any scientific value'.[157] Just like Murray, in his *Grammar* Elworthy dissects and tabulates West Somerset grammar according to formal parts of speech: nouns, adjectives, pronouns, verbs (at great length), adverbs, prepositions, conjunctions, and interjections. The treatment is exhaustive, and analogous to contemporary grammars of Latin, or of Old English. To give a sense

---

[156] Elworthy, *The West Somerset Word-Book*, pp. 105–6.
[157] Mayberry, 'Elworthy, Frederick Thomas'.

of the scale and rationale of this treatment: eight and a half pages are devoted to noun plurals, and Elworthy records the full system of West Somerset dialect, not simply the features in which the dialect diverges from Standard English (such as the basic pattern of plurals in *s*, *z*, and *ez*, and mutation plurals such as *tèo·dh* > *tai·dh* 'teeth' and *gèo·z* > *gee·z* 'geese'). But he is especially careful to point out distinctive features, such as nouns ending in *-lf* which form their plural with *-lfs* rather than *-lvs* (for example, *wuolfs*, not *wolves*), nouns which show double plurals (such as *bee·ŭstezez* 'beasts' and *vuy·stezez* 'fists'), and, finally, the curious fact that 'many diseases are spoken of only in the plural', such as *muul·igruubz* 'stomach-ache', *chaul·iwaubulz* 'diarrhoea', and, even worse, *wuy·ul skwuurts* 'excessive diarrhoea'.[158]

After grammatical information, in the glossary entries, comes the definition. All three glossarists supply compact, efficient definitions, though Elworthy, in keeping with his more exhaustive approach, also includes a Latin botanical gloss (*Pyrethum Parthenium*—contrast Peacock on *buzzard-clock*) and cross-references (to *feather-few* and *race-iron*). Elworthy alone, as in Murray's *OED*, subdivides an entry according to different senses (though should the various *buttons* perhaps be listed as separate words?), in contrast to Holland's practice, where it is not clear from his entry whether the hatting term *buy a father* is a different sense or not to the meaning 'to give a shilling for beer as a treat to workpeople'. Elworthy is also the only glossarist to give a frequency label (*button-stockings* is 'very com[mon]', he notes), but Holland's glossary is especially valuable for the manner in which it plots geographical distribution, tagging *buttybrew* as a word recorded in Bredbury and *buzzock* as coming from Runcorn (Elworthy combines frequency with geography in his information that *buzznacking* is 'heard sometimes in this district; common in South Devon').

The role of illustrative quotations in helping to communicate meaning is clearly important. Here again, Elworthy is the most thorough, though Peacock supplies a quotation from one of Tennyson's dialect poems to illustrate *buzzard-clock* (and elsewhere in his glossary, Peacock quotes his own novel, *Ralf Skirlaugh*). Holland simply offers a more circumlocutory definition to explain *butty*, but elsewhere in his glossary he does include snippets of local talk to act as illustrations—just as Elworthy does here, for *buttons* sense 2 and *buzz*. What Elworthy offers for *buttrace/buttress* is something different, though: not examples of contemporary speech, but rather a series of quotations from historical (printed) works: Cotgrave and Spiers were lexicographers (seventeenth- and nineteenth-century), and Thomas Tusser a sixteenth-century poet, whose *Five Hundred Pointes of Good Husbandrie* was reprinted by the English Dialect Society in 1878. This desire to quote older works in order to cast light on present-day dialect was, as we have seen, both a common practice in Victorian dialect study (as in the footnotes that William Gaskell added to his wife's *Mary Barton*) and also an exemplification of one of its fundamental perceptions—namely, that regional dialects often preserved older words and senses that had been lost from the standard

---

[158] Frederic Thomas Elworthy, *An Outline of the Grammar of the Dialect of West Somerset*, English Dialect Society 19 (London: English Dialect Society, 1877), pp. 4–13 (first published in *Transactions of the Philological Society* 1877–9, 143–257).

180 The Victorians and English Dialect

language. To cite older parallels was to demonstrate the antiquity (and, thus, venerability) of regional dialects, and the glossaries of the English Dialect Society are liberally sprinkled with quotations from medieval and early modern texts, many of them inserted by Skeat, who performed this service for glossarists without the necessary learning.[159]

But what we do not see in any of our fifteen sample entries, it may be noted, is an attempt to engage with etymology: nothing is said about where a word may have come from, or what its original form or derivation may have been. This absence, too, is the result of a deliberate policy on Skeat's part.

Richard Garnett had earlier opined that 'every glossarist is, *ex officio*, an etymologist', but Alexander Ellis took the opposite view, insisting that 'no one can be an etymologist if he is not also somewhat of a phonologist', and therefore 'it is really lamentable to read the etymologies in our provincial glossaries. They are no part of the glossary maker's business'.[160] Certainly, Skeat had striven hard to keep this impulse in check among contributors to the English Dialect Society (and we should remember that Skeat was the leading etymologist among the English philologists of his generation). The last sentence of his 1873 *Rules and Directions for Word-Collectors* declares: 'Etymologies are best avoided'.[161] This uncompromising assertion was then glossed, and justified, at greater length in his first annual report:

> Why, in the "Rules", do we say that "etymology" is not desired? Is it meant that etymology is to be ignored? Not so, but it may as well be left to a later period, as it can always be supplied afterwards, and it forms no real part of a word-collector's duty. The worst of etymology is, that it enables a word-collector to evade his real work; he speculates upon the word till he forgets to say what he *practically* knows about it, and even (as is common) allows the supposed etymology to distort his definition of the meaning. Yet he, and only he, can supply the true sense, the true use, the exact locality, the statements as to whether it is common or uncommon, as to what class of people use it, and the like practical details which form the only true scientific basis for study. Really good and faithful observers may thus do work which is humbler in appearance, but nobler and more unselfish in reality. They contribute sound knowledge in place of brilliant speculation, and it is to such word-collectors that we are most thankful.[162]

All three glossarists being examined here comply closely, if not invariably, with Skeat's recommendation: Holland, for instance, informs his readers in his preface that 'I have, throughout the Glossary, carefully abstained from derivations', and Elworthy is similarly relieved that 'upon the slippery slope of etymology I have been

---

[159] See, for example, Ross, Stead, and Holderness, *Glossary of Words Used in Holderness*, p. iv; Chamberlain, *Glossary of West Worcestershire Words*, p. xii; *English Dialect Society: Eleventh Annual Report*, p. 2.

[160] Garnett, *Philological Essays*, p. 54; Ellis, 'Eleventh Annual Address', p. 4, and 'First Annual Address', p. 20.

[161] [Skeat], *Rules and Directions for Word-Collectors*, p. 4.

[162] *English Dialect Society: First Report*, pp. 4–5; see also Skeat, 'Report on the English Dialect Society', p. 19.

careful not to tread'.[163] The temptation to speculate is fiercely repressed: Holland, to give one example, merely records the existence of the Macclesfield exclamation *filliloo*—'the meaning of which I am totally unable to explain'.[164]

Questions of phonetics have been left till last: for the English Dialect Society, these were both the most challenging and the most disputed of all the questions of method. In the samples from our three glossarists, we can see that Holland gives no phonetic information at all, and Peacock supplies the pronunciation for a single item (*buttrise*), whereas Elworthy provides phonetic transcriptions for every word, as an essential item of information; and he also writes some of his illustrative quotations in phonetic notation.

It is not an exaggeration to say that, at times, the mission of the English Dialect Society was marked by a tug-of-war between the phoneticians and the lexicologists, and that, on the whole, the lexicologists won—though this was as much on the grounds of expediency as principle. Leading the attack for the phoneticians—in a curiously defeatist way, however—was Alexander Ellis, supported by Henry Sweet. Ellis' view, as we saw in Chapter 2, was that phonetic study must be primary; but in him, this was combined with an aspersive conviction of the inadequacy of most regional workers, and his writings, like those of Sweet, are full of complaints on this score.

'Collecting country words is looked upon as an amusement', Ellis lamented, 'not as laying a brick in the temple of science; and, curiously enough, an accurate appreciation of their sounds is one of the last things thought of, and one which few glossarists give themselves any trouble about'.[165] And elsewhere: 'Let eni wun luok at our gloseriz and see hou impos·ibl it iz too komprihen·d dhem [Let any one look at our glossaries and see how impossible it is to comprehend them]'.[166] And again: 'Our clergy and their schoolmasters and educated men generally are so supremely ignorant of phonetics, and seem so incapable of beating any notion of it into their brains, that I have often been in utter despair'.[167] Such views were amply echoed by Sweet, dismissive of 'the wretched attempts at writing the sounds of our dialects made by educated men of the present day', and complaining (in 1884, when over forty English Dialect Society volumes had been published) that 'even our best dialectal work gives little more than a rough discrimination of the elementary sounds; sentence-stress, intonation, and, generally speaking, the higher phonetic analysis of our dialects are almost ignored'.[168] (Sweet also thought the Society should not spend its time reprinting old

---

[163] Holland, *Glossary of Words Used in the County of Chester*, p. vi; Elworthy, *The West Somerset Word-Book*, p. x.

[164] Holland, *Glossary of Words Used in the County of Chester*, p. 123; see, though, Wright (ed.), *English Dialect Dictionary*, II, 357.

[165] Ellis, *On Early English Pronunciation*, IV, 1087, n. 2.

[166] Ellis, 'On Glosik', p. 93.

[167] Ellis, 'Eleventh Annual Address', p. 27. See also Sanders, 'Alexander John Ellis', pp. 549–50.

[168] Sweet, *History of English Sounds*, p. 19, and *Collected Papers*, p. 50. See also H. C. Wyld, 'The Study of Living Popular Dialects and its Place in the Modern Science of Language', *Transactions of the Yorkshire Dialect Society* 6 (1904), 5–31, at pp. 21–5.

182 The Victorians and English Dialect

glossaries.[169]) One further lament is worth quoting at length, as this makes plain the hierarchical nature of Ellis' views, in which everyone should know their place (with himself, implicitly, at the top):

> Not only do dialectologists not know how to represent the sounds they hear, but they do not in general know the purpose for which words and idioms have to be collected [...] Word-collectors are not generally philosophic linguists. Their business is to hand over the materials in a trustworthy form, unadulterated with superficial and superfluous additions, containing what is wanted and *no more*, to those who *are* philosophic linguists. Perhaps when collectors review the hard work which the latter have to go through to reach probably a very moderate result, they may be induced to stay their "prentice han's". But this is not enough. They must be drilled into becoming real workers that can ease off the pressure on the architect who builds with their bricks, and into becoming good 'clerks of the works', to carry out that architect's conceptions.[170]

From one point of view, perhaps, this is not so different from Skeat's recommendations concerning etymology, but it has an astringency, and a sheep-and-goats division, which is not found in Skeat's writings; moreover, the convictions of Ellis and Sweet can give the impression that dialect-collection must attain Ellis-like standards of phonetic competence or else be deemed worthless.

Skeat took a different view. In his scholarship, he was, of course, fully conscious of the importance of phonetics; but he was also of the pre-Neogrammarian generation of philologists, and was inclined to take the word rather than the sound as his fundamental unit of analysis. He did not share Ellis' all-or-nothing conviction that the same notation had to be used by every collector: he was 'convinced that the difficulties of word-collecting have been greatly under-rated' in various ways, and endeavoured to steer a middle course, wishing to achieve the manageable rather than fail to attain the ideal.[171] So under Skeat's leadership, Ellis' Glossic was adopted as the notation of choice (rather than his more complex Palaeotype), and a copy of Ellis' pamphlet, *Varieties of English Pronunciation*, setting out the system, was sent to every Society member.[172] But although—to Ellis' delight—Skeat promoted the use of Glossic among the Society's collectors, he nonetheless allowed that 'if, after a fair trial, you cannot write down what you intend or do not know the correct sound, the only remaining plan is to leave a blank space after the word'; in other words, collections without phonetic representations were still of value to the Society.[173] This approach was continued under Nodal's leadership, with also, perhaps, an

---

[169] See Henry Sweet to J. H. Nodal 18 April 1884, Manchester, John Rylands Research Institute and Library, GB 133 JHN 1/117.

[170] Ellis, 'Third Annual Address', p. 450.

[171] Skeat, 'English Dialects', p. 385, and 'Report on the English Dialect Society', pp. 12–13; see also Murray, *Caught in the Web of Words*, pp. 84–6.

[172] Skeat, 'Preface', in Sweet, *History of English Sounds*, p. vii.

[173] [Skeat], *Rules and Directions for Word-Collectors*, pp. 1–2; Ellis, 'Tenth Annual Address', pp. 271–2.

The English Dialect Society **183**

added awareness of the multiple audiences the Society was catering for.[174] Further-more, Thomas Hallam was often on hand to lend his expertise as a sort of emergency phonetic taskforce, and we find him parachuting in with Glossic contributions to a number of the Society's glossaries, including Edith Chamberlain's *Glossary of West Worcestershire Words*.[175] But the Society's publications show great variability in their treatment of pronunciation, and in whether or not Ellis' Glossic system is used.

In the light of all this, we can return to the practice of our three glossarists. Even from a sample of only fifteen words, we can see that Holland gives the least fine-grained phonetic information. His preface is honest: 'With respect to the spelling of words', he writes, 'I have endeavoured, as far as possible, to represent the pronunci-ation phonetically; but as I have never mastered the glossic system of sounds, I have been obliged to give the words according to the usual recognized rules of English spelling'.[176] Peacock gives the Glossic form for one word—*buttrise*, presumably on the grounds that the pronunciation of the second syllable is ambiguous—but many pages of his glossary are free from phonetic notation. The introduction to his first (1877) edition says nothing whatsoever about pronunciation, except for a half-page footnote by Skeat, who is thanked by Peacock for having 'added the "glossic"' to a small number of words.[177] This note has disappeared from the second edition, though the 1889 introduction does contain some guidance (Glossic-free) on pronunciation; but Peacock's comments that, for example, 'the vowel sounds of many of the words are still in a fluent state' are not likely to have satisfied a dedicated phonetician.[178] But Elworthy, as we can see, is at the opposite end of the scale, scrupulously giving the Glossic form for every word, and including a 'Key to Glossic Spelling' at the start of his *Word-Book* (at the same time, though, like Holland and Peacock, he also has to devise an appropriate headword spelling in the standard alphabet for words hith-erto existing only orally: the Glossic *chaul·iwaubulz* or *chaul·iwaub·lz*, for instance, becomes *chollywabbles*).[179]

Elworthy had over a decade of phonetic study and expert guidance behind him by the time his *Word-Book* was published. His 1875 publication, *The Dialect of West Somerset*, forms the first, phonetic part of his tripartite scheme, and it contains a lib-eral quantity of notes inserted by Ellis, leaving no doubt as to whose is the guiding hand. The Glossic rendering in this 1875 work was the result of a mammoth session of pronunciation practice: Elworthy explained that 'having previously arranged the words in groups, each word was pronounced by me to Mr Ellis, often many times, in an examination extending over five days, and he assigned the vowels as well as he

---

[174] Sanders, 'Alexander John Ellis', p. 758.

[175] See Chamberlain, *Glossary of West Worcestershire Words*, pp. xix–xxiii.

[176] Holland, *Glossary of Words Used in the County of Chester*, p. iv. See also Sanders, 'Alexander John Ellis', pp. 443–4.

[177] Edward Peacock, *Glossary of Words Used in the Wapentakes of Manley and Corringham, Lincolnshire*, English Dialect Society 15 (London: English Dialect Society, 1877), p. iv.

[178] Peacock, *Glossary of Words Used in the Wapentakes of Manley and Corringham* (1889), p. xi. See, though, Ellis, *On Early English Pronunciation*, V, 1743–7/311–15.

[179] Elworthy, *The West Somerset Word-Book*, pp. xlvii–xlviii, 130.

184 The Victorians and English Dialect

could'.[180] But by the time of the second, grammatical publication of 1876–7, it is Murray who has become Elworthy's phonetic mentor and supplier of learned footnotes; and Murray, unlike Ellis, visited Somerset in Elworthy's company and 'studied the pronunciation on the spot'.[181]

A particular dilemma, as dialect collectors had recognized from at least the early nineteenth century, was what to do about words that differed from Standard English in punctuation alone. Should such words properly be regarded as dialectal? Should they be included in a glossary? If so, any word list would have to expand many times over, and more distinctive dialect words and senses would be buried in such a mass. 'It has been rather difficult to know to what extent the local pronunciation of ordinary English words should be admitted', Holland confessed. Inevitably, the solution had to be a fudge: 'There was no fixed rule possible, so I have used my judgment in these cases, by admitting words of which the pronunciation seemed to me to be sufficiently removed from the accepted pronunciation, omitting those in which the difference was slight'.[182] Many glossarists chose to give a separate section either at the beginning or end of their work, listing Standard English words with their dialect pronunciation (and with no further information, such as definition or illustration).[183] Elworthy's *Word-Book* ends with a twenty-page 'List of the common literary words, used in West Somerset, which are not pronounced by dialect speakers as in Standard English', and the contents of his earlier 1875 *Dialect of West Somerset* perform the same function (the days of the week, for example, run *Muun·dĕe, Chùe·zdĕe, Wai·nzdĕe, Dhuuz·dĕe, Vruy·dĕe, Zad·urdĕe, Zin·dĕe*).[184] Holland does not include such a list of common words, but he does offer an appendix on 'The Pronunciation of Place and Family Names'—with Glossic transcriptions supplied by Thomas Hallam (Cholmondeley and Cholmondeston, for instance, are *Chùm·li* and *Chuur·mstun*).[185]

Elworthy's *Word-Book* was issued in 1886, the final part of Holland's *Glossary* also in 1886, and the second edition of Peacock's *Glossary* in 1889. Elworthy wrote in his preface that 'the various workers of the [English] Dialect Society are of the greatest use to each other, by reason of their bringing the folk-speech of different localities into a sort of focus; and thus they suggest to an observer what he should look for in his own'.[186] But for how much longer should the English Dialect Society go on? In his annual report for 1874, Skeat had written that 'the work of the Society is now in full swing'; and he imagined that a period of ten years 'may see the most important part of our work done'.[187] Four years later, Nodal ventured that 'by a determined effort on

---

[180] Elworthy, *The Dialect of West Somerset*, p. 29. See also Ellis, *On Early English Pronunciation*, V, 1577–87/145–55; Sanders, 'Alexander John Ellis', p. 444.

[181] Elworthy, *Outline of the Grammar of the Dialect of West Somerset*, p. 3.

[182] Holland, *Glossary of Words Used in the County of Chester*, p. iv.

[183] See, for example, Ross, Stead, and Holderness, *Glossary of Words Used in Holderness*, pp. 12–16; Mrs [Angelina] Parker, 'Supplement to the Glossary of Words Used in Oxfordshire', in Walter W. Skeat (ed.), *Original Glossaries*, English Dialect Society 32 (London: English Dialect Society, 1881), pp. 65–104, at pp. 69–71; see also Skeat, 'Report on the English Dialect Society', p. 17.

[184] Elworthy, *The Dialect of West Somerset*, p. 48.

[185] Holland, *Glossary of Words Used in the County of Chester*, p. 429.

[186] Elworthy, *The West Somerset Word-Book*, p. v.

[187] *English Dialect Society: Second Report*, p. 7.

The English Dialect Society **185**

the part of the Society's workers it seems likely that the whole can be accomplished within the next four or five years', and in 1883 there was talk of wrapping up the Society in 1888, fifteen years after foundation.[188] But in 1888 it was reported that 'more manuscript is in the hands of the Society's printers than at any previous period'.[189] Nonetheless, the annual report the following year contained the announcement: 'It has now been arranged to bring the Society to a close in 1892', and this intention was repeated the following year.[190] The reason for this was that work on the long-anticipated 'General Dialect Dictionary' had now begun, using materials collected by the Society—as we will see in Chapter 6. So in January 1892, as the 1893 report explained, 'the Committee decided to take steps for the winding-up of the Society's work'.[191] However, what happened next was that 'numerous communications were received urging continuance on the ground that much good and available material remains unpublished and offers of other original glossaries were still being made'. Therefore, 'it was [. . .] decided to maintain the Society for a few years longer'.[192] But after a decade and a half of service, Nodal and Milner were ready to step down from their roles as Secretary and Treasurer. The same annual report—the last to be issued, in fact—also records the deaths of a number of members of the Society who had been giant figures in the world of dialect over the previous few decades: Alfred Tennyson, Alexander Ellis, Louis Lucien Bonaparte, and Lancashire's own Edwin Waugh.[193]

Having, in the words of R. O. Heslop, 'passed its maturity in the bracing air of the North', the Society was formally transferred from Manchester to Oxford, where the great dialect dictionary was being prepared.[194] And so the final annual general meeting to be held in Manchester took place on Monday, 12 June 1893, in the Central Free Library on King Street. It was an opportunity for thanks to be given to Nodal and Milner, and to Manchester more generally. Alderman Joseph Thompson, unavoidably absent, wrote to Nodal that 'it is not always given to us to be connected with a movement that has done so much good and so little harm as the E. D. S', and 'the credit is due to you [i.e. Nodal], the treasurer, and the zealous labourers in the philological vineyard'.[195] H. T. Crofton, presiding in the chair, expressed what perhaps others were feeling too, that 'personally he was rather sorry that the head-quarters of the Society were to be removed from Manchester'; the annual meetings, he said, 'had been as pleasant as any he had attended'.[196] Skeat, also absent, expressed his 'deep sense of the obligations which the Society is under to the long-continued and helpful services of the retiring Secretary and Treasurer', celebrated again how 'the kindly people of the City of Manchester came to our assistance at a difficult juncture', and singled

---

[188] *English Dialect Society: Sixth Report*, p. 13; *English Dialect Society: Tenth Annual Report*, pp. 4–5; see also Skeat, 'Report on the English Dialect Society', p. 19.

[189] *English Dialect Society: Fourteenth Report*, p. 2.

[190] *English Dialect Society: Fifteenth Report*, p. 2; *English Dialect Society: Sixteenth Report*, pp. 1–2.

[191] *English Dialect Society: Seventeenth Report*, p. 1.

[192] *English Dialect Society: Seventeenth Report*, pp. 1–2.

[193] *English Dialect Society: Seventeenth Report*, p. 3.

[194] R. Oliver Heslop, 'Dialect Notes from Northernmost England', *Transactions of the Yorkshire Dialect Society* 5 (1903), 7–31, at p. 30.

[195] *English Dialect Society: Seventeenth Report*, p. 7.

[196] *English Dialect Society: Seventeenth Report*, p. 8.

186   The Victorians and English Dialect

out Nodal in particular for 'his untiring energy in the performance of his unpaid yet onerous duties'.[197]

Nodal and Milner both made speeches in reply, and Milner's was especially full. It might be asked, he said, 'why the Society came to Manchester at all'. The reason was as follows:

> It came to the city because at that time there was in Lancashire and Manchester a greater interest displayed with regard to the study of dialects than there was in the University of Cambridge, where the Society was first carried on under the direction of Professor Skeat. Why then was the society going to Oxford? It was not because the interest in dialects had diminished in Lancashire and Manchester, but because that interest had increased in our English Universities. How much of the greater interest shown by the Universities in dialectal study was owing to the work of the Society it would be difficult to say.[198]

This was a modest way for Milner and Nodal to sign off from their leadership duties. But the clear implication of Milner's statement was that it was precisely because of the work of the English Dialect Society that the study of dialect, nation-wide, was in such a lively and coherent state, at the professional level as well as the amateur. Financed by regional enthusiasts, driven forward by local workers all over the country, and for most of its existence administered out of Manchester, the English Dialect Society had more than upheld the tradition of regional philology being a devolved and democratic pursuit, and not simply the preserve of a small number of scholars. In Milner's formulation, the universities were just beginning to catch up with what the provinces had already known.

---

[197] *English Dialect Society: Seventeenth Report*, p. 8.
[198] *English Dialect Society: Seventeenth Report*, p. 9.

5
Folklore and the Past

Histories of England

Victorian philology was a historically minded discipline. Not only did it devote itself to studying the languages of the past, it also studied the languages of the present for the purpose of understanding the past; and philological methods offered a unique and powerful tool for historical discovery. Richard Chenevix Trench believed that the history of England, social and political, could effectively be recovered from the English language alone: 'there are vast harvests of historic lore garnered often in single words', he wrote.[1] The present chapter will ask what historical discoveries Victorian philologists believed they could make from the scrutiny of regional dialect. What could dialect study reveal about England's past? What might it disclose about medieval culture, on either a regional or national scale? And what might it show more locally and socially about the lives, practices, and enduring beliefs of the speakers of dialect? In other words, what was the connection between regional philology and another new, Victorian field of study—folklore?

We will begin on the national scale. In a draft lecture or article on the value of 'the study of provincialisms', Thomas Hallam wrote that:

> An acquaintance with their etymology would effectually prevent a very great portion of the unwarrantable, <u>unlearned</u>, sarcastic, & scornful remarks which are made in reference to those speaking the provincial dialects, and therefore prevent a great deal of ill-feeling at present produced in society. I believe, there are many having a tolerable education, who think that these provincialisms are either mere vulgar corruptions of modern English, or so to speak mere barbarisms—words, &c. having no authority either historically or etymologically. But a proper investigation of the subject would show that they are quite mistaken—that a many of these provincialisms have an excellent etymology—are veritable relics of antiquity—have been handed down thro' bygone centuries from the Anglo-Saxon, Danish, or British periods. When viewed in this light the cause for sarcastic criticism entirely vanishes.[2]

As we saw in Chapter 1, the dignity and value of regional dialect was massively boosted by the historical demonstration that many dialect words were ancient and

---

[1] Trench, *On the Study of Words*, p. 49.
[2] Oxford, Bodleian Libraries, MS Eng. lang. d. 22, fol. 64. See also Drury, 'Aural Community and William Barnes as Earwitness', pp. 443–4.

The Victorians and English Dialect. Matthew Townend, Oxford University Press. © Matthew Townend (2024).
DOI: 10.1093/oso/9780198888123.003.0006

188   The Victorians and English Dialect

venerable—'*old* English rather than *bad* English', in Trench's phrase.[3] Trench also recognized the hybrid nature of contemporary English, and the importance of the changes brought about by the contact between speakers (or readers) of English and speakers (or texts) of other languages—through migration, learning, conquest, and empire. 'No language has shown itself less exclusive', Trench insisted, 'none has thrown open its arms wider'.[4]

This was a common conviction. 'Our mixed descent is embodied in our provincialisms', J. R. Wise wrote in 1865, and James Britten and Robert Holland believed they could track the successive impact of Britons, Saxons, and Danes on the naming of English plants.[5] When the Manchester professor Thomas Northcote Toller addressed the AGM of the English Dialect Society in 1884, he told his audience that:

> Owing to the successive waves of immigration and conquest there was a greater variety of dialect in the United Kingdom than in some other countries, and it was nowhere stronger than in this district and the north of England generally, where they were not afraid of expending some lung-power upon their words.[6]

So what might the 'old words' of the English dialects reveal about the history of contact and settlement?

The Anglo-Saxon element in regional speech was central and foundational; the dialects of the nineteenth century could not be understood without a sound knowledge of Old English. As we saw in Chapter 1, John Yonge Akerman and (especially) William Barnes were in the vanguard of this Saxonizing dialectology, and Barnes' 1844 'Dissertation on the Dorset Dialect of the English Language' in many ways represents its apogee as well. Barnes' 'Dissertation' opens with an extended account of the region's history in the Anglo-Saxon period, and then makes every effort to correlate the linguistic forms of the contemporary dialect with those of Old English. There is no need to repeat the arguments and examples given in the earlier chapter; it is sufficient to restate that the evidence was indisputable, and the consequences profound, in the demonstration of the Anglo-Saxon provenance of English regional dialects.

As Fred Elworthy remarked, the resemblance between Old English and modern dialect was not solely a question of vocabulary, but also of phonology and grammar:

> A comparison of our present dialectal pronunciation of many literary words with their forms in Early and Middle English, will prove how very slow phonetic changes have been in the past, at least in the spoken language of the people. The same holds good [. . .] with respect to many forms of grammar and syntax which have long become obsolete in literature.[7]

---

[3] Trench, *English Past and Present*, p. 84.
[4] Trench, *English Past and Present*, p. 45.
[5] [Wise], 'The Poetry of Provincialisms', p. 30; Britten and Holland, *Dictionary of English Plant-Names*, pp. xiv–xv.
[6] *English Dialect Society: Eleventh Annual Report*, p. 12.
[7] Elworthy, *The West Somerset Word-Book*, p. vi.

A few supplementary examples will help to make this case. In his 1844 'Dissertation', Barnes points out the absence of the personal pronoun *him* from western dialect:

> The accusative case of *he* [in Dorset dialect] is *en* not *him*, the Anglo-Saxon *hine*. 'He aærde hine up'. 'He raised him up'.[8]

So Dorset *en* is not a 'vulgar corruption' of Modern English *him*, as might ignorantly have been supposed; rather, it has a different genealogy, and descends from the Old English masculine accusative singular pronoun *hine* (as demonstrated by Barnes' Old English example). Standard English (and other regional dialects) had gone one way in the post-Conquest period, generalizing the Old English dative *him* as the object form of the masculine pronoun; western dialects had gone the other way, generalizing the accusative *hine*. It was only the study of Old English which revealed this, and which validated the western form as a 'relic of antiquity' and not a 'corruption'.

Barnes' insistence on this point of grammar was supported by later dialect workers. G. P. R. Pulman, of the 'Axe-Yarty district', includes *en* in the glossary to his *Rustic Sketches*, citing the Old English etymology: yet another piece of evidence that, as he puts it in his introduction, 'the great root of nearly all our provincial dialects [. . .] is the Saxon language', and that 'the "uncouth" and "vulgar" phraseology (as "gentility" sometimes calls it) of those who lead their toilful lives "remote from towns", are the remains of the tongue which Alfred spoke'.[9] Alexander Ellis, in *The Existing Phonology of English Dialects*, acclaims *en* for *him* as a 'remarkable survival'.[10] And Elworthy gives a characteristically precise analysis, with an etymological footnote added by James Murray.[11] Personal pronouns were always a good hunting ground for dialectologists, and the humble monosyllable *en* was revelatory. Similar revelations could be found in other footnotes that Murray supplied to Elworthy's *Outline of the Grammar of the Dialect of West Somerset*: for example, 'It is interesting to find *tho* ["then"] still existing in the Old West-Saxon land. From Northern English it disappeared eight centuries ago'; or 'The accentuation of wassail, taking us back to the Anglo-Saxon wæs hæl! is very interesting, and doubtless, embodies a genuine tradition'.[12] The claims for antiquity should not be elevated to an absolute principle, though, and Elworthy's *Outline* also records features where Somerset grammar is, in fact, less conservative than Standard English: for instance, as Elworthy and Murray note, although in its verb system Somerset dialect has preserved the prefix *a-* on past participles (from Old English *ge-*), it has also seen the loss of almost all so-called strong verbs, unlike Standard English (as seen in such past tense forms as *vaa·l(d* and *zing(d*, compared to Standard English—and Old English—*fell* and *sang*).[13]

---

[8] Barnes, *Poems in the Broad Form of the Dorset Dialect*, p. 13.
[9] Pulman, *Rustic Sketches*, pp. v, vi, 65.
[10] Ellis, *On Early English Pronunciation*, V, 1475/43.
[11] Elworthy, *Outline of the Grammar of the Dialect of West Somerset*, pp. 33, 37, 39 n. 2, and *The West Somerset Word-Book*, p. 232.
[12] Elworthy, *Outline of the Grammar of the Dialect of West Somerset*, pp. 86–7 n. 1, 100 n. 1.
[13] Elworthy, *Outline of the Grammar of the Dialect of West Somerset*, pp. 43–9.

190   The Victorians and English Dialect

Improbable as it may seem, a proper understanding of Old English grammar could be one tool in the sincere championing of marginalized or belittled communities, as in the work of Barnes and Pulman; and the cultural or political meaning of Old English could be geographically dependent. To return again to Toller's speech to the English Dialect Society in Manchester:

> A phrase that might still be heard in Lancashire was, "Sithee lad", but it had dropped out of the book language, and was heard in the streets only. Yet only a few days ago, when examining a translation of the Psalms made before the Conquest, he [i.e. Toller] noticed that the educated Churchman who had glossed them invariably translated *Ecce* by *Sehthe*—the very word a Manchester lad might still be heard using in conversation with his playmates.[14]

This observation elicited 'Applause' from his listeners: Toller knew how to spot connections between Old English and modern dialect in a manner that was contextually meaningful.

The account given so far may suggest that the beneficial relations between Old English and modern dialects primarily went in one direction—that is, that the understanding of modern dialects gained enormously from the advancing knowledge of Old English in the nineteenth century. But there were effects in the opposite direction as well. For one thing, awareness of modern dialect differences served to sharpen the question of whether or not the Anglo-Saxon period was also marked by dialectal diversity. It would seem unlikely that the evolution of modern dialect differences should be wholly a post-medieval phenomenon; what was the evidence for different dialects in medieval English?

This question was pursued for both Old and Middle English; and in effect, the determining of dialect differences in medieval England and in modern England was one and the same investigation, often undertaken by the same scholars. The antiquarian Thomas Wright, in his 1857 *Dictionary of Obsolete and Provincial English*, had explained modern differences as being long-standing inheritances:

> There can be no doubt that the peculiar characteristics, or, we may say, the organic differences of dialect, are derived more or less from a diversity of tribe among the Anglo-Saxon settlers in our island; for, as far as our materials allow us to go, we can trace these diversities in Anglo-Saxon times.[15]

On the whole, the more expert philologists who followed him were inclined to agree. Ellis' view was that 'the Saxon and Danish tribes which came to our shores of course already spoke dialectally', and J. G. Goodchild thought that 'the various dialects of the Angles [. . .] were probably as diverse in their day as are the dialects of the

---

[14] *English Dialect Society: Eleventh Annual Report*, p. 12.
[15] Wright, *Dictionary of Obsolete and Provincial English*, p. v.

parts the Angles came from diverse at the present day'.[16] Important studies of Old English dialects were made by Henry Sweet and H. M. Chadwick, Skeat's successor as Professor of Anglo-Saxon at Cambridge.[17]

The scholarly value of studying modern dialects at the same time as medieval ones was proved even more strongly for the Middle English (post-Conquest) period, especially in the work of the Rev. Richard Morris (1833–94). Largely self-educated (his own father was a hatter and his wife's father a coachman), Morris was for most of his life a schoolteacher, and in the 1860s and 1870s, in a series of editions for the Early English Text Society, he advanced the knowledge of Middle English dialects more than any other scholar working at the time.[18] One of the texts that Morris was engaged in editing was the *Cursor Mundi* (*The Runner of the World*), a massive poem that narrates the Christian history of the world over nearly thirty thousand lines; in the end, the edition required no fewer than seven volumes from the Early English Text Society (1879–93) and it proved a treasure trove for the makers of the *OED*: one contributor sent in over forty thousand different slips from the poem, and eventually it became the second-most cited work in the *Dictionary* after the Bible.[19] In 1874, Morris became President of the Philological Society (succeeding Ellis and preceding Sweet), and in his 1876 address he spent some time demonstrating the mutual relations between medieval and regional philology; this section of his address was reprinted by the English Dialect Society under the title *On the Survival of Early English Words in our Present Dialects*. Drawing his evidence mostly from the English Dialect Society glossaries published to date, Morris explains that 'numerous words in our dialects belong to a former period, and render them more archaic than the standard English [. . .] This archaic character makes all provincial glossaries very helpful to students of our earlier literature'.[20] The *Cursor Mundi* supplies several examples:

> In the Cursor Mundi we meet with the phrase '*throd* and thriven'. The North-country dialects alone explain it by their use of *throdden*, to thrive, grow; *throddy*, plump; cf. Icelandic *þróask*, to wax, grow.[21]

Morris is easily able to supply many more examples in which 'dialects alone explain it'.

---

[16] Ellis, *On Early English Pronunciation*, IV, 1318; Goodchild, 'Traditional Names of Places in Edenside', p. 51.

[17] Sweet, *Collected Papers*, pp. 185–211; H. M. Chadwick, 'Studies in Old English', *Transactions of the Cambridge Philological Society* 4.2 (1899), 85–265. See further Richard Dance, 'H. M. Chadwick and Old English Philology', in Michael Lapidge (ed.), *H. M. Chadwick and the Study of Anglo-Saxon, Norse and Celtic in Cambridge*, Cambrian Medieval Celtic Studies 69/70 (Aberystwyth: Department of Welsh, Aberystwyth University, 2015), pp. 83–97.

[18] See J. S. Cotton, 'Morris, Richard (1833–1894)', rev. John D. Haigh, in *Oxford Dictionary of National Biography* [www.oxforddnb].

[19] Charlotte Brewer, '*OED* Sources', in Lynda Mugglestone (ed.), *Lexicography and the OED: Pioneers in the Untrodden Forest* (Oxford: Oxford University Press, 2000), pp. 40–58, at pp. 46–7; Gilliver, *The Making of the Oxford English Dictionary*, p. 201.

[20] Morris, *On the Survival of Early English Words in our Present Dialects*, pp. 7–8.

[21] Morris, *On the Survival of Early English Words in our Present Dialects*, p. 9.

192 The Victorians and English Dialect

Other scholars had the same experience, of modern dialects supplying the key to understanding medieval vocabulary. A speech by Joseph Hall, headmaster of Hulme Grammar School in Oldham and an editor of Middle English texts, was relayed in the English Dialect Society annual report for 1884:

> The interest in dialect work was sure to increase as time goes on, especially in connection with the study of Old and Middle English. He thought this had not been worked out in any way hitherto, and the explanation of Middle English words, particularly in old books, which puzzled people at present, would be found largely in dialectal words.[22]

So, for example, the baffling form *hrinde* in *Beowulf* line 1363, applied to the trees at Grendel's mere, was emended to *hrimge* ('rimy') by late nineteenth-century editors until Elizabeth Mary Wright pointed out that modern northern dialects preserve a word *rindy* ('frosty'), surely the same word—a helping lexical hand, as it were, stretched back from contemporary dialect over almost a thousand years to make sense of the unique text of *Beowulf*.[23] For Middle English, J. R. Wise had written that 'the phrases of our old poets now linger only in the mouths of our peasants. The echo of Piers Plowman's voice still rings not so very far from his own Malvern Hills', and Skeat's editorial labours on the many manuscripts of Langland's poem were informed by his dialect studies, just as his dialect studies were informed by his editing of *Piers*.[24] As a result, references to *Piers Plowman* crop up in unexpected places in English Dialect Society glossaries, inserted by Skeat for mutual illumination between medieval and modern.[25] Skeat's Chaucerian learning also protrudes in such glossaries: readers of the *Holderness Glossary*, for example, looking up the word *sconce* ('a subterfuge; a pretext'), might have been surprised to find a note stating that 'Chaucer makes use of the expression *ascaunce* in the same sense, which is explained by the Rev. W. W. Skeat, in the Glos[sary] to the *Man of Lawes Tale*, Clar[endon] Press edition, and nowhere else'.[26] The abundant evidence of contemporary dialect could also aid in the localization of medieval texts: scholars of Yorkshire literature were hopeful that modern dialect forms could serve to confirm (or disprove) the attribution of the 'Towneley Plays' to Wakefield, while on the other side of the Pennines the localization of *Sir Gawain and the Green*

---

[22] *English Dialect Society: Twelfth Annual Report*, p. 10.

[23] See Elizabeth Mary Wright, 'Bêowulf l. 1363: *ofer þæm hongiað hrinde bearwas*', *Englische Studien* 30 (1901), 341–3; Wright (ed.), *English Dialect Dictionary*, V, 116; Skeat, *English Dialects*, pp. 7–9; Wright, *Rustic Speech and Folk-Lore*, pp. 67–8; R. D. Fulk, Robert E. Bjork and John D. Niles (eds), *Klaeber's Beowulf* (Toronto: University of Toronto Press, 2008), p. 399.

[24] [Wise], 'The Poetry of Provincialisms', p. 39; Brewer, *Editing Piers Plowman*, pp. 152–5, 173–4, 327.

[25] See, for example, C. Clough Robinson, *A Glossary of Words Pertaining to the Dialect of Mid-Yorkshire*, English Dialect Society 14 (London: English Dialect Society, 1876), p. 115; Peacock, *Glossary of Words Used in the Wapentakes of Manley and Corringham* (1877), p. 95; Edward Sutton, 'North Lincolnshire Words', in Walter W. Skeat (ed.), *Original Glossaries*, English Dialect Society 32 (London: English Dialect Society, 1881), pp. 113–22, at p. 117.

[26] Ross, Stead, and Holderness, *Glossary of Words Used in Holderness*, p. 119. See also, for example, Robinson, *Glossary of Words Pertaining to the Dialect of Mid-Yorkshire*, pp. 39, 63, 131.

Knight (for which Morris produced the standard nineteenth-century edition) was from the beginning tied up with questions of dialect vocabulary.[27]

It was natural, also, that early modern literature, and the works of Shakespeare in particular, should be drawn into such dialectal discussions. Many of the English philologists of the nineteenth century, not least F. J. Furnivall and Alexander Ellis, were ardent Shakespeareans, and did not see an abrupt break between medieval and Renaissance scholarship. Could dialect study make a contribution to the understanding of Shakespeare's language or biography? In 1859, Thomas Wright and James Orchard Halliwell produced a revised edition of Robert Nares' 1822 glossary of early modern literature, and two years later J. R. Wise published *Shakspere: His Birthplace and Its Neighbourhood*, an investigation that includes a chapter on 'The Provincialisms of Shakspere' as well as a 'Glossary of Words still used in Warwickshire to be found in Shakspere'.[28] Wise's argument is that Shakespeare's vocabulary and phraseology are 'still to be heard in the mouths of the Warwickshire peasantry, who now more than anybody else, "Speak the tongue / That Shakespeare spake"'; in other words, contemporary dialect now offered the most immediate access to Shakespeare's own language.[29] Among the examples that Wise proffers are *boltered* 'clotted, caked' (as in *blood-boltered*, in *Macbeth* IV.1), *claw* 'to flatter' (in *Love's Labours Lost* IV.2), and *deck* with the sense 'a hand of cards', rather than 'a pack' (in *Henry VI* V.1).[30] Other philologists followed the same path. James Murray gave a paper to the Philological Society which 'illustrated Shakspere's usages from modern dialects', and a number of his footnotes to Elworthy's grammatical *Outline* draw attention to parallels between Somerset dialect and Shakespeare's English.[31] Thomas Hardy made notes on the dialect forms which he encountered when reading Shakespeare.[32] And in his 1876 presidential address, Richard Morris declared confidently that 'many of Shakespeare's words may be explained by a reference to provincial glossaries'.[33] One such glossary was Isabella Francis' collection of *South Warwickshire Provincialisms* (1876), published by the English Dialect Society: Skeat introduced the work by noting that nearly all of Francis' words were 'collected in the village of Tysoe, near Kineton, and possess considerable interest from the fact that this village is only some fifteen miles from Stratford-upon-Avon'.[34] The trend continued: in the Edwardian period,

---

[27] See Skeat and Nodal, *Bibliographical List*, pp. 110–11; Richard Dance, *Words Derived from Old Norse in Sir Gawain and the Green Knight: An Etymological Survey*, Publications of the Philological Society 50, 2 vols (Oxford: Philological Society, 2018), I, 9–24, 54–63.

[28] Robert Nares, *A Glossary; or, Collection of Words, Phrases, Names, and Allusions to Customs, Proverbs, Etc, which have been thought to require illustration, in the works of English authors, particularly Shakespeare and his contemporaries*, new ed., rev. James O. Halliwell and Thomas Wright, 2 vols (London: Smith, 1859), and see Hultin, '"To Shine with Borrowed Splendour"', pp. 131–2; John R. Wise, *Shakspere: His Birthplace and Its Neighbourhood* (London: Smith, Elder, and Co., 1861), pp. 103–15, 149–58.

[29] Wise, *Shakspere*, p. 104; see also 'The Poetry of Provincialisms', p. 31.

[30] Wise, *Shakspere*, pp. 105, 113, 151.

[31] Ellis, 'Second Annual Address', p. 210; Elworthy, *Outline of the Grammar of the Dialect of West Somerset*, pp. 39 n. 2, 83 n.1, 90 n.1.

[32] Taylor, *Hardy's Literary Language and Victorian Philology*, p. 164.

[33] Morris, *On the Survival of Early English Words in our Present Dialects*, p. 11.

[34] Walter W. Skeat (ed.), *Original Glossaries*, English Dialect Society 12 (London: English Dialect Society, 1876), p. 122. See also G. F. Northall, *A Warwickshire Word-Book, Comprising Obsolescent and Dialect*

194   The Victorians and English Dialect

C. T. Onions, about to become the fourth editor of the *Oxford English Dictionary*, published his *Shakespeare Glossary* in 1911, and Elizabeth Mary Wright gave a compact analysis in her 1913 book, *Rustic Speech and Folk-Lore* (declaring, like Morris, that 'most of the obsolete Shakespearian words can still be traced in the dialects').[35] Such scholars were not, on the whole, arguing that words found in Shakespeare were unique to Warwickshire—dialect collectors were well aware that many words were found widely—but they did insist on the value of modern dialects for explicating early Modern English, since regional dialects retained words and senses that had been lost from Standard English.

In *Rustic Speech and Folk-Lore*, Elizabeth Mary Wright characterized the Old English element in English regional dialects as their 'backbone'.[36] But the context in which Wright made this statement is highly important. 'We have often been told', she writes, 'or we have read in newspaper reviews and suchlike works, that the rustic vernacular is indigenous to the soil, mostly raw material in the rough, but entirely a native product'. There is a degree of truth in this, she acknowledges, as she points to the Old English element. But she continues, significantly: 'when we examine the whole [dialect] vocabulary in detail, we find it contains a very considerable admixture of foreign elements'—especially loanwords from French and Old Norse. Skeat made similar comments in his 1912 textbook, *English Dialects*: 'There is a widely prevalent notion that the speakers of English Dialects employ none but native words', he remarked, before proceeding to dispel this myth with a chapter, like Wright, on 'Foreign Elements in the Dialects'.[37]

In particular, the significant French element in English dialects, Skeat complained, had been 'almost invariably overlooked'.[38] Both Skeat and Wright give long lists of French-derived dialect terms, drawn from a variety of regions, such as *arain* 'a spider', *asprous* 'raw, inclement', *boco* 'a large quantity, principally of fish' (from *beaucoup*), *fammel* 'to starve, famish', *goo* 'taste, relish', *jigget* 'to ride or walk at a jog-trot, to shake, to dance up and down', *keev* 'a large tub', *parl(e)* 'to talk, converse', and *urchin* 'hedgehog'.[39] The point being made by Skeat and Wright is clear: the study of regional dialect, although it may have been founded on the knowledge of Old English, also involved an engagement with the French element in the English vocabulary: it did not stand apart from it, as some sort of native resistance.

Words, Colloquialisms, Etc., Gathered from Oral Relation, and Collated with Accordant Works, English Dialect Society 79 (London: English Dialect Society, 1896).

[35] See C. T. Onions, *A Shakespeare Glossary* (Oxford: Clarendon Press, 1911), p. iv; Wright, *Rustic Speech and Folk-Lore*, pp. 54–61, at p. 54. See now, for example, David Kathman, 'Shakespeare and Warwickshire', in Paul Edmondson and Stanley Wells (eds), *Shakespeare Beyond Doubt: Evidence, Argument, Controversy* (Cambridge: Cambridge University Press, 2013), pp. 121–32; Rosalind Barber, 'Shakespeare and Warwickshire Dialect', *Journal of Early Modern Studies* 5 (2016), 91–118; Manfred Markus, 'The Survival of Shakespeare's Language in English Dialects (on the Basis of *EDD Online*)', *English Studies* 98 (2017), 881–96.

[36] Wright, *Rustic Speech and Folk-Lore*, p. 96.

[37] Skeat, *English Dialects*, p. 82.

[38] Skeat, *English Dialects*, p. 94.

[39] Wright, *Rustic Speech and Folk-Lore*, pp. 96–101; see also Skeat, *English Dialects*, pp. 93–8.

Folklore and the Past   **195**

In any case, earlier dialectologists had perhaps not overlooked the French element quite as much as Skeat suggested. Anna Gurney, back in the 1850s, had been struck by the Norfolk use of *woash*, a wagoner's call, 'to make his horses turn off', and proposed a derivation from the French *gauche* 'left'.[40] Britten and Holland had no difficulty in demonstrating French influence on plant names: not only obvious national terms such as *dandelion*, but also local instances such as *framboys*, 'an old Dorsetshire name for the raspberry'.[41] And Fred Elworthy, in his *West Somerset Word-Book*, sometimes allows himself to comment on etymology when it is a French-derived word that is at stake: examples cited include *summer* 'a horizontal beam or joist' (from French *sommier*), used as a technical term for 'the longitudinal parts of the bottom of a wagon' and 'the large beam on the top of a cider-press', the verb *versy* 'to read out of the Bible verses in turn' (from *verseiller*), and the striking word *hogo* 'stink, strong smell', which Elworthy derives from French *haut gout*.[42]

Again, phonology was important as well as vocabulary. For William Barnes, multilingual awareness could explain apparent irregularities in local pronunciation. One of the most familiar patterns was the presence of initial *v* in Dorset dialect where Standard English had *f*: *veed* against *feed*, *vetch* against *fetch*, and so on. But, Barnes notes, 'the Dorset does not hold V for F in words that are brought in from other and not Teutonic languages. We must say *Factory, false, family, famine, figure*, in Dorset, as well as in English'.[43] Elworthy thought the same for Somerset, distinguishing *vuy·ul* 'a rasp' (from Old English *feol*) from *fuy·ul* 'bills' (from French *file*), and James Murray observed similar patterns in southern Scotland.[44] Elworthy also believed that French loans in dialect often remained closer to the original pronunciation than the Standard English forms, citing Somerset *júlau·fur* 'gilliflower' (from French *giroflée*) and *mau·njur* 'manger' (from French *mangeoire*).[45] The latter receives an unusually full note: 'This is a good example of the conservatism of dialectal pronunciation', Elworthy writes, 'as well as a link in the chain of evidence of the direct importation of Norm[an] Fr[ench] words into this part of England, probably by or through the retainers of the Norman barons'. Other scholars were similarly attentive to the phonology of French-derived words. Nearly twenty per cent of the words in Alexander Ellis' Classified Word List for which pronunciation needed to be elicited for *The Existing Phonology*, were labelled 'Romance'; he wasn't just in search of Old English words.[46] Skeat's own daughter Bertha (1861–1948), later a headmistress, published with the English Dialect Society an 1884 tract entitled *A Word-List Illustrating the Correspondence of Modern English with Anglo-French Vowel-Sounds*. And

---

[40] Gurney, 'Norfolk Words', p. 38.

[41] Britten and Holland, *Dictionary of English Plant-Names*, pp. xv, 193.

[42] Elworthy, *The West Somerset Word-Book*, pp. 345, 727, 801.

[43] Barnes, *Glossary of the Dorset Dialect*, p. 8.

[44] Elworthy, *The West Somerset Word-Book*, pp. ix, 253; Murray, *The Dialects of the Southern Counties of Scotland*, p. 141.

[45] Elworthy, *The West Somerset Word-Book*, pp. x, 285, 466.

[46] Ellis, *On Early English Pronunciation*, V, 23*–24*.

196 The Victorians and English Dialect

Skeat himself thought that 'there is no greater literary disgrace to England than the fact that there is no reasonable dictionary in existence of Anglo-French'.[47]

The quest for the Celtic element in English dialects was more frustrating. Skeat and Elizabeth Mary Wright, in their end-of-the-period overviews, both manage to give a list of likely candidates for words borrowed out of Celtic into the English dialects, but the material is thinner than for other strata of language, and Wright's tone is almost apologetic: 'the number of Celtic words in the English dialects is relatively small', she writes, 'even if under the common term Celtic we group together Gaelic, Welsh, and Old Cornish words'.[48] Skeat further explains that while, until recently, 'it was very easy to give a wild guess that an obscure word was "Celtic"', those unsystematic old days are now past, and moreover: 'The fact is that there is no such language as "Celtic"; it is the name of a group of languages, including "British" or Welsh, Cornish, Breton, Manx, Gaelic, and Irish; and it is now incumbent on the etymologist to cite the exact forms in one or more of these on which he relies, so as to adduce some semblance of proof'. The result of such philological method, needless to say, was 'an extraordinary shrinkage in the number of alleged Celtic words'.[49] Among the items advanced by Skeat and Wright are *bannock* 'an oat or barley cake', *brock* 'a badger', *combe* 'the head of a valley', and *galore* 'in abundance'; but it is hard to insist that such words are strictly dialectal, quite apart from the question as to whether they are medieval entrants into English or more recent.[50]

But one subset of apparently Celtic vocabulary did become very celebrated. These were the remarkable 'sheep-scoring' numerals, the counting systems used by shepherds to tally up their flock: *yan, tyan, tethera, methera, pimp*, as the set recorded in Borrowdale in Cumberland begins, or *eän, teän, tethera, methera, mip*, according to the one from Weardale in County Durham. The philologist and antiquarian Isaac Taylor, of Settrington in Yorkshire, became intrigued by these numerals, as did Alexander Ellis, who gave transcriptions of them into both Palaeotype and Glossic, and set his network of informants to work to collect and supply him with as many versions as possible: this resulted in a paper to the Philological Society in which no fewer than forty-five different versions are listed, mostly from the northern counties of England (though occurrences in America gave extra cause for thought).[51] James Murray was interested, and supplied examples, as did Henry Bradley, and other contributions came from Mary Powley and from Ellis' key helpers J. G. Goodchild and C. Clough Robinson.[52] Another version was provided by Sophia De Morgan, former tutor of Ada Lovelace and mother of William De Morgan and Mary De Morgan. Even Max Müller joined in. Outside of Ellis' record, Edward Peacock's *Manley and Corringham Glossary*, in its second edition, ends with a one-page appendix on 'Numerals

---

[47] Skeat, *English Dialects*, p. 96.
[48] Wright, *Rustic Speech and Folk-Lore*, p. 105.
[49] Skeat, *English Dialects*, pp. 83–4.
[50] Skeat, *English Dialects*, pp. 85–6; Wright, *Rustic Speech and Folk-Lore*, pp. 105–7.
[51] See Ellis, 'On Palaeotype', pp. 37–8, 'On Glosik', p. 17, and 'The Anglo-Cymric Score', *Transactions of the Philological Society* 1877, 316–72. See further Sanders, 'Alexander John Ellis', pp. 855–65.
[52] See Murray, *Caught in the Web of Words*, p. 73; Henry Bradley, *Collected Papers* (Oxford: Clarendon Press, 1928), pp. 159–64.

Used in Lincolnshire for Sheep-Scoring' ('This particular list was got from an old shepherd at Winteringham, who ran through the numbers very rapidly, making a slight pause at every fifth word').[53] In the Lake District, the Rev. Thomas Ellwood of Torver near Coniston collected eight different versions, and made a special study of the language of Cumbrian sheep-farming; his conclusions were popularized in travel books by the Rev. H. D. Rawnsley, one of the founders of the National Trust and a major influence on Beatrix Potter's Herdwick environmentalism.[54]

Ellis termed these numerals 'the Anglo-Cymric score': 'score' because they ran up to the number 20, and 'Anglo-Cymric' because, in the view of Ellis and other scholars, 'these numerals are Anglicised Welsh with curious interpolations'.[55] But 'Cymric' was chosen in preference to 'Welsh' in the interests of ambiguity: the distribution of the recorded examples suggested an origin, or centre of gravity, in the north-west of England, so Ellis left it deliberately unclear 'whether Cymric means simply Welsh, or both Welsh and Cumbrian'. Were these numerals, then, to be explained as a recent import from Wales into the north of England, or (more romantically) as a pre-Saxon survival of the Celtic language of Cumbria? Many scholars, such as Ellwood, favoured the latter option; Ellis preferred to leave the question open.[56]

If the Celtic element in English dialects was found to be frustratingly elusive, such was not the case for the final historical stratum to be considered: the Old Norse element, the result of Viking or Scandinavian settlement in the north and east of the country from the ninth century on. Dialect study was in the vanguard of the Victorian rediscovery of England's Viking past, and the quantity of material that suddenly came to light was massive.[57] Just as the dialect studies of such figures as Barnes sometimes formed part of a broader interest in the Anglo-Saxon past, so the interest in the Norse element in dialect could be part of a larger cultural movement, sometimes called 'Old Northernism', expressed variously through archaeology and antiquarianism, translations of Old Norse, and reverential pilgrimages to Scandinavia.[58] And as with the impact of Bosworth's 1838 *Dictionary* on studies of the Old English element in regional dialects, so we can point to two major publications that opened up the Norse element. The first was the translation into English, in 1852, of *An Account of the Danes and Norwegians in England, Scotland, and Ireland* by the Danish archaeologist

---

[53] Peacock, *Glossary of Words Used in the Wapentakes of Manley and Corringham* (1889), p. 636.

[54] See Townend, *The Vikings and Victorian Lakeland*, pp. 203–8; Alan G. Crosby, 'Folklore, Customs and Traditions', in Michael Winstanley (ed.), *Revealing Cumbria's Past: 150 Years of the Cumberland and Westmorland Antiquarian and Archaeological Society*, Cumberland and Westmorland Antiquarian and Archaeological Society Extra Series 45 (Kendal: Cumberland and Westmorland Antiquarian and Archaeological Society, 2016), pp. 153–74, at pp. 160–3. See also Ellis, *On Early English Pronunciation*, V, 1981–2/549–50; and Linda Lear, *Beatrix Potter: A Life in Nature* (London: Penguin, 2007), pp. 52–4, 139–41.

[55] Ellis, 'The Anglo-Cymric Score', p. 319.

[56] See, for example, Wright, *Rustic Speech and Folk-Lore*, p. 327. See further Michael Barry, 'Traditional Enumeration in the North Country', *Folk Life* 7 (1969), 75–91; Juhani Klemola, 'The Origins of the Northern Subject Rule: A Case of Early Contact?', in Hildegard L. C. Tristram (ed.), *The Celtic Englishes II* (Heidelberg: Winter, 2000), pp. 329–46, at pp. 342–5.

[57] See Townend, 'The Vikings and the Victorians and Dialect'.

[58] See Wawn, *The Vikings and the Victorians*; Townend, *The Vikings and Victorian Lakeland*; Tim William Machan, *Northern Memories and the English Middle Ages*, Manchester Medieval Literature and Culture 34 (Manchester: Manchester University Press, 2020).

198   The Victorians and English Dialect

J. J. A. Worsaae: this surveyed a diverse range of evidence in magisterial fashion, and advocated that 'the natives of the lands which they subdued [should account] it an honour to descend from the bold natives of the North'.[59] Worsaae included a section on dialect evidence for Scandinavian settlement, and where the great archaeologist led, regional philologists soon followed: in Cumbria, Robert Ferguson (mayor and later MP for Carlisle, and author of *The Northmen in Cumberland and Westmoreland* in 1856), and in Yorkshire, J. C. Atkinson, whose 1868 *Cleveland Glossary*, in its introduction, works outwards, and backwards, from its key linguistic observation—the parallels between Cleveland dialect and modern Scandinavian languages—in order to reconstruct the region's Viking Age history and heritage.[60]

The second major publication was the 1874 *Icelandic-English Dictionary* ('Icelandic' is here equivalent to 'Old Norse', the two languages being exceptionally similar, especially in grammar and morphology), co-credited to Gudbrand Vigfússon and Richard Cleasby, but really a new work prepared by Vigfússon on Cleasby's earlier foundations. This was a huge breakthrough: puzzling items of local vocabulary could now be identified by reference to their Old Norse etymons, and the true extent of the Norse influence on regional vocabulary could be appreciated for the first time. The impact of 'Cleasby-Vigfússon' was immediate and extensive. Richard Morris' 1876 explication of the vocabulary of the *Cursor Mundi* (such as *throd*) is clearly indebted to it, as are the few etymological notes which Edward Peacock slipped into the 1877 edition of his *Manley and Corringham Glossary* (for example, the entry for *near* 'the kidney of an animal' directs the reader's attention to 'Icel. *nýru*', and that for *ramming* 'big, fine' to 'Icel. *ramr*').[61] Skeat went through the whole dictionary to draw up *A List of English Words the etymology of which is illustrated by comparison with Icelandic, prepared in the form of an appendix to Cleasby and Vigfússon's Icelandic-English Dictionary* (1876); he also published a series of notes on Norse-derived dialect terms in *Notes and Queries*, and later gave a disarmingly honest account of his methodology: 'I found the etymology of the provincial words [. . .] in the Icelandic Dictionary'.[62] That was all that was required; the words were now ready and waiting. And Skeat was not the only person to read Cleasby-Vigfússon all through (seven hundred pages long, in small print and double columns): in the Lake District, Thomas Ellwood also read it cover to cover, in order to spot Norse etymologies.[63]

---

[59] J. J. A. Worsaae, *An Account of the Danes and Norwegians in England, Scotland, and Ireland* (London: Murray, 1852), p. xxii.

[60] See Townend, 'The Vikings and the Victorians and Dialect'.

[61] See, for example, Peacock, *Glossary of Words Used in the Wapentakes of Manley and Corringham* (1877), pp. 177, 201.

[62] Skeat, *A Student's Pastime*, p. lxxii; see also pp. 92, 214; Walter W. Skeat, *A List of English Words the etymology of which is illustrated by comparison with Icelandic, prepared in the form of an appendix to Cleasby and Vigfússon's Icelandic-English Dictionary* (Oxford: Clarendon Press, 1876). See also Skeat, *Etymological Dictionary of the English Language*, pp. 750–1.

[63] T. Ellwood, 'Notes upon some of the older Word Forms to be found in comparing the language of Lakeland with the language of Iceland', *Transactions of the Cumberland and Westmorland Antiquarian and Archaeological Society*, 1st Series 9 (1887), 383–92, at p. 385.

Folklore and the Past **199**

Let us consider two regional workers who, like Ferguson, Atkinson, and Ellwood, pursued Norse connections in their own patch of the country with energy and insight: G. S. Streatfeild and Mary Powley.

George Sidney Streatfeild was born in 1844 and died in 1921. In the 1870s he was Vicar of Louth in Lincolnshire, and in 1884 he published *Lincolnshire and the Danes*. The primary evidence from which he constructs both his picture of Viking Lincolnshire and his romantic awareness of its lingering after-effects is not archaeological or textual, but linguistic, in the form of dialect vocabulary and local place names. Like Atkinson in Cleveland, Streatfeild shows a remarkable acumen, and if his answers aren't always convincing, then the questions that he asks are unusually astute: he suggests, for example, that if field name surveys 'were done for every parish in the county, it is likely, not only that many very interesting Danish names might be discovered, but also that Old Norse words, long obsolete in Lincolnshire, might be rescued from oblivion', and he is interested in surnames, too ('our very shop fronts are amongst the links that connect the times we live in with the age and presence of the viking').[64] Streatfeild's preface is attractively downbeat: his book, he writes, is likely to find few readers, on account of its 'tedious details and technicalities', and he is not even an evangelist for his chosen county of Lincolnshire, opining that the county 'excites less interest than any other in the mind of an average Englishman'.[65]

Streatfeild never joined the English Dialect Society, and this is itself a sign of just how much local activity must have been going on in England in the 1870s and 1880s, often unrecorded in the census-like lists of contributors to the Society and Ellis' *Existing Phonology*. *Lincolnshire and the Danes* concludes with a sixty-page 'Glossary' ('put forward with the greatest possible diffidence') of Lincolnshire dialect words for which Streatfeild proposes an Old Norse origin. Streatfeild fully acknowledges his debts to the prior work of scholars such as Atkinson and Peacock; but it is also clear that he has done valuable collecting work for himself, with his copy of Cleasby-Vigfússon at hand for guidance. A fair number of Streatfeild's words pertain to farming, such as *cush, cush, cush-a-cow* 'the call for a cow', for which Streatfeild points to 'Icel. *kussa*, a cow (a colloquial diminutive)', or *farwelted* 'overthrown' ('said of sheep when thrown on their back'), for which he derives the second element from Old Norse *velta* 'to roll over' and wonders whether the first element might come from *fé, fjár* 'sheep'.[66] J. H. Nodal, reviewing the work for the English Dialect Society, commented that 'it is a glossary with limitations'—the main one being that Streatfeild has prioritized looking for Old Norse origins, when Old English ones might be equally plausible—but it is also a glossary with strengths, and it attests to the Old Northern excitements that might animate regional philology.[67] 'The Lincolnshire Glossary', Streatfeild declares proudly, 'is still rich in specimens

---

[64] G. S. Streatfeild, *Lincolnshire and the Danes* (London: Kegan Paul, Trench, and Co., 1884), pp. 187, 274.

[65] Streatfeild, *Lincolnshire and the Danes*, pp. viii, 1.

[66] Streatfeild, *Lincolnshire and the Danes*, pp. 323, 327.

[67] *English Dialect Society: Eleventh Annual Report*, p. 3.

200   The Victorians and English Dialect

from the Old Norse, and forms a living link of connection between our modern English and the ancient literature of the North'.[68]

Mary Powley's 1875 collection *Echoes of Old Cumberland* includes a number of dialect poems, but the role that regional language plays in her poetry is somewhat different from that of most other dialect writers. For Powley, writing in Langwathby in Cumberland, dialect constitutes one of the main markers of local identity, and her poetry, philologically informed, foregrounds this fact and meditates on what it might mean in terms of culture and history—but it does so without necessarily using dialect itself as its main medium. As she states in her preface, some of her poems 'were written to preserve in remembrance, and in their proper connection, expressive old words'.[69] The key phrase is 'in their proper connection': words are rooted and used in particular places and for particular purposes, and the connection they reveal, when viewed philologically, is often an historical one. Powley is very strong on how a modern word—or a place name—might act as 'the echo of a thought', thus revealing the 'inner life' of its previous users in a 'Gothic truth of speech'.[70]

For Powley, these echoes were often Scandinavian. In the poem 'Eden's Story', concerning the River Eden, Powley proceeds via a contemplation of the Norse element in local dialect:

> The burden of the Eden's song
> > Brings echoes of the Northern seas;
> > And oft, quaint rustic speech may throng
> > The thought with hints and memories.[71]

Powley contrasts the lack—as it was believed at the time—of archaeological evidence for the Scandinavian settlement ('no sculptures theirs', she writes in another stanza) with the evidence of spoken language. It is 'rustic speech' that reveals history, and also provokes thought. And local place names do the same—'where mead, and grove, and rock retaineth / Names each hath borne, a thousand years', the same stanza declares. 'On an Ancient Grave' makes the same point: 'the name of one hamlet' (namely, Melmerby) conjures up a vision of Viking Age history, guaranteeing that, although 'his deeds are forgotten [. . .] tradition still points where dwelt Melmor the Dane'.[72] Again, the potency, and the access, lies in and through 'our rude Northern tongue, unenfeebled by time'. Another poem, 'England, the Meadow Land', turns on a single item of dialect vocabulary: the northern term *ing*, meaning 'meadow', is another Scandinavian loanword (from Old Norse *eng*), as Powley herself points out in a lengthy footnote ('In Langwathby, there is a parcel of joint proprietorship named *open Ings*'). Rejecting the standard etymology of 'England' as 'land of the Angles (or English)', she builds a poem out of the conceit that the first element is really this item

---

[68] Streatfeild, *Lincolnshire and the Danes*, p. 275.
[69] Powley, *Echoes of Old Cumberland*, p. iv.
[70] Powley, *Echoes of Old Cumberland*, pp. 13–15 ('Memory and Grief').
[71] Powley, *Echoes of Old Cumberland*, pp. 120–2.
[72] Powley, *Echoes of Old Cumberland*, pp. 59–63.

of northern dialect ('England! Methinks thou wert The Meadow Land, / To olden rovers of the North seas known').[73] Powley's works therefore provide us with an interesting counterpart to the more famous dialect poetry of Barnes and Tennyson. The 'intense localization' of which Hardy wrote (with reference to Barnes) can obviously be communicated through the medium of dialect composition; but Powley's poetry suggests that this is not the only way in which a commitment to local culture (and the local past) can be expressed through a celebration of local language—and her poetry also reveals to us the intensity, and perceptiveness, with which some regional philologists contemplated the local Scandinavian past.

Philology and folklore

Let us return to sheep for a moment. Other poems in Mary Powley's *Echoes of Old Cumberland* offer a celebration of local practices and events, such as the great fair at Brough Hill, and a number take as their subject the distinctive Cumbrian culture of sheep farming. Such poems often include a scattering of dialect words: the poem 'The Heaf on the Fell', for example, contains *brattling* ('rushing; clattering') and *wreckling* ('the youngest or smallest in a litter'), as well as *heaf* itself ('accustomed pasture-ground'), a celebrated term on which Powley wrote at length in *Notes and Queries*.[74] So in Powley's writings, the study of dialect and the study of local culture are in many ways two sides of the same coin, all part of the same intellectual activity.

We should also revisit the 'sheep-scoring numerals' which Ellis catalogued for the Philological Society. As Ellis' paper makes clear, sheep-counting was in fact only one of the uses to which this enumeration system was being put, and his informants often reported that they, or their local sources, knew it rather from its use in knitting (for counting stitches), from childcare (for calming babies), or from children's games (for counting who was 'it', and suchlike). In Ellis' view, this represented a degradation for the score, a sinking down from its earlier 'high estate' of shepherds' culture to the lesser world of 'old women', 'nurses, mothers, etc', and 'schoolboys'.[75] But there is, of course, another way of looking at this. The sources cited by Ellis' informants include 'an old woman', 'an old lady', 'school children', 'servants', '[a] housemaid', 'a peasant woman', someone's 'grandmother', and the 'old nurse' of Ellis' wife.[76] These are all sections of the population who were far from prominent in the hierarchies of Victorian society. The Anglo-Cymric score may or may not have reached back to an antique world of Celtic-speaking shepherds; but what it was definitely giving access to, right under the collectors' noses, was a kind of alternative body of culture, subterranean rather than celebrated, and circulating through a variety of oral contexts and

---

[73] Powley *Echoes of Old Cumberland*, pp. 67–70.
[74] Powley, *Echoes of Old Cumberland*, pp. 114–19. See also [Mary Powley], 'The Heaf', *Notes and Queries* 4th Series 10 (14 September 1872), 201–3, 4th Series 11 (11 January 1873), 38–40, and 4th Series 11 (18 January 1873), 57–8.
[75] Ellis, 'The Anglo-Cymric Score', p. 340.
[76] Ellis, 'The Anglo-Cymric Score', pp. 347, 348, 349, 352, 353, 355, 357.

202 The Victorians and English Dialect

exchanges. The numerals may or may not have been medieval history, but they were certainly contemporary folklore; and dialect and folklore went hand in hand, as we will now see.

The Victorian study of folklore grew out of the earlier, Romantic-era enthusiasm for 'popular antiquities', a taste that united the antiquary, the religionist, the mythologist—and the dialect collector. The very word 'folklore', when it arrived to bring focus to such a heterogeneous enthusiasm, was philological in design. The word was coined, as a deliberate term, by William John Thoms (1803–85), writing in 1846 in the *Athenaeum* (under the pseudonym of Ambrose Merton) on the subject of 'what we in England designate as Popular Antiquities, or Popular Literature (though by-and-bye it is more a Lore than a Literature, and would be most aptly described by a good Saxon compound, Folk-Lore—*the Lore of the People*)'.[77] Thoms, who was a clerk and later assistant librarian in the House of Lords, was inspired by Jacob Grimm's *Deutsche Mythologie*; so his designation of the pursuit as 'folk-lore' (with or without the hyphen) was proposed in cognizance of the new philology issuing out of Germany.[78] In 1849, Thoms founded the journal *Notes and Queries*, which became an essential space for many antiquarian and historical inquiries, including dialect study. The compound 'folk-speech', as a term for dialect, is clearly modelled on Thoms' coinage of 'folk-lore', and the shift from the terminology of 'provincialisms' to that of 'folk-speech' in itself encapsulates an attitudinal change.

The Folklore Society was founded in 1878, as a national organization, and its journal, at first called *The Folk-Lore Record* and later simply *Folk-Lore*, became the major publication outlet for debates and reports.[79] As its beginnings in 'popular antiquities' indicate, folklore studies was in origin a historical discipline, but in the 1870s and 1880s its leading voices came under the spell of the cultural evolutionism that derived from Darwin's *Origin of Species* and E. B. Tylor's *Primitive Culture*, so that the discipline took a strongly anthropological turn: core figures included George Lawrence Gomme and Andrew Lang. Here, there were two key paradigms.[80] The first was the idea of the fossil-like 'survival': in Tylor's own definition, survivals were 'processes, customs, opinions, and so forth, which have been carried on by the force of habit into a new state of society, different from that in which they had their original home, and they thus remain as proofs and examples of an older condition of culture out of which

---

[77] [William J. Thoms], 'Folk-Lore', *The Athenaeum* 22 August 1846, 862–3, at p. 862.

[78] On Thoms, see Dorson, *The British Folklorists*, pp. 75–90; Jonathan Roper, 'Thoms and the Unachieved "Folk-Lore of England"', *Folklore* 118 (2007), 203–16, '"Our National Folk-Lore": William Thoms as Cultural Nationalist', in Krishna Sen and Sudeshna Chakravarti (eds), *Narrating the (Trans) Nation: The Dialectics of Culture and Identity* (Kolkata: Dasgupta and Co., 2008), pp. 60–74, and 'England—The Land Without Folklore?'; Arthur Sherbo, 'Thoms, William John (1803–1885)', in *Oxford Dictionary of National Biography* [www.oxforddnb].

[79] See Chris Wingfield and Chris Gosden, 'An Imperialist Folklore? Establishing the Folk-Lore Society in London', in Timothy Baycroft and David Hopkin (eds), *Folklore and Nationalism in Europe During the Long Nineteenth Century* (Leiden: Brill, 2012), pp. 255–74.

[80] See, for example, Dorson, *The British Folklorists*, pp. 193–7; Stocking, *Victorian Anthropology*; Gillian Bennett, 'Geologists and Folklorists: Cultural Evolution and "The Science of Folklore"', *Folklore* 105 (1994), 25–37; Colls, *Identity of England*, pp. 245–57; Peter Mandler, 'Looking Around the World', in Adelene Buckland and Sadiah Qureshi (eds), *Time Travelers: Victorian Encounters with Time and History* (Chicago: University of Chicago Press, 2020), pp. 24–41.

a newer has been evolved'.[81] The second key paradigm was a suspension of the usual principles of time and space, so that 'peasant' cultures at home, and so-called 'savage' cultures abroad, might both supply evidence for primitive society, and thus (Tylor again) there might be 'scarce a hand's breadth difference between an English plough-man and a negro of Central Africa', meaning that 'the European may find among the Greenlanders or Maoris many a trait for reconstructing the picture of his own prim-itive ancestors'.[82] (Notwithstanding the extreme hierarchism of this view, it should perhaps be noted that Tylor, a Quaker by upbringing, was a dedicated champion of 'monogenesis', and viewed differences between peoples in terms of culture, not biol-ogy: 'it appears both possible and desirable', he argued, 'to eliminate considerations of hereditary varieties or races of man, and to treat mankind as homogeneous in nature, though placed in different grades of civilization'.)[83]

Comparable beliefs about survivalism and primitivism are not hard to find among nineteenth-century writers on rural dialect; J. R. Wise, for example, thought that 'our peasantry still remain in many respects in an early stage of society', and of course the fundamental claim that dialect was '*old* English rather than *bad* English' could have more than a hint of survivalism about it ('like so many of our so-called "dialect words"', wrote J. C. Atkinson of one term, 'it is only a survival of the older English').[84] Among the major philologists, the closest analogue to the theoretical folklorists such as Gomme and Lang was probably Alexander Ellis, even though he seems to have had little interest in folklore itself. 'We have to go out of ourselves', he argued, 'to see the phenomena in others before we can appreciate their significance. And hence the necessity of collecting foreign materials in abundance, to understand our home growth'.[85] Like the anthropological folklorists, Ellis operated at a national level, unag-itated by local piety, and like them he believed that there were parallels between various manifestations of 'primitive culture': as we saw in Chapter 2, he made con-nections between peasant dialect and 'lingue franche, camp speech, savage talk'.[86] Ellis saw such forms of language as giving access to early culture, but we should note that it was not exactly in terms of ossified 'survivals' or decontextualized fos-sils: rather, what dialect offered to Ellis, or so he believed, was language in a state of origin and becoming, a sort of laboratory that enabled linguistic change to be studied in progress.

So although philology and anthropological folklore were adjacent (and, at times, overlapping) disciplines, even at the national level they were not the same thing. Max Müller, in his pioneering and hugely ambitious 'comparative mythology', took the philological methods of comparative reconstruction and argued that just as the

---

[81] Edward B. Tylor, *Primitive Culture: Researches into the Development of Mythology, Philosophy, Religion, Language, Art, and Custom*, 4th ed., 2 vols (London: Murray, 1903), I, 16.

[82] Tylor, *Primitive Culture*, I, 7, 21.

[83] Tylor, *Primitive Culture*, I, 7. See further Stocking, *Victorian Anthropology*, pp. 219–28; Wingfield, 'Is the Heart at Home?', pp. 33–4.

[84] [Wise], 'The Poetry of Provincialisms', p. 31; J. C. Atkinson, *Forty Years in a Moorland Parish: Reminiscences and Researches in Danby in Cleveland* (London: Macmillan, 1891), p. 181 n. 1.

[85] Ellis, 'Eleventh Annual Address', p. 147.

[86] Ellis, 'First Annual Address', p. 19.

204 The Victorians and English Dialect

parent form of all the Indo-European languages could be rediscovered, so too could early Indo-European culture and society—and mythology and religion, too.[87] There are obvious resemblances here with some of the principles and practices of anthropological folklore, especially on the grand scale. But Müller had many criticisms to make of the anthropologists, and thought that what they really needed to do was to learn some languages.[88] Andrew Lang, in return, rejected the invitation to subscribe to the *English Dialect Dictionary*, declaring that 'English dialects are of a wonderful hideousness, and one sees only too much of them in novels. For these reasons I am not anxious to be connected in any way with a work on Dialects'.[89]

Furthermore, when we move from debates about folklore at a national level to examine more local or regional investigations by those we might call 'dialect-folklorists', there are at least four differences to observe. The first is that the local workers were usually highly active in fieldwork and collection, whereas the major actors in the national debate, often based in London, tended to be 'armchair' folklorists, concerned rather with synthesizing and theorization.[90] The second is that local dialect-folklorists often stood apart from the national debates about survivalism and cultural evolutionism; those were not necessarily the paradigms that drove their activities, and they often had more affinity with old-style gatherers of 'popular antiquities'.[91] The third is that, as a result of this, local collectors rarely had much interest in the non-European materials which increasingly occupied the anthropological folklorists towards the end of the nineteenth century.[92] And the fourth, very importantly, is that the dialect-folklorists were often themselves part of the culture that they collected and studied, or at least partially so: they were locally resident, long familiar with the language and practices they were recording, and very frequently animated by a spirit of conservation and love rather than (or as well as) scientific analysis.[93] What was important was simply to collect the material and celebrate it, not to theorize its place in the evolution of human culture. Moreover, as we saw in the long quotation from Hallam at the start of this chapter, regional philologists were often at pains to demonstrate that non-standard dialects were the very opposite of 'barbaric' or 'savage'—that they were, in fact, coherent and regular and hallowed by antiquity. From the point of view of the modern reader, it is hard not to conclude that, while

---

[87] Müller, *Lectures on the Science of Language*, p. 236. See further, for example, Tom Shippey, 'A Revolution Reconsidered: Mythography and Mythology in the Nineteenth Century', in Tom Shippey (ed.), *The Shadow-Walkers: Jacob Grimm's Mythology of the Monstrous*, Medieval and Renaissance Texts and Studies 291 (Tempe: Arizona Center for Medieval and Renaissance Studies, 2005), pp. 1–28; Colin Kidd, *The World of Mr Casaubon: Britain's Wars of Mythography, 1700–1870* (Cambridge: Cambridge University Press, 2016), esp. pp. 213–15.

[88] See Dorson, *The British Folklorists*, pp. 166–9; Stocking, *Victorian Anthropology*, pp. 305–11.

[89] Quoted in Wright, *The Life of Joseph Wright*, II, 378.

[90] See Dorson, *The British Folklorists*, pp. 316–31; Wingfield and Gosden, 'An Imperialist Folklore?', pp. 267–9.

[91] See John Ashton, 'Beyond Survivalism: Regional Folkloristics in Late-Victorian England', *Folklore* 108 (1997), 19–23.

[92] See Dorson, *The British Folklorists*, pp. 332–91; Gillian Bennett, 'Folklore Studies and the English Rural Myth', *Rural History* 4 (1993), 77–91, at pp. 88–9.

[93] Roper, 'Thoms and the Unachieved "Folk-Lore of England"', p. 210; see also Colls, *Identity of England*, pp. 268–9.

Folklore and the Past **205**

many of the theories of the national figures have now passed away or become period pieces, much of the work of the regional collectors has retained or even increased its value.

Nonetheless, the affinities between dialect study and folklore study were extremely close, and it could be hard to say where one ended and the other began. Many students of folk-speech were students of folklore too, and many dialect glossaries—not least English Dialect Society ones—contain sections on 'Customs' or 'Superstitions' or 'Sayings' or 'Proverbs'.[94] In the case of sayings and proverbs, it was especially hard to say which discipline they belonged to: Skeat had urged members of the English Dialect Society to collect and contribute 'provincial proverbs' as well as provincial words, and one of the Society's volumes was G. F. Northall's *Folk-Phrases of Four Counties* (1894); but successive editions of the Folklore Society's official *Handbook of Folklore* also gave guidance on how and why to collect 'Proverbs and Riddles' and 'Proverbial Rhymes and Local Sayings'.[95] Pithy, idiomatic phrases were hard to resist, and promised to reveal the quiddity of a local culture, from Elworthy's simile 'hairy as a badger' to Edith Chamberlain's 'Look for summer on the top of an oak tree'.[96]

Many regional workers combined an interest in dialect with an interest in folklore. Anne Elizabeth Baker, for example, whose work was discussed in Chapter 1, had originally planned a separate publication on folk customs, but eventually incorporated her material into her *Glossary of Northamptonshire Words and Phrases* as an appendix.[97] We examined J. C. Atkinson's *Glossary of the Cleveland Dialect* (1868) in Chapter 1, but he is now better known for his *Forty Years in a Moorland Parish* (1891), in which he proposed that the 'original customs' of certain practices surviving on the North York Moors—such as 'running for the ribbon' at weddings—might be 'largely, as well as safely, inferred [...] from the memorials engraved on the tablets of the folk-speech'—that is, from dialect words and phrases.[98] One of the last pieces of writing done by William Barnes was the provision of a lengthy 'Fore-Say' or preface to John Symonds Udal's *Dorsetshire Folk-Lore* (this introductory essay was not actually published until 1922, thirty-eight years after Barnes' death, so drawn out was Udal's progress).[99] And the relationship between Barnes and Udal was reciprocal:

---

[94] See, for example, Henry Smith and C. Roach Smith, 'A Glossary of Words in Use in the Isle of Wight', in Walter W. Skeat (ed.), *Original Glossaries*, English Dialect Society 32 (London: English Dialect Society, 1881), pp. 1–64, at pp. 49–64; Chamberlain, *Glossary of West Worcestershire Words*, pp. 37–40 (and see also *Up Hill and Down Dale*, II, 105–6); Holland, *Glossary of Words Used in the County of Chester*, pp. 443–57. See also Wright, *Rustic Speech and Folk-Lore*, pp. 158–90; Roper, 'Folklore in the Glossaries of the English Dialect Society'.

[95] *English Dialect Society: First Report*, p. 2; George Laurence Gomme, *The Handbook of Folklore*, Publications of the Folklore Society 20 (London: Folklore Society, 1890), pp. 159–63; Charlotte Sophia Burne, *The Handbook of Folklore*, rev. ed., Publications of the Folklore Society 73 (London: Sidgwick and Jackson, 1914), pp. 280–91.

[96] Elworthy, *The Grammar of the Dialect of West Somerset*, p. 22; Chamberlain, *Glossary of West Worcestershire Words*, p. 38. See further Wright, *Rustic Speech and Folk-Lore*, pp. 158–90, and also Manfred Markus, 'As drunk as muck. The Role and Logic of Similes in English Dialects on the Basis of Joseph Wright's *English Dialect Dictionary*', *Studia Neophilologica* 82 (2010), 203–16.

[97] Baker, *Glossary of Northamptonshire Words and Phrases*, I, xvi, and II, 417–39.

[98] Atkinson, *Forty Years in a Moorland Parish*, p. 207.

[99] William Barnes, 'Fore-Say', in John Symonds Udal, *Dorsetshire Folk-Lore* (Hertford: Austin and Sons, 1922), pp. 1–16.

206 The Victorians and English Dialect

the younger man, professionally a barrister, supplied Barnes with words for the final version of his Dorset glossary.[100]

Baker's dilemma, of whether to publish dialect and folklore as one collection or two, was shared by other workers. Georgina Jackson's massive *Shropshire Word-Book* was, in fact, originally intended to be one of a pair: Book I (the *Word-Book*) was on the subject of dialect, and Book II would address folklore. But illness prevented Jackson from undertaking Book II herself, and her collection of materials on Shropshire folklore, gathered in the course of her 'dialecting tours', was passed to her friend Charlotte Burne (who grew up in Edgmond in Shropshire) to bring to publication as *Shropshire Folk-Lore: A Sheaf of Gleanings* (1883), a comparably monumental work of over six hundred pages.[101] As with Jackson's *Word-Book*, Skeat read the volume at the preparation stage, and 'enriched [its] pages with valuable notes and corrections, both etymological and otherwise'.[102] Burne was the first woman to be president of the Folklore Society, and she produced the revised edition of the Society's *Handbook of Folklore* in 1914; Ellis' *Existing Phonology* also reveals that she sent him dialect information for Newport in Shropshire.[103] Edward Peacock, indecisive over the same dilemma, included folklore content in the first edition of his *Manley and Corringham Glossary*, but then chose to remove such content from the second edition: his intention—not realized—was to produce a separate volume on *The Folk-Lore of Lincolnshire*, to be published by the Folklore Society.[104] So, for example, the first edition of the *Manley and Corringham Glossary* contains an entry on *eggs*—hardly a dialect word, of course, and what Peacock's entry discusses instead is a whole series of popular beliefs ('It is unlucky to set a hen upon an even number of eggs [. . .] If eggs are carried over running water, they will have no chicks in them [. . .] If egg-shells are thrown into the fire it hinders the eggs from laying'). In the second edition, the entry for *eggs* has been removed from the word list and all this cultural information has gone.[105] Among other English Dialect Society glossarists, Margaret Courtney followed her 1880 *West Cornwall Glossary* with a companion volume on *Cornish Feasts and Folk-Lore* ten years later, and Angelina Parker, author of the *Oxfordshire Glossary* and supplement, collected traditions and gave lectures on local folklore well into the twentieth century.[106]

---

[100] Baxter, *The Life of William Barnes*, pp. 278–9; Chedzoy, *The People's Poet*, pp. 187–8.

[101] Jackson, *Shropshire Word-Book*, p. 523; Charlotte Sophia Burne (ed.), *Shropshire Folk-Lore: A Sheaf of Gleanings, from the collections of Georgina F. Jackson* (London: Trübner, 1883), p. vii. See further Gordon Ashman and Gillian Bennett, 'Charlotte Sophia Burne: Shropshire Folklorist, First Woman President of the Folklore Society, and First Woman Editor of *Folklore*. Part 1: A Life and Appreciation', *Folklore* 111 (2000), 1–21; Gillian Bennett, 'Charlotte Sophia Burne: Shropshire Folklorist, First Woman President of the Folklore Society, and First Woman Editor of *Folklore*. Part 2: Update and Preliminary Bibliography', *Folklore* 112 (2001), 95–106.

[102] Burne (ed.), *Shropshire Folk-Lore*, p. viii.

[103] Ellis, *On Early English Pronunciation*, V, 1910–12/478–80.

[104] Peacock, *Glossary of Words Used in the Wapentakes of Manley and Corringham* (1889), p. ix; Stephen Miller, 'The Lost Publications of the Folk-Lore Society', *Folklore* 124 (2013), 226–35, at pp. 227, 230.

[105] See Peacock, *Glossary of Words Used in the Wapentakes of Manley and Corringham* (1877), pp. 97–8, and (1889), p. 189.

[106] See Oxford, Bodleian Libraries, MSS Eng. lang. d. 69–76, and Angelina Parker, 'Oxfordshire Village Folklore (1840–1900)', *Folklore* 24 (1913), 74–91, and see further Ruano-García, 'The Contribution of Angelina Parker to the *English Dialect Dictionary*'.

Such examples lead to the obvious conclusion that many of the participants in the English Dialect Society were also highly active as writers on folklore: to look at the membership lists of the Folklore Society alongside those of the English Dialect Society is to see many names in common. James Britten over-promised a set of publications to the Folklore Society, just as he had done for the English Dialect Society, before his attention shifted to pro-Catholic campaigning.[107] Thomas Satchell, also a member of both societies, similarly failed to deliver a catalogue of local names of 'British Fishes, Marine Animals, and Fishing Appliances' to the English Dialect Society, and an ambitious *Bibliography of Folk-Lore* to the Folklore Society.[108] A more productive member of both societies was Fred Elworthy. After completing his three-part study of West Somerset dialect in the 1880s, Elworthy increasingly turned his attention to folklore topics, and became a member of the Folklore Society's Council: his main works in the field were a monograph on *The Evil Eye* (1895) and a related collection of essays, *Horns of Honour* (1900). He was a collector, and donated a number of Somerset and Devon objects to the Pitt Rivers Museum in Oxford; he was also a near-neighbour of E. B. Tylor, both being resident in Wellington in Somerset.[109]

Indeed, the beginnings of the Folklore Society are usually traced to a call to arms in *Notes and Queries*, issued by a dedicated member of the English Dialect Society, Eliza Gutch. Born Eliza Hutchinson in Lincolnshire in 1840, she married a York solicitor, John James Gutch, in 1868, and their properties within the city were extensive.[110] Over seven decades, Eliza Gutch published hundreds of short articles in the journal *Notes and Queries*: her first, in 1860 aged 20, was on children's games, and her last, in 1928 aged 87, was on an association between Tennyson and York.[111] Her contributions were signed with the pen name 'St Swithin', a pseudonym taken from her birthday—15 July—but also one with calendrical folklore attached to it (concerning weather prognostication). One of her notes was headed 'A Folk-Lore Society', and reads as follows (in total):

I am not alone in thinking it high time that steps should be taken to form a society for collecting, arranging, and printing all the scattered bits of folk-lore which we read of in books and hear of in the flesh. Such a society should not confine its labours to the folk-lore of our own land, but should have members and workers everywhere.[112]

---

[107] Miller, 'The Lost Publications of the Folk-Lore Society', pp. 227–8, 230.

[108] *English Dialect Society: Sixth Report*, pp. 8–9; Miller, 'The Lost Publications of the Folk-Lore Society', pp. 227–8.

[109] 'E. B.', 'Obituary: Frederic Thomas Elworthy', *Folklore* 19 (1908), 109–10; Wingfield, 'Is the Heart at Home?', p. 36 n. 18; Roper, 'Folklore in the Glossaries of the English Dialect Society', pp. 191–3.

[110] [Anon], 'In Memoriam: [Mrs] Eliza Gutch, (1840–1931)', *Folklore* 41 (1930), 301; Jacqueline Simpson and Steve Roud, *A Dictionary of English Folklore* (Oxford: Oxford University Press, 2000), p. 158.

[111] 'St Swithin' [Eliza Gutch], 'Children's Drama', *Notes and Queries* 2nd Series 10 (1 September 1860), 168, and 'A Glimpse of Tennyson', *Notes and Queries* 155 (7 July 1928), 7.

[112] 'St Swithin' [Eliza Gutch], 'A Folk-Lore Society', *Notes and Queries* 5th Series 5 (12 February 1876), 124.

208   The Victorians and English Dialect

The lively correspondence that followed—reminiscent of the correspondence over the idea of a dialect society five years earlier—led to the foundation of the Folklore Society two years later.[113] Gutch herself contributed a number of longer articles to the Society's journal, and edited three volumes for its 'County Folk-Lore Series'.[114] Gutch was a member of the English Dialect Society from beginning to end, and contributed Lincolnshire words to its collections; when she died in 1931, she was also the last remaining founder member of the Folklore Society.[115]

What exactly did Victorians mean by 'folklore'? The term was a capacious one, ranging from survivalist relics, to place legends, to vanishing features of everyday life; and often there was an implicit contrast between the community or class that was producing or preserving the material labelled as 'folklore' (rural, traditional, working class) and the more elite or educated society that it was being defined against (urban, contemporary, middle or upper class): the contrast between dialect speech and Standard English—and Victorian consciousness of that contrast—forms a very apposite analogy. Regional philologists who combined an interest in dialect with an interest in folklore tended to take a word-based rather than pronunciation-based approach to their investigations: they were interested in words, objects, practices, beliefs—not phonology. So here are four of the main areas in which regional workers collected words and folklore together.

First, flora and fauna. J. H. Nodal, writing in the English Dialect Society report for 1882, drew the members' attention to 'an important fact—that a large amount of work remains to be done in rural England, if competent and willing observers could only be found, not only in regard to the names of flowers and plants, but of animals, birds, fishes, insects, the aspects of the seasons, and the occupations and incidents of rural life'.[116] This was an enormously productive field for dialect and folklore collectors. Many dialect collectors were also natural historians of one sort or another—such as J. C. Atkinson and G. S. Streatfeild—and J. R. Wise believed that 'it is especially in reference to natural objects that the real poetry of provincialisms is seen'.[117]

The major work on flora was Britten and Holland's *Dictionary of English Plant-Names*, published by the English Dialect Society, a six-hundred-page compendium that lists plant names in alphabetical order, giving county distributions wherever possible and painstakingly correlating vernacular names with identifications in botanical Latin. But many regional glossaries offered a more local gathering of plant lore. So, for example, William Dickinson, in his *Glossary of Words and Phrases Pertaining to the Dialect of Cumberland* (1878) includes an introductory list of 'Cumberland names of British plants'. This extends over five pages, and those under the letter A include:

---

[113] See Dorson, *The British Folklorists*, pp. 202–5; Wingfield and Gosden, 'An Imperialist Folklore?', pp. 261–3.

[114] See Miller, 'The Lost Publications of the Folklore Society', p. 229, and 'The County Folk-Lore Series (Volumes 1–7) of the Folk-Lore Society', *Folklore* 124 (2013), 327–44.

[115] *English Dialect Society: First Report*, p. 10; *English Dialect Society: Second Report*, p. 11; *English Dialect Society: Third Report*, p. 10.

[116] *English Dialect Society: Tenth Annual report*, p. 2.

[117] [Wise], 'The Poetry of Provincialisms', p. 34.

Agrostemma Githago	...	Popple
Allium ursinum	...	Ramps
Anagallis arvensis	...	Poor man's weather-glass
Angelica sylvestris	...	Water kesh, Kesks[118]

These plants are now probably best known by the names of corncockle, wild garlic, scarlet pimpernel, and wild angelica.[119] The Latin index to Britten and Holland's *Dictionary* catalogues alternative names for the same plant, and enables us to see that the scarlet pimpernel, for example, was known by at least twenty-three different names across the country, many arising from its tendency to close up when atmospheric pressure falls, thereby predicting bad weather: *bird's eye* in Buckinghamshire and Oxfordshire, for instance, *John-go-to-bed-at-noon* in Northamptonshire, *shepherd's calendar* in Devon and *shepherd's sundial* in Suffolk, *sunflower* in Cumberland, and *wink-a-peep* in Cheshire, Shropshire, and Staffordshire.[120] But plant names were highly variable, and Britten and Holland also record that *bird's eye*, for example, was used as the name of twelve other plants as well, and not just *anagallis arvensis* (such as the *veronica chamaedrys* or germander speedwell, *myosotis palustris* or water forget-me-not, and *stellaria holostea* or greater stitchwort).[121]

Bird-names were covered by Charles Swainson's *Provincial Names and Folk Lore of British Birds* (1885)—tellingly, a joint publication between the English Dialect Society and the Folklore Society—and later H. Kirke Swann's *Dictionary of English and Folk-Names of British Birds* (1913). One well-known example, now made famous by Hopkins' poem, is *windhover* as a name for the kestrel, a name found in the south and west of England, according to Swainson, with variant forms elsewhere being the *windbibber* (Kent), *windsucker* (also Kent), and *windcuffer* (Orkney).[122] The regional names of insects also proved highly fertile. Anna Gurney reported that in Norfolk the ladybird was known as 'Bishop Barnabee', claiming that it was 'in heathen times sacred to Frigga', and Ernest Adams addressed the Philological Society with a paper 'On the Names of the Wood-Louse': according to Adams, these included *cheese-lip*, *grammar-sow* (in Cornwall), *kitchen-ball, lobstrouse-louse* (in the north of England), *lock-chester* (in Oxfordshire), *maggy-many-feet, monkey-pee* (in Kent, with an etymology from Latin *multipes* 'many-footed'), and *tiggy-hog* (in Northamptonshire).[123] And while James Britten never produced his intended dictionary of 'the English Names of Animals, Reptiles, and Insects', regional glossaries still provide an abundance of material.[124] Atkinson's *Cleveland Glossary*, for example, parades a variety of

---

[118] William Dickinson, *A Glossary of Words and Phrases Pertaining to the Dialect of Cumberland*, English Dialect Society 20 (London: English Dialect Society, 1878), p. xviii.

[119] Information from the Royal Horticultural Society (www.rhs.org.uk).

[120] Britten and Holland, *Dictionary of English Plant-Names*, pp. 43, 280, 428, 429, 459, 495, 566.

[121] Britten and Holland, *Dictionary of English Plant-Names*, p. 43.

[122] Charles Swainson, *Provincial Names and Folk Lore of British Birds*, English Dialect Society 47 (London: English Dialect Society, 1885), pp. 140–1. See also [Wise], 'The Poetry of Provincialisms', p. 40; Wright (ed.), *English Dialect Dictionary*, VI, 503–4; H. Kirke Swann, *A Dictionary of English and Folk-Names of British Birds* (London: Witherby and Co., 1913), p. 258; Hopkins, *The Major Works*, p. 132.

[123] Gurney, 'Norfolk Words', p. 29; Ernest Adams, 'On the Names of the Wood-Louse', *Transactions of the Philological Society* 1860–1, 8–19.

[124] *English Dialect Society: Seventh Annual Report*, p. 6.

210   The Victorians and English Dialect

clock-names: the *black-clock* or black-beetle, *lady-clock* or ladybird, and *water-clock* or water-beetle, as well as the more uncertain *bracken-clock* 'a small brown-sharded beetle, often found about the bracken, or ferns generally'.[125]

The vocabulary and folklore of the natural world leads closely onto our second field, that of agriculture. The romantic J. R. Wise claimed—perhaps tongue-in-cheek—that 'a Derbyshire peasant uses eight different terms for a pigsty', and once more there was a dedicated volume, again by James Britten: his 1880 *Old Country and Farming Words: Gleaned from Agricultural Books* (published by the English Dialect Society). Britten worked at the British Museum, and so he was perfectly placed to produce such works as this, which excerpted dialect vocabulary from over seventy printed volumes, many of them hard to obtain; such labours led J. H. Nodal to praise Britten's 'tireless industry' and 'the minute care, the accuracy, and the abounding knowledge which characterize [his] work'.[126] But most collectors were engaged in contemporary fieldwork rather than antiquarian trawling, and the yield was prodigious: an astonishing array of finely distinguished terms for the qualities of land, agricultural implements, animal behaviour, annual practices, and so on. The reader of Dickinson's *Cumberland Glossary*, for example, could learn about the repertoire of local terms for hedging (see *cockgard*, *steak and reyse*, and *stower and yedder*); Dickinson (1798–1882) was a farmer and landowner himself, as well as an active dialect poet for over half a century.[127] Terms for animal husbandry—sheep, cattle, horses—were especially prolific, and highly characteristic of pre-mechanized farming. Let us take, as an example, the *Glossary of Words in Use in the Isle of Wight* (1881), compiled by Major Henry Smith, and brought to publication after his death by his brother, C. Roach Smith. The latter writes of his brother, the glossary's compiler, that he was 'endowed with a remarkably retentive memory; with a thoughtful and reflective mind; born in a farm-house; I might say, born to the plough; passing his early years in the midst of farm-labourers, and engaged in the various duties of farm life'.[128] The following is a selection—and only a small selection—of the words referring to animal husbandry in Smith's collection: *azew* 'not giving milk', *bodyhoss* 'the horse in a team nearest the hindmost, or the shafts', *culls* 'the worst sheep taken from a flock', *gambrul* 'a wooden implement generally used to open the hinder legs of pigs for taking out the entrails', *hatch-on* 'to fasten the horses to the plough', *hoss-stopples* 'holes made by horses in wet land', *not-cow* and *not-sheep* 'a cow without horns' and 'a sheep without horns', *purr-lamb* 'a male lamb', *thiltugs* 'chains attached to the collar of the thill or shaft horse', and *zooul* 'a stake to fasten sheep-hurdles'.[129]

Such agricultural vocabulary leads us to our third field of words—technical terminology drawn from trades and professions. In this context, Georgina Jackson's

---

[125] Atkinson, *Glossary of the Cleveland Dialect*, pp. 48, 62, 107, 301.

[126] [Wise], 'The Poetry of Provincialisms', p. 32; *English Dialect Society: Eighth Annual Report*, p. 1; *English Dialect Society: Ninth Annual Report*, p. 2.

[127] Dickinson, *Glossary of Words and Phrases Pertaining to the Dialect of Cumberland*, pp. 19, 94, 95. See further William Dickinson, *Uncollected Literary Remains*, ed. W. Hodgson (Carlisle: Coward, 1888).

[128] Smith and Smith, 'Glossary of Words in Use in the Isle of Wight', p. xi.

[129] Smith and Smith, 'Glossary of Words in Use in the Isle of Wight', pp. 2, 4, 8, 12, 14, 16, 23, 26, 37, 45.

account of word-collecting in the 1870s, in her *Shropshire Word-Book*, is worth quoting at length:

> It was my wont on dialecting tours, when I had been settled in head-quarters for a day or two, and had made friends with the good folk there, to begin my work by having a chat with the village blacksmith about his tools, the implements he was making or repairing, and so forth. Often on these occasions I was met with some such remark as, 'Yo' seemen to know summat about 'em, Ma'am. I could shewn yo' a noud-fashioned tool sich as I dar' say yo' never sid before.' And then would be brought out of some dark hole or corner an obsolete agricultural implement, and all its parts and uses would be explained to me, and measurements given. And so I learnt all about *that*, and picked up many words and sounds into the bargain.
>
> The wheelwright would then be visited, and the terms of his craft acquired in like manner. The butcher would allow me to go into his shop to see how the great joints 'slench', 'lift', &c—were cut for his country customers. Some neighbouring farmer and his wife would be pleased to shew me the farm-yard, the poultry-yard, and the dairy, and thus I learnt the lore they had to teach.[130]

In this account Jackson combines together both the antique ('an obsolete agricultural implement') and the current ('the terms of his craft'). Her *Word-Book* contains an extraordinary section on weights and measures, for example, recording the divergent systems for weighing and measuring wheat, barley, oats, beans, peas, malt, flour, bran, potatoes, apples, pears, damsons, cheese, and butter in eleven different Shropshire markets.[131] Such practices, clearly, were arcane and highly localized, but they were not obsolete or unimportant.

Fred Elworthy, recording in Somerset, also strove to view local life and work with an eye that was both contemporary and historicist. 'I have [. . .] endeavoured to give clear definitions of words', he explained, 'and where they related to anything of a technical character I have tried to describe the object, so that those who come after us may be able to know precisely what the article now is'.[132] This remarkable perspective, viewing the present from the historicist viewpoint of the future, informs Elworthy's research: 'certain well-known names of common articles', he writes, 'have been inserted as a sort of legacy to the future—these are now obsolescent, and probably in a few years will be quite forgotten—*e.g.* pattens, gambaders, &c'.[133] *Gambaders* are explained as 'a kind of leather shield or case for the legs of a horseman', and *pattens* as 'a kind of clogs worn by women which rest on iron oval rings, and so keep the feet quite two inches from the ground'; for the latter, Elworthy adds that 'they were much

---

[130] Jackson, *Shropshire Word-Book*, pp. x–xi.
[131] Jackson, *Shropshire Word-Book*, pp. lxxxiv–xciii.
[132] Elworthy, *The West Somerset Word-Book*, p. vii.
[133] Elworthy, *The West Somerset Word-Book*, p. viii.

212   The Victorians and English Dialect

worn within the writer's memory, but are now only to be found in out-of-the-way places and on the stage.'[134]

To many fieldworkers at the intersection of dialect and folklore, it was especially important to make a record of significant regional industries. Elworthy, whose family wealth came through ownership of a Somerset woollen mill, was alert to the language of wool and textile manufacture.[135] In Northumberland, in a major piece of research, Richard Oliver Heslop made a thorough record of the vocabulary of coal mining. Heslop (1842–1916) was an iron merchant, whose eight-hundred-page *Northumberland Words* was published in two volumes by the English Dialect Society in 1892–3.[136] Heslop took special care to record the region's industrial vocabulary, and he drew extensively on W. E. Nicholson's *Glossary of Terms Used in the Coal Trade of Northumberland and Durham* (1888), itself a revision of an earlier work, with identical title, by G. C. Greenwell.[137] Accordingly, Heslop includes entries for such terms as *engine-pit* 'the shaft of a colliery in which the pumps are worked' and *engine-plane* 'at a colliery, a level main road', *metal-coal* 'coal containing pyrites', and *outshifts* 'in mining, shifts worked by sinkers outside the shaft, for which a less wage is paid', as well as less obviously technical, but still highly specific, words such *jowlin* 'the cracking, rending sound heard when the props are removed from a mine working', *ootbye* 'towards the bottom of the shaft of a pit', and *pricker* 'a thin pointed rod made of yellow metal, and used for placing and adjusting a blasting cartridge'.[138] Some definitions lead the reader along a chain of entries: *makins* 'the small coals hewn out in kirving and nicking; or the slack and dirt made in drilling a hole in the coal', inevitably leads to reference to *kirvin-and-nickin* 'in coal mining, the preparatory operations for bringing down the *jud* or top', which in turn leads to *jud* 'the portion of coal at which the hewer is working, kirved, nicked, and ready to be brought down'.[139] Nor does Heslop confine his industrial vocabulary to mining: he also includes many other words drawn from the working life of the region, such as *can* 'the allowance of beer claimed by keelmen', *ockeril* 'a little cabin or resting place where the men at a rolling mill had each his own seat for resting and eating chance meals between heats', and *plater* 'the man who has charge of putting on ship-plates'.[140]

In Cheshire, Robert Holland sought out information about, variously, salt mining, tanning, silk and felt manufacture, and hatting.[141] Terms from tanning to be found in his *Cheshire Glossary* include *bate-shaving*, *beam*, *butt*, *crop-hide*, *hand-hook*, and

---

[134] Elworthy, *The West Somerset Word-Book*, pp. 278, 558.

[135] See, for example, Elworthy, *Outline of the Grammar of the Dialect of West Somerset*, p. 72 n.1; see also Ogilvie, *The Dictionary People*, pp. 77–9.

[136] See Colls, 'The New Northumbrians', pp. 156–7, 162–3.

[137] R. Oliver Heslop, *Northumberland Words: A Glossary of Words Used in the County of Northumberland and on the Tyneside*, 2 vols, English Dialect Society 66, 68 (London: English Dialect Society, 1892–3), p. xxviii.

[138] Heslop, *Northumberland Words*, pp. 266, 409, 513, 476, 516, 551.

[139] Heslop, *Northumberland Words*, pp. 410, 426, 464.

[140] Heslop, *Northumberland Words*, pp. 127, 508, 541.

[141] See *English Dialect Society: Eighth Annual Report*, pp. 2–3; Holland, *Words Used in the County of Chester*, p. v; Robert Holland to J. H. Nodal 5 October 1883, Manchester, John Rylands Research Institute and Library, GB 133 JHN 1/60.

unhair, while Cheshire's silk industry supplies *cane, danter, gate, half-timer*, and *quill*; and weaving terms more generally include *heald, leease, reed, sheead*, and *swift*.[142] But it is hatting and salt mining which are especially generative of local industrial vocabulary. Holland's *Glossary* contains nearly forty terms from the hatting trade, from *anglesea* and *basket* ('the name given to a peculiar curl of the hat brim' and 'a flat crossing of twigs used to press down the layers of wool or fur'), through *flake* and *goose* ('a small wicker grating used for collecting the bowed wool' and 'an implement used in the curling of hat brims'), to *walk-pin* and *yeoman* ('a round piece of wood thickest in the middle and tapered off at each end, used to press the water out of hat bodies' and 'the difference in size of a hat crown between the band or head part and the top of the crown').[143] But even this rich vocabulary is dwarfed by that of salt mining, from which Holland includes more than 150 terms: the letter B alone supplies over twenty, for example, including *barnacles* 'a pair of chains with two hooks to hook on each side of the tub when drawing rock salt', *basses* 'clinkers formed in the furnace', *benching* 'getting the bed of rock salt down to the "sole" of the mine after the roofing drift has been made', *boiler* 'the name given to the men who make stoved and butter salt', *breasters* 'lumps of salt placed between distinct lots to separate them', and *broth* 'a liquor made by boiling calves' feet, glue, &c., used for clarifying the brine, and put in after the new brine has been run into a pan'.[144] Such work practices, and the workers engaged in them, are viewed closely in terms of the experience of labour, and not remotely as picturesque figures in a landscape: Holland's hatting terms, for example, include *garrett* 'a meeting of workpeople', *knock off shop* 'to pass a resolution to refuse taking out any more work until a real or supposed grievance has been remedied', and, requiring most explanation, *small-gang* ('When any man, or big bully, has made himself intolerable to the boys amongst the hands, they take measures to *small-gang* him. Upon the principle that union is strength, they watch or make their opportunity, and all at once, or by relays, fall upon the oppressor, till, as a matter of course, they get him down, and give him a most severe beating; thus revenging the past, and securing a future of peace').[145] There is also *wack* 'a name given to materials which have been pilfered by workmen during the course of manufacture'.[146]

Industrial emphases such as these were not unique to Holland's or Heslop's work: the English Dialect Society, for example, reprinted a number of glossaries on Derbyshire lead mining, and Georgina Jackson, in her *Shropshire Word-Book*, also took a special interest in mining vocabulary.[147] Such records give the lie to the idea that Victorian collectors were only interested in country traditions, in constructing an 'English rural myth'; rather, they are reminiscent of Hopkins' celebration in 'Pied Beauty', his praise-poem on the multifariousness of creation, of 'all trades, their gear

---

[142] Holland, *Glossary of Words Used in the County of Chester*, pp. 22, 24, 51, 87, 155, 374; pp. 55, 95, 139, 154, 276; pp. 160, 200, 284, 310, 349.
[143] Holland, *Glossary of Words Used in the County of Chester*, pp. 8, 21, 125, 146, 380, 399.
[144] Holland, *Glossary of Words Used in the County of Chester*, pp. 20, 21, 27, 36, 44, 47.
[145] Holland, *Glossary of Words Used in the County of Chester*, pp. 139, 193, 324.
[146] Holland, *Glossary of Words Used in the County of Chester*, p. 379.
[147] See Walter W. Skeat (ed.), *Reprinted Glossaries*, English Dialect Society 5 (London: English Dialect Society, 1874); Jackson, *Shropshire Word-Book*, p. xv.

214   The Victorians and English Dialect

and tackle and trim'.[148] It is true that regional philologists were habitually more interested in language that they perceived to be old rather than new, and that some scholars could take a negative view of urban dialects, but there were many who gathered industrial vocabulary just as assiduously as they did agricultural.[149] This was a journey into the industries of Victorian England, not an escape from them. The two points of England most associated with regional dialect were the west and the north; and while the language and culture of Dorset and Devon and Somerset were usually perceived as rural and agricultural, those of Lancashire and Yorkshire were often urban and industrial.

And of course, much of this industrial vocabulary does not represent 'folklore' in the sense of arcane customs or archaic belief: it is simply life as lived by the working classes of the nineteenth century, a vocabulary and existence captured by dialect collectors in much the same way that Henry Mayhew had earlier recorded the details of labouring life in London. Fred Elworthy presented his *West Somerset Word-Book* as a 'labour of love', and reflected that 'the work [. . .] has brought me into closer contact with my humbler neighbours than any other pursuit could have done; so that I have become familiar not only with their forms of speech but with their mode of thought'.[150] Indeed, it is notable how Elworthy aligns himself with the local dialect speakers he is studying through his use of the first person pronoun: 'we are very fond of the termination *ĕesh*', he writes, or 'the termination *n*, *en*, or *ĕen* is very common with us'.[151] *Us*—not *them*. It is not a coincidence that many dialect collectors, such as Charlotte Ellis in Leicestershire, were committed to political reform and social welfare.

Our fourth and final field of vocabulary, though, is perhaps more stereotypically 'folkloric'—namely, words that reveal supernatural beliefs. T. S. Eliot, writing in 1920, put a low valuation on 'our trolls and pixies' and suggested that, effaced by Christian culture in Britain, they 'were perhaps no great loss in themselves'.[152] But other students of culture, working a few decades earlier, took a very different view, and dialect-folklorists recorded a vast population of—as the so-called *Denham Tracts* put it in an exhilarating list—'ghosts, boggles, bloody-bones, spirits, demons, ignis fatui, brownies, bugbears, black dogs, spectres, shellycoats, scarecrows, witches, wizards, barguests, Robin-Goodfellows, hags, night-bats, scrags, breaknecks, fantasms, hobgoblins, hobhoulards, boggy-boes, dobbies, hob-thrusts, fetches, kelpies, warlocks', and so on and so on for another hundred types.[153] As this teeming catalogue suggests, many wights and spectres haunt the pages of Victorian dialect glossaries,

---

[148] Hopkins, *The Major Works*, pp. 132–3. See, for example, Bennett, 'Folklore Studies and the English Rural Myth'.

[149] See further, for example, Peter Wright, *The Language of British Industry* (London: Macmillan, 1974).

[150] Elworthy, *The West Somerset Word-Book*, p. xii; see further Roper, 'Folklore in the Glossaries of the English Dialect Society', pp. 195–6.

[151] Elworthy, *Outline of the Grammar of the Dialect of West Somerset*, p. 18.

[152] T. S. Eliot, *The Sacred Wood: Essays on Poetry and Criticism* (London: Faber and Faber, 1997), p. 133.

[153] James Hardy (ed.), *The Denham Tracts: A Collection of Folklore by Michael Aislabie Denham*, 2 vols, Publications of the Folklore Society 29, 35 (London: Folklore Society, 1892–5), II, 77. See further Dorson, *The British Folklorists*, pp. 291–3; Peter Gilliver, Jeremy Marshall, and Edmund Weiner, *The Ring of Words: Tolkien and the Oxford English Dictionary* (Oxford: Oxford University Press, 2006), pp. 145–9.

Folklore and the Past **215**

and fairy lore—or 'goblindom', as Laurence Gomme's 1890 *Handbook of Folklore* called it—could be discovered in all manner of traditional words and names. Britten and Holland's *Dictionary of English Plant-Names*, for example, lists no fewer than seventeen different plant or flower names containing the word *fairy* or *fairies* (Fairy Bell, Fairy Butter, Fairy Cap, Fairy Cheeses, Fairy Cups, and so on).[154]

An especially common figure is the *boggle* or *boggart*: uncanny, shape-shifting, and most definitely to be avoided, the boggle was liable to be encountered on deserted roads and in remote places.[155] Ben Brierley recalled from his childhood how 'older boys met on winter nights, and told "boggart-tales" until they were so frightened that their parents had to fetch them home at bedtime'.[156] The enlarged version of F. K. Robinson's *Whitby Glossary* records a whole suite of *boggle*-compounds, suggesting something of how this elusive, mutable figure could form a core part of world view and vocabulary: *boggle-beck* 'the haunted stream', *boggle-blunder'd* 'bewildered in the dark by having lost one's road', and *boggle-chass'd* 'pursued by the *boggle* or barguest, as people in the dark have been scared by "something" tracking their footsteps'. We learn something—but only something—of the boggle's appearance and presence: *boggle-gloor* 'the glare of the barguest, or the "saucer-eyed" being', and *boggle-howl* 'the unearthly yell of the barguest'.[157] Terms such as *boggle-flay'd* 'scared by the boggle' expand into more idiomatic expressions or even psychological diagnoses: *boggle-fits* 'nervous depressions; dismal apprehensions', *boggle-hunter* 'one who "meets troubles half way", or harasses himself with imaginary difficulties', and *boggle-press'd* 'oppressed by the nightmare; "hag-ridden"'.

The boggle was perhaps the most persistent and prominent of (in Elizabeth Mary Wright's description) 'all those imaginary beings that peopled the darkness of long ago'—Grendel-like presences, glimpsed out of the corner of the eye or sensed over the shoulder.[158] But there were many other manifestations out there too, not least a terrifying array of 'nursery bogies', invoked to discipline and deter children. On the Isle of Wight, according to Smith and Smith, recalcitrant children were threatened that 'I'll zend the *mumpoker* ater ye', while in Cheshire Robert Holland records the terrors of Jinny Green-teeth and Nelly Long Arms: both of these haunted ponds or wells, and local children were warned that, if they went too close to the water, '*Jinny Green-teeth* should have them' or '*Nelly Long Arms* would pull them in'.[159]

---

[154] Gomme, *Handbook of Folklore*, pp. 30–8; Britten and Holland, *Dictionary of English Plant-Names*, p. 173.

[155] See, for example, Wright (ed.), *English Dialect Dictionary*, I, 326–8; Wright, *Rustic Speech and Folk-Lore*, pp. 192–5; Jennifer Westwood and Jacqueline Simpson, *The Lore of the Land: A Guide to England's Legends, from Spring-Heeled Jack to the Witches of Warboys* (London: Penguin, 2005), pp. 560–1; Simon Young, 'Joseph Wright Meets the Boggart', *Folk Life* 56 (2018), 1–13, and *The Boggart: Folklore, History, Place-Names and Dialect* (Exeter: Exeter University Press, 2022).

[156] Brierley, *Home Memories*, p. 9.

[157] F. K. Robinson, *A Glossary of Words Used in the Neighbourhood of Whitby*, English Dialect Society 9, 13 (London: English Dialect Society, 1875–6), p. 21.

[158] Wright, *Rustic Speech and Folk-Lore*, p. 191.

[159] Smith and Smith, 'Glossary of Words in Use in the Isle of Wight', p. 22; Holland, *Glossary of Words Used in the County of Chester*, pp. 182, 238. See further Wright, *Rustic Speech and Folk-Lore*, pp. 197–9; Katharine Briggs, *A Dictionary of Fairies: Hobgoblins, Brownies, Bogies and Other Supernatural Creatures*

216 The Victorians and English Dialect

Not far behind the boggle in its near-ubiquity in dialect glossaries, but potentially more homely, was the *hobthrush* or equivalent, defined by Wright as a 'drudging goblin' and explained by Dickinson in his *Cumberland Glossary* as 'a hobgoblin having the repute of doing much useful work unseen and unheard during the night, if not interfered with, but discontinuing or doing mischief if crossed or watched, or endeavoured to be coaxed or bribed to work in any way but his own' (though *hobthrush* was also yet another dialect term for the wood-louse, found for instance in Swaledale in Yorkshire).[160] Many hobs or hobthrushes, naturally enough, were associated with particular places. One especially famous one, who could cure the *kink-cough* or whooping cough, lived at Hob Hole at Runswick Bay on the Yorkshire coast, and both F. K. Robinson and J. C. Atkinson recorded the rhyme that was needed to solicit his help: 'Hob-hole Hob! Mah bairn's getten t' kin'-cough:/Tak' 't off! Tak' 't off!'[161]

Atkinson's awareness of the supernatural presences in his area of country led not simply to glossary-making but also to storytelling. Philology, folklore, and narrative had been intertwined since the time of the Brothers Grimm, and a number of dialect-folklorists could see the connection between their scholarly pursuits and the writing or recording of fairy tales. For example, Sidney Oldall Addy (1848–1933) was a solicitor in Sheffield who published an important *Glossary of Words Used in the Neighbourhood of Sheffield* with the English Dialect Society in 1888, and then a volume of *Household Tales with Other Traditional Remains* in 1895 (the idiom 'household tales' is modelled on the Grimms' *hausmärchen*); his convinced view was that 'the collection of dialect leads us into folklore, as well as into important questions of philology'.[162] Atkinson's efforts were akin to Addy's in some respects, but were both more consciously creative and also more closely tied to specific places. In the same year, 1891, Atkinson published both *Forty Years in a Moorland Parish*, his classic of folkloric antiquarianism, and also a collection of stories called *The Last of the Giant Killers; or The Exploits of Sir Jack of Danby Dale*. In *The Last of the Giant Killers*, Atkinson takes fairy-tale traditions in the vicinity of Danby, especially those associated with specific places, and strings them together as a (semi-)coherent set of stories around the archetypal figure of Jack (who happens, incidentally, to marry Little Red Riding Hood in the course of his adventures). It is strategically unclear as to which elements of the narrative are Atkinson's own invention—clearly, quite a lot are—but

---

(London: Penguin, 1976), pp. 242, 313; Westwood and Simpson, *The Lore of the Land*, pp. 620, 696–7; Simon Young, 'In Search of Jenny Greenteeth', *Gramarye* 16 (2019), 24–38.

[160] Wright, *Rustic Speech and Folk-Lore*, pp. 201–2; Dickinson, *Glossary of Words and Phrases Pertaining to the Dialect of Cumberland*, p. 47; Adams, 'On the Names of the Wood-Louse', pp. 17–19; John Harland, *A Glossary of Words Used in Swaledale, Yorkshire*, English Dialect Society 3 (London: English Dialect Society, 1873), p. 16. See further Briggs, *Dictionary of Fairies*, 222–3; Carolyne Larrington, *The Land of the Green Man: A Journey through the Supernatural Landscapes of the British Isles* (London: Tauris, 2015), pp. 142–50.

[161] Atkinson, *Glossary of the Cleveland Dialect*, p. 262; Robinson, *Glossary of Words Used in the Neighbourhood of Whitby*, p. xii. See further Westwood and Simpson, *The Lore of the Land*, pp. 827–30.

[162] Sidney Oldall Addy, 'The Collection of English Dialect', *Transactions of the Yorkshire Dialect Society* 8 (1906), 23–33, at p. 32. On Addy, see Ashton, 'Beyond Survivalism', pp. 21–2; Bennett, 'Folklore Studies and the English Rural Myth', pp. 85–6; Simpson and Roud, *Dictionary of English Folklore*, pp. 2–3; Roper, 'Folklore in the Glossaries of the English Dialect Society', pp. 193–4.

Folklore and the Past   **217**

equally there is no doubt of the fundamental continuity between the tales in *The Last of the Giant Killers*, the words in the *Cleveland Glossary*, and the traditions in *Forty Years in a Moorland Parish*.

Let us take as an example the final story in the collection, 'How Sir Jack Restored Its Head to the Headless Hart of the Hart Leap'. This takes as its point of beginnings the place name 'The Hart Leap', between Great Fryup and Glaisdale, around which Atkinson weaves a story of a giant stag and a series of bloody killings, a chain of events which Jack is only able to bring an end to through the help of 'the elf-maidens of the Glaisdale Swangs' and 'the fay-flames from the round House near Giant Wade's grave', as well as possession of a very useful seeing-stone or 'all-kenner'.[163] The Wild Hunt or 'Gabriel-ratchet' is at the centre of the tale, the unseen, baying hounds that rush overhead and bring death and terror: 'sometimes they were called "corpse-hounds", and sometimes by other names that meant the same, and in English might be written "lych-whelps", "lych-hounds", "corpse-trackers", or the like; and even our own home name, or "Gaab'rl ratchet"'; and this last 'home name' does indeed receive a very full discussion in Atkinson's *Cleveland Glossary*.[164] Atkinson presents his own narrator-persona as a seeker-out of old traditions, as he claims to piece together the story: 'all this and more I heard at different times and from different people', he writes, and he credits one particular tradition-bearer, a man called Reuben, whom Atkinson knew 'a long while ago' and who lived 'at an out-of-the-way house, in a wild part of Commondale, called Skelderskew'.[165] Local words are foregrounded as well as local place names and local traditions—*belantered, cleugh, fleeing-ask, hagworm, strike*—as Atkinson combines folklore and fairy tale with philology and antiquarianism to tell his stories of 'this one-time fairy-haunted country'.[166]

Folkloric fiction

The stories of Addy and Atkinson take us back to the question of dialect and fiction, last considered in Chapter 3. There we saw how the provincial novel and indus-trial novel of the 1840s to 1860s foregrounded regional dialect in a contemporary and often urban setting. But we also saw the beginnings of a distinctive strand of regional fiction, in the form of *Adam Bede* and *Sylvia's Lovers*, in which a more rural setting is preferred, and an element of historical distance is introduced, so that the language and culture of the characters are being examined as something differ-ent from that of the readers of such books. In the final section of this chapter, we will move forward into the later decades of the nineteenth century, and explore the

---

[163] J. C. Atkinson, *The Last of the Giant Killers; or The Exploits of Sir Jack of Danby Dale* (London: Macmillan, 1891), pp. 224, 228.

[164] Atkinson, *The Last of the Giant Killers*, p. 201; Atkinson, *Glossary of the Cleveland Dialect*, pp. 203–4. See further Wright, *Rustic Speech and Folk-Lore*, pp. 195–6; Westwood and Simpson, *The Lore of the Land*, pp. 670–1; Larrington, *The Land of the Green Man*, pp. 97–104.

[165] Atkinson, *The Last of the Giant Killers*, p. 196.

[166] Atkinson, *Glossary of the Cleveland Dialect*, pp. 39, 105, 188, 240, 432; Atkinson, *The Last of the Giant Killers*, p. 244.

218 The Victorians and English Dialect

development of what might be called 'folkloric fiction': that is, fiction in which rural folklore and dialect play a prominent part, and in which the traditions of the Victorian regional novel meet those of the historical novel, and are informed by the perspectives and discourses of nineteenth-century folklore study. We will examine novels by three writers, all associated with the west of England: R. D. Blackmore, Sabine Baring-Gould, and (finally and most fully) Thomas Hardy.

Lorna Doone by Richard Doddridge Blackmore was published in 1869, and was a formative influence on the regional historical novels of the later nineteenth century. By turns pastoral, historical, regional, romantic, and melodramatic, it also formed a bridge between the novels of Walter Scott and certain 'New Romance' writers such as Robert Louis Stevenson.[167] Blackmore himself (1825–1900) was a lawyer, teacher, and (most of all) fruit farmer in Teddington in Middlesex, as well as the author of over a dozen works of fiction.[168] He was highly regarded: as a novelist, Gerard Manley Hopkins for one rated him above George Eliot.[169]

Lorna Doone is set in the 1680s, at the time of the 'Monmouth Rebellion'. Its location (mostly) is Exmoor, on the border between Devon and Somerset—where Blackmore had spent some of his formative years—and its protagonist and narrator is John Ridd, a west-country farmer. He falls in love with the mysterious Lorna Doone, held captive in a secret valley by the outlaw Doone clan. Eventually John rescues her, and she is revealed to be not a member of the Doone family after all, but a wealthy aristocrat who had been captured by them as a child. The central plot idea, therefore, is that of the outlaw clan, and certain real-life local legends seem to lie behind Blackmore's telling of the story: Arthur Munby, an old friend of Blackmore's, wrote in his diary in 1871 that 'his "Lorna Doone" has been a great success and has had (what is the best success) the effect of arousing among the people on the spot a keen interest in their own legends'; the novel also generated a whole tourist industry.[170] Blackmore also packs his narrative with a variety of folkloric motifs and episodes, including a visit to a wise woman, a headless ghost, and a belief in pixies, while occasional footnotes assert the antiquarian veracity of the traditions reported.[171] These folklore elements form part of Blackmore's fundamental technique of historical distancing, as he contrives to make the past seem different from the present, even at the same time as he uses his novel about the past to explore various present concerns.

Blackmore's narrative accentuates a number of different layers of historical difference. One is implicit, between the 1680s and the 1860s (except where the occasional footnotes make it explicit), and Blackmore plays the historical novelist's game of including objects and customs which are unremarkable at the time of composition

---

[167] See, for example, John Bowen, 'The Historical Novel', in Patrick Brantlinger and William B. Thesing (eds), *A Companion to the Victorian Novel* (Oxford: Wiley Blackwell, 2005), pp. 244–59, at pp. 256–7.
[168] See Charlotte Mitchell, 'Blackmore, Richard Doddridge (1825–1900)', in *Oxford Dictionary of National Biography* [www.oxforddnb].
[169] Hopkins, *Correspondence*, II, 826 (28 October 1886).
[170] Hudson, *Munby: Man of Two Worlds*, p. 295; see Nicola J. Watson, *The Literary Tourist* (Basingstoke: Palgrave Macmillan, 2006), pp. 163–8.
[171] See R. D. Blackmore, *Lorna Doone: A Romance of Exmoor*, ed. Sally Shuttleworth (Oxford: Oxford University Press, 2008), pp. 136–43, 246, 301, 318 n.

but were novelties at the time of the novel's setting (so his seventeenth-century characters marvel over the new-fangledness of potatoes, cigars, pointer dogs, potters' treadmills, and even carts with wheels).[172] But even within the first person narrative of John Ridd, Blackmore opens up a space for awareness of change through his conceit that the story is being written by John Ridd in his old age, sometime in the early 1700s and thus several decades after the events of the novel ('nowadays it is very different', he writes).[173] This permits Ridd to ponder on the past like a proto-Victorian, an antiquarian proxy with interests in rural customs and—importantly—language. So the nativization of potatoes is marked linguistically (Ridd writes of 'the root called "batata" (a new but good thing in our neighbourhood, which our folk have turned into "taties")'), and Blackmore's narrator is alert to lexical change: Ridd relates, for instance, that '[Lorna] was too young to answer me, in the style some maidens would have used; the manner, I mean, which now we call from a foreign word "coquettish"'.[174] Ridd is thus something of an anachronistic philologist, offering nineteenth-century insights in an early eighteenth-century text, for example on the etymologies of the place names of Devon.[175] These interests are really Blackmore's, of course, and the prose (and especially the dialogue) of *Lorna Doone* is a fascinating example of the kind of historically sensitive, period-appropriate language that novelists might attempt to use in the wake of the rise of philology. Blackmore tries very hard at this—*foughten, gotten, lanthorn, liefer*—and if at times he tips over into a stagey faux-archaism (John Ridd really does say 'Gadzooks' at one point), his sustained endeavour is still a very creditable one, especially for a pre-*OED* writer.[176]

Blackmore's care with dialect is immense, both in finding the right language for individual characters, and in distinguishing different grades of dialect speech and dialect speaker. The majority of the characters speak Exmoor dialect, and this is differentiated from the Cornish speech of Gwenny Carfax, Lorna's 'handmaid'.[177] Mocking or sneering at dialect is never tolerated, no matter who does it:

> While I was gazing at all these things, with wonder and some sadness, Lorna turned upon me lightly (as her manner was) and said,—
> 'Where are the new-laid eggs, Master Ridd? Or hath blue hen ceased laying?'
> I did not altogether like the way in which she said it, with a sort of a dialect, as if my speech could be laughed at.
> 'Here be some', I answered, speaking as if in spite of her.[178]

Blackmore's general practice, as for other Victorian novelists, is to give major characters a light, suggestive dressing of dialect, and to retain the heaviest use for minor characters, even those from the same social class: so, for example, an unnamed

---

[172] See Blackmore, *Lorna Doone*, pp. 75, 160–1, 469, 477, 487.
[173] Blackmore, *Lorna Doone*, p. 181.
[174] Blackmore, *Lorna Doone*, p. 130.
[175] See Blackmore, *Lorna Doone*, pp. 22, 137.
[176] Blackmore, *Lorna Doone*, pp. 16, 17, 18, 50, 66.
[177] See, for example, Blackmore, *Lorna Doone*, pp. 293–4, 405, 592.
[178] Blackmore, *Lorna Doone*, p. 147; see also p. 14.

220   The Victorians and English Dialect

Somerset militia-man turns up and says 'Plaise zur [. . .] hus tould Harfizers, as a wor no nade of un, now King's man hiszel wor coom, a puppose vor to command us laike'.[179] Dialect-heavy minor characters, even named ones such as Ridd's servant John Fry, are rarely given lengthy speeches (Ridd admits that, in his narrative, he has 'robbed [John Fry] of many speeches'), and on the one occasion when Fry is permitted to tell a long story, Ridd explains, as Blackmore's narrator, that 'I dare not write down some few of his words, because they are not convenient, for dialect or other causes; and that I cannot find any way of spelling many of the words which I do repeat, so that people, not born on Exmoor, may know how he pronounced them' (Fry begins: 'I wor over to Exeford in the marning [. . .] for to zee a little calve, Jan, as us cuddn't get thee to lave house about').[180]

The novel is full of dialect words: a sample of just a few pages supplies *brewis*, *fern-web, galanies, prog, speckots*, and *stickle*.[181] Elizabeth Mary Wright was especially struck by Blackmore's use of the word *tallat* or *tallet* 'a hay-loft', which she considered an early loanword from Celtic into Old English, and before that a loanword from Latin into Celtic: 'the remarkable point about the preservation of this word', she wrote, 'is that it never once occurs in the whole range of English literature down to the nineteenth century, when Blackmore introduced it in his *Lorna Doone*'.[182] But especially significant for understanding the new development that *Lorna Doone* represents are those many occurrences where Blackmore marks out the dialect term by punctuation (quotation marks or inverted commas, according to the edition), and then provides a gloss for the uncomprehending reader who may be remote, non-dialect-speaking, and perhaps urban. There are many examples: 'we were come to a long deep "goyal", as they call it on Exmoor'; 'I caught a "whacker" (as we called a big fish at Tiverton)'; '[I] saw their hats under the rampart of ash, which is made by what we call "splashing"'; 'no man could "keep yatt" (as we say)'; 'quick she had always been, and "peart" (as we say on Exmoor)'; 'soaked and sodden, and, as we call it, "mucksy"'; and 'he stuck fast in a "dancing-bog", as we call them upon Exmoor'.[183] We have already met this practice in Gaskell's *Sylvia's Lovers*, and what it signals is important: the presentation of dialect to a non-dialectal audience via a mode that might be called antiquarian or even anthropological. Here, the approach is mediated through John Ridd's first person narrative; but there is no reason why such a method might not equally be adopted by an omniscient narrator, as in *Sylvia's Lovers*.

A visit to London makes John Ridd conscious—but not ashamed—of his 'west-country twang', and the contrastive effects of a number of episodes set in the capital serve to heighten the celebratory (though not uncritical) presentation of Exmoor life.[184] Blackmore's novel includes a number of set-piece scenes of rural life, supremely

---

[179] Blackmore, *Lorna Doone*, p. 457.
[180] Blackmore, *Lorna Doone*, pp. 313, 314.
[181] Blackmore, *Lorna Doone*, pp. 52–8, 666.
[182] Blackmore, *Lorna Doone*, p. 444; Wright, *Rustic Speech and Folk-Lore*, p. 105. See further A. L. Mayhew, '"Tallet", a West-Country Word', *Notes and Queries* 8th Series 4 (2 December 1893), 450–1; Wright (ed.) *English Dialect Dictionary*, VI, 23.
[183] Blackmore, *Lorna Doone*, pp. 29 (and see also 137), 60, 300, 321, 365, 373, 391.
[184] Blackmore, *Lorna Doone*, p. 213.

a harvest chapter on 'reaping' and 'revelling', complete with rhymes, rituals, and a grand harvest supper, climaxing in the singing of an 'Exmoor Harvest-Song' (full text included, albeit in Standard English).[185] What *Lorna Doone* bequeathed to subsequent writers was a model for fiction which was regional and rural in setting, historical in orientation, and rich in local dialect, folklore, and customs—with a dash of melodrama to speed the narrative along.

A second novel to consider is *Red Spider* by Sabine Baring-Gould, published a decade and a half later, in 1887. Baring-Gould (1834–1924) was an extraordinarily prolific writer, whose list of published volumes runs well into three figures—quite apart from his duties as 'squarson' (squire and parson) of Lew Trenchard in Devon.[186] Born one year before Skeat, and two years before Murray, he was a talented linguist who could speak five languages by the age of 15, and in the 1850s and 1860s, like others of his generation, he developed a range of historical and philological interests, not least an early, and unusually deep, knowledge of Old Norse language and literature— including a pioneering trip round Icelandic saga sites in 1861.[187] He wrote dozens of religious books, including a fifteen-volume set of *Lives of the Saints* (1872–7); biographies; travel books; and nearly fifty works of fiction, from short-story collections to three-volume novels. He is most famous now (in addition to his composition of the hymn 'Onward, Christian Soldiers') for his activities and writings as a folklorist, above all his efforts as a collector of west-country folk songs.[188]

An interest in regional dialect, not surprisingly, features in Baring-Gould's work from an early stage. His first full-length novel, *Through Flood and Flame* (1868), is marked by the use of Yorkshire dialect—the result of seven years in Yorkshire as a curate. His well-known novel *Mehalah* (1880) shows Essex dialect—the result of his time as rector of East Mersea. But after his return to Devon in 1881, it was the dialect and traditions of his family area that came to dominate his work.

Baring-Gould regarded *Red Spider* as his finest novel, and in time it was even adapted into an opera. The story is set in Baring-Gould's own area of Devon, and tells of the rivalry between two land-holders, Hillary Nanspian and Taverner Langford, viewed mostly from the perspective of Honor Luxmore, the capable daughter of the local carrier. Regional dialect is drawn to the reader's attention in the second paragraph of the story, telling of Hillary Nanspian:

> When he ate a particularly good apple, he collected the pips for sowing, put them in a paper cornet, and wrote thereon, 'This here apple was a-eated of I on—' such and

---

[185] Blackmore, *Lorna Doone*, pp. 220–8.

[186] See Bickford H. C. Dickinson, *Sabine Baring-Gould: Squarson, Writer and Folklorist, 1834–1924* (Newton Abbot: David and Charles, 1970), pp. 176–85.

[187] See Andrew Wawn, 'The Grimms, the Kirk-Grims, and Sabine Baring-Gould', in Andrew Wawn (ed.), *Constructing Nations, Reconstructing Myth: Essays in Honour of T. A. Shippey*, Making the Middle Ages 9 (Turnhout: Brepols, 2007), pp. 215–42, and 'Sabine Baring-Gould and Iceland: A Re-evaluation', in Marie Wells (ed.), *The Discovery of Nineteenth-Century Scandinavia* (Norwich: Norvik Press, 2008), pp. 27–42.

[188] See Martin Graebe, *As I Walked Out: Sabine Baring-Gould and the Search for the Folk Songs of Devon and Cornwall* (Oxford: Signal Books, 2017); Roud, *Folk Song in England*, pp. 93–8.

222 The Victorians and English Dialect

such a day, 'and cruel good he were too'. (*Cruel*, in the West, means no more than 'very'.)[189]

The short sentence written by Nanspian packs in several features of dialect grammar ('a-' as prefix on past participles, 'I' as object case, and 'were' as third person singular indicative), a couple of syntactic points ('This here' as a deictic, and sentence-fronting of the complement 'cruel good'), and an item of dialect vocabulary ('cruel')—quite apart from the narrator's desire to comment explicitly on this last point. Such passages of high-density dialect occur frequently in the novel, although, as in *Lorna Doone*, they tend to be associated with particular characters, rather than being evenly distributed. Quite how authentic Baring-Gould's depiction of Devon dialect may be is up for dispute: his own grandson thought that 'being multilingual himself and not having spent his early boyhood in Devon, he was apt to use words and phrases that he had heard in Yorkshire and Essex, just as he himself, as he freely admitted, used Danish or Dutch words when speaking German'.[190]

It is, however, the habit of narratorial comment or glossing that merits further attention, and which connects closely with what we have just seen in *Lorna Doone*. Like Blackmore, Baring-Gould inserts his glosses and comments prominently into the main text of the novel. Sometimes, as in the instance of 'cruel' above, these are quite discursive: for example, 'the rafters of the old house, the beams of the cattle-sheds, the posts of the gates, the very rails ("shivers", as they were locally called), the flooring ("plancheon" locally), all were of oak, hard as iron'; or 'he found himself lying on the hay in the little "linney", or lean-to shed, of his father'.[191] Often, though, the glosses are simply given parenthetically, with minimal fuss (and usually only at the time of first occurrence). But because, by definition, dialect terms normally occur in the direct speech of the local protagonists, rather than in the narrator's own prose (as happens in *Lorna Doone*), the narrator's Standard English glosses have to keep breaking into the characters' dialect utterances: for example, 'I will keep the fire up with a mote (tree-stump)'; or 'in our barton field the sweet water comes out at the well, and the riddam (ferruginous red water) at the alders'; or 'folks far away see a great light on Broadbury, and say we be swaling (burning gorse) up here'.[192] Sometimes, even, there is a sort of reverse glossing, in which the Standard English term is used in the narrative, but the comment or parenthesis supplies the local variant: for example, 'behind her, seen through the door, was a bank of bushes and pink foxgloves, "flopadocks" is the local name', and 'she threw down her pitchfork ("heable" in the local dialect)'.[193] At times, this can be presented almost in terms of a guide to a foreign language, especially when marked by the Latin word *vulgo*, as in 'he wanted to know whether he had bought the crockery—*vulgo* "cloam"—as desired', and 'the

---

[189] Sabine Baring-Gould, *Red Spider* (Stroud: Nonsuch, 2007), p. 14
[190] Dickinson, *Sabine Baring-Gould*, pp. 145–6.
[191] Baring-Gould, *Red Spider*, pp. 15, 95.
[192] Baring-Gould, *Red Spider*, pp. 137, 151, 206.
[193] Baring-Gould, *Red Spider*, pp. 129, 187–8.

Folklore and the Past **223**

antagonists have their legs wreathed with haybands (*vulgo* skillibegs)'.[194] The use of *vulgo* (meaning 'in the vernacular') to signal a different language goes back at least to the practice of medieval Latin chronicles, with which Baring-Gould would have been familiar. In overall effect, these in-text glosses represent an intensification of the practice and perspective seen in *Sylvia's Lovers* and *Lorna Doone*. By identifying the Standard English glosses with the interventions of the narrator, Baring-Gould places the reader, with the narrator, on the outside of the culture that is being depicted: the world of Nanspian and Langford is being held up as an object for inquiry, and displayed as being full of well-justified interest.

In other words, the dialect element in *Red Spider* is viewed from a folkloric perspective. Baring-Gould was a distinguished scholar of folklore, and in *Red Spider* he heavily and self-consciously lays on the local flavour in terms of old and vanishing customs: the story contains fairs and festivals, Devon wrestling, the hunt for a witch supposedly transformed into a hare, the evil eye, a Hand of Glory, corpse-candles, weather-prognostics, and a whole series of scenes set at a prehistoric tumulus named after a local murderer. The very title of the work is folkloric: in local belief, a red spider was a money-spinner, a creature of good omen, though here 'Red Spider' is also the nickname of Honor Luxmore, the central female character.

Baring-Gould's use of dialect thus fits very intelligibly into his broader commitment to a vanishing rural culture; and as such, a novel like *Red Spider* marks a further consolidation of a literary form that combines philology, folklore, and regionalism in both its narrative content and its attitude towards time and place. The parallels with Thomas Hardy, our third and final novelist, are obvious, and do not need to be laboured. Oddly, Baring-Gould himself claimed never to have read Hardy's novels, though later he was an admirer of his poetry, while among Baring-Gould's works, Hardy shows knowledge of his folk song collection, *Songs of the West* (1905).[195] The Hardy novel we shall set alongside *Lorna Doone* and *Red Spider* here is *The Woodlanders* (1887), though many other works could have been chosen. But first we should consider Hardy's fictions more broadly, for his relationships with dialect and folklore, and the interconnections between the two.

The use of dialect in Hardy's novels and short stories has been well studied.[196] Like Blackmore and George Eliot, he observes a careful gradation in the density of

---

[194] Baring-Gould, *Red Spider*, pp. 114, 198.
[195] Dickinson, *Sabine Baring-Gould*, pp. 144–5; Thomas Hardy, *Collected Letters*, ed. Richard Little Purdy and Michael Millgate, 7 vols (Oxford: Clarendon Press, 1978–88), III, 247, 283.
[196] See, for example, Ulla Baugner, *A Study of the Use of Dialect in Thomas Hardy's Novels and Short Stories*, Stockholm Theses in English 7 (Stockholm: Stockholm University, 1972); Patricia Ingham, 'Thomas Hardy and the Dorset Dialect', in E. G. Stanley and Douglas Gray (eds), *Five Hundred Years of Words and Sounds: A Festschrift for Eric Dobson* (Woodbridge: Boydell and Brewer, 1983), pp. 84–91, and 'Dialect in the Novels of Hardy and George Eliot'; Page, 'Hardy and the English Language', pp. 163–5; Page, *Speech in the English Novel*, pp. 71–7; Elliott, *Thomas Hardy's English*, esp. pp. 36–109; Chapman, *The Language of Thomas Hardy*, pp. 112–24; Taylor, *Hardy's Literary Language and Victorian Philology*; Andrew R. Cooper, '"Folk-speech" and "book English": re-presentations of dialect in Hardy's novels', *Language and Literature* 3 (1994), 21–41; Gatrell, *Thomas Hardy's Vision of Wessex*, pp. 202–25, and 'Dialect'; Will Abberley, *English Fiction and the Evolution of Language, 1850–1914* (Cambridge: Cambridge University Press, 2015), pp. 121–7; Gregory Tate, 'Thomas Hardy's Pure English', *Victorian Literature and Culture* 50 (2022), 521–47.

224   The Victorians and English Dialect

his dialect representation, with the language of his major characters usually much less strongly marked than that of their supporting cast. Partly this is the result of a literary calculation, a desire to reach readers far removed from the Dorset he was writing about; but partly it is also a consequence of Hardy's habit of focalizing his fictions not through agricultural labourers, but rather through the more professional or independent members of the village community. Such families, according to *Tess of the D'Urbervilles*, 'formed the backbone of the village life in the past' and were 'the depositaries of the village traditions'.[197] We examined Hardy's championing of dialect words in his poetry in Chapter 3, but arguably the use of dialect takes on a different, more social meaning within the world of Hardy's fiction, one related rather to class, education, and perception than to the shaping of the author's own literary language. Chapter 1 of this book adduced the famous passage in *Tess of the D'Urbervilles* which contrasts the mental and linguistic world of Tess with that of her mother; elsewhere, at the wedding of Fancy Day (a schoolteacher) and Dick Dewy (the son of a 'tranter' or carrier) in *Under the Greenwood Tree* (1872), the narrator reports that 'the propriety of every one was intense, by reason of the influence of Fancy, who, as an additional precaution in this direction had strictly charged her father and the tranter to carefully avoid saying "thee" and "thou" in their conversation, on the plea that those ancient words sounded so very humiliating to persons of newer taste'.[198] A further example, more serious, is the generational and educational contrast between Elizabeth-Jane and her father Michael Henchard in *The Mayor of Casterbridge*:

> In time it came to pass that for "fay" she said "succeed"; that she no longer spoke of "dumbledores" but of "humble bees"; no longer said of young men and women that they "walked together", but that they were "engaged"; that she grew to talk of "greggles" as "wild hyacinths"; that when she had not slept she did not quaintly tell the servants next morning that she had been "hag-rid", but that she had "suffered from indigestion".[199]

From an early point in his fame, Hardy was either called upon, or felt obliged, to comment on the use of dialect in his novels: to members of the English Dialect Society in 1877 (as we saw in the previous chapter), he explained that, while he had 'scarcely preserved peculiarities of accent and trifling irregularities with such care as could have been wished for purposes of critical examination, the characteristic words which occur are in every case genuine, as heard from the lips of the natives'; to readers of the *Athenaeum* the following year, he asserted that that 'if a writer attempts to exhibit on paper the precise accents of a rustic speaker he disturbs the proper balance of a true representation by unduly insisting upon the grotesque element; thus

---

[197] Hardy, *Tess of the D'Urbervilles*, p. 339. See further, for example, Merryn Williams and Raymond Williams, 'Hardy and Social Class', in Norman Page (ed.), *Thomas Hardy: The Writer and his Background* (London: Bell and Hyman, 1980), pp. 29–40, at pp. 30–2.

[198] Hardy, *Tess of the D'Urbervilles*, p. 28, and *Under the Greenwood Tree*, ed. Simon Gatrell, new ed. (Oxford: Oxford University Press, 2013), p. 173.

[199] Thomas Hardy, *The Mayor of Casterbridge*, ed. Dale Kramer (Oxford: Oxford University Press, 2004), p. 121.

directing attention to a point of inferior interest, and diverting it from the speaker's meaning, which is by far the chief concern where the aim is to depict the men and their natures rather than their dialect forms'; and in the *Spectator* in 1881, he wrote that 'the rule of scrupulously preserving the local idiom, together with the words which have no synonym among those in general use, while printing in the ordinary way most of those local expressions which are but a modified articulation of words in use elsewhere, is the rule I usually follow; and it is, I believe, generally recognised as the best, where every such rule must of necessity be a compromise'.[200] In this last piece, Hardy asserted himself further and insisted: 'It must, of course, be always a matter for regret that, in order to be understood, writers should be obliged thus slightingly to treat varieties of English which are intrinsically as genuine, grammatical, and worthy of the royal title [i.e. the Queen's English] as is the all-prevailing competitor which bears it; whose only fault was that they happened not to be central, and therefore were worsted in the struggle for existence, when a uniform tongue became a necessity among the advanced classes of the population'. It is not hard to discern here the influence of William Barnes: only two years earlier, in his review of a new edition of Barnes' *Poems of Rural Life in the Dorset Dialect*, Hardy had published the first of his several tributes to the older writer—though the idea of a 'struggle for existence' seems a distinctively Hardyan note.[201]

'Things were like that in Wessex', Hardy wrote in the General Preface to the 1912 collected edition of his novels; 'the inhabitants lived in certain ways, engaged in certain occupations, kept alive certain customs, just as they are shown doing in these pages'.[202] But when were things like that? When was Wessex, exactly? Hardy is often evasive—no doubt intentionally so—about the chronological setting of his stories, and contrary indicators are often in tension. Some of his fiction, most obviously *Under the Greenwood Tree*, seems to be pitched a generation or two previously, in the 1820s and 1830s; and that was also the period that Hardy drew on when searching old copies of the *Dorset County Chronicle* for plot elements.[203] Other novels—*Tess*, perhaps—seem to be claiming a more contemporary setting; but if this is the case, is Hardy deliberately selecting for depiction features of (near-)contemporary rural life which he knows are recessive, on their way out—like Fred Elworthy with his recording of *pattens* and *gambaders*? In any case, it is important to realize that Hardy's concept of 'Wessex' did not spring into existence fully formed, from the time of his earliest fictions; rather, it emerged piecemeal, as real place names were gradually replaced by 'Wessex' ones, geography was altered and maps were added, and a consistency of mood and treatment was slowly cultivated. Arguably, 'Wessex' only reached its full realization after Hardy's novel-writing days were over, in the revisions and

---

[200] Millgate (ed.), *Thomas Hardy's Public Voice*, pp. 11, 14, 29.

[201] See Millgate (ed.), *Thomas Hardy's Public Voice*, pp. 16–27, 65–71, 291–7; Hardy, *Complete Poetical Works*, II, 212–13 ('The Last Signal').

[202] Harold Orel (ed.), *Thomas Hardy's Personal Writings: Prefaces, Literary Opinions, Reminiscences* (Lawrence: University of Kansas Press, 1966), p. 46.

[203] See Michael Millgate, *Thomas Hardy: His Career as a Novelist* (New York: Random House, 1971), pp. 237–43.

226   The Victorians and English Dialect

prefaces to the successive editions of his works (especially the Osgood, McIlvaine collected edition in 1895, and the Macmillan collected edition in 1912).[204]

The historian J. W. Burrow, invoking Hardy by name, wrote of 'the romantic intensification of antiquarianism into a kind of imaginative archaeology' in the later nineteenth century.[205] 'Romantic intensification' is a good phrase, and ties in well with Hardy's own observations about the need to move away from the tenets of classic Victorian realism and metropolitanism. Many of the artistic memoranda included in his posthumous biography (issued under the name of Florence Hardy, but essentially written by Hardy himself) make points to this effect. So, for example, in 1880, rejecting the view of Matthew Arnold, Hardy writes:

> Arnold is wrong about provincialism, if he means anything more than a provincialism of style and manner in exposition. A certain provincialism of feeling is invaluable. It is of the essence of individuality, and is largely made up of that crude enthusiasm without which no great thoughts are thought, no great deeds done.[206]

And in 1890: 'Art is a disproportioning—(*i.e.* distorting, throwing out of proportion)—of realities, to show more clearly the features that matter in those realities, which, if merely copied or reported inventorially, might possibly be observed, but would more probably be overlooked. Hence "realism" is not Art'.[207] These are broad, experimental statements about questions of viewpoint and narrative, but they illuminate how Hardy sought to advance the provincial novel from some of its earlier forms, and they also contextualize his engagement with traditions, folklore, and local stories.

In an early chapter of *Jude the Obscure*, Hardy writes of the fields of Jude's home village that 'to every clod and stone there really attached associations enough and to spare—echoes of songs from ancient harvest-days, of spoken words, and of sturdy deeds'.[208] And in his 1901 interview with William Archer, Hardy was asked: 'I suppose, now, you can yourself remember many of the old customs—the relics of paganism—that you have described?' To which Hardy replied: 'Oh, yes. They survived well into my time. I have seen with my own eyes things that many people believe to have been extinct for centuries'.[209] Hardy's attitude to the rich folkloric materials which he builds into his fiction is not simple or straightforward; and it seems likely that his perspectives changed over the decades, as signalled by the gradual elaboration of 'Wessex'.[210] Often conscious of modern thought, Hardy can at times

---

[204] See Simon Gatrell, 'Wessex', in Dale Kramer (ed.), *The Cambridge Companion to Thomas Hardy* (Cambridge: Cambridge University Press, 1999), pp. 19–37, and *Thomas Hardy's Vision of Wessex*.

[205] J. W. Burrow, *A Liberal Descent: Victorian Historians and the English Past* (Cambridge: Cambridge University Press, 1981), p. 67.

[206] Florence Hardy, *The Early Life of Thomas Hardy, 1840–1891* (London: Macmillan, 1928), p. 189.

[207] Hardy, *The Early Life of Thomas Hardy*, p. 299.

[208] Hardy, *Jude the Obscure*, p. 9.

[209] Archer, 'Real Conversations', p. 31.

[210] See Ruth A. Firor, *Folkways in Thomas Hardy* (Philadelphia: University of Pennsylvania Press, 1931); Joanna Cullen Brown (ed.), *Hardy's People: Figures in a Wessex Landscape* (London: Allison and Busby, 1991); Jan Jedrzejewski, 'Folklore', in Norman Page (ed.), *Oxford Reader's Companion to*

(especially, perhaps, in the 1870s) seem like a Tylor or a Gomme, viewing local customs in terms of obsolescence and survivalism, and implying a dispassionate, scientific attitude to folklore.[211] But this is not his most characteristic or most enduring position. Rather, he has a much greater resemblance to someone like Elworthy: abreast of contemporary theory, certainly, but also loyally attached to a particular corner of the country, with a strong strand of conservation and even celebration. When J. S. Udal's *Dorsetshire Folk-Lore*, with its posthumous 'Fore-Say' by William Barnes, was eventually published by subscription in 1922, Hardy's name could be found as one of the subscribers, side by side with other local enthusiasts—vicars, retired military men, and assorted antiquaries.[212] Moreover, Hardy himself stood in a much closer relation to 'the folk' than the theorists of the Folklore Society did—not only as an empathetic recorder, but also through his family connections.[213]

The Woodlanders is a good novel to choose for analysis precisely because it does not contain a big rural or folkloric set piece, such as the sheep-shearing supper in *Far From the Madding Crowd* or the skimmington ride in *The Mayor of Casterbridge*. It shows the usual indeterminacy of date, with pointers both to a more recent and to a more remote setting. Almost the only absolute date is a reference to 'the great November gale of 1824', though how long ago this happened is not clear, while the 'new law' about divorce, which Mr Melbury for a time places such faith in, is hard to date definitively.[214] The strongest signal for a near-contemporary setting is the statement that Mrs Charmond's American lover had left the United States after the end of the Civil War, and that this was some years previous.[215] Supporting indicators include Mrs Charmond's smoking of cigarettes, which is presented as being self-consciously modern, and the fact that the man-trap which Timothy Tangs sets is viewed from an antiquarian angle (and indeed, man-traps now form part of a historical collection at Mrs Charmond's Hintock House).[216] On the other hand, the novel begins on 'a bygone winter's day', in a period which is explicitly contrasted with 'now', and Edred Fitzpiers' studies of German philosophy seem not especially contemporary—whereas some decades earlier they could well have been avant-garde.[217]

This refusal to be pegged to the real-world calendar is clearly deliberate on Hardy's part, and within the novel—whenever it is set—there is a further sense of a pastness that is starting to recede and be lost. Mr Melbury tells 'ancient timber-stories', and Robert Creedle recalls 'ancient days, when there was battles, and famines, and

---

Hardy (Oxford: Oxford University Press, 2000), pp. 142–5; Michael A. Zeitler, *Representations of Culture: Thomas Hardy's Wessex and Victorian Anthropology* (New York: Lang, 2007); Jacqueline Dillion, *Thomas Hardy: Folklore and Resistance* (London: Palgrave Macmillan, 2016).

[211] Andrew Radford, 'Folklore and Anthropology', in Phillip Mallett (ed.), *Thomas Hardy in Context* (Cambridge: Cambridge University Press, 2013), pp. 210–220, esp. p. 215.

[212] Udal, *Dorsetshire Folk-Lore*, p. iv.

[213] Dillion, *Thomas Hardy: Folklore and Resistance*, pp. 14–18, 25–8.

[214] Thomas Hardy, *The Woodlanders*, ed. Dale Kramer (Oxford: Oxford University Press, 2005), pp. 167, 243, 253, and 356–7.

[215] Hardy, *The Woodlanders*, p. 137.

[216] Hardy, *The Woodlanders*, pp. 169–70, 316–17, 320.

[217] Hardy, *The Woodlanders*, pp. 5, 31, 111, 118, 128.

228   The Victorians and English Dialect

hang-fairs, and other pomps'.[218] In the novel's opening scene, the narrator remarks on the 'discontinuance' of the old use of coffin-stools, so that such items of furniture, although they are still to be found (as in Marty South's cottage), are now being used for other purposes.[219] The waggons in Melbury's barns are 'built on those ancient lines whose proportions have been ousted by modern patterns', and moreover, Melbury is 'among the last to retain horse-bells' in the neighbourhood.[220] Wealthy industrialists are buying up old manor houses in the vicinity—'as they do nowadays', Giles Winterborne comments.[221] And there is a detail that seems straight out of Elworthy's *West Somerset Word-Book* (published the previous year): Marty is wearing pattens as she walks to Sherborne-Abbas ('click, click, click, went the pattens; and she did not turn her head'), and the nature of her footwear is foregrounded by Winterborne's surprise, when he overtakes her (the surprise is not that Marty is wearing pattens, but rather that she should choose to walk such a long distance in them; either way, this enables Hardy to linger on this feature of Marty's costume).[222] Elworthy, it may be recalled, declared that the wearing of pattens was 'now only to be found in out-of-the-way places and on the stage'.[223] Is Hardy's Little Hintock an 'out-of-the-way place' or a version of 'the stage', or perhaps something of both?

This is not a rural community in stasis. One of the prominent themes of *The Woodlanders*, as in other novels by Hardy, is the contrast between the old ways of the country and the new ways that are arriving, often in the form of conspicuously modern characters from beyond the vicinity (in *The Woodlanders*, Fitzpiers and Mrs Charmond). The remoteness of the Hintocks, its 'woodland sequestration' and distance in time as well as space, is repeatedly stressed: the novel tells the story, the narrator says, of 'old-fashioned people in the rural districts' and 'old-fashioned woodland forms of life'.[224] Is this a Tylorian distance, though? The mediating character, caught in a state of troubled in-betweenness, is Grace Melbury, 'trained and tilled into foreignness of view' through her education, but still open to the strengths and attractions of her former home and way of life.[225] She is present at, but does not participate in, the communal hemp-sewing on Midsummer Eve, and the narrator tells us that 'by contrast with her life of late years [the proceedings] made her feel as if she had receded a couple of centuries in the world's history'.[226] The collision in mentalities is genuine, but 'a couple of centuries' seems merely to indicate old-fashionedness, not some sort of pre-historic survivalism. In the early parts of the novel, Hardy lays on some allusions to Norse mythology as part of his associational repertoire for the Hintocks ('the fabled Jarnvid wood', and so on), and at a later point Winterborne is classed as a 'ceorl', an Anglo-Saxon term; but Hardy stops far short of offering the

---

[218] Hardy, *The Woodlanders*, pp. 68, 124.
[219] Hardy, *The Woodlanders*, pp. 9–10.
[220] Hardy, *The Woodlanders*, pp. 16, 87.
[221] Hardy, *The Woodlanders*, p. 206.
[222] Hardy, *The Woodlanders*, pp. 31–2; see also p. 26.
[223] Elworthy, *The West Somerset Word-Book*, pp. 278, 558.
[224] Hardy, *The Woodlanders*, pp. 39, 144, 165.
[225] Hardy, *The Woodlanders*, p. 100. See further, for example, pp. 156, 201, 267.
[226] Hardy, *The Woodlanders*, p. 132.

Hintocks as a portrait of 'primitive culture'.[227] The anonymous reviewer for the *Saturday Review* thought that Little Hintock represented 'an almost primitive form of society'—but that 'almost' is important, and there is, in fact, no impassable gulf, no 'Ginning-Gap', between the residents of Little Hintock and the likes of Fitzpiers.[228] As Winterborne tells him, 'Why shouldn't a Hintock girl, taken early from home and put under proper instruction, become as finished as any other young lady if she's got brains and good looks to begin with.'[229] Grace herself shares the same view: she cannot tolerate Fitzpiers feeling 'as if [he] belonged to a different species from the people who are working in that yard'.[230] This is a Tylorian belief in monogenesis, a conviction that differences reside in culture not biology, but it does not in itself cast the Hintocks into a 'primitive' or 'savage' light: the customs and traditions of the area are antiquated but not prehistoric, as in 'the superstitious freaks or frolicsome scrimmages between sweethearts that still survived in Hintock from old-English times'.[231]

The Midsummer Eve hemp-sewing, in which the young women of the community hope to gain a vision of their future husbands, is the closest *The Woodlanders* comes to supplying a major folkloric custom to compare with the mumming play in *The Return of the Native* or the skimmington ride in *The Mayor of Casterbridge*.[232] It is an old tradition, but it is also self-consciously a game—not a meaningless 'survival'. That Grace chooses to come along as a spectator, and Fitzpiers joins in the pursuit itself, suggests that the event has a communal function, and is even open to newcomers; and some of the women who participate have come over from Great Hintock for the purpose.[233] Other local traditions are less prominently threaded through the novel: Marshcombe Bottom is 'popularly supposed to be haunted by spirits', and the party of bark-rippers tell ghost stories and 'sundry narratives [. . .] only to be accounted for by supernatural agency'; and Suke Damson sings a 'local ballad' when she is hiding in the haycock on Midsummer Eve.[234]

In terms of dialect itself, *The Woodlanders* forms a fitting conclusion to this chapter, as it exemplifies, almost to order, the state of dialect engagement in the 1880s. Hardy's usual gradation of speakers is observed, with Grammer Oliver and other choric figures showing the heaviest dialect, passing through Marty and Winterborne and Mr Melbury in a median position, to Grace's Standard English (and beyond that, Fitzpiers and Mrs Charmond). Grammer Oliver—who can only sign her name with a cross—still says *'Ch* for *I* and *er* for *he* (and *'Ch woll* for *I will*), but hers are not the only pronouns worth attending to: John Upjohn says *'a* for *she*, and Robert Creedle uses the celebrated *en* for *him*, from Old English *hine* ('not that I should call

---

[227] Hardy, *The Woodlanders*, pp. 15, 19, 48, 86, 248. See further Heather O'Donoghue, *Old Norse-Icelandic Literature: A Short Introduction* (Oxford: Blackwell, 2004), pp. 179–81.

[228] R. G. Cox (ed.), *Thomas Hardy: The Critical Heritage* (London: Routledge and Kegan Paul, 1970), p. 150; Hardy, *The Woodlanders*, p. 15.

[229] Hardy, *The Woodlanders*, p. 107.

[230] Hardy, *The Woodlanders*, pp. 107, 161; see also pp. 145, 166.

[231] Hardy, *The Woodlanders*, p. 320.

[232] See Dillion, *Thomas Hardy: Folklore and Resistance*, pp. 168–71.

[233] Hardy, *The Woodlanders*, p. 131.

[234] Hardy, *The Woodlanders*, pp. 125, 135, 228.

230   The Victorians and English Dialect

'n maister by rights, for his father growed up side by side with me').[235] Grammer Oliver's speech is marked by dialect vocabulary as well as grammar, including *projick*, *rozums*, *wherrit*, *woak* (very Barnesian), *chimmer*, and *chevy*, a Hopkins word ('If you only knew how he do chevy me round the chimmer in my dreams you'd pity me', she says to Grace).[236] Other local words cluster in the speech of comparable figures such as Creedle, Upjohn, and Melbury's other employees (*bruckle*, *glutch*, *kex*, *lewth*, *nesh*, *teuny*, and many more).[237] The presence of foreign loanwords, insisted upon by Skeat and Elizabeth Mary Wright as an important feature of English dialects, is also well illustrated. Grammer Oliver comments of the Midsummer Eve excitements that: 'I've seen such larries before', and the origin of *larry* is Latin *alarum* (also giving Standard English *alarm*).[238] *Randy* is a widespread and well-established dialect term, meaning (in Barnes' 1886 definition) 'a merry-making; an uproar'.[239] Following Winterborne's unsuccessful party, Creedle suggests that 'bachelor-men shouldn't give randys', and later John Upjohn reminisces that 'I've knowed men drowse off walking home from randies'.[240] But the etymology becomes apparent from the fuller form used by Mr Melbury, who comments of Winterborne's at-home that 'this means a regular randy-voo'—indicating derivation from French *rendezvous*.[241]

As for Hardy as narrator, his practices are often akin to those of Blackmore and Baring-Gould, with the use of punctuation and glosses to explain local vocabulary to a non-local readership. So, for example, 'drong', 'hag-rid', and 'tole' are all marked out as being alien to the narrator's usual vocabulary, and 'toiled' is additionally noted as being a 'local and better word', while explicit glosses include 'great straw "cheeses" as they were called', and 'here called "old-man's-beard" from its aspect later in the year' (for wild clematis).[242] Linking the linguistic and the cultural, and standing at the heart of *The Woodlanders*, is Hardy's respectful anatomy of the language, labour, and lore of wood-craft and apple-growing. He supplies technical accounts of various skills and operations, and glosses their vocabulary: 'a bundle of the straight smooth hazel rods called spar-gads', '"shrouding" as they called it at Hintock', 'a heap of rendlewood—as barked oak was here called'.[243] This fieldworker-like record is equivalent to Robert Holland's catalogue of terms from salt mining, and R. O. Heslop's of those from coal mining, both of which were being collected and preserved at the same time that Hardy was writing *The Woodlanders*—and parallel also to Hopkins' celebration of 'all trades'. And in a climactic passage, it is the idea of language that Hardy reaches for in order to communicate Marty and Winterborne's kinship in wood-craft: 'The casual glimpses which the ordinary population bestowed upon that wondrous

---

[235] Hardy, *The Woodlanders*, pp. 68, 108, 109, 330.

[236] Hardy, *The Woodlanders*, pp. 45, 108–9, 117, 222.

[237] Hardy, *The Woodlanders*, pp. 26, 66, 293, 328–9.

[238] Hardy, *The Woodlanders*, p. 132. See Wright (ed.), *English Dialect Dictionary*, III, 526; Ingham, 'Thomas Hardy and the Dorset Dialect', p. 86; Elliott, *Thomas Hardy's English*, p. 45.

[239] Barnes, *Glossary of the Dorset Dialect*, p. 91; Wright (ed.), *English Dialect Dictionary*, V, 32–3.

[240] Hardy, *The Woodlanders*, pp. 73, 192.

[241] Hardy, *The Woodlanders*, p. 65. See Wright, *English Dialect Dictionary*, V, 31 (*randivoose*); Elliott, *Thomas Hardy's English*, pp. 91–2.

[242] Hardy, *The Woodlanders*, pp. 133, 158, 176, 182, 268, 318.

[243] Hardy, *The Woodlanders*, pp. 9, 84, 244; see further pp. 23–4, 122, 154.

world of sap and leaves called the Hintock woods had been with these two, Giles and Marty, a clear gaze. They had been possessed of its finer mysteries as of commonplace knowledge; had been able to read its hieroglyphs as ordinary writing [. . .] They had planted together, and together they had felled; together they had, with the run of the years, mentally collected those remoter signs and symbols which seen in few were of runic obscurity, but all together made an alphabet'.[244] So it is fitting that the novel should end with dialect speech, and with these two exemplars of the language of the Hintock woods. As she stands at the grave of Giles Winterborne, Marty South's elegy is marked by the region's grammar and vocabulary, as well as by the concerns of its local 'trade', right through to the novel's last, moving sentence: 'Whenever I plant the young larches I'll think that none can plant as you planted; and whenever I split a gad, and whenever I turn the cider-wring I'll say none could do it like you. If ever I forget your name let me forget home and heaven . . . But no, no, my love, I never can forget 'ee; for you was a good man, and did good things!'[245]

Hardy's *The Woodlanders* and Baring-Gould's *Red Spider*, in their different ways, show how a distinctive genre of folkloric fiction had developed by the penultimate decade of the nineteenth century. Both were published in 1887, and by that date the English Dialect Society had been in existence for nearly a decade and a half, and had issued over fifty volumes. It was time, its directors believed, to embark on the great task that had been envisaged from its foundation—namely, to bring together the miscellaneous evidences of glossaries, novels, and poetry to create a single, consolidated dialect dictionary for the whole of the country. So it is to the story and contents of the *English Dialect Dictionary*—in many ways, the culmination of regional philology in Victorian England—that we must turn in our final chapter.

[244] Hardy, *The Woodlanders*, pp. 297–8.
[245] Hardy, *The Woodlanders*, p. 331.

6
The *English Dialect Dictionary*

From Society to *Dictionary*

The *English Dialect Dictionary*, edited by Joseph Wright and published in six volumes between 1898 and 1905, is the last of the three great monuments of Victorian dialect study, following Ellis' *Existing Phonology* and the publications of the English Dialect Society.

The production of such a dictionary had been a central part of the plan right from the beginning of the English Dialect Society, and the Society had only been existence for six years before there began to be calls for it to hurry up. In March 1879, an article appeared in *Notes and Queries* headed 'Wanted—an English Dialect Dictionary'. This praised the work done to date, but went on:

> May I venture, then, to express the hope that the E. D. S. will consider itself, before long, in a position to gather all the results of its work and of the researches of others into one magnificent monument of scholarship, an English Dialect Dictionary? May I dare to hope that before very long the philologist and the lover of English may be able to find the matter now scattered and buried in hundreds of volumes arranged, in all the "sweet simplicity" of alphabetical order, in one great lexicon?[1]

The author of this call was the Rev. Anthony Lawson Mayhew (1842–1916). Born in Suffolk, Mayhew became chaplain of Wadham College, Oxford, the year after his *Notes and Queries* piece, and remained there for the rest of his career. He had a long-standing interest in English philology, awakened as a schoolboy through the reading of Trench's work: later he produced revised editions of Trench's *On the Study of Words* (1888) and *English Past and Present* (1889). Mayhew's further publications included *A Concise Dictionary of Middle English* (1888, with Skeat as co-author), *A Synopsis of Old English Phonology* (1891), and, for the Early English Text Society, an edition of the *Promptorium Parvulorum* (1908), an English-Latin dictionary of the fifteenth century. He became a close acquaintance of James Murray, who suggested him as a possible second editor for the *Oxford English Dictionary*.[2] He was also an old college friend of the cleric Francis Kilvert (1840–79), and is the only person to whom

---

[1] A. L. Mayhew, 'Wanted—an English Dialect Dictionary', *Notes and Queries* 5th Series 11 (29 March 1879), 260.

[2] See Murray, *Caught in the Web of Words*, pp. 239–40; Richard W. Bailey, '"This Unique and Peerless Specimen": The Reputation of the *OED*', in Lynda Mugglestone (ed.), *Lexicography and the OED: Pioneers in the Untrodden Forest* (Oxford: Oxford University Press, 2000), pp. 207–27, at pp. 220–2; Gilliver, *The Making of the Oxford English Dictionary*, pp. 185–7.

The Victorians and English Dialect. Matthew Townend, Oxford University Press. © Matthew Townend (2024).
DOI: 10.1093/oso/9780198888123.003.0007

234   The Victorians and English Dialect

Kilvert is known to have shown his famous diary during his lifetime: on reading it, Mayhew especially enjoyed Kilvert's account of his pilgrimage to meet William Barnes in 1874 (Kilvert was a devotee of Barnes' poetry, regarding him as 'the great idyllic Poet of England', and on his visit, he found him 'a very remarkable man and a very remarkable-looking man, half hermit, half enchanter', and also 'a self-taught man, a distinguished philologist, [who] is said to understand seventeen languages').[3] Kilvert's diary contains a very full account of staying with Mayhew and his family in Oxford in 1878, and afterwards he passed to his friend a collection of Radnorshire words he had gathered, which Mayhew then published in *Notes and Queries*.[4]

Mayhew's 1879 piece in *Notes and Queries*, calling for work to begin on an *English Dialect Dictionary*, did not go unnoticed; Eliza Gutch, for one, wrote in to second his views, insisting that 'the E. D. S. will but half finish the work it is carrying on so satisfactorily if it should allow itself to be dissolved [. . .] without effecting the compilation spoken of by [Mayhew]'.[5] These calls for action provoked a long, considered response from Skeat.[6] Such requests were premature, he insisted; the English Dialect Society had only recently hit its stride, and 'the work of collection *must* come first'. Moreover, it would be unwise, he suggested, to begin the task of a dialect dictionary before Murray's *OED* had begun publication, and before the right editor had been found ('we want a leader', said Skeat, 'and the rest will follow', while making it clear that that leader and editor would not be him).

So when was the right time to begin? The first instalment of the *OED* did not appear until 1884, and Murray's view, communicated to Skeat in the early 1880s, was that another ten years of English Dialect Society collection and publication was needed before work could properly begin on a dialect dictionary. Skeat was unconvinced, but events proved that Murray's instinct was correct.[7] The other major issue was money—above all, money to pay an editor to do the work. A 'tentative offer' from a London publisher was reported in 1881, but this was rejected by Skeat, who subsequently opened negotiations with Cambridge University Press.[8] 'What [the English Dialect Society] wanted', Skeat told its members, 'was for somebody to give them £5,000, and then he thought the thing would be done'.[9]

---

[3] William Plomer (ed.), *Kilvert's Diary: Selections from the Diary of the Rev. Francis Kilvert*, 3 vols, rev. ed. (London: Cape, 1969), II, 437–43, III, 213. See further Teresa Williams and Alison Williams, 'The Reverend Anthony Lawson Mayhew', *The Kilvert Society Newsletter* May 1980, 2–6; Chedzoy, *The People's Poet*, pp. 182–3; A. L. Le Quesne, 'Kilvert, (Robert) Francis (1840–1879)', rev. Brenda Colloms, in *Oxford Dictionary of National Biography* [www.oxforddnb].

[4] Plomer (ed.), *Kilvert's Diary*, III, 308–22, 411; A. L. Mayhew, 'Some Radnorshire Words', *Notes and Queries* 5th Series 10 (10 August 1878), 105. See further Frederick Grice, 'Kilvert and Folklore', *Folklore* 85 (1974), 199–201.

[5] 'St Swithin' [Eliza Gutch], 'Wanted—an English Dialect Dictionary', *Notes and Queries* 5th Series 11 (12 April 1879), 294–5, at p. 294.

[6] Walter W. Skeat, 'An English Dialect Dictionary', *Notes and Queries* 5th Series 11 (31 May 1879), 421–2; also printed in *English Dialect Society: Ninth Annual Report*, pp. 10–11.

[7] *English Dialect Society: Eleventh Annual Report*, p. 11.

[8] *English Dialect Society: Ninth Annual Report*, p. 9; *English Dialect Society: Eleventh Annual Report*, p. 11.

[9] *English Dialect Society: Eleventh Annual Report*, p. 11.

The *English Dialect Dictionary*   235

But even if the money could be found, was the English Dialect Society necessarily best placed to be the producer of such a dictionary? Alexander Ellis, thinking of the *OED* rather than the proposed *EDD*, suggested to the Philological Society that it was better for a dictionary to be made by a single editor, rather than a collective society:

> Several things, indeed, make me inclined to think that a Society is less fitted to compile a dictionary than to get the materials collected. We want too much tyrannical power in an editor to suit the requirements of a Society. He must be allowed to have his own way thoroughly, or he will probably make no way at all. But materials must be collected by numbers.[10]

This was also the view taken by the leading figures of the English Dialect Society— most importantly, Skeat and Nodal. Skeat had declared as much in his 1879 riposte to Mayhew, and he repeated such comments at the annual meeting of the Society in 1884:

> The work would clearly have to be done, and this society must have something to do with it. It was, however, quite impossible that they could undertake the printing of such a book.[11]

Skeat accordingly began to focus his attention on the two major challenges of finding enough money and finding the right editor, and in 1886 he returned to these questions:

> I wish again to bring before the members of the English Dialect Society the scheme which I have already once mentioned, viz.: the advisability of attempting to raise a fund for the printing of an English Dialect Dictionary [. . .] As nothing has as yet been offered us, I think the time has come when we must attempt to raise the money by a general subscription. Even if no one else contributes to this object, I feel that I must at any rate do so myself; but being unable to command the sum required, I cannot do more than contribute the hundredth part of it.[12]

So Skeat contributed £50, and offered to 'draw up a prospectus' and act 'as Secretary and Treasurer of the English Dialect Dictionary Fund'. What was needed was a wealthy industrialist to step forward, though there was some talk, as a stop-gap, of redirecting annual subscriptions from the Society to the new dictionary.

The following year, it was reported that just under £300 had been raised so far, although half of this was in the form of pledges for the future rather than cash in hand.[13] Nonetheless, Skeat felt able to press ahead and appoint an editor: the Rev. Abram Smythe Palmer (1844–1917). Palmer was a Doctor of Divinity who had

---

[10] Ellis, 'Third Annual Address', p. 354.
[11] *English Dialect Society: Eleventh Annual Report*, p. 11.
[12] *English Dialect Society: Thirteenth Report*, pp. 6–7; see also pp. 17–18.
[13] *English Dialect Society: Fourteenth Report*, p. 4.

236 The Victorians and English Dialect

lectured at Trinity College Dublin, and was now resident in Woodford in London. His bibliography looks heterogeneous: volumes on Biblical and linguistic history predominate, but he was also a belated champion of Max Müller's mythological arguments, and later the author of *The Ideal of a Gentleman* (1908).[14] At the time of his appointment by Skeat, he was best known for his *Folk-Etymology: A Dictionary of Verbal Corruptions or Words Perverted in Form or Meaning, by False Derivation or Mistaken Analogy* (1882), and he had once been suggested as a possible extra editor for the *OED*.[15]

Palmer is rather a forgotten figure; the *English Dialect Dictionary* now tends to be associated exclusively with the name of his triumphant successor as editor, whom we will meet shortly. But he set to work with energy, and had soon recruited nearly a hundred helpers to act as readers or collectors, a quarter of whom were women.[16] No doubt under Skeat's guidance, Palmer began to issue annual reports, just as the English Dialect Society had done—listing helpers, setting out the programme of work, and auditing the finances. Some of these helpers were familiar names— Charlotte Ellis, Thomas Ellwood, W. D. Parish—who were also busy with the English Dialect Society and/or Ellis' *Existing Phonology* (as well as their own work), but there were many new names as well, suggesting a reservoir of assistance that had not as yet been fully tapped. The programmatic reading of published sources, for the purpose of excerpting words, was a new development in dialect study, though of course the method was borrowed from the Philological Society's practice with its own dictionary. Palmer's readers were able to borrow the works they needed from the EDS Library: the chief librarian of the Manchester Free Libraries reported that 'he had had a large correspondence with its [i.e. the *EDD*'s] workers who had required books [. . .] and this showed that there was an enthusiasm felt in the work which it was most gratifying to see'; indeed, the supplementary catalogue of the EDS Library was prepared in 1888 'more especially in order to assist the Editor of the English Dialect Dictionary and his workers in the prosecution of their task'.[17]

One of the new names on Palmer's list of helpers was 'HOPKINS, REV. G. M., S. J., University College, S. Stephen's Green, Dublin', who was listed as contributing 'a collection of specimens and illustrations of the Anglo-Irish Dialect'.[18] This seems to have been the first time that Hopkins made connection with the philological community centred on the English Dialect Society. We know from his correspondence that Hopkins wrote to Skeat concerning certain entries in his *Etymological Dictionary*, and at the same time he offered to collect Irish words; although Hopkins' letters to Skeat are not extant, the reply that Skeat sent back does survive.[19] Hopkins wrote to his mother that: 'I am making a collection of Irish words and phrases for the great

---

[14] See Dorson, *The British Folklorists*, pp. 182–6.
[15] Gilliver, *The Making of the Oxford English Dictionary*, p. 153.
[16] *English Dialect Society: Fourteenth Report*, p. 4.
[17] *English Dialect Society: Fourteenth Report*, p. 8; *English Dialect Society: Fifteenth Report*, p. 1.
[18] *The English Dialect Dictionary: Second Annual Report* (no place of publication, 1889), p. 14 (King's College London Archives, GB0100 KCLCA Skeat 11/2).
[19] See Hopkins, *Correspondence*, II, 861–2 (20 February 1887), 867–8 (10–11 March 1887), 875–6 (6–7 April 1887), and 923 (Skeat to Hopkins, 27 February 1888).

English Dialect Dictionary and am in correspondence with the editor.[20] It is unclear whether Hopkins was in direct contact with Palmer, or whether he was under the misapprehension that Skeat was the editor—but since nearly one hundred words submitted by Hopkins (who died in 1889) did eventually find their way into the text of the *English Dialect Dictionary*, we may assume some form of unrecorded contact between Hopkins and Palmer.[21]

Palmer's 1889 report, which includes Hopkins' name, records who was reading material for the dictionary, and it reveals an impressive programme of work.[22] It was not simply a case of needing volunteers to read through poetry and fiction and gather dialect vocabulary; more laboriously, the contents of all previous glossaries, not least those published by the English Dialect Society, had to be copied out onto individual slips of paper of uniform size and format, in order to facilitate the future compilation of dictionary entries. Only a small number of glossaries were excluded from this requirement, namely the biggest and most magisterial, which instead would be checked routinely as standard works of reference: those by Atkinson (Cleveland), Baker (Northamptonshire), Elworthy (Somerset), Jackson (Shropshire), and Peacock (Lincolnshire).[23] This systematic 'slipping' of English Dialect Society glossaries was arguably the most important outcome of Palmer's editorship; as we will see, such glossaries formed the core material out of which the *English Dialect Dictionary* was eventually to be compiled.

So who was reading what? To pick a few examples, beginning with some of the women readers: Rotha Busk, of Portman Square in London, was reading early modern drama (Dekker and Middleton, Beaumont and Fletcher); Eliza Felicia Burton, of Shadwell Lodge, Carlisle, was reading an enormous range of northern dialect texts (Samuel Bamford, Ben Brierley, W. M. Egglestone, and so on); Mary Combs, in Leytonstone in Essex, was reading Tennyson's 'Northern Farmer' poems and Gilbert White's *Natural History of Selborne*; Charlotte Ellis was reading various antiquarian works on Leicestershire, as well as some Ben Brierley and George Eliot for good measure; Elizabeth Mary Greg of Handforth near Manchester was tackling Holland's *Cheshire Glossary*; Eliza Gutch, in York, was reading various Yorkshire works, including F. K. Robinson's *Whitby Glossary* and C. Clough Robinson's *Leeds Glossary*; Sarah Kirby, of Kensington in London, was reading a dozen novels by Dickens, as well as a variety of other works, including Jerome K. Jerome's *Idle Thoughts of an Idle Fellow*; Miss Frances Thompson, in Settle in Yorkshire, was reading *Wuthering Heights, Sylvia's Lovers*, and Mrs Humphrey Ward's *Robert Elsmere*, while her older sister Rachel was busy with such works as J. Jackson Wray's *Nestleton Magna* and Isaac Binns' *Laffable Adventers a Tom Wallop*, as well as Isabella Banks' *Wooers and*

---

[20] Hopkins, *Correspondence*, II, 924–5 (13 March 1888).

[21] See Wright (ed.), *English Dialect Dictionary*, I, xii; White, 'G. M. Hopkins's Contribution to the *English Dialect Dictionary*'.

[22] *English Dialect Dictionary: Second Annual Report*, pp. 6–25.

[23] *English Dialect Dictionary: Second Annual Report*, p. 4; *The English Dialect Dictionary: Third Annual Report* (no place of publication, 1890), p. 6 (King's College London Archives, GB0100 KCLCA Skeat 11/2). See also A. Smythe Palmer, 'The "English Dialect Dictionary"', *Notes and Queries* 7th Series 8 (9 November 1889), 363–4.

Winners: A Yorkshire Story; and Mabel Peacock in Lincolnshire was re-reading her own *Tales and Rhymes in the Lindsey Folk-Speech*. Among the management, Abram Smythe Palmer and his wife had loaded themselves up with an enormous number of books to work through (from Sheridan Le Fanu's *Uncle Silas* to G. S. Streatfeild's *Lincolnshire and the Danes*), though the reader with the longest list was E. W. Prevost (1851–1920), a Carlisle-born scientist and writer who was reading works mostly with a Cumberland provenance (including Mary Powley's *Echoes of Old Cumberland* and William Dickinson's *Cumberland Glossary*, of which he would later produce a revised edition). Skeat was listed conjointly with the rest of his family, and collectively the household reading list included *Lorna Doone*, Mabel Peacock's *Tales and Rhymes* (again), and Baring-Gould's *Red Spider*. Several important authors had their works spread across a number of readers, with Hardy's fiction being read variously by George Fielding Blandford (*Under the Greenwood Tree*), George Dartnell (*Far From the Madding Crowd* and *Wessex Tales*), Gertrude Hope (*The Trumpet-Major*), Sarah Kirby (*The Hand of Ethelberta*), and Skeat and his family (*Under the Greenwood Tree*, again). The works of Edwin Waugh were also shared across half a dozen readers—another indication that, as earlier in Milner and Nodal's *Lancashire Glossary*, Lancashire dialect was, to some degree, being codified in his image.

Skeat's choice of Palmer as editor, did, however, receive fierce criticism from the belligerent pen of Mayhew. In a merciless article in *Notes and Queries*, Mayhew reviewed various entries in Palmer's *Folk-Etymology*, and demonstrated that the author was guilty of more than a few instances of 'false derivation' himself ('These guesses are without value [...] There is not the slightest evidence [...] It is absurd in the highest degree [...]' and so on). Mayhew offered these notes, he said, 'in order that those who are interested in the proposed "Dialect Dictionary" may be in a position to judge how far the newly appointed editor is duly qualified for undertaking so great and difficult a work'.[24] Palmer responded with matching sarcasm in what was becoming a public spat: 'Mr Mayhew no doubt is right. He would have made a far better editor himself. Few of us can lay claim to that immunity from mistake which he happily enjoys'.[25] All Skeat could do was to try to put on a brave face, and to take some of the blame himself ('I find that two of the mistakes attributed to Mr Palmer are my own', he graciously wrote).[26] But he also, it seems, felt he had no option but to acknowledge Palmer's inadequacy: what Palmer was doing, he explained, was 'really the work of a sub-editor; but obviously it would be absurd to give him the title of sub-editor so long as no editor is appointed to do the final work'. Skeat lamented: 'It will [...] be extremely difficult to find another Dr Murray, and I confess that I do not know where to look'. But he was clearly fed up with Mayhew's sniping, explaining that '[what] we most want just now are money for our fund and expressions of good will. But the raising of difficulties will not help us at all'.

---

[24] A. L. Mayhew, 'Notes on Mr A. S. Palmer's "Folk-Etymology"', *Notes and Queries* 7th Series 3 (23 April 1887), 322–3.

[25] A. Smythe Palmer, [no title], *Notes and Queries* 7th Series 3 (7 May 1887), 365.

[26] Walter W. Skeat, 'The English Dialect Dictionary', *Notes and Queries* 7th Series 3 (7 May 1887), 365.

The appointment of Palmer was perhaps an uncharacteristic misstep on Skeat's part.

It is thus unlikely to be a coincidence that, only a couple of months after Mayhew's stinging critique, and even when Palmer was still new in his job, Skeat should be making his first approaches to a much more promising candidate: Joseph Wright. The invitation was to the point:

> We hope to have some day a big Dialect Dictionary. Mr Palmer is provisional editor *pro tem*, for collection of material. But we want a good man for final editor. He should be a phonetician, a philologist, & shd. have some dialect knowledge. I cannot tell whether you consider it within your power or not. Do you think you could do it: & if so, will you undertake it?[27]

Palmer served two and a half years as editor (or sub-editor) of the *English Dialect Dictionary*, from early 1887 to late 1889, drawing a salary of £100 a year; and then the money ran out. Skeat's 'English Dialect Dictionary Fund' never really got off the ground, and only managed to raise a total of £521-14-10, a mere tenth of the £5,000 thought to be required—and over £200 of this came from Skeat himself. There was £60 from Fitzedward Hall, £50 from T. L. Kington-Oliphant, and £30 from H. T. Crofton. J. R. Wise, gravely ill, wrote to Skeat to enclose £10 for the Dictionary Fund, and Mayhew (to do him justice) also contributed £10, but no other donation reached double figures.[28] Nor were the publishing prospects any better, as Cambridge University Press declined to undertake the role of publisher.[29]

Wright's initial reply to Skeat does not survive, and it is not possible to pinpoint the date on which he formally took over from Palmer as editor. In the English Dialect Society report for 1888 (issued in 1889), members were informed that 'Dr Wright is likely to take a leading part in the compilation of the Dictionary, in which his proficiency in phonology will be of great value', and a similar statement was included in the *English Dialect Dictionary* report for 1889 (issued in 1890, after Palmer had ceased to be paid).[30] By early 1889, though, we know that Wright was telling friends privately that he would take on the task.[31]

The appointment of Palmer was perhaps an uncharacteristic misstep on Skeat's part. But the first editor still deserves considerable credit, not least for the reading programme he oversaw: the collections and contacts that Wright inherited, as he would discover, were not compromised or unusable, and they supplied a firm foundation on which to build. In addition to the excerpting of dialect fiction and poetry, Palmer could report that 'almost all the known glossaries of the different dialects

---

[27] Quoted in Wright, *The Life of Joseph Wright*, II, 353 (13 June 1887).

[28] J. R. Wise to W. W. Skeat 7 April 1887, King's College London Archives, GB0100 KCLCA Skeat 1/14. See *The English Dialect Dictionary: First Annual Report* (no place or date of publication), pp. 7–8 (King's College London Archives, GB0100 KCLCA Skeat 11/2); *English Dialect Dictionary: Second Annual Report*, pp. 25–6; *English Dialect Dictionary: Third Annual Report*, p. 8; *The English Dialect Dictionary: Fourth Report* (no place or date of publication), pp. 2–3 (King's College London Archives, GB0100 KCLCA Skeat 11/2).

[29] See *English Dialect Dictionary: Third Annual Report*, p. 8, though see also *English Dialect Dictionary: Fourth Report*, p. 2.

[30] *English Dialect Society: Fifteenth Report*, p. 3; *English Dialect Dictionary: Second Annual Report*, p. 6.

[31] Wright, *The Life of Joseph Wright*, II, 353.

240 The Victorians and English Dialect

have been transcribed—a word to a slip'; and altogether the quantity of slips that Palmer had accumulated amounted to over a million in number and approximately one ton in weight.[32] Moreover, when Palmer had been appointed as editor, he had received from the English Dialect Society various unpublished materials, ranging from Mary Powley's collection of Cumberland dialect terms to a never-quite-finished digest of dialect articles in *Notes and Queries*.[33] Some of this material had already been worked through, and now it was handed over to Wright as he took control. This all looked very promising. However, Skeat reported to the dictionary's supporters that 'the material, valuable as it is, does not appear to Professor Wright sufficient to enable him to make a beginning of preparing for the press'.[34] This realization may partly have been brought about by Wright's attempt to draw up a specimen page for the dictionary, to explore presentation and coverage; this was printed by Cambridge University Press (at Skeat's expense) but not made public.[35] So when Wright took over, the materials were good, insofar as they went—but they did not go far enough. And in addition to a new reading and collection programme, everything else—funding, staffing, and publishing—would have to begin again under Wright's editorship.

At around the same time, as we saw at the end of Chapter 4, the running of the English Dialect Society was formally transferred from Manchester to Oxford. Nodal and Milner stepped down as Secretary and Treasurer, and their roles were taken by Wright and Mayhew; Wright wrote to them that 'you have both done a good deal more for the grand and glorious cause of English Dialectology than any other two Englishmen' (though Wright's appreciation of Milner's work soon waned when he looked at the accounts and membership list, both of which he judged in need of an overhaul).[36] In reporting this transfer, in the seventeenth—and last—annual report of the Society, it was further announced that, in the move from Manchester to Oxford, 'the Committee has also been strengthened'.[37] This strengthening involved in particular the addition of a number of university-based scholars, marking a professional as well as geographical shift from its existence in Manchester: A. S. Napier in Oxford, W. P. Ker in London, and Julius Zupitza in Berlin. James Murray also became a committee member, and Skeat was formally designated as President.

So we should now make a fuller acquaintance with Joseph Wright himself, before we turn to his labours on the great dictionary that he produced.[38] In fact, Wright's life

---

[32] *English Dialect Dictionary: Third Annual Report*, p. 3; Wright, *The Life of Joseph Wright*, II, 355. See further Ann Thompson, 'Joseph Wright's Slips', *Transactions of the Yorkshire Dialect Society* 108 (2008), 12–21.

[33] See *English Dialect Society: Tenth Annual Report*, p. 7; *English Dialect Society: Fifteenth Report*, p. 2; *English Dialect Dictionary: Third Annual Report*, p. 5.

[34] *English Dialect Dictionary: Fourth Report*, p. 1.

[35] *English Dialect Dictionary: Fourth Report*, p. 2; Wright, *The Life of Joseph Wright*, II, 354; Joseph Wright to J. H. Nodal 31 October 1894, Manchester, John Rylands Research Institute and Library, GB 133 JHN 1/129/29.

[36] Joseph Wright to J. H. Nodal 20 December 1892, Manchester, John Rylands Research Institute and Library, GB 133 JHN 1/129/5 (courtesy of The University of Manchester).

[37] *English Dialect Society: Seventeenth Report*, p. 2.

[38] For biography, see Wright, *The Life of Joseph Wright*; C. H. Firth, 'Joseph Wright, 1855–1930', in Michael Lapidge (ed.), *Interpreters of Early Medieval Britain* (London: British Academy, 2002), pp. 119–35

story is still so astonishing that it can be hard to believe that it is true; even in his own lifetime, he was abundantly fêted as an extraordinary exemplar of Victorian autodidacticism and self-help. Born into poverty in 1855, with a childhood that included a spell in a workhouse, Wright grew up in an area he sometimes identified as Thackley, sometimes as Windhill, sometimes as Idle (all now part of the Bradford conurbation). He was first employed at the age of 6, as a donkey-boy at a nearby quarry, and a year later, aged 7, he started at Titus Salt's famous mill at Saltaire, working as a 'doffer' (a 'doffer', as Wright was to define it in the *EDD* forty years later, was 'a boy or girl employed in a factory to remove the full bobbins from the throstle-frame and replace them by empty ones').[39] Wright's father, a weaver and quarryman, died in 1866, and it was his resourceful mother who exerted the greater parental influence on him; she taught herself to read in her mid-forties, and it was remembered that 'her one luxury was a frequent cup of strong tea'.[40] As a young West Riding mill-worker, Wright, like his mother, could not read or write—he was 'never a day at school in [his] life', he later said—until he started to teach himself to read, aged 15, using the Bible and Bunyan's *Pilgrim's Progress* as his textbooks.[41] But after that, his progress was extraordinary. At 18 he started running his own night school, teaching the 'three Rs' to other boys and men, and by 21 he had saved enough money to leave his mill work and seek out German learning. He crossed the Channel, and then walked from Antwerp to Heidelberg, to study German and mathematics for a few months at the university there. Back in Britain, he taught at schools in Bradford, Wrexham, and Margate, learning ever more languages as he went (French, German, Latin, Greek, and Welsh were his first five), before returning to Heidelberg in 1882. This time, he intended to stay, and to study mathematics, but he was encouraged instead to direct his attention to comparative philology, and in Germany he added to his linguistic repertoire Old English, Old Saxon, Old High German, Middle High German, Gothic, Old Norse, Russian, Bulgarian, Lithuanian, and Sanskrit.[42] The result, in 1885, was a PhD on 'The qualitative and quantitative changes in the Indo-Germanic vowel system in Greek'.[43] It was only fifteen years since he had been an illiterate mill-worker in Yorkshire.

These were the years of the Neogrammarian revolution in German philology, and Wright was well connected, moving to Leipzig in 1886 and producing an English version of the first volume of Karl Brugmann's *Elements of the Comparative Grammar of the Indo-Germanic Languages* (*Grundriss der vergleichenden Grammatik der*

(first published in *Proceedings of the British Academy* 18 (1932), 423–38); R. W. Holder, *The Dictionary Men: Their Lives and Times* (Bath: Bath University Press, 2004), pp. 228–67; Arnold Kellett, 'Wright, Joseph (1855–1930)', in *Oxford Dictionary of National Biography* [www.oxforddnb]. See also Manfred Markus, Clive Upton, and Reinhard Heuberger (eds), *Joseph Wright's English Dialect Dictionary and Beyond: Studies in Late Modern English Dialectology* (Frankfurt am Main: Lang, 2010); David Crystal, *The Disappearing Dictionary: A Treasury of Lost English Dialect Words* (London: Macmillan, 2015).

[39] Wright (ed.), *English Dialect Dictionary*, II, 107.

[40] Wright, *The Life of Joseph Wright*, I, 20, 22.

[41] Joseph Wright to J. H. Nodal 14 January 1893, Manchester, John Rylands Research Institute and Library, GB 133 JHN 1/129/4 (courtesy of The University of Manchester).

[42] Wright, *The Life of Joseph Wright*, I, 75.

[43] Wright, *The Life of Joseph Wright*, I, 85–6; J. P. C. Toalster, 'Joseph Wright, PhD (Heidelberg)', *Transactions of the Yorkshire Dialect Society* 101 (2001), 47–9.

indogermanischen Sprachen)—though one of its readers, the fastidious Hopkins, thought that it was 'translated badly'.[44] In 1887—the year of Skeat's first approach to him—Wright moved to London, and then in 1888 to Oxford, having been invited by Max Müller to take up a teaching position there. And in Oxford he remained, until his death in 1930: in 1901 he succeeded Müller as Professor of Comparative Philology, having been deputy professor since 1891. Memoirs and reminiscences make it clear that Wright was regarded as not simply a learned or admirable figure, but also a lovable one; he was held in a great deal of affection as well as respect.[45] J. R. R. Tolkien, one of Wright's pupils (and in time, one of the executors of his will) later recalled 'the vastness of Joe Wright's dining-room table (when I sat alone at one end learning the elements of Greek philology from glinting glasses in the further gloom)'.[46] Moreover, in his own person Wright straddled both national (and international) university scholarship and local, place-based enthusiasm: he never turned his back on his Yorkshire origins, or concealed his illiterate, working-class beginnings, any more than he forgot his accent; and both Bradford and Oxford were proud to claim his as their own.[47]

Wright married Elizabeth Mary Lea, herself a philologist, in 1896, and the grand house they built in Oxford was called 'Thackley', after his place of birth; but the great grief of the Wrights' otherwise blissful marriage was the death of their two children at a young age, in 1902 and 1908. Elizabeth Mary Wright began to gather materials for her husband's biography while he was still alive, and her two-volume *Life of Joseph Wright* was published in 1932, two years after his death (there was also an abridged version, called *The Story of Joseph Wright*, in 1934). The moral lesson which one reviewer took from the biography was that 'Wright's scholarship was not merely a profession but in a real sense a function of his character, and that the self-discipline which made possible his great achievement was not on the side of suppression but all in favor of an integration of his robust humanity with his austere ideal of the scholar's life'.[48] Another reader of Wright's biography, drawing similar conclusions, was Virginia Woolf. 'Old Joseph Wright & Lizzie Wright are people I respect', she wrote in her diary in 1932. 'He was a maker of dialect dixeries [i.e. dictionaries]: he was a workhouse boy—his mother went charing'. She reflected further: 'I sometimes would like to be learned myself. About sounds & dialects [...] The triumph of learning is that it leaves something done solidly for ever. Everybody knows now about dialect', she concluded, 'owing to his dixery'.[49] Woolf subsequently transposed Wright into fiction, in

---

[44] Hopkins, *Correspondence*, II, 984 (1 March 1889). See further Plotkin, *The Tenth Muse*, pp. 96–7. On Brugmann, see Anna Morpurgo Davies, 'Karl Brugmann and Late Nineteenth-Century Linguistics', in Theodora Bynon and F. R. Palmer (eds), *Studies in the History of Western Linguistics, in Honour of R. H. Robins* (Cambridge: Cambridge University Press, 1986), pp. 150–71.

[45] See, for example, Gilbert E. Gunner, 'Joseph and Elizabeth Mary Wright—a Memory and a Tribute', *Transactions of the Yorkshire Dialect Society* 85 (1985), 14–16.

[46] Tolkien, *The Monsters and the Critics*, p. 238.

[47] Joyce, *Visions of the People*, pp. 210–11.

[48] H. S. V. J., review of Elizabeth Mary Wright, *The Life of Joseph Wright*, *Journal of English and Germanic Philology* 32 (1933), 618–19, at p. 619.

[49] Virginia Woolf, *The Diary of Virginia Woolf, Volume IV: 1931–1935*, ed. Anne Olivier Bell (London: Hogarth Press, 1982), pp. 115–16.

The *English Dialect Dictionary*   **243**

the minor character of Sam Robson in *The Years* (1937), a working-class man turned Oxford professor, whom the more central character Kitty Malone visits in the 1880 chapter of the novel:

> 'The moor at the back of our house', said Mr Robson, seeing her look at a picture.
> It struck Kitty that the accent with which he spoke was a Yorkshire accent. In looking at the picture he had increased his accent.[50]

Robson seems to have been a schoolteacher before becoming an Oxford don, and the identification with Wright is consolidated by the formative influence of his mother:

> Here Sam, who stood in the background fiddling with his watch-chain, stepped forward and indicated with his stubby forefinger the picture of an old woman looking rather over life size in the photographer's chair.
> 'My mother', he said [...]
> 'You're very like her, Mr Robson', was all [Kitty] could find to say. Indeed they had something of the same sturdy look; the same piercing eyes; and they were both very plain. He gave an odd little chuckle.
> 'Glad you think so', he said. 'Brought us all up. Not one of them a patch on her though'.[51]

As Kitty leaves, the thought comes to her that: 'You are the nicest man I have ever met'.[52]

Making the *English Dialect Dictionary*

Before we can move forward with the story of Wright's editing of the *English Dialect Dictionary*, we need first to review his engagement with dialect in the years preceding his editorship. Henry Sweet believed that the ideal dialect investigator would themselves be a speaker of that dialect—as well as possessing a command of phonetics and other necessary philological skills.[53] Joseph Wright surely conformed to Sweet's ideal more fully than any other individual of his period and profession, and there are two pre-*EDD* publications on dialect to consider—one minor, and one major.

The minor work is an 1891 article on 'English Dialects' (written in German, as 'Englische Mundarten'), published in the first volume of Hermann Paul's *Grundriss der germanischen Philologie* (1891). The article is mostly a review and digest of prior works on English dialectology, appraised with a stringency of philological judgement

---

[50] Virginia Woolf, *The Years*, ed. Hermione Lee (Oxford: Oxford University Press, 1992), pp. 67–8. See further Rowena Fowler, 'Virginia Woolf: Lexicographer', *English Language Notes* 39 (2002), 54–70, at pp. 57–8; Natasha Periyan, '"Altering the structure of society": an institutional focus on Virginia Woolf and working-class education in the 1930s', *Textual Practice* 32 (2018), 1301–23, at pp. 1304–12.

[51] Woolf, *The Years*, pp. 69–70.

[52] Woolf, *The Years*, p. 71.

[53] Sweet, *Collected Papers*, pp. 126–7.

244 The Victorians and English Dialect

that pulls no punches. Wright's view is that 'amongst the numerous dialect glossaries which have been compiled and published, there are relatively few which are of real significance for the researcher in the field of the phonology and history of the English language'.[54] The glossaries picked out for special praise are Atkinson on Cleveland ('a rich and valuable collection'), Holland on Cheshire ('valuable contribution to English dialectology'), Darlington on South Cheshire ('very valuable and reliable work'), Baker on Northamptonshire ('a very important work'), and, as usual, Jackson on Shropshire ('very comprehensive, precise, and invaluable for English dialectology') and Elworthy on West Somerset (similarly, 'very full, precise, and invaluable for English dialectology').[55] But Wright was more severe on questions of phonology and morphology. Although Ellis' *Existing Phonology* is declared to be 'magnificent', and Murray's *Dialect of the Southern Counties of Scotland* is acclaimed as 'the only grammar written from a historical point of view', most publications—including, by implication, most of the publications of the English Dialect Society—are condemned wholesale: 'In many glossaries and dictionaries there is an introductory chapter on the phonology and occasionally the grammar of the dialect in question. Yet these introductions are in by far the majority of cases utterly worthless'.[56] As can be seen, Wright was more than capable of academic acerbity, at least at this stage in his career.

Wright's major pre-*EDD* publication was his *Grammar of the Dialect of Windhill in the West Riding of Yorkshire* (1892). Wright's name first features in the records of the English Dialect Society in the annual report for the years 1885–6, where one of the works offered for publication is:

The Dialect of Idle and Windhill, in the West Riding of Yorkshire (three miles from Bradford). By J. Wright, MA, PhD.[57]

The report praises Wright for being a member of 'the most advanced "new school" of philologists', and his proposed volume 'will help to settle many general questions of English phonetics, such as the close and open *o* and the medial *th*, besides giving a sound historical and phonetic treatment of the dialect and all its peculiarities'. Two years later, the English Dialect Society report also announced that Wright would prepare for the Society a new edition of Thomas Batchelor's *Orthoëpical Analysis of the Dialect of Bedfordshire* (1809), but only his *Grammar of the Dialect of Windhill* ever appeared.[58]

The crucial word in the title is 'grammar': this is a grammar, not a glossary, and what Wright means by a grammar is a study of morphology and (above all) phonology, viewed from a historical point of view. Nearly two-thirds of the analysis in the *Windhill Grammar* are devoted to historical phonology, of which three-quarters are

---

[54] Graham Shorrocks, 'English Dialects: A Translation of Joseph Wright's "Englische Mundarten"', *Transactions of the Yorkshire Dialect Society* 89 (1990), 10–19, at p. 11 (first published in *Journal of English Linguistics* 21 (1988), 127–36).

[55] Shorrocks, 'English Dialects', pp. 13–15.

[56] Shorrocks, 'English Dialects', pp. 11, 16.

[57] *English Dialect Society: Thirteenth Report*, p. 3.

[58] *English Dialect Society: Fifteenth Report*, pp. 2–3.

The *English Dialect Dictionary* **245**

given to vowels: the core chapters run 'The Old English Equivalents of the Windhill Vowels in Accented Syllables', 'The Vowels Treated Historically', 'The French Element', 'The Vowels in Unaccented Syllables', and 'The Consonants'. Wright organizes his analysis on a vowel-by-vowel basis, and traces both the origins of Windhill vowels backwards into Old English, and the evolution of Old English vowels forwards into Windhill dialect: for example, short *i* in Windhill dialect is shown to descend from no fewer than twelve different vowels in Old English, and Old English short *o* has evolved into eight possible vowels in Windhill dialect, depending on sound changes and phonetic context.[59] Hence the chapter on 'The French Element' is not concerned with vocabulary, as one might have expected, but rather with the evolution of the new vowel sounds introduced into English through French loanwords. Wright's preface stresses that the book is intended for 'specialists in English philology', enticing them with such promises as that 'the present grammar will, I trust, help to throw some light upon Old English vowel quantities' and that 'in the chapter on the consonants the chief interest naturally lies in the gutturals'.[60]

The big chapters on phonology are followed by five more on morphology. Again, the perspective is historical, placing the grammar of Old English alongside that of the Windhill dialect, and tracing the connections between the two: so, for example, 'the strong form **ðem** ["them"] is from OE **ðǣm** (**ðām**), the dat[ive] plural of the demonstrative pronoun **sē, sēo, ðæt**, whereas the weak forms **əm, m** are from OE **heom**, the dat[ive] plural of the personal pronoun **hē, hēo, hit**'.[61] But alongside such tracing of continuities, Wright also notes the ways in which Windhill grammar is actually less, rather than more, conservative than Standard English, such as the loss of initial *h-*, the disappearance of *whom*, and the absence of the subjunctive.[62] He is also alert to questions of variation, and what these might mean in terms of language contact and change: the coexistence of multiple forms of the reflexive pronoun (for example, *misen, misel, miseln* 'myself') leads Wright to suggest that 'such a variety of forms must be quite modern, and is probably due to importation from neighbouring dialects'.[63]

Is there no interest in vocabulary? The *Windhill Grammar* does in fact end with a forty-page index, but although each entry is glossed, this is still effectively an index to help in the study of phonology and grammar rather than lexis or semantics, as the first half-dozen words under F will serve to show: *fādin* 'farthing', *fadm* 'fathom', *fāə(r)* 'far', *faiə(r)* 'fire', *fail* 'file', *fain* 'fine' (all words found also in Standard English, with identical meanings).[64] Nonetheless, even though such material is not foregrounded, it is possible to find more local vocabulary cited within the *Grammar* (usually as a demonstration of a certain phonetic or grammatical feature): so, for instance, examples of nouns that only occur in the plural form include *laps* 'a kind of woollen waste

---

[59] Joseph Wright, *A Grammar of the Dialect of Windhill, in the West Riding of Yorkshire*, English Dialect Society 67 (London: English Dialect Society, 1892), pp. 14–15, 39–42.
[60] Wright, *Grammar of the Dialect of Windhill*, pp. v–vii.
[61] Wright, *Grammar of the Dialect of Windhill*, p. 119 (bold original).
[62] Wright, *Grammar of the Dialect of Windhill*, pp. 102, 125, 145.
[63] Wright, *Grammar of the Dialect of Windhill*, p. 123.
[64] Wright, *Grammar of the Dialect of Windhill*, p. 223.

246   The Victorians and English Dialect

made in spinning', *loks* 'small pieces of wool which have been detached from the fleece', and *noilz* 'the short hairs taken out of the wool by the combing machine'.[65] Just occasionally, too, Wright permits his lexical curiosity to be (almost) self-justifying, unrelated to any grammatical point, for example in a discussion of the names for different sorts of marbles (in the children's game), or 'the relation, if any', between Windhill *bleg* and Standard English *blackberry*.[66] And there are also a few moments at which Wright allows his impersonal tone to lapse, and he himself becomes a first-person witness: he recalls, for example, how 'þ and ð were regularly used among the younger Windhill people, but **f** and **v** were still generally used in Thackley and Idle, which are only about a mile distant from W[indhill]. I well remember how we used to twit the Thackley and Idle people about the pronunciation of these sounds: **faklə** *Thackley*, **fiŋk** *think*, **fēd** *third*, [...] **smivi** *smithy*, etc'.[67] Wright is unafraid at times to use the pronoun *we* ('we [...] always use **ðə** before **loəd** when it means *God*'), and there is even a note of reminiscence: at least one sentence begins 'When I was a lad [...]'.[68] The book is dedicated to Wright's mother, and the main body of the grammar is followed by fifty pages of 'Specimens': poems and stories taken from local almanacs and authors, such as Ben Preston, and transcribed by Wright into phonetic notation. He also includes, for good measure, updated Windhill versions of Ellis' Comparative Specimen and Dialect Test.[69]

It is indisputable that Wright's *Grammar of the Dialect of Windhill* set new standards for English regional philology: the methods and scholarship which Wright used elsewhere to analyse and expound medieval languages are here deployed in the service of Yorkshire dialect (in 1886 the eminent scholar Ferdinand Holthausen had joined Wright for a time in Windhill: he later recalled that 'we studied dialect [...] we discovered almost daily new sound-laws and etymologies').[70] His work was recognized from the start as offering something distinctive to English dialect study—something arriving from the universities of Germany—though this claim has sometimes been over-staked. Wright's wife later declared the *Windhill Grammar* to be 'the first Grammar of its kind in England: a scientific study of a living dialect intended to be useful to philologists'.[71] But this is an exaggeration: although not explicitly Neogrammarian in their emphasis on the centrality and regularity of sound change, Murray's *Dialect of the Southern Counties of Scotland* (1873) and Elworthy's *Outline of the Grammar of the Dialect of West Somerset* (1876–7) both pre-date the *Windhill Grammar* by over a decade and a half, and of course Ellis' *Existing Phonology* had appeared in 1889. Nonetheless, the *Windhill Grammar* is a remarkable work, and its influence (and its somewhat mythic reputation) was to be greatly enhanced by the later appearance of the *English Dialect Dictionary*, which then sent

---

[65] Wright, *Grammar of the Dialect of Windhill*, p. 109.
[66] Wright, *Grammar of the Dialect of Windhill*, pp. 99, 115.
[67] Wright, *Grammar of the Dialect of Windhill*, p. 91.
[68] Wright, *Grammar of the Dialect of Windhill*, pp. 112, 118.
[69] Wright, *Grammar of the Dialect of Windhill*, pp. 170–5, and see Ellis, *On Early English Pronunciation*, V, 1820–6/388–94.
[70] Wright, *The Life of Joseph Wright*, I, 85.
[71] Wright, *The Life of Joseph Wright*, I, 138.

The *English Dialect Dictionary* **247**

later researchers back to Wright's English Dialect Society monograph as a template for future work.

Wright's *Windhill Grammar* appeared more than five years after Skeat first approached him about the *English Dialect Dictionary*; and actual editorial work on the dictionary did not begin for at least another couple of years after that. There were two main reasons for this delay: first, because Wright took a long time to mull over the project before he fully committed to it; and second, because the greatest challenge, at least to begin with, was financial. Wright did not want the dictionary to peter out, or have to be stopped due to lack of funds; the money question needed to be resolved before the editorial work could begin.

Wright himself required income to act as editor—or rather, since he was already drawing a university salary, he required funds with which to cover the working costs of the dictionary; by the start of 1896, he reckoned that he had spent nearly £1,500 of his own money.[72] Some assistance came from the government, in recognition of the project's national importance. An application to Arthur Balfour as First Lord of the Treasury resulted in Wright receiving an allocation of £200 a year till the project's end, first as a grant from the Royal Bounty Fund and then in the form of a Civil List pension.[73] There were also some other gifts and bequests. Thomas Hallam died in September 1895, and his obituary in the *Manchester City News* recorded that '[his] one regret was in his last moments that he had not lived to see the issue of the great Dialect Dictionary'.[74] But his will—which appointed Wright, Mayhew, and Skeat as executors—did bequeath a portion of his residuary estate for the publication of the *EDD*. Wright had written to J. H. Nodal, when Hallam had been unwell the previous year, that 'he is a precious jewel the <u>likes</u> of which we shall <u>never</u> see again'.[75]

All this helped; but it remained a challenge to cover the cost of the dictionary's compilation and printing. After a series of publishers failed to show interest—not just Cambridge University Press, but also Oxford University Press, John Murray, and A. and C. Black—Wright made the bold decision to shoulder the risk himself, by taking on the cost of publication.[76] This he would do through the gathering of subscriptions, and he set about the task with typical vigour. 'Although I am not a business man', Wright wrote to Nodal, 'I have a strong feeling for the "<u>methodical</u>" and promptness in the despatch of business matters'.[77] Wright sent out three thousand handwritten letters and fifty thousand prospectuses, soliciting individuals and institutions to act as subscribers. By April 1895, he could report that 280 subscribers had been recruited; by May, five hundred, and by June, six hundred. At the start of 1896, the number

---

[72] Joseph Wright to J. H. Nodal 5 January 1896, Manchester, John Rylands Research Institute and Library, GB 133 JHN 1/129/30.

[73] See Wright, *The Life of Joseph Wright*, II, 391–7, 407–12.

[74] [Anon], 'Thomas Hallam'.

[75] Joseph Wright to J. H. Nodal 9 January 1894, Manchester, John Rylands Research Institute and Library, GB 133 JHN 1/129/15 (courtesy of The University of Manchester).

[76] Wright, *The Life of Joseph Wright*, II, 362–4, 366–7.

[77] Joseph Wright to J. H. Nodal 2 February 1894, Manchester, John Rylands Research Institute and Library, GB 133 JHN 1/129/20 (courtesy of The University of Manchester).

248 The Victorians and English Dialect

stood at just over nine hundred.[78] Many had been contacted via the subscription list for Skeat's Oxford edition of Chaucer—another indication of the intertwining of medieval studies and regional philology.[79] The cost of subscription was 1 guinea a year, for which subscribers would receive two half-yearly instalments at a reduced cost—or 2 guineas a year for the limited 'Special Edition' on handmade paper.[80] The work would be printed at Oxford's Clarendon Press, with Henry Frowde formally designated as publisher, but the Delegates of the Press were adamant that they were to be free of liability; all the hazard lay with Wright himself.[81]

A partial subscription list for the *EDD* was included in Volume I of the dictionary, but an unpublished ledger, dating from 1896 and surviving among Wright's papers, records a fuller list of names and addresses. It is a witness to Wright's efficacy in generating a broad support base and also to public interest in his project. Many of the glossarists of the English Dialect Society subscribed, of course, as did many steadfast supporters of the Society, such as Charlotte Ellis, Eliza Gutch, and Arthur Munby. Eminent writers and public figures ranged from W. E. Gladstone and J. C. Ryle to J. M. Barrie, Robert Bridges, and William Morris. There was a wide range of university scholars—not just philologists, but also those in adjacent disciplines such as F. W. Maitland and George Saintsbury. Wright's success in gaining institutional subscriptions—a more stable income source than individual subscribers—is especially notable. To take only a sample of those listed under the letter B, such institutions included: The Bala Theological College Library in North Wales, Barking Public Library, Barrow-in-Furness Free Public Library, Basle University Library, Battersea Public Library, Bedford Literary and Scientific Institute and General Library, Bedford Modern School, Belfast Free Public Library, Benares College in India, Bingley Free Library, Birkenhead Free Public Library, Birmingham Oratory Library, Blackburn Free Library, Blackpool Free Public Library, Blundell's School in Devon, Bonn University Library, Bootle Free Public Library, Boston Public Library in Massachusetts, Bournemouth Public Library, Bowdoin College Library in Maine, Bradfield College Library in Berkshire, Bradford Historical and Antiquarian Society, Brasenose College Library in Oxford, Brighton Public Library, Bryn Mawr College Library in Pennsylvania, Burnley Literary and Philosophical Society, Burton-on-Trent Public Library, and Bury Public Library and Art Gallery.[82]

Wright's talent for publicity was also evident in his success in assembling a list of over one hundred 'Patrons', eminent public figures who were willing to lend their name (and thus, their implicit support) to the project.[83] Queen Victoria herself headed the list, followed by the Archbishops of Canterbury and York, multiple

---

[78] Wright, *The Life of Joseph Wright*, II, 372–4, 392.

[79] Wright, *The Life of Joseph Wright*, II, 379.

[80] Wright, *The Life of Joseph Wright*, II, 372; [Walter W. Skeat], *The English Dialect Society's Last Notice* (no place or date of publication), p. 2 (King's College London Archives, GB0100 KCLCA Skeat 11/1).

[81] Wright, *The Life of Joseph Wright*, II, 367–9; on Frowde, see Martin Maw, 'Frowde, Henry (1841–1927)', in *Oxford Dictionary of National Biography* [www.oxforddnb].

[82] Oxford, Bodleian Libraries, MS Eng. lang. c. 12; see also Wright (ed.), *English Dialect Dictionary*, I, 857–64.

[83] See Wright, *The Life of Joseph Wright*, II, 370, and Plate XXI.

The *English Dialect Dictionary*   **249**

other bishops and members of the House of Lords, and then an 1890s 'Who's Who' of professors, MPs, and writers and scholars, including old *OED* hands such as Furnivall, Henry Hucks Gibbs, and Fitzedward Hall, philologists such as Müller, Skeat, and Toller, and miscellaneous figures with interests in the English past, such as Sabine Baring-Gould, William Morris, and E. B. Tylor.

With publicity, finances, and publishing arrangements falling into place, Wright could at last turn to the actual compilation of the dictionary. In 1895, he started to assemble a core team of workers. These were mostly female: the *English Dialect Dictionary* was, to all intents and purposes, written by women. Although Wright was the editor and coordinator, responsible for the final form and content of what was sent to the printer, he seems to have done little in terms of actually writing entries.[84] This was done instead by a group of six 'senior assistants', all women. Female workers played a significant role in the *OED* under James Murray, but Wright's dependence on his six senior assistants went far beyond this.[85] His first appointment was Jane Bella Partridge (1869–1958), who served from 1895 to 1897. Born in Alvechurch in Worcestershire, she was educated at University College, Aberystwyth, and was recommended to Wright by the Professor of English Philology there, C. H. Herford.[86] After her work on the *EDD*, Partridge became a schoolteacher in Bournemouth and later a journalist in Gloucestershire.[87] Partridge was present from the start, being involved in the establishment of the dictionary's working practices, and later in 1895 she was joined by two other senior assistants, Mary Dormer Harris (1867–1936) and Agnes Horatia Frances Hart (probably 1868–1936). Harris only stayed for a year, but she came from helping Murray on the *OED* (as his first female assistant), and may have given Wright useful insider information on work practices in the 'Scriptorium'.[88] A graduate of Lady Margaret Hall, Oxford (where she gained a First in English), and already the author of an article in the *English Historical Review*, Harris subsequently went on to a distinguished career as a local historian of Warwickshire, with her published works including a four-part edition of the *Coventry Leet Book* for the Early English Text Society; she was also highly active in, variously, the suffragist movement, the Workers' Educational Association, and Leamington amateur dramatics (as both playwright and performer).[89] Agnes Hart was the daughter of Horace Henry Hart, Controller (that is, head printer) of Oxford University Press, and was a governess prior to her work on the *EDD*; her time on the staff lasted for two years, before a breakdown in her mental health, requiring residential care, brought her work to an

---

[84] Wright, *The Life of Joseph Wright*, II, 381.

[85] See Peter Gilliver, 'Thoughts on Writing a History of the *Oxford English Dictionary*', *Dictionaries* 34 (2013), 175–83, at p. 180, and *The Making of the Oxford English Dictionary*, pp. 212, 250; Russell, *Women and Dictionary Making*, pp. 149–69, 173–81; Ogilvie, *The Dictionary People*, pp. 292–310.

[86] Wright, *The Life of Joseph Wright*, II, 379.

[87] Census information from *Ancestry*: www.ancestry.co.uk.

[88] Gilliver, *The Making of the Oxford English Dictionary*, pp. 238–9.

[89] See Jean Field, *Mary Dormer Harris: The Life and Works of a Warwickshire Historian* (Studley: Brewin Books, 2002); see also Mary Dormer Harris, *Plays and Essays*, ed. Florence Hayllar (Leamington Spa: Courier Press, no date of publication).

250   The Victorians and English Dialect

end.[90] Next to join the team, in 1896, was Lilian Jane Yates (1872–1955), who had read History and Law at Girton College, Cambridge, and who became the longest-serving assistant on the dictionary, remaining until its completion in 1905 (with one year away as Girton's librarian).[91] The final two members of Wright's group of six senior assistants were Alice Beatrice Covernton (1876–1972), who worked from 1897 to 1903, and Edith Mary Miller (1870–1929), who worked from 1899 to the end. Beatrice Covernton, studying at Royal Holloway College in London, also gained a First in the Oxford Honours School of English; after working on the *EDD*, she became a teacher at Cheltenham Ladies' College and later worked at Bedford College, London.[92] Edith Miller, who likewise gained a First in English from Oxford, was a friend and former pupil of Edith Mary Wright (and next-door neighbour of W. A. Craigie, third editor of the *Oxford English Dictionary*); later, she became a schoolteacher and also sub-warden of the Lady Margaret Hall Settlement in Lambeth. In 1881 Miller and her sister had made the acquaintance of Lewis Carroll, and Carroll remained a friend and correspondent until his death.[93]

These were the six women who wrote the *English Dialect Dictionary*, although— since the letters of the alphabet were not divided up between them—it is not possible to specify which assistants drafted which entries, except in the broad terms of coordinating their periods of service with the dictionary's schedule of progress and publication.[94] Four of the six were recent graduates in English (at least three at First Class standard), having studied Old and Middle English and, no doubt, received a fair grounding in historical philology. But as Partridge recalled, 'not one of the staff was a dialect speaker'—though she herself did supply the dictionary with a substantial collection of words for north-east Worcestershire, and Mary Dormer Harris provided a handful of Warwickshire words.[95] There were also a number of 'unskilled' junior assistants, and further help was sometimes provided by George Ostler, an Oxford University Press employee who assisted with proofreading and other tasks when Wright was short-staffed.[96] Until 1902, A. L. Mayhew also worked on the dictionary in the mornings, and Elizabeth Mary Wright contributed in a multitude of ways.[97]

Four of the six senior assistants provided reminiscences when Elizabeth Mary Wright was preparing the biography of her husband, and Jane Partridge's memoirs provide by far the fullest account of what working on the dictionary was like.[98] The dictionary's premises were located at the Clarendon Press, on Walton Street in

---

[90] See Martin Maw, 'Hart, Horace Henry (1840–1916)' in *Oxford Dictionary of National Biography* [www.oxforddnb]; *Ancestry* [www.ancestry.co.uk].
[91] Wright, *The Life of Joseph Wright*, II, 388.
[92] Wright, *The Life of Joseph Wright*, II, 388–9.
[93] Wright, *The Life of Joseph Wright*, II, 389–91; Morton N. Cohen (ed.), *The Letters of Lewis Carroll*, 2 vols (London: Macmillan, 1979), esp. I, 443 n.1.
[94] Wright, *The Life of Joseph Wright*, II, 380–1.
[95] Wright, *The Life of Joseph Wright*, II, 383; Wright (ed.), *English Dialect Dictionary*, I, xi (listed erroneously as 'J. W. Partridge'), VI [Bibliography], 61–2 (as 'J. B. Partridge').
[96] Wright, *The Life of Joseph Wright*, II, 379, 389.
[97] Wright, *The Life of Joseph Wright*, II, 380, 399–402.
[98] See Wright, *The Life of Joseph Wright*, II, 380–8.

The *English Dialect Dictionary* **251**

Oxford, and comprised a large communal room known as 'the Workshop', and a separate, connected office for Wright. The Workshop was soon filled with dictionaries, dialect novels, and the one and a half million slips which had accumulated by this point.[99] Hours were regular, from 9.00 to 5.30, and an institution fondly remembered by all participants was the daily afternoon tea at 4.00, with lots of cake—a detail that Virginia Woolf later seized upon for her portrait of Sam Robson in *The Years* ('"Tell Jo we're not sparing the cake", said Mr Robson, cutting himself a slice of that craggy-looking object').[100]

Wright's *Windhill Grammar* had been the sixty-seventh volume to be published by the English Dialect Society (out of eighty). The last few years of the Society, in publication terms, were highly productive: the final four subscriptions generated thirteen volumes. But once the personnel and working arrangements for making the *English Dialect Dictionary* were in place, Wright took the view that the Society was no longer needed as a separate operation, and so it was formally dissolved at the end of 1896. A *Complete List of Publications* was printed—you could buy the full set of eighty volumes for £22-2-0—and Skeat issued an elegiac *Last Notice* to the members who remained:

> Now that THE ENGLISH DIALECT DICTIONARY is at last well started, the object for which the Society was originally established is practically attained. In future, all collections of local words, properly written out so as to give each word (with its meaning, locality, and some guide to its pronunciation), can be forwarded in manuscript to Professor J. Wright [. . .] for immediate insertion in The Dialect Dictionary, instead of going through the now unnecessary process of being previously printed [. . .][101]

But it was natural that Skeat should want to sign off with a message of thanks, and not just practical arrangements:

> In conclusion, I beg leave, in the name of the Society, to thank all the members for their hearty support, and to acknowledge much assistance from many well-wishers both within and without the Society. Since the Society was founded in June, 1873, up to the close of 1896, work has been accomplished of which we all have some reason to be proud, notwithstanding many shortcomings and occasional errors for which we trust that posterity will, on the whole, forgive us.[102]

Was the winding-up of the English Dialect Society a sensible move or not? In spite of the vibrant publication programme, Wright seems to have taken the view that he had inherited the Society in a somewhat dilapidated state, at least in terms of the extent of its membership; and he may have thought that a fresh start, tied specifically

---

[99] Wright, *The Life of Joseph Wright*, 378, 398.
[100] See Wright, *The Life of Joseph Wright*, II, 382, 388, 390; Woolf, *The Years*, p. 68.
[101] [Skeat], *The English Dialect Society's Last Notice*, p. 1.
[102] [Skeat], *The English Dialect Society's Last Notice*, p. 3.

252   The Victorians and English Dialect

to the needs of the *EDD*, was the better course. In any case, he had already set up structures to draw on the same wells of regional enthusiasm that the Society had earlier accessed, encouraging the establishment of local dictionary committees (for example, in Bradford, Bristol, Hull, Manchester, and Newcastle) to help with the collection of words and reading of sources.[103] Similarly, just as he had elicited subscribers, so Wright also sent out multiple circulars asking for assistance, and he used local newspapers to broadcast the project.[104] Indeed, it was not unknown for Wright to sit up all night, writing letters and stuffing envelopes; his wife thought that 'perhaps he had never lost the effects of early training in the monotonous labour of "doffing" bobbins in the spinning-room of a Yorkshire mill'.[105]

The temptation is to tell the story of the *English Dialect Dictionary* as a heroic one-man struggle; but that is not how it was. The extraordinary nature of Wright's achievement is not diminished by acknowledging that, as editor and entrepreneur, he sat at the top of a pyramid of personnel, and that it was his senior assistants who compiled the entries, with hundreds of other voluntary helpers also supplying materials and guidance. So with our awareness of the human actors in the dictionary now established, we should turn to Wright's policy decisions on questions of content and inclusion, and then to an examination of the actual entries in the dictionary.

Dialect lexicography (1): contents

Questions of what to include and what to exclude were present from the start. In his 1879 plea, 'Wanted—an English Dialect Dictionary', Mayhew had not hesitated to offer his own opinion: 'The work should be strictly an English Dialect Dictionary, admitting to its word-list provincialisms only. The English of books, whether Old English, Middle English, or Elizabethan, should only be introduced to illustrate the provincial word'.[106] That is to say, the projected dictionary should turn its back on the earlier convention, best exemplified by Halliwell's dictionary of 1847, of collecting 'archaic' and 'provincial' words together in one list, as if they were the same thing.

T. N. Toller had told the annual general meeting of the English Dialect Society in 1889 that 'dialects had in many cases been the asylum for words which were the exiles and outlaws of the ordinary dictionary, but the people fell back upon them'.[107] Toller's phrase 'the exiles and outlaws of the ordinary dictionary', while investing dialect words with a touch of rebellion or outsider status, also raised a central question for the projected *English Dialect Dictionary*: what should its relationship be with the *Oxford English Dictionary*?

---

[103] See Wright, *The Life of Joseph Wright*, II, 356–7, 361, 363, 376; see also Joseph Wright to J. H. Nodal 6 October 1894, 29 October 1894, Manchester, John Rylands Research Institute and Library, MS 1/129/26, 1/129/28.

[104] Wright, *The Life of Joseph Wright*, II, 355.

[105] Wright, *The Life of Joseph Wright*, II, 404; see also Joseph Wright to J. H. Nodal 24 January 1894, Manchester, John Rylands Research Institute and Library, GB 133 JHN 1/129/18.

[106] Mayhew, 'Wanted—an English Dialect Dictionary', p. 260.

[107] *English Dialect Society: Fifteenth Report*, p. 9.

The *English Dialect Dictionary* **253**

To answer this question, we need to consider the treatment of dialect words in the *OED* itself; and there is a complex back story on this issue. As we saw in Chapter 1, in the 1840s the Philological Society had made some attempts at collecting dialect vocabulary, and in the 1860s and 1870s, some members of the Society were energetic in dialect study, with the Society's *Transactions* including a good deal of important work on English dialects (for example, by Murray, Elworthy, and Robert Backhouse Peacock). As we have also seen, Trench's 1857 lectures *On Some Deficiencies in our English Dictionaries* argued clearly for the exclusion of dialect vocabulary from the Society's dictionary, proposing that '*provincial* or *local* words stand on quite a different footing from *obsolete*', as their very provincialism means that 'they have no right to a place in a Dictionary of the English tongue'.[108] The sole justification for an exception to this principle, Trench thought, was where 'a word may be local or provincial now, which was once current over the whole land': such words should be admitted, he argued, 'not [. . .] in right of what they now are, but of what they once have been; not because they now survive in some single district, but because they once lived through the whole land'.[109]

The Philological Society's 1859 *Proposal for the Publication of a New English Dictionary* affirmed Trench's position, explaining that 'as soon as a standard language has been formed, which in England was the case after the Reformation, the lexicographer is bound to deal with that alone', and hence 'works written subsequently to the Reformation for the purpose of illustrating provincial dialects' should be excluded.[110] However, the route from Trench's principles to Murray's practices was by no means direct. The *Canones Lexicographici*, a document drawn up under Herbert Coleridge's leadership in 1859–60, listed among its categories for inclusion, '*Provincial and Local Words*, where their existence can be vouched for by any creditable authority', and the *Canones* made a special case for departing from Trench's precepts and admitting such words ('as the claims of Philology, in such a work as this, must be looked upon as paramount to all others, we have resolved to give [dialect words] place in the pages of the Main Dictionary, whether furnished or not with the otherwise indispensable passport of a quotation').[111] This decision was supported by a paper to the Philological Society by Derwent Coleridge (Samuel Taylor Coleridge's son, and Herbert Coleridge's uncle): 'The question', he wrote, 'is not whether a dialectic word belongs to the standard currency of the language, but whether, on other grounds it deserves to be recorded [. . .] For etymological purposes, and as bearing upon the ancient literature or language of the country, [dialect] has a *great* value'.[112] At the

---

[108] Trench, *On Some Deficiencies*, p. 12.

[109] Trench, *On Some Deficiencies*, p. 12.

[110] *Proposal for the Publication of a New English Dictionary by the Philological Society* (London: Trübner, 1859), p. 3.

[111] Herbert Coleridge et al, 'Canones Lexicographici; or Rules to be Observed in Editing the New English Dictionary of the Philological Society', *Transactions of the Philological Society* 1859, Part II, 1–12, at pp. 4, 11.

[112] Derwent Coleridge, 'Observations on the Plan of the Society's Proposed New English Dictionary', *Transactions of the Philological Society* 1860, 152–68, at p. 164; see Benzie, *Dr F. J. Furnivall*, p. 90 n. 66; Crowley, *Politics of Discourse*, pp. 104–5.

254   The Victorians and English Dialect

start of the 1860s, Furnivall was telling Robert Backhouse Peacock that 'we wanted Provincialisms collected for our book', and many of the early sub-editors were also generous in including dialect vocabulary in the materials they assembled; but in 1877 the Delegates of Oxford University Press, when negotiations were in train for them to act as publishers, expressed reservations about the presence of dialect words in the proposed dictionary.[113]

James Murray was appointed as editor in 1879, having made his philological reputation primarily as a dialect scholar. (The second editor of the *OED*, Henry Bradley, was also respected as a dialectologist, and Joseph Wright consulted him over Sheffield dialect.)[114] The 'Directions to Readers for the Dictionary', which Murray issued soon after his appointment, say nothing about dialect explicitly; Murray's instructions simply urge readers to 'make a quotation for *every* word that strikes you as rare, obsolete, old-fashioned, new, peculiar, or used in a peculiar way', and in particular to 'take special note of passages which show or imply that a word is either new and tentative, or needing explanation as obsolete or archaic'.[115] There is nothing in these instructions that would seem to exclude dialect vocabulary from the general call. Arguably, the position of dialect in Murray's thinking for the *OED* does not become fully clear until the publication of the first instalment in 1884, and the appearance of his 'General Explanations'. This prefatory essay contains Murray's famous compass-style visualization of English vocabulary: 'Common' is placed at the centre, with 'Literary' and 'Colloquial' above and below, and five spokes radiating outwards ('Scientific', 'Foreign', 'Dialectal', 'Slang', and 'Technical'). 'Dialectal' is placed in the 'Colloquial' lower half, and between the spokes for 'Foreign' and 'Slang'. The 'General Explanations' set out Murray's policies on the treatment of dialect, and merit quoting at length:

> Down to the Fifteenth Century the language existed only in dialects, all of which had a literary standing: during this period, therefore, words and forms of all dialects are admitted on an equal footing into the Dictionary. Dialectal words and forms which occur since 1500 are not admitted, except when they continue the history of a word or sense once in general use, illustrate the history of a literary word, or have themselves a certain literary currency, as is the case with many modern Scottish words. It is true that the dialectal words are mostly genuine English, and that they are an essential part of the contents of a *Lexicon totius Anglicitatis*; but the work of collecting them has not yet been completed; and, even when they shall have been collected, the phonetic variety in which they exist in different localities, and the want of any fixed written forms round which to group the variations, will require a method of treatment different from that applicable to the words of the literary language, which have an accepted uniform spelling and an approximately uniform pronunciation.[116]

---

[113] Furnivall, 'Prefatory Notice', p. iii; Peacock, 'On Some Leading Characteristics of Northumbrian', p. 233; Gilliver, *The Making of the Oxford English Dictionary*, pp. 69, 93.

[114] See Wright, *Grammar of the Dialect of Windhill*, p. 112.

[115] Murray, *Caught in the Web of Words*, p. 347.

[116] Murray, 'General Explanations', p. xviii.

The *English Dialect Dictionary*   255

This is a passage rich in insight and wisdom. According to Murray, dialectal vocabulary is distinct from, but not inferior to, the standard language; it has just as much claim to be counted within a complete lexicon of English as the standard variety; but it cannot usually be accommodated within the *Oxford English Dictionary*: first, because of what we might call the headword problem, which we will return to—under which 'fixed written forms' could one organize the material?—and second, because 'the work of collecting [...] has not yet been completed' (the English Dialect Society was just over ten years old at the time of Murray's writing). But Murray also recognizes that categories blur, and exceptions can be made to include certain dialect words ('when they continue the history of a word or sense once in general use, illustrate the history of a literary word, or have themselves a certain literary currency'). But the central principle, ultimately derived from Trench, of including pre-1500 dialect vocabulary (on the grounds that no standard form of English then existed) but excluding most post-1500 dialect, may mean, oddly, that medieval dialect is more systematically represented in the *OED* than modern dialect.[117]

One consequence of Murray's decision to exclude most dialect terms was that a substantial quantity of dialect vocabulary which had been collected by readers for the *OED* was no longer needed. And so, as J. H. Nodal relayed to English Dialect Society members in his report for 1881, 'a large number of quotations and references to dialectal words and forms in authors subsequent to 1600 had been accumulated at Mill Hill [i.e. Murray's London home], of which Dr Murray and his assistants would not make use in the New English Dictionary. These they kindly proposed to put aside and reserve for the use of the Editor of the Dialect Dictionary'.[118] Thus although the road from 1857 to 1884 was bumpy, by the time Murray had begun to publish the instalments of the *OED*, and Wright had agreed to take on the editorship of the *EDD*, a broadly complementary relationship had been established between the two dictionaries. In terms of their overlapping schedules, the *OED* had reached the middle of the letter F at the start of the *EDD*'s publication programme, while the *OED* was able to start drawing on the published *EDD* as a resource from the letter J onwards.[119] In other words, the *EDD* lexicographers could make use of the *OED* for the earlier part of the alphabet, while subsequently the *OED* lexicographers could draw on the *EDD* for a somewhat longer stretch of the later part. A sample check of the first thirty separate words in the *EDD* under F reveals that ten are included in the first edition of the *OED* and twenty are excluded (counting exclusions on the basis of the

[117] See further Martyn F. Wakelin, 'The Treatment of Dialect in English Dictionaries', in Robert Burchfield (ed.), *Studies in Lexicography* (Oxford: Clarendon Press, 1987), pp. 156–77, at pp. 169–73; Anne Curzan, 'The Compass of the Vocabulary', in Lynda Mugglestone (ed.), *Lexicography and the OED: Pioneers in the Untrodden Forest* (Oxford: Oxford University Press, 2000), pp. 96–109, at pp. 104–5; Mugglestone, *Lost for Words*, pp. 107–8.
[118] *English Dialect Society: Ninth Annual Report*, p. 11.
[119] See Jenny McMorris, 'Appendix I: OED Sections and Parts', in Lynda Mugglestone (ed.), *Lexicography and the OED: Pioneers in the Untrodden Forest* (Oxford: Oxford University Press, 2000), pp. 228–31; Roper, 'The Clergyman and the Dialect Speaker', p. 118. See further Philip Durkin, 'The *English Dialect Dictionary* and the *Oxford English Dictionary*: A Continuing Relationship Between Two Dictionaries', in Manfred Markus, Clive Upton, and Reinhard Heuberger (eds), *Joseph Wright's English Dialect Dictionary and Beyond: Studies in Late Modern English Dialectology* (Frankfurt am Main: Lang, 2010), pp. 201–18.

256 The Victorians and English Dialect

absence from the *OED* of the *EDD* word or sense, or the lack of a cross-reference in the *OED* to the Standard English form), while a comparable sample for the first thirty words under N produces nine inclusions and twenty-one exclusions. What even such a modest sampling shows is that, not surprisingly, a significant number of words were included in both dictionaries (usually with the label '*dial.*' in the *OED*). The *EDD*, by its very nature, contains many dialect words not to be found in the *OED*, whereas the *OED* probably contains few dialect terms not to be found in the *EDD*. A comparison between the two dictionaries also shows that Wright and his assistants did not hesitate to adopt definitions more or less wholesale from the *OED*: among our samples, see, for instance, *facy*, which the *OED* defines as 'characterised by "face"; insolent, impudent', a phrasing directly echoed—that is to say, copied—by the *EDD*'s 'insolent, impudent'.[120]

In terms of historical coverage, Murray's *Oxford English Dictionary* had its own very clear principles of inclusion: all words recorded in English from the mid-twelfth century onwards were included, with attention given also to pre-twelfth-century histories for such words where they existed. The chronological range of Wright's *English Dialect Dictionary* was more circumscribed: its subtitle announces it as 'the complete vocabulary of all dialect words still in use, or known to have been in use during the last two hundred years'. This circumscription was part of the complementary relationship with the *OED*, with its commitment to a thorough coverage of pre-1500 dialect—though at least in theory, dialect terms of the sixteenth or early seventeenth century might fall between the two stools and be included in neither dictionary.

Wright's geographical remit is also important, and is explained in the preface he supplied for Volume I of the *EDD* in 1898: in the opening sentence of this, he repeats the phrasing of the dictionary's subtitle ('all dialect words still in use [. . .]') and further specifies that this is 'in England, Ireland, Scotland, and Wales'.[121] So Wright's *English Dialect Dictionary* is 'English' in the same way as Skeat and Nodal's English Dialect Society: although, proportionally, most attention is given to the dialects of England, it also treats the English dialects of Scotland, Ireland, and Wales as falling within its proper view (but not, of course, the Celtic languages of those countries). Beyond Britain and Ireland, though, coverage becomes much more patchy, as Wright acknowledges in a lengthy explanation in his preface:

> [The *EDD*] also includes American and Colonial dialect words which are still in use in Great Britain and Ireland, or which are to be found in early-printed books and glossaries. After some experience it became clear that this plan was absolutely necessary in order to avoid admitting into the Dictionary words for which I had not full and reliable evidence. It is difficult enough to obtain information about the pronunciation and exact usage of many words in the United Kingdom, and it would have been still more difficult to obtain such information from abroad.[122]

---

[120] Wright (ed.), *English Dialect Dictionary*, II, 274.

[121] Wright (ed.), *English Dialect Dictionary*, I, v.

[122] Wright (ed.), *English Dialect Dictionary*, I, v. See further Javier Ruano-García, 'On the Colonial Element in Joseph Wright's *English Dialect Dictionary*', *International Journal of Lexicography* 32 (2019), 38–57.

The *English Dialect Dictionary*   257

That is to say, a different type of proof was needed for the inclusion of global English varieties, through the confirmation of either print or domestic usage. A similar ambivalence had animated the English Dialect Society: although Skeat and Nodal's *Bibliographical List* contains sections on 'Americanisms', 'The English Language in India', and 'China-English Dialect' (the last two very brief), the Society never actually published any volumes on dialect outside of Britain and Ireland; the offer of a Barbados word list, for example, had come to nothing.[123] (By contrast, Ellis' *On Early English Pronunciation* does pay some attention to overseas English.)[124]

A more difficult question that faced Wright over inclusion concerned slang—as recognized also in Murray's compass of the English language, in which 'Dialectal' is placed between 'Foreign' and 'Slang'. Palmer's first report as the editor of the *EDD* indicates how the scope of the dictionary was conceived at the beginning: 'the conclusion has gradually been forced upon us', Palmer wrote, 'that we shall have to take in every description of folk-speech—not only, dialect words proper—but slang, cant, vulgar and colloquial expressions, *all, in fact, that are not literary English*.'[125] But an addendum by Skeat to the second report (issued when Wright had already been approached) struck a note of caution: 'It may turn out that it is absolutely necessary to *exclude* from the Dialect Dictionary words which absolutely belong to *slang* and *vulgarisms*; but this will not affect the *collection* of such words'.[126]

Victorian philologists and dialect collectors often had an ambiguous or conflicted attitude towards slang, and the topic deserves discussion. Where—if anywhere— should one draw the line between dialect and slang? Alexander Ellis pronounced axiomatically that 'slang is only a form of dialect', and in expounding his spelling system of Glossic, he collocated 'nashenel deialek·tik [national dialectic]' with 'difek·tiv sluvnli uterensez [defective slovenly utterances]', proposing that the latter at least 'shuod bi very kairfuoli studid in aurder too bee korek·ted [should be very carefully studied in order to be corrected]'; elsewhere in the same paper he brackets together 'proavin·shel deialekts and vulgar·itiz [provincial dialects and vulgarities]' and writes of the 'korek·shen ov difek·tiv, sluvnli, proavin·shel uterensez [correction of defective, slovenly, provincial utterances]'.[127] As we saw in Chapter 2, Ellis thought that regional accents would need to be lost in order to introduce a reformed spelling system and so 'facilitat[e] intercourse between man and man'—a loss, perhaps, that might be mourned less if provincial speech was viewed as 'slovenly' and 'defective'.[128]

Here, though, is Richard Morris, the great Early English Text Society editor and surveyor of Middle English dialects, commenting on a recent news story: 'In a case tried in the police courts the other day, a woman spoke of having "*nicked* a watch". I find this, to us, horribly vulgar word, in common use among boys'. (Morris was

---

[123] See Skeat and Nodal, *A Bibliographical List*, pp. 166–70, 172; *English Dialect Society: Second Report*, p. 11.

[124] See Ellis, *On Early English Pronunciation*, IV, 1058–70, 1217–30, V, 1668–80/236–48.

[125] *English Dialect Dictionary: First Annual Report*, p. 3; see also *English Dialect Dictionary: Second Annual Report*, p. 3.

[126] *English Dialect Dictionary: Second Annual Report*, p. 6.

[127] Ellis, *On Early English Pronunciation*, I, 19, and 'On Glosik', pp. 98–9, 110 n.1.

[128] Ellis, *On Early English Pronunciation*, II, 630.

258   The Victorians and English Dialect

a schoolmaster, well familiar with boys' slang.) So far this anecdote sounds as if its conclusion will be a standard disapproval of demotic language, inviting a shudder on the part of the reader at the use of such vocabulary. But Morris continues his musings on the verb *to nick* as follows: 'It occurs in various dialects with the sense of to cheat, steal; and it curiously enough turns up in the Cursor.'[129] A word that might initially be perceived as 'horribly vulgar' can, in fact, be reappraised and rehabilitated on at least two grounds: its distribution in modern dialects, and its occurrence in a medieval text (the *Cursor Mundi*). So Victorian philologists, as Morris' anecdote suggests, were well aware that contemporary slang could have a medieval provenance—just like dialect. Inspired by Cleasby and Vigfússon's *Icelandic-English Dictionary*, for example, A. L. Mayhew published a short piece on 'Some Slang Expressions Illustrated from the Icelandic' in which he offered medieval etymologies for a whole range of modern terms (*to drub, funk, gift of the gab, a wigging*, and several more).[130] Did this alter the perception of such words and phrases?

Dialect scholars thus seem to have been torn two ways over slang. W. E. A. Axon thought there was a readily discernible 'difference between provincial words and mere vulgarisms'.[131] Skeat and Nodal, though, included a lengthy section on 'Slang and Cant' in their *Bibliographical List*: this suggests that slang was viewed at one and the same time as being both closely connected with dialect but also able to be differentiated from it.[132] It is therefore not surprising that some glossarists acknowledged the inclusion of slang in their collections, while others were insistent that what they had collected was dialect alone—or even suggested that there was a sort of distinctive local slang which really qualified as dialect. So, for example, the compilers of the *Holderness Glossary* state that 'they have been careful to admit no words excepting such as can be considered genuinely dialectal', with 'technical trade terms, slang, and exotics having been avoided'; but then they qualify this by adding 'excepting where they are peculiar to the district' (an example might be *bangin* 'great in size', used as a superlative).[133] William Dickinson includes *cum-atable* 'attainable' in his *Cumberland Glossary*, but adds the comment 'Query a modern coinage?' (he also includes *banger* 'anything great', with the example 'It is a banger').[134] R. O. Heslop, in his *Northumberland Glossary*, labels a number of words as 'cant' to indicate slang, such as *piker* 'the nose', *scufter* 'a policeman', *smasher* 'anything of huge or gross dimensions', and *winkers* 'the eyes'.[135] When, in the 1890s, Mabel Peacock and her brothers tried to solicit material for a never-completed 'Lincolnshire Place-Name and Dialect Dictionary', their prospectus was careful to define dialect 'in a wide sense to include

---

[129] Morris, *On the Survival of Early English Words in our Present Dialects*, p. 9.
[130] A. L. Mayhew, 'Some Slang Expressions Illustrated from the Icelandic', *Notes and Queries* 5th Series 4 (11 September 1875), 206.
[131] Axon, *George Eliot's Use of Dialect*, p. 42.
[132] Skeat and Nodal, *A Bibliographical List*, pp. 157–65.
[133] Ross, Stead, and Holderness, *Glossary of Words Used in Holderness*, pp. iii, 26.
[134] Dickinson, *Glossary of Words and Phrases Pertaining to the Dialect of Cumberland*, pp. 5 (italics removed), 23.
[135] Heslop, *Northumberland Words*, pp. 536, 609, 661, 791.

The *English Dialect Dictionary*   **259**

colloquialisms, vulgarisms, slang, and mispronunciations, everything which is not good literary English'.[136]

Fred Elworthy states that he omits 'ordinary colloquialisms' from his *West Somerset Word-Book*, while noting that 'many glossaries contain such words': among his examples of excluded terms are *all to smash, cross-patch, stone-blind, spick and span,* and *transmogrify*.[137] But Elworthy also claims that while there is a good deal of 'coarseness' in rural dialect, there is no real obscenity, and the dialect collector does not need to censor or bowdlerize their word list: 'The reason is that there is nothing to suppress; the people are simple, and although there is a super-abundance of rough, coarse language, yet foul-mouthed obscenity is a growth of cities, and I declare I have never heard it'.[138] Modern scholars have expressed scepticism about this; swearing may well be under-reported in nineteenth-century dialect and folklore collections.[139] Certainly, the repertoire of interjections said to be 'expressive of anger, in various degrees' recorded by C. Clough Robinson in his *Mid-Yorkshire Glossary* seems suspiciously mild: the list runs *Od rabit! Od zounds! Drat! Od rat! Blame! Dash! Burn! Deng!* and *Zolch!*[140]

A central question was age. As we have seen repeatedly, regional dialect was often valued for its antiquity: derivation from medieval forms of language was held to validate the dignity and ancestry of regional dialect, and provided a weapon for those who wished to defend non-standard speech against its critics and assailants. So did new, fresh, expressive regional words and phrases, which could not be derived from Old English or Old Norse, count as dialect as well—or only as slang? This was a real dilemma for Victorian philologists, given not only their historicist orientation but also their arguments for the value of dialect. Henry Sweet's contrarian appraisal of dialects might have seemed heretical to some, but it did at least offer a means of viewing innovations in a positive light: 'The fact is', he wrote, 'that dialects generally change and reconstruct themselves with far greater ease than the literary languages, whose growth is impeded in many ways. It is in their independent developments, rather than in their archaisms, that their real value seems to me to lie'.[141] But this was not the view of most dialect scholars.

Regrettably, the few introductory pages of Wright's 1898 preface to the *EDD* are a far cry from the mission statement offered by Murray's 'General Explanations' for the *OED*. Wright says nothing about slang, or about his policies for inclusion and exclusion in this area, even though '*slang*' and '*colloq*'. are two of the usage labels he employs within the dictionary itself (being applied to about two per cent of entries,

---

[136] Elder (ed.), *The Peacock Lincolnshire Word Books*, p. 18.
[137] Elworthy, *West Somerset Word-Book*, p. vii.
[138] Elworthy, *West Somerset Word-Book*, p. xii.
[139] Waller, 'Democracy and Dialect, Speech and Class', p. 9; Roper, 'England—The Land Without Folklore?', p. 247.
[140] Robinson, *Glossary of Words Pertaining to the Dialect of Mid-Yorkshire*, p. lviii.
[141] Sweet, *Collected Papers*, p. 131.

260   The Victorians and English Dialect

it has been calculated).[142] In his writings, though, Wright does quite often use the phrase 'pure dialect', an expression which seems to denote a local variety that is historically consistent and not marked by either modern admixture or conspicuous innovation.[143] Elizabeth Mary Wright records that her husband found 'any exaggerated expression, or common colloquialism—apart from dialect—distasteful' and that he 'disliked slang of any sort'.[144] But Victorian dictionaries of slang were among the core resources used in the making of the *EDD*, especially the earlier parts of John S. Farmer and W. E. Henley's historicist, multi-volume *Slang and Its Analogues Past and Present* (1890–1914).[145] The first volume of the *EDD* (covering A–C) contains many items labelled as '*slang*', including *barker* 'a pistol, firearm', *broads* 'playing-cards', *bub* 'intoxicating liquor of any kind', *button* 'one of the persons engaged in the thimble-rigging swindle; a decoy of any kind', *cabbage* 'to appropriate surreptitiously, to pilfer, rob', and *chummy* 'a chimney-sweep; the small boy formerly made to climb chimneys'.[146] Many of the occurrences are compounds or phrases, such as *(to upset the) apple-cart*, *back-swap* 'to cry off a bargain', *(to save one's) bacon*, and *catgut-scrapers* 'an orchestra, players on stringed instruments', and there is also a significant presence of public school slang (including *bake* 'to sit or lie at ease', *barter* 'a half-volley at cricket', and *cargo* 'a hamper of good things sent from home', all from Winchester College).[147] Few of the items marked as '*slang*' are simplexes for which a medieval etymology can be supplied; the majority are creative or metaphorical redeployments of common vocabulary, or lexemes of unknown origin.[148] They are often restricted in register or discourse (such as the language of crime); the slang words of the *EDD* also have more urban or metropolitan associations than most of the other vocabulary in the dictionary, as well as being of a more recent origin.

Mention of Farmer and Henley's *Slang and Its Analogues* moves us on to the question of the sources which were used to compile the *English Dialect Dictionary*.[149] The *EDD*'s second subtitle on its title pages announces that the dictionary was 'founded on the publications of the English Dialect Society and on a large amount of material never before printed'. Wright's 1898 preface states that over three thousand works had been 'read and excerpted', and the final volume of the *EDD*, published in 1905, contained a full bibliography, subdivided into counties like Skeat and Nodal's earlier listing.[150] Some of the rarer items had been accessed via Louis Lucien Bonaparte's

---

[142] Marta Degani and Alexander Onysko, 'Giving Voice to Local Cultures: Reflections on the Notion of "Dialect" in the *English Dialect Dictionary*', in Roberta Facchinetti (ed.), *English Dictionaries as Cultural Mines* (Newcastle: Cambridge Scholars, 2012), pp. 55–72, at pp. 67–8.

[143] See for example, Wright (ed.), *English Dialect Dictionary*, I, v, and VI, *English Dialect Grammar*, iv; see also Petyt, *The Study of Dialectology*, pp. 84–5.

[144] Wright, *The Life of Joseph Wright*, II, 605.

[145] See Julie Coleman, *A History of Slang and Cant Dictionaries, Volume III: 1859–1936* (Oxford: Oxford University Press, 2008).

[146] Wright (ed.), *English Dialect Dictionary*, I, 166, 408, 424, 468, 478, 602.

[147] Wright (ed.), *English Dialect Dictionary*, I, 65, 111, 122–3, 137, 175, 521, 542.

[148] See Julie Coleman, *The Life of Slang* (Oxford: Oxford University Press, 2012), pp. 26–48.

[149] See Manfred Markus, 'Joseph Wright's *English Dialect Dictionary* and Its Sources', in Ingrid Tieken-Boon van Ostade and Wim van der Wurff (eds), *Current Issues in Late Modern English* (Bern: Lang, 2009), pp. 263–82.

[150] Wright (ed.), *English Dialect Dictionary*, I, vi.

The *English Dialect Dictionary*   **261**

library, which had been made available to Wright, but many were purchased and shelved in the Workshop on Walton Street; Elizabeth Mary Wright recalled that 'the number of dialect novels was not to be counted! [Joseph Wright] had bought whole sets of the classic authors such as Hardy, George Eliot, the Brontës, Blackmore, Stevenson, Scott, Barrie, Crockett, Galt, &c., and scores of others, good, bad, and indifferent, anything which contained even a smattering of dialect here and there' (and she herself, in reading such novels for the *EDD*, soon 'became an adept at skipping the standard English').[151]

The reading of sources and drafting of entries threw up countless queries. As Jane Partridge later recalled, the correspondents whom Wright and his assistants wrote to 'were of all sorts and conditions—country gentlemen, clergy, mill-workers, farmers, students, enthusiasts of all sorts, both scholars and homely folk'.[152] In its published form, the *English Dialect Dictionary* includes three different lists of helpers: at the start of the first volume, there is a 'List of Voluntary Readers', a 'List of Unprinted Collections of Dialect Words', and a 'List of Correspondents'; and at the end of the last volume there is a consolidated 'List of Correspondents and of Unprinted Collections of Dialect Words'.[153] The collectors and correspondents are usually identified in the dictionary by initials, so that, by consulting the key of initials, we can see who contributed which words and offered guidance on which topics.

The resources of the *English Dialect Dictionary* are now able to be unlocked as never before, thanks to the development of an online version at the University of Innsbruck, under the direction of Manfred Markus.[154] This means that, through online searching, we can now locate the contributions of individual correspondents across the dictionary, and can even reassemble the 'unprinted collections' that are distributed across the letters of the alphabet.[155] So a simple search reveals, for example, that sixty-nine words submitted or elucidated by Charlotte Ellis are included in the text of the *EDD*, compared to only twelve words by Arthur Munby. Gerard Manley Hopkins' collection of Irish vocabulary yields ninety-five words in the published dictionary.[156] Mary Powley's 'MS collections on the Cumberland dialect'—at first put together for the English Dialect Society, then, after her death, passed to Abram Smythe Palmer by Powley's brother, and then passed on in turn to Wright—turn out to be especially extensive.[157] The initials 'M. P.' occur over eight hundred times in the *English Dialect Dictionary*, and although a proportion relate to Mabel Peacock's Lincolnshire contributions, the great majority are tagged to Powley's Cumberland words. Powley's collection, to repeat, had never previously been published (in the form, say, of an English Dialect Society glossary): it only survives

---

[151] Wright, *Life of Joseph Wright*, II, 378, 400.

[152] Wright, *The Life of Joseph Wright*, II, 384.

[153] Wright (ed.), *English Dialect Dictionary*, I, ix–xiv, VI [Bibliography], 60–2. See also Degani and Onysko, 'Giving Voice to Local Cultures', p. 58.

[154] https://eddonline4-proj.uibk.ac.at/edd/ and see Manfred Markus, *English Dialect Dictionary Online: A New Departure in English Dialectology* (Cambridge: Cambridge University Press, 2021).

[155] See Markus, *English Dialect Dictionary Online*, pp. 62–3.

[156] See White, 'G. M. Hopkins's *Contribution to the English Dialect Dictionary*'.

[157] *English Dialect Dictionary: Third Annual Report*, p. 4.

262   The Victorians and English Dialect

in a dispersed state, threaded through the six volumes of the published *EDD*, and so it is only now, through the search functions of the online *EDD*, that it can be reconstructed as a coherent assemblage. There are many other major collections embedded in the *EDD* that are now able to be reassembled: for instance, Thomas Holderness, editor of the *Driffield Observer* and one of the three authors of the *Holderness Glossary*, supplied Wright with an enormously expanded collection, and for East Riding words the label '*MS. add.* (T. H.)' is a very common one through the dictionary. Angelina Parker similarly supplemented her English Dialect Society publications with an enlarged collection of Oxfordshire words for the *EDD*.[158]

Just as unpublished collections can now be systematically identified and reconstituted, so too can the letters written to Wright and his assistants—an especially important possibility, as Wright does not seem to have preserved the correspondence he received as a consolidated archive. Let us continue with the initials T. H., for in Wright's lists they refer not only to Thomas Holderness (and sometimes Thomas Hallam too), but also to Thomas Hardy. Jane Partridge's memoirs recall that Dorset was found to be 'a dialect blank', with especially poor collections, and so 'in our difficulty we wrote to Thomas Hardy, explaining the position, and asking him if he could tell us of someone able and willing to help us'.[159] According to Partridge, Hardy put the dictionary workers in touch with Henry Joseph Moule, curator of the Dorset County Museum in Dorchester (and the initials 'H. J. M' accordingly appear next to many Dorset words), but the published text of the *EDD* attests that Hardy also helped directly: he is listed among Wright's correspondents, and his initials are cited as the authority for a number of definitions and glosses. So, for example, *wring-down* is included in the *EDD* as 'a cider-making term', the sole source for which is a quotation from *Far From the Madding Crowd*: 'She had just got off her mare to look at the last wring-down of cider for the year'.[160] But then a note follows: 'A single process of the screw from the top of the press to the bottom after charging with fresh pomace. Also the result from such process (T. H.)'. Similarly, one of the meanings of *twank* is 'to utter peevish sighs; to whine, complain', a sense which is illustrated by a quotation from *The Mayor of Casterbridge* ('A poor twanking woman like her'); again, this is followed by an explanation from Hardy: 'To "querk" is to complain without good cause; to "twank" is to complain with real cause (T. H.)'.[161] Only two letters seem to survive from Hardy to Wright, glossing the words *chaw (high)* and *trangleys*; by comparison with the published entries for these words (in which 'T. H.' is cited), we can see that Wright seems to have incorporated Hardy's explanations word for word.[162] Hardy's clarificatory contributions in the *EDD* have never been extracted and collected together; if they were, what they would amount to would be both an addition

---

[158] See Ruano-García, 'The Contribution of Angelina Parker to the *English Dialect Dictionary*'.
[159] Wright, *The Life of Joseph Wright*, II, 384.
[160] Wright (ed.), *English Dialect Dictionary*, VI, 554.
[161] Wright (ed.), *English Dialect Dictionary*, VI, 279.
[162] Hardy, *Collected Letters*, II, 168, III, 42–3; Wright (ed.), *English Dialect Dictionary*, I, 570, VI, 221.

The *English Dialect Dictionary*   263

to Hardy's known correspondence, and also a modest but noteworthy collection of glosses by one of the most important writers of the century.[163]

Dialect lexicography (2): entries

The best way to appreciate the lexicographical practices in the finished *English Dialect Dictionary* is to look at an entry—though it has been noted that the entries in the *EDD* 'demonstrate a great deal of internal heterogeneity and complexity'.[164] So here is the word *lallack*:

> **LALLACK**, *v.* and *sb.* Nhb. Lakel. Yks. Wor. Also written **lalack** Lakel.[2]; and in forms **laleek** Nhb.[1] Cum.; **lallik** Lakel.[2]; **lallock** n.Yks.[3]; **lalluck** s.Wor. [la·lək.]
>
> 1. *v.* To idle about, to go gossiping from house to house. Lakel.[2], s.Wor. (F. W. M. W.) See **Lall**, *v.*[1]; cf. **lollock**.
> 2. To hang the tongue loosely from the mouth; to put out the tongue. Cf. **lall**, *v.*[2]
>   **Cum.** Leuk at thur sheep laleekan the'r tongues oot (J.D.). **e.Yks.**[1] Brazzant huzzy lallackt her tung oot at mă, *MS. add.* (T. H.)
>   Hence **Lalliker**, *sb.* the tongue.
>   **Lakel.**[2] Lal oot thi lalliker.
> 3. *sb. pl.* Play, frolic.
>   **Nhb.**[1] Run away oot and get your laleeks.
>   Hence **Lallocking** or **Laleeking**, (1) *sb.* unrestrained junketing or scampering; (2) *ppl. adj.* boisterous.
>   (1) **n.Yks.**[3] (2) **Nhb.**[1] That dog's a greet laleekin animal.[165]

There is a lot to unpack here, beginning with the form of the so-called 'headword'. For dialect lexicographers, producing an alphabetical word list was far from straightforward, as this entry for *lallack* makes clear. Since the term was essentially a spoken word until the period of nineteenth-century dialect-collecting, and had no history of appearing in print in any sort of standard spelling, Wright had to choose a single headword form from the various candidates: his sources offered him not only *lallack*, but also *lalack, laleek, lallik, lallock*, and *lalluck*.[166] Some of these forms might just be spelling variants, as different authors and collectors had recorded the

---

[163] See further Ingham, 'Thomas Hardy and the Dorset Dialect', p. 88; Taylor, *Hardy's Literary Language and Victorian Philology*, pp. 121–2.

[164] Manfred Markus and Reinhard Heuberger, 'The Architecture of Joseph Wright's *English Dialect Dictionary*: Preparing the Computerised Version', *International Journal of Lexicography* 20 (2007), 355–68, at p. 366; see also Manfred Markus, 'The Complexity and Diversity of the Words in Wright's *English Dialect Dictionary*', in Manfred Markus et al (eds), *Middle and Modern English Corpus Linguistics: A Multi-Dimensional Approach* (Amsterdam: Benjamins, 2012), pp. 209–24, and Degani and Onysko, 'Giving Voice to Local Cultures', pp. 59–65.

[165] Wright (ed.), *English Dialect Dictionary*, III, 509.

[166] See Clive Upton, 'Regional and Dialect Dictionaries', in Philip Durkin (ed.), *The Oxford Handbook of Lexicography* (Oxford: Oxford University Press, 2015), pp. 381–92, at pp. 387–8; see also Van Keymeulen, 'The Dialect Dictionary', p. 46.

264 The Victorians and English Dialect

oral word according to their own transcription, but others might indicate variation in pronunciation. One option would be to multiply the headwords with a system of cross-references (for example, by inserting '**Laleek**, see **Lallack**'), but although Wright does do this sometimes, on this occasion he has chosen not to include separate headwords for the five other variant spellings of *lallack*; and to do so for all variants of all words would, of course, enlarge the length and complexity of the dictionary enormously. But inconsistencies inevitably arise. One of the *EDD*'s Lakeland sources (designated 'Lakel.²') spells the word as *lallik*, and this source also includes the derivative *lalliker* 'the tongue'; yet Wright does not respell this derivative as *lallacker*. Similarly, Wright gives the noun and adjective forms as *lallocking* or *laleeking*, not *lallacking*, though he does give a standard *-ing* ending, even though the supporting quotation has *-in* (*laleekin*). The issue facing Wright, for many of the words in his dictionary, was not that there was one standard spelling to use as a base form and then several dialectal spellings to record as variants (which would be difficult enough); rather, none of the spellings were standard or dominant, and so in each instance Wright and his assistants had to make a decision as to which form to choose as their headword.

The problem was long-standing, and had been recognized by earlier nation-wide lexicographers. James Orchard Halliwell, in his *Dictionary of Archaic and Provincial Words* (1847) had largely side-stepped the issue, precisely by entering multiple dialect variants as separate headwords.[167] Thomas Wright, in his 1857 *Dictionary of Obsolete and Provincial English*, explains that to record all variants 'would be to increase the dictionary twofold or threefold', and so his habitual practice has been to include 'the word only under the form in which it occurs most usually, or which seems most correct'.[168] James Murray, as we have seen, partly justified the exclusion of dialect words from the *OED* on the grounds that such words 'require a method of treatment different from that applicable to the words of the literary language, which have an accepted uniform spelling'.[169]

But the coexistence of variant forms was not the only challenge in producing an alphabetical word list; other aspects of regional phonology meant that the template of Standard English alphabeticization could not simply be carried over. So, for example, the presence or absence of initial *w* in certain forms of dialect speech also required a decision: in Elworthy's *West Somerset Word-Book*, the equivalents of Standard English *wood* and *wool* (and similar words) appear under O as *ood* and *ool*, while contrariwise in William Barnes' poetry Standard English *oak* appears as Dorset *woak* (as in the poem 'The Vield Path', which we examined in Chapter 3).[170] A further question was what to do about silent <h>, and how far dialect collectors should ignore the template of standard spelling when attempting a more phonetic transcription of unwritten words. Alexander Ellis observed that 'glossary writers put in the *h* as a

---

[167] See Hultin, '"To Shine with Borrowed Splendour"', pp. 122, 129, 140–2.
[168] Wright, *Dictionary of Obsolete and Provincial English*, p. vi.
[169] Murray, 'General Explanations', p. xviii.
[170] Elworthy, *The West Somerset Word-Book*, pp. 538–9.

The *English Dialect Dictionary*   265

matter of habit, even where they know that no dialect speaker uses it'.[171] For example, John Harland's *Swaledale Glossary* (1873) shows a systematic discrepancy between its headword forms and its pronunciations under the letter H, as in the following sequence of words:

Hobthrush, [ob·thruosh] *sb.* a wall-louse.
Hocker, [ok·ur] *v.* to clamber; applied specially to cattle climbing on each other's backs.
Holm, [oaw·m] *sb.* a meadow near a river.[172]

But other glossarists take the opposite course, which can lead to a counter-intuitive alphabetical order. So, for instance, Robert Holland, under the letter E, offers the entry: 'ELLO, *interj.* an exclamation of astonishment'.[173] This is, obviously, the word *hello*, as spoken in Cheshire; but Holland's *Glossary* does not indicate it as such. Even more thoroughly, in his 1892 *Windhill Grammar*, Joseph Wright noted that 'initial **h** has disappeared in the W[indhill] dialect'.[174] This means that words which are alphabeticized under <h> in a dictionary of Standard English are distributed across all five vowels in Wright's index: for example, *ās* 'house', *evi* 'heavy', *iəl* 'to heal', *olə* 'hollow', and *unt* 'to hunt' (Wright's phonetic alphabeticization also, of course, ignores the presence of silent <h> in Standard English, as in *onə(r)* 'honour').[175] One can see why, according to Jane Partridge's memoirs, Wright's assistants on the *English Dialect Dictionary* found the vowel A to be an extremely difficult letter to begin with, and longed to move on to the consonant B.[176] (For information: Holland's *ello* does not make it into the *EDD*, whereas Barnes' *woak* and Elworthy's *ood* and *ool* are given as cross-references, to *oak*, *wood*, and *wool*.)[177]

If we return to the entry for *lallack* in the *EDD*, we can see that, following the range of forms, Wright indicates the word's pronunciation, in square brackets and bold print: [**la·lək**]. Except where the pronunciation might seem self-evident, this is a policy throughout the *EDD*, although the existence of variant pronunciations in different parts of the country is a repeated challenge (so that sometimes more than one pronunciation is given, as for example with [**i·ntēk, i·ntak**], recognizing variable vowel length in the second syllable of *intake* or *intak*).[178] Such pronunciations are given in Wright's own spelling system—'a simple phonetic scheme, specially formulated for the purpose', as he explains in his preface.[179] Given Wright's Neogrammarian training, and the phonological emphasis of his *Windhill Grammar*, it is at first surprising how little attention is given to phonetic matters in the entries of the *EDD*;

---

[171] Ellis, *On Early English Pronunciation*, V, 2265/833.
[172] Harland, *Glossary of Words Used in Swaledale*, p. 16.
[173] Holland, *Glossary of Words Used in the County of Chester*, p. 114.
[174] Wright, *Grammar of the Dialect of Windhill*, p. 102.
[175] Wright, *Grammar of the Dialect of Windhill*, pp. 216, 222, 228, 237, 237, 252.
[176] Wright, *The Life of Joseph Wright*, II, 383; see also Markus, *English Dialect Dictionary Online*, p 3.
[177] Wright (ed.), *English Dialect Dictionary*, IV, 352, VI, 530
[178] Wright (ed.), *English Dialect Dictionary*, III, 326.
[179] Wright (ed.), *English Dialect Dictionary*, I, v; and see xvii.

266 The Victorians and English Dialect

on the whole, this is a Skeat-like prioritization of words over sounds. But as we will see shortly, the major, lexicographical part of Wright's grand dialect project—the six volumes of the *EDD*—was by no means the element on which he placed most value.

Wright's *EDD* entries supply grammatical information (*v.* = verb, *sb.* = substantive or noun, *ppl.* = participle, and so on), and divide definitions into senses and subsenses (the verb form of *lallack*, for example, is divided into two separate meanings, distinguished from a further, nominal form).[180] Moreover, Wright's *EDD*—like Murray's *OED*—also includes compound or phrasal forms under the umbrella headword (though the relatively brief entry for *lallack* does not demonstrate this). So, for example, the entry under the headword **Fairy** lists forty-three different senses 'in comb[ination]': *fairies' butter, fairy dart, fairy hair, fairy hillocks, fairypaths, fairy petticoats, fairypipes, fairy stirrup*, and many others.[181] Or more prosaically, the dozen combinations involving **Gob** 'the mouth' include *gobfight* 'a wordy quarrel', *gobmeat* 'food', *gobslotch* 'a greedy person', and *gobwind* 'an eructation'.[182] The entry for **Long** almost exclusively comprises compounds and combinations—no fewer than 174 in all, running from *long acher* 'a cut through the nail of the little finger, caused by the sickle slipping' to *longwund* 'of stories: tedious; involved', with a further twenty-two bird names in *long-* (such as *longneb* 'the snipe' and *longtail* 'the linnet') and eight phrases or sayings (for example, *long in the lugs*, meaning 'sharp-eared, quick in hearing').[183]

One absence in the entry for *lallack* may also be noted: there is no etymology. In his 1879 aspirations for an ideal dialect dictionary, A. L. Mayhew had insisted that 'the etymology should be given in each case, where known; or reference should be made, where possible, to some kindred word in a book language, the dictionaries of which would supply further information'.[184] Set against this, there was a long history of warning against the rash derivation of dialect terms, dating back to Skeat's 1873 caution to the word-collectors of the English Dialect Society that 'etymologies are best avoided'.[185] It is therefore little surprise to find that the practice of the *EDD* falls somewhere between the desires of Mayhew and the reservations of Skeat. Wright's preface includes the claim that entries will give 'the etymology so far as it relates to the immediate source of each word', but the apparent confidence of this is undercut by a subsequent, more honest confession:

---

[180] See further Manfred Markus, 'What Did Joseph Wright Mean by *Meaning*? The Complexity of Lexical Semantics in the *English Dialect Dictionary Online*', *International Journal of English Studies* 20 (2020), 1–25.

[181] Wright (ed.), *English Dialect Dictionary*, II, 284–6.

[182] Wright (ed.), *English Dialect Dictionary*, II, 665–6; see further Morris, *On the Survival of Early English Words in our Present Dialects*, pp. 3–4.

[183] Wright (ed.), *English Dialect Dictionary*, III, 646–51. See further Alexander Onysko, 'Phrases, Combinations and Compounds in the *English Dialect Dictionary* as a Source of Conceptual Metaphors and Metonymies in Late Modern English Dialects', in Manfred Markus, Clive Upton, and Reinhard Heuberger (eds), *Joseph Wright's English Dialect Dictionary and Beyond: Studies in Late Modern English Dialectology* (Frankfurt am Main: Lang, 2010), pp. 131–53.

[184] Mayhew, 'Wanted—an English Dialect Dictionary', p. 260.

[185] [Skeat], *Rules and Directions for Word-Collectors*, p. 4.

The *English Dialect Dictionary*   267

In the etymological part of the dictionary, it must not be assumed that where no etymology is given there has been no attempt to find one. The very opposite is the case.
It has often happened that dozens of dictionaries, special glossaries, and articles in
philological journals have been carefully searched without any satisfactory results. In
all such instances I have preferred to give nothing rather than a mere guess.[186]

If we keep browsing a little further into the L section of the dictionary, we find that, as
a sample, of the twenty-eight headwords beginning **loa-** (excluding cross-references),
only eight receive any etymological comment, set in square brackets at the end of the
entry.[187] Few of even these, however, offer a straightforward, authoritative derivation
in the manner of the *OED*, and it seems that the *EDD* is most inclined to suggest
etymologies for dialect terms which are possible loanwords (Wright's preface flags up
words derived from Norse and French); but even here there is a tentativeness about
many of the suggestions, which often amount more to a body of potential evidence
than a definitive ruling.[188] So etymology is not a core element of *EDD* entries in the
way that pronunciation is.

The next element to note in *EDD* entries is geographical distribution. In the entry
for *lallack*, the opening information specifies 'Nhb. Lakel. Yks. Wor.' and also 'Cum.',
and later subsections of the entry explain which features of the word, or which examples, derive from which of these areas. Four of these five designations are counties
(Northumberland, Yorkshire, Worcestershire, and Cumberland), and the county is
Wright's basic unit of organization, especially for England (for Scotland especially, a
more catch-all 'Sc.' is often used, signalling Wright's dependence on John Jamieson's
1808 *Etymological Dictionary of the Scottish Language*).[189] 'Lakel.' (Lakeland), however, is a looser, regional label rather than a county one, and the *EDD* frequently
employs such larger regional labels. As a number of commentators have observed,
there is a pronounced northern slant to the contents of the *EDD*, and the regional
abbreviation 'n.Cy' or N.Cy' (that is, 'North Country') occurs far more frequently
than any other regional marker. In terms of county citations, Wright's own Yorkshire
is way out in front, receiving nearly three times as many notices as the next most
numerous (which is Lancashire, receiving 27,957 citations compared to Yorkshire's
colossal 76,661).[190]

We should next add into the picture Wright's system for the citation of sources.
As can be seen, the entry for *lallack* references as sources **e.Yks.[1], Lakel.[2], Nhb.[1]**,

---

[186] Wright (ed.), *English Dialect Dictionary*, I, v–vi.
[187] Wright (ed.), *English Dialect Dictionary*, III, 631–5.
[188] See further Emil Chamson, 'Etymology in the *English Dialect Dictionary*', in Manfred Markus
et al (eds), *Middle and Modern English Corpus Linguistics: A Multi-Dimensional Approach* (Amsterdam:
Benjamins, 2012), pp. 225–40.
[189] On Jamieson's dictionary, see Susan Rennie, *Jamieson's Dictionary of Scots: The Story of the First Historical Dictionary of the Scots Language* (Oxford: Oxford University Press, 2012), and 'The First Scottish
'National' Dictionary: John Jamieson's Etymological Dictionary of the Scottish Language (1808/1825),
in Sarah Ogilvie and Gabriella Safran (eds), *The Whole World in a Book: Dictionaries in the Nineteenth
Century* (Oxford: Oxford University Press, 2020), pp. 110–30.
[190] Degani and Onysko, 'Giving Voice to Local Cultures', pp. 63–5.

268   The Victorians and English Dialect

and **n.Yks.**[3], as well as the initialled individuals F. M. W. W., J. D., and T. H. Both sets of abbreviations can be unlocked through Wright's indexes: the three individuals are F. M. W. Woodward, J. Denwood, and Thomas Holderness, and the four printed sources are Ross, Stead, and Holderness' *Holderness Glossary*, Bryham Kirkby's *Lakeland Words* (1898), Heslop's *Northumberland Words*, and Harland's *Swaledale Glossary*. As can be seen, glossaries routinely used in the *EDD* are given abbreviations on a county basis (and in bold): **n.Yks.**[3], for instance, is the *Holderness Glossary*, while **n.Yks.**[1] is Atkinson's *Cleveland Glossary* and **n.Yks.**[2] is Robinson's *Whitby Glossary*. This system of bibliographical referencing was worked out with much trial and thought by Wright, in an attempt to save space by maximal compression; and its efficiency is undeniable when we meet such strings of references as, for example, '**w.Yks.**[1245], **ne.Lan.**[1], **Chs.**[1], **nw.Der.**[1]' in the entry for *alablaster* (a variant of *alabaster*)—seven glossaries crammed into only half a line of print.[191] But there is a potential problem here as well, which is that the source glossaries have lost their local specificity in the process of being given county designations.[192] Does it make sense to treat Cleveland dialect and Swaledale dialect as if they are part of the same thing, the dialect of north Yorkshire, or is it their 'intense localization' (to use Hardy's phrase) which is more important? Moreover, the unaware reader who simply consults the entries and does not check what the bibliographical abbreviations stand for, might gain the impression that a dialect item is attested county-wide, rather than being much more locally restricted (for example, to Cleveland or to Swaledale). There are many words in the *EDD* which receive only a single reference, but such references are county-based, which might be taken to imply a county-wide distribution. The tension is well exemplified by the word *dannikins*, which is given the label 'Yks.' but defined as 'the name of the feast or wake held at Bolsterstone in Bradfield on Holy Thursday and several succeeding days'. A single source is cited, **w.Yks.**[2], which is the supplement to Sidney Addy's *Sheffield Glossary*; and this (quoted by the *EDD*) records that the word 'was in common use about Bolsterstone and Oughtibridge fifty or sixty years ago'.[193] So the entry, derived from Addy, makes it clear that this was a highly restricted term, found only in one narrowly defined place; but Wright's system of reference disguises the localism of Addy's Sheffield-specific glossary under the designation of '**w.Yks.**[2]', and further generalizes this very specific term under the county label of 'Yks.' Clearly, Wright needed to devise a consistent system of reference, especially to allow the wider distribution of more frequent words to be appraised; but it is possible to think that Skeat may have been wise not to commit the English Dialect Society to a county-by-county survey, and to keep open a more variable scale.

The actual quotations and citations are the last element of the typical *EDD* entry to look at. The entry for *lallack* includes five quotations or citations, of which two are unpublished and three published. The unpublished examples are from Denwood (J.

---

[191] Wright (ed.), *English Dialect Dictionary*, I, 35.

[192] Petyt, *The Study of Dialect*, p. 81; Burton and Ruthven, in Barnes, *Poems in the Broad Form of the Dorset Dialect*, p. lv; Penhallurick, 'Dialect Dictionaries', p. 305.

[193] Wright (ed.), *English Dialect Dictionary*, II, 21; Sidney Oldall Addy, *A Supplement to the Sheffield Glossary*, English Dialect Society 62 (London: English Dialect Society, 1891), pp. 16–17.

D.) and Holderness (T. H., an addition to **e.Yks.**[1]), and the published ones are from *Lakeland Words, Northumberland Words*, and the *Swaledale Glossary*. For the first two of these, the *EDD* takes an illustrative quotation; for the third, no quotation is given and the glossary is simply cited as the source for the word. If one checks the entry for *lallocking* in Harland's *Swaledale Glossary*, one sees that no illustrative quotation is given there either, and the entry comprises solely a definition: 'unrestrained junketing, or scampering'—and this, word for word, is the definition given in the *EDD* also.[194]

From this, we can observe at least three points. The first is that citations of prior glossaries by abbreviation alone (as for **n.Yks.**[3] in the entry for *lallack*) function as much as references as quotations—in other words, as signposts telling the reader where fuller information might be sought (and often found).[195] The second point is that definitions in prior glossaries were sometimes taken over verbatim into the *EDD*. Indeed, not much checking is required to discover that the copying of prior definitions into the *EDD*, either word for word or with minor tweaks, was not an occasional practice, but a core activity.[196] In the previous chapter, for example, we encountered the flavourful series of *boggle*-compounds included in F. K. Robinson's enlarged *Whitby Glossary* (*boggle-beck, boggle-blunder'd, boggle-chass'd*, and so on): nearly all of Robinson's entries are taken over into the *EDD* in recognizable form (so, for example, *boggle-hunter* 'one who "meets troubles half way"', or harasses himself with imaginary difficulties' in the *Whitby Glossary* becomes 'one who harasses himself with imaginary difficulties' in the *EDD*).[197] The task of producing the *EDD*, we might conclude, was in many ways as much a labour of copying and editing as it was of gathering and analysing. Of course, for words or senses recorded only in one or two sources, this was unavoidable: Wright's team had no way of forming an independent judgement on the meaning or usage of such items.

The third point to note is that the glossaries of the English Dialect Society were, quite rightly, among the most important resources available to Wright and his assistants; but this was something of a mixed blessing for the future prospects of such glossaries. Climactic achievements can act as inadvertent barriers too, screening off the lesser achievements that went before, and giving the false impression that earlier works may have been rendered redundant. So even as Wright's mighty dictionary granted to the future an unparalleled word-hoard of dialect lexicography, it also contributed to the neglect of most of the regional glossaries that had preceded it. Wright's *English Dialect Dictionary* became the go-to publication; and while some major works (such as those by Baker, Elworthy, Holland, Jackson, and Peacock) retained some regional purchase, briefer glossaries (by Chamberlain, Dickinson, Parker, and others) became almost wholly forgotten. So it is important to state that such glossaries

---

[194] Harland, *Glossary of Words Used in Swaledale*, p. 17.

[195] Markus, 'Joseph Wright's *English Dialect Dictionary* and Its Sources', pp. 268–9; Michael Adams, 'Regional Varieties of Language', in John Considine (ed.), *The Cambridge World History of Lexicography* (Cambridge: Cambridge University Press, 2019), pp. 509–29, at p. 513.

[196] See further, though, Roper, 'The Clergyman and the Dialect Speaker', pp. 116–18.

[197] Robinson, *Glossary of Words Used in the Neighbourhood of Whitby* (1876), p. 21; Wright (ed.), *English Dialect Dictionary*, I, 328.

270   The Victorians and English Dialect

retain their independent value and contain an abundance of material not included in the *EDD*: not only their discursive introductions and guides to grammar and culture, but also many of the illustrative quotations given for individual entries.[198]

Some sources were used very extensively, as the online *EDD* now permits us to see. We have noted already the high use made of some manuscript collections, such as those by Mary Powley and Thomas Holderness. The late seventeenth-century unpublished *Etymologicon Anglicanum*, compiled by the clergyman White Kennett, is cited nearly two thousand times in the *EDD* (Kennett's manuscript was well known to the English Dialect Society as a potential source).[199] On the whole, literary works (that is, poetry and fiction) don't show such high rates of use, and some well-known works are cited with surprising infrequency—though an obvious proviso here is that, lacking access to the original slips collected for the *EDD*, we can't know whether the published citations reflect faithfully the proportions of the available slips, or whether the *EDD*, as an editorial policy, has systematically downplayed the use of literary sources in preference for other forms of evidence. Eliot's *Adam Bede*, for example, is cited eighty-eight times in the text of the *EDD*, and Gaskell's *Sylvia's Lovers* sixty-nine times. Baring-Gould's *Red Spider* receives sixty citations. Among Hardy's works, there is some variability: *The Woodlanders*, for example, is cited thirty-seven times and *Far From the Madding Crowd* as many as 108; but *Jude the Obscure* features only seventeen times, and *Under the Greenwood Tree* seems to receive a mere four citations—especially surprising when we recall that, according to early reports, this short work was supposedly being read by two different volunteers for the *EDD* (George Fielding Blandford and Skeat and his family). Tennyson scores better, with over two hundred citations. William Barnes receives over five hundred credits, but this includes his glossaries as well as his poetry. In fact, the creative writers who rate highest in terms of citation in the *EDD*—far higher than those we might think of as the major dialect novelists of the period, such as Eliot, Gaskell, and Hardy—are the northern writers of working-class humour and pathos: Edwin Waugh is cited over nine hundred times in the dictionary, and Ben Brierley nearly one thousand times.[200] In this respect, then, Wright's practice in the *EDD* is very different from that of Ellis in *The Existing Phonology*, who excluded the evidence of Brierley and Waugh as well as other northern writers.[201] (There is, however, a difference in the use made of literary works in the *EDD*, in that a high proportion of their citations involve the inclusion of

---

[198] See, for example, Markus, 'Joseph Wright's *English Dialect Dictionary* and Its Sources', pp. 270–1; Roper, 'Folklore in the Glossaries of the English Dialect Society', pp. 200–2; Beal, 'The Contribution of the Rev. Joseph Hunter's *Hallamshire Glossary*'.

[199] See *English Dialect Society: First Report*, p. 3; *English Dialect Society: Second Report*, p. 8; Javier Ruano-García, 'Digging into the English Dialect Dictionary: The Contribution of MS Lansd. 1033', *International Journal of Lexicography* 26 (2013), 176–89; Kennett, *Etymological Collections of English Words*, pp. 80–1, 85–7; see also Javier Ruano-García, 'Towards an Understanding of Joseph Wright's Sources: White Kennett's Parochial Antiquities (1695) and the English Dialect Dictionary', in Manfred Markus et al (eds), *Middle and Modern English Corpus Linguistics: A Multi-Dimensional Approach* (Amsterdam: Benjamins, 2012), pp. 241–56.

[200] See also Javier Ruano-García, 'Late Modern Lancashire English in lexicographical context: representations of Lancashire speech and the *English Dialect Dictionary*', *English Today* 28.4 (2012), 60–8.

[201] Ellis, *On Early English Pronunciation*, V, 1798/366.

The *English Dialect Dictionary*   271

illustrative quotations, whereas glossaries are often just cited as references, with no quotation.)

Nonetheless, the use of glossaries in the *EDD* dwarfs that of poetry and fiction in terms of sheer frequency. So, for example, the glossary in G. S. Streatfeild's *Lincolnshire and the Danes* is cited over four hundred times, and major glossaries receive many times this number of citations. Atkinson's *Cleveland Glossary* is cited over five thousand times and Anne Elizabeth Baker's *Northamptonshire Glossary* over six thousand times. Among the larger glossaries of the English Dialect Society, Elworthy's *West Somerset Word-Book* and Peacock's *Manley and Corringham Glossary* are each cited over seven thousand times, and F. K. Robinson's *Whitby Glossary* over nine thousand. Holland's *Cheshire Glossary* reaches five figures, with over eleven thousand citations. Even the briefer glossaries are thoroughly utilized: Edith Chamberlain's *West Worcestershire Glossary* receives more than one thousand citations, and Angelina Parker's *Oxfordshire Glossary* more than two thousand. Such figures, especially when contrasted with the much lower numbers for literary works, serve to demonstrate again the truth of the claim made in the *EDD*'s subtitle, that the dictionary was 'founded on the publications of the English Dialect Society'.

Dialect lexicography (3): adjuncts

Unlike most other grand scholarly projects resulting in multi-volume publications, the *English Dialect Dictionary* was completed on time and on budget. Wright thought the *EDD* would take him ten years to complete overall, an estimate later revised to eight years for the dictionary proper, followed by a period of work on ancillary materials.[202] As Wright planned, the first part or fascicle was published in 1896, and the first complete volume (A–C) in 1898; and thereafter two fascicles appeared regularly in January and July of each year. In spite of S being the largest letter, the *English Dialect Dictionary* actually speeded up as it moved towards the later part of the alphabet: from 1902 the publication rate was doubled, to four fascicles a year, and the final pages of the dictionary were sent to the printers in 1903 (with the final volume, covering T–Z, reaching subscribers in early 1905).[203] The finished dictionary included 65,000 entries across 4,500 pages (double columns, folio size).[204] Wright's wife believed that 'few men have spent more time and found more real enjoyment in hard work than he did', while Wright himself claimed (at least in his bachelor days) that 'the only pleasure I have in life is work'.[205] The final entry in the dictionary

---

[202] Wright, *The Life of Joseph Wright*, II, 397, 423; see also p. 415.
[203] Wright, *The Life of Joseph Wright*, II, 419–21, 434.
[204] See Markus and Heuberger, 'The Architecture of Joseph Wright's *English Dialect Dictionary*', p. 357; Degani and Onysko, 'Giving Voice to Local Cultures', p. 58; Adams, 'Regional Varieties of English', p. 513; Markus, *English Dialect Dictionary Online*, p. 2.
[205] Wright, *The Life of Joseph Wright*, II, 401; Joseph Wright to J. H. Nodal 14 January 1893, Manchester, John Rylands Research Institute and Library, GB 133 JHN 1/129/4 (courtesy of The University of Manchester).

272 The Victorians and English Dialect

was *zwodder*, an obsolete Somerset word meaning 'a drowsy, stupid state of body or mind'—hardly a word one would associate with Wright himself.[206]

But the sixth volume of the dictionary didn't just stop at *zwodder*. It also included a 179-page 'Supplement', adding words which had been omitted from earlier volumes, and a brief list of 'Corrigenda'.[207] In the latter, a significant number of words receive the gratifying emendation of either 'Delete *Obs*'. or 'Delete [not known to our correspondents]'—that is to say, evidence had come to light to suggest that words originally so designated were not in fact obsolete or unknown after all, but were still familiar and in use (such as *cobblilty* 'milk and oatmeal porridge', *codnop* 'a foolish fellow', and *dewgs* 'scraps, rags, shreds, small pieces'). There were some typos that needed attention, but remarkably few: under *bunter*, for example, '*For* A dun cow *read* A dun crow', and under *doss*, '*For* tightening poops *read* tightening hoops'.[208] Volume VI further included the dictionary's bibliography and indexes of helpers, and finally, very importantly, it also included the 'English Dialect Grammar'. (In the final months in the Workshop, the two remaining senior assistants were Lilian Yates and Edith Miller: Yates worked on compiling the bibliography, while Miller helped Wright with the grammar.)[209]

Back in 1878, Henry Sweet had longed for 'that great desideratum—a Comparative Grammar of the living English dialects, a work which would throw the greatest light on the standard language, as well as on the dialects of Middle English'.[210] There were elements of such a grammar in Ellis' *Existing Phonology of English Dialects*, but the work was exceptionally difficult to navigate and is mostly concerned with pronunciation.[211] From the start of his editorship, Wright had intended for 'a Comprehensive Comparative Grammar of all the English Dialects in the United Kingdom' to be a core part of the dictionary's mission, and he believed that 'for future students of philology this would prove the most important part of the work'.[212] It is not evident, though, that this has been the case in the subsequent century and more, and the readership for the dictionary—professional as well as casual—has probably always outstripped that for the grammar.

The *English Dialect Grammar* was published simultaneously in two different formats: in folio size, to be bound up in Volume VI of the *EDD* (187 pages) and in octavo size, as a self-standing publication (696 pages). The *Grammar* is subdivided into numbered sections: 1–2 are introductory, 3–20 give an overview of pronunciation, and then the main body of the work traces the historical evolution of vowels (21–235) and consonants (236–367) from Old English and French to the dialects of the present day. Finally, there is a chapter (368–445) on 'Accidence', which is strongly reminiscent of the comparable section in Wright's *Windhill Grammar* and also Elworthy's *Outline*

---

[206] Wright (ed.), *English Dialect Dictionary*, VI, 596.
[207] See Manfred Markus, 'The Supplement to the *English Dialect Dictionary*: Its Structure and Value as Part of *EDD Online*', *International Journal of Lexicography* 32 (2019), 58–67.
[208] Wright (ed.), *English Dialect Dictionary*, VI, Supplement, 179.
[209] Wright, *The Life of Joseph Wright*, II, 388, 390.
[210] Sweet, *Collected Papers*, p. 97.
[211] See, for example, Ellis, *On Early English Pronunciation*, V, 25*, 2266–7/834–5.
[212] Wright, *The Life of Joseph Wright*, II, 423.

of the Grammar of the Dialect of West Somerset (with accidence here signifying morphology and some features of syntax). But these numbered sections form less than half the length of the book: more pages are taken up by the index that follows, which supplies a list of words with the varying county pronunciations indicated, together with references to the preceding numbered sections where the relevant vowels or consonants are discussed (and Wright explains that he did in fact compile the *Grammar* from the index, rather than the other way round). So an entry in the index looks like this:

> **Meadow**, 135, 229—*medə* sw.Nhb., Dur. Wm.+*mīdə*, Yks. Lan. I.Ma. Chs. Stf. Der. Lin.
> Rut. Lei. Shr. Oxf. Ken. Sus. me.Wil. e.Dev.
> *mèdə* w.Frf. e.Per.
> *mēdə* n.Ayr.
> *midə* Keb. E.Suf. w.Som.
> *mīdi* Lth. Edb.
> *mīdə* s.Ayr. Peb. Ant. S.Nhb. Dur. Wm.[213]

Seven different pronunciations are given for the word *meadow*, with their county distributions indicated. As can be surmised, Wright's *Grammar* is overwhelmingly phonological, and in its vowel-by-vowel presentation in its main body, it stands in a genealogical relation to formal Neogrammarian grammars—such as Brugmann's *Comparative Grammar of the Indo-Germanic Languages*, which Wright had translated into English.

In spite of its presence in Volume VI, the connection between the *English Dialect Grammar* and the *English Dialect Dictionary* was not as close or as inevitable as might at first appear. The word *meadow* is, of course, a Standard English one, and Wright's whole word list in his index is Standard English too (a run of entries under D, for example, goes **Deep, Deer, Delay, Delight, Deliver, Den, Depth, Desire**). What is the reason? Wright does not give much away in his preface, but he does state the following:

> At one time I intended to base my material for the Phonology of the grammar chiefly upon non-literary words [...] But on further consideration it became clear that such a plan would not prove satisfactory, because very few genuine dialect words extend over a large area [...] I therefore decided to base my material for the most part upon words which occur both in the literary language and in the dialects.[214]

What this means is that most of the *English Dialect Grammar* was not, in fact, compiled from the resources of the *English Dialect Dictionary* at all. Instead, as a sort of Plan B, Wright was obliged to draw up a word list (the basis for his index) and then

---

[213] Wright (ed.), *English Dialect Dictionary*, VI, *English Dialect Grammar*, 141.
[214] Wright (ed.), *English Dialect Dictionary*, VI, *English Dialect Grammar*, iii.

274 The Victorians and English Dialect

send out a questionnaire to over one thousand correspondents, asking them to 'write down accurately the dialect pronunciation' that was known to them.[215] He then supplemented this postal survey (which produced 'only a comparatively small number' of responses) with targeted solicitations and a number of in-person research trips; in these excursions, Wright even made some pioneering experiments with sound recordings, to assemble a collection of dialect voices.[216] (Dialectologists had, naturally, been aware of the potentiality of sound recordings for some time: Ellis had made some experiments with a phonograph in 1878, and in *The Existing Phonology* he metaphorically praised the detailed transcriptions of J. G. Goodchild as 'wonderful phonographs, so to speak'; Wright's own phonograph and wax cylinders are now preserved in the History of Science Museum in Oxford.)[217] So really, in the *English Dialect Grammar*, Wright was repeating the research mission of Ellis and Hallam twenty years earlier, on a smaller scale, in less detail, but with a more ruthless efficiency; and he acknowledges as much at certain points, expressing his 'great indebtedness to [Ellis'] monumental work', which he 'found invaluable for checking and supplementing my own material', and explaining that 'in a great measure' he had followed Ellis' classification of dialects.[218] But Wright's *English Dialect Grammar* has a sparseness of presentation which is very different from the baroque complexity of *The Existing Phonology*: where Ellis has a whole section on Sam Weller and 'Dickens' London English', for example, Wright simply states that 'There are no examples in the dialects of initial **w** being changed to **v** before a following vowel'.[219]

The *English Dialect Grammar* was the first of three adjunct or ancillary works which were intended to be generated from, or to accompany, the *English Dialect Dictionary*. The second and third can be more rapidly dealt with, especially as the second did not, in the event, come to fruition.

Early in the compilation of the *EDD*, Skeat had urged Wright to produce a 'small octavo one-volume *epitome*' of the whole dictionary, on the grounds that such an abridged version had the potential to sell very well (and would also forestall anyone else from plundering Wright's material to do exactly the same thing).[220] Wright followed Skeat's advice closely, taking unbound pages of the dictionary as they were printed, cutting them into single columns, and pasting them onto large folio sheets. He then edited the text into a simplified, streamlined version, including additions from the 'Supplement' (and also, it seems, with an intention to omit all illustrative quotations). But for whatever reason—perhaps financial, perhaps professional—Wright never published his shortened version of the *EDD*, and the unprinted text of his abridgement remains among his papers in the Bodleian Library, bound up

---

[215] Wright (ed.), *English Dialect Dictionary*, VI, *English Dialect Grammar*, iv.
[216] See Wright, *The Life of Joseph Wright*, II, 423–34.
[217] Ellis, *On Early English Pronunciation*, V, 1436/4; Sanders, 'Alexander John Ellis', pp. 676–9.
[218] Wright (ed.), *English Dialect Dictionary*, VI, *English Dialect Grammar*, v, 1.
[219] Ellis, *On Early English Pronunciation*, V, 1660–1/228–9; Wright (ed.), *English Dialect Dictionary*, VI, *English Dialect Grammar*, 57 (§236).
[220] Wright, *The Life of Joseph Wright*, II, 435.

The third product of the *English Dialect Dictionary* was the work of Elizabeth Mary Wright, not her husband. Back in the late 1870s, Eliza Gutch, in correspondence in *Notes and Queries*, had suggested that a simple alphabetical list was not an appropriate form in which to present a dictionary of English dialect: her proposal was that the dictionary 'should be in two parts, division i. containing dialect words with definitions in standard English, division ii. standard English words with dialect equivalents'.[222] Gutch's first part, in other words, would be a normal, alphabetical dictionary—which is what Joseph Wright produced—but her second part would be a concordance or thesaurus of dialect vocabulary. As she pointed out, such a method of arrangement could be found, for example, in Britten and Holland's *Dictionary of English Plant-Names*, and she mused: 'how pleasant it would be to be able to ascertain at a glance all the various folk-names of anything which might be the subject of inquiry!'[223] Twenty-five years later, as Wright's dictionary approached completion, Gutch renewed her call for the *EDD* also to generate a 'Dictionary of English Dialect Synonyms'. She appealed:

> I suppose there are few of us who have not at some time wanted to know all the dialect equivalents of a stook, a donkey, a shed, or of something else; and though it may not be altogether profitless, it is certainly time-consuming labour in a busy age to have to examine every precious page of the 'E. D. D'. to pick out the poor dozen words of which we may be in search.[224]

Gutch's appeals seem to have elicited minimal response.[225] But something of what she desired finally appeared ten years later in the form of a very substantial book. Elizabeth Mary Wright's *Rustic Speech and Folk-Lore* (1913) remains the best discursive demonstration of the *EDD*'s riches, being effectively a kind of companion volume to it. As we have seen repeatedly, *Rustic Speech and Folk-Lore* often provides a distillation of nineteenth-century regional philology and folklore. The contents of Wright's book move from more narrowly linguistic topics (etymology, archaism, grammar) to more cultural or societal ones (later chapters include 'Birth, Marriage, and Death Customs', 'Customs Connected with Certain Days and Seasons', and 'Weather Lore and Farming Terms'). It was assembled overwhelmingly out of the *English Dialect Dictionary* itself, rather than out of the prior sources that had gone into the making of

---

[221] Oxford, Bodleian Libraries, MSS Eng. lang. d. 77–106. See Lynda Mugglestone, *Dictionaries: A Very Short Introduction* (Oxford: Oxford University Press, 2011), pp. 114–15.

[222] [Gutch], 'Wanted—an English Dialect Dictionary', pp. 294–5.

[223] [Gutch], 'Wanted—an English Dialect Dictionary', p. 295. See also Van Keymeulen, 'The Dialect Dictionary', pp. 41–2.

[224] 'St Swithin' [Eliza Gutch], 'A Dictionary of English Dialect Synonyms', *Notes and Queries* 9th Series 12 (5 December 1903), 444.

[225] See 'St Swithin' [Eliza Gutch], 'A Dictionary of English Dialect Synonyms', *Notes and Queries* 10th Series 2 (2 July 1904), 18.

276   The Victorians and English Dialect

the *EDD*.[226] It is a dense book—effectively a set of lists presented in discursive format, or a lexicon masquerading as a monograph—but it goes a long way towards meeting Gutch's desire. So, for example, a typical paragraph in the weather lore chapter contains the following:

> It is a sign of coming wet weather [. . .] if the *packmen* [snails] are about (War.); If paddocks crowk in t'pow [pool] at neet, We may expect baith win' an' weet (Cum.); if a peacock cries frequently (Dev.); if you meet a *shiny-back* (War.), or common garden beetle; if you kill a *rain-clock* [beetle], or *rain-bat* (n.Cy. Wor.), an *egg-clock* [cockchafer] (Lan.), or *God's horse* [the sun-beetle] (Cum.).[227]

The abbreviations are those used also in the *EDD*; and bibliographical sources for Wright's material can all be found in the parent dictionary. *Rustic Speech and Folk-Lore* is an amazing digest—though one curious flaw is that it lacks an index, which could have enhanced its utility greatly.

Across its publication period, the instalments of the *English Dialect Dictionary* were rapturously received. When the first fascicle was printed in 1896, *Notes and Queries* led the way in giving it a warm welcome. 'Most sincerely do we congratulate the English Dialect Society upon the beginning of its important task', the anonymous reviewer declared, perhaps not realizing that the beginning of the *Dictionary* had marked the end of the Society. 'It is only within years comparatively recent that the notion of collecting the variations of folk-speech has commended itself to English scholarship', the reviewer reflected; but 'Dr Wright and his assistants are to be congratulated upon the manner in which their task has been, up to the present, accomplished'.[228] Later reviews were similarly complimentary: by 1900 (Volume II, D–G), the journal was acclaiming the dictionary as 'this great and important work', and rhapsodizing that 'to dip into the volume is an unwearying delight, and we could go on quoting till columns were filled'.[229] The reviewer also wished to draw a contrast with the ongoing *OED*, suggesting that for Murray's dictionary, because of the continuous evolution of language, 'the earlier letters must necessarily be incomplete before the last letters are finished', and thus something like a rolling re-editing might be needed. Wright's *EDD*, on the other hand, was likely to be a once-for-all undertaking, and none too soon: 'Dialect will never greatly enlarge its borders; rather will it in the end die out'. The 1902 review thought that 'it suffices to say that to the philologist and to the student of local customs the dictionary is indispensable', and the 1903 one marvelled that 'the case [. . .] is unique of a work of primary importance and of immense labour not only being published within the time promised, but largely in advance of it'.[230] The 1904 review thought that 'the production of the dictionary

---

[226] See Roper, 'Folklore in the Glossaries of the English Dialect Society', pp. 203–4.
[227] Wright, *Rustic Speech and Folk-Lore*, pp. 314–15.
[228] Review in *Notes and Queries* 8th Series 10 (1 August 1896), 107.
[229] Review in *Notes and Queries* 9th Series 6 (18 August 1900), 138–9.
[230] Reviews in *Notes and Queries* 9th Series 9 (5 April 1902), 279, and 9th Series 11 (11 April 1903), 298–9.

affords exemplary proof of what may be hoped when the cultivated leisure of academic life is backed up by public spirit and sufficing means'—though it seems unlikely that Wright would have defined his own regimen of extreme hard work as 'cultivated leisure'.[231] But it was not just scholarly publications that rejoiced in the appearance of the dictionary: on a return home to Windhill, Wright was especially gladdened to learn that at the library of the Saltaire Institute, the *EDD* was 'more in demand than any other work in the reference department'.[232]

The dictionary as a whole was dedicated to Skeat. When the final volume was printed in 1905, Wright wrote to the older man to acclaim him—and not Wright himself—as 'the father and real originator' of the dictionary, and the whole-page dedication in the *EDD* itself was effusive: 'To the Rev. Professor W. W. Skeat, Litt. D., D. C. L./Founder and President of The English Dialect Society/Editor of "Chaucer", "Piers Plowman", and "The Bruce",/The unwearied Worker in the varied Field of English Scholarship To whose patient industry and contagious enthusiasm in connexion with the laborious task of accumulating dialect material, the possibility of compiling an adequate Dictionary of English Dialects is mainly due'.[233] But Skeat returned the compliment, in a retrospective in *Notes and Queries,* in which he attributed the completion of the dictionary squarely to 'the zeal and genius of its editor'—as well as giving 'heartfelt thanks' for the role the journal had played in supporting dialect studies since the inception of the English Dialect Society, more than thirty years previously.[234]

Wright's last word, spoken to his wife on his death-bed in 1930, was 'Dictionary'.[235] This was not the egotism of a senior scholar preening himself on his eminence, but rather, as Elizabeth Mary Wright explained, a lover's acknowledgement of the part that the *EDD* had played in their own early life together: the great dictionary was a shared achievement, not an individual one, and it was rooted in love. To quote Virginia Woolf again, writing in her diary: 'Old Joseph Wright & Lizzie Wright are people I respect [. . .] The triumph of learning is that it leaves something done solidly for ever. Everybody knows now about dialect, owing to his dixery'.[236]

---

[231] Review in *Notes and Queries* 10th Series 1 (12 March 1904), 218–19.
[232] Wright, *The Life of Joseph Wright*, II, 413.
[233] Wright, *The Life of Joseph Wright*, ii, 437; Wright (ed.), *English Dialect Dictionary*, I, iii.
[234] Skeat, 'The English Dialect Dictionary' (1905), 381.
[235] Wright, *The Life of Joseph Wright*, II, 682.
[236] Woolf, *Diary, Volume IV*, pp. 115–16.

Epilogue

Philology's Aftermath

The *English Dialect Dictionary* marks the climax of Victorian dialect study, and of the story of regional philology which we have been following in this book. But even as it represented the end point of nineteenth-century labours, it stimulated a number of new beginnings, albeit on a smaller scale or with a different set of priorities.

In 1896 Wright had brought the English Dialect Society to an end, having set up substitute reading committees to support the making of the *EDD*. These reading committees were themselves wound up once the *EDD* had commenced its programme of publication; but the committee in Wright's home city of Bradford, on the grounds that 'the field of research was by no means exhausted', reconstituted itself into a new, regionally focused dialect society, the first of its kind: the Yorkshire Dialect Society, founded in 1897.[1] The honorary Vice-Presidents included J. C. Atkinson, W. W. Skeat, and (of course) Wright himself, and the President was the Marquess of Ripon—Liberal politician and former Viceroy of India—who, in his inaugural address, reprised many of the core arguments made in favour of dialect study over the past fifty years:

> Why should we make a study of those dialects which we admit are departing? The answer is very simple—because they are closely connected with the history of our country and the history of our language [. . .] Everything which brings before us the past of our country, what its people were and what they have been, the lives they lived and the tongue they talked—all this is of the deepest interest, especially in days like these, when it has come to be recognised by students of history that the real history of a people does not consist merely in the doings of its sovereign or statesmen, its great soldiers or sailors, but also in all that concerns the lives, the progress, the speech, and the industry of the people.[2]

The Society was a local, grassroots organization, but it maintained connections with university scholarship: speakers in the Society's first decade included H. M. Chadwick (Cambridge), H. C. Wyld (Liverpool and later Oxford), and F. W. Moorman (Leeds). An important innovation came in 1904, when the Society enjoyed 'Sol: A Farce in the Baildon Dialect' by John Metcalfe, as the first 'carrying out of an enterprise which has frequently been suggested', namely that 'examples of the dialects of

---

[1] S. K. Craven, 'Report', *Transactions of the Yorkshire Dialect Society* 1 (1898), 41.
[2] Marquis of Ripon [George Robinson], 'Inaugural Address', *Transactions of the Yorkshire Dialect Society* 1 (1898), 3–6, at pp. 4–5.

The Victorians and English Dialect. Matthew Townend, Oxford University Press. © Matthew Townend (2024).
DOI: 10.1093/oso/9780198888123.003.0008

280 The Victorians and English Dialect

various districts of our county should be written by those acquainted with them and published by the Society.[3] This inclusion of original dialect compositions was the final ingredient in the Society's enduring formula—and one copied by other regional dialect societies that were founded in its wake (such as the Lakeland Dialect Society and the Lancashire Dialect Society).[4]

Within universities, Wright's *English Dialect Grammar*, in alliance with his earlier *Windhill Grammar*, was enormously influential on the next three decades of dialectology, in Britain, Germany, and Scandinavia, supplying a template for a series of research projects, especially PhDs and comparable awards that examined a local dialect from a dominantly phonological point of view.[5] One of these—a 1923 Oxford dissertation examined by Wright himself—was by Harold Orton, on the phonology of Byers Green in County Durham.[6] Twenty years later, Orton (1898–1975), by then based at the University of Leeds, became the driving force behind the 'Survey of English Dialects', the leading research project in English dialectology in the second half of the twentieth century.[7] But Wright himself did not produce any further sustained work on English dialect after the *English Dialect Dictionary*, even though the linguistic textbooks he co-wrote with his wife often pay attention to dialectal variation and refer back to the *English Dialect Grammar*.[8]

In addition to the completion of the *English Dialect Dictionary*, the flourishing of the Yorkshire Dialect Society, and the proliferation of Windhill-style research projects, the early years of the twentieth century saw the publication of two important summaries or textbooks, W. W. Skeat's *English Dialects* in 1911 and Elizabeth Mary Wright's *Rustic Speech and Folk-Lore* in 1913. But there were also deaths. Skeat, the founder of the English Dialect Society and the dedicatee of the *English Dialect Dictionary*, died in 1912, to be eulogized by W. P. Ker, in an echo of the *EDD* dedication, as 'the unwearied athlete of philology'.[9] Henry Sweet also died in 1912, and then James Murray in 1915. It was the end of an era, and the deaths of Skeat, Sweet, and Murray mark the passing of the heroic generation of English philologists who were born in the 1830s and 1840s and felt the glamour of the new science of language in the 1850s and 1860s.

---

[3] John Metcalfe, 'Sol: A Farce in the Baildon Dialect', *Transactions of the Yorkshire Dialect Society* 6 (1904), 31–43, at p. 31.

[4] See Arnold Kellett and Ian Dewhirst (eds), *A Century of Yorkshire Dialect: Selections from the Transactions of the Yorkshire Dialect Society* (Otley: Smith Settle, 1997).

[5] See Petyt, *The Study of Dialect*, pp. 81–8; see also Wyld, 'The Study of Living Popular Dialects'.

[6] See Katie Wales and Clive Upton, 'Celebrating Variation: Harold Orton and Dialectology, 1898–1998', *English Today* 56.4 (1998), 27–33, esp. pp. 27–9.

[7] For publications, see Eugen Dieth, 'A New Survey of English Dialects', *Essays and Studies* 32 (1946), 74–104; Harold Orton et al, *Survey of English Dialects*, 13 vols (Leeds: Arnold and Son, 1962–71); Harold Orton and Nathalia Wright, *A Word Geography of England* (London: Seminar Press, 1974); Harold Orton, Stewart Sanderson, and John Widdowson (eds), *The Linguistic Atlas of England* (London: Croom Helm, 1978); Clive Upton, Stewart Sanderson, and John Widdowson, *Word Maps: A Dialect Atlas of England* (London: Croom Helm, 1987); Clive Upton, David Parry, and J. D. A. Widdowson, *Survey of English Dialects: The Dictionary and Grammar* (London: Routledge, 1994). For scholarship, see, for example, Wakelin, *English Dialects*, pp. 51–8; Petyt, *The Study of Dialect*, pp. 88–93; Penhallurick, *Studying Dialect*, pp. 28–38.

[8] Joseph Wright and Elizabeth Mary Wright, *An Elementary Historical New English Grammar* (Oxford: Oxford University Press, 1924), p. vi.

[9] W. P. Ker, *Collected Essays*, ed. Charles Whibley, 2 vols (London: Macmillan, 1925), II, 223.

World events were also marking the end of an era, with the coming of war in 1914. Progress on the *Oxford English Dictionary* was slowed not only by the death of Murray, but also by the loss of staff to the war effort.[10] Some philologists and lexicographers were co-opted into Admiralty Intelligence in London (the nearest equivalent, perhaps, of the Second World War's Bletchley Park); a Belgian refugee was recruited to work on the dictionary in Oxford; and some proofs were even corrected in dug-outs on the Western Front.[11] Thomas Hardy, another of the generation of Skeat, Sweet, and Murray, reflected on the war in 'The Pity of It', written in April 1915:

> I walked in loamy Wessex lanes, afar
> From rail-track and from highway, and I heard
> In field and farmstead many an ancient word
> Of local lineage like 'Thu bist', 'Er war',
> 'Ich woll', 'Er sholl', and by-talk similar,
> Even as they speak who in this month's moon gird
> At England's very loins, thereunto spurred
> By gangs whose glory threats and slaughters are.
>
> Then seemed a Heart crying: 'Whosoever they be
> At root and bottom of this, who flung this flame
> Between kin folk kin tongued even as are we,
>
> 'Sinister, ugly, lurid be their fame;
> May their familiars grow to shun their name,
> And their breed perish everlastingly.'[12]

Hardy's sonnet offers a distinctively philological, and even dialectological, protest against the war. It begins by emphasizing the antiquity of Wessex dialect ('many an ancient word'), and the rural remoteness of its speakers, untouched by modern communications ('afar / From rail-track and from highway'). The grammatical forms of the verbs 'to be' and 'will' and 'shall' are those anatomized in such works such as Barnes' Dorset 'Dissertation' and Elworthy's Somerset *Outline*, and represented by Hardy himself in his fiction (it may be recalled that Grammer Oliver in *The Woodlanders* says *'Ch woll*).[13] But the mid-poem turn links Wessex dialect with varieties of German, and acclaims speakers of German as 'kin folk' on the grounds that they are 'kin tongued' to Wessex speakers: in other words, the 'pity of it', in Hardy's poem, is to be perceived on the grounds of linguistic comparativism. It was a perception

---

[10] Gilliver, *The Making of the Oxford English Dictionary*, pp. 325–6.
[11] See Mugglestone, *Lost for Words*, pp. 197–8; Gilliver, *The Making of the Oxford English Dictionary*, pp. 331 n. 5, 335–6.
[12] Hardy, *Complete Poetical Works*, II, 294.
[13] See, for example, Barnes, *Poems in the Broad Form of the Dorset Dialect*, p. 14; Elworthy, *Outline of the Grammar of the Dialect of West Somerset*, p. 60; Hardy, *The Woodlanders*, p. 108, and see also Gatrell, *Thomas Hardy's Vision of Wessex*, p. 221.

282   The Victorians and English Dialect

of long standing among Victorian dialectologists: back in 1877, the annual report of the English Dialect Society had recorded that an agreement of cooperation had been reached between the Society and the newly founded Low-German Dialect Society—'the old kith and kin'.[14]

In Devon in 1918, local landholder and historian Cecil Torr had nineteen German prisoners of war allotted to work on his farmland. In his *Small Talk at Wreyland*, a three-volume collection of memoirs and musings, he also reflected that 'the German are our kith and kin'. But his philological thoughts were a little different from Hardy's: 'The prisoners spoke such different dialects', he recalled, 'that they could hardly understand each other, and the Yorkshire of the corporal in charge of them was not exactly like our Devonshire'.[15] Torr (1857–1928) had well-established interests in dialect and the history of English, and his *Small Talk* volumes are full of observations on local language. (One of the sitting rooms in his house at Wreyland was called the Tallet, the Celtic loanword whose occurrence in *Lorna Doone* had so excited Elizabeth Mary Wright.)[16] 'Devonshire speech is not capricious', he reflected, 'but has a syntax of its own. The classic phrase is 'her told she'. A pious person told me that 'us didn't love He, 'twas Him loved we' [...] A complete Grammar might be compiled'.[17] Torr thought that it would be useful for children to learn Grimm's Law at school, though he feared the excesses of 'fonetic fanatics' when it came to spelling reform—'there would be as many written languages as there are dialects now'.[18] Torr was not unique in finding dialectal interest in the language of POWs: in Berlin, the distinguished Alois Brandl, an old friend of Furnivall, was involved in a project to record the speech of British prisoners.[19]

For philologists, though, Anglo-German connections were not just linguistic but often professional too, and here the crisis caused by the war was severe and long-lasting. The inability to consult German academics hampered progress on the *OED*.[20] Joseph Wright, in the early months of the war, had endeavoured to express his goodwill by organizing welfare visits and gifts to wounded German soldiers in hospital in Oxford, but he was soon warned away by the authorities; and though he was insistent, in a letter to a widowed German mother, that there was no 'strong national feeling against the German people', nonetheless in the immediate aftermath of the war he confessed that 'he would feel uncomfortable were he to meet his former friends in Germany'.[21] Henry Bradley of the *OED* was also deeply distressed by the breakdown of English-German relations, and troubled by how best to resume them; one

---

[14] *English Dialect Society: Fourth Report*, p. 4.
[15] Cecil Torr, *Small Talk at Wreyland*, 3 vols (Cambridge: Cambridge University Press, 1918–23), II, 53.
[16] Torr, *Small Talk at Wreyland*, I, 16.
[17] Torr, *Small Talk at Wreyland*, I, 55.
[18] Torr, *Small Talk at Wreyland*, III, 39, 103
[19] See Wakelin, *English Dialects*, p. 48; Andrew D. Evans, *Anthropology at War: World War I and the Science of Race in Germany* (Chicago: University of Chicago Press, 2010), pp. 134–5.
[20] Gilliver, *The Making of the Oxford English Dictionary*, pp. 325–6.
[21] Wright, *The Life of Joseph Wright*, II, 459–63, 646.

olive branch, offered in 1925, was a *festschrift* from German academics in honour of Wright's seventieth birthday.[22]

But by 1925, the damage had been done, and English philology itself had become one of the lesser casualties of the Great War. In an article published the previous year, J. R. R. Tolkien had written that, in post-war conditions: 'Not only is the great contribution of German-speaking scholars liable to be foolishly belittled, but 'philology' itself, conceived as a purely German invention, is in some quarters treated as though it were one of the things that the late war was fought to end'.[23]

This was not a joke.[24] In the late nineteenth and early twentieth century, at least as a university subject, philology had often been viewed as dominantly a German discipline.[25] H. C. Wyld wrote in 1904 that 'it is a melancholy fact for us Englishmen to reflect upon, that English Philology is not a home-grown product, but has been imported from Germany'. Wyld himself had studied in Germany, at Bonn and Heidelberg, and believed that 'if, say, ten English Philologists were suddenly wanted as Professors of the English language [...] most of them also would have to be imported from Germany'.[26] Tolkien thought that the supposed German domination of English philology was a myth (he had not studied in Germany, but rather had been taught by Joseph Wright at Oxford, and then learned his trade on the *OED* under Henry Bradley), and he believed moreover that 'the philological instinct is [...] as universal as is the use of language'.[27] But by the early 1920s, English philology was under attack, and in retreat.

One cause was the much-discussed report on *The Teaching of English in England* (1921), better known as the 'Newbolt Report' after its committee chairman, the poet Sir Henry Newbolt.[28] This government report quoted approvingly the view of Sir Walter Raleigh, the first Professor of English Literature at Oxford (appointed 1904), that 'English literature could be the basis of a liberal education, but needed to be freed from slavery to philology and phonology'—especially the type of philology which Raleigh characterized as 'hypothetical sound-shiftings in the primeval German forests'.[29] Much of the problem, according to the report, arose from the fact that English philologists 'had either been trained in Germany or were under the influence of German educational ideals and methods'—or 'the alien yoke of Teutonic

---

[22] See Robert Bridges, 'A Memoir', in Henry Bradley, *Collected Papers* (Oxford: Clarendon Press, 1928), pp. 1–56, at pp. 36–8; Wright, *The Life of Joseph Wright*, II, 651–6.

[23] Tolkien, 'Philology: General Works', pp. 36–7.

[24] See Shippey, *The Road to Middle-earth*, p. 10.

[25] Morpurgo Davies, *Nineteenth-Century Linguistics*, pp. 226–9.

[26] Wyld, 'The Study of Living Popular Dialects', p. 30.

[27] Tolkien, 'Philology: General Works', p. 37; see also Chambers, *Concerning Certain Great Teachers of the English Language*.

[28] See, for example, Palmer, *The Rise of English Studies*, pp. 179–85; Chris Baldick, *The Social Mission of English Criticism, 1848–1932* (Oxford: Clarendon Press, 1983), pp. 92–8; Matthews, *The Making of Middle English*, pp. 187–90; Stefan Collini, *Public Moralists: Political Thought and Intellectual Life in Britain 1850–1930* (Oxford: Clarendon Press, 1991), pp. 364–68; Momma, *From Philology to English Studies*, pp. 185–7; Lawrie, *The Beginnings of University English*, pp. 149–57.

[29] *The Teaching of English in England, being the Report of the Departmental Committee Appointed by the President of the Board of Education into the Position of English in the Educational System of England* (London: His Majesty's Stationery Office, 1921), p. 218.

philology', as another critic put it.[30] The solution, the report recommended, was to make more detailed and technical forms of philology ('investigating sound-shiftings, changes in the form of words, variations of dialect, and the inter-relation of languages') into predominantly a postgraduate pursuit.[31] A countervailing voice was that of W. P. Ker, Professor of English at University College London: when called upon to provide evidence to the Newbolt committee, Ker gave his view that philology was not a pernicious German invention, but rather that 'the division between philology and literature had been made too absolute', and that 'historical grammar and the history of the language ought not to be regarded as a philological side of the study distinct from the history of literature'.[32] Ker's own expertise seamlessly combined 'Lit.' with 'Lang.', and now, on publication of *The Teaching of English in England*, he performed a public burning of the report in his college courtyard.[33]

But stigmatization as a tainted, German discipline was not the only reason why philology was in retreat in Britain in the period after the First World War. Revolutionary changes were also afoot in the theorization of language study, a rethinking as momentous and far-reaching as that which had marked the rise of the new philology itself almost a century earlier. The Swiss scholar Ferdinand de Saussure (1857–1913) had been trained in the methods of Neogrammarian philology at Leipzig, and gained a high reputation as a comparative Indo-Europeanist. But the posthumous publication of his lectures as the *Course in General Linguistics* (*Cours de linguistique générale*, 1916) set in train a process of wholesale re-theorization, most famously in the distinctions that Saussure made between *langue* and *parole*, and between diachrony and synchrony, and also in his core proposition that the linguistic 'sign' was arbitrary, in the sense that the relationship between the signifier and the signified was not inherent or motivated.[34] The new linguistics that arose in the 1920s and 1930s—often now categorized as 'structuralist'—tended to be synchronic rather than diachronic, more concerned with the systems of *langue* than the examples of *parole*. As Anna Morpurgo Davies has written, in the nineteenth century, 'core linguistics [. . .] was historical linguistics'.[35] But no longer: post-Saussurean language study often defined itself as being non-historicizing and thus as not philology; and the inter-war disciplines of both

---

[30] *The Teaching of English in England*, p. 216; Basil Willey, quoted in Baldick, *The Social Mission of English Criticism*, p. 87.

[31] *The Teaching of English in England*, p. 221.

[32] *The Teaching of English in England*, p. 218; see also R. W. Chambers, *The Teaching of English in the Universities of England*, English Association Pamphlet 53 (Oxford: English Association, 1922). On Ker, see R. W. Chambers, 'W. P. Ker, 1855–1923', in Michael Lapidge (ed.), *Interpreters of Early Medieval Britain* (Oxford: British Academy, 2002), pp. 139–52 (first published in *Proceedings of the British Academy* 11 (1924–5), 413–26; revised version also in Chambers, *Man's Unconquerable Mind*, pp. 386–406); R. W. Chambers, 'Ker, William Paton (1855–1923)', rev. A. S. G. Edwards, in *Oxford Dictionary of National Biography* [www.oxforddnb].

[33] Palmer, *The Rise of English Studies*, p. 130; John Dover Wilson, *Milestones on the Dover Road* (London: Faber and Faber, 1969), pp. 97–8; Baldick, *The Social Mission of English Criticism*, p. 94.

[34] See, for example, Jonathan Culler, *Ferdinand de Saussure* (Ithaca: Cornell University Press, 1986); John E. Joseph, *Saussure* (Oxford: Oxford University Press, 2012).

[35] Morpurgo Davies, *Nineteenth-Century Linguistics*, p. 301.

literature and linguistics often sought to distance themselves from their common nineteenth-century ancestor.[36]

But philology did not wholly disappear. H. C. Wyld wrote in 1921 that 'the subject-matter of English Philology possesses a strange fascination for the man in the street' (though in Wyld's pessimistic view, 'almost everything that he thinks and says about it is incredibly and hopelessly wrong').[37] The *OED* was still going, and over the decades had come to be recognized as a national monument: in 1897, it had been dedicated to Queen Victoria; in 1908, Herbert Asquith, as Prime Minister, nominated Murray for a knighthood; and in 1928, when the dictionary was finally completed, another Prime Minister, Stanley Baldwin, presided at the celebratory banquet, and the senior surviving editor, W. A. Craigie, was also awarded a knighthood. The very last entry in the first edition of the *OED*, we might note, was a dialect word: *zyxt*, an obsolete Kentish form of the second person singular of the verb 'to see'.

In 1963, the Cumbrian author Norman Nicholson wrote that 'dialect is already becoming not the language of the people but a literary language evolved from the vernacular past'.[38] But this was already true in the inter-war period, if not even earlier. By the twentieth century, the heyday of dialect poetry—Barnes, Tennyson, Waugh—lay in the past, and the genre would increasingly be associated with the conservationist instincts of such bodies as the Yorkshire Dialect Society.[39] But the so-called Georgian poets, often venerators of Hardy, placed a significant emphasis on the regional, the rural, and the colloquial, seen for example in John Masefield's *The Everlasting Mercy* (1911), the early works of Edmund Blunden, and the poetry of Edward Thomas.

The use of dialect in Edwardian fiction shows no clear break with Victorian practice: in D. H. Lawrence's *Sons and Lovers* (1913), for instance, the speech of the miner Walter Morel is full of Nottinghamshire dialect (*clunch, sluther, barkled up, chelp*), and before their courtship his wife, from the south of England, 'had never been "thee'd" and "thou'd" before'.[40] But it may be that inter-war rural fiction does start to show a qualitative difference, due to its increasing distance from the nineteenth-century, pre-urban, agricultural world: the note of nostalgia or wistfulness grows keener, and the sense of the rural past as a distinctive period, with its own literary flavour (again, often inspired by Hardy), grows ever more defined.[41] Such a claim could be explored in the works of a number of writers (including important children's authors, such as Alison Uttley), but the most eminent example is probably Mary

---

[36] Harpham, 'Roots, Races, and the Return to Philology', pp. 50–2; Momma, *From Philology to English Studies*, pp. 187–92.

[37] H. C. Wyld, *English Philology in English Universities: An Inaugural Lecture* (Oxford: Clarendon Press, 1921), p. 10.

[38] Norman Nicholson, *The Lakes* (London: Hale, 1977 [first published as *Portrait of the Lakes*, 1963]), p. 80.

[39] See, for example, Jane Hodson, 'The Problem with Dialect Poetry', in Claire Hélie, Elise Brault-Dreux, and Emilie Loriaux (eds), *No Dialect Please, You're A Poet: English Dialect in Poetry in the 20th and 21st Centuries* (London: Routledge, 2019), pp. 57–72.

[40] D. H. Lawrence, *Sons and Lovers*, ed. David Trotter (Oxford: Oxford University Press, 1995), pp. 16, 23, 25, 42, 70.

[41] See further, for example, Glen Cavaliero, *The Rural Tradition in the English Novel, 1900–1939* (Basingstoke: Palgrave Macmillan, 1977); Dominic Head, *Modernity and the English Rural Novel* (Cambridge: Cambridge University Press, 2017).

286 The Victorians and English Dialect

Webb's *Precious Bane* (1924). *Precious Bane* is the *Lorna Doone* of the 1920s: intense and evocative, historically earnest, but with a touch of pastiche and melodrama. Like *Lorna Doone*, it was also very successful: when it was included in Webb's posthumous collected works in 1928, the novel gained a prime ministerial introduction penned by Baldwin.[42]

Precious Bane is set in early nineteenth-century Shropshire, and tells the story of Prue Sarn and her brother Gideon, a Heathcliffian anti-hero. Prue's first-person narration plays the common trick, as did John Ridd's in *Lorna Doone*, of noting the early appearance of familiar things ('one of the new-fangled weaving machines I hear tell of', for example), as well as safeguarding the good standing of lead characters by giving them anachronistically enlightened views ('we knew all his spells and what-nots were but foolish games').[43] Packed to bursting point with folkloric tropes and motifs, the novel includes a local wise man, sin-eating, funeral cakes, bee-lore, hare-lore, fairy-lore, prognostications, curses, ballads, May Day ploughing, the attempted drowning of a witch, Wild Edric, the Seven Whistlers, and a series of very Hardy-like set-pieces, such as a hiring fair and a harvest feast.[44] Both Prue's narrative voice, and the characters' dialogue, is marked by the heavy use of dialect, grammatical as well as lexical, and many local terms receive explicit glosses: 'we called the dragon-fly the ether's mon or ether's nild'; 'we started swiving, that is reaping, at the beginning of August-month'; 'he always said harroost, it being the old way of saying harvest'; and so on.[45] There is also a delight in expressive vocabulary: 'how can a man govern the land as canna govern his own womankind, but lets his girl go about like a ripstitch-rantipole?'[46]

Webb's foreword to the novel gives thanks to 'the authors of *Shropshire Folk Lore*' for a couple of rhymes and also 'for the verification of various customs which I had otherwise only known by hearsay'.[47] The source acknowledged here is Charlotte Sophia Burne's *Shropshire Folk-Lore* (1883), assembled out of Georgina Jackson's collections, as we saw in Chapter 5. But Webb's foreword may be under-crediting her debt to Burne and Jackson, who can be shown to be the direct source of a number of *Precious Bane*'s folkloric elements, not simply a means of verification. At one point in the narrative, for example, Prue explains the local card game of 'Costly Colours'— 'how you counted, and of the trumps, and how three of a suit was a *prial*, and four of a suit was a *Costly*, and how you could *mog*, or change, your cards'—and it is no surprise to find Burne and Jackson explaining that Costly Colours was a Shropshire 'specialty', even though 'few now play or understand this old-fashioned game', and also including

---

[42] On Webb, see Thomas Moult, *Mary Webb: Her Life and Work* (London: Cape, 1932); Gladys Mary Coles, *The Flower of Light: A Biography of Mary Webb* (London: Duckworth, 1978).

[43] Mary Webb, *Precious Bane* (London: Virago, 1978), pp. 19, 218.

[44] See further W. K. McNeil, 'The Function of Legend, Belief and Custom in *Precious Bane*', *Folklore* 82 (1971), 132–46; Simon White and Owen Davies, 'Tradition and Rural Modernity in Mary Webb's Shropshire: *Precious Bane* in Context', *The Space Between: Literature and Culture, 1914–1945* 15 (2019) [www.spacebetweenjournal.org].

[45] Webb, *Precious Bane*, pp. 189, 196, 199.

[46] Webb, *Precious Bane*, p. 77

[47] Webb, *Precious Bane*, p. 7.

Epilogue **287**

a three-page account of its rules and terms.[48] But not only has Webb (wisely) consulted Burne and Jackson's *Shropshire Folk-Lore* in her historical reconstruction; she has also made extensive use of Jackson's earlier *Shropshire Word-Book* (1879–81) for her dialect vocabulary. So—taking the examples above—Jackson's glossary includes entries for *ether's mon* and *ether's nild*, for *swive*, and for *harroost*, and under *rantipole* she includes the illustrative example 'Whad a great rompin', rip-stitch rantipole that girld is'.[49] So while there is no doubting Webb's commitment to the landscape and heritage of Shropshire, nor the power of her story, it is apparent that she is working at a greater remove from rural language and customs than her Victorian predecessors in the regional novel, with more book learning and less fieldwork.

Inevitably, all this was potentially ripe for parody, and that parody duly arrived in the form of Stella Gibbons' *Cold Comfort Farm*, which takes aim not only at the writings of Webb, but also at D. H. Lawrence, Sheila Kaye-Smith, and others. Gibbons mocks the highly wrought nature prose of such authors ('Frond leapt on root and hare on hare. Beetle and finch-fly were not spared'); and in the contest that is staged in *Cold Comfort Farm* between tradition and modernity, it is modernity—with its technology and optimism—that wins triumphantly.[50] Prominent in Gibbons' satire is a whole vocabulary of (invented) dialect terms: for farm implements ('the scranlet of his plough', 'his pruning-snoot and reaping-hook', 'the rennet-post near the horse-trough'), domestic utensils ('a snood full of coarse porridge'), local plants and flowers (*dog's-fennel, beard's-crow, sukebind*), and insults or endearments ('a capsy wennet', 'my own wild marsh-tigget').[51] As we have seen throughout this book, these were precisely the sorts of fields that Victorian glossarists had recorded so assiduously. But Gibbons has not just invented words which sound like plausible omissions from the *English Dialect Dictionary*; she has also anatomized (and exaggerated) dialectal grammar with acumen. So, for example, she parodies the type of non-standard plurals which so excited Fred Elworthy (*bosomses and barnses, beasten-housen*), and she knows that personal pronouns are of prime interest and flavour: *Cold Comfort Farm* is full of constructions such as *oursen* and *hissen*, and *you'm* and *she'm*, with *a* for *she* and (Barnes' favourite) *un* for *him*; but these are often pushed beyond their normal grammatical limits, so that, for instance, *un* stands for *she* as well as *him* ('un came to say good-bye to me before un took the twelve-thirty train from Godmere with un's husband-to-be').[52]

So Gibbons knew was she was parodying, linguistically as well as generically. *Cold Comfort Farm* was published in 1932—the same year, we might note, as Elizabeth Mary Wright's biography of her husband, and perhaps the date might be taken to mark the passing of a certain un-ironic earnestness about dialect, a further break with the world of Victorian collectors and celebrants. But although philology, as a word

---

[48] Webb, *Precious Bane*, p. 104; Burne, *Shropshire Folk-Lore*, pp. 527, 647–9.

[49] Jackson, *Shropshire Word-Book*, p. 344; see also pp. 135, 196, 426.

[50] Stella Gibbons, *Cold Comfort Farm* (London: Penguin, 2011), p. 45; Chris Baldick, *The Modern Movement*, Oxford English Literary History 10 (Oxford: Oxford University Press, 2004), pp. 294–5.

[51] Gibbons, *Cold Comfort Farm*, pp. 34, 38, 40, 42, 46, 55, 64, 219.

[52] Gibbons, *Cold Comfort Farm*, pp. 39, 43, 56, 80, 88, 108, 111, 131, 215; see Elworthy, *Outline of the Grammar of the Dialect of West Somerset*, pp. 4–13.

288   The Victorians and English Dialect

and concept, has been declining steadily in public prominence for the last hundred years, there are still indicators that Tolkien's conviction, that the 'philological instinct' is widespread or even universal, may have something to recommend it; and this is as true of an appetite for regional dialect as it is for any other form of linguistic engagement. The popularity of Robert Macfarlane's book *Landmarks* (2015), for example, is one sign of an ongoing desire for dialect, as is the success of the BBC/British Library's 'Voices' project and the Cambridge University 'English Dialects' app—quite apart from the continuing, and evolving, discipline of academic dialectology.[53]

Seamus Heaney, in his prize-winning translation of *Beowulf* (1999), made much of the role of non-standard language in giving speakers and writers an entry into what he called their own 'voice-right'.[54] As one such 'loophole' into language, Heaney's introduction celebrates the connection between the Old English verb *þolian* 'to suffer, endure', encountered in the text and glossary of *Beowulf*, and the Ulster word *thole*. Heaney writes that 'although at first [*þolian*] looked completely strange with its *thorn* symbol instead of the familiar *th*, I gradually realized that it was not strange at all, for it was the word that older and less educated people would have used in the country where I grew up', and thus the occurrence of the word *þolian* in *Beowulf* served as a demonstration to Heaney that modern *thole* 'was not just a self-enclosed family possession but an historical heritage'.[55] He dubs this moment of revelation 'illumination by philology', and Heaney's pleasure in the word *thole*—personal, linguistic, political, aesthetic—would have made perfect sense to the Victorian collectors and dialect defenders whom we have encountered in this book.[56] Indeed, *thole* itself, with its Old English etymology, was a word that was frequently noticed, and Wright's *English Dialect Dictionary* supplies a very full entry, with multiple examples from Scotland, Northern Ireland, and the north of England.[57] As this and other 'loopholes' might suggest, although the nineteenth century was the great era of regional philology, there is abundant evidence that the 'philological instinct' endures, and so does an interest in dialect, and everything it might mean.

---

[53] See Robert Macfarlane, *Landmarks* (London: Hamilton, 2015); Jonnie Robinson, *A Thesaurus of English Dialect and Slang: England, Wales and the Channel Islands* (Cambridge: Cambridge University Press, 2021).

[54] Seamus Heaney, *Beowulf: A New Translation* (London: Faber and Faber, 1999), p. xxiii.

[55] Heaney, *Beowulf*, p. xxv.

[56] Heaney, *Beowulf*, pp. xxv–xxvi.

[57] Wright (ed.), *English Dialect Dictionary*, VI, 97–8. See also, for example, Robinson, *Glossary of Words Pertaining to the Dialect of Mid-Yorkshire*, pp. 143–4; Nodal and Milner, *Glossary of the Lancashire Dialect*, p. 262; Dickinson, *Glossary of Words and Phrases Pertaining to the Dialect of Cumberland*, p. 103; William Hugh Patterson, *A Glossary of Words in Use in the Counties of Antrim and Down*, English Dialect Society 28 (London: English Dialect Society, 1880), p. 105; Thomas Clarke, 'Anglo-Saxon as an Aid to the Study of Dialects', *Transactions of the Yorkshire Dialect Society* 1 (1898), 18–25, at p. 21.

Bibliography

Unpublished and archival sources

London, King's College
Papers of Walter W. Skeat: GB0100 KCLCA Skeat.

Manchester, John Rylands Research Institute and Library
Papers of J. H. Nodal: GB 133 JHN.

Oxford, Bodleian Libraries
Papers of Thomas Hallam: MSS Eng. lang. c. 1–4, d. 1–64, e. 1–5, g. 1–53, 55–79.
Papers of Joseph Wright and Elizabeth Mary Wright: MSS Eng. lang. c. 12–14, d. 77–128, e. 13–15, f. 3, Eng. lett. c. 329, d. 347, Eng. misc. a. 15, b. 117(R), c. 566–7, Top. Oxon. b. 267.
Letters to Joseph Wright and Elizabeth Mary Wright: MS Eng. lett. d. 125.
Letters from J. C. Atkinson to James Murray: MS Murray 1/2, Folder 1.
Papers of Angelina Parker: MSS Eng. lang. d. 69–76.

Other
Will of Thomas Hallam, 5 September 1895 [www.gov.uk/search-will-probate].

Published and online sources

Aarsleff, Hans, *The Study of Language in England, 1780–1860*, 2nd ed. (Minneapolis: University of Minnesota Press, 1983).

Abberley, Will, 'Race and Species Essentialism in Nineteenth-Century Philology', *Critical Quarterly* 53 (2011), 45–60.

Abberley, Will, *English Fiction and the Evolution of Language, 1850–1914* (Cambridge: Cambridge University Press, 2015).

Acland, Robin, 'Mary Powley (1811–1882)', *Cumberland and Westmorland Antiquarian and Archaeological Society Newsletter* 40 (Summer 2002), 9–10.

Adams, Ernest, 'On the Names of the Wood-Louse', *Transactions of the Philological Society* (1860–1), 8–19.

Adams, Michael, 'Regional Varieties of Language', in John Considine (ed.), *The Cambridge World History of Lexicography* (Cambridge: Cambridge University Press, 2019), pp. 509–29.

Adamson, Sylvia, 'Literary Language', in Suzanne Romaine (ed.), *The Cambridge History of the English Language: Volume IV, 1776–1997* (Cambridge: Cambridge University Press, 1999), pp. 589–692.

Addy, Sidney Oldall, *A Supplement to the Sheffield Glossary*, English Dialect Society 62 (London: English Dialect Society, 1891).

290 Bibliography

Addy, Sidney Oldall, 'The Collection of English Dialect', *Transactions of the Yorkshire Dialect Society* 8 (1906), 23–33.

Akerman, John Yonge, *A Glossary of Provincial Words and Phrases in Use in Wiltshire* (London: Smith, 1842).

Aldrich, Richard, 'Payne, Joseph (1801–1876)', in *Oxford Dictionary of National Biography* [www.oxforddnb].

Alexander, Christine, and Margaret Smith (eds), *The Oxford Companion to the Brontës* (Oxford: Oxford University Press, 2006).

Alexander, Michael, *Medievalism: the Middle Ages in Modern England* (New Haven: Yale University Press, 2007).

Alter, Stephen G., *Darwinism and the Linguistic Image: Language, Race, and Natural Theology in the Nineteenth Century* (Baltimore: Johns Hopkins University Press, 1999).

Ancestry: https://www.ancestry.co.uk

Anderson, Peter M., 'A New Light on *Early English Pronunciation*', *Transactions of the Yorkshire Dialect Society* 14 (1977), 32–41.

[Anon], 'A New Society', *The Athenaeum* 14 May 1870, 643.

[Anon], 'Thomas Hallam', *Manchester City News* 5 October 1895.

[Anon], 'In Memoriam: [Mrs] Eliza Gutch, (1840–1931)', *Folklore* 41 (1930), 301.

Applegate, Celia, *A Nation of Provincials: The German Idea of Heimat* (Berkeley: University of California Press, 1990).

Archer, William, 'Real Conversations', in Martin Ray (ed.), *Thomas Hardy Remembered* (London: Routledge, 2007), pp. 28–37.

Ashman, Gordon, and Gillian Bennett, 'Charlotte Sophia Burne: Shropshire Folklorist, First Woman President of the Folklore Society, and First Woman Editor of *Folklore*. Part 1: A Life and Appreciation', *Folklore* 111 (2000), 1–21.

Ashton, John, 'Beyond Survivalism: Regional Folkloristics in Late-Victorian England', *Folklore* 108 (1997), 19–23.

Atherton, Carol, 'The Organisation of Literary Knowledge: The Study of English in the Late Nineteenth Century', in Martin Daunton (ed.), *The Organisation of Knowledge in Victorian Britain* (Oxford: Oxford University Press, 2005), pp. 219–34.

Atherton, Mark, "To observe things as they are without regard to their origin': Henry Sweet's General Writings on Language in the 1870s', *Henry Sweet Society for the History of Linguistic Ideas Bulletin* 51.1 (2008), 41–58.

Atherton, Mark, 'Imaginative Science: The Interactions of Henry Sweet's Linguistic Thought and E. B. Tylor's Anthropology', *Historiographia Linguistica* 37 (2010), 31–73.

Atkinson, Diane, *Love and Dirt: The Marriage of Arthur Munby and Hannah Cullwick* (London: Macmillan, 2003).

Atkinson, J. C., 'On the Dialect of Cleveland in the North Riding of Yorkshire', *Transactions of the Philological Society* (1867), 326–57.

Atkinson, J. C., *A Glossary of the Cleveland Dialect: Explanatory, Derivative, and Critical* (London: Smith, 1868).

Atkinson, J. C., 'On the Danish Element in the Population of Cleveland, Yorkshire', *Journal of the Ethnological Society of London* 2 (1869–70), 351–66.

Atkinson, J. C., 'Provincial Glossary', *Notes and Queries*, 9 April 1870, 363.

Atkinson, J. C., 'On the Danish Aspect of the Local Nomenclature of Cleveland', *Journal of the Anthropological Institute of Great Britain and Ireland* 3 (1874), 115–20.

Atkinson, J. C., *Forty Years in a Moorland Parish: Reminiscences and Researches in Danby in Cleveland* (London: Macmillan, 1891).

Atkinson, J. C., *The Last of the Giant Killers; or The Exploits of Sir Jack of Danby Dale* (London: Macmillan, 1891).

Auden, W. H., *The Dyer's Hand and Other Essays* (London: Faber and Faber, 1963).

Axon, William E. A., *Folk Song and Folk-Speech of Lancashire, on the Ballads and Songs of the County Palatine, with Notes on the Dialect in which many of them are written, and an Appendix on Lancashire Folk-Lore* (Manchester: Tubbs and Brook, 1870).

Axon, William E. A., *George Eliot's Use of Dialect*, English Dialect Society 33 (London: English Dialect Society, 1881).

Bacon, Alan (ed.), *The Nineteenth-Century History of English Studies* (Aldershot: Routledge, 1998).

Bailey, Isabel, 'Thompson, Pishey (1785–1862)', in *Oxford Dictionary of National Biography* [www.oxforddnb].

Bailey, Richard W., *Nineteenth-Century English* (Ann Arbor: University of Michigan Press, 1996).

Bailey, Richard W., "This Unique and Peerless Specimen': The Reputation of the *OED*', in Lynda Mugglestone (ed.), *Lexicography and the OED: Pioneers in the Untrodden Forest* (Oxford: Oxford University Press, 2000), pp. 207–27.

Baker, Anne Elizabeth, *Glossary of Northamptonshire Words and Phrases*, 2 vols (London: Smith, 1854).

Baldick, Chris, *The Social Mission of English Criticism, 1848–1932* (Oxford: Clarendon Press, 1983).

Baldick, Chris, *The Modern Movement*, Oxford English Literary History 10 (Oxford: Oxford University Press, 2004).

Bankert, Dabney A., *Philology in Turbulent Times: Joseph Bosworth, His Dictionary, and the Recovery of Old English* (Turnhout: Brepols, 2023).

Barber, Rosalind, 'Shakespeare and Warwickshire Dialect', *Journal of Early Modern Studies* 5 (2016), 91–118.

Baring-Gould, Sabine, *Red Spider* (Stroud: Nonsuch, 2007).

Barnes, William, *Se Gefylsta (The Helper): An Anglo-Saxon Delectus*, 2nd ed. (London: Smith, 1857).

Barnes, William, *Tiw; or, A View of the Roots and Stems of the English as a Teutonic Tongue* (London: Smith, 1862).

Barnes, William, *A Grammar and Glossary of the Dorset Dialect* (Berlin: Philological Society, 1863).

Barnes, William, *An Outline of English Speech-Craft* (London: Kegan Paul and Co., 1878).

Barnes, William, *A Glossary of the Dorset Dialect with a Grammar of its Word Shapening and Wording* (London: Trübner, 1886).

Barnes, William, 'Fore-Say', in John Symonds Udal, *Dorsetshire Folk-Lore* (Hertford: Austin and Sons, 1922), pp. 1–16.

Barnes, William, *Poems in the Broad Form of the Dorset Dialect*, ed. T. L. Burton and K. K. Ruthven, Complete Poems of William Barnes I (Oxford: Oxford University Press, 2013).

Baron, Dennis E., *Going Native: The Regeneration of Saxon English*, Publications of the American Dialect Society 69 (Tuscaloosa: University of Alabama Press, 1982).

Barry, Michael, 'Traditional Enumeration in the North Country', *Folk Life* 7 (1969), 75–91.

Bate, Jonathan, *John Clare: A Biography* (London: Picador, 2003).

Baugh, George C., 'Jackson, Georgina Frederica (1823/4–1895)', in *Oxford Dictionary of National Biography* [www.oxforddnb].

Baugner, Ulla, *A Study of the Use of Dialect in Thomas Hardy's Novels and Short Stories*, Stockholm Theses in English 7 (Stockholm: Stockholm University, 1972).

Baxter, Lucy, *The Life of William Barnes, Poet and Philologist* (London: Macmillan, 1887).

Beal, Joan C., *An Introduction to Regional Englishes* (Edinburgh: Edinburgh University Press, 2010).

Beal, Joan C., 'The Contribution of the Rev. Joseph Hunter's *Hallamshire Glossary* (1829) to Wright's *English Dialect Dictionary*', in Manfred Markus, Clive Upton, and Reinhard

292 Bibliography

Heuberger (eds), *Joseph Wright's English Dialect Dictionary and Beyond: Studies in Late Modern English Dialectology* (Frankfurt am Main: Lang, 2010), pp. 39–48.

Beal, Joan C., 'Northern English and Enregisterment', in Sylvie Hancil and Joan C. Beal (eds), *Perspectives on Northern Englishes*, Topics in English Linguistics 96 (Berlin: De Gruyter, 2017), pp. 17–39.

Beetham, Margaret, '"Healthy Reading": The Periodical Press in late Victorian Manchester', in Alan J. Kidd and K. W. Roberts (eds), *City, Class and Culture: studies of social policy and cultural production in Victorian Manchester* (Manchester: Manchester University Press, 1985), pp. 167–92.

Bennett, Gillian, 'Folklore Studies and the English Rural Myth', *Rural History* 4 (1993), 77–91.

Bennett, Gillian, 'Geologists and Folklorists: Cultural Evolution and "The Science of Folklore"', *Folklore* 105 (1994), 25–37.

Bennett, Gillian, 'Charlotte Sophia Burne: Shropshire Folklorist, First Woman President of the Folklore Society, and First Woman Editor of *Folklore*. Part 2: Update and Preliminary Bibliography', *Folklore* 112 (2001), 95–106.

Benson, Larry D. (ed.), *The Riverside Chaucer*, 3rd ed. (Oxford: Oxford University Press, 1988).

Benzie, William, *Dr F. J. Furnivall: A Victorian Scholar Adventurer* (Norman: Pilgrim Books, 1983).

Bickley, F. L., 'Sebastian Evans (1830–1909)', rev. Rowena Williams, in *Oxford Dictionary of National Biography* [www.oxforddnb].

Blackmore, R. D., *Lorna Doone: A Romance of Exmoor*, ed. Sally Shuttleworth (Oxford: Oxford University Press, 2008).

Blake, N. F., *Non-Standard Language in English Literature* (London: Deutsch, 1981).

Blandford, George Fielding, 'Provincial Glossary', *Notes and Queries*, 9 April 1870, 363–4.

Bonaparte, Prince Louis Lucien, 'On the Dialects of Monmouthshire, Herefordshire, Worcestershire, Gloucestershire, Berkshire, Oxfordshire, South Warwickshire, South Northamptonshire, Buckinghamshire, Hertfordshire, Middlesex, and Surrey, with a New Classification of the English Dialects', *Transactions of the Philological Society* 16 (1876), 570–81.

Bosworth, J[oseph], *A Dictionary of the Anglo-Saxon Language* (London: Longmans et al, 1838).

Bowen, John, 'The Historical Novel', in Patrick Brantlinger and William B. Thesing (eds), *A Companion to the Victorian Novel* (Oxford: Wiley Blackwell, 2005), pp. 244–59.

Bowers, John M., *Tolkien's Lost Chaucer* (Oxford: Oxford University Press, 2019).

Bradley, Henry, *Collected Papers* (Oxford: Clarendon Press, 1928).

Bradley, Henry, 'Bosworth, Joseph (1787/8–1876)', rev. John D. Haigh, in *Oxford Dictionary of National Biography* [www.oxforddnb].

Brewer, Charlotte, *Editing Piers Plowman: the evolution of the text*, Cambridge Studies in Medieval Literature 28 (Cambridge: Cambridge University Press, 1996).

Brewer, Charlotte, 'Walter William Skeat (1835–1912)', in Helen Damico (ed.), *Medieval Scholarship: Biographical Studies on the Formation of a Discipline. Volume 2: Literature and Philology* (New York: Garland, 1998), pp. 139–49.

Brewer, Charlotte, '*OED* Sources', in Lynda Mugglestone (ed.), *Lexicography and the OED: Pioneers in the Untrodden Forest* (Oxford: Oxford University Press, 2000), pp. 40–58.

Brewer, Charlotte, *Treasure-House of the Language: The Living OED* (New Haven: Yale University Press, 2007).

Bridges, Robert, 'A Memoir', in Henry Bradley, *Collected Papers* (Oxford: Clarendon Press, 1928), pp. 1–56.

Bridges, Robert, and Henry Bradley, *Correspondence of Robert Bridges and Henry Bradley 1900–1923* (Oxford: Clarendon Press, 1940).

[Brierley, Ben], *Ab-o'th'-Yate's Dictionary; or, Walmsley Fowt Skoomester* (Manchester: Heywood, 1881).

Brierley, Ben, *Ab-o'th'-Yate Sketches and Other Short Stories*, ed. James Dronsfield, 3 vols (Oldham: Clegg, 1896).

Brierley, Ben, *Home Memories and Out of Work* (Bramhall: Reword, 2002).

Briggs, Katharine, *A Dictionary of Fairies: Hobgoblins, Brownies, Bogies and Other Supernatural Creatures* (London: Penguin, 1976).

Britten, James, and Robert Holland, *A Dictionary of English Plant-Names*, English Dialect Society 22, 26, 45 (London: English Dialect Society, 1886).

Brook, G. L., *English Dialects* (London: Deutsch, 1963).

Brook, G. L., *The Language of Dickens* (London: Deutsch, 1970).

Brown, Joanna Cullen (ed.), *Hardy's People: Figures in a Wessex Landscape* (London: Allison and Busby, 1991).

Brundage, Anthony, and Richard A. Cosgrove, *British Historians and National Identity: From Hume to Churchill* (London: Pickering and Chatto, 2014).

Burne, Charlotte Sophia (ed.), *Shropshire Folk-Lore: A Sheaf of Gleanings, from the collections of Georgina F. Jackson* (London: Trübner, 1883).

Burne, Charlotte Sophia, *The Handbook of Folklore*, rev. ed., Publications of the Folklore Society 73 (London: Sidgwick and Jackson, 1914).

Burnley, David, *The Language of Chaucer* (Basingstoke: Macmillan, 1989).

Burns, Tom Scott, *Canon Atkinson and his Country* (Leeds: Rigg, 1986).

Burrow, J. W., *Evolution and Society: A Study in Victorian Social Theory* (Cambridge: Cambridge University Press, 1966).

Burrow, J. W., 'The Uses of Philology in Victorian England', in Robert Robson (ed.), *Ideas and Institutions of Victorian Britain: Essays in Honour of George Kitson Clark* (London: Bell and Sons, 1967), pp. 180–204.

Burrow, J. W., *A Liberal Descent: Victorian Historians and the English Past* (Cambridge: Cambridge University Press, 1981).

Burton, T. L., and K. K. Ruthven, 'Dialect Poetry, William Barnes and the Literary Canon', *English Literary History* 76 (2009), 309–41.

Calhoon, Robert M., 'Boucher, Jonathan (1738–1804)', in *Oxford Dictionary of National Biography* [www.oxforddnb].

Campion, G. Edward, *A Tennyson Dialect Glossary, with the dialect poems*, 3rd ed. (Lincoln: Lincolnshire and Humberside Arts, 1976).

[Carr, William], *Horæ Momenta Cravenæ, or, the Craven Dialect* (London: Hurst, Robinson, and Co., 1824).

Catalogue of the English Dialect Library (Manchester: English Dialect Society, 1880).

Cavaliero, Glen, *The Rural Tradition in the English Novel, 1900–1939* (Basingstoke: Palgrave Macmillan, 1977).

Chadwick, Ellis H., *Mrs Gaskell: Haunts, Homes, and Stories*, rev. ed. (London: Pitman and Sons, 1913).

Chadwick, H. M., 'Studies in Old English', *Transactions of the Cambridge Philological Society* 4.2 (1899), 85–265.

Chamberlain, Edith L., *A Glossary of West Worcestershire Words*, English Dialect Society 36 (London: English Dialect Society, 1882).

Chamberlain, Edith L., *Up Hill and Down Dale: A Tale of Country Life*, 3 vols (London: Remington, 1884).

Chambers, J. K., and Peter Trudgill, *Dialectology*, 2nd ed. (Cambridge: Cambridge University Press, 1998).

Chambers, R. W., *The Teaching of English in the Universities of England*, English Association Pamphlet 53 (Oxford: English Association, 1922).

Chambers, R. W., *Concerning Certain Great Teachers of the English Language: An Inaugural Lecture Delivered in University College, London* (London: Arnold and Co., 1923).

294 Bibliography

Chambers, R. W., *Man's Unconquerable Mind* (London: Cape, 1939).

Chambers, R. W., 'W. P. Ker, 1855–1923', in Michael Lapidge (ed.), *Interpreters of Early Medieval Britain* (Oxford: British Academy, 2002), pp. 139–52.

Chambers, R. W., 'Ker, William Paton (1855–1923)', rev. A. S. G. Edwards, in *Oxford Dictionary of National Biography* [www.oxforddnb].

Chamson, Emil, 'Etymology in the *English Dialect Dictionary*', in Manfred Markus et al (eds), *Middle and Modern English Corpus Linguistics: A Multi-Dimensional Approach* (Amsterdam: Benjamins, 2012), pp. 225–40.

Chapman, Raymond, *The Language of Thomas Hardy* (Basingstoke: Macmillan, 1990).

Chapple, J. A. V., and Arthur Pollard (eds), *The Letters of Mrs Gaskell* (Manchester: Manchester University Press, 1966).

Chaudhuri, Nirad C., *Scholar Extraordinary: The Life of Professor the Rt. Hon. Friedrich Max Müller, P. C.* (London: Chatto and Windus, 1974).

Chedzoy, Alan, *The People's Poet: William Barnes of Dorset* (Stroud: History Press, 2010).

Cheshire, Jim, *Tennyson and Mid-Victorian Publishing: Moxon, Poetry, Commerce* (London: Palgrave Macmillan, 2017).

Christy, Miller, 'Ellis, John (1789–1862)', rev. Alan R. Griffin, in *Oxford Dictionary of National Biography* [www.oxforddnb].

Clarke, Thomas, 'Anglo-Saxon as an Aid to the Study of Dialects', *Transactions of the Yorkshire Dialect Society* 1 (1898), 18–25.

Coates, Jennifer, *Women, Men and Language: a sociolinguistic account of sex differences in languages* (London: Longman, 1986).

Cohen, Morton N. (ed.), *The Letters of Lewis Carroll*, 2 vols (London: Macmillan, 1979).

Cole, Malcolm. *'Be Like Daisies': John Ruskin and the Cultivation of Beauty at Whitelands College*, Ruskin Lecture 1992 (St Albans: Guild of St George, 1992).

Coleman, Julie, *A History of Slang and Cant Dictionaries, Volume III: 1859–1936* (Oxford: Oxford University Press, 2008).

Coleman, Julie, *The Life of Slang* (Oxford: Oxford University Press, 2012).

Coleridge, Derwent, 'Observations on the Plan of the Society's Proposed New English Dictionary', *Transactions of the Philological Society* (1860), 152–68.

Coleridge, Herbert, et al, 'Canones Lexicographici; or Rules to be Observed in Editing the New English Dictionary of the Philological Society', *Transactions of the Philological Society* (1859), Part II, 1–12.

Coles, Gladys Mary Coles, *The Flower of Light: A Biography of Mary Webb* (London: Duckworth, 1978).

[Collier, John], *The Works of Tim Bobbin, Esq. in Prose and Verse* (Manchester: Heywood, 1862).

Collini, Stefan, *Public Moralists: Political Thought and Intellectual Life in Britain 1850–1930* (Oxford: Clarendon Press, 1991).

Colls, Robert, *Identity of England* (Oxford: Oxford University Press, 2002).

Colls, Robert, 'The New Northumbrians', in Robert Colls (ed.), *Northumbria: History and Identity 547–2000* (Chichester: Phillimore, 2007), pp. 151–77.

Colls, Robert, and Philip Dodd (eds), *Englishness: Politics and Culture 1880–1920* (London: Croom Helm, 1986).

Considine, John, *Small Dictionaries and Curiosity: Lexicography and Fieldwork in Post-Medieval Europe* (Oxford: Oxford University Press, 2017).

Cooper, Andrew R., '"Folk-speech" and 'book English': re-presentations of dialect in Hardy's novels', *Language and Literature* 3 (1994), 21–41.

Cooper, Paul, 'Russian Dolls and Dialect Literature: The Enregisterment of Nineteenth-Century 'Yorkshire' Dialects', in Patrick Honeybone and Warren Maguire (eds), *Dialect Writing and the North of England* (Edinburgh: Edinburgh University Press, 2020), pp. 126–46.

Cooper, Thompson, 'Baker, Anne Elizabeth (1786–1861); rev. Paul Stamper, in *Oxford Dictionary of National Biography* [www.oxforddnb].

Cooper, Thompson, 'Forby, Robert (1759–1825); rev. John D. Haigh, in *Oxford Dictionary of National Biography* [www.oxforddnb].

Cotton, J. S., 'Morris, Richard (1833–1894); rev. John D. Haigh, in *Oxford Dictionary of National Biography* [www.oxforddnb].

Courtney, W. P., 'Pulman, George Philip Rigney (1819–1880); rev. Ian Maxted, in *Oxford Dictionary of National Biography* [www.oxforddnb].

Cox, R. G. (ed.), *Thomas Hardy: The Critical Heritage* (London: Routledge and Kegan Paul, 1970).

Craven, S. K., 'Report', *Transactions of the Yorkshire Dialect Society* 1 (1898), 41.

Crawforth, Hannah, *Etymology and the Invention of English in Early Modern Literature* (Cambridge: Cambridge University Press, 2013).

Crook, David, 'Hunter, Joseph (1783–1861); in *Oxford Dictionary of National Biography* [www.oxforddnb].

Crosby, Alan G., 'Folklore, Customs and Traditions', in Michael Winstanley (ed.), *Revealing Cumbria's Past: 150 Years of the Cumberland and Westmorland Antiquarian and Archaeological Society*, Cumberland and Westmorland Antiquarian and Archaeological Society Extra Series 45 (Kendal: Cumberland and Westmorland Antiquarian and Archaeological Society, 2016), pp. 153–74.

Cross, J. W. (ed.), *George Eliot's Life as Related in her Letters and Journals*, 4 vols (Leipzig: Tauchnitz, 1885).

Crowley, Tony, *The Politics of Discourse: The Standard Language Question in British Cultural Debates* (Basingstoke: Macmillan, 1989).

Crystal, David, 'Early Interest in Shakespeare: Original Pronunciation', *Language and History* 56 (2013), 5–17.

Crystal, David, *The Disappearing Dictionary: A Treasury of Lost English Dialect Words* (London: Macmillan, 2015).

Culler, Jonathan, *Ferdinand de Saussure* (Ithaca: Cornell University Press, 1986).

Cunningham, Valentine (ed.), *The Victorians: An Anthology of Poetry and Poetics* (Oxford: Blackwell, 2000).

Curzan, Anne, 'The Compass of the Vocabulary', in Lynda Mugglestone (ed.), *Lexicography and the OED: Pioneers in the Untrodden Forest* (Oxford: Oxford University Press, 2000), pp. 96–109.

Dance, Richard, 'H. M. Chadwick and Old English Philology', in Michael Lapidge (ed.), *H. M. Chadwick and the Study of Anglo-Saxon, Norse and Celtic in Cambridge*, Cambrian Medieval Celtic Studies 69/70 (Aberystwyth: Department of Welsh, Aberystwyth University, 2015), pp. 83–97.

Dance, Richard, *Words Derived from Old Norse in Sir Gawain and the Green Knight: An Etymological Survey*, Publications of the Philological Society 50, 2 vols (Oxford: Philological Society, 2018).

Darwin, Charles, *The Descent of Man, and Selection in Relation to Sex*, 2nd ed., The Works of Charles Darwin 21–22 (London: Pickering and Chatto, 1989).

Darwin, Charles, *The Origin of Species*, ed. Gillian Beer (Oxford: Oxford University Press, 1996).

Degani, Marta, and Alexander Onysko, 'Giving Voice to Local Cultures: Reflections on the Notion of 'Dialect' in the *English Dialect Dictionary*', in Roberta Facchinetti (ed.), *English Dictionaries as Cultural Mines* (Newcastle: Cambridge Scholars, 2012), pp. 55–72.

Dickens, Charles, *'Gone Astray' and Other Papers from Household Words 1851–59*, ed. Michael Slater, Dent Uniform Edition of Dickens' Journalism 3 (London: Dent, 1998).

Dickens, Charles, *Hard Times*, ed. Paul Schlicke (Oxford: Oxford University Press, 2006).

296 Bibliography

Dickinson, Bickford H. C., *Sabine Baring-Gould: Squarson, Writer and Folklorist, 1834–1924* (Newton Abbot: David and Charles, 1970).

Dickinson, William, *A Glossary of Words and Phrases Pertaining to the Dialect of Cumberland*, English Dialect Society 20 (London: English Dialect Society, 1878).

Dickinson, William, *Uncollected Literary Remains*, ed. W. Hodgson (Carlisle: Coward, 1888).

Dieth, Eugen, 'A New Survey of English Dialects', *Essays and Studies* 32 (1946), 74–104.

Dillion, Jacqueline, *Thomas Hardy: Folklore and Resistance* (London: Palgrave Macmillan, 2016).

Dorson, Richard M., *The British Folklorists: A History* (London: Routledge and Kegan Paul, 1968).

Dowling, Linda, 'Victorian Oxford and the Science of Language', *Publications of the Modern Languages Association* 97 (1982), 160–78.

Dronsfield, James, 'Preface: Ben Brierley', in Ben Brierley, *Ab-o'th'-Yate Sketches and Other Short Stories*, ed. James Dronsfield, 3 vols (Oldham: Clegg, 1896), I, v–xxv.

Drury, Annmarie, 'Aural Community and William Barnes as Earwitness', *Victorian Poetry* 56 (2018), 433–53.

Duncan, Ian, 'The Provincial or Regional Novel', in Patrick Brantlinger and William B. Thesing (eds), *A Companion to the Victorian Novel* (Oxford: Blackwell, 2002), pp. 318–35.

Durkin, Philip, 'The *English Dialect Dictionary* and the *Oxford English Dictionary*: A Continuing Relationship Between Two Dictionaries', in Manfred Markus, Clive Upton, and Reinhard Heuberger (eds), *Joseph Wright's English Dialect Dictionary and Beyond: Studies in Late Modern English Dialectology* (Frankfurt am Main: Lang, 2010), pp. 201–18.

E. B., 'Obituary: Frederic Thomas Elworthy', *Folklore* 19 (1908), 109–10.

Ebbatson, Roger, *Landscape and Literature 1830–1914: Nature, Text, Aura* (London: Palgrave Macmillan, 2013).

Edney, Sue, '"Times be Badish vor the Poor": William Barnes and his Dialect of Disturbance in the Dorset "Eclogues"', *English* 58 (2009), 206–29.

Edney, Sue, 'Recent Studies in Victorian English Literary Dialect and its Linguistic Connections', *Literature Compass* 8.9 (2011), 660–74.

Edney, Sue, 'William Barnes's Place and Dialects of Connection', in Kirstie Blair and Mina Gorji (eds), *Class and the Canon: Constructing Labouring-Class Poetry and Poetics, 1780–1900* (Basingstoke: Palgrave Macmillan, 2013), pp. 190–210.

Edney, Sue, 'The "Boggle" in the "Waäste": Meaning and Mask in Tennyson's Dialect Poems', in Claire Hélie, Elise Brault-Dreux, and Emilie Loriaux (eds), *No Dialect Please, You're A Poet: English Dialect in Poetry in the 20th and 21st Centuries* (London: Routledge, 2019), pp. 26–37.

Elder, Eileen (ed.), *The Peacock Lincolnshire Word Books 1884–1920* (Scunthorpe: Scunthorpe Museum Society, 1997).

Eliot, George, *Selected Critical Writings*, ed. Rosemary Ashton (Oxford: Oxford University Press, 1992).

Eliot, George, *Adam Bede*, ed. Carol A. Martin (Oxford: Oxford University Press, 2008).

Eliot, T. S., *The Sacred Wood: Essays on Poetry and Criticism* (London: Faber and Faber, 1997).

Elliott, Ralph W. V., *Thomas Hardy's English* (Oxford: Blackwell, 1984).

Ellis, Alexander J., 'On Palaeotype; or, the Representation of Spoken Sounds for Philological Purposes by Means of the Ancient Types', *Transactions of the Philological Society* (1867), Supplement I, 1–52.

Ellis, Alexander J., *On Early English Pronunciation, with Especial Reference to Shakspere and Chaucer*, 5 vols, Early English Text Society, Extra Series 2, 7, 14, 23, 56 (London: Philological Society, Early English Text Society, and Chaucer Society, 1869–89).

Ellis, Alexander J., 'On Glosik, A Neu Sistem ov Ingglish Spelling, Proapoa.zd faur Konkur.ent Eus, in Aurder too Remidi dhi Difek,ts, widhou.t Ditrak.ting from dhi Valeu ov Our Prezent Aurthog.rafi', *Transactions of the Philological Society* (1870–1), 89–118.

Ellis, Alexander J., 'First Annual Address of the President to the Philological Society, Delivered at the Anniversary Meeting, Friday, 17th May, 1872', *Transactions of the Philological Society* (1873–4), 1–34.

Ellis, Alexander J., 'Second Annual Address of the President to the Philological Society, Delivered at the Anniversary Meeting, Friday, 16th May, 1873', *Transactions of the Philological Society* (1873–4), 201–52.

Ellis, Alexander J., 'Third Annual Address of the President to the Philological Society, Delivered at the Anniversary Meeting, Friday, 15th May, 1874', *Transactions of the Philological Society* (1873–4), 354–460.

Ellis, Alexander J., 'The Anglo-Cymric Score', *Transactions of the Philological Society* (1877), 316–72.

Ellis, Alexander J., 'Tenth Annual Address of the President to the Philological Society, Delivered at the Anniversary Meeting, Friday, 20th May, 1881', *Transactions of the Philological Society* (1881), 252–321.

Ellis, Alexander J., 'Eleventh Annual Address of the President to the Philological Society, Delivered at the Anniversary Meeting, Friday, 19th May, 1882', *Transactions of the Philological Society* (1882–4), 1–148.

Ellis, Alexander J., *Report on Dialectal Work*, English Dialect Society 49 (London: English Dialect Society, 1885).

Ellis, Alexander J., *Second Report on Dialectal Work*, English Dialect Society 55 (London: English Dialect Society, 1887).

Ellis, Alexander J., *English Dialects – Their Sounds and Homes*, English Dialect Society 60 (London: English Dialect Society, 1890).

Ellwood, T., 'Notes upon some of the older Word Forms to be found in comparing the language of Lakeland with the language of Iceland', *Transactions of the Cumberland and Westmorland Antiquarian and Archaeological Society*, 1st Series 9 (1887), 383–92.

Elworthy, Frederic Thomas, *The Dialect of West Somerset*, English Dialect Society 7 (London: English Dialect Society, 1875).

Elworthy, Frederic Thomas, *An Outline of the Grammar of the Dialect of West Somerset*, English Dialect Society 19 (London: English Dialect Society, 1877).

Elworthy, Frederic Thomas, *The West Somerset Word-Book: A Glossary of Dialectal and Archaic Words and Phrases Used in the West of Somerset and East Devon*, English Dialect Society 50 (London: English Dialect Society, 1886).

The English Dialect Dictionary Online: https://eddonline4-proj.uibk.ac.at/edd/

The English Dialect Dictionary: First Annual Report (no place or date of publication).

The English Dialect Dictionary: Second Annual Report (no place of publication, 1889).

The English Dialect Dictionary: Third Annual Report (no place of publication, 1890).

The English Dialect Dictionary: Fourth Report (no place or date of publication).

The English Dialect Library: Catalogue Part II (Works Added from 1880 to 1888) (London: English Dialect Society, 1888).

English Dialect Society: First Report, for the Year 1873 (no place or date of publication).

English Dialect Society: Second Report, for the Year 1874 (no place or date of publication).

English Dialect Society: Third Report, for the Year 1875 (no place or date of publication).

English Dialect Society: Notice to Members. March, 1876 (no place or date of publication).

English Dialect Society: Fourth Report, for the Year 1876 (no place or date of publication).

English Dialect Society: Fifth Report, for the Year 1877 (no place or date of publication).

English Dialect Society: Sixth Report, for the Year 1878 (no place or date of publication).

English Dialect Society: Seventh Annual Report, for the Year 1879 (no place or date of publication).

English Dialect Society: Eighth Annual Report, for the Year 1880 (no place or date of publication).

298 Bibliography

English Dialect Society: Ninth Annual Report, for the Year 1881 (no place or date of publication).

English Dialect Society: Tenth Annual Report, for the Year 1882 (no place or date of publication).

English Dialect Society: Eleventh Annual Report, for the Year 1883 (no place or date of publication).

English Dialect Society: Twelfth Annual Report, for the Year 1884 (no place or date of publication).

English Dialect Society: Thirteenth Report, for the Years 1885 and 1886 (no place or date of publication).

English Dialect Society: Fourteenth Report, for the Year 1887 (no place or date of publication).

English Dialect Society: Fifteenth Report, for the Year 1888 (no place or date of publication).

English Dialect Society: Sixteenth Report, for the Year 1889 (no place or date of publication).

English Dialect Society: Seventeenth Report, for the Three Years, 1890, 1891, and 1892 (no place or date of publication).

Eustace, S. S., 'The Meaning of the Palaeotype in A. J. Ellis's *On Early English Pronunciation 1869–89*', *Transactions of the Philological Society* (1969), 31–79.

Evans, Andrew D., *Anthropology at War: World War I and the Science of Race in Germany* (Chicago: University of Chicago Press, 2010).

Evans, Arthur Benoni, *Leicestershire Words, Phrases, and Proverbs*, ed. Sebastian Evans, English Dialect Society 31 (London: English Dialect Society, 1881).

Everett, Dorothy, 'Chambers, Raymond Wilson (1874–1942)', rev. John D. Haigh, in *Oxford Dictionary of National Biography* [www.oxforddnb].

Farrant, John H., 'Grose, Francis (*bap.* 1731, *d.* 1791)', in *Oxford Dictionary of National Biography* [www.oxforddnb].

Faulkner, Mark, 'Gerald of Wales and Standard Old English', *Notes and Queries* 58 (2011), 19–24.

Ferguson, Susan L., 'Drawing Fictional Lines: Dialect and Narrative in the Victorian Novel', *Style* 32 (1998), 1–17.

Field, Jean, *Mary Dormer Harris: The Life and Works of a Warwickshire Historian* (Studley: Brewin Books, 2002).

Firor, Ruth A., *Folkways in Thomas Hardy* (Philadelphia: University of Pennsylvania Press, 1931).

Firth, C. H., 'Joseph Wright, 1855—1930', in Michael Lapidge (ed.), *Interpreters of Early Medieval Britain* (London: British Academy, 2002), pp. 119–35.

Forby, Robert, *The Vocabulary of East Anglia; an attempt to record the vulgar tongue of the twin sister counties, Norfolk and Suffolk, as it existed in the last twenty years of the eighteenth century, and still exists; with proof of its antiquity from etymology and authority*, 2 vols (London: Nichols and Son, 1830).

Fowler, Rowena, 'Virginia Woolf: Lexicographer', *English Language Notes* 39 (2002), 54–70.

Freeman, Arthur, and Janet Ing Freeman, 'Phillipps, James Orchard Halliwell (1820–1889)', in *Oxford Dictionary of National Biography* [www.oxforddnb].

Freeman, Michael, *Victorians and the Prehistoric: Tracks to a Lost World* (New Haven: Yale University Press, 2004).

Fulk, R. D., Robert E. Bjork and John D. Niles (eds), *Klaeber's Beowulf* (Toronto: University of Toronto Press, 2008).

Furnivall, Frederick J., 'Prefatory Notice', in Robert Backhouse Peacock, *A Glossary of the Dialect of the Hundred of Lonsdale, North and South of the Sands, in the County of Lancaster* (London: Philological Society, 1869), pp. iii–vi.

Fynes, R. C. C., 'Müller, Friedrich Max (1823–1900)', in *Oxford Dictionary of National Biography* [www.oxforddnb].

Garnett, Richard, 'Memoir of the late Rev. Richard Garnett', in Richard Garnett, *Philological Essays* (London: Williams and Norgate, 1859), pp. i–xvi.

Garnett, Richard, 'Garnett, Richard (1789–1850)', rev. John D. Haigh, in *Oxford Dictionary of National Biography* [www.oxforddnb].

Garnett, Richard, *Philological Essays* (London: Williams and Norgate, 1859).

Gaskell, Elizabeth, *North and South*, ed. Angus Easson (Oxford: Oxford University Press, 1998).

Gaskell, Elizabeth, *Mary Barton*, ed. Shirley Foster (Oxford: Oxford University Press, 2006).

Gaskell, Elizabeth, *Sylvia's Lovers*, ed. Francis O'Gorman (Oxford: Oxford University Press, 2014).

Gatrell, Simon, 'Wessex', in Dale Kramer (ed.), *The Cambridge Companion to Thomas Hardy* (Cambridge: Cambridge University Press, 1999), pp. 19–37.

Gatrell, Simon, 'Dialect', in Norman Page (ed.), *Oxford Reader's Companion to Hardy* (Oxford: Oxford University Press, 2001), pp. 96–8.

Gatrell, Simon, *Thomas Hardy's Vision of Wessex* (London: Palgrave Macmillan, 2003).

Geary, Patrick J., *The Myth of Nations: The Medieval Origins of Europe* (Princeton: Princeton University Press, 2002).

Gibbons, Stella, *Cold Comfort Farm* (London: Penguin, 2011).

Gibson, Alexander Craig, *The Folk-Speech of Cumberland and Some Districts Adjacent* (London: Smith, 1869).

Gill, Stephen (ed.), *William Wordsworth* (Oxford: Oxford University Press, 1984).

Gill, Stephen, *Wordsworth and the Victorians* (Oxford: Clarendon Press, 1998).

Gilliver, Peter, 'Appendix II: *OED* Personalia', in Lynda Mugglestone (ed.), *Lexicography and the OED: Pioneers in the Untrodden Forest* (Oxford: Oxford University Press, 2000), pp. 232–52.

Gilliver, Peter, 'Harvesting England's ancient treasure: dialect lexicography and the Philological Society's first plans for a national dictionary', *Dictionaries* 32 (2011), 82–92.

Gilliver, Peter, 'Thoughts on Writing a History of the *Oxford English Dictionary*', *Dictionaries* 34 (2013), 175–83.

Gilliver, Peter, *The Making of the Oxford English Dictionary* (Oxford: Oxford University Press, 2016).

Gilliver, Peter, Jeremy Marshall, and Edmund Weiner, *The Ring of Words: Tolkien and the Oxford English Dictionary* (Oxford: Oxford University Press, 2006).

Gilmour, Robin, 'Regional and Provincial in Victorian Literature', in R. P. Draper (ed.), *The Literature of Region and Nation* (New York: Palgrave Macmillan, 1989), pp. 51–60.

Gladstone, Jo, "New World of English Words': John Ray, FRS, the Dialect Protagonist, in the Context of his Times (1658–1691)', in Peter Burke and Roy Porter (eds), *Language, Self, and Society: A Social History of Language* (Cambridge: Cambridge University Press, 1991), pp. 115–53.

Gomme, George Laurence, *The Handbook of Folklore*, Publications of the Folklore Society 20 (London: Folklore Society, 1890).

Goodchild, J. G., 'Traditional Names of Places in Edenside', *Transactions of the Cumberland and Westmorland Antiquarian and Archaeological Society* 6 (1881–83), 50–76.

Görlach, Manfred, *English in Nineteenth-Century England: An Introduction* (Cambridge: Cambridge University Press, 1999).

Goulden, R. J. 'Smith, John Russell (1810–1894)', in *Oxford Dictionary of National Biography* [www.oxforddnb].

Graebe, Martin, *As I Walked Out: Sabine Baring-Gould and the Search for the Folk Songs of Devon and Cornwall* (Oxford: Signal Books, 2017).

Green, Alice Stopford, 'Canon Atkinson: Scholar, Thinker, and Lover of the Country', *The Bookman* (May 1900), 49–51.

Green, J. Hanson, 'Yorkshire Dialect as Spoken in the West Riding During the Fifteenth and Nineteenth Centuries', *Transactions of the Yorkshire Dialect Society* 2 (1899), 54–68.

300 Bibliography

Grice, Frederick, 'Kilvert and Folklore', *Folklore* 85 (1974), 199–201.

Grose, Francis, *A Provincial Glossary, with a Collection of Local Proverbs, and Popular Superstitions* (London: Hooper, 1787).

Guest, Harriet, 'The Deep Romance of Manchester: Gaskell's *Mary Barton*', in K. D. M. Snell (ed.), *The Regional Novel in Britain and Ireland, 1800–1990* (Cambridge: Cambridge University Press, 1998), pp. 78–98.

Gunner, Gilbert E., 'Joseph and Elizabeth Mary Wright – a Memory and a Tribute', *Transactions of the Yorkshire Dialect Society* 85 (1985), 14–16.

Gurney, Anna, 'Norfolk Words', *Transactions of the Philological Society* (1855), 29–39.

[Gutch, Eliza], 'Children's Drama', *Notes and Queries* 2nd Series 10 (1 September 1860), 168.

[Gutch, Eliza], 'A Folk-Lore Society', *Notes and Queries* 5th Series 5 (12 February 1876), 124.

[Gutch, Eliza], 'Wanted – an English Dialect Dictionary', *Notes and Queries* 5th Series 11 (12 April 1879), 294–5.

[Gutch, Eliza], 'A Dictionary of English Dialect Synonyms', *Notes and Queries* 9th Series 12 (5 December 1903), 444.

[Gutch, Eliza], 'A Dictionary of English Dialect Synonyms', *Notes and Queries* 10th Series 2 (2 July 1904), 18.

[Gutch, Eliza], 'A Glimpse of Tennyson', *Notes and Queries* 155 (7 July 1928), 7.

Guy, Josephine M., '"The Chimneyed City': Imagining the North in Victorian Literature', in Katherine Cockin (ed.), *The Literary North* (Basingstoke: Palgrave Macmillan, 2012), pp. 22–37.

Haigh, John D., 'Kemble, John Mitchell (1807–1857)', in *Oxford Dictionary of National Biography* [www.oxforddnb].

Hakala, Taryn, 'Working Dialect: Nonstandard Voices in Victorian Literature' (unpublished PhD, University of Michigan, 2010).

Hakala, Taryn, 'A Great Man in Clogs: Performing Authenticity in Victorian Lancashire', *Victorian Studies* 52 (2010), 387–412.

Hakala, Taryn, 'Linguistic Self-Fashioning in Elizabeth Gaskell's *Mary Barton*', in Jane Hodson (ed.), *Dialect and Literature in the Long Nineteenth Century* (Abingdon: Routledge, 2017), pp. 146–61.

Hakala, Taryn, 'Dialect', *Victorian Literature and Culture* 46 (2018), 649–52.

Halliwell, James Orchard, *A Dictionary of Archaic and Provincial Words: Obsolete Phrases, Proverbs, and Ancient Customs, from the Fourteenth Century* (London: Smith, 1847).

Hardy, Florence, *The Early Life of Thomas Hardy, 1840–1891* (London: Macmillan, 1928).

Hardy, James (ed.), *The Denham Tracts: A Collection of Folklore by Michael Aislabie Denham*, 2 vols, Publications of the Folklore Society 29, 35 (London: Folklore Society, 1892–5).

Hardy, Thomas, *Collected Letters*, ed. Richard Little Purdy and Michael Millgate, 7 vols (Oxford: Clarendon Press, 1978–88).

Hardy, Thomas, *Complete Poetical Works*, ed. Samuel Hynes, 5 vols (Oxford: Clarendon Press, 1982–95).

Hardy, Thomas, *Tess of the D'Urbervilles*, ed. Juliet Grindle and Simon Gatrell (Oxford: Oxford University Press, 1988).

Hardy, Thomas, *Jude the Obscure*, ed. Patricia Ingham (Oxford: Oxford University Press, 1996).

Hardy, Thomas, *The Mayor of Casterbridge*, ed. Dale Kramer (Oxford: Oxford University Press, 2004).

Hardy, Thomas, *The Woodlanders*, ed. Dale Kramer (Oxford: Oxford University Press, 2005).

Hardy, Thomas, *Under the Greenwood Tree*, ed. Simon Gatrell, new ed. (Oxford: Oxford University Press, 2013).

Hargreaves, John A., 'Waugh, Edwin (1817–1890)', in *Oxford Dictionary of National Biography* [www.oxforddnb].

Harland, John, *A Glossary of Words Used in Swaledale, Yorkshire*, English Dialect Society 3 (London: English Dialect Society, 1873).

Harpham, Geoffrey Galt, 'Roots, Races, and the Return to Philology', *Representations* 106 (2009), 34–62.

Harris, Mary Dormer, *Plays and Essays*, ed. Florence Hayllar (Leamington Spa: Courier Press, no date of publication).

Head, Dominic, *Modernity and the English Rural Novel* (Cambridge: Cambridge University Press, 2017).

Heaney, Seamus, *Beowulf: A New Translation* (London: Faber and Faber, 1999).

Herford, C. H., 'Wedgwood, Hensleigh (1803–1891)', rev. John D. Haigh, in *Oxford Dictionary of National Biography* [www.oxforddnb].

Hermeston, Rod, 'Metaphor and Indexicality in *The Pitman's Pay*: The Ambivalence of Dialect', in Patrick Honeybone and Warren Maguire (eds), *Dialect Writing and the North of England* (Edinburgh: Edinburgh University Press, 2020), pp. 168–87.

Heselwood, Barry, *Phonetic Transcription in Theory and Practice* (Edinburgh: Edinburgh University Press, 2013).

Heslop, R. Oliver, *Northumberland Words: A Glossary of Words Used in the County of Northumberland and on the Tyneside*, 2 vols, English Dialect Society 66, 68 (London: English Dialect Society, 1892–3).

Heslop, R. Oliver, 'Dialect Notes from Northernmost England', *Transactions of the Yorkshire Dialect Society* 5 (1903), 7–31.

Hilton, Tim, *John Ruskin: The Later Years* (New Haven: Yale University Press, 2000).

Hodson, Jane, *Dialect in Film and Literature* (Basingstoke: Macmillan, 2014).

Hodson, Jane, 'Talking Like a Servant: What nineteenth century novels can tell us about the social history of the language', *Journal of Historical Sociolinguistics* 2 (2016), 27–46.

Hodson, Jane (ed.), *Dialect and Literature in the Long Nineteenth Century* (Abingdon: Routledge, 2017).

Hodson, Jane, 'The Problem with Dialect Poetry', in Claire Hélie, Elise Brault-Dreux, and Emilie Loriaux (eds), *No Dialect Please, You're A Poet: English Dialect in Poetry in the 20th and 21st Centuries* (London: Routledge, 2019), pp. 57–72.

Hodson, Jane, "Did She Say Dinner, Betsey, at This Taam o'Day?': Representing Yorkshire Voices and Characters in Novels 1800–1836', in Patrick Honeybone and Warren Maguire (eds), *Dialect Writing and the North of England* (Edinburgh: Edinburgh University Press, 2020), pp. 188–210.

Hodson, Jane, and Alex Broadhead, 'Developments in Literary Dialect Representation in British Fiction 1800–1836', *Language and Literature* 22 (2013), 315–32.

Holder, R. W., *The Dictionary Men: Their Lives and Times* (Bath: Bath University Press, 2004).

Holland, Bernard, *The Lancashire Hollands* (London: Murray, 1917).

Holland, Edgar Swinton, *A History of the Family of Holland of Mobberley and Knutsford in the County of Chester*, ed. William Fergusson Irvine (Edinburgh: Ballantyne Press, 1902).

Holland, Robert, *A Glossary of Words Used in the County of Chester*, English Dialect Society 44, 46, 51 (London: English Dialect Society, 1884–6).

Hollingworth, Brian (ed.), *Songs of the People: Lancashire Dialect Poetry of the Industrial Revolution* (Manchester: Manchester University Press, 1977).

Hollingworth, Brian, 'From Voice to Print: Lancashire Dialect Verse, 1800–70', *Philological Quarterly* 92 (2013), 289–308.

Hollingworth, Brian, 'Edwin Waugh: The Social and Literary Standing of a Working-Class Icon', in Kirstie Blair and Mina Gorji (eds), *Class and the Canon: Constructing Labouring-Class Poetry and Poetics, 1780–1900* (Basingstoke: Palgrave Macmillan, 2013), pp. 174–90.

Hollingworth, Brian, 'Axon, William Edward Armytage (1846–1913)', in *Oxford Dictionary of National Biography* [www.oxforddnb].

302 Bibliography

Honey, John, '"Talking Proper": Schooling and the Establishment of English "Received Pronunciation"', in Graham Nixon and John Honey (eds), *An Historic Tongue: Studies in English Linguistics in Memory of Barbara Strang* (London: Routledge, 1988), pp. 209–27.

Honeybone, Patrick, and Warren Maguire (eds), *Dialect Writing and the North of England* (Edinburgh: Edinburgh University Press, 2020).

Hooper, Walter (ed.), *They Stand Together: The Letters of C. S. Lewis to Arthur Greeves (1914–1963)* (London: Collins, 1979).

Hopkin, David, 'Regionalism and Folklore', in Xosé M. Núñez Seixas and Eric Storm (eds), *Regionalism and Modern Europe: Identity Construction and Movements from 1890 to the Present Day* (London: Bloomsbury, 2018), pp. 43–64.

Hopkins, Gerard Manley, *The Major Works*, ed. Catherine Phillips (Oxford: Oxford University Press, 2002).

Hopkins, Gerard Manley, *Correspondence*, ed. R. K. R. Thornton and Catherine Phillips, 2 vols, Collected Works of Gerard Manley Hopkins I–II (Oxford: Oxford University Press, 2013).

Hopkins, Gerard Manley, *Diaries, Journals, and Notebooks*, ed. Lesley Higgins, Collected Works of Gerard Manley Hopkins III (Oxford: Oxford University Press, 2015).

Horgan, D. M., 'Popular Protest in the Eighteenth Century: John Collier (Tim Bobbin), 1708–1786', *Review of English Studies* New Series 48 (1997), 310–31.

Horobin, Simon, 'J. R. R. Tolkien as a Philologist: A Reconsideration of the Northernisms in Chaucer's *Reeve's Tale*', *English Studies* 82 (2001), 97–105.

Horobin, Simon, *Does Spelling Matter?* (Oxford: Oxford University Press, 2013).

Howatt, A. P. R., and H. G. Widdowson, *A History of English Language Teaching*, 2nd ed. (Oxford: Oxford University Press, 2004).

Hudson, Derek, *Munby: Man of Two Worlds. The Life and Diaries of Arthur J. Munby 1828–1910* (London: Murray, 1972).

Huk, David, *Ben Brierley 1825–1896* (Manchester: Richardson, 1995).

Hultin, Neil C., '"To Shine with Borrowed Splendour": J. O. Halliwell-Phillipps, Thomas Wright, and Victorian Lexicography', *Dictionaries* 16 (1995), 109–50.

Hunter, Fred, 'Morley, Henry (1822–1894)', in *Oxford Dictionary of National Biography* [www.oxforddnb].

Hunter, Joseph, *The Hallamshire Glossary* (London: Pickering, 1829).

Ingham, Patricia, 'Dialect in the Novels of Hardy and George Eliot', in George Watson (ed.), *Literary English Since Shakespeare* (Oxford: Oxford University Press, 1970), pp. 347–63.

Ingham, Patricia, 'Thomas Hardy and the Dorset Dialect', in E. G. Stanley and Douglas Gray (eds), *Five Hundred Years of Words and Sounds: A Festschrift for Eric Dobson* (Woodbridge: Boydell and Brewer, 1983), pp. 84–91.

Ingham, Patricia, 'Dialect as 'Realism': *Hard Times* and the Industrial Novel', *Review of English Studies* New Series 37 (1986), 518–27.

Ingham, Patricia, 'The Language of Dickens', in David Paroissien (ed.), *A Companion to Charles Dickens* (Oxford: Oxford University Press, 2008), pp. 126–41.

Irace, Kathleen, 'Mak's Sothren Tothe: A Philological and Critical Study of the Dialect Joke in the *Second Shepherd's Play*', *Comitatus: A Journal of Medieval and Renaissance Studies* 21 (1990), 38–51.

Jackson, Georgina F., *Shropshire Word-Book: A Glossary of Archaic and Provincial Words, Etc, Used in the County* (London: Trübner, 1879).

Jacobs, Willis D., *William Barnes, Linguist* (Albuquerque: University of New Mexico Press, 1952).

Jedrzejewski, Jan, 'Folklore', in Norman Page (ed.), *Oxford Reader's Companion to Hardy* (Oxford: Oxford University Press, 2000), pp. 142–5.

Johnston, Judith, *George Eliot and the Discourses of Medievalism*, Making the Middle Ages 6 (Turnhout: Brepols, 2006).

Jones, Bernard, 'William Barnes, the Philological Society up to 1873 and the New English Dictionary', in Juhani Klemola, Merja Kytö, and Matti Rissanen (eds), *Speech Past and Present: Studies in English Dialectology in Memory of Ossi Ihalainen* (Frankfurt am Main: Lang, 1996), pp. 80–100.

Jones, Bernard, *William Barnes: The Philological Society and the English Dialect Society* (Gillingham: Meldon House, 2010).

Jones, Chris, *Fossil Poetry: Anglo-Saxon and Linguistic Nativism in Nineteenth-Century Poetry* (Oxford: Oxford University Press, 2018).

Joseph, John E., *Saussure* (Oxford: Oxford University Press, 2012).

Joyce, Patrick, *Visions of the People: Industrial England and the Question of Class 1848–1914* (Cambridge: Cambridge University Press, 1991).

Joyce, Patrick, 'The People's English: Language and Class in England c. 1840–1920', in Peter Burke and Roy Porter (eds), *Language, Self, and Society: A Social History of Language* (Cambridge: Polity Press, 1991), pp. 154–90.

Joyce, Patrick, *Democratic Subjects: The Self and the Social in Nineteenth-Century England* (Cambridge: Cambridge University Press, 1994).

Kathman, David, 'Shakespeare and Warwickshire', in Paul Edmondson and Stanley Wells (eds), *Shakespeare Beyond Doubt: Evidence, Argument, Controversy* (Cambridge: Cambridge University Press, 2013), pp. 121–32.

Keith, W. J., 'Thomas Hardy's Edition of William Barnes', *Victorian Poetry* 15 (1977), 121–31.

Kellett, Arnold, 'Wright, Joseph (1855–1930)', in *Oxford Dictionary of National Biography* [www.oxforddnb].

Kellett, Arnold, and Ian Dewhirst (eds), *A Century of Yorkshire Dialect: Selections from the Transactions of the Yorkshire Dialect Society* (Otley: Smith Settle, 1997).

Kelly, J., 'The 1847 Alphabet: An Episode of Phonotypy', in R. E. Asher and Eugénie J. A. Henderson (eds), *Towards a History of Phonetics* (Edinburgh: Edinburgh University Press, 1981), pp. 248–64.

Kemble, J. M., 'Surrey Provincialisms', *Transactions of the Philological Society* (1854), 83–4.

Kennett, White, *Etymological Collections of English Words and Provincial Expressions*, ed. Javier Ruano-García (Oxford: Oxford University Press, 2018).

Ker, W. P., *Collected Essays*, ed. Charles Whibley, 2 vols (London: Macmillan, 1925).

Kerswill, Paul, 'Dialect Formation and Dialect Change in the Industrial Revolution: British vernacular English in the nineteenth century', in Laura Wright (ed.), *Southern English Varieties Then and Now* (Berlin: De Gruyter, 2018), pp. 8–38.

Kidd, Alan J., and K. W. Roberts (eds), *City, Class and Culture: studies of social policy and cultural production in Victorian Manchester* (Manchester: Manchester University Press, 1985).

Kidd, Colin, *The World of Mr Casaubon: Britain's Wars of Mythography, 1700–1870* (Cambridge: Cambridge University Press, 2016).

Kingsley, Charles, *The Water-Babies*, ed. Robert Douglas-Fairhurst (Oxford: Oxford University Press, 2013).

Klemola, Juhani, 'The Origins of the Northern Subject Rule: A Case of Early Contact?', in Hildegard L. C. Tristram (ed.), *The Celtic Englishes II* (Heidelberg: Winter, 2000), pp. 329–46.

Kretzschmar, William A., Jr, 'Dialectology and the History of the English Language', in Donka Minkova and Robert Stockwell (eds), *Studies in the History of the English Language: A Millennial Perspective*, Topics in English Linguistics 39 (Berlin: De Gruyter, 2002), pp. 79–108.

Kretzschmar, William A., Jr, 'Linguistic Atlases', in Charles Boberg, John Nerbonne, and Dominic Watt (eds), *The Handbook of Dialectology* (Oxford: Wiley Blackwell, 2017), pp. 57–72.

304 Bibliography

Kumar, Krishan, *The Making of English National Identity* (Cambridge: Cambridge University Press, 2003).

Kuper, Adam, *The Invention of Primitive Society: Transformations of an Illusion* (London: Routledge, 1988).

Lapidge, Michael, 'Walter William Skeat, 1835–1912', in Michael Lapidge (ed.), *Interpreters of Early Medieval Britain* (London: British Academy, 2002), pp. 37–47.

Lapidge, Michael, 'Introduction: The Study of Anglo-Saxon, Norse and Celtic in Cambridge, 1878–1999', in Michael Lapidge (ed.), *H. M. Chadwick and the Study of Anglo-Saxon, Norse and Celtic in Cambridge* (Aberystwyth: Department of Welsh, Aberystwyth University, 2015), pp. 1–58.

Larrington, Carolyne, *The Land of the Green Man: A Journey through the Supernatural Landscapes of the British Isles* (London: Tauris, 2015).

Lawrence, D. H., *Sons and Lovers*, ed. David Trotter (Oxford: Oxford University Press, 1995).

Lawrie, Alexandra, *The Beginnings of University English: Extramural Study, 1885–1910* (London: Palgrave Macmillan, 2014).

Lear, Linda, *Beatrix Potter: A Life in Nature* (London: Penguin, 2007).

Lee, Sidney, 'Wise, John Richard de Capel (1831–1890)', rev. Giles Hudson, in *Oxford Dictionary of National Biography* [www.oxforddnb].

Le Quesne, A. L., 'Kilvert, (Robert) Francis (1840–1879), rev. Brenda Colloms, in *Oxford Dictionary of National Biography* [www.oxforddnb].

Levine, Philippa, *The Amateur and the Professional: Antiquarians, Historian and Archaeologists in Victorian England, 1838–1886* (Cambridge: Cambridge University Press, 1986).

[Lewis, George Cornewall], *A Glossary of Provincial Words used in Herefordshire and some of the Adjoining Counties* (London: Murray, 1839).

Local, John K., 'Making a Transcription: the evolution of A. J. Ellis's Palaeotype', *Journal of the International Phonetic Association* 13.1 (1983), 2–12.

Loriaux, Emilie, 'From 'Zome Other Geäme' to 'Another Joy' in William Barnes's Poetry: Composing, Translating and/or Rewriting', *The Hardy Society Journal* 10 (2014), 61–71.

Loriaux, Emilie, 'Thomas Hardy's Use of the Dorset Dialect: 'A Memory of William Barnes'', *The Thomas Hardy Journal* 32 (2016), 104–12.

Lowenthal, David, *George Perkins Marsh: Prophet of Conservation* (Seattle: University of Washington Press, 2003).

McCauley, Larry, '"Eawr Folk": Language, Class, and English Identity in Victorian Dialect Poetry', *Victorian Poetry* 39 (2001), 287–300.

McDonagh, Josephine, 'Rethinking Provincialism in Mid-Nineteenth-Century Fiction: *Our Village* to *Villette*', *Victorian Studies* 55 (2013), 399–424.

Macfarlane, Robert, *Landmarks* (London: Hamilton, 2015).

Machan, Tim William, *Northern Memories and the English Middle Ages*, Manchester Medieval Literature and Culture 34 (Manchester: Manchester University Press, 2020).

MacMahon, Michael K. C., 'Thomas Hallam and the Study of Dialect and Educated Speech', *Transactions of the Yorkshire Dialect Society* 83 (1983), 19–31.

MacMahon, Michael K. C., 'James Murray and the Phonetic Notation in the *New English Dictionary*', *Transactions of the Philological Society* (1985), 72–112.

MacMahon, Michael K. C., 'Palaeozoic and Palaeotype: A Note on John George Goodchild (1844–1906)', *The Henry Sweet Society Newsletter* 10 (1988), 7–9.

MacMahon, Michael K. C., 'Henry Sweet (1845–1912)', in Helen Damico (ed.), *Medieval Scholarship: Biographical Studies on the Formation of a Discipline. Volume 2: Literature and Philology* (New York: Garland, 1998), pp. 167–75.

MacMahon, Michael K. C., 'Phonology', in Suzanne Romaine (ed.), *The Cambridge History of the English Language: Volume IV, 1776–1997* (Cambridge: Cambridge University Press, 1999), pp. 373–535.

MacMahon, Michael K. C., 'Pronunciation in the *OED*', in Lynda Mugglestone (ed.), *Lexicography and the OED: Pioneers in the Untrodden Forest* (Oxford: Oxford University Press, 2000), pp. 172–88.

MacMahon, Michael K. C., 'Ellis [*formerly* Sharpe], Alexander John (1814–1890), in *Oxford Dictionary of National Biography* [www.oxforddnb].

MacMahon, Michael K. C., 'Sweet, Henry (1845–1912)', in *Oxford Dictionary of National Biography* [www.oxforddnb].

McMorris, Jenny, 'Appendix I: *OED* Sections and Parts', in Lynda Mugglestone (ed.), *Lexicography and the OED: Pioneers in the Untrodden Forest* (Oxford: Oxford University Press, 2000), pp. 228–31.

McNeil, W. K., 'The Function of Legend, Belief and Custom in *Precious Bane*', *Folklore* 82 (1971), 132–46.

Maguire, Warren, 'Mapping *The Existing Phonology of English Dialects*', *Dialectologia et Geolinguistica* 20 (2012), 84–107.

Maguire, Warren, 'Phonological Analysis of Early-Nineteenth-Century Tyneside Dialect Literature: Thomas Wilson's *The Pitman's Pay*', in Patrick Honeybone and Warren Maguire (eds), *Dialect Writing and the North of England* (Edinburgh: Edinburgh University Press, 2020), pp. 243–65.

Maguire, Warren, '"Mr A. J. Ellis – the pioneer of scientific phonetics in England" (Sweet 1877, vii): an examination of Ellis's data from the northeast of England' [http://www.lel.ed.ac.uk/EllisAtlas/Maguire2003.pdf].

Maguire, Warren, 'An Atlas of Alexander J. Ellis's *The Existing Phonology of English Dialects*' [http://www.lel.ed.ac.uk/EllisAtlas/].

Mandelbrote, Scott, 'Ray [*formerly* Wray], John (1627–1705)', in *Oxford Dictionary of National Biography* [www.oxforddnb].

Mandler, Peter, 'Looking Around the World', in Adelene Buckland and Sadiah Qureshi (eds), *Time Travelers: Victorian Encounters with Time and History* (Chicago: University of Chicago Press, 2020), pp. 24–41.

Manias, Chris, *Race, Science, and the Nation: Reconstructing the Ancient Past in Britain, France, and Germany* (London: Routledge, 2013).

Markus, Manfred, 'Joseph Wright's *English Dialect Dictionary* and Its Sources', in Ingrid Tieken-Boon van Ostade and Wim van der Wurff (eds), *Current Issues in Late Modern English* (Bern: Lang, 2009), pp. 263–82.

Markus, Manfred, 'As drunk as muck. The Role and Logic of Similes in English Dialects on the Basis of Joseph Wright's *English Dialect Dictionary*', *Studia Neophilologica* 82 (2010), 203–16.

Markus, Manfred, 'The Complexity and Diversity of the Words in Wright's *English Dialect Dictionary*', in Manfred Markus et al (eds), *Middle and Modern English Corpus Linguistics: A Multi-Dimensional Approach* (Amsterdam: Benjamins, 2012), pp. 209–24.

Markus, Manfred, 'The Survival of Shakespeare's Language in English Dialects (on the Basis of *EDD Online*)', *English Studies* 98 (2017), 881–96.

Markus, Manfred, 'The Supplement to the *English Dialect Dictionary*: Its Structure and Value as Part of *EDD Online*', *International Journal of Lexicography* 32 (2019), 58–67.

Markus, Manfred, 'What Did Joseph Wright Mean by *Meaning*? The Complexity of Lexical Semantics in the *English Dialect Dictionary Online*', *International Journal of English Studies* 20 (2020), 1–25.

Markus, Manfred, *English Dialect Dictionary Online: A New Departure in English Dialectology* (Cambridge: Cambridge University Press, 2021).

Markus, Manfred, and Reinhard Heuberger, 'The Architecture of Joseph Wright's *English Dialect Dictionary*: Preparing the Computerised Version', *International Journal of Lexicography* 20 (2007), 355–68.

306 Bibliography

Markus, Manfred, Clive Upton, and Reinhard Heuberger (eds), *Joseph Wright's English Dialect Dictionary and Beyond: Studies in Late Modern English Dialectology* (Frankfurt am Main: Lang, 2010).

Marshall, William, 'An Eisteddfod for Yorkshire? Professor Moorman and the Uses of Dialect', *Yorkshire Archaeological Journal* 83 (2011), 199–217.

Martin, Carol A., 'Rural Life', in Margaret Harris (ed.), *George Eliot in Context* (Cambridge: Cambridge University Press, 2013), pp. 256–63.

Matthews, David, *The Making of Middle English, 1765–1910* (Minneapolis: University of Minnesota Press, 1999).

Matthews, David, *Medievalism: A Critical History* (Cambridge: Brewer, 2015).

Matthews, Stephen, *Josiah Relph of Sebergham: England's First Dialect Poet* (Carlisle: Bookcase, 2015).

Maw, Martin, 'Frowde, Henry (1841–1927)', in *Oxford Dictionary of National Biography* [www.oxforddnb].

Maw, Martin, 'Hart, Horace Henry (1840–1916)' in *Oxford Dictionary of National Biography* [www.oxforddnb].

Mayberry, T. W., 'Elworthy, Frederic Thomas (1830–1907)', in *Oxford Dictionary of National Biography* [www.oxforddnb].

Mayhew, A. L., 'Some Slang Expressions Illustrated from the Icelandic', *Notes and Queries* 5th Series 4 (11 September 1875), 206.

Mayhew, A. L., 'Some Radnorshire Words', *Notes and Queries* 5th Series 10 (10 August 1878), 105.

Mayhew, A. L., 'Wanted – an English Dialect Dictionary', *Notes and Queries* 5th Series 11 (29 March 1879), 260.

Mayhew, A. L., 'Notes on Mr A. S. Palmer's 'Folk-Etymology'', *Notes and Queries* 7th Series 3 (23 April 1887), 322–3.

Mayhew, A. L., '"Tallet", a West-Country Word', *Notes and Queries* 8th Series 4 (2 December 1893), 450–1.

Melchers, Gunnel, 'Mrs Gaskell and Dialect', in Mats Rydén and Lennart A. Björk (eds), *Studies in English Philology, Linguistics and Literature, Presented to Alarik Rynell 7 March 1978*, Stockholm Studies in English 46 (Stockholm: Almqvist & Wiksell, 1978), pp. 112–24.

Melchers, Gunnel, ''An' I 'oäps as 'e beänt boöklarn'd: but 'e dosn' not coom fro' the shere: Alfred Tennyson's dialect poetry and insider/outsider readers and writers', in Jane Hodson (ed.), *Dialect and Literature in the Long Nineteenth Century* (Abingdon: Routledge, 2017), pp. 51–64.

Metcalfe, John, 'Sol: A Farce in the Baildon Dialect', *Transactions of the Yorkshire Dialect Society* 6 (1904), 31–43.

Millar, A. H., 'Neaves, Charles, Lord Neaves (1800–1876)', rev. Robert Shiels, in *Oxford Dictionary of National Biography* [www.oxforddnb].

Miller, Stephen, 'The Lost Publications of the Folk-Lore Society', *Folklore* 124 (2013), 226–35.

Miller, Stephen, 'The County Folk-Lore Series (Volumes 1–7) of the Folk-Lore Society', *Folklore* 124 (2013), 327–44.

Millgate, Michael, *Thomas Hardy: His Career as a Novelist* (New York: Random House, 1971).

Millgate, Michael (ed.), *Thomas Hardy's Public Voice: The Essays, Speeches, and Miscellaneous Prose* (Oxford: Clarendon Press, 2001).

Millgate, Michael, *Thomas Hardy: A Biography Revisited* (Oxford: Oxford University Press, 2004).

Milner, George, 'Introductory Essay, On the Dialect of Lancashire Considered as a Vehicle for Poetry', in Edwin Waugh, *Poems and Songs*, ed. George Milner (Manchester: Heywood, no date of publication).

Milnes, Kenneth, 'Trench, Richard Chevenix (1807–1886)', in *Oxford Dictionary of National Biography* [www.oxforddnb].

Milroy, James, *The Language of Gerard Manley Hopkins* (London: Deutsch, 1977).

Mitchell, Charlotte, 'Blackmore, Richard Doddridge (1825–1900)', in *Oxford Dictionary of National Biography* [www.oxforddnb].

Momma, Haruko, *From Philology to English Studies: Language and Culture in the Nineteenth Century* (Cambridge: Cambridge University Press, 2012).

Momma, Haruko, 'The Newly-Found Kemble Notebook and an Old English *Hildebrandslied*: A Mirror of the New Philology in the 1830s', *Poetica* 86 (2016), 87–106.

Montgomery, Chris, and Emma Moore (eds), *Language and a Sense of Place: Studies in Language and Region* (Cambridge: Cambridge University Press, 2017).

Moorman, F. W., *Plays of the Ridings* (London: Elkin Mathews, 1919).

Morpurgo Davies, Anna, 'Karl Brugmann and Late Nineteenth-Century Linguistics', in Theodora Bynon and F. R. Palmer (eds), *Studies in the History of Western Linguistics, in Honour of R. H. Robins* (Cambridge: Cambridge University Press, 1986), pp. 150–71.

Morpurgo Davies, Anna, *Nineteenth-Century Linguistics*, History of Linguistics IV (London: Longman, 1998).

Morris, Richard, 'Fifth Annual Address of the President to the Philological Society, Delivered at the Anniversary Meeting, Friday, the 19th of May, 1876', *Transactions of the Philological Society* (1876), 273–397.

Morris, Richard, *On the Survival of Early English Words in Our Dialects*, English Dialect Society 11 (London: English Dialect Society, 1876).

Moult, Thomas, *Mary Webb: Her Life and Work* (London: Cape, 1932).

Mugglestone, Lynda, 'A. J. Ellis, 'Standard English' and the Prescriptive Tradition', *Review of English Studies* New Series 39 (1988), 87–92.

Mugglestone, Lynda, 'Alexander Ellis and the virtues of doubt', in M. J. Toswell and E. M. Tyler (eds), *Studies in English Language and Literature: 'Doubt Wisely': Papers in Honour of E. G. Stanley* (London: Routledge, 1996), pp. 85–98.

Mugglestone, Lynda, 'John Walker and Alexander Ellis: Antedating *RP*', *Notes and Queries* 44 (1997), 103–7.

Mugglestone, Lynda (ed.), *Lexicography and the OED: Pioneers in the Untrodden Forest* (Oxford: Oxford University Press, 2000).

Mugglestone, Lynda, *Lost for Words: The Hidden History of the Oxford English Dictionary* (New Haven: Yale University Press, 2005).

Mugglestone, Lynda, *'Talking Proper': The Rise of Accent as Social Symbol*, 2nd ed. (Oxford: Oxford University Press, 2007).

Mugglestone, Lynda, *Dictionaries: A Very Short Introduction* (Oxford: Oxford University Press, 2011)

Mugglestone, Lynda (ed.), *The Oxford History of English*, rev. ed. (Oxford: Oxford University Press, 2012).

Mugglestone, Lynda, 'Nodal, John Howard (1831–1909)', in *Oxford Dictionary of National Biography* [www.oxforddnb].

Müller, F. Max, *Lectures on the Science of Language* (London: Longmans, Green and Co., 1861).

Müller, F. Max, *Lectures on the Science of Language: Second Series* (London: Longmans, Green, and Co., 1864).

Munby, Arthur, *Ann Morgan's Love: A Pedestrian Poem* (London: Reeves and Turner, 1896).

Munro, John James (ed.), *Frederick James Furnivall: A Volume of Personal Record* (Oxford: Oxford University Press, 1911).

Murray, James A. H., *The Dialects of the Southern Counties of Scotland: Its Pronunciation, Grammar, and Historical Relations* (London: Philological Society, 1873).

Murray, James A. H., 'General Explanations', in James A. H. Murray (ed.), *A New English Dictionary on Historical Principles: Part 1: A–Ant* (Oxford: Clarendon Press, 1884), pp. xvii–xxiv.

308 Bibliography

Murray, K. M. Elisabeth, *Caught in the Web of Words: James A. H. Murray and the Oxford English Dictionary* (New Haven: Yale University Press, 1977).

Nares, Robert, *A Glossary; or, Collection of Words, Phrases, Names, and Allusions to Customs, Proverbs, Etc, which have been thought to require illustration, in the works of English authors, particularly Shakespeare and his contemporaries*, new ed., rev. James O. Halliwell and Thomas Wright, 2 vols (London: Smith, 1859).

Neaves, Charles, *A Glance at Some of the Principles of Comparative Philology as Illustrated by the Latin and Anglian Forms of Speech* (Edinburgh: Blackwood and Sons, 1870).

[Neaves, Charles], *Songs and Verses, Social and Scientific*, 4th ed. (Edinburgh: Blackwood and Sons, 1875).

Nesbit, E., *In Homespun* (London: Lane, 1896).

Nicholson, Albert, 'Gibson, Alexander Craig (1813–1874)', rev. Angus J. L. Winchester, in *Oxford Dictionary of National Biography* [www.oxforddnb].

Nicholson, Norman, *The Lakes* (London: Hale, 1977).

Niles, John D., *The Idea of Anglo-Saxon England 1066–1901: Remembering, Forgetting, Deciphering, and Renewing the Past* (Chichester: Wiley Blackwell, 2015).

Nodal, John H., and George Milner, *A Glossary of the Lancashire Dialect* (Manchester: Manchester Literary Club, 1875–82).

Northall, G. F., *A Warwickshire Word-Book, Comprising Obsolescent and Dialect Words, Colloquialisms, Etc., Gathered from Oral Relation, and Collated with Accordant Works*, English Dialect Society 79 (London: English Dialect Society, 1896).

O'Donoghue, Heather, *Old Norse-Icelandic Literature: A Short Introduction* (Oxford: Blackwell, 2004).

Ogilvie, Sarah, 'A Nineteenth-Century Garment Throughout: Description, Collaboration, and Thorough Coverage in the *Oxford English Dictionary* (1884–1928)', in Sarah Ogilvie and Gabriella Safran (eds), *The Whole World in a Book: Dictionaries in the Nineteenth Century* (Oxford: Oxford University Press, 2020), pp. 54–72.

Ogilvie, Sarah, *The Dictionary People: the unsung heroes who created the Oxford English Dictionary* (London: Chatto and Windus, 2023).

Olender, Maurice, *The Languages of Paradise: Race, Religion and Philology in the Nineteenth Century*, trans. Arthur Goldhammer (Cambridge, MA: Harvard University Press, 1992).

Onions, C. T., *A Shakespeare Glossary* (Oxford: Clarendon Press, 1911).

Onysko, Alexander, 'Phrases, Combinations and Compounds in the *English Dialect Dictionary* as a Source of Conceptual Metaphors and Metonymies in Late Modern English Dialects', in Manfred Markus, Clive Upton, and Reinhard Heuberger (eds), *Joseph Wright's English Dialect Dictionary and Beyond: Studies in Late Modern English Dialectology* (Frankfurt am Main: Lang, 2010), pp. 131–53.

Orel, Harold (ed.), *Thomas Hardy's Personal Writings: Prefaces, Literary Opinions, Reminiscences* (Lawrence: University of Kansas Press, 1966).

Orton, Harold, et al, *Survey of English Dialects*, 13 vols (Leeds: Arnold and Son, 1962–71).

Orton, Harold, and Nathalia Wright, *A Word Geography of England* (London: Seminar Press, 1974).

Orton, Harold, Stewart Sanderson, and John Widdowson (eds), *The Linguistic Atlas of England* (London: Croom Helm, 1978).

Pacey, Robert (ed.), *'Yours Sincerely Mabel Peacock': Fragments of a Lincolnshire Friendship. Letters from Mabel Peacock to John Ostler Nicholson written between 1893 and 1915*, rev. ed. (Burgh le Marsh: Old Chapel Lane Books, 2001).

Page, Norman, 'Hardy and the English Language', in Norman Page (ed.), *Thomas Hardy: The Writer and his Background* (London: Routledge and Kegan Paul, 1980), pp. 151–72.

Page, Norman, *Speech in the English Novel*, 2nd ed. (London: Palgrave Macmillan, 1988).

Palmer, A. Smythe, [no title], *Notes and Queries* 7th Series 3 (7 May 1887), 365.

Palmer, A. Smythe, 'The 'English Dialect Dictionary'', *Notes and Queries* 7th Series 8 (9 November 1889), 363–4.

Palmer, D. J., *The Rise of English Studies: An Account of the Study of English Language and Literature from its Origins to the Making of the Oxford English School* (Oxford: Oxford University Press, 1965).

Parker, Angelina, 'Supplement to the Glossary of Words Used in Oxfordshire', in Walter W. Skeat (ed.), *Original Glossaries*, English Dialect Society 32 (London: English Dialect Society, 1881), pp. 65–104.

Parker, Angelina, 'Oxfordshire Village Folklore (1840–1900)', *Folklore* 24 (1913), 74–91.

Patterson, William Hugh, *A Glossary of Words in Use in the Counties of Antrim and Down*, English Dialect Society 28 (London: English Dialect Society, 1880).

Payne, Joseph, 'Provincial Glossary', *Notes and Queries*, 9 April 1870, 362–3.

Peacock, Edward, *Glossary of Words Used in the Wapentakes of Manley and Corringham, Lincolnshire*, English Dialect Society 15 (London: English Dialect Society, 1877).

Peacock, Edward, *A Glossary of Words Used in the Wapentakes of Manley and Corringham, Lincolnshire*, 2nd ed., English Dialect Society 58, 59 (London: English Dialect Society, 1889).

Peacock, Robert Backhouse, 'On Some Leading Characteristics of Northumbrian; and on the Variations in its Grammar from that of Standard English, with their Probable Etymological Sources', *Transactions of the Philological Society* (1862–3), 232–63.

Pearsall, Derek, 'Frederick James Furnivall (1825–1910)', in Helen Damico (ed.), *Medieval Scholarship: Biographical Studies on the Formation of a Discipline. Volume 2: Literature and Philology* (New York: Garland, 1998), pp. 125–38.

Penhallurick, Robert, 'On Dialectology', in Robert Penhallurick (ed.), *Debating Dialect: Essays on the Philosophy of Dialect Study* (Cardiff: University of Wales Press, 2000), pp. 116–24.

Penhallurick, Robert, 'Dialect Dictionaries', in A. P. Cowie (ed.), *The Oxford History of English Lexicography*, 2 vols (Oxford: Oxford University Press, 2008), II, 290–313.

Penhallurick, Robert, *Studying Dialect* (London: Bloomsbury, 2018).

Periyan, Natasha, '"Altering the structure of society": an institutional focus on Virginia Woolf and working-class education in the 1930s', *Textual Practice* 32 (2018), 1301–23.

Peterson, William S., 'Furnivall, Frederick James (1825-1910)', in *Oxford Dictionary of National Biography* [www.oxforddnb].

Petyt, K. M., *Emily Bronte and the Haworth Dialect: A Study of the Dialect Speech in 'Wuthering Heights'* (Keighley: Yorkshire Dialect Society, 1970).

Petyt, K. M., *The Study of Dialect: An Introduction to Dialectology* (London: Deutsch, 1980).

Petyt, K. M., 'A survey of dialect studies in the area of Sedbergh & District History Society'; [http://centre-for-english-traditional-heritage.org/TraditionToday6/TT6_Petyt_Dialects.pdf].

Phillipps, K. C., *Language and Class in Victorian England* (Oxford: Blackwell, 1984).

Plomer, William (ed.), *Kilvert's Diary: Selections from the Diary of the Rev. Francis Kilvert*, 3 vols, rev. ed. (London: Cape, 1969).

Plotkin, Cary H., *The Tenth Muse: Victorian Philology and the Genesis of the Poetic Language of Gerard Manley Hopkins* (Carbondale: Southern Illinois University Press, 1989).

Plotz, John, 'The Provincial Novel', in Stephen Arata et al (eds), *A Companion to the English Novel* (Oxford: Wiley Blackwell, 2015), pp. 360–72.

Poetry of the Lancashire Cotton Famine: http://cottonfaminepoetry.exeter.ac.uk/

Posner, Rebecca, 'Sir George Cornewall Lewis: statesman and 'new philologist'', *Historiographia Linguistica* 17 (1990), 339–56.

Poussa, Patricia, 'Ellis's "Land of *Wee*": A Historico-Structural Re-evaluation', *Neuphilologische Mitteilungen* 96 (1995), 295–307.

310 Bibliography

Poussa, Patricia, 'Dickens as Sociolinguist: Dialect in *David Copperfield*', in Irma Taavitsainen, Gunnel Melchers, and Päivi Pahta (eds), *Writing in Nonstandard English* (Amsterdam: Benjamins, 1999), pp. 27–44.

Power, D'A., 'Blandford, George Fielding (1829–1911)', rev. Nick Hervey, in *Oxford Dictionary of National Biography* [www.oxforddnb].

[Powley, Mary], 'The Heaf', *Notes and Queries* 4th Series 10 (14 September 1872), 201–3, 4th Series 11 (11 January 1873), 38–40, and 4th Series 11 (18 January 1873), 57–8.

Powley, Mary, *Echoes of Old Cumberland* (London: Bemrose and Sons, 1875).

Preest, David (trans.), *William of Malmesbury: The Deeds of the Bishops of England (Gesta Pontificum Anglorum)* (Woodbridge: Boydell, 2002).

Proposal for the Publication of a New English Dictionary by the Philological Society (London: Trübner, 1859).

Pulman, G. P. R., *Rustic Sketches; being Rhymes on Angling and Other Subjects Illustrative of Rural Life, &c, in the Dialect of the West of England; with Notes and a Glossary* (London: Bell, 1853).

Radford, Andrew, 'Folklore and Anthropology', in Phillip Mallett (ed.), *Thomas Hardy in Context* (Cambridge: Cambridge University Press, 2013), pp. 210–20.

Raines, Melissa, 'Language', in Margaret Harris (ed.), *George Eliot in Context* (Cambridge: Cambridge University Press, 2013), pp. 176–82.

Ray, John, *A Collection of English Words* (London: Bruges, 1674).

Readman, Paul, 'The Place of the Past in English Culture c.1890–1914', *Past and Present* 186 (2005), 147–99.

Readman, Paul, *Storied Ground: Landscape and the Shaping of English National Identity* (Cambridge: Cambridge University Press, 2018).

Rennie, Simon, "This 'Merikay War': Poetic Responses in Lancashire to the American Civil War', *Journal of Victorian Culture* 25 (2020), 126–43.

Rennie, Susan, *Jamieson's Dictionary of Scots: The Story of the First Historical Dictionary of the Scots Language* (Oxford: Oxford University Press, 2012).

Rennie, Susan, 'The First Scottish 'National' Dictionary: John Jamieson's Etymological Dictionary of the Scottish Language (1808/1825), in Sarah Ogilvie and Gabriella Safran (eds), *The Whole World in a Book: Dictionaries in the Nineteenth Century* (Oxford: Oxford University Press, 2020), pp. 110–30.

Roberts, D. S., 'Thomas De Quincey's 'Danish Origin of the Lake Country Dialect'', *Transactions of the Cumberland and Westmorland Antiquarian and Archaeological Society*, 2nd Series 99 (1999), 257–65.

Robins, Robert Henry, 'Against the Establishment: Sidelines on Henry Sweet', in Mark Janse (ed.), *Productivity and Creativity: Studies in General and Descriptive Linguistics in Honor of E. M. Uhlenbeck* (Berlin: De Gruyter, 1998), pp. 167–78.

Robinson, Amy J., 'The Victorian Provincial Novel', *Literature Compass* 12 (2015), 548–54.

Robinson, C. Clough, *A Glossary of Words Pertaining to the Dialect of Mid-Yorkshire*, English Dialect Society 14 (London: English Dialect Society, 1876).

Robinson, Eric, and David Powell (eds), *The Later Poems of John Clare 1837–1864*, 2 vols (Oxford: Clarendon Press, 1984).

[Robinson, F. K.], *A Glossary of Yorkshire Words and Phrases, Collected in Whitby and the Neighbourhood* (London: Smith, 1855).

Robinson, F. K., *A Glossary of Words Used in the Neighbourhood of Whitby*, English Dialect Society 9, 13 (London: English Dialect Society, 1875–6).

[Robinson, George], 'Inaugural Address', *Transactions of the Yorkshire Dialect Society* 1 (1898), 3–6.

Robinson, Jonnie, *A Thesaurus of English Dialect and Slang: England, Wales and the Channel Islands* (Cambridge: Cambridge University Press, 2021).

Romaine, Suzanne (ed.), *The Cambridge History of the English Language: Volume IV, 1776–1997* (Cambridge: Cambridge University Press, 1999).

Roper, Jonathan, 'Thoms and the Unachieved "Folk-Lore of England"', *Folklore* 118 (2007), 203–16.

Roper, Jonathan, '"Our National Folk-Lore": William Thoms as Cultural Nationalist', in Krishna Sen and Sudeshna Chakravarti (eds), *Narrating the (Trans) Nation: The Dialectics of Culture and Identity* (Kolkata: Dasgupta and Co., 2008), pp. 60–74.

Roper, Jonathan, 'English Purisms', *Victoriographies* 2 (2012), 44–59.

Roper, Jonathan, 'William Barnes and Frisian Forefathers', *Leeds Studies in English* 43 (2012), 9–20.

Roper, Jonathan, 'England – The Land Without Folklore?', in Timothy Baycroft and David Hopkin (eds), *Folklore and Nationalism in Europe During the Long Nineteenth Century* (Leiden: Brill, 2012), pp. 227–53.

Roper, Jonathan, 'The Clergyman and the Dialect Speaker: some Sussex examples of a nineteenth century research tradition', in Laura Wright (ed.), *Southern English Varieties Then and Now* (Berlin: De Gruyter, 2018), pp. 110–31.

Roper, Jonathan, 'Folklore in the Glossaries of the English Dialect Society', in Jonathan Roper (ed.), *Dictionaries as Sources of Folklore Data*, Folklore Fellows' Communications 321 (Helsinki: Suomalainen Tiedeakatemia, 2020), pp. 189–208.

Ross, Frederick, Richard Stead, and Thomas Holderness, *A Glossary of Words Used in Holderness in the East-Riding of Yorkshire*, English Dialect Society 16 (London: English Dialect Society, 1877).

Roud, Steve, *Folk Song in England* (London: Faber and Faber, 2017).

The Royal Horticultural Society: https://www.rhs.org.uk

Ruano-García, Javier, 'Late Modern Lancashire English in lexicographical context: representations of Lancashire speech and the *English Dialect Dictionary*', *English Today* 28.4 (2012), 60–8.

Ruano-García, Javier, 'Towards an Understanding of Joseph Wright's Sources: White Kennett's *Parochial Antiquities* (1695) and the *English Dialect Dictionary*', in Manfred Markus et al (eds), *Middle and Modern English Corpus Linguistics: A Multi-Dimensional Approach* (Amsterdam: Benjamins, 2012), pp. 241–56.

Ruano-García, Javier, 'Digging into the *English Dialect Dictionary*: The Contribution of MS Lansd. 1033', *International Journal of Lexicography* 26 (2013), 176–89.

Ruano-García, Javier, 'On the Colonial Element in Joseph Wright's *English Dialect Dictionary*', *International Journal of Lexicography* 32 (2019), 38–57.

Ruano-García, Javier, 'The Contribution of Angelina Parker to the *English Dialect Dictionary*', *Dictionaries* 41.2 (2020), 1–24.

Russell, Dave, *Looking North: Northern England and the National Imagination* (Manchester: Manchester University Press, 2004).

Russell, Lindsay Rose, *Women and Dictionary Making: Gender, Genre, and English Language Lexicography* (Cambridge: Cambridge University Press, 2018).

Salisbury, Jesse, *A Glossary of Words and Phrases used in S. E. Worcestershire* (London: Salisbury, 1893).

Salmon, Paul, 'Max Müller and the Origin of Language', in Vivien Law and Werner Hüllen (eds), *Linguists and Their Diversions: A Festschrift for R. H. Robins on His 75th Birthday* (Münster: Nodus, 1996), pp. 333–60.

Sanders, Robert Alan, 'Alexander John Ellis: A Study of a Victorian Philologist' (unpublished PhD, Memorial University, 1977).

Scott, Patrick Greig, '"Flowering in a Lonely Word": Tennyson and the Victorian Study of Language', *Victorian Poetry* 18 (1980), 371–81.

Scragg, Donald (ed.), *Textual and Material Culture in Anglo-Saxon England: Thomas Northcote Toller and the Toller Memorial Lectures* (Cambridge: Brewer, 2003).

312 Bibliography

Scragg, Donald, 'Toller, Thomas Northcote (1844–1930)', in *Oxford Dictionary of National Biography* [www.oxforddnb].

Scruton, William, 'Ben Preston', *Transactions of the Yorkshire Dialect Society* 4 (1902), 41–3.

Shaw, George Bernard, *Pygmalion: A Romance in Five Acts* (London: Penguin, 2000).

Sheils, William Joseph, 'Church, Community and Culture in Rural England, 1850–1900: J. C. Atkinson and the Parish of Danby in Cleveland', in Simon Ditchfield (ed.), *Christianity and Community in the West: Essays for John Bossy* (Aldershot: Ashgate, 2001), pp. 260–77.

Sheils, William Joseph, 'Nature and Modernity: J. C. Atkinson and Rural Ministry in England c. 1850–1900', in Peter Clarke and Tony Claydon (eds), *God's Bounty? The Churches and the Natural World* (Woodbridge: Boydell and Brewer, 2010), pp. 366–95.

Sheils, William Joseph, 'Atkinson, John Christopher (1814–1900)', in *Oxford Dictionary of National Biography* [www.oxforddnb].

Shepherd, Valerie, 'Anne Elizabeth Baker's *Glossary of Northamptonshire Words and Phrases* and John Clare's 'rustic idiom'', *John Clare Society Journal* 15 (1996), 69–75.

Sherbo, Arthur, 'Thoms, William John (1803–1885)', in *Oxford Dictionary of National Biography* [www.oxforddnb].

Shippey, Tom, 'Goths and Huns: the rediscovery of the Northern cultures in the nineteenth century', in Andreas Haarder et al (eds), *The Medieval Legacy: A Symposium* (Odense: Odense University Press, 1982), pp. 51–69.

Shippey, Tom, *The Road to Middle-earth*, rev. ed. (London: HarperCollins, 2005).

Shippey, Tom, 'A Revolution Reconsidered: Mythography and Mythology in the Nineteenth Century', in Tom Shippey (ed.), *The Shadow-Walkers: Jacob Grimm's Mythology of the Monstrous*, Medieval and Renaissance Texts and Studies 291 (Tempe: Arizona Center for Medieval and Renaissance Studies, 2005), pp. 1–28.

Shorrocks, Graham, 'English Dialects: A Translation of Joseph Wright's "Englische Mundarten"', *Transactions of the Yorkshire Dialect Society* 89 (1990), 10–19.

Shorrocks, Graham, 'A. J. Ellis as Dialectologist: A Reassessment', *Historiographia Linguistica* 18 (1991), 321–34.

Shorrocks, Graham, 'Non-Standard Dialect Literature and Popular Culture', in Juhani Klemola, Merja Kytö, and Matti Rissanen (eds), *Speech Past and Present: Studies in English Dialectology in Memory of Ossi Ihalainen* (Frankfurt am Main: Lang, 1996), pp. 385–411.

Simpson, Jacqueline, and Steve Roud, *A Dictionary of English Folklore* (Oxford: Oxford University Press, 2000).

Singleton, Antony, 'The Early English Text Society in the Nineteenth Century: An Organizational History', *Review of English Studies* New Series 56 (2005), 90–118.

Sisam, Kenneth, 'Skeat, Walter William (1835–1912)', rev. Charlotte Brewer, in *Oxford Dictionary of National Biography* [www.oxforddnb].

Sisson, C. J., 'Raymond Wilson Chambers, 1874–1942', in Michael Lapidge (ed.), *Interpreters of Early Medieval Britain* (London, 2002), pp. 221–33.

Skeat, Walter W., 'Provincial Glossary', *Notes and Queries*, 19 March 1870, 302–3.

Skeat, Walter W., 'English Dialects', *Notes and Queries*, 10 May 1873, 385–6.

Skeat, Walter W., 'English Dialect Society', *Notes and Queries* 17 May 1873, 406–7.

Skeat, Walter W., 'English Dialect Society', *Notes and Queries*, 1 November 1873, 341–2.

Skeat, Walter W., 'Preface', in Henry Sweet, *A History of English Sounds from the Earliest Period*, English Dialect Society 4 (London: English Dialect Society, 1874), pp. v–xi.

Skeat, Walter W. (ed.), *Reprinted Glossaries*, English Dialect Society 5 (London: English Dialect Society, 1874).

Skeat, Walter W., *A List of English Words the etymology of which is illustrated by comparison with Icelandic, prepared in the form of an appendix to Cleasby and Vigfússon's Icelandic-English Dictionary* (Oxford: Clarendon Press, 1876).

Skeat, Walter W. (ed.), *Original Glossaries*, English Dialect Society 12 (London: English Dialect Society, 1876).

Skeat, Walter W., 'An English Dialect Dictionary', *Notes and Queries* 5th Series 11 (31 May 1879), 421–2.

Skeat, Walter W., *An Etymological Dictionary of the English Language* (Oxford: Clarendon Press, 1882).

Skeat, Walter W., 'Report on the English Dialect Society', in Alexander J. Ellis, 'Eleventh Annual Address of the President to the Philological Society, Delivered at the Anniversary Meeting, Friday, 19th May, 1882', *Transactions of the Philological Society* 1–148 (1882–4), pp. 10–20.

Skeat, Walter W., 'The English Dialect Dictionary', *Notes and Queries* 7th Series 3 (7 May 1887), 365.

Skeat, Walter W. (ed.), *The Complete Works of Geoffrey Chaucer: Volume 5: Notes to the Canterbury Tales* (Oxford: Clarendon Press, 1894).

Skeat, Walter W., *A Student's Pastime* (Oxford: Clarendon Press, 1896).

Skeat, Walter W., 'The English Dialect Dictionary', *Notes and Queries* 10th Series 4 (11 November 1905), 381.

Skeat, Walter W., *English Dialects from the Eighth Century to the Present Day* (Cambridge: Cambridge University Press, 1912).

[Skeat, Walter W.], *English Dialect Society* (no place or date of publication).

[Skeat, Walter W.], *English Dialect Society: Rules and Directions for Word-Collectors* (no place or date of publication).

[Skeat, Walter W.], *The English Dialect Society's Last Notice* (no place or date of publication).

Skeat, Walter W., and Thomas Hallam (eds), *Two Collections of Derbicisms, Containing Words and Phrases in a Great Measure Peculiar to the Natives and Inhabitants of the County of Derby, by Samuel Pegge, A. M.*, English Dialect Society 78 (London: English Dialect Society, 1896).

Skeat, Walter W., and J. H. Nodal (eds), *A Bibliographical List of the Works that have been Published, or are Known to Exist in MS, Illustrative of the Various Dialects of English*, English Dialect Society 3, 8, 18 (London: English Dialect Society, 1873–7).

Smith, D. A., 'Lewis, Sir George Cornewall (1806–1863)', in *Oxford Dictionary of National Biography* [www.oxforddnb].

Smith, D. N., 'Wright, William Aldis (1831–1914)', rev. David McKitterick, in *Oxford Dictionary of National Biography* [www.oxforddnb].

Smith, Henry, and C. Roach Smith, 'A Glossary of Words in Use in the Isle of Wight', in Walter W. Skeat (ed.), *Original Glossaries*, English Dialect Society 32 (London: English Dialect Society, 1881), pp. 1–64.

Snell, K. D. M. (ed.), *The Regional Novel in Britain and Ireland, 1800–1990* (Cambridge: Cambridge University Press, 1998).

Snell, K. D. M., *The Bibliography of Regional Fiction in Britain and Ireland, 1800–2000* (Aldershot: Routledge, 2002).

Sorensen, Janet, *Strange Vernaculars: How Eighteenth-Century Slang, Cant, Provincial Languages, and Nautical Jargon Became English* (Princeton: Princeton University Press, 2017).

Spencer, Brian, 'Elizabeth Gaskell and the Dialect of Whitby', *Transactions of the Yorkshire Dialect Society* 20.101 (2001), 40–5.

Spencer, Helen, 'F. J. Furnivall's Six of the Best: The *Six-Text Canterbury Tales* and the Chaucer Society', *Review of English Studies* New Series 66 (2015), 601–23.

Spenser, Edmund, *Poetical Works*, ed. J. C. Smith and E. De Selincourt (Oxford: Oxford University Press, 1912).

Sperling, Matthew, 'Richard Chenevix Trench (1807–1886)', in Jay Parini (ed.), *British Writers XIX* (New York: Cengage Gale, 2013), pp. 317–34.

Sperling, Matthew, *Visionary Philology: Geoffrey Hill and the Study of Words* (Oxford: Oxford University Press, 2014).

Spevack, Marvin, *James Orchard Halliwell-Phillipps: The Life and Works of the Shakespearean Scholar and Bookman* (New Castle, DE: Oak Knoll, 2001).

314 Bibliography

Stainsby, Michael, *More than an Ordinary Man: Life and Society in the Upper Esk Valley, 1830–1910* (Helmsley: North York Moors National Park Authority, 2006).

Stamper, Paul, 'Baker, George (1781–1851)', in *Oxford Dictionary of National Biography* [www.oxforddnb].

Stanley, Liz, 'Munby, Arthur Joseph (1828–1910)', in *Oxford Dictionary of National Biography* [www.oxforddnb].

Stitt, Megan Perigoe, *Metaphors of Change in the Language of Nineteenth-Century Fiction: Scott, Gaskell, and Kingsley* (Oxford: Clarendon Press, 1998).

Stock, Jonathan P. J., 'Alexander J. Ellis and His Place in the History of Ethnomusicology', *Ethnomusicology* 51 (2007), 306–25.

Stocking, George W., Jr, *Victorian Anthropology* (New York: Free Press, 1987).

Streatfeild, G. S., *Lincolnshire and the Danes* (London: Kegan Paul, Trench, and Co., 1884).

Sutton, C. W., 'Brierley, Benjamin [Ben] (1825–1896)', in *Oxford Dictionary of National Biography* [www.oxforddnb].

Sutton, Edward, 'North Lincolnshire Words', in Walter W. Skeat (ed.), *Original Glossaries*, English Dialect Society 32 (London: English Dialect Society, 1881), pp. 113–22.

Swainson, Charles, *Provincial Names and Folk Lore of British Birds*, English Dialect Society 47 (London: English Dialect Society, 1885).

Swann, H. Kirke, *A Dictionary of English and Folk-Names of British Birds* (London: Witherby and Co., 1913).

Sweet, Henry, *A History of English Sounds from the Earliest Period*, English Dialect Society 4 (London: English Dialect Society, 1874).

Sweet, Henry, *Collected Papers*, ed. H. C. Wyld (Oxford: Clarendon Press, 1913),

Tate, Gregory, 'Thomas Hardy's Pure English', *Victorian Literature and Culture* 50 (2022), 521–47.

Taylor, Dennis, 'Victorian Philology and Victorian Poetry', *Victorian Newsletter* 53 (1978), 13–16.

Taylor, Dennis, *Hardy's Literary Language and Victorian Philology* (Oxford: Clarendon Press, 1993).

Taylor, Dennis, 'The Victorian Philological Contexts of Hardy's Poetry', in Phillip Mallett (ed.), *Thomas Hardy in Context* (Cambridge: Cambridge University Press, 2013), pp. 231–41.

The Teaching of English in England, being the Report of the Departmental Committee Appointed by the President of the Board of Education into the Position of English in the Educational System of England (London: His Majesty's Stationery Office, 1921).

Tennyson, Alfred, *Poems*, ed. Christopher Ricks, 3 vols, 2nd ed. (London: Longman, 1987).

Thompson, Ann, 'Joseph Wright's Slips', *Transactions of the Yorkshire Dialect Society* 108 (2008), 12–21.

Thompson, Michael Welman, 'Wright, Thomas (1810–1877)', in *Oxford Dictionary of National Biography* [www.oxforddnb].

Thompson, Pishey, *The History and Antiquities of Boston* (Boston: Noble, 1856).

[Thoms, William J.], 'Folk-Lore', *The Athenaeum* 22 (August 1846), 862–3.

Thorpe, Lewis (trans.), *Gerald of Wales: The Journey through Wales and The Description of Wales* (Harmondsworth: Penguin, 1978)

Tilling, Philip M., 'Local Dialect and the Poet: A Comparison of the Findings in the *Survey of English Dialects* with Dialect in Tennyson's Lincolnshire Poems', in Martyn F. Wakelin (ed.), *Patterns in the Folk Speech of the British Isles* (London: Athlone Press, 1972), pp. 88–108.

Toalster, J. P. C., 'Joseph Wright, PhD (Heidelberg)', *Transactions of the Yorkshire Dialect Society* 101 (2001), 47–9.

Tolkien, J. R. R., 'Philology: General Works', *The Year's Work in English Studies* 4 (1923), 20–37.

Tolkien, J. R. R., 'Chaucer as a Philologist', *Transactions of the Philological Society* (1934), 1–70.

Tolkien, J. R. R. *The Monsters and the Critics and Other Essays*, ed. Christopher Tolkien (London: Allen and Unwin, 1983).

Torr, Cecil, *Small Talk at Wreyland*, 3 vols (Cambridge: Cambridge University Press, 1918–23).

Toswell, M. J., 'Anna Gurney: The Unknown Victorian Medievalist', *Poetica* 86 (2016), 69–86.

Townend, Matthew, *The Vikings and Victorian Lakeland: the Norse medievalism of W. G. Collingwood and his contemporaries*, Cumberland and Westmorland Antiquarian and Archaeological Society Extra Series 34 (Kendal: Cumberland and Westmorland Antiquarian and Archaeological Society, 2009).

Townend, Matthew, 'The Vikings and the Victorians and Dialect', in Richard Dance, Sara Pons-Sanz, and Brittany Schorn (eds), *The Legacy of Medieval Scandinavian Encounters with England and the Insular World* (Turnhout: Brepols, forthcoming).

Trench, Richard Chenevix, *On Some Deficiencies in Our English Dictionaries* (London: Parker and Son, 1857).

Trench, Richard Chenevix, *On the Study of Words. English Past and Present*, Everyman's Library 788 (London: Dent, no date of publication).

Triggs, Tony D., 'Pitman, Sir Isaac (1813–1897)', in *Oxford Dictionary of National Biography* [www.oxforddnb].

Turley, Richard Marggraf, 'Tennyson and the Nineteenth-Century Language Debate', *Leeds Studies in English* New Series 28 (1997), 123–40.

Turner, James, *Philology: The Forgotten Origins of the Modern Humanities* (Princeton: Princeton University Press, 2014).

Tylor, Edward B., *Primitive Culture: Researches into the Development of Mythology, Philosophy, Religion, Language, Art, and Custom*, 4th ed., 2 vols (London: Murray, 1903).

Umbach, Maiken, 'Nation and Region: Regionalism in Modern European Nation-States', in Timothy Baycroft and Mark Hewitson (eds), *What is a Nation? Europe 1789–1914* (Oxford: Oxford University Press, 2006), pp. 63–80.

Upton, Clive, 'Modern Regional English in the British Isles', in Lynda Mugglestone (ed.), *The Oxford History of English*, rev. ed. (Oxford: Oxford University Press, 2012), pp. 379–414.

Upton, Clive, 'Regional and Dialect Dictionaries', in Philip Durkin (ed.), *The Oxford Handbook of Lexicography* (Oxford: Oxford University Press, 2015), pp. 381–92.

Upton, Clive, Stewart Sanderson, and John Widdowson, *Word Maps: A Dialect Atlas of England* (London: Croom Helm, 1987).

Upton, Clive, David Parry, and J. D. A. Widdowson, *Survey of English Dialects: The Dictionary and Grammar* (London: Routledge, 1994).

Utz, Richard, 'Enthusiast or Philologist? Professional Discourse and the Medievalism of Frederick James Furnivall', *Studies in Medievalism* 11 (2001), 189–212.

Van Arsdel, Rosemary T., 'Banks, Isabella Varley [*née* Isabella Varley; *known as* Mrs G. Linnaeus Banks] (1821–1897)', in *Oxford Dictionary of National Biography* [www.oxforddnb].

Van Keymeulen, Jacques, 'The Dialect Dictionary', in Charles Boberg, John Nerbonne, and Dominic Watt (eds), *The Handbook of Dialectology* (Oxford: Wiley Blackwell, 2017), pp. 39–56.

van Wyhe, John, 'The Descent of Words: Evolutionary Thinking 1780–1880', *Encounter* 29.3 (2005), 94–100.

Vaughan, C., 'Memoir', in F. W. Moorman, *Tales, Songs and Plays of the Ridings* (London: Elkin Mathews, 1921), pp. 7–20.

Vicinus, Martha, *The Industrial Muse: A Study of Nineteenth Century Working-Class Literature* (London: Croom Helm, 1974).

Vicinus, Martha, *The Ambiguities of Self-Help: Concerning the Life and Work of the Lancashire Dialect Writer Edwin Waugh* (Littleborough: Kelsall, 1983).

Vickery, A. Roy, 'James Britten: A Founder Member of the Folklore Society', *Folklore* 89 (1978), 71–4.

Viereck, Wolfgang, 'The English Dialect Society and its Dictionary', *Transactions of the Yorkshire Dialect Society* 70 (1970), 28–33.

316 Bibliography

Waddington-Feather, John, 'The Dialect of *Shirley*', *Brontë Studies* 27 (2002), 235–9.

Wagner, Susanne, 'Late Modern English: Dialects', in Alexander Bergs and Laurel J. Brinton (eds), *English Historical Linguistics: An International Handbook*, 2 vols (Berlin: De Gruyter, 2012), I, 915–38.

Waithe, Marcus, 'William Barnes: Views of Field Labour in Poems of Rural Life', in Matthew Bevis (ed.), *The Oxford Handbook of Victorian Poetry* (Oxford: Oxford University Press, 2013), pp. 460–74.

Wakelin, Martyn F., *English Dialects: An Introduction* (London: Athlone Press, 1972).

Wakelin, Martyn F., 'The Treatment of Dialect in English Dictionaries', in Robert Burchfield (ed.), *Studies in Lexicography* (Oxford: Clarendon Press, 1987), pp. 156–77.

Wales, Katie, *Northern English: A Cultural and Social History* (Cambridge: Cambridge University Press, 2006).

Wales, Katie, 'Dickens and Northern English: Stereotyping and "Authenticity" Re-considered', in Sylvie Hancil and Joan C. Beal (eds), *Perspectives on Northern Englishes*, Topics in English Linguistics 96 (Berlin: De Gruyter, 2017), pp. 41–60.

Wales, Katie, and Clive Upton, 'Celebrating Variation: Harold Orton and Dialectology, 1898–1998', *English Today* 56.4 (1998), 27–33.

Watson, Nicola J., *The Literary Tourist* (Basingstoke: Palgrave Macmillan, 2006).

Wawn, Andrew, 'George Stephens, Cheapinghaven and Old Northern Antiquity', *Studies in Medievalism* 7 (1995), 1–42.

Wawn, Andrew, *The Vikings and the Victorians: Inventing the Old North in Nineteenth-Century Britain* (Cambridge: Brewer, 2000).

Wawn, Andrew, 'The Grimms, the Kirk-Grims, and Sabine Baring-Gould', in Andrew Wawn (ed.), *Constructing Nations, Reconstructing Myth: Essays in Honour of T. A. Shippey*, Making the Middle Ages 9 (Turnhout: Brepols, 2007), pp. 215–42.

Wawn, Andrew, 'Sabine Baring-Gould and Iceland: A Re-evaluation', in Marie Wells (ed.), *The Discovery of Nineteenth-Century Scandinavia* (Norwich: Norvik Press, 2008), pp. 27–42.

Wawn, Andrew, 'Stephens, George (1813–1895)', in *Oxford Dictionary of National Biography* [www.oxforddnb].

Weaver, Sarah, 'Victorian Philology and the Metaphors of Language', *Literature Compass* 12 (2015), 333–43.

Weaver, Sarah, *Tennyson's Notebook Glossary and Rhyme Lists*, Tennyson Society Monographs 17 (Lincoln: Tennyson Society, 2019).

Waller, P. J., 'Democracy and Dialect, Speech and Class', in P. J. Waller (ed.), *Politics and Social Change in Modern Britain: Essays Presented to A. F. Thompson* (Brighton: Harvester Press, 1987), pp. 1–33.

Webb, Mary, *Precious Bane* (London: Virago, 1978).

Westwood, Jennifer, and Jacqueline Simpson, *The Lore of the Land: A Guide to England's Legends, from Spring-Heeled Jack to the Witches of Warboys* (London: Penguin, 2005).

Wetherall, David, 'The Growth of Archaeological Societies', in Vanessa Brand (ed.), *The Study of the Past in the Victorian Age* (Oxford: Oxbow, 1998), pp. 21–34.

White, Norman, 'G. M. Hopkins's Contribution to the *English Dialect Dictionary*', *English Studies* 68 (1987), 325–35.

White, Norman, *Hopkins: A Literary Biography* (Oxford: Oxford University Press, 1992).

White, Simon, and Owen Davies, 'Tradition and Rural Modernity in Mary Webb's Shropshire: *Precious Bane* in Context', *The Space Between: Literature and Culture, 1914–1945* 15 (2019) [www.spacebetweenjournal.org].

Wiley, Raymond A. (ed.), *John Mitchell Kemble and Jakob Grimm: A Correspondence, 1832–1852* (Leiden: Brill, 1971).

Wiley, Raymond A., 'Anglo-Saxon Kemble: The Life and Works of John Mitchell Kemble, 1807–1857: Philologist, Historian, Archaeologist', *Anglo-Saxon Studies in Archaeology and History* 1 (1979), 165–263.

Williams, Merryn, and Raymond Williams, 'Hardy and Social Class', in Norman Page (ed.), *Thomas Hardy: The Writer and his Background* (London: Bell and Hyman, 1980), pp. 29–40.

Williams, Teresa, and Alison Williams, 'The Reverend Anthony Lawson Mayhew', *The Kilvert Society Newsletter*, May 1980, 2–6.

Wilson, John Dover, *Milestones on the Dover Road* (London: Faber and Faber, 1969).

Winchester, Simon, *The Meaning of Everything: The Story of the Oxford English Dictionary* (Oxford: Oxford University Press, 2003).

Wingfield, Chris, 'Is the Heart at Home? E. B. Tylor's Collections from Somerset', *Journal of Museum Ethnography* 22 (2009), 22–38.

Wingfield, Chris, and Chris Gosden, 'An Imperialist Folklore? Establishing the Folk-Lore Society in London', in Timothy Baycroft and David Hopkin (eds), *Folklore and Nationalism in Europe During the Long Nineteenth Century* (Leiden: Brill, 2012), pp. 255–74.

Wise, John R., *Shakspere: His Birthplace and Its Neighbourhood* (London: Smith, Elder, and Co., 1861).

[Wise, John R.], 'The Poetry of Provincialisms', *Cornhill Magazine*, July 1865, 30–42.

Woolf, Virginia, *The Diary of Virginia Woolf, Volume IV: 1931–1935*, ed. Anne Olivier Bell (London: Hogarth Press, 1982).

Woolf, Virginia, *The Years*, ed. Hermione Lee (Oxford: Oxford University Press, 1992).

Worsaae, J. J. A., *An Account of the Danes and Norwegians in England, Scotland, and Ireland* (London: Murray, 1852).

Wrenn, Charles, 'Henry Sweet', *Transactions of the Philological Society* (1946), 177–210.

Wright, Elizabeth Mary, 'Bêowulf l. 1363: *ofer þæm hongiað hrinde bearwas*', *Englische Studien* 30 (1901), 341–3.

Wright, Elizabeth Mary, *Rustic Speech and Folk-Lore* (London: Oxford University Press, 1913).

Wright, Elizabeth Mary, *The Life of Joseph Wright*, 2 vols (London: Oxford University Press, 1932).

Wright, Joseph, *A Grammar of the Dialect of Windhill, in the West Riding of Yorkshire*, English Dialect Society 67 (London: English Dialect Society, 1892).

Wright, Joseph (ed.), *English Dialect Dictionary*, 6 vols (Oxford: Frowde, 1898–1905).

Wright, Joseph, and Elizabeth Mary Wright, *An Elementary Historical New English Grammar* (Oxford: Oxford University Press, 1924).

Wright, Peter, *The Language of British Industry* (London: Macmillan, 1974).

Wright, Peter, 'Alexander J. Ellis: *On Early English Pronunciation* Part V: Key Dialect Tool or Forgotten Antique?', *Journal of the Lancashire Dialect Society* 34 (1985), 3–10.

Wright, Thomas, *Dictionary of Obsolete and Provincial English* (London: Bohn, 1857).

Wright, William Aldis, 'Provincial Glossary', *Notes and Queries*, 12 March 1870, 271.

Wrigley, Chris, 'Barnes, William (1801–1886)', in *Oxford Dictionary of National Biography* [www.oxforddnb].

Wroth, W. W., 'Akerman, John Yonge (1806–1873)', rev. Nilanjana Banerji, in *Oxford Dictionary of National Biography* [www.oxforddnb].

Wyld, H. C., 'The Study of Living Popular Dialects and its Place in the Modern Science of Language', *Transactions of the Yorkshire Dialect Society* 6 (1904), 5–31.

Wyld, H. C., *English Philology in English Universities: An Inaugural Lecture* (Oxford: Clarendon Press, 1921).

Young, Robert J. C., *The Idea of English Ethnicity* (Oxford: Blackwell, 2008).

318 Bibliography

Young, Simon, 'Joseph Wright Meets the Boggart', *Folk Life* 56 (2018), 1–13.

Young, Simon, 'In Search of Jenny Greenteeth', *Gramarye* 16 (2019), 24–38.

Young, Simon, *The Boggart: Folklore, History, Place-Names and Dialect* (Exeter: Exeter University Press, 2022).

Zeitler, Michael A., *Representations of Culture: Thomas Hardy's Wessex and Victorian Anthropology* (New York: Lang, 2007).

Zietlow, Paul, 'Thomas Hardy and William Barnes: Two Dorset Poets', *Publications of the Modern Language Association* 84 (1969), 291–303.

Index

Abberley Hall 165
Aberystwyth 249
accent *see* phonetics and phonology
Acle 149
Adams, Ernest 209
Addy, Sidney Oldall 155, 216–17, 268
Ælfric 29, 30, 146
agriculture *see* farming
Akerman, John Yonge 29–30, 35, 76, 120, 188
Alfred the Great, King 29, 30, 31, 34
Allingham, William 170
Allsopp, A. Percy 157
Almondbury 165
Alvechurch 249
America, United States of 71, 161, 163, 166, 196, 227, 248, 256–7
Ancrene Wisse 50, 53
Anglo-Saxon *see* Old English
Anglo-Saxon Chronicle 32–3
Anglo-Saxons 1–2, 23, 28–35, 69, 105, 187–91, 228
see also Old English
animal names 157, 207, 208–10, 216, 265
Annfield Plain 87
anthropology 68–9, 70, 95, 109, 202–5, 220, 227, 228–9
antiquarianism 17, 18–19, 22–5, 43, 47, 51–2, 71, 91, 111–12, 129, 146–7, 151–2, 160, 165, 166, 173–4, 197, 202, 210–11, 217, 218–19, 220, 226–9
Antrim 273, 288
archaism 18–19, 25–7, 37–9, 41–2, 53, 104, 106, 111, 123, 132–41, 150, 179–80, 187–9, 191, 219, 224, 252, 254, 259, 275, 281
Archer, William 136–7, 140, 226
Ardeley 97
Arden, Mrs Douglas 128
Arnold, Matthew 226
Ashcroft, Mary 80, 81, 90
Ashton-under-Lyme 75
Asquith, Herbert 285
Athenaeum magazine 76, 145, 159, 202, 224
Atkinson, Ann 167
Atkinson, Edward L. 47
Atkinson, J. C. 47–55, 58, 72, 88, 117, 144, 148, 154, 198, 199, 203, 205, 208, 209–10, 216–17, 237, 244, 268, 271, 279
Auden, W. H. 3, 36
Austen, Jane 91
Australia 166
autodidacticism 9–10, 30, 74–5, 113, 136, 173, 191, 234, 241–3

Axon, William E. A. 119–20, 130, 148, 152, 161, 162, 258
Ayenbite of Inwyt 152
Aylesbury 91
Ayrshire 273

Bagshaw, Robert 76
Bailey, John Eglinton 160
Baker, Anne Elizabeth 23–5, 44, 118, 154, 205–6, 237, 244, 269, 271
Baker, George 23–4
Baker, Thomas 161
Bala 248
Baldwin, Stanley 285, 286
Balfour, Arthur 247
Bamford, Samuel 115, 130, 237
Banks, George 167
Banks, Isabella 167–8, 170, 237–8
Barbados 157, 257
Baring-Gould, Sabine 218, 221–3, 230, 231, 238, 249, 270
Barking 248
Barnes, William 30–5, 38, 40, 42, 44–5, 62, 75, 76, 92, 120, 121–6, 127, 130, 132, 135, 138, 139–41, 148, 152, 154, 171, 188–90, 195, 197, 201, 205–6, 225, 227, 230, 234, 264, 270, 281, 285, 287
Barrie, J. M. 248, 261
Barrow-in-Furness 248
Batchelor, Thomas 27, 244
Bath 18
Battersea 248
Beaumont, Francis 237
Bede 29, 30
Bede, Cuthbert *see* Bradley, Edward
Bedford 248
Bedfordshire 27, 94, 157, 164, 244
Beeby, Miss 91
Belfast 248
Belgrave 87, 88, 168
Bell, Alexander Graham 58
Bell, Alexander Melville 58–9, 63, 70, 87
Benson, Edward White 165
Beowulf 192, 288
Berkshire 27, 92, 164, 248
Bewdley 80, 81, 90
Bingley 248
Binns, Isaac 154, 170, 237
bird names 153, 156, 208–10
Birkenhead 248
Birmingham 162, 166, 248

320 Index

Birstall 154
Blackburn 166, 248
Blackmore, R. D. 103, 218–21, 222, 223, 230, 238, 261, 282, 286
Blackmore, Vale of 125
Blackpool 248
Blandford, George Fielding 144, 238, 270
Blunden, Edmund 285
Boase, G. C. 152
Bobbin, Tim *see* Collier, John
Bolsterstone 268
Bolton 166
Bonaparte, Louis Lucien 92–3, 148, 152, 162, 163, 165, 185, 260–1
Bonaparte, Napoleon 92
Booth, William H. 82
Bootle 248
Borrowdale 196
borrowing *see* loanwords
Boston 22–3
Bosworth, Joseph 28–9, 30, 31, 166, 197
Bottesford 173
Boucher, Jonathan 25–6, 41–2
Bournemouth 248, 249
Bradfield (Yorkshire) 268
Bradford 118, 166, 241, 242, 244, 248, 252
Bradley, Edward 119
Bradley, Henry 7, 10, 31, 196, 254, 282, 283
Bradshaw, Henry 166
Brandl, Alois 282
Bredbury 177, 179
Breton 196
Bridges, Robert 10, 32, 139–40, 248
Bridgnorth 80
Brierley, Ben 103, 113–16, 119, 130, 131, 133, 170, 215, 237, 270
Brighton 166, 248
Bristol 166, 252
British Museum 21, 174, 210
Britten, James 153, 157, 174, 188, 195, 207, 208–9, 210, 215, 275
Brockett, John Trotter 21
Brontë, Charlotte 103, 109
Brontë, Emily 101, 103, 109, 110, 237
Brontë, Patrick 109
Brontë sisters 101, 109, 261
Brown, Ford Madox 160
Brugmann, Karl 241–2, 273
Buckingham 91
Buckinghamshire 91, 92, 152, 209
Buckle, Miss 91
Bulgarian 241
Bunyan, John 241
Burne, Charlotte Sophia 205, 206, 286–7
Burnett, Frances Hodgson 101
Burnley 248
Burns, Robert 17, 113, 130
Burton, Eliza Felicia 237
Burton-on-Trent 248
Bury 248

Busk, Rotha 237
Buxton (Norfolk) 80
Byers Green 280
Byron, Lord 113

Calland, Miss 91
Cambridge 150–1, 160, 161–2, 164
Cambridgeshire 80, 81, 110
Cambridge University 9, 47–8, 61, 62, 102, 126, 144, 146, 163, 165, 166, 171, 186, 191, 250, 279
Camelford 92
Campbell, Georgiana Mary Elizabeth 167–8
Canterbury 165
Carlisle 44, 108, 198, 237, 238
Carr, William 26, 42–3, 76
Carroll, Lewis 250
Cartmell, James 151
Celtic languages 34, 36, 54, 132, 196–7, 201, 220, 256, 282
Celts 51–2, 105, 187–8, 196–7
  see also Celtic languages
Chadwick, H. M. 191, 279
Chadwick, Martha 75
Chamberlain, Edith Laxon 121, 155, 168–70, 183, 205, 269, 271
Chambers, R. W. 10, 14
Chapel-en-le-Frith 74–5, 76, 88, 92, 157
Chaucer, Geoffrey 11, 15, 71, 73, 76, 95, 102, 106, 116, 118, 126, 146, 172, 192, 248, 277
Chaucer Society 71, 84, 144, 152
Chelmsford 88, 149
Chelsea 91
Chertsey 22
Cheshire 16, 76, 77, 151, 155, 156, 158, 165, 173–4, 176–84, 209, 212–13, 215, 237, 244, 265, 268, 271, 273
Chester 158
Chesterfield 155
Chetham Society 131, 160
China 161, 163, 257
Cholmondeley 184
Cholmondeston 184
Chope, Richard Pearse 155
Chorlton 75
Civil List pensions 48, 130, 158, 247
Clare, John 24–5, 118
Cleasby, Richard 198, 199, 258
clergy 30, 36, 47–9, 86, 90–1, 94, 106, 109–10, 118–19, 128, 143, 144, 146, 151, 155, 157, 164–5, 167, 181, 191, 197, 227, 233, 235–6, 248–9, 261
Cleveland 48–55, 58, 117, 154, 198, 205, 209–10, 216–17, 237, 244, 268, 271
Clifton 151
Cockayne, Thomas Oswald 145–6
Cockayne Hatley 94
Cockney 89, 95, 110, 118, 274
Cole, R. E. 155
Coleridge, Derwent 253
Coleridge, Herbert 253

Coleridge, Samuel Taylor 253
collecting *see* crowdsourcing; fieldwork
Collier, John 57–8, 110, 120, 130, 152
Collins, Wilkie 101
colonialism 68–9, 157, 163, 202–3, 204, 256–7
Combs, Mary 237
Commondale 217
Coniston 197
Cope, William H. 155
Cornish 196
Cornwall 152, 155, 164, 168–9, 206, 209, 219
Corringham 173–4, 176–84, 196–7, 198, 206, 237, 271
Cotgrave, Randle 177, 179
Cotton Famine, Lancashire 130
Couch, Thomas Quiller 155
Courtney, Leonard Henry 169
Courtney, Margaret Ann 155, 168–9, 206
Courtney, W. P. 152
Coventry 249
Covernton, Alice Beatrice 250
Coxe, H. O. 166
Craigie, W. A. 250, 285
Crane, Walter 134
Craven 26, 42
Crewkerne 120
Crockett, S. R. 261
Crofton, H. T. 185, 239
Cromer 22
Crossley, James 160
crowdsourcing 76, 85–6, 88, 151, 174, 236–8, 252, 261–2, 273–4
Crudgington 80
Cumberland 21, 25, 26, 43–4, 89, 108, 121, 130, 152, 167, 196, 197, 198, 200–1, 208–9, 210, 216, 238, 240, 258, 261–2, 263, 267, 276, 285, 288
see also Lakeland
Cumberland and Westmorland Antiquarian and Archaeological Society 43
Cursor Mundi 191, 198, 258
Curteis, Bessy 167–8
Cust, H. C. 94

Danby 47–55, 144, 216–17
Danes *see* Vikings
Danish 32, 34, 50–1, 53, 68, 222
Darlington, Thomas 155, 165, 244
Dartnell, George E. 155, 238
Darwin, Charles 11–12, 54, 134, 202
Day, Cecilia M. 110
Day, Edward 110
Dekker, Thomas 237
De Quincey, Thomas 17
De Morgan, Mary 196
De Morgan, Sophia 196
De Morgan, William 196
Denham, Michael Aislabie 214
Denmark 162, 166, 197–8
Denwood, J. 263, 268–9
Derby, Earl of 82

Derbyshire 20, 74–5, 79, 83, 87, 88, 92, 119, 155, 157, 210, 213, 268, 273
Devon 91, 101, 102, 120–1, 138, 153, 155, 156, 165, 178, 179, 189–90, 207, 209, 218–23, 248, 273, 276, 282
Dickens, Charles 82, 95, 101, 103, 110, 113, 115, 118, 237, 274
Dickinson, William 152, 208–9, 210, 216, 238, 258, 269
diglossia 45, 77–8, 89, 90, 121–6, 130–1
Disraeli, Benjamin 82
Domesday Book 52
Doncaster 18
Dorchester 30, 262
Dorset 30–5, 45–6, 86, 92, 120–6, 134–7, 138, 140, 152, 161, 188–90, 195, 205–6, 223–31, 262–3, 264, 281–2
Douglas, Miss 151
Downes, Miss 110
Dublin 36, 138, 141, 165, 236
Durham 87
Durham, County 87, 110, 119, 196, 212, 273, 280
Dutch 222

Earle, John 166
Early English Text Society 51, 71, 84, 87, 126, 143–4, 146, 148, 151–2, 173, 191, 233, 249, 257
Easington 110
Easther, A. 154, 155
East Mersea 221
Edgmond 206
Edinburgh 273
editing 51, 53, 87, 121–2, 144, 146, 159, 161, 169, 173, 175, 191–3, 233, 249, 277
Edmondbyers 87
education 42–6, 62, 64, 78, 86, 90, 96, 105, 131, 132, 137, 143–4, 146, 150, 157, 165–6, 175, 224, 283–4
see also schools and schoolteachers
Egglestone, William Morley 119, 237
Eliot, George 103, 109, 111–13, 115, 116, 119–20, 127, 130, 131, 141, 161, 170, 217, 218, 223, 237, 261, 270
Eliot, T. S. 214
Ellis, Alexander John 4, 39, 61–73, 74, 76–99, 104, 109–10, 117, 118–19, 120, 128–9, 130, 145, 147–8, 149, 150, 151, 153, 154, 158, 161, 162, 164, 166, 167–9, 180–3, 185, 189, 190, 191, 193, 195, 196–7, 199, 201–2, 203, 206, 235, 236, 244, 246, 257, 264–5, 270, 272, 274
see also Existing Phonology of English Dialects, The
Ellis, Charlotte 87, 88, 168, 171, 214, 236, 237, 248, 261
Ellis, John 168
Ellwood, Thomas 197, 198–9, 236
elocution 58, 72, 75–6
Elworthy, Frederic Thomas 45, 117, 173–84, 188–9, 193, 195, 205, 207, 211–12, 214, 225, 227, 228, 237, 244, 246, 253, 259, 264, 269, 271, 272–3, 281, 287

322   Index

Emerson, Ralph Waldo 36
empire *see* colonialism
English Dialect Dictionary 75, 117, 118, 141, 148,
 158, 185, 204, 231, 233–77, 279, 287, 288
English Dialect Grammar 272–4, 280
English Dialect Society 1, 65, 74, 88, 99, 121, 141,
 143–86, 188, 190, 191, 192, 193, 195, 199,
 205–10, 212–13, 216, 224, 231, 233–40, 244–7,
 248, 251–2, 255, 256–7, 260–2, 266, 276–7, 279,
 282
 see also glossaries
Englishness 146–7, 148, 188, 247, 279
English studies 9–10, 249–50, 282–5
enregisterment 101
Epsom 25
Essex 17, 47, 88, 90, 149, 164, 221, 222, 237
Ethnological Society of London 49
etymology 16, 23, 28, 36, 49–51, 54, 105–6, 180–1,
 187–201, 209, 230, 246, 253, 260, 266–7, 275
 see also Celtic languages; Normans and Norman
 Conquest; Old English; Old Norse
Evans, Arthur Benoni 155, 168
Evans, Sebastian 155, 168, 171
evolution 11–12, 68, 69, 202–4
Existing Phonology of English Dialects, The 72,
 83–99, 109–10, 118–19, 120, 128–9, 147–8, 151,
 153, 154, 161, 164, 167–9, 189, 195, 199, 206,
 236, 244, 246, 270, 272, 274
Exmoor 155, 218–21

Failsworth 113
fairies *see* supernatural beliefs
fairy tales 91, 216–17
Faraday, Michael 5
Farmer, John S. 260
farming 30, 74–5, 78, 108, 135, 173–4, 178, 196–7,
 199, 201–2, 210, 218, 226, 261, 275, 287
Farndon 151
Faunthorpe, John Pincher 91
Faversham 91
Ferguson, Robert 198, 199
Fernilee 75
Ffarington, Susan Maria 91
fiction 45, 54–5, 82, 101–21, 131, 161, 170, 173, 174,
 216–31, 237–8, 242–3, 251, 261, 270, 285–7
field names 199
fieldwork 20, 24, 27, 46–7, 58, 64–5, 73, 74–83, 85–7,
 88–9, 93–4, 144, 148–50, 155, 167, 171–2, 174,
 180–4, 196–7, 199, 204, 206, 210–11, 213–14,
 230, 234, 236–7, 240, 246, 251–2, 254–5, 257,
 261–2, 274, 287
 see also crowdsourcing
First World War 281–3
fishing 22, 94, 120, 144, 157
Fishwick, Henry 160
FitzGerald, Edward 144, 148, 157, 171
Fitzhugh, Alice 80
Flagg 75
Flateyjarbók 50
Fleay, F. G. 165

Fletcher, John 237
Folkestone 94, 165
folklore 2–3, 25, 47, 51–2, 81, 108–9, 111–12, 146–7,
 153, 156, 167, 178, 187, 203–31, 259, 268,
 275–6, 286–7
Folklore Society 156, 202, 205, 206–8, 209, 227
Forby, Robert 23, 58, 76
Forfarshire 273
Frampton, Miss 109–10
France 67
Francis, Isabella 151, 167, 193
Freeman, E. A. 71
French 36, 86, 132, 194–6, 230, 241, 245, 267, 272
 see also Normans and Norman Conquest
French, E. 151, 165
Friend, Hilderic 156, 165
Frisian 34
Frodsham 174
Frowde, Henry 248
Furness 155, 248
Furnivall, F. J. 26, 48, 51, 54, 105, 126, 128, 148, 151,
 166, 169, 193, 249, 254, 282

Gaelic 196
Gainsborough 91
Galt, John 261
Garnett, Richard 20–1, 25, 28, 30, 76, 102, 117, 180
Garstang 88
Gaskell, Elizabeth 54–5, 103, 104–9, 113, 115,
 116–17, 131, 170, 174, 179, 217, 220, 237, 270
Gaskell, William 76, 105–6, 108, 109, 110, 120, 179
geology 36, 68, 89
Gerald of Wales 15
German 71, 222, 241, 281–2
Germany 63, 67, 111, 166, 202, 240, 241–2, 248, 280,
 281–4
Gibbons, Stella 287
Gibbs, Henry Hucks 166, 249
Gibson, Alexander Craig 121
Gilliéron, Jules 67–8
Gladstone, W. E. 130, 248
Glaisdale 217
Glenfield 87
glossaries 1–3, 18–25, 26, 29–30, 32, 42–3, 44, 48–55,
 57–8, 64, 76, 89, 106, 108, 110, 116, 117–18,
 120–1, 125, 131–3, 134, 135, 143–4, 150, 152–9,
 160, 167–71, 172–85, 192, 193, 195, 196–7,
 199–200, 205–6, 209–16, 230, 231, 237–8,
 239–40, 244, 258–9, 260–2, 264–5, 267–71,
 286–7
Glossic alphabet 62, 63–6, 76, 89, 99, 145, 149, 158,
 168, 170, 182–4, 196, 257
Gloucestershire 92, 94, 109, 249
Goddard, E. H. 155
Gomme, George Lawrence 202–3, 205, 215, 227
Goodchild, J. G. 89, 91, 94, 98, 148, 151, 154, 190–1,
 196, 274
Gothic 241
Gower, Granville Leveson 155, 165

grammar 20, 27–8, 31, 33–4, 38–9, 45, 49–50, 53, 54, 86, 93, 94, 104, 107, 112, 123–4, 129, 139, 149, 153, 172, 175–6, 178–9, 188–9, 222, 229–30, 231, 244–6, 266, 270, 272–4, 275, 281, 282, 286, 287
Grasmere 154
Great Fryup 217
Great Stukeley 81
Great Yarmouth 94, 165
Greek 37, 68, 76, 241, 242
Greenwell, G. C. 212
Greg, Elizabeth Mary 237
Grimm, Brothers 216
Grimm, Jacob 4, 7, 12, 20, 53, 202
Grimm's Law 6–7, 282
Grose, Francis 17, 20
Guildford 22, 165
Gurney, Anna 22, 195, 209
Gutch, Eliza 207–8, 234, 237, 248, 275–6
Gutch, John James 207

Hagley 169
Hailstone, Edward 166
Hall, Fitzedward 166, 239, 249
Hall, Joseph 162, 192
Hallam, Thomas 73–83, 84, 86, 88, 91, 92, 93–4, 97–8, 99, 105, 119, 131, 147, 148, 151, 154, 155, 156–7, 158, 162, 167, 169–70, 183, 184, 187–8, 204, 247, 262, 274
Hallamshire 18–19, 21, 43, 58, 125, 134, 157
Halliwell, James Orchard 26–8, 41–2, 58, 106, 148, 166, 193, 252, 264
Halton Holegate 128
Hampshire 106–7, 109, 117, 134, 155
Handforth 237
Hannington 110
Hardingstone 80
Hardy, Florence 226
Hardy, Thomas 7, 30, 31, 35, 45–6, 69, 101, 103, 121–2, 125, 127, 133–7, 138, 140, 141, 144, 161, 193, 201, 218, 223–31, 238, 261, 262–3, 268, 270, 281–2, 285–6
Harland, John 154, 176, 265, 268–9
Harrington 110
Harris, Mary Dormer 249, 250
Harrison, E. P. 110
Harrison, William 165
Hart, Agnes Horatia Frances 249–50
Hart, Horace Henry 249
Hartland 155
Hartlebury 110
Haviland, Misses 110
Haworth 109
Heaney, Seamus 288
Henley, W. E. 260
Herefordshire 19–20, 80, 81, 92, 94
Herford, C. H. 249
Hertfordshire 92, 102
Heslop, Richard Oliver 155, 165, 212, 230, 258, 268–9

Higgins, Henry 57, 58, 60, 79
historicism 1–2, 10–12, 36–7, 39, 40, 49–52, 60, 67, 69–70, 71, 73, 103, 105–6, 108–9, 111–12, 115–16, 146–7, 159–60, 172, 179–80, 187–231, 244–5, 249, 256, 259–60, 284–5
Holderness 1–3, 19, 44, 88, 154, 156, 165, 178, 192, 258, 262, 268
Holderness, Thomas 1–3, 19, 44, 154, 258, 262, 263, 268–9, 270
Holland, Robert 153, 154, 155, 156, 158, 173–4, 176–84, 188, 195, 208–9, 212–13, 215, 230, 237, 244, 265, 269, 271, 275
Holloway, William 26
Holt, Robert 163
Holthausen, Ferdinand 246
Hope, Gertrude 238
Hopkins, Gerard Manley 7, 32, 37, 133–4, 137–41, 209, 213–14, 218, 230, 236–7, 242, 261
Huddersfield 154, 155, 165
Hull 165, 252
Hunter, Joseph 18–19, 21, 25, 43, 58, 76, 125, 134, 157
Huntingdon 81
Huntingdonshire 80, 81, 97, 154, 164
Huxley, Thomas 82

Iceland 221
Icelandic 53, 71
Idle 241, 244, 246
India 161, 168, 248, 257, 279
Indo-European 4, 8, 66, 204, 284
intelligibility 15, 16, 48–9, 96, 105–6, 114–15, 119, 225, 257
International Phonetic Association 61, 93
Ireland 87, 141, 148, 161, 162, 163, 236–7, 248, 256–7, 261, 288
Irish 196
isoglosses 93
Italian 86

Jackson, Georgina F. 158, 167, 171–2, 206, 210–11, 213, 237, 244, 269, 286–7
Jackson, William 154
Jamieson, John 267
Jerome, Jerome K. 237
Johnson, Louisa H. 109
Johnson, Samuel 25, 75
Jones, Joseph 165
Jones, Sir William 66
Jutland 53

Kaye-Smith, Sheila 287
Kemble, John Mitchell 22, 126
Kennett, White 17, 28, 270
Kensington 95, 237
Kent 91, 94, 151, 152, 155, 209, 273, 285
Ker, W. P. 166, 240, 280, 284
Kilvert, Francis 233–4
Kineton 90, 193
King, Edward Bolton 167

324 Index

Kingsley, Charles 101, 174
King's Lynn 94
Kington–Oliphant, T. L. 166, 239
Kipling, Rudyard 136, 165
Kirby, Sarah 237–8
Kirby Bedon 110
Kirkby, Bryham 268–9
Kirkby Stephen 118
Kirkcudbrightshire 273
Kirton 173
Knatchbull-Hugessen, Herbert 91
Knighton, William 80
Knutsford 174

Lakeland 17, 197, 198, 263–4, 267–9
Lakeland Dialect Society 280
Lambeth 250
Lancashire 54, 57–8, 75, 77, 83, 87, 88, 91, 102,
    104–7, 108, 110, 113–16, 118–19, 129–33, 138,
    152, 155–7, 160, 163, 165, 185–6, 190, 197, 238,
    267, 268, 273, 276, 288
Lancashire Dialect Society 280
Lanchester 87
Lang, Andrew 202–4
Langland, William 11, 50–1, 53, 146, 192, 277
language change 4, 8, 18, 20, 21, 42–3, 45–6, 49–51,
    52, 67–8, 95, 97, 122, 134, 150, 155, 175–6, 203,
    219
Langwathby 43–4, 200
Latin 10, 33, 36, 37, 55, 64, 68, 76, 132, 178, 208–9,
    220, 222–3, 230, 233, 241
Lawrence, D. H. 285, 287
Lawson, Robert 155
Layamon 30, 53
Leader, R. E. 154
Leamington Spa 249
Leasam 168
Ledbury 81, 94
Leeds 17, 89, 118, 166, 237
Leeds, University of 102, 279, 280
Lees, Thomas 155
Le Fanu, Sheridan 238
Leicester 87
Leicestershire 20, 87, 155, 168, 171, 214, 237, 261,
    273
Lewes 156
Lewis, C. S. 11
Lewis, George Cornewall 19–20, 28, 57
Lew Trenchard 221
lexicography 16–17, 25–9, 40–2, 49–52, 75, 76, 116,
    140, 146, 148–50, 173–84, 197–8, 233–77
    see also glossaries
Leyland 91
Leytonstone 237
libraries 148, 160, 161, 162–3, 164, 166, 169, 202,
    236, 248, 250, 277
Lincolnshire 22–23, 27, 43, 83, 87, 91, 121, 126–9,
    155, 173–4, 176–84, 198, 199–200, 206, 207–8,
    237–8, 258–9, 261, 271, 273
Lindisfarne Gospels 51

Lithuanian 241
Liverpool 166
loanwords 53, 132, 175–6, 188, 194–201, 220, 230,
    245, 267, 282
localism 51–2, 68–9, 88, 95–6, 106–7, 121–5, 137,
    138, 179, 180, 190, 199, 200–1, 203, 204–5, 211,
    216–17, 218, 227, 242, 245–6, 251–2, 258, 267–8
    see also regionalism
London 15, 60, 62, 77, 86, 89, 95, 102, 104, 113,
    114–15, 118, 145, 159, 161, 164, 165–6, 168,
    204, 214, 220, 236, 237, 240, 242, 250, 281
    see also Cockney; Philological Society of London
Lonsdale 54
Loughborough 87
Lothian 273
Louth 199
Lovelace, Ada 196
Lumby, J. R. 166

Macclesfield 181
Macfarlane, Robert 288
Macmillan, Alexander 165
Magnússon, Eiríkr 71, 166
Maitland, F. W. 248
Man, Isle of 152, 163, 196, 273
Manchester 74, 75–6, 78, 79, 82, 104–7, 108, 113,
    115, 119, 130, 131–3, 151, 159–63, 164, 166,
    185–6, 188, 190, 236, 237, 240, 252
Manchester Literary Club 115–16, 119–20, 131,
    155–6, 160
Manley 173–4, 176–84, 196–7, 198, 206, 237, 271
Manx 196
maps 92–4
Margate 241
Market Drayton 80
Market Harborough 87
Market Weighton 119
Marsh, George 138
Masefield, John 285
mathematics 61–2, 75, 146, 241
Mathwin, Henry 159
Mattishall 91
Maurice, F. D. 5
Mayhew, Anthony Lawson 74, 233–5, 238–9, 240,
    247, 250, 252, 258, 266
Mayhew, Henry 214
medievalism 37, 53, 73, 87, 95, 105–6, 111, 126, 133,
    137–8, 152, 159–60, 166, 171, 180, 187–201,
    202, 223, 246, 248, 253, 258–9
Melmerby 200
Mere 30
Metcalfe, John 279
Middle English 15, 38, 50–1, 53, 71, 73, 76, 101–2,
    106, 118, 126–7, 134, 138, 146, 152, 173, 188,
    190–3, 198, 233, 250, 252, 254–5, 256, 257–8
Middle High German 241
Middlesex 87, 92, 154, 218
Middleton, Thomas 237
military 17, 154, 165, 168, 227
Mill, John Stuart 5

Miller, Edith Mary 250, 272
Milner, George 115–16, 131–3, 135, 148, 155, 156–7, 160, 164, 185–6, 238, 240
Milnrow 131
Milverton 90
mining 90, 94, 157, 212–13, 230
Mirk, John 173
Mitchell, George 95
Mobberley 174
Monmouth 94
Monmouthshire 87, 92
Montacute 95
Moody, D. L. 82
Moorman, F. W. 102, 279
Morley, Henry 165–6
Morris, Richard 139, 191, 193–4, 198, 257–8
Morris, William 7, 71, 137, 248, 249
Moule, Henry Joseph 262
Much Cowarne 81, 94
Müller, Friedrich Max 5–7, 12, 31, 35, 36, 39, 46, 53, 67, 126, 134, 138, 196, 203–4, 236, 242, 249
Mullett, John 81, 83
multilingualism 13, 21, 31, 194–201, 204, 221, 222, 234, 241
Munby, Arthur Joseph 171–2, 173–4, 218, 248, 261
Murray, James 5, 7, 8–9, 12, 39, 42, 44, 46, 48, 60, 62, 64, 76, 83, 84, 85, 87, 93, 96, 97, 117, 130, 148, 157, 165, 175, 178, 179, 184, 189, 193, 195, 196, 221, 233, 234, 238, 240, 244, 246, 249, 253, 254–7, 259, 264, 266, 276, 280–1, 285

Napier, A. S. 10, 166, 240
Nares, Robert 193
nationalism 12–13, 41, 247, 279, 283–4, 285
  see also Englishness
Native American languages 63
nativism 32, 132, 194
  see also purism
Neaves, Charles 6–7
Neogrammarians 9, 67–8, 69, 70, 182, 241–2, 246, 265, 273, 284
Nesbit, E. 118
Nettleship, J. 165
Newbolt, Henry 283
Newbolt Report 283–4
Newcastle upon Tyne 89, 155, 166, 252
Newport (Shropshire) 206
New Zealand 166
Nicholson, Norman 285
Nicholson, W. E. 212
Nodal, John Howard 131–3, 150–1, 155, 156–7, 160–3, 164, 169, 171, 174, 178, 182, 184–6, 199, 208, 210, 235, 238, 240, 247, 255, 256–7, 258, 260
Norbury 76
Norfolk 22, 23, 27, 58, 80, 91, 93, 94, 110, 146, 149, 195, 209
Normans and Norman Conquest 1–2, 23, 35, 36, 194–6
Northall, G. F. 205

Northampton 24, 80
Northamptonshire 23–5, 44, 80, 83, 87, 92, 110, 118, 154, 205, 209, 237, 244, 271
Northumberland 86, 88, 89, 94, 119, 155, 165, 212, 258, 263, 267–9, 273
Norwegian 53
Norwich 94
Notes and Queries journal 143–4, 152, 159, 173, 198, 201, 202, 207, 233–4, 238, 240, 275, 276–7
Nottingham 81, 83, 166
Nottinghamshire 285

'observer's paradox' 77, 89
Old English 15, 21, 22, 23, 28–35, 36, 37, 38, 50, 51, 53, 54, 60, 71, 76, 86, 95, 105–6, 120–1, 123, 126–7, 132, 134, 138, 146, 160, 178, 188–91, 192, 197, 199, 220, 228, 229, 233, 241, 245, 250, 252, 256, 259, 272, 288
Old High German 241
Old Norse 11, 16–17, 22, 23, 36, 50–1, 52–3, 54, 71, 86, 129, 132, 134, 138, 162, 191, 194, 197–201, 221, 228–9, 241, 258, 259, 267
Oldham 113, 165, 192
Onions, C. T. 194
Orkney 209
orthography *see* spelling
Orton, Harold 280
Ostler, George 250
Oswestry 88
Oughtibridge 268
Oundle 80
Oxford 151, 164, 169, 185–6, 234, 240, 250–1, 261, 282, 283
Oxford, University of 3, 5, 9, 10, 28, 61, 74, 79, 166, 169, 185–6, 207, 233, 242–3, 248, 249–51, 274, 279, 280
Oxford English Dictionary 7–9, 12, 40–2, 46, 48, 54, 60, 69, 75, 76, 135, 136, 143, 166, 168, 175, 179, 191, 194, 219, 233, 234–5, 236, 249, 250, 252–6, 259, 264, 266, 276, 281, 282, 283, 285
Oxfordshire 86, 92, 169, 206, 209, 262, 271, 273

palaeontology 36, 68
Palaeotype alphabet 62, 63, 64, 71, 76, 89, 93, 94, 99, 128, 182, 196
Palmer, Abram Smythe 235–40, 257, 261
Parish, W. D. 156, 236
Parker, Angelina 168–9, 206, 262, 269, 271
Parker, George 169
Parliament, Members of 19, 91, 157, 165, 167, 168, 168, 198, 249
Partridge, Jane Bella 249–51, 261, 262, 265
Patmore, Coventry 30
Paul, Hermann 243
Payne, Joseph 144, 165
Peacock family 173, 258–9
Peacock, Edward 121, 173–4, 176–84, 196–7, 198, 199, 206, 237, 269, 271
Peacock, Mabel 173, 238, 258–9, 261
Peacock, Robert Backhouse 54, 72–3, 253–4

326 Index

Pearl 126
Pegge, Samuel 155
Pembrokeshire 151, 273
Penrith 43, 167
Penwith 168
Penzance 168
perceptual dialectology 92, 170, 224
personal names 52
Perthshire 273
Peterloo 115
Piers Plowman see Langland, William
Philological Society of London 9, 19, 22, 40–2, 48,
    49, 54, 60, 63, 66, 69–70, 71, 72, 76, 77, 84, 89,
    92, 96, 109, 139, 143–4, 150, 151–2, 159, 165,
    167, 175, 191, 193, 196, 201, 209, 235, 236, 253
philology 3–14, 19–21, 35, 36–7, 39, 47–55, 66–71,
    89, 95–6, 105–6, 111, 114, 115–16, 120–1, 125,
    126, 127, 129–30, 132–4, 137–8, 146, 162, 166,
    181–3, 187–8, 200, 202, 203–5, 219, 223, 231,
    241–2, 249–50, 253, 272–3, 280–5, 287–8
phonetic alphabets 55, 58–9, 60–1, 62, 76, 90, 104,
    181–2, 265
    see also Glossic alphabet; Palaeotype alphabet
phonetics and phonology 27–8, 29, 38–9, 45, 48–9,
    55, 57–99, 104, 107, 112, 118, 122–4, 131, 138,
    145, 149, 153, 175–6, 178, 181–4, 188, 195, 208,
    239, 243–7, 251, 254–5, 256, 257, 263–6, 272–4,
    280, 282, 283–4
phonograph recording 274
phonotypy 62–3
Pitman, Isaac 58, 62, 63, 75, 113
place names 51–2, 88, 89, 90, 129, 153, 199–201, 217,
    219, 225
plant names 153, 156, 174, 178, 179, 188, 195,
    208–10, 215, 230, 246, 275, 287
Plymouth 168
poetry 6–7, 24–5, 32, 34, 36, 43–4, 62, 76, 118–19,
    120–41, 144, 167, 171–2, 200–1, 210, 231, 234,
    237–8, 270, 281–2, 285
Potter, Beatrix 197
Powley, Mary 43–4, 45, 88, 130, 167, 196, 199–201,
    238, 240, 261–2, 270
Powley family 167, 261
Preece, Francis 80
prescriptivism 40
Preston 110
Preston, Ben 118, 246
Prevost, E. W. 238
Price, Stephen 95
primitivism 67–9, 202–5, 228–9
Promptorium Parvulorum 51, 233
pronunciation *see* phonetics and phonology
proverbs 43, 111–12, 129, 170, 205
publishers 26, 30, 49, 71, 78, 84, 105, 115, 120, 127,
    152, 153, 155–6, 158, 165, 234, 239, 240, 247–8,
    249–51, 254, 271–2
Pulman, G. P. R. 120–1, 189–90
purism 32–5, 42, 78, 96, 115, 117, 125, 132, 134, 260
Pyrford 22

Radnorshire 234
railways and mobility 42–4, 46, 52, 65, 74, 75, 78,
    79–80, 88, 105, 112, 143–4, 146, 150, 158, 168,
    169, 170, 175, 281
Raine, James 166
Raines, F. R. 131
Raleigh, Walter 283
Randolph, H. 90
Rask, Rasmus 4, 7
Rawnsley, H. D. 197
Ray, John 16–17, 18, 28, 43
Received Pronunciation 96
Reform Movement 61
regionalism 13, 22–5, 103, 114–15, 139, 146–7,
    153–5, 176, 204–5, 212–13, 221, 223, 227, 252,
    267–8, 285–7
    see also localism
Relph, Josiah 130
Ridings, Elijah 113
Riehl, Wilhelm Heinrich von 111
Ripley 22
Robinson, C. Clough 89, 91, 118, 148, 152, 154, 196,
    237, 259
Robinson, Francis Kildale 49–50, 88, 108, 148, 154,
    215–16, 237, 268, 269, 271
Robinson, George 279
Rochdale 130, 131
Romani language 161, 163
Rose, W. F. 157
Ross 94
Ross, Frederick 1–3, 19, 44, 154, 258, 268
Rothbury 88
Rowntree, John Stephen 165
Royal Bounty Fund 247
Royal Institution 5–6, 166
Royal Literary Fund 158
Royal Society 16, 17
Runcorn 177, 179
Runswick Bay 216
Ruskin, John 71, 91
Rutland 87, 119, 164, 273
Rye 168
Ryle, J. C. 248

Saintsbury, George 248
Salisbury 33
Salisbury, Jesse 156
Salt, Titus 241
Saltaire 241, 277
Samlesbury Hall 165
Sanskrit 5, 6, 31, 66, 68, 241
Satchell, Thomas 207
Saussure, Ferdinand de 284
Sawston 81, 83
schools and schoolteachers 30, 44, 60, 61, 75, 91, 157,
    158, 164–6, 181, 191, 192, 195, 224, 241, 243,
    248, 249–50, 258, 260
Scotland 42, 60, 64, 87, 92, 93, 148, 157, 161, 163,
    178, 195, 209, 244, 246, 256, 267, 273, 288

Scots language 60, 86, 254
Scott, Robert Falcon 47
Scott, Walter 37, 117, 174, 218, 261
Scotter 91
Searle, W. G. 166
servants 77, 78, 90, 101
Settle 237
Settrington 196
Shaftesbury, Lord 82
Shakespeare, William 23, 26, 39, 71, 85, 106, 144, 162, 165, 193–4
Shaw, George Bernard 57, 58, 60–1, 62
sheep-scoring numerals 196–7, 201–2
Sheffield 18, 154, 155, 165, 166, 216, 254, 268
Shifnal 172
shorthand 58, 75, 113
Shropshire 20, 80, 88, 158, 171–2, 206, 209, 210–11, 213, 237, 244, 273, 286–7
Sir Gawain and the Green Knight 192–3
Sittingbourne 151
Skeat, Bertha 195
Skeat, Walter William 7, 9, 11, 17, 39, 48, 51, 58, 74, 90, 102, 117, 119–20, 145–59, 160, 161–2, 163, 164, 166, 168, 169, 178, 180–3, 184, 185–6, 191, 192, 193, 194, 195–6, 198, 205, 206, 221, 230, 234–40, 242, 247, 248, 249, 251, 256–7, 258, 260, 266, 268, 270, 277, 279, 280
Skelton, John 23
Skipton 165
slang 19, 24, 107, 161, 163, 254, 257–60
slips 149, 151, 158, 237, 240, 251, 270
Smiles, Samuel 170
Smith, C. Roach 210, 215
Smith, Henry 210, 215
Smith, John Russell 26, 27, 28–9, 30, 49, 152
Society of Antiquaries 18, 29
sociolinguistics 80, 91, 97, 245
Somersby 126, 128, 129
Somerset 27, 45, 90, 94, 95, 102, 117, 120–1, 157, 173–84, 189–90, 193, 195, 207, 211–12, 214, 218–21, 228, 237, 244, 246, 259, 264, 271, 272–3, 281
Song of Solomon 76, 92, 163
sound change 6–7, 9, 40, 60, 67, 70, 84, 97, 245–6, 283–4
spelling 15, 58–9, 62–6, 71–3, 83–4, 88, 95–6, 114, 115, 117, 123–4, 127–8, 135, 165, 183, 184, 220, 244, 254–5, 257, 263–5, 282
Spenser, Edmund 106, 134
Spiers, Alexander 177, 179
Spilsby 129
Staffordshire 20, 83, 87, 119, 209, 273
Standard English 4, 15, 17, 31, 32–4, 38–40, 41–2, 44, 53, 54, 57, 59, 72–3, 81–2, 89, 96, 102, 104, 114, 116, 121–6, 130–1, 133, 135, 137, 140, 149, 175, 184, 187, 189, 194, 195, 208, 221, 222–3, 225, 229, 230, 245–6, 253–6, 261, 264–5, 272–4, 275
Stanhope 119
Stead, Richard 1–3, 19, 44, 88, 154, 165, 258, 268

Steel, Joseph 118
Stephens, George 162, 166
Stevenson, Joseph 25
Stevenson, Robert Louis 218
Stockport 160
Stoke Lacy 94
Stourport 81
Stratford-upon-Avon 167, 193
Stratmann, F. H. 166
Streatfeild, George Sidney 199–200, 208, 238, 271
Stretton 119
Strood 91
structuralist linguistics 284–5
Sturminster Newton 30
Suffolk 23, 58, 87, 144, 157, 209, 233, 273
Sunderland 94
supernatural beliefs 3, 214–17, 218, 223, 226, 229, 266, 269, 286
surnames 81, 199
Surrey 22, 25, 92, 102, 155, 165
Survey of English Dialects 280
survivalism 202–5, 208, 227, 228–9
Sussex 156, 168, 273
Swainson, Charles 153, 156, 209
Swaledale 154, 176, 216, 265, 268–9
Swann, H. Kirke 209
Swedish 53
Sweet, Henry 7, 9, 11, 46, 58–9, 60–1, 62, 70, 72, 84, 86, 97, 98–9, 166, 175, 181–2, 191, 243, 259, 272, 280
Swinburne, Algernon Charles 26, 136
Switzerland 248

Taddington 75, 76
Taylor, Isaac 196
Teddington 218
Tennyson, Alfred 30, 71, 126–9, 141, 171, 177, 179, 185, 201, 207, 237, 270, 285
Tetbury 109
Thackley 241, 246
Thaxted 90
Thomas, Edward 285
Thompson, Frances 237
Thompson, Joseph 159, 185
Thompson, Pishey 22–3, 43
Thompson, Rachel 237
Thoms, William John 202
Thoresby, Ralph 17
Tilshead 109
Titsey Place 165
Tolkien, J. R. R. 3, 5, 47, 102, 242, 283, 288
Tollemache, Miss 110
Toller, Thomas Northcote 28, 160, 188, 190, 249, 252
Torquay 166
Torr, Cecil 282
Torver 197
Towneley Plays 50–1, 53, 102, 192

trades and industries 80, 90, 107, 113, 129–30, 134, 157, 165, 178, 196–7, 210–14, 224, 230–1, 241, 245–6, 258, 261
Trench, Richard Chenevix 35–42, 46, 58, 76, 106, 165, 187–8, 203, 233, 253, 255
Trollope, Anthony 103
Truro 165
Turnbull, Thomas 165
Tusser, Thomas 177, 179
Tylor, E. B. 68, 202–3, 207, 227, 228–9, 249
Tyrrell, Sarah 90
Tysoe 151, 167, 193

Udal, John Symonds 205–6, 227
uniformitarianism 67, 70
universities 5, 9–10, 47–8, 74, 147, 151, 160, 164–6, 186, 188, 236, 240, 241–2, 246, 248–50, 279–80, 282–5
    see also Cambridge University; English studies; Leeds, University of; Oxford, University of
Upton-on-Severn 155
Uttley, Alison 285

Victoria, Queen 6, 248
Vigfússon, Gudbrand 198, 199, 258
Vikings 1–2, 15, 22, 31, 52–3, 69, 105, 187–8, 190, 197–201
    see also Old Norse

Wakefield 51, 192
Wales 87, 92, 93, 148, 151, 152, 163, 197, 234, 248, 249, 256, 273
Wales, Prince of 82
Walker, John 75
Walker, Miss 110
Ward, Mary Augusta 237
Warminster 168
Warrington 166
Warwickshire 20, 90, 92, 111, 119, 151, 163, 167, 193–4, 249, 250, 276
Washington, George 25
Waterloo, battle of 113
Watson, John 58
Waugh, Edwin 103, 119, 130–3, 138, 141, 160, 162, 170, 185, 238, 270, 285
Weardale 196
Webb, Mary 285–7
Webb, W. T. 157
Webster, Noah 25
Wedgwood, Hensleigh 54, 166
Wedmore 94
Wellington 175, 207
Welsh 20, 138, 196–7, 241
Wendover 91
Wenker, Georg 67–8
West Bromwich 166
Westminster 36
Westmorland 21, 26, 87, 118, 154, 197, 198, 273
    see also Lakeland

Weybridge 22
Weymouth, R. F. 165
Whaley Bridge 75
Whewell, William 62
Whitby 48, 49, 55, 88, 107–9, 117, 154, 165, 215, 237, 268, 269, 271
White, Gilbert 237
Whitelands Training College 91
Whittington 155
Wight, Isle of 27, 210, 215
Wilberforce, Samuel 82
Wilkins, A. S. 160
William of Malmesbury 15
Wilson, Thomas 119, 130
Wiltshire 29–30, 89, 109, 120, 155, 168, 273
Windhill 241, 244–7, 251, 265, 272, 277, 280
Windsor 113
Windsor Castle 148, 166
Winterborne Came 30, 120
Winteringham 197
Wise, J. R. 134, 150, 163, 172–3, 188, 192, 193, 203, 208, 210, 239
Wood Ditton 110
Woodward, F. M. W. 263, 268
Woolf, Virginia 242–3, 251, 277
Worcestershire 20, 80, 92, 110, 121, 155, 156, 165, 169–70, 183, 249, 250, 263, 267, 271, 276
Worden Hall 91
Wordsworth, William 17–18, 132
Worsaae, J. J. A. 197–8
Wray, James Jackson 118–19, 237
Wrexham 241
Wreyland 282
Wright, Dufton 241
Wright, Elizabeth Mary 10, 40, 117–18, 192, 194, 196, 215–16, 220, 230, 242, 246, 250, 252, 260, 271, 275–6, 277, 280, 282, 287
Wright, Joseph 74, 118, 151, 233, 239–77, 279–80, 282–3, 288
Wright, Sarah Ann 241, 243, 246
Wright, Thomas 26, 35, 42, 190, 193, 264
Wright, William Aldis 143–5, 148, 150, 157
Wülcker, Richard Paul 166
Wyld, Henry Cecil 279, 283, 285
Wythburn 154

Yates, Lilian Jane 250, 272
York 15, 165, 171, 207, 237
Yorkshire 1–3, 16, 18–19, 21, 26, 42–3, 44, 47–55, 58, 83, 87, 89, 102, 107–9, 117, 118–19, 125, 129–30, 134, 144, 152, 153–4, 157, 163, 165, 170, 171, 176, 178, 192, 196, 198, 205, 209–10, 215, 216–17, 221, 222, 237, 240–3, 244–7, 258–9, 262, 263, 265, 267–8, 271, 273, 277, 279–80, 282, 288
Yorkshire Dialect Society 279–80, 285

Zupitza, Julius 166, 240